A Guide and Reference with Readings

D0144333

reference

need research help?

need design help?

need proofreading help?

reader

need more examples?

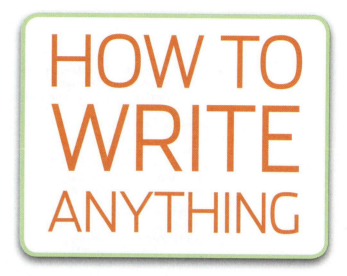

HOW TO WRITE ANYTHING

A Guide and Reference with Readings

John J. Ruszkiewicz
UNIVERSITY OF TEXAS, AUSTIN

Jay Dolmage
WEST VIRGINIA UNIVERSITY

BEDFORD/ST. MARTIN'S
Boston ◆ New York

For Bedford/St. Martin's

Executive Editor: Leasa Burton
Senior Developmental Editor: Ellen Darion
Senior Production Editor: Deborah Baker
Senior Production Supervisor: Dennis J. Conroy
Marketing Manager: Molly Parke
Editorial Assistants: Melissa Cook and Sarah Guariglia
Copyeditors: Mary Lou Wilshaw–Watts and Linda McLatchie
Art Director and Text Design: Anna Palchik
Cover Design: Nancy Goulet
Composition: Aptara
Printing and Binding: RR Donnelley and Sons

President: Joan E. Feinberg
Editorial Director: Denise B. Wydra
Editor in Chief: Karen S. Henry
Director of Marketing: Karen Melton Soeltz
Director of Editing, Design, and Production: Marcia Cohen
Assistant Director of Editing, Design, and Production: Elise Kaiser
Managing Editor: Elizabeth M. Schaaf

Library of Congress Control Number: 2008925889

Manufactured in the United States of America.

4   3   2   1   0   9
f   e   d   c   b   a

For information, write: Bedford/St. Martin's, 75 Arlington Street, Boston, MA 02116
(617–399–4000)

ISBN–10: 0–312–53278–4
ISBN–13: 978–0–312–53278–9

Acknowledgments:

"2007 Porsche 911 Turbo." Excerpt from article published in *Road & Track*, June 2006. Copyright © 2006. Reprinted with permission of the publisher.
Natalie Angier. "Almost Before We Spoke, We Swore." Originally published in *The New York Times*. Copyright © 2005 by The New York Times. Reprinted by permission of the author.
Stephanie Armour. "More Families Move in Together during Housing Crisis." *USA Today* February 2, 2009. USA TODAY is a division of Gannett Co., Inc. Reprinted with permission. http://www.usatoday.com.

Acknowledgments and copyrights are continued at the back of the book on pages 900–10, which constitute an extension of the copyright page. It is a violation of the law to reproduce these selections by any means whatsoever without the written permission of the copyright holder.

Preface

How to Write Anything: A Guide and Reference with Readings is not a humble title. You might wonder whether any book, especially one designed expressly as a guide for college writers, should promise so much. The simple answer is *no*; the more intriguing one is *maybe*.

What, after all, do writers do when they face an assignment? They try to grasp what the project entails; they look for examples of the genre; they wrestle with basic language and research skills. *How to Write Anything* guides college writers through these stages for their most common academic and professional assignments. In doing so, it lays out strategies to follow in any situation that requires purposeful writing.

But rarely do different writers work in the same order, and the same writer is likely to follow different paths for different projects. *How to Write Anything* doesn't define a single process of writing or imagine that all students using it will have the same skills and interests. Instead, a modular chapter organization and an innovative system of cross references encourage students to navigate the book's materials to find exactly the information they want at the level of specificity they need—which pretty much sums up the rationale for the book. If many college guides to composition test the patience of teachers and students alike by their sheer size and kitchen-sink approach to instruction, *How to Write Anything* is both more focused and more flexible, marrying the rich perspectives of a full rhetoric and reader to the efficiency of a brief handbook.

A Guide, Reference, and Reader

The Guide, in Parts 1 and 2, covers a wide range of genres that instructors frequently assign in composition classes or that students encounter in other undergraduate courses. Each chapter lays out the basics of a genre, such as narrative or argument, then redefines the writing process as a flexible series of rhetorical choices—Exploring Purpose and Topic; Understanding Audience; Finding and Developing Materials; Creating a Structure; and Choosing a Style and Design. These choices provide students with a framework for writing in any situation and in any genre, and encourage writers to explore the range of possibilities within genres. The explanations here are direct, practical, and economical. If writers do need more help with a particular topic, targeted cross references make it easy to find in the Reference section.

The Reference section (Parts 3 through 9) covers key aspects of the writing process—with separate parts devoted to Ideas; Shaping and Drafting; Style; Revising and Editing; Research and Sources; Media and Design; and Common Errors. While the topics will seem familiar to most writing instructors, the fresh and lively material here is designed to expand points introduced in the Guide. For instance, a writer might turn to these sections to find specific techniques for generating ideas or arguments or guidance for making a formal style feel more friendly. The organization of *How to Write Anything* lets students quickly find what they need without getting bogged down in other material.

Part 10, the Reader, is an anthology of 50 additional contemporary selections organized by genres covered in the Guide. Drawn from a variety of sources such as print and online journals, books, scholarly and popular magazines, blogs, graphic novels, and government reports, the readings offer both solid models for writing as well as compelling topics for students to respond to. Some examples include Kelefa Sanneh's report on hip-hop music from New Orleans, the Union of Concerned Scientists' proposal to address global warming, Lynda Barry's comic literacy narrative, Douglas Kellner's critique of Michael Jordan, and evaluations of everything from cell phone ringtones to organic food to reality television shows. The Reader includes new content from established authors such as Michael Pollan, Camille Paglia, Joyce Carol Oates, and Deborah Tannen, as well as newer voices such as Naomi Klein, Ira Sukrungruang, and Rob Sheffield. Headnotes provide context for all readings in the text, and selections in the reader are followed by analysis questions and writing assignments, which feature cross references from the questions back to the Guide and Reference sections of the book. These readings, and the questions that follow them, are designed to help students more deeply consider and use the major genres in *How to Write Anything*.

A Flexible Writing Process

Writers get started, develop ideas, and revise in different ways. *How to Write Anything* acknowledges this by asking students to think about their *own* process and what they need help with. Rather than merely walking them through a lockstep, linear writing sequence, the text encourages students to actively choose the order of topics that best fits their situation.

At the beginning of each Guide chapter, "How to Start" questions anticipate where students get stuck when writing and direct them to specific materials within the chapter for help. For example, one writer might need advice about finding a topic, while another will already have a topic but need help with audience, or developing or organizing ideas.

In this hyperlinked era, we know how important it is for supporting information to be intuitive, easy to find, and, above all, relevant and useful. With this in mind, the cross references between the Guide, Reference, and Reader sections target only the topics that students are most likely to need help with for the assignment at hand. The cross references' simple language and unobtrusive design result in clean, uncluttered pages that make it easy for students to find the exact help they need and to stay focused on their own writing. For a visual explanation of how these elements work, see the "How to Use This Book" tutorial on pages xlvi–xlvii.

Professional and Student Writing

How to Write Anything: A Guide and Reference with Readings contains over 80 readings, more than 30 in the Guide chapters and 50 in the Reader. Selections are carefully chosen to illustrate key principles and show how genres change in response to different contexts and audiences. Writers intuitively look to such models to understand patterns of composition or points of rhetoric, style, and mechanics. So every chapter in the Guide includes many complete examples of the genres under discussion, most of these texts annotated to show how they meet criteria set down in *How to Write Anything*. Each of the assignments offered at the end of these chapters is tied to a particular reading in the chapter, so students can use the sample texts both as models and as springboards for discussion and exploration.

Just as important, the models in *How to Write Anything* are approachable. The readings offered for each chapter of the book reveal the diversity of contemporary writing being done in these genres. Some represent the work of published professionals; others show how college students themselves have approached similar assignments. The student samples are especially inventive—chosen to motivate undergraduates to take comparable risks with their own writing. Together, the readings and exercises suggest to writers not just the rules for each genre, but also the many creative possibilities of working in these genres.

"How To" Visual Tutorials

Throughout the book, students will recognize a world they already live in, one which assumes that composing occurs in more than just words. But learning occurs in more than just words too. Savvy readers of telegraphic text messages and quick-cut visuals will no doubt appreciate the direct yet context-rich advice in the book's "How To" Visual Tutorials. Through drawings, photographs, and screen shots, these tutorials show step-by-step instructions for challenging topics, ranging from how to browse the Internet for ideas to how to cite a variety of materials in both MLA and APA formats.

The Visual Tutorials are just one example of *How to Write Anything*'s appealing visual style, a style well-suited to readers accustomed to blogging, texting, and using the Internet. The variety of illustrations and humorous visual commentary here can't help but draw readers in and keep them interested.

Invitation to Write

How to Write Anything was designed and edited to be compact and readable. But it retains a personal voice, frank and occasionally humorous, on the grounds that a textbook without character won't convince students that their own prose should have a style adapted to real audiences. And if some chapters operate like reference materials, they still aren't written coldly or dispassionately—not even the section on Common Errors.

So if *How to Write Anything* seems like an ambitious title, maybe it's because learning to write should be a heady enterprise, undertaken with confidence and optimism. Our hope is that this book will encourage students to grasp the opportunities that the writing affords and gain the satisfaction that comes from setting ideas (and words) into motion.

Acknowledgments

The following reviewers were very helpful through several drafts of this book:

Angela K. Albright, NorthWest Arkansas Community College; Glenn Blalock, Baylor University; Patricia Boyd, Arizona State University; Miriam Chirico, Eastern Connecticut State University; Ron Christiansen, Salt Lake Community College; Michelle Cox, Bridgewater State College; Mark Crane, Utah Valley State College; Anthony Edgington, University of Toledo; Caroline L. Eisner, University of Michigan; Jessica Fordham Kidd, University of Alabama; Maureen Fitzpatrick, Johnson County Community College; Hank Galmish, Green River Community College; John Gides, California State University–Northridge; Steffen Guenzel, The University of Alabama; Virginia Scott Hendrickson, Missouri State University; Lynn Lewis, University of Oklahoma; Leigh A. Martin, Community College of Rhode Island; Sandie McGill Barnhouse, Rowan-Cabarrus Community College; Miles McCrimmon, J. Sargeant Reynolds Community College; Erica Messenger, Bowling Green State University; Mary Ellen Muesing, University of North Carolina–Charlotte; Mark Reynolds, Jefferson Davis Community College; Bridget F. Ruetenik, Penn State Altoona; Wendy Sharer, East Carolina University; Marti Singer, Georgia State University; William H. Thelin, University of Akron; James G. Van Belle,

Edmonds Community College; Carol Westcamp, University of Arkansas–Fort Smith; Kelli Wood, El Paso Community College; and Mary K. Zacharias, San Jacinto College Central.

All books are collaborations, but we have never before worked on a project that more creatively drew upon the resources of an editorial team and publisher. *How to Write Anything* began with the confidence of Joan Feinberg, president of Bedford/St. Martin's, that we could develop a groundbreaking brief rhetoric. She had the patience to allow the idea to develop at its own pace and then assembled an incredible team to support it. We are grateful for the contributions of Denise Wydra, Editorial Director; Karen Henry, Editor in Chief; and Leasa Burton, Senior Executive Editor. We are also indebted to the designers who labored over *How to Write Anything* at greater length and with more care than we have ever seen in thirty years of publishing: Anna Palchik, Art Director and designer of the text; Deborah Baker, Senior Production Editor; and designer Nancy Goulet. Special thanks to Sarah Guariglia, who conceived the Visual Tutorials and took the photographs, and to Peter Arkle for his drawings. They all deserve credit for the distinctive and accessible visual style of *How to Write Anything*.

For their marketing efforts, we are grateful to the guidance offered by Karen Melton Soeltz, Karita dos Santos, and Molly Parke. And for all manner of tasks including art research, coordinating reviews, and permissions, we thank Melissa Cook.

But our greatest debt is to Ellen Darion, who was our splendid editor on this lengthy project: always confident about what we could accomplish, patient when chapters went off-track, and perpetually good-humored. If *How to Write Anything* works, it is because Ellen never wavered from our original high aspirations for the book. Her hand is in every chapter, every choice of reading, and every assignment. She and Leasa Burton also oversaw the complex design and created its splendid Visual Tutorials.

Finally, we are extraordinarily grateful to our former students whose papers or paragraphs appear in *How to Write Anything*. Their writing speaks for itself, but we have been inspired, too, by their personal dedication and character. These are the sort of students who motivate teachers, and so we are very proud to see their work published in *How to Write Anything*: Marissa

Dahlstrom, Manasi Deshpande, Micah T. Eades, Ryan Hailey, Wade Lamb, Cheryl Lovelady, Shane McNamee, Melissa Miller, Matthew Nance, Ricky Patel, Miles Pequeno, Heidi Rogers, Tobias Salinger, Kanaka Sathasivan, Scott Standley, and Annie Winsett.

John J. Ruszkiewicz
Jay Dolmage

Correlation to the Council of Writing Program Administrators' (WPA) Outcomes Statement

How to Write Anything helps students build proficiency in the four categories of learning that writing programs across the country use to assess their work: rhetorical knowledge; critical thinking, reading, and writing; writing processes; and knowledge of conventions. For a complete, detailed correlation to specific WPA outcomes, see the instructor's manual, *Teaching with How to Write Anything*, at bedfordstmartins.com/howtowrite.

Note on MLA Documentation

The MLA documentation in this book conforms to the *MLA Handbook for Writers of Research Papers*, Seventh Edition (2009). This guide for undergraduate and high school students was published in spring 2009.

Classroom and Professional Support

CompClass for How to Write Anything: A Guide and Reference with Readings <bedfordstmartins.com/compclass> is the first online course space shaped by the needs of composition students and instructors. In *CompClass*, students can read assignments, do their work, and see their grades all in one place; and instructors can easily monitor student progress and give feedback right away. Along with the *How to Write Anything e-Book*, *CompClass* comes preloaded with the innovative digital content that Bedford/St. Martin's is known for. To order *CompClass* packaged with *How to Write Anything: A Guide and Reference with Readings*, use ISBN-10: 0-312-61146-3/ISBN-13: 978-0-312-61146-0.

Re:Writing Plus <bedfordstmartins.com/rewritingplus> neatly gathers our collections of premium digital content into one online library for composition. Check out hundreds of model documents; *i•cite visualizing sources,* which brings research to life through animation, tutorials, and hands-on practice; and *Peer Factor,* the first ever peer-review game. New for January 2009: *VideoCentral,* where real writers talk about what it means to write at work, at school, and to change the world. Available stand-alone or packaged at a discount with the print book. To order *Re:Writing Plus* packaged with *How to Write Anything: A Guide and Reference with Readings,* use ISBN-10: 0-312-61079-3/ISBN-13: 978-0-312-61079-1.

How to Write Anything e-Book <bedfordstmartins.com/howtowrite> is available online, all the time. Easy to search and use, the e-book is integrated with all the free resources available on the book companion site. Available stand-alone or packaged for free with the print book. To order the *How to Write Anything: A Guide and Reference with Readings e-Book* packaged with the print book, use ISBN-10: 0-312-61147-1/ISBN-13: 978-0-312-61147-7.

Book Companion Site <bedfordstmartins.com/howtowrite> for *How to Write Anything: A Guide and Reference with Readings* includes a wealth of free resources, additional examples of the genres covered in the book, checklists for analyzing each genre, the complete instructor's manual, and more.

Teaching with HOW TO WRITE ANYTHING: A GUIDE AND REFERENCE WITH READINGS. Also available on the book companion site, the instructor's manual features sample syllabi, thorough coverage of each genre treated in the book, correlations to the Council of Writing Program Administrators' (WPA) Outcomes Statement, and more. Each chapter also includes teaching tips, suggestions for prompting class discussion, and additional writing activities and assignments.

Brief Contents

guide

reference

reader

Contents

guide

Part 1   Genres   2

2   Report   40

8   Rhetorical Analysis   222

Part 2   Special Assignments   252

9   Essay Examination   254

10   Position Paper   260

reference

reader

How to... Use this book

1 Use the book's inside front cover to find your assignment.

| 3 | Argument | 68 |

How to Write Anything

how to start

guide

need a form for your writing?
already got an assignment?

reference

need help getting started?

stuck in the middle?

want to improve your draft?

ready to revise?

2 Choose a place to start in the chapter.

How to start
- Need a **topic**? See page 74.

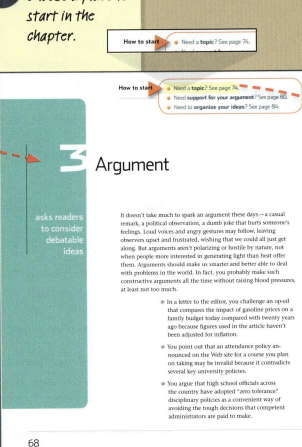

How to start
- Need a **topic**? See page 74.
- Need **support for your argument**? See page 80.
- Need to **organize your ideas**? See page 84.

3 Argument

asks readers to consider debatable ideas

It doesn't take much to spark an argument these days—a casual remark, a political observation, a dumb joke that hurts someone's feelings. Loud voices and angry gestures may follow, leaving observers upset and frustrated, wishing that we could all just get along. But arguments aren't polarizing or hostile by nature, not when people more interested in generating light than heat offer them. Arguments should make us smarter and better able to deal with problems in the world. In fact, you probably make such constructive arguments all the time without raising blood pressures, at least not too much.

- In a letter to the editor, you challenge an op-ed that compares the impact of gasoline prices on a family budget today compared with twenty years ago because figures used in the article haven't been adjusted for inflation.

- You point out that an attendance policy announced on the Web site for a course you plan on taking may be invalid because it contradicts several key university policies.

- You argue that high school officials across the country have adopted "zero tolerance" disciplinary policies as a convenient way of avoiding the tough decisions that competent administrators are paid to make.

68

3 Find your starting point.

▶ topic

4 Follow links to chapters with more help.

You are here!

Exploring purpose and topic

▶ topic

In a college assignment, you could be asked to write an argument or be given a topic area to explore, but you probably won't be told what your claim should be. That decision has to come from you, drawing on your knowledge, experiences, and inclinations. So choose topics about which you genuinely care—not issues routinely defined in the media as controversial. You'll likely do a more credible job defending your choice *not* to wear a helmet when cycling than explaining, one more time, why the environment should concern us all. And if environmental matters do roil you, stake your claim on a specific ecological problem—perhaps from within your community—that you might actually change by the power of your rhetoric. ○

If you really are stumped, the Yahoo Directory's list of "Issues and Causes"—with topics from *abortion* to *zoos*—offers problems enough to keep both liberal Susan Sarandon *and* conservative Jon Voight busy to the end of the century. To find it, click on "Society and Culture" on the site's main Web directory (http://dir.yahoo.com). ("Society and Culture" itself offers a menu of intriguing topic areas.) Once you have an issue or even a specific claim, you'll need to work it like bread dough.

Arguments take many different forms, but finger-pointing is rarely a good persuasive tool.

get an idea
p. 308

17 Brainstorming

find a topic/
get an idea

A great deal of thinking occurs at the beginning of a project or assignment. How exactly will you fill ten or twenty pages with your thoughts on Incan architecture, the life cycle of dung beetles, or what you did last summer? What hasn't already been written about religion in America, cattle in Africa, or the cultural hegemony of iTunes? What do you do when you find yourself clueless or stuck or just overwhelmed by the possibilities—or lack thereof? Simple answer: Brainstorm.

Put a notion on the table and see where it goes—and what you might do with it or learn about it. Toy with an idea like a kitten with a catnip mouse. Push yourself to think through, around, over, and under a proposition. Dare to be politically incorrect or, alternatively, so conventional that your good behavior might scare even your elders.

But don't think of brainstorming as disordered and muddled. Consider the metaphor itself: Storms are awesomely organized events. They generate power by physical processes so complex that we're just beginning to understand them. Similarly, a first-rate brainstorming session spins ideas from the most complex chemistry in our bodies, the tumult of the human brain.

Naturally, you'll match brainstorming techniques to the type of writing you hope to produce. Beginning a personal tale about a trip to Wrigley Field, you might make a list of sensory details to jog your memory—the smell of hot dogs, the catcalls of fans, the green

guide

Genres

part one

Need a form that you don't see here? Try "Special Assignments," p. 252.

How to start
- Need a **topic**? See page 9.
- Need to choose the right **details**? See page 12.
- Need to **organize the events** in your story? See page 14.

1 Narrative

describes events in people's lives

You may never have been asked to write a narrative, but chances are you've shared bits and pieces of your life story in writing. In doing so, you've written personal narratives. *Personal* does not necessarily mean you're baring your soul. Instead, it implies that you're telling a story from a unique perspective, providing details only you could know and insights only you could have.

- You want more people to think about bicycling to work, so you share your own experiences as an urban cyclist.

- Your application for a scholarship must include a personal statement of no more than five hundred words explaining how your life has prepared you for a career as a pharmacist.

- To work at the campus writing center, you prepare a literacy biography explaining your own experiences with writing and language.

- Your insurance company demands a detailed explanation of your most recent traffic accident— the one involving your mother's Caravan and a Starbucks that formerly served your neighborhood.

- A community group is collecting stories about the lives of local citizens, past and present, and you decide to tell your grandparents' story.

UNDERSTANDING NARRATIVES.   Narratives may describe almost any human activity that writers choose to share with readers: school, family, work experiences, personal tragedies, travel, sports, growing up, relationships, and so on. Stories can be told in words or through other media, including photographs, film, songs, cartoons, and more. Expect a narrative you write to do the following.

Tell a story.   In a narrative, something usually happens. Maybe all you do in the paper is reflect on a single moment when something peculiar caught your attention. Or your story could follow a simple sequence of events—the classic road-trip script. Or you might spin a tale complicated enough to seem like an actual plot, with a connected beginning, middle, and end. In every case, though, you need to select specific events that serve your purpose in writing, whatever it may be. Otherwise you're just rambling.

StoryCorps Story-Booth   StoryCorps is a national project of Sound Portraits Productions meant to inspire people to record one another's stories in sound. Photo of the Story-Corps StoryBooth, courtesy of StoryCorps. Learn more at www.storycorps.net.

Make a point—usually.   Your point may depend on your specific reason for writing a narrative. If your insurance agent asks about your recent auto wreck, she probably just wants to know who hit whom and how you are involved in the incident. But most narratives will be less cut-and-dry and more reflective, enabling you to connect with audiences more subtly—to amuse, enlighten, and, perhaps, even to change them. ○ Some narratives are therapeutic too, enabling you to confront personal issues or to get a weight off your chest.

Observe details closely.   What makes a narrative memorable and brings it to life are its details—the colors, shapes, textures, sounds, and smells that you convey to readers through language or other media. Those physical impressions go a long way toward convincing readers that a story is credible and honest. They assure readers that you were close enough to an experience to have an insider's perspective. So share your reactions with readers, conveying specific information as events unfurl. But don't fall back on clichés to make your points. Give readers evidence that the story really belongs to you.

Sara Smith, a college student, keeps a journal both to explore ideas that are important to her and so skill have a reservoir of events and memories for writing assignments. Does this journal entry suggest any paper topics to you?

My Dad friended me last night. How lame is that? Last month he didn't know how to send an e-mail and all of a sudden he has his own page on Facebook. It's really sad, it's worse than sad, it's pathetic. He's lonely. Has no friends. So he puts up a picture of us — a father and his very happy daughter, both with the Albert Einstein crazy hair except his is grey and mine is brown, both beaming — to show people what a good family guy he is. There should be an age limit or something, for Facebook.

develop a thesis
p. 336

Wall Street Journal columnist Peggy Noonan uses narrative to introduce her argument that Americans need a common language to ensure they can work out problems together. More than just an opening anecdote, the personal narrative is key to her argument—it both engages readers and raises the issue of a single national language above mere politics. In particular, note how Noonan's descriptive details shift as her story of a meeting on a city street develops.

From "We Need to Talk"

Peggy Noonan

July 6, 2007

It is late afternoon in Manhattan on the Fourth of July, and I'm walking along on Lexington and 59th, in front of Bloomingdale's. Suddenly in my sight there's a young woman standing on a street grate. She is short, about 5 feet tall, and stocky, with a broad brown face. She is, I think, Latin American, maybe of Indian blood. She has a big pile of advertisements in her hand, and puts one toward me. "MENS SUITS NEW YORK—40% to 60% Off Sale!—Armani, Canali, Hugo Boss, DKNY, Zegna. TAILOR ON PREMISES. EXCELLENT SERVICE. LARGE SELECTION." Then the address and phone number.

> Uses factual details to describe subject, a woman distributing advertising fliers.

You might have seen this person before. She's one of a small army of advertisement giver-outers in New York. Which means her life right now consists of standing in whatever weather and trying to give passersby a thing most of them don't want. If this is her regular job, she spends most of her time being rebuffed or ignored by busy people blurring by. You should always take an advertisement, or ten, from the advertisement giver-outers, just to give them a break, because once they give out all the ads, they can go back and get paid. So I took the ad and thanked her and walked on.

> Second paragraph provides contextual information and describes a simple action.

And then, half a block later, I turned around. I thought of a woman I'd met recently who had gone through various reverses in life and now had a new job, as a clerk in the back room of a store. She was happy to

> Turning around marks a shift in thought and action.

have it, a new beginning. But there was this thing: They didn't want to pay for air conditioning, so she sweltered all day. This made her want to weep, just talking about it. Ever since that conversation, I have been so grateful for my air conditioning. I had forgotten long ago to be grateful for it.

Anyway, I look back at the woman on the street grate. It's summer and she's in heavy jeans and a black sweatshirt with a hood. On top of that, literally, she's wearing a sandwich board—MENS SUITS NEW YORK. Her hair is long and heavy, her ponytail limp on her shoulders. She's out here on a day when everybody else, as she well knows—the streets are not crowded—is at a ball game or the beach. Everyone else is off.

So I turned around and went back. I wanted to say something—I don't know what, find out where she was from, encourage her. I said hello, and she looked at me and I patted her arm and said, "Happy Fourth of July, my friend." She was startled and then shy, and she smiled and made a sound, and I realized: She doesn't speak English. "God bless you," I said, because a little while in America and you know the word *God* just as ten minutes in Mexico and you learn the word *Dios*. And we both smiled and nodded and I left.

I went into Bloomingdale's and wrote these words: "We must speak the same language so we can hearten each other."

The question of whether America should have an "official language," of whether English should be formally declared our "national language," is bubbling, and will be back, in Congress, the next few sessions.

Exploring purpose and topic

Writing a narrative on your own, you usually don't have to search for a topic. You know what events you want to record in a journal or diary or what part of your life you want to share in e-mails with friends. You'll know your audience well enough, too, to tune your story to the people likely to read it.

Assigned to write a narrative in school, you face different choices. Typically, such an assignment directs you to narrate an event that has changed or shaped you. Or perhaps an instructor requests a story that explores an aspect of your personality or reveals something about the communities to which you belong. Consider the following strategies when no topic ideas present themselves.

topic ◀

Brainstorm, freewrite, build lists, and use memory prompts to find a topic for a narrative. Talk with others, too, about their choices of subjects or share ideas on a class Web site. Trading ideas might jog your own memory about an incident or moment worth retelling.

Choose a manageable subject. You may be drawn to those life-changing events so obvious they seem cliché: deaths, graduations, car wrecks, winning hits, or first love. But understand that to make such topics work, you have to make them fresh for readers who've likely under-gone similar experiences—or seen the movie. If you find an angle on such familiar events that belong specifically to you and can express it originally, you might take the risk. ⭕

Alternatively, you can opt to narrate a slice of life rather than the whole side of beef—your toast at a wedding rather than the three-hour reception, a single encounter on a road trip rather than the entire cross-country adven-ture, or the scariest part of the night you were home alone when the power went out, rather than a minute-by-minute description. Beginning with your general topic, mine it for the dozens of more manageable stories within.

get an idea
p. 308

Understanding your audience

People like to read other people's stories, so the audiences for narratives are large, diverse, and receptive. (Even many diarists secretly hope that someone someday will find and read the confidential story of their lives.) Most of these eager readers probably expect a narrative to make some point or reveal an insight. Typically, they hope to be moved by the piece, to learn something from it, or perhaps to be amused by it.

You can capitalize on those expectations, using stories to introduce ideas that readers might be less open to if presented more formally (see Peggy Noonan's "We Need to Talk," p. 7).

Sometimes, however, your audience is quite specific. For instance, people within well-defined social, political, ethnic, or religious groups often write to share the experiences of their lives. Women and members of minority groups have used such narratives to document the adversities they face or to affirm their solidarity. Similarly, members of religious groups recall what it was like to grow up Jewish or Catholic or Baptist—and their readers appreciate when a story hits a familiar note. Of course, the best of these personal narratives often attract readers from outside the target audience too. ○

Of course, you might decide finally that the target audience of a narrative is yourself. Even then, be demanding. Think about how your story might sound ten or twenty years from now. Whatever the audience, you have choices to make.

A Classic Narrative Arc
You'll need to decide where to start your story and where to stop. The plan shown in this illustration is effective because the action unfolds in a way that meets audience expectations.

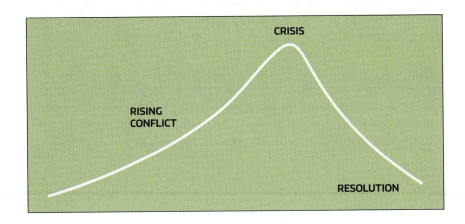

CRISIS

RISING CONFLICT

RESOLUTION

respect your readers
p. 374

Select events that will keep readers engaged.   Consider what parts of your topic will matter to readers. Which events represent high points in the action or moments that could not logically be omitted? Select those and consider cutting the others. Build toward a few major moments in the story that support one or two key themes.

Pace the story effectively.   Readers do want the story to move ahead, but not always at the same speed. Early on, they may want to learn about the characters involved in the action or to be introduced to the setting. You can slow the narrative to fill in these details and also to set up expectations for what will follow. For instance, if a person plays a role later in the story, introduce him or her briefly in the early paragraphs. If a cat matters, show the cat. But don't dwell on incidentals: Keep the story moving.

Tailor your writing to your intended readers.   An informal story written for peers may need brisk action as well as slang and dialogue to sound convincing—though you shouldn't use rough language for cheap effects. In a narrative written for an academic audience, you should slow the pace and use neutral language. But don't be too cautious. You still want the story to have enough texture to make your experiences seem authentic.

For instance, when writing a personal statement for an application to an academic program, keep a tight rein on the way you present yourself. O Here, for example, is a serious anecdote offered in an application to graduate school. You could easily imagine it told much more comically to friends.

> During my third year of Russian, I auditioned for the role of the evil stepsister Anna in a stage production of *Zolushka*. Although I welcomed the chance to act, I was terrified because I could not pronounce a Russian *r*. I had tried but was only able to produce an embarrassing sputter. Leading up to the play, I practiced daily with my professor, repeating "ryba" with a pencil in my mouth. When the play opened, I was able to say "*Kakoe urodstvo!*" with confidence. This experience gave me tremendous pride, because through it I discovered the power to isolate a problem, seek the necessary help, and ultimately solve it. I want to pass this power along to others by becoming a Russian language instructor.
>
> —Melissa Miller

refine your tone
p. 374

Finding and developing materials

▶ develop
details

When you write about an event soon after it occurs—for instance, an accident report for an insurance claim—you might have the facts fresh in mind. Yet even in such cases, evidence helps back up your recollections. That's why insurance companies encourage drivers to carry a disposable camera in their cars in case they have a collision. The photo freezes details that human memory, especially under pressure, could ignore or forget. Needless to say, when writing about events in the more distant past, other memory prompts will help.

Consult documents.   A journal, if you keep one, provides a handy record for personal narratives such as a job history or family chronicle. Even a daily planner or PDA (personal digital assistant) might hold the necessary facts to reconstruct a series of events: Just knowing when certain meetings occurred jogs your thinking.

Consult images.   Photographs and videos provide material for personal narratives of all sorts. Not only do they document people and places, but they may also generate ideas, calling to mind far more than just what appears in the images. In writing a personal narrative, such prompts may stimulate your memory about past events and, just as important, the feelings those events generated. Visual images also remind you of the physical details—the shapes, colors, and textures—that add authenticity to a narrative and assure readers you're a sharp observer.

Trust your experiences.   In gathering materials for a narrative (or searching for a subject), you may initially be skeptical about your credentials for the assignment: you might think, "What have I done worth writing about"? ⭘ Most people underestimate their own expertise. First-year college students, for example, are usually experts about high school or certain kinds of music or hanging out at the mall or dealing with difficult parents. You don't have to be a celebrity to observe life or have something to say about it.

find a topic
p. 308

Here's humorist David Sedaris—who's made a career writing about his very middle-class life from his unique personal perspective—describing the problem:

> When I was teaching—I taught for a while—my students would write as if they were raised by wolves. Or raised on the streets. They were middle-class kids and they were ashamed of their background. They felt like unless they grew up in poverty, they had nothing to write about. Which was interesting because I had always thought that poor people were the ones who were ashamed. But it's not. It's middle-class people who are ashamed of their lives. And it doesn't really matter what your life was like, you can write about anything. It's just the writing of it that is the challenge. I felt sorry for these kids, that they thought that their whole past was absolutely worthless because it was less than remarkable.

—David Sedaris, interviewed in *January Magazine*, June 2000

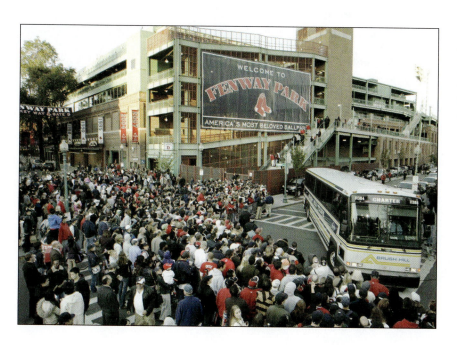

Photographs such as this one taken at a celebration after the Boston Red Sox won the 2007 World Series may recall not only the scene but also the moment the photo was taken, who was there, and so on.

Creating a structure

▶ organize
events

Don't be intimidated by the idea of organizing a narrative. ⭕ You know a great deal about narrative structure from watching films or TV. All the complex plot devices you see in dramas or comedies—from foreshadowing to flashback, even to telling a story backward (as in the film *Memento*)—can be adapted to narratives you create in prose. But you need to plan ahead, know how many words or pages you have to tell your story, and then be sure you connect your incidents with effective transitional words and phrases.

Consider a simple sequence.   In a simple sequence, one event follows another chronologically. This structure has its complications, but it's a natural choice for narrative. Journals and diaries probably have the simplest sequential structures, with writers just recording one event after another without connecting them by anything much more than a date.

> First event
>
> Next event
>
> Next event
>
> Final event

Build toward a climax.   Narratives become much more complex if you want to present a set of incidents that lead to a *climax* or an *epiphany*. A climax is the moment when the action of a story peaks, takes an important turn, or is resolved. An epiphany is a moment of revelation when a writer or character suddenly sees events in a new light.

> First event
>
> Next event
>
> Next event
>
> Climax and/or epiphany
>
> Final event

connect ideas
p. 350

Narratives can have both structural features and often do—it's only logical that a major event in life would trigger heightened awareness or new understanding. In creating a structure for this kind of narrative, you can begin by deciding what that important event will be and then choosing other elements and incidents that lead up to or explain it. Everything not connected to that moment should probably be cut from the story. O

Similarly, when you want a narrative to make a specific point, include only events and incidents that reinforce your theme, directly or indirectly. Cut any actions that don't contribute to that point, however much you love them. Or refocus your narrative on the moment you do love.

Use images to tell a story.   In some cases, you may use images to accompany your narrative or to illustrate a sequence of events. O An illustrated timeline is a simple form of this kind of narrative, as are baby books or yearbooks. More complex stories about your life or community can be told by combining your words and pictures in photo-essays or other media productions.

Fisherman with His Catch, a 32-inch, 18-pound Striped Bass   Note how the photograph conveys far more than the numerical statistics alone would.

revise for details
p. 386

think visually
p. 500

Choosing a style and design

Narratives are usually written in middle or low styles. That's because both styles nicely mimic the human voice through devices such as contractions and colloquialisms. Both styles are also comfortable with *I*, the point of view of many stories. A middle style may work in reaching academic or professional audiences. But a low style, dipping into slang and unconventional speech, can more accurately capture many moments in life and so feel more authentic. It's your choice.

Style is important because narratives get their energy and textures from sentence structures and vocabulary choices. In general, narratives require tight but evocative language — *tight* to keep the action moving, *evocative* to capture the gist of events. In a first draft, run with your ideas and don't do much editing. Flesh out the skeleton as you have designed it and then go back to see that the story works technically: Characters should be introduced and developed, locations identified and colored, events clearly explained and sequenced, key points made memorably and emphatically. You'll likely need several drafts to get these major items into shape.

Then look at your language and allow plenty of time for it. Begin with Chapter 32, "Vigorous, Clear, Economical Style." When you get the language right, your readers get the impression that you have observed events closely. Here are some options for your narrative.

Need help seeing the big picture? See "How to Revise Your Work" on pp. 390–91.

Don't hesitate to use first person—*I*. Most personal narratives are about the writer and so use first-person pronouns without apology. ○ (Third-person perspective tends to be used by essayists and humorists.)

A narrative often must take readers where the *I* has been, and using the first-person pronoun helps make writing authentic. Consider online journalist Michael Yon's explanation of why he reports on the Iraq War using *I* rather than a more objective third-person perspective:

> I write in first person because I am actually there at the events I write about. When I write about the bombs exploding, or the smell of blood, or the bullets snapping by, and I say *I*, it's because I was there. Yesterday a sniper shot at us, and seven of my neighbors were injured by a large bomb. These

are my neighbors. These are soldiers. . . . I feel the fire from the explosions, and am lucky, very lucky, still to be alive. Everything here is first person.

−Glenn Reynolds, *An Army of Davids*

Use figures of speech such as similes, metaphors, and analogies to make memorable comparisons. *Similes* make comparisons by using *like* or *as: He used his camera* like *a rifle. Metaphors* drop the *like* or *as* to gain even more power: *His camera was a rifle aimed at enemies.* An *analogy* extends the comparison: *His camera became a rifle aimed at his imaginary enemies, their private lives in his crosshairs.*

People use comparisons eagerly, some so common they've been reduced to invisible clichés: *hit me like a ton of bricks; dumb as an ox; clear as a bell.* Use similes and metaphors in a narrative fresher than these and yet not contrived or strained. Here's science writer Michael Chorost effortlessly using both a metaphor (*spins up*) and a simile (*like riding a roller coaster*) to describe what he experiences as he awaits surgery.

I can feel the bustle and clatter around me as the surgical team spins up to take-off speed. It is like riding a roller coaster upward to the first great plunge, strapped in and committed.

−*Rebuilt: How Becoming Part Computer Made Me More Human*

In choosing verbs, favor active rather than passive voice. Active verbs propel the action (*Agnes signed the petition*) while passive verbs slow it down by an unneeded word or two (*The petition was signed by Agnes*). ⭕

Since narratives are all about movement, build sentences around strong and unpretentious verbs. Edit until you get down to the bone of the action and produce sentences as effortless as these from Joseph Epstein, describing the pleasures of catching plagiarists. ⭕ Verbs are highlighted in this passage; you'll find only one passive verb *is followed* in the mix.

In thirty years of teaching university students I never encountered a case of plagiarism, or even one that I suspected. Teachers I've known who have caught students in this sad act report that the capture gives one an odd sense of power. The power derives from the authority that resides behind the word *gotcha*. This is followed by that awful moment—a veritable sadist's

improve your sentences
p. 378

avoid plagiarism
p. 431

Mardi Gras—when one calls the student into one's office and points out the odd coincidence that he seems to have written about existentialism in precisely the same words Jean-Paul Sartre used fifty-two years earlier.

—"Plagiary, It's Crawling All Over Me," *Weekly Standard*, March 6, 2006

> The difference between the almost right word and the right word is really a large matter—it's the difference between the lightning bug and the lightning.

—Mark Twain

Use powerful and precise modifiers.   In most cases, one strong word is better than several weaker ones (*freezing* rather than *very cold*; *doltish* rather than *not very bright*).   ◉ Done right, proper modifiers can even make you hungry.

My friend Barbara got the final stretch of the trip, a southwestern route of burritos and more burritos: with and without rice, with and without sour cream, planned burritos and serendipitous burritos.

We pulled off the highway near Odessa, Texas, to hunt down a Taco Villa and, across the street, espied something called JumBurrito, an even smaller Texas chain. Taco Villa's grilled chicken burrito had a profusion of chicken that indeed tasted grilled, while JumBurrito's combination burrito redeemed dull beef with vibrant avocado.

Neither approximated the majesty of the burrito I loved most, which I ate in Dallas, at a Taco Cabana. A great burrito is a balancing act, and the proportions of ground beef, beans, sour cream, and diced tomatoes in Taco Cabana's plump, heavy Burrito Ultimo (three Wet Naps) were spot on.

—Frank Bruni, "Life in the Fast-Food Lane," *New York Times*, May 24, 2006

Use dialogue to propel the narrative and to give life to your characters.   What people say and how they say it can reveal a great deal about them without much commentary from you. But be sure the words your characters speak sound natural: *No* dialogue is better than awkward dialogue. Dialogue ordinarily requires quotation marks and new paragraphs for each change of speaker. But keep the tags simple: You don't have to vary much from *he said* or *she said*.

"My dear Mr. Bennet," said his lady to him one day, "have you heard that Netherfield Park is let at last?"

Mr. Bennet replied that he had not.

"But it is," returned she; "for Mrs. Long has just been here, and she told me all about it."

Mr. Bennet made no answer.

improve your sentences
p. 378

"Do not you want to know who has taken it?" cried his
wife, impatiently.
"*You* want to tell me, and I have no objection to hearing it."
This was invitation enough.

–Jane Austen, *Pride and Prejudice*

**If you are using dialogue —
say it aloud as you write it.
Only then will it have the
sound of speech.**
—John Steinbeck

Develop major characters through language *and* action.   Search for
the precise adjectives and adverbs to describe their looks (*cheery, greedily*)
and their manners (*tight, conceitedly, smarmy*) or, even better, have them
reveal their natures by their actions (*glancing in every mirror; ignoring the staff
to fawn over the bigwigs*). In fact, you'll probably need to do both. Here's how
one writer describes a classmate (ouch!) with whom she is partnered on a
group project:

> Jane dragged me to her dorm one weekend to help her crunch the
> numbers. Her phone started ringing, but she told me to ignore it. The
> answering machine clicked on as a whiny, southern voice pleaded, "Jane,
> honey, where *are* yew? Daddy and I have been trying to reach you for three
> days, but you haven't answered your dorm or cell phones. Please, call us
> so we'll know that you're okay. We love you very much, Sweetie."
>   Jane's annoyance rivaled the desperation in her mother's voice. She
> had always claimed to love her family, but she barely batted an eye at her
> mom's concern for her well-being. "I don't have time for her right now,"
> Jane stated coldly as she continued typing.
>
> –Bettina Ramon, "Ambition Incarnate"

Develop the setting to set the context and mood.   Show readers
where and when events are occurring if the setting makes a difference—and
that will be most of the time. Location (Times Square; dusty street in Gallup,
New Mexico; your bedroom), as well as climate and time of day (cool dawn,
exotic dusk, broiling afternoon), will help readers get a fix on the story. But
don't churn out paragraphs of description just for their own sake; readers
will skate right over them. Consider, too, whether photographs attached to
the narrative might help readers grasp the setting and situation. Don't use
images as an excuse to avoid writing; rather, consider how they complement
text, and so may have a legitimate place in your story. **O**

think visually
p. 500

Examining models

LITERACY NARRATIVE   Such a piece typically narrates the processes by which a person learns to read or write or acquires an intellectual skill or ability. In "Strange Tools," author Richard Rodriguez explains how he developed his habits of reading. The selection is from *Hunger of Memory* (1981), in which Rodriguez explains how his life has followed the pattern of "the scholarship boy," described by Richard Hoggart as a youth from a lower-class background whose pursuit of education separates him from his community.

Strange Tools

RICHARD RODRIGUEZ

Sets the scene.

From an early age I knew that my mother and father could read and write both Spanish and English. I had observed my father making his way through what, I now suppose, must have been income tax forms. On other occasions I waited apprehensively while my mother read onion-paper letters airmailed from Mexico with news of a relative's illness or death. For both my parents, however, reading was something done out of necessity and as quickly as possible. Never did I see either of them read an entire book. Nor did I see them read for pleasure. Their reading consisted of work manuals, prayer books, newspapers, recipes.

Richard Hoggart imagines how, at home,

> . . . [The scholarship boy] sees strewn around, and reads regularly himself, magazines which are never mentioned at school, which seem not to belong to the world to which the school introduces him; at school he hears about and reads books never mentioned at home. When he brings those books into the house they do not take their place with other books which the family are reading, for often there are none or almost none; his books look, rather, like strange tools.

Hoggart's "scholarship boy" is a key theme in Rodriguez's work.

In our house each school year would begin with my mother's careful instruction: "Don't write in your books so we can sell them at the end of the year." The remark was echoed in public by my teachers, but only in part: "Boys and girls, don't write in your books. You must learn to treat them with great care and respect."

OPEN THE DOORS OF YOUR MIND WITH BOOKS, read the red and white poster over the nun's desk in early September. It soon was apparent to me that reading was the classroom's central activity. Each course had its own book. And the information gathered from a book was unquestioned. READ TO LEARN, the sign on the wall advised in December. I privately wondered: What was the connection between reading and learning? Did one learn something only by reading it? Was an idea only an idea if it could be written down? In June, CONSIDER BOOKS YOUR BEST FRIENDS. Friends? Reading was, at best, only a chore. I needed to look up whole paragraphs of words in a dictionary. Lines of type were dizzying, the eye having to move slowly across the page, then down, and across. . . .The sentences of the first books I read were coolly impersonal. Toned hard. What most bothered me, however, was the isolation reading required. To console myself for the loneliness I'd feel when I read, I tried reading in a very soft voice. Until: "Who is doing all that talking to his neighbor?" Shortly after, remedial reading classes were arranged for me with a very old nun.

At the end of each school day, for nearly six months, I would meet with her in the tiny room that served as the school's library but was actually only a storeroom for used textbooks and a vast collection of *National Geographics*. Everything about our sessions pleased me: the smallness of the room; the noise of the janitor's broom hitting the edge of the long hallway outside the door; the green of the sun, lighting the wall; and the old woman's face blurred white with a beard. Most of the time we took turns. I began with my elementary text. Sentences of astonishing simplicity seemed to me lifeless and drab: "The boys ran from the rain. . . . She wanted to sing. . . . The kite rose in the blue." Then the old nun would read from her favorite books, usually biographies of early American presidents. Playfully she ran through complex sentences, calling the words alive with her voice, making it seem that the author somehow was speaking directly to me. I smiled just to listen to her. I sat there and sensed for the very first time some possibility of fellowship between a reader and a writer, a communication, never *intimate* like that I heard spoken words at home convey, but one nonetheless *personal*.

One day the nun concluded a session by asking me why I was so reluctant to read by myself. I tried to explain; said something about the way written words made me feel all alone—almost, I wanted to add but didn't, as when I spoke to myself in a room just emptied of furniture. She studied my face as I spoke; she seemed to be watching more than listening. In an uneventful voice she replied that I had nothing to fear. Didn't I realize that reading would open up whole new worlds? A book could open doors for me. It could introduce me to people and show me places I never imagined existed. She gestured toward the bookshelves. (Bare-breasted African women danced, and the shiny hubcaps of automobiles on the back covers of the *Geographic* gleamed in my mind.) I listened with respect. But her words were not very influential. I was thinking then of another consequence of literacy, one I was too shy to admit but nonetheless trusted. Books were going to make me "educated." *That* confidence enabled me, several months later, to overcome my fear of the silence.

In fourth grade I embarked upon a grandiose reading program. "Give me the names of important books," I would say to startled teachers. They soon found out that I had in mind "adult books." I ignored their suggestion of anything I suspected was written for children. (Not until I was in college, as a result, did I read *Huckleberry Finn* or *Alice's Adventures in Wonderland.*) Instead, I read *The Scarlet Letter* and Franklin's *Autobiography*. And whatever I read I read for extra credit. Each time I finished a book, I reported the achievement to a teacher and basked in the praise my effort earned. Despite my best efforts, however, there seemed to be more and more books I needed to read. At the library I would literally tremble as I came upon whole shelves of books I hadn't read. So I read and I read and I read: *Great Expectations*; all the short stories of Kipling; *The Babe Ruth Story*; the entire first volume of the *Encyclopaedia Britannica* (A–ANSTEY); the *Iliad*; *Moby-Dick*; *Gone with the Wind*; *The Good*

> Most action occurs in Rodriguez's thoughts.

Earth; Remond; Forever Amber; The Lives of the Saints; Crime and Punishment; The Pearl. . . . Librarians who initially frowned when I checked out the maximum ten books at a time started saving books they thought I might like. Teachers would say to the rest of the class, "I only wish the rest of you took reading as seriously as Richard obviously does."

But at home I would hear my mother wondering, "What do you see in your books?" (Was reading a hobby like her knitting? Was so much reading even healthy for a boy? Was it the sign of "brains"? Or was it just a convenient excuse for not helping around the house on Saturday mornings?) Always, "What do you see . . . ?"

What *did* I see in my books? I had the idea that they were crucial for my academic success, though I couldn't have said exactly how or why. In the sixth grade I simply concluded that what gave a book its value was some major idea or theme it contained. If that core essence could be mined and memorized, I would become learned like my teachers. I decided to record in a notebook the themes of the books that I read. After reading *Robinson Crusoe,* I wrote that its theme was "the value of learning to live by oneself." When I completed *Wuthering Heights,* I noted the danger of "letting emotions get out of control." Rereading these brief moralistic appraisals usually left me disheartened. I couldn't believe that they were really the source of reading's value. But for many more years, they constituted the only means I had of describing to myself the educational value of books.

In spite of my earnestness, I found reading a pleasurable activity. I came to enjoy the lonely good company of books. Early on weekday mornings, I'd read in my bed. I'd feel a mysterious comfort then, reading in the dawn quiet—the bluegray silence interrupted by the occasional churning of the refrigerator motor a few rooms away or the more distant sound of a city bus beginning its run. On weekends I'd go to the public library to read, surrounded by old men and women. Or, if the weather was fine, I would take my books to the park and read in the shade of a tree. A warm summer evening was my favorite reading time. Neighbors would leave for vacation and I would water their lawns. I

Margin notes:

Growing skill as a reader causes conflict for Rodriguez.

Getting older, Rodriguez examines why he reads.

Rodriguez concludes by raising doubts about the skills he has acquired.

would sit through the twilight on the front porches or in backyards, reading to the cool, whirling sounds of the sprinklers.

I also had favorite writers. But often those writers I enjoyed most I was least able to value. When I read William Saroyan's *The Human Comedy,* I was immediately pleased by the narrator's warmth and the charm of his story. But as quickly I became suspicious. A book so enjoyable to read couldn't be very "important." Another summer I determined to read all the novels of Dickens. Reading his fat novels, I loved the feeling I got—after the first hundred pages—of being at home in a fictional world where I knew the names of the characters and cared about what was going to happen to them. And it bothered me that I was forced away at the conclusion, when the fiction closed tight, like a fortune-teller's fist—the futures of all the major characters neatly resolved. I never knew how to take such feelings of a novel's meaning. Still, there were pleasures to sustain me after I'd finish my books. Carrying a volume back to the library, I would be pleased by its weight. I'd run my fingers along the edge of the pages and marvel at the breadth of my achievement. Around my room, growing stacks of paperback books reinforced my assurance.

I entered high school having read hundreds of books. My habit of reading made me a confident speaker and writer of English. Reading also enabled me to sense something of the shape, the major concerns, of Western thought. (I was able to say something about Dante and Descartes and Engels and James Baldwin in my high school term papers.) In these various ways, books brought me academic success as I hoped that they would. But I was not a good reader. Merely bookish, I lacked a point of view when I read. Rather, I read in order to acquire a point of view. I vacuumed books for epigrams, scraps of information, ideas, themes—anything to fill the hollow within me and make me feel educated. When one of my teachers suggested to his drowsy tenth-grade English class that a person could not have a "complicated idea" until he had read at least two thousand books, I heard the remark without detecting either its irony or its very complicated truth. I merely determined to compile a list of all the books I had ever read. Harsh with myself, I included only once a title I might have read several times. (How, after all, could one read a book more than once?) And I included only those books over a hundred pages in length. (Could anything shorter be a book?)

There was yet another high school list I compiled. One day I came across a newspaper article about the retirement of an English professor at a nearby state college. The article was accompanied by a list of the "hundred most important books of Western Civilization." "More than anything else in my life," the professor told the reporter with finality, "these books have made me all that I am." That was the kind of remark I couldn't ignore. I clipped out the list and kept it for the several months it took me to read all of the titles. Most books, of course, I barely understood. While reading Plato's *Republic,* for instance, I needed to keep looking at the book jacket comments to remind myself what the text was about. Nevertheless, with the special patience and superstition of a scholarship boy, I looked at every word of the text. And by the time I reached the last word, relieved, I convinced myself that I had read *The Republic.* In a ceremony of great pride, I solemnly crossed Plato off my list.

MEMOIR   In the following essay, Miles Pequeno uses a narrative about a chess match to describe a changing relationship with his father. The paper was written in response to an assignment in an upper-division college writing class.

Pequeno 1

Miles Pequeno

Professor Mitchell

English 102

May 12, 20--

Check. Mate?

"Checkmate! Right? You can't move him anywhere, right? I got you again!" I couldn't control my glee. For good measure, I even grabbed my rook, which stood next to his king, and gave him a posthumous beating. The deposed king tumbled from the round table and onto the hardwood floor with a thud. The sound of sure victory. Being eight, it was easy to get excited about chess. It gave me not only at least a few minutes of Dad's attention and approval, but the comfort of knowing I'd taste victory every time. Either Dad was letting me always win, or I was the prodigy he wanted me to be. I always liked to believe it was the latter.

> Narrative opens with dialogue and action.

The relationship I had with my father was always complicated. I loved him and he loved me; that much was understood. But his idea of fatherhood was a little unorthodox (or maybe too orthodox, I'm not sure which). We didn't play catch in the yard, but he did make flash cards to teach me my multiplication tables when I was still in kindergarten. He didn't take me to Astros games, but he made sure I knew lots of big words from the newspaper. We were close, but only on his terms.

> Uses particular details to explain relationship with father.

Pequeno 2

Save for the ever-graying hair near his temples, he looks much the same now as he did when I was little: round belly, round face, and big brown eyes that pierced while they silently observed and inwardly critiqued. His black hair, coarse and thick, and day-or-two-old beard usually gave away his heritage. He came to our suburb of Houston from Mexico when he was a toddler, learned English watching Spider-Man cartoons, and has since spent his life catching up, constantly working at moving up in the world. Even more was expected of me, the extension of his hard work and dreams for the future. I had no idea at the time, but back when I was beating him at chess as a kid, I myself was a pawn. He was planning something.

Then a funny thing happened. After winning every game since age eight, the five-year win streak ended. I lost. This time, Dad had decided to take off the training wheels. Just as he was thrust into the real world unceremoniously with my birth when he was but eighteen years old, I was forced to grow up a little early, too. The message was clear: Nothing is being handed to you anymore, Son.

This abrupt lesson changed my outlook. I no longer wanted to make Dad proud; I wanted to equal or better him. I'd been conditioned to seek his attention and approval, and then the rug was pulled from beneath my feet. I awoke to the realization that it was now my job to prove that the student could become the teacher.

I spent time after school every day playing chess against the artificial intelligence of my little Windows 95 computer. I knew what problems I had to correct because Dad was sure to point them out in the days after forcing that first loss. I had trouble using my queen. Dad always either knocked her out early or made me too afraid to put her in play. The result was my king slaughtered time and time

---

Using first person, Pequeno draws on personal experience to describe and characterize father.

Notice how a metaphor here (*training wheels*) blossoms into an analogy about growing up.

Provides background information here important later in story.

Pequeno 3

again as his bride, the queen, sat idle on the far side of the board.

Our chess set was made of marble, with green and white hand-carved pieces sitting atop the thick, round board. Dad kept the set next to the TV and, most nights, we'd take it down from the entertainment center and put it on the coffee table in front of the sofa, where we sat side by side and played chess while halfway paying attention to the television. One night after Mom's spaghetti dinner, I casually walked into the living room to find Dad sitting sipping a Corona and watching the Rockets game. Hakeem Olajuwon was having a great night. Usually, if Dad was really into something on TV, we'd go our separate ways and maybe play later. This night, I picked up the remote control from the coffee table. Off.

"Let's play," I said resolutely. I grabbed the marble chess set, with all the pieces exactly where I had put them in anticipation of this game. The board seemed heavier than usual, carrying it to the coffee table. I sat down next to him on the sofa and stared at the pieces, suddenly going blank. The bishops might as well have been knights. I froze as Dad asked me what color I wanted. Traditionally, this had been merely a formality. I'd always picked white before because I wanted to have the first move. That was the rule: *White moves first, green next.*

"Green."

Then it all came back to me. The certainty of my declaration surprised him. He furrowed his brows slightly and leaned back just enough to show good-natured condescension.

"You sure? That means I go first."

"I'm sure. Take white."

So he began his attack. He started off controlling one side of the board, slowly advancing. The knights led the charge, with the

> Paragraph sets the physical scene for climactic chess match.

> First dialogue since opening signals rising action.

> "Combat" metaphor in next few paragraphs moves story forward.

Pequeno 4

pawns waiting in the wings to form an impenetrable wall around the royal family, who remained in their little castle of two adjacent spaces.

Every move was made with painful precision. Now and then after my moves, he'd sigh and sink a little into the sofa. He'd furrow those big black brows, his eyes darting quickly from one side of the board to the other, thinking two or three moves ahead. Some of his mannerisms this time were completely new, like the hesitation of his hand as he'd reach for a piece and then jerk it back quickly, realizing that my strategy had shut more than a few doors for him.

Eventually I worked up the courage to thrust the queen into action. She moved with great trepidation at first, never attacking, merely sneaking down the board. In the meantime, Dad's advancing rooks and knights were taking out my line of pawns, which I'd foolishly put too far into play. Every risk either of us took was clearly calculated. Sometimes he'd mutter to himself, slowly realizing this game wasn't as usual.

Things were looking good. Even if I didn't win, I'd already won a victory by challenging him. But that wasn't what I had practiced for. It wasn't why I'd turned off the television, and it certainly wasn't why I was concentrating so hard on these white-and-green figurines.

I was locked in. This was more than father and son. This was an epic battle between generals who knew each other well enough to keep the other at bay. But I was advancing. Sure, there were losses, but that was the cost of war. I had a mission.

My queen finally reached his king unharmed.

"Check."

I uttered the word silently. As the game had progressed, gaining intensity and meaning, there was no conversation. In its place were sporadic comments, muttered with deference. So when I said

Another extended analogy.

Pequeno 5

"check," I made sure not to make a big deal of it. I said it quietly, softly. I didn't want to jinx myself with bragging, and I certainly didn't want to get too excited and break my own concentration. As his king scrambled for a safe hiding place my knights continued their advance. I had planned for this stage of the game several moves before, which was apparently at least one move more than Dad was thinking ahead. Check again. More scrambling, and another check. It seemed I had him cornered. Then. . . .

"Check." It wasn't the first time I had him in check, and I didn't expect it to be the last in this game.

"Mate," he whispered, faint hints of a smile beginning to show on the corners of his mouth, pushing his cheeks up slightly. I hadn't realized that I had won until he conceded defeat with that word. Raising his eyebrows, he leaned back into the cushion of the sofa. He looked a little tired.

"Mate?" I wasn't sure he was right. I didn't let myself believe it until I stared at these little marble men. Sure enough, his desperate king was cornered.

"Good game, Son."

And that was it. There was his approval right there, manifesting itself in that smile that said "I love you" and "you sneaky son of a bitch" at the same time. But I didn't feel like any more of a man than I had an hour before. In fact, I felt a little hollow. So I just kept my seat next to him, picked up the remote control again, and watched the Rockets finish off the Mavericks. Business as usual after that. I went back to my room and did some homework, but kept the chess game at the forefront of my mind.

Note that story climax occurs mostly through dialogue.

Father's smile signals change in father-son relationship.

Pequeno 6

"Wait a second. Had he let me win? Damn it, I'd worked so hard just for him to toy with me again, even worse than when he'd let me beat him before. No, there's no way he let me win. Or maybe he did. I don't know."

I walked back into the living room.

"Rematch?"

So we played again, and I lost. It didn't hurt, though. It didn't feel nearly as bad when he first took off the training wheels. This was a different kind of defeat, and it didn't bother me one bit. I had nothing left to prove. If I'd lost, so what? I'd already shown what I could do.

But what if he'd let me win?

Again, so what? I had made myself a better player than I was before. I didn't need him to pass me a torch. I'd taken the flame myself, like a thirteen-year-old Prometheus. After that night, I was my own man, ready for everything: high school, my first girlfriend, my parents' divorce, my first job, moving away to college, starting a career. I never lost the feeling that I could make everything work if I just chose the right moves. I still live by that principle.

> Initial doubts about followup match lead to *epiphany* in final paragraph— sudden moment of insight.

GRAPHIC NOVEL (EXCERPT)　　In *Persepolis* (2003), Marjane Satrapi uses the medium of graphic novel to narrate the story of her girlhood in Iran. As she grew up, she witnessed the overthrow of the shah and the Islamic Revolution, and the subsequent war with Iraq. The selection on the following pages describes life under the shah.

"The Letter," translated by Mattias Ripa and Blake Ferris, from *Persepolis: The Story of a Childhood* by Marjane Satrapi, translated by Mattias Ripa and Blake Ferris, copyright © 2003 by L'Association, Paris, France. Used by permission of Pantheon Books, a division of Random House, Inc.

HE TOOK PHOTOS EVERY DAY. IT WAS STRICTLY FORBIDDEN. HE HAD EVEN BEEN ARRESTED ONCE BUT ESCAPED AT THE LAST MINUTE.

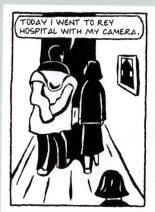

TODAY I WENT TO REY HOSPITAL WITH MY CAMERA.

PEOPLE CAME OUT CARRYING THE BODY OF A YOUNG MAN KILLED BY THE ARMY. HE WAS HONORED LIKE A MARTYR. A CROWD GATHERED TO TAKE HIM TO THE BAHESHTE ZAHRA CEMETERY.

THEN THERE WAS ANOTHER CADAVER, AN OLD MAN CARRIED OUT ON A STRETCHER. THOSE WHO DIDN'T FOLLOW THE FIRST ONE WENT OVER TO THE OLD MAN, SHOUTING REVOLUTIONARY SLOGANS AND CALLING HIM A HERO.

HERE IS ANOTHER MARTYR.

WELL, I WAS TAKING MY PHOTOS WHEN I NOTICED AN OLD WOMAN NEXT TO ME. I UNDERSTOOD THAT SHE WAS THE WIDOW OF THE VICTIM. I HAD SEEN HER LEAVE THE HOSPITAL WITH THE BODY.

PLEASE! STOP IT! STOP IT!

WHAT? WHAT IS IT?

STOP IT!

WHO ARE YOU?

HIS WIDOW!

ARE YOU A ROYALIST?

NO, BUT MY HUSBAND DIED OF CANCER...

1. **Literacy Narrative:** After reading Richard Rodriguez's "Strange Tools" (p. 20), write a literacy narrative of your own, recalling teachers or assignments that helped (or hindered) you in learning to read or write. Describe books that changed you or ambitions you might have to pursue a writing or media career. However, you don't have to be an aspiring writer to make sense of this assignment. Remember that there are many kinds of literacy. The narrative you write may be about your encounters with paintings, films, music, fashion, architecture, or maybe even video games.

2. **Memoir:** Using Miles Pequeno's "Check. Mate?" as a model (p. 26), compose a short narrative describing how an individual (like Pequeno's father) changed your life or made you see the world in a different way. Make sure readers gain a strong sense both of this person and your relationship to him or her.

3. **Reflection:** Make a point about your school or community the way Peggy Noonan does in her piece about Manhattan on the Fourth of July ("We Need to Talk," p. 7). If appropriate, supplement the narrative with a photo.

4. **Visual Narrative:** *Persepolis* (p. 32) demonstrates that a story can be told in various media: This graphic novel even became an animated film in 2007. Using a medium other than words alone, tell a story from your own life or from your community. Draw it, use photographs, craft a collage, create a video, record interviews, or combine other media suited to your nonfiction tale.

5. **Reflection:** Narrate your experiences about a *place*—from the past or present—that show why this environment is an important part of your life. You can introduce readers to characters you met there, thoughts or emotions the place evokes, or incidents that occurred in this setting, whether it is a coffeehouse, stage, newspaper office, club, or even a library. You can tell this story in words, in a photoessay, or in a video.

How to start

- Need a **topic**? See page 45.
- Need to **find information**? See page 48.
- Need to **organize that information**?
  See page 50.

2 Report

provides readers with reliable information

You've been preparing reports since the second grade when you probably used an encyclopedia to explain why volcanoes erupt or who Franklin Roosevelt was. Today, the reports you write may be more ambitious.

- You research a term paper on global warming, trying to separate scientific evidence from political claims.

- You write up the results of your chemistry, biology, or physics labs hoping your words do less damage than the experiments did.

- You write a sports column for your campus newspaper, describing the complexities of NCAA regulations on major collegiate sports. You focus on recruiting.

- You prepare a PowerPoint presentation for your history class to show that weather—more than English naval tactics—doomed the Spanish Armada of 1588.

- You study the annual reports issued by a major company for the past decade to compare growth projections with actual performance.

UNDERSTANDING REPORTS.   As you might guess, reports make up one of the broadest genres of writing. If you use Google to search the term online, you will turn up an unwieldy two billion items, beginning with the *Drudge Report* and moving on to sites that cover everything from financial news to morbidity studies. Such sites may not resemble the term papers, presentations, and lab reports you'll typically prepare for school. But they'll share at least some of the goals you'll have when drafting academic reports.

Stephen Colbert parodies the concept of *report* in his nightly putdown of pompous cable-TV pundits, *The Colbert Report*. *Time*, on the other hand, promises to provide readers with accurate information about the aftermath of Katrina in a "special report." But does the magazine undermine its objectivity by rendering a verdict on the cover: "It's pathetic"?

Present information.   Obviously, people read reports to discover what they don't already know or confirm what they do. They expect what they read to be timely and accurate. And sometimes, the information or data you present *will* be new (as in *news*), built from recent events or the latest research. But just as often, your reports will repackage data from existing sources. *Are cats and dogs really color-blind?* The answer to such a question is already out there for you to find—if you know where to look.

Find reliable sources.   The heart and soul of any report will be reliable sources that provide or confirm information—whether they are "high government officials" quoted anonymously in news stories or articles listed in the bibliographies of college term papers. If asked to write a report about a topic new to you, immediately plan to do library and online research. O

But the information in reports is just as often generated by careful experiments and observations. Even personal experience may sometimes provide material for reports, though anecdotes need corroboration to be convincing.

Aim for objectivity.   Writers and institutions (such as newspapers or government agencies) know that they'll lose credibility if their factual presentations seem incomplete or biased. Of course, smart readers understand that reports on contentious subjects—global warming, intelligent design, or stem-cell research, for example—may lean one way or another. In fact, you may develop strong opinions based on the research you've done. But readers of reports usually prefer to draw their own conclusions.

Present information clearly.   Readers expect material in reports and reference material to be arranged (and perhaps illustrated) for their benefit. O So when you present information, state your claims quickly and support them with data. You'll gain no points for surprises, twists, or suspense in a report. In fact, you'll usually give away the game on the first page of most reports by announcing not only your thesis but also perhaps your conclusions.

find a topic
p. 308

think visually
p. 500

This very brief report—actually a news item—from *Astronomy* magazine explains a recent astronomical discovery. Brief as it is, it shows how reports work.

Uranus's Second Ring-Moon System

LAURA LAYTON

Saturn isn't the only planet to harbor a complex ring structure. In 1986, NASA's *Voyager 2* spacecraft sent back images of a family of ten moons and a system of rings orbiting Uranus. New images from the Hubble Space Telescope (HST) increase those numbers.

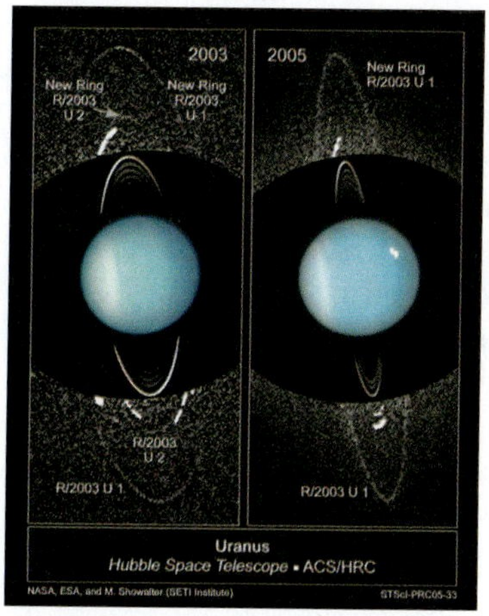

On December 22, planetary astronomer Mark Showalter of the SETI Institute and Jack Lissauer of the NASA Ames Research Center announced the discovery of two additional moons and two large outer rings. HST's Advanced Camera for Surveys (ACS) imaged new moons Cupid and Mab as well as two faint, dusty rings from July 2003 through August 2005.

Newly discovered moon Cupid orbits in the midst of a swarm of inner moons known as the Portia group, so named after the group's largest moon. The Portia group lies just outside Uranus's inner ring system and

The Hubble telescope imaged Uranus's two newly discovered rings in 2003 and 2005. *NASA, ESA, and M. Showalter of the SETI Institute.*

Title is simple, factual.

Opening paragraphs present new information and sources.

Facts are presented clearly and objectively.

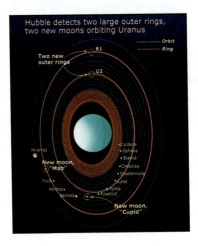

Hubble detects two large outer rings,
two new moons orbiting Uranus

The features and locations of Uranus's
known moons and rings.   *NASA, ESA, and
A. Field of STScI.*

inside the planet's larger, classical moon group of Belinda, Perdita, Puck, and Miranda. Mab, the smaller of the two newly detected moons, orbits outside the inner moon group and Cupid, but interior to Uranus's four outer moons.

A second ring system was also detected around Uranus and imaged by Hubble. Rings R/2003 U 1 and R/2003 U 2 (R1 and R2, respectively) both lie outside the orbit of the inner ring system. Researchers believe micron-size dust is a main constituent of these rings.

What is not clear is how these rings formed. Meteoroid impacts on Uranus's moons that eject fine dust may feed the rings or collisions among existing rings may produce new ones. Either way, the moons' small sizes and surface areas keep any ejected material from falling back to their surfaces and reaccreting. According to Showalter, "Dust material is coming off of Mab and spreading out to make this [R1] ring." It's not apparent what body provides the material for the inner (R2) ring. Lissauer theorizes that a disrupted moon may have been a source.

Showalter believes Uranus's ring-moon system is unstable and exhibits chaotic evolution. Since the last observations were made, Uranus's moons changed orbit. This has long-term implications for Uranus's ring-moon system. "Long-term changes to the system include collisions and crossing ring systems," adds Lissauer.

One thing is for sure, says Lissauer — "Our solar system is a dynamic place."

—*Astronomy*, December 28, 2005

Images and captions illustrate discovery.

Authorities are quoted.

Exploring purpose and topic

When assigned a report, think about the kinds of information you need to present. Will your report merely answer a factual question about a topic and deliver basic information? Or are you expected to do a more in-depth study? Or might the report deliver new information based on your own recent research or experiments? Consider your various options as you select a topic.

topic ◀

Answer questions.   For this kind of report, include basic facts and, perhaps, an overview of key features, issues, or problems. Think of an encyclopedia as a model: When you look up an article there, you usually aren't interested in an exhaustive treatment of a subject.

Assigned a report intended to answer basic questions, you can choose topics that would otherwise seem overly ambitious. So long as all that readers expect is an overview, not expertise, you could easily write two or three fact-filled pages on "Memphis and the Blues" or "The Battle of Marathon" by focusing on just a few key figures, events, and concepts. Given this opportunity, select a topic that introduces you to new ideas or perspectives—this could, in fact, be the rationale for the specific assignment.

Review what is already known about a subject.   Instructors who ask you to write five- or ten-page reports on specific subjects in a field—for example, to explain banking practices in Japan or to describe current trends in museum architecture—doubtless know plenty about those subjects

Field research is one way to deliver new information.

already. They want you to look at the topic in some depth to increase what you know. But the subject may also be evolving rapidly because of ongoing research or current events.

So consider updating an idea introduced in a lecture or textbook: You might be surprised by how much you can add to what an instructor has presented. If workers are striking in Paris again, make that a focal point of your general report on European Union economic policies; if your course covers globalism, consider how a world community made smaller by jet travel complicates the response to epidemic diseases. In considering topics for in-depth reports, you'll find "research guides"especially helpful. O You may also want to consult librarians or experts in the field you're writing about. O

Report new knowledge.   Many schools encourage undergraduates to conduct original research in college. In most cases, this work is done under the supervision of an instructor in your major field, and you'll likely choose a topic only after developing expertise in some area. For a look at research topics students from different schools have explored, use Google to search "undergraduate research journal."

If you have trouble finding a subject for a report, try the brainstorming techniques suggested in Chapter 17, both to identify topic ideas and to narrow them to manageable size.

Establish credibility.   Because they draw on sources, speak in reasonable tones, and document their claims, reports often seem more respectable than even responsible editorials or op-ed pieces. Not surprisingly then, people and organizations use reports to boost their credibility. On the Web site of any major group embroiled in controversy you will usually find—if you look hard enough—reports, white papers, fact sheets, and other data to back up the organization's major claims. Most credible groups feel an obligation to provide such information. Academic reports you write may serve this func-tion, providing the solid facts and evidence for ideas you will explore later in more advanced work.

refine your search
p. 406

ask for help
p. 325

Understanding your audience

You probably know that you should tailor any report to its potential readers. Well-informed audiences expect detailed reports that use technical language, but if your potential audience includes a range of readers, from experts to amateurs, design your work to suit them all. Perhaps you can use headings to ease novices through your report while simultaneously signaling to more knowledgeable readers what sections they might skip. ⭕ Make audience-sensitive moves like this routinely, whenever you are composing.

But sometimes it's not the content that you must tailor for potential readers: It's how readers perceive *you*. They'll look at you differently, according to the expertise you bring to the project. What are the options?

Suppose you are the expert. This may be the typical pose of most professional writers of reports, smoothly presenting material they know well enough to teach. But knowledgeable people still often make two common mistakes in presenting information. Either they assume an audience is as informed as they are, and so omit the very details and helpful transitions that many readers need, or they underestimate the intelligence of their readers and consequently weary them with trivial and unnecessary explanations. ⭕ Readers want a confident guide but also one who knows when—*and when not*—to define a term, provide a graph, or supply some context.

Suppose you are the novice. In a typical academic report, you're likely dealing with material relatively new to you. Your expertise on language acquisition in childhood may be only a book chapter and two journal articles thick, but you may still have to write ten pages on the topic to pass a psychology course. Moreover, you not only have to provide information in a report but you also have to convince an expert reader—your instructor— that you have earned the credentials to write about this subject.

Suppose you are the peer. For some reports, your peers may be your primary audience. That's often the case with oral presentations in class. You know that an instructor is watching and likely grading the content— including your topic, organization, and sources. But that instructor may also be watching how well you adapt that material to the interests and capabilities of your colleagues. ⭕

Tips for Writing Credible Reports

- Choose a serious subject you know you can research.
- Model the project on professional reports in that area.
- Select sources recognized in the field.
- Document those sources correctly.
- Use the discipline's technical vocabulary and conventions.

design your work p. 517

respect your readers p. 374

understand oral reports p. 298

Finding and developing materials

▶ find information

Once you have settled on a research topic and thesis, plan to spend time online, in a library, or in the field gathering the data you need for your report. Look beyond reference works such as dictionaries and encyclopedias toward resources used or created by experts in the field, including scholarly books published by university presses, articles in professional journals, government reports (also known as white papers), oral histories, and so on. Find materials that push you well beyond what you knew at the outset of the project. The level of the works you read may intimidate you initially, but that's a signal that you are learning something new—an outcome your instructor probably intended.

Sometimes, you will write reports based on information you discover yourself, either under the controlled conditions of a scientific experiment or through interviews, fieldwork, polling, or news-gathering. ○ It's not easy to summarize all the rules that govern such work. They vary from major to major, and some you learn in courses devoted to research methods. But even informal field research requires systematic procedures and detailed record keeping so that you can provide readers with data they can verify. To get reports right, follow these basic principles.

Need help finding relevant sources? See "How to Browse for Ideas" on pp. 312–13.

Base reports on the best available sources.   You can't just do an online search on a topic and hope for the best. The quality of material on Web sites (and in libraries, for that matter) varies widely. You will embarrass yourself quickly if you don't develop procedures and instincts for evaluating sources. Look for materials—including data such as statistics and photo-graphic reproductions—supported by major institutions in government, business, and the media and offered by reliable authors and experts. For academic papers, take your information whenever possible from journals and books published by university presses and professional organizations. ○

With Web materials, track them back to their original sources. Use the Google search engine for "Korean War," for instance, and you find an item that seems generic—except that its URL indicates a military location (.mil). Opening the URL, however, you discover that a government institution— the Naval Historical Center—supports the site. So its information is likely to be credible but will reflect the perspectives of the Department of the Navy. That's information you need to know as you read material from the site.

understand lab reports
p. 290

find reliable sources
p. 415

Some Online Sites for Locating Facts and Information

- **Alcove 9: An Annotated List of Reference Sites** (http://www.loc .gov/rr/main/alcove9/) A collection of online reference sites maintained by the Library of Congress.

- **Bartleby.com: Great Books Online** (http://www.bartleby.com/) Includes online versions of key reference and literary works, from *Gray's Anatomy* to the *Oxford Shakespeare*.

- **Biography on A&E** (http://www.biography.com/search/) A collection of 25,000 brief biographies, from Julius Caesar to Orlando Bloom.

- **Fedstats** (http://www.fedstats.gov/) *The* site for finding information gathered by the federal government. Also check out FirstGov.gov (http:// www.firstgov.gov/).

- **The Internet Public Library** (http://www.ipl.org) Provides links to material on most major academic fields and subjects. Includes reference collections as well.

- **The World Factbook** (http://www.cia.gov/cia/publications/factbook/ index.html) Check here for data about any country—compiled by the CIA.

Base reports on multiple sources.   Don't rely on a limited or narrow selection of material. Not all ideas or points of view deserve equal coverage, but neither should you take any particular set of claims for granted. Above all, avoid the temptation to base a report on a single source, even one that *is* genuinely excellent. You may find yourself merely paraphrasing the material, not writing a report of your own.

Fact-check your report.   It's a shame to get the big picture in focus in a report and then lose credibility because you slip up on a few easily verifiable facts. In a lengthy project, these errors might seem inevitable or just a nuisance. But misstatements can take on a life of their own and become lore— like the initial and exaggerated reports of crime and mayhem during Hurricane Katrina. So take the extra few minutes it requires to get details right.

Creating a structure

▶ organize
information

How does a report work? Not like a shopping mall—where the escalators and aisles are designed to keep you wandering and buying, deliberately confused. Not like a mystery novel that leads up to an unexpected climax, or even like an argument, which steadily builds in power to a memorable conclusion. Instead, reports lay all their cards on the table right at the start and hold no secrets. They announce what they intend to do and then do it, providing clear markers all along the way.

Clarity doesn't come easily; it only seems that way when a writer has been successful. You have to know a topic intimately to explain it to others. Then you need to choose a pattern that supports what you want to say. Among structures you might choose for drafting a report are the following, some of which overlap.

Organize by date, time, or sequence.   Drafting a history report, you may not think twice about arranging your material chronologically: In 1958, the USSR launched *Sputnik,* the first Earth satellite; in 1961, the USSR launched a cosmonaut into Earth orbit; in 1969, the United States put two men on the moon. This structure puts information into a relationship readers understand immediately as a competition. You'd still have blanks to fill in with facts and details to tell the story of the race to the moon, but a chronological structure helps readers keep complicated events in perspective.

By presenting a simple sequence of events, you can use time to organize many kinds of reports, from the scoring in football games to the movement of stock markets to the flow of blood through the human heart. ○

Organize by magnitude or order of importance.   Many reports present their subjects in sequence, ranked from biggest to smallest (or vice versa); most important to least important; most common/frequent to least; and so on. Such structures assume, naturally, that you have already done the research to position the items you expect to present. At first glance, reports of this kind might seem tailored to the popular media: "10 Best Restaurants in Seattle," "100 Fattest American Cities." But you might also use such a structure to report on the disputed causes of a war, the multiple effects of a stock-market crash, or even the factors responsible for a disease.

shape your work
p. 340

Organize by division.   It's natural to organize some reports by division—
that is, by breaking a subject into its major parts. A report on the federal
government, for example, might be organized by treating each of its three
branches in turn: executive, legislative, and judicial. A report on the Elizabethan stage might examine the separate parts of a typical theater: the
heavens, the balcony, the stage wall, the stage, the pit, and so on. Of course,
you'd then have to decide in what order to present the items, perhaps
spatially or in order of importance. You might even use an illustration to
clarify your report.

The Swan Theatre
The architectural layout
of this Elizabethan theater,
shown in this 1596 sketch
by Johannes de Witt,
might suggest the struc-
ture of a report describing
the theater.

Organize by classification.   Classification is the division of a group of concepts or items according to specified and consistent principles. Reports organized by classification are easy to set up when you borrow a structure that is already well established—such as those below. A project becomes more difficult when you try to create a new system—perhaps to classify the various political groups on your campus or to describe the behavior of participants in a psychology experiment.

- **Psychology** (by type of study): abnormal, clinical, comparative, developmental, educational, industrial, social

- **Plays** (by type): tragedy, comedy, tragicomedy, epic, pastoral, musical

- **Nations** (by form of government): monarchy, oligarchy, democracy, dictatorship

- **Passenger cars** (by engine placement): front engine, mid engine, rear engine

- **Dogs** (by breed group): sporting, hound, working, terrier, toy, nonsporting, herding

Organize by position, location, or space.   Organizing a report spatially is a powerful device for arranging ideas—even more so today, given the ease with which material can be illustrated. O A map, for example, is a report organized by position and location. But it is only one type of spatial structure.

You use spatial organization in describing a painting from left to right, a building from top to bottom, a cell from nucleus to membrane. A report on medical conditions might be presented most effectively via cutaways that expose different layers of tissues and organs. Or a report on an art exhibition might follow a viewer through a virtual 3-D gallery.

Organize by definition.   Typically, definitions begin by identifying an object by its "genus" and "species" and then listing its distinguishing features, functions, or variations. This useful structure is the pattern behind most entries in dictionaries, encyclopedias, and other reference works.

think visually
p. 300

It can be readily expanded too, once the genus and species have been established: *Ontario* is a *province of Canada* between Hudson Bay and the Great Lakes. That's a good start, but what are its geographical features, history, products, and major cities—all the things that distinguish it from other provinces? You could write a book, let alone a report, based on this simple structure.

Organize by comparison/contrast.   You've been comparing and contrasting probably since the fourth grade, but that doesn't make this principle of organization any less potent for college-level reports. O You compare and contrast to highlight distinctions that might otherwise not be readily apparent. Big differences are usually uninteresting: That's why *Consumer Reports* doesn't test Nikon SLRs against disposable cameras. But the differences between Nikons and Canons? That might be worth exploring.

Organize by thesis statement.   Obviously, you have many options for organizing a report; moreover, a single report might use several structural patterns. So it helps if you explain early in a project what its method of organization will be. That idea may be announced in a single thesis sentence, a full paragraph (or section), or even a PowerPoint slide. O

SENTENCE ANNOUNCES STRUCTURE

In the late thirteenth century, Native Puebloans may have abandoned their cliff dwellings for several related reasons, including an exhaustion of natural resources, political disintegration, and, most likely, a prolonged drought.

−Kendrick Frazier, *People of Chaco: A Canyon and Its Culture*

PARAGRAPH EXPLAINS STRUCTURE

In order to detect a problem in the beginning of life, medical professionals and caregivers must be knowledgeable about normal development and potential warning signs. Research provides this knowledge. In most cases, research also allows for accurate diagnosis and effective intervention. Such is the case with Cri Du Chat Syndrome (CDCS), also commonly known as Cat Cry Syndrome.

−Marissa Dahlstrom, "Developmental Disorders: Cri Du Chat Syndrome"

understand evaluation
p. 102

develop a thesis
p. 336

Choosing a style and design

Reports are typically written in a formal or *high* style—free of emotional language that might make them sound like arguments. ○ To separate fact from opinion, scientific and professional reports usually avoid *I* and other personal references as well as devices such as contractions and dialogue. Reports in newspapers, magazines, and even encyclopedias may be less formal: You might detect a person behind the prose. But the style will still strive for impartiality, signaling that the writer's opinions are (or, at least, *should* be) less important than the facts reported.

Why tone down the emotional, personal, or argumentative temper of the language in reports? It's a matter of audience. The moment readers suspect that you are twisting language to advocate an agenda or moving away from a sober recital of facts, they will question the accuracy of your report. So review your drafts to see if a word or phrase might be sending wrong signals to readers. Give your language the appearance of neutrality, balance, and perspective.

Present the facts cleanly.   Get right to the point and answer key questions directly: *Who? What? Where? When? How? Why?* Organize paragraphs around topic sentences so readers know what will follow. Don't go off on tangents. Keep the exposition controlled and focus on data. When you do, the prose will seem coolly efficient and trustworthy.

Keep out of it.   Write from a neutral, third-person perspective, avoiding the pronouns *I* and *you*. Like all guidelines, this one has exceptions, and it certainly doesn't apply across the board to other genres of writing. But when perusing a report, readers don't usually care about the writer's personal opinion unless that writer's individual experiences are part of the story.

Avoid connotative language.   Maintaining objectivity is not easy because language is rife with *connotations*—the powerful cultural associations that may surround words, enlarging their meanings and sometimes imposing value judgments. Connotations make *shadowy* and *gloomy* differ from *dark*; *porcine* and *tubby*, from *overweight*. What's more, words' connotations are not the same for every reader. One person may have no problem with a

define your
style p. 366

term like *slums,* but another person living in *low-income housing* may beg to differ. Given the minefield of potential offenses that writing can be, don't use loaded words when more neutral terms are available and just as accurate. Choose *confident,* not *overweening* or *pompous;* try *corporate official* rather than *robber baron*—unless, of course, the more colorful term fits the context.

Cover differing views fairly, *especially* those you don't like.   The neutrality of reports is often a fiction. You need only look at the white papers or fact sheets on the Web sites of various groups to appreciate how data presentation can sometimes be biased. But a report you prepare for a course or a professional situation should represent a good-faith effort to run the bases on a subject, touching all its major points. An upbeat report on growth in minority enrollment on your campus might also have to acknowledge areas where achievements have been lagging. A report on the economic boom that occurred during Bill Clinton's presidency (1993–2001) might also have to cover the dot-com bust and slide into recession at the end of his term.

Pay attention to elements of design.   Clear and effective design is particularly important in reports. ○ If your paper runs more than a few pages and readily divides into parts, consider using headings or section markers to help readers follow its structure and locate information. Documents such as term papers and lab reports may follow specific formulas, patterns, and templates that you will need to learn.

   Much factual information is best presented graphically. This is especially the case with numbers and statistics. So learn to create or incorporate charts, graphs, photos, and illustrations, and also captions into your work. Software such as Microsoft Word can create modest tables and simple graphics; generate more complex tables and graphs with software such as Excel. And remember that any visual items should be purposeful, not ornamental.

design your work
p. 517

Examining models

INFORMATIVE REPORT In "Gene-Altered Foods: A Case Against Panic," health and nutrition expert Jane E. Brody summarizes what is known about genetically modified foods to correct false impressions about them. The article originally appeared in the *New York Times*.

Gene-Altered Foods: A Case Against Panic

Jane E. Brody

December 5, 2000

Ask American consumers whether they support the use of biotechnology in food and agriculture and nearly 70 percent say they do. But ask the question another way, "Do you approve of genetically engineered (or genetically modified) foods?" and two-thirds say they do not.

Yet there is no difference between them. The techniques involved and the products that result are identical. Rather, the words "genetic" and "engineer" seem to provoke alarm among millions of consumers.

The situation recalls the introduction of the MRI (for magnetic resonance imaging), which was originally called an NMR, for nuclear magnetic resonance. The word *nuclear* caused such public concern, it threatened to stymie the growth of this valuable medical tool.

The idea of genetically modified foods, known as GM foods, is particularly frightening to those who know little about how foods are now produced and how modern genetic technology, if properly regulated, could result in significant improvements by reducing environmental hazards, improving the nutritional value of foods, enhancing agricultural productivity, and fostering the survival worldwide of small farms and the rural landscape.

Without GM foods, Dr. Alan McHughen, a biotechnologist at the University of Saskatchewan, told a recent conference on agricultural biotechnology at Cornell, the earth will not be able to feed the ever-growing billions of people who inhabit it.

> Thesis: People don't understand GM foods and fear what they don't understand.

Still, there are good reasons for concern about a powerful technology that is currently imperfectly regulated and could, if inadequately tested or misapplied, bring on both nutritional and environmental havoc. To render a rational opinion on the subject and make reasoned choices in the marketplace, it is essential to understand what genetic engineering of foods and crops involves and its potential benefits and risks.

GENETICS IN AGRICULTURE

People have been genetically modifying foods and crops for tens of thousands of years. The most commonly used method has involved crossing two parents with different desirable characteristics in an effort to produce offspring that express the best of both of them. That and another approach, inducing mutations, are time-consuming and hit-or-miss and can result in good and bad characteristics.

Genetic engineering, on the other hand, involves the introduction into a plant or animal or micro-organism of a single gene or group of genes that are known quantities, genes that dictate the production of one or more desired elements, for example, the ability to resist the attack of insects, withstand herbicide treatments, or produce foods with higher levels of essential nutrients.

Since all organisms use the same genetic material (DNA), the power of the technique includes the ability to transfer genes between organisms that normally would never interbreed.

Thus, an antifreeze gene from Arctic flounder has been introduced into strawberries to extend their growing season in northern climates. But contrary to what many people think, this does not make the strawberries "fishy" any more than the use of porcine insulin turned people into pigs.

Dr. Steven Kresovich, a plant breeder at Cornell, said, "Genes should be characterized by function, not origin. It's not a flounder gene but a cold tolerance gene that was introduced into strawberries."

As Dr. McHughen points out in his new book, *Pandora's Picnic Basket: The Potential and Hazards of Genetically Modified Foods,* people share about 7,000 genes with a worm called *C. elegans.* The main

---

Headings mark off key topics in report.

Explains how genetic engineering works.

Sources add authority.

difference between organisms lies in the total number of genes their cells contain, how the genes are arranged, and which ones are turned on or off in different cells at different times.

CURRENT AND POTENTIAL BENEFITS

An insecticidal toxin from a bacterium called *Bacillus thuringiensis.* (Bt) has been genetically introduced into two major field crops, corn and cotton, resulting in increased productivity and decreased use of pesticides, which means less environmental contamination and greater profits for farmers. For example, by growing Bt cotton, farmers could reduce spraying for bollworm and budworm from seven times a season to none. Bt corn also contains much lower levels of fungal toxins, which are potentially carcinogenic.

"The genetic introduction of herbicide tolerance into soybeans is saving farmers about $200 million a year by reducing the number of applications of herbicide needed to control weed growth," said Leonard Gianessi, a pesticide analyst at the National Center for Food and Agricultural Policy, a research organization in Washington.

Genetically engineered pharmaceuticals are already widely used, with more than 150 products on the market. Since 1978, genetically modified bacteria have been producing human insulin, which is used by 3.3 million people with diabetes.

Future food benefits are likely to accrue directly to the consumer. For example, genetic engineers have developed golden rice, a yellow rice rich in beta carotene (which the body converts to vitamin A) and iron. If farmers in developing countries accept this crop and if the millions of people who suffer from nutrient deficiencies will eat it, golden rice could prevent widespread anemia and blindness in half a million children a year and the deaths of one million to two million children who succumb each year to the consequences of vitamin A deficiency.

Future possibilities include peanuts or shrimp lacking proteins that can cause life-threatening food allergies, fruits and vegetables with

Offers five paragraphs of evidence in support of GM foods.

longer shelf lives, foods with fewer toxicants and antinutrients, meat and dairy products and oils with heart-healthier fats, and foods that deliver vaccines.

REAL AND POTENTIAL RISKS

GM foods and crops arrived without adequate mechanisms in place to regulate them. Three agencies are responsible for monitoring their safety for consumers, farmers, and the environment: the Food and Drug Administration, the Department of Agriculture, and the Environmental Protection Agency. But the drug agency says its law does not allow it to require premarket testing of GM foods unless they contain a new substance that is not "generally recognized as safe."

For most products, safety tests are done voluntarily by producers. The recent recall of taco shells containing GM corn that has not been approved for human consumption was done voluntarily by the producer. The agency is now formulating new guidelines to test GM products and to label foods as "GM-free," but says it lacks a legal basis to require labeling of GM foods.

"In the current environment, such a label would be almost a kiss of death on a product," said Dr. Michael Jacobson, director of the Center for Science in the Public Interest, a nonprofit consumer group. "But it may be that the public is simply not going to have confidence in transgenic ingredients if their presence is kept secret."

The introduction of possible food allergens through genetic engineering is a major concern. If the most common sources of food allergens—peanuts, shellfish, celery, nuts, milk, or eggs—had to pass through an approval process today, they would never make it to market.

But consumers could be taken unaware if an otherwise safe food was genetically endowed with an allergen, as almost happened with an allergenic protein from Brazil nuts. Even if known allergenic proteins are avoided in GM foods, it is hard to predict allergenicity of new proteins.

Remains objective, reporting both sides: GM foods still need regulation.

> Explains that technology poses real risks.

A potentially serious environmental risk involves the "escape" of GM genes from crops into the environment, where they may harm innocent organisms or contaminate crops that are meant to be GM-free.

Dr. Jacobson concluded, "Now is the time, while agricultural biotechnology is still young, for Congress and regulatory agencies to create the framework that will maximize the safe use of these products, bolster public confidence in them, and allow all of humankind to benefit from their enormous potential." Two congressional bills now under discussion can do much to assure safer use of agricultural biotechnology, he said.

> Reports that Congress can act to address these risks.

ACADEMIC REPORT   Academic reports often support clear and straightforward thesis statements. The following short report does that in explaining the dual mission of Frank Gehry's celebrated Guggenheim Museum Bilbao. The paper below is not only based on sources but also on information gathered at the museum, in Spain's Basque Country.

Winsett 1

Annie Winsett

Professor Sidor

Writing 200

5 December, 20--

Inner *and* Outer Beauty

The Guggenheim Bilbao, designed by North American architect Frank Gehry (b. 1929), is a recent addition to the Solomon R. Guggenheim Foundation, a conglomeration of museums dedicated to modern American and European art. Home to several

> Thesis suggests a paper with two parts.

Winsett 2

permanent works and host to visiting expositions, the Guggenheim Bilbao is itself an artistic wonder, perhaps more acclaimed than any of the art it houses. In design, the building meets the requirements of a proper museum, but it also signifies the rejuvenation of Spain's Basque country.

Like any museum, the Guggenheim Bilbao is dedicated to preserving and presenting works of art. Paintings and sculptures are here to be protected. So the thick glass panes of the Bilbao serve not only to let in natural light, but also provide escape for the heat generated by the titanium outsides of the structure. The unconventional metal plating of the Guggenheim, guaranteed to last up to one hundred years, actually ensures its survival as well. Similarly, the floor material will be able to withstand the many visitors to come.

Fig. 1. The Guggenheim Museum Bilbao

Winsett offers a photograph to convey Bilbao's extraordinary design.

Winsett 3

First section of paper explains how the avant-garde building functions as a museum.

Even though the outside of the Guggenheim Bilbao appears to be composed of irregular forms only, the interior houses nineteen functional galleries. The alternating rooms and curving walkways around a central atrium provide an extensive journey through the world of art. So the unusual exterior structure actually allots a vast amount of wall and floor display space and serves the wide variety of art it houses more than adequately.

"But" at beginning of paragraph signals that report is moving into its second section.

But the Guggenheim Bilbao was created to do more. In 1991, having noted the economic depression facing one of its main industrial cities, the Basque Country government proposed that the Solomon R. Guggenheim Foundation locate its next museum in Bilbao ("History" 1). As part of a massive revitalization involving the city's port, railways, and airport, the new museum would enhance the cultural identity of the city. Perhaps a conventional structure would have met the need for societal enrichment.

Yet the Basque government achieved much more by selecting a design by Frank Gehry. Designed with computers, the museum presents an original and striking three-dimensional form not possible using conventional design methods. From above, it appears that its metal-coated solids extend from a central skylight in the shape of a flower ("Guggenheim"). The building also suggests a ship on the river's shore with edges that swoop upward in a hull-like fashion. The "scales" of metal that surround the structure's steel frame are like those of a fish. Undoubtedly, the design references the museum's coastal and riverside environment.

Paper uses several online sources.

Report explains how museum represents city of Bilbao.

Whatever its intended form, Gehry's building captures the spirit of a renewed Bilbao in the twenty-first century. For instance, Gehry managed to incorporate the city's mining industries in the

Winsett 4

structural materials. The titanium plates reflect both the beautiful Basque sky and the core of the Basque economy. Also crucial is the tourism such an incomparable structure might generate. Though most of Gehry's works incorporate the unique materials and forms seen in Bilbao, the Guggenheim is individual and original. And travelers have flocked here to experience the futuristic titanium masterpiece. As hoped, Bilbao and the Basque Country have earned a revived place in the international community. At the 2004 Venice Biennial, the Basque Country was recognized for the most successful urban regeneration project in the world, at the heart of which was the Guggenheim museum ("Culture").

Winsett 5

Works Cited

"Culture." *Euskadi.net.* Eusko Jaurlaritza-Gobierno Vasco (Basque
    Govt.), 17 Mar. 2005. Web. 7 Nov. 2006.

"Guggenheim Bilbao Museum." *Bilbao Metropoli-30.* Assn. for the
    Revitalization of Metropolitan Bilbao, 2006. Web. 30 Oct. 2006.

"History of the Guggenheim Museum Bilbao." *Guggenheim Bilbao.*
    Solomon R. Guggenheim Foundation, 26 Oct. 2006. Web. 29
    Oct. 2006.

VISUAL REPORT

Like many items published today, "Blood Cells for Sale" uses both words and an image (in this case carefully annotated) to convey information clearly and memorably. The two-page spread originally appeared in the November 2007 issue of *Scientific American*.

Blood Cells for Sale

There's More to Blood Banking Than Just Bagging Blood

EMILY HARRISON • PHOTOGRAPH BY CARY WOLINSKY

This is not a bag of blood. Granted, it did begin as a blood donation, drawn from the arm of a volunteer donor in Massachusetts. Within hours of collection, though, that precursory pint of warm whole blood had been centrifuged, fractionated, and decanted into a red blood cell concentrate laced with a cocktail of chemical buffers and nutrients. The ruddy yield, shown here, is one chilled unit of processed blood product, suitable for a patient desperately in need of red cells. Such units—screened, packaged, and tracked through their life cycles in keeping with the dictates of the U.S. Food and Drug Administration—are manufactured with assembly-line efficiency to optimize the safety and utility of a precious, limited resource.

A half-liter unit of whole blood, when spun, separates into layers. The 275-milliliter top layer of lemon-yellow plasma is rich in platelet cells, which are principal to blood clotting. The 225-ml bottom layer of red cells (erythrocytes), which shuttle oxygen and carbon dioxide around the body, is skimmed with a slick of the immune system's white cells (leukocytes). Because different patients need varying boosts for different blood functions, packaging these layers separately lets each whole blood donation help several people. And reducing unnecessary biological material, such as the leukocytes in the red cell concentrate, lowers the risk that a patient's immune system will reject a transfusion.

Synthetic blood replacements, which would carry no disease risk and could be manufactured in surplus, have an enormous potential market. Although several are in development, nothing can yet take the place of genuine blood cells grown by the human body.

COST OF LIVING

The product of 24 hours of processing, this unit of leukocyte-reduced AS-3 red cells costs $220. A typical kidney transplant surgery requires 1–2 units; a heart transplant requires 4–6. Car accident victims consume as many as 20 units.

Keeping Tabs
A unique bar code on each package lets blood banks monitor their inventory and anonymously link each unit to donor information in a central database. The same bar code labels four small tubes of blood collected at the time of donation and sent to testing laboratories for disease screening and blood typing.

Sanguine Expiration
Red cells endure 42 days at 1 to 6 degrees Celsius, over a month longer than platelets last at their optimal temperature of 20 to 24 degrees C. If a temporary glycerol preservative is added to the red cells, they can be frozen for up to one year, but the stress of being frozen and having the glycerol washed out reduces their post-thaw shelf life to one day.

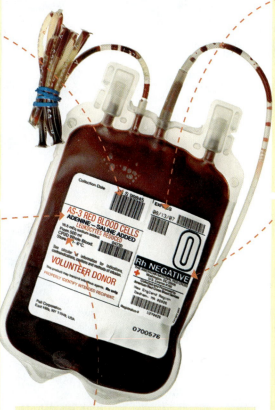

Sustainable Envelopment
Living red cells have needs, even in refrigerated storage. The preservative AS-3 provides them with sodium citrate, sodium phosphate, adenine, sodium chloride, and dextrose, which act as anticoagulants, maintain the cells' structural integrity, and sustain their metabolism. AS-3 also dilutes the red cell concentrate so that it flows freely through tubes and needles into blood vessels.

Type Treatment
Blood type is determined by sugar-and-protein chains, called antigens, that tag the red cells' surfaces. The body rejects cells bearing antigens that do not match its own, so the most universally useful blood type of transfusions is O negative—which carries neither the common A and B antigens nor the Rh antigen. If researchers could pin down a procedure for stripping blood cells of their antigens, it could expand the usefulness and safety of the blood supply.

Clot Stopper
Once outside the body, blood has a natural tendency to clot and dry. To counter that, an anticlotting solution called CP2D is added to the whole blood at the time of donation.

VISUAL REPORT   This report by Michael Kupperman originally appeared in *The Believer* magazine.

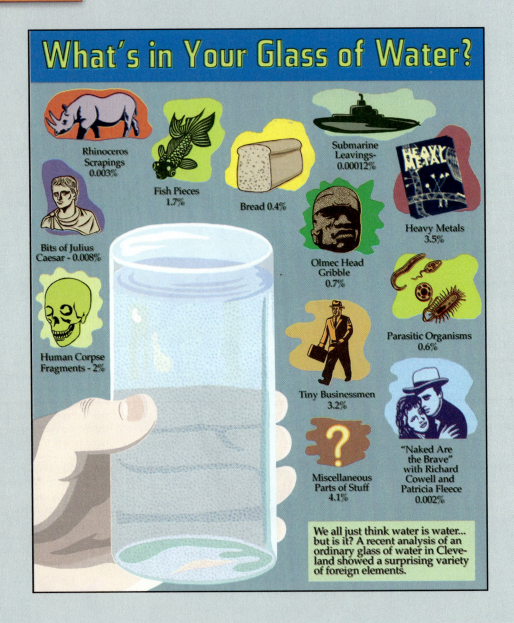

Assignments

1. **Informative Report:** Jane E. Brody draws on her expertise in health and nutrition to write "Gene-Altered Foods: A Case Against Panic" (p. 56). Write a similar report on a subject you already know a great deal about, using your experience to correct false impressions general readers less knowledgeable than you might have about the topic. Be certain to look for new information to keep the report fresh and to base all claims you make on reputable sources and authorities.

2. **Visual Report:** Design a report that, like "Blood Cells for Sale" (p. 64) and "What's in Your Glass of Water?" (facing page), combines words and images to convey information. Use charts, photographs, drawings, diagrams, annotations, and so on. Your word processor or more specialized graphic software (like PowerPoint or InDesign) will help you produce a handsome but sensible project.

3. **Academic Report:** Write a factual academic report based on subjects or ideas in courses outside your major—in other words, on topics generally new to you. Like Annie Winsett in "Inner *and* Outer Beauty" (p. 60), narrow your subject to a specific claim that you can explain in several pages. Use respectable sources and document them in proper Modern Language Association (MLA) or American Psychological Association (APA) style. (For MLA style, see p. 437; for APA style, see p. 474.)

4. **Informative Report:** Imagine that you've been asked to prepare a report on some natural phenomena (like the rings of Uranus, see p. 43) to a group of ninth graders—one of the toughest audiences in the world. In a brief report, engage them with a topic of your choosing, perhaps reflecting your own interest in an offbeat subject. Design the report as a paper, oral presentation, or Web site and base it on reliable sources, which you should cite in some form within the report.

How to start

- Need a **topic**? See page 74.
- Need **support for your argument**? See page 80.
- Need to **organize your ideas**? See page 84.

3 Argument

asks readers to consider debatable ideas

It doesn't take much to spark an argument these days—a casual remark, a political observation, a dumb joke that hurts someone's feelings. Loud voices and angry gestures may follow, leaving observers upset and frustrated, wishing that we could all just get along. But arguments aren't polarizing or hostile by nature, not when people more interested in generating light than heat offer them. Arguments should make us smarter and better able to deal with problems in the world. In fact, you probably make such constructive arguments all the time without raising blood pressures, at least not too much.

- In a letter to the editor, you challenge an op-ed that compares the impact of gasoline prices on a family budget today compared with twenty years ago because figures used in the article haven't been adjusted for inflation.

- You point out that an attendance policy announced on the Web site for a course you plan on taking may be invalid because it contradicts several key university policies.

- You argue that high school officials across the country have adopted "zero tolerance" disciplinary policies as a convenient way of avoiding the tough decisions that competent administrators are paid to make.

UNDERSTANDING ARGUMENTS.   Arguments come in many shapes to serve different purposes. Subsequent chapters in this section cover some forms often assigned in the classroom, including *causal analyses*, *proposals*, and *literary analyses*. But even less specialized arguments have distinctive features. In your projects, you'll aim to do the following.

Offer levelheaded and disputable claims.   You won't influence audiences by making points no one cares about or calls into question. In any argument, something clear and specific ought to be at stake. Maybe you want to change readers' minds about an issue or reaffirm what they already believe. In either case, you'll need a well-defined and appropriately qualified point, either stated or implied, if you expect to influence levelheaded audiences. ○

Poster by Ben Shahn, 1968   This poster illustrates the words of British pacifist and parliamentarian John Morley (1838–1923). Note how the style of Shahn's typography and crayon figure complement each other to make a memorable argument out of Morley's sober observation.

Ben Shahn, "You have not converted a man because you have silenced him." 1968. Offset lithograph, 45 inches x 30 inches (114.2 x 76.2 cm). Smithsonian American Art Museum, Washington, D.C. , USA © Estate of Ben Shahn / Licensed by VAGA, New York, NY. Photo credit: Smithsonian American Art Museum, Washington, D.C. / Art Resource, NY. / Art Resource, NY.

○
develop a thesis
p. 336

Offer good reasons to support a claim.   Without evidence and supporting reasons, a claim is just an assertion—and little better than a shout or a slogan. Slogans do have their appeal in advertising and politics. But they don't become arguments until they are developed through full-bodied thinking and supported by a paper trail of evidence.

Respond to opposing claims and points of view.   You won't be able to make a strong case until you can honestly paraphrase the logic of those who see matters differently. ⭕ And, in your own arguments, you will seem smarter and more fair when you acknowledge these other *reasonable* opinions even as you refute them. Also be prepared to address less rational claims temperately, but firmly.

Use language strategically—and not words only.   Opinions clothed in good sense still need to dress for the occasion. You have to find the right words and images to carry a case forward. Fortunately, you have many options to make words memorable. Design is increasingly important, too: Your choice of medium may ultimately determine who sees your message. ⭕

It goes without saying that many appeals you encounter daily do not measure up to the criteria of serious argument. We've all been seduced by claims just because they are stylish, hip, or repeated so often that they begin to seem true. But if much persuasion doesn't seem fair or sensible, that's all the more reason to reach for a higher standard.

Do you think this Nike advertisement is more than just a slogan? If so, what argument do you think it makes?

⭕ restate ideas
p. 428

⭕ work with visuals
p. 504

Here's an argument by writer and editor Robert Kuttner that raises serious questions about the uses college admissions officers make of school rankings and the consequent effects of their actions on students. Kuttner's word choices leave little doubt how strongly he feels about the subject. But the piece also gains power from the way it is written: The author invites readers to share his outrage. Kuttner also offers colleges a simple avenue for change: *Just say* no.

American Prospect

Posted: February 27, 2006
From: Robert Kuttner

College Rankings or Junk Science?

Connotative words (*feverish, infecting*) suggest Kuttner's view.

It's approaching that season when students and their parents anxiously await college admissions decisions. But increasingly, an equally feverish process is infecting the other side of the transaction and distorting the process of who gets financial aid.

Colleges these days engage in an ever-more-frantic competition for "rankings," driven almost entirely by the annual *U.S. News & World Report* issue on "America's Best Colleges." *U.S. News* is so dominant that when a dean boasts that his school is ranked in the top ten or a president's bonus is based on whether his college makes it into the top fifty he invariably refers to *U.S. News*.

Massive efforts by admissions departments, deans, and college presidents are devoted to gaming the *U.S. News* ranking system, published every August. This includes everything from manipulating who is considered a part-time student (which raises the reported performance of full-time students) to giving students temporary research jobs in order to raise the placement score reported to *U.S. News*. But the easiest single way to raise rankings is by enrolling students with ever-higher SAT scores.

Explains the problem he sees with *U.S. News*'s college rankings.

Doesn't name specific sources in article.

If the average score of your entering freshman class increases, the *U.S. News* ranking will probably improve, too. And if your ranking goes up, the presumed prestige of the college will follow. More kids will apply, more applicants will choose your college rather than brand X, and, best of all, more families will pay sticker price.

This competition spawns many evils that should shame a higher-education system devoted to intellectual honesty. But perhaps the worst thing about it is what the ranking obsession is doing to the allocation of financial aid. More and more scholarship money is being shifted from aid based on financial need to aid based on "merit."

Explains how rankings influence admissions policies.

That sounds nice — who could be opposed to merit? But to-day's "merit scholarships" are primarily bait to attract students with very high SAT scores who don't need the aid. The flip side is less aid available to students from less affluent families, who can't at-tend college without aid, or who must sacrifice academic work to paid jobs, or who graduate with staggering debt loads.

Anticipates potential objection to his argument.

There is, of course, a limited pot of financial aid. One reason tuitions keep relentlessly rising is that some of the tuition money goes to underwrite financial-aid budgets. That would be defensi-ble, even laudable if colleges were "taxing" affluent families in order to redistribute aid money to less affluent ones. But when higher tuitions spin off scholarships for other affluent kids intended mainly to raise rankings, the result is to doubly raise barriers to poor and middle-class kids, with both higher tuition barriers and diminished aid.

One result: poorer performance by poorer kids. Forty percent of all college students from the most affluent quarter of the popula-tion get a bachelor's degree within five years. For kids in the bot-tom income quarter, the figure is just six percent, according to a new book, *Strapped*, by Tamara Draut.

Finally names a source.

Another consequence: Affluent families pass their affluence along to their children. According to studies by Anthony P. Carnevale and Steven J. Rose, nearly three-quarters of students at elite universities are from the wealthiest quarter of the population. Just 3 percent are from the bottom quarter.

Offers more evidence for claim.

The *U.S. News* process for ranking colleges and universities has been almost universally condemned by specialists as junk science. Publishing a data-rich guide to colleges is a service. What's bogus is the supposed ranking. As any statistician will tell you, you can't reasonably combine entirely unrelated variables (test scores, reputation, placements, spending per student, student aid, etc.) into a single linear index. Worse, the criteria and their weightings are arbitrary. It's hard enough for colleges to come up with financial aid based on need, without a spurious ranking contest creating inducements to subsidize the already privileged.

> Appeals to authority (*any statistician*) to undercut rankings.

The data sent by colleges to *U.S. News* are self-reported and unaudited. Also, many of the factors are entirely subjective to begin with. One dean told me that when she rates reputations of other comparable graduate schools, she hasn't a clue how to rate more than a few. There is also the all-too-human temptation to downgrade the near competition.

> Kuttner's thesis: He endorses action against college rankings.

Oregon's Reed College, for more than a decade, has stopped cooperating with *U.S. News*. The college's president, Colin Diver, writing in the *Atlantic*, reported that liberation from this annual hazing has freed Reed to "pursue our own educational philosophy, not that of some magazine." Reed has thrived.

Others should follow Reed's lead and just boycott this travesty.

Exploring purpose and topic

▶ topic

In a college assignment, you could be asked to write an argument or be given a topic area to explore, but you probably won't be told what your claim should be. That decision has to come from you, drawing on your knowledge, experiences, and inclinations. So choose topics about which you genuinely care—not issues routinely defined in the media as controversial. You'll likely do a more credible job defending your choice *not* to wear a helmet when cycling than explaining, one more time, why the environment should concern us all. And if environmental matters do roil you, stake your claim on a specific ecological problem—perhaps from within your community—that you might actually change by the power of your rhetoric. ⚪

If you really are stumped, the Yahoo Directory's list of "Issues and Causes"—with topics from *abortion* to *zoos*—offers problems enough to keep both liberal Susan Sarandon *and* conservative Jon Voight busy to the end of the century. To find it, click on "Society and Culture" on the site's main Web directory (http://dir.yahoo.com). ("Society and Culture" itself offers a menu of intriguing topic areas.) Once you have an issue or even a specific claim, you'll need to work it like bread dough.

Arguments take many different forms, but finger-pointing is rarely a good persuasive tool.

74

get an idea
p. 308

Learn *much* more about your subject.   Do basic library and online research to get a better handle on it—*especially* when you think you already have all the answers. Chances are, you don't.

State a preliminary claim, if only for yourself.   Some arguments fail because writers never examine their own thinking. Instead, they wander around their subjects, throwing out ideas or making contradictory assertions, hoping perhaps that readers will assemble the random parts. To avoid this misdirection, begin with a *claim*—a complete sentence that states a position you will then have to defend. Though you will likely change this initial claim, such a statement will keep you on track as you explore a topic. Even a simple sentence helps:

> College ranks published annually by *U.S. News & World Report* do more harm than good.
>
> Westerners should be less defensive about their cultures.
>
> People who oppose gay marriage don't know what they are talking about.

Qualify your claim to make it reasonable.   As you learn more about a subject, revise your topic idea to reflect the complications you encounter. Your tentative thesis will likely grow longer, but the topic will actually narrow because of the issues and conditions you've specified. You'll also have less work to do, thanks to qualifying expressions such as *some, most, a few, often, under certain conditions, occasionally, when necessary,* and so on. Other qualifying expressions are highlighted below.

> The statistically unreliable college ratings published by *U.S. News* usually do more harm than good to students because they lead admissions officers to award scholarships on the basis of merit rather than need.
>
> Westerners should be more willing to defend their cultural values and intellectual achievements if they hope to defend freedom against its enemies.
>
> Many conservative critics who oppose gay marriage unwittingly undermine their own core principles, especially monogamy and honesty.

Examine your core assumptions.   Claims may be supported by reasons and evidence, but they are based on assumptions. *Assumptions* are the principles and values on which we ground our beliefs and actions. Sometimes those assumptions are controversial and stand right out. At other times, they're so close to us, they seem invisible—they are part of the air we breathe. Expect to spend a paragraph defending any assumptions your readers might find controversial. ○

CLAIM

The statistically unreliable college ratings published by *U.S. News & World Report* usually do more harm than good to students because they lead admissions officers to award scholarships on the basis of merit rather than need.

ASSUMPTION

Alleviating need in our society is more important than rewarding merit. [Probably controversial]

CLAIM

Westerners should be more willing to defend their cultural values and intellectual achievements if they hope to defend freedom against its enemies.

ASSUMPTION

Freedom needs to be defended at all costs.
[Possibly noncontroversial for some audiences in many democracies]

CLAIM

Many conservative critics who oppose gay marriage unwittingly undermine their own core principles, especially monogamy and honesty.

ASSUMPTION

People should be consistent about their principles.
[Probably noncontroversial]

develop ideas
p. 346

Understanding your audience

Retailers know audiences. In fact, they go to great lengths to pinpoint the groups most likely to buy their fried chicken or video games. They then tailor their images and advertising pitches to those specific customers. You'll play to audiences the same way when you write arguments—if maybe a little less cynically.

Understand that you won't ever please everyone in a general audience, even if you write bland, colorless mush—because then some readers will regard you as craven and spineless. In fact, how readers imagine you *as the person presenting an argument* may determine their willingness to consider your claims at all.

Specific topics simply touch groups of readers differently, so you will need to consider a variety of approaches when imagining the audiences for your arguments.

Consider and control your ethos.

People who study persuasion describe the character that writers create for themselves within an argument as their *ethos*—the voice and disposition they choose to give their case. It is a powerful concept, worth remembering. Surely you recognize when writers are coming across as, let's say, appealingly confident or stupidly nasty. And don't you respond in kind, giving ear to the likable voice and dismissing the malicious one? A few audiences—like those for political blogs—may actually prefer a writer with a snarky ethos. But most readers respond better when writers seem reasonable, knowledgeable, and fair—neither insulting those who disagree with them nor making those who share their views embarrassed to have them on their side.

Control your ethos in an argument by adjusting the style, tone, and vocabulary: For instance, contractions can make you seem friendly (or too casual); an impressive vocabulary suggests that you are smart (or maybe just pompous); lots of name-dropping makes you seem hip (or perhaps pretentious). You may have to write several drafts to find a suitable ethos for a particular argument. ○ And, yes, your ethos may change from paper to paper, audience to audience.

> Need help supporting your argument? See "How to Use the Writing Center" on pp. 328–29.

Consider your own limits.   If you read newspapers and magazines that mostly confirm your own political views, you might be in for a wake-up call when you venture an opinion beyond your small circle of friends. Tread softly. There are good reasons people don't talk politics at parties. When you do argue about social, political, or religious issues, be respectful of those who work from premises different from your own.

Consider race and ethnicity.   The different lives people live as a result of their heritage plays a role in many claims you might make about education, politics, art, religion, or even athletics. Be sensitive without being gutless. ◐

Consider gender and sexual orientation.   These issues almost always matter, often in unexpected ways. Men and women, whether straight or gay, don't inhabit quite the same worlds. But, even so, you shouldn't argue, either, as if all men and all women think the same way—or should. False assumptions about gender can lead you into a minefield.

Gender attitudes develop early, along with some argument strategies.

respect your readers
p. 374

Consider income and class.   People's lives are often defined by the realities of their economic situations—and the assumptions that follow from privilege, poverty, or something in between. Think it would be just dandy to have an outdoor pool on campus or a convenient new parking garage? You may find that not everyone is as eager or as able as you to absorb the costs of such proposals to improve campus life. And if you intend to complain about fat cats, ridicule soccer moms, or poke fun at rednecks, is it because you can't imagine them among your readers?

Consider religion and spirituality.   Members of different organized religions manage to insult each other almost without trying, more so now perhaps as religion routinely takes center stage in the political and diplomatic arena. People within the same denomination often hold incompatible views. And the word *atheist* can engender negative reactions in certain audiences. It takes skill and good sense to keep the differences in mind when your topic demands it.

Consider age.   Obviously, you'd write differently for children than for their parents on almost any subject, changing your style, vocabulary, and allusions. But consider that people at different ages really have lived different lives. The so-called greatest generation never forgot the Depression; youngsters today will remember the destruction of the World Trade Center Towers on September 11, 2001, and the school shootings in Littleton, Colorado. They'll grow up with different attitudes, values, heroes, and villains. A writer has to be savvy enough to account for such differences when constructing an argument.

Finding and developing materials

You could write a book by the time you've completed the research for some arguments. Material is out there on every imaginable subject, and the research techniques you use to prepare a report or term paper should work for arguments too. Since arguments often deal with current events and topics, start with a resource such as the Yahoo "Issues and Causes" directory mentioned earlier. Explore your subject, too, in *LexisNexis,* if your library gives you access to this huge database of newspaper articles. **O**

▶ develop
support

As you gather materials, though, consider how much space you have to make your argument. Sometimes a claim has to fit within the confines of a letter to the editor, an op-ed column in a local paper, or a fifteen-minute PowerPoint lecture. Aristotle, still one of the best theorists on persuasion, thought arguments *should* be brief, with speakers limiting examples to the *minimum* necessary to make a case—no extra points for piling on. So gather big, and then select only the best stuff for your argument.

List your reasons.   You'll come up with reasons to support your claim almost as soon as you choose a subject. Write those down. Then start reading and continue to list new reasons as they arise, not being too fussy at this point. Be careful to paraphrase these ideas so that you don't inadvertently plagiarize them later.

Then, when your reading and research are complete, review your notes and try to group the arguments that support your position. It's likely you'll detect patterns and relationships among these reasons, and an unwieldy initial list of potential arguments may be streamlined into just three or four—which could become the key reasons behind your claim. Study these points and look for logical connections or sequences. Readers will expect your ideas to converge on a claim or lead logically toward it. **O**

ORIGINAL

Why ethanol won't solve our energy problems

- Using ethanol in cars actually increases NOx emissions.
- Ethanol requires more energy to make it than it produces.
- Ethanol reduces range: You can't drive as far on a gallon.
- Ethanol can plug up fuel systems of older cars.
- Ethanol produces much less energy per gallon than gas.
- Creating ethanol contributes to global warming.

refine your search
p. 406

shape your work
p. 340

- Ethanol is cheaper than gas only because of massive farm subsidies.
- Ethanol harms performance in cars.
- Ethanol damages engines.
- Everyone's just on another eco bandwagon.
- Ethanol drives up crop prices, and thus food prices.

STREAMLINED

Why ethanol won't solve our energy problems

- Ethanol hurts performance of vehicles significantly.
- Ethanol is expensive to produce.
- Ethanol harms the environment.

Assemble your hard evidence.   Gather examples, illustrations, testimony, and numbers to support each main point. Record these items as you read, photocopying the data or downloading it carefully into labeled files. Take this evidence from the most reputable sources and keep track of all bibliographical information (author, title, publication info, URL) just as you would when preparing a term paper—even if you aren't expected to document your argument. You want that data on hand in case your credibility is later challenged.

If you borrow facts from a Web site, do your best to track the information down to its actual source. For example, if a blogger quotes statistics from the U. S. Department of Agriculture, take a few minutes to find the table or graph on the USDA Web site itself and make sure the numbers are reported accurately. ○

Think of hard evidence as a broad category that might also include photographs, video clips, or physical objects. Audiences do have a fondness for smoking guns—those pieces of indisputable evidence that clinch an argument. If you find one, use it.

Cull the best quotations.   You've done your homework for an assignment, reading the best available sources. So prove it in your argument by quoting from them intelligently. Choose quotations that do one or more of the following:

○

analyze claims and
evidence p. 420

- Put your issue in focus or context.
- Make a point with exceptional power and economy.
- Support a claim or piece of evidence that readers might doubt.
- State an opposing point well.

Copy passages that appeal to you, but don't plan on using all of them. An argument that is a patchwork of quotations reads like a patchwork of quotations—which is to say, *boring.*

Be scrupulous about getting the quotations right. That's easier now than in the past because files can be copied and downloaded electronically. But you still need to use such passages fairly and be prepared to cite and document them. O

Find counterarguments.   If you study your subject thoroughly, you'll come across plenty of honest disagreement. List all the reasonable objections that you can find to your claim, either to your basic argument or to any controversial evidence you expect to cite. When possible, cluster these objections to reduce them to a manageable few. Decide which you must refute in detail, which you might handle briefly, and which you can afford to dismiss. O

Ethanol counterarguments

- Ethanol is made from corn, a renewable resource.
- Ethanol is available today.
- Ethanol is locally made, not imported.
- Using ethanol decreases CO emissions.

Consider emotional appeals.   Nuclear power plants produce electricity without contributing significantly to global warming. But don't expect Americans who recall the Three Mile Island accident in 1979 to put aside their fears about atomic power readily, even to preserve the environment. Emotions play a powerful role in many arguments, a fact you cannot

understand citation
styles p. 435

develop ideas
p. 346

afford to ignore when a claim you make stirs up strong feelings. Questions to answer include the following:

- What emotions might be raised to support my point?
- How might I responsibly introduce such feelings: through words, images, color, sound?
- How might any feelings my subject arouses work contrary to my claims or reasons?

Well-chosen visuals add power to an argument. A writer trying to persuade readers not to buy fur might include this photo in an article. How would this image influence you, as a reader?

Creating a structure

▶ organize
ideas

It's easy to sketch a standard structure for arguments: One that leads from claim to supporting reasons to evidence and even accommodates a counter-argument or two.

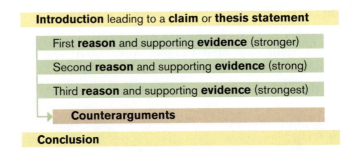

The problem is you won't read many effective arguments, either in or out of school, that follow this template. The structure isn't defective, just too simple to describe the way arguments really move when ideas matter. Some controversies need lots of background to get rolling; some require detours to resolve other issues first; and a great many arguments work best when writers simply lay out the facts and allow readers to draw their own conclusions—or be nudged toward them.

You won't write a horrible paper if you use the traditional model because all the parts will be in place. Thesis? Check. Three supporting reasons? Check. Counterarguments? Check. But your argument will sound exactly like what it is: A writer going through the motions instead of engaging with ideas. Here's how to get your ideas to breathe in an argument—while still hitting all the marks.

Spell out what's at stake. When you write an argument, you start a disagreement, so you'd better explain why. ○ Do you hope to fix a looming problem? Then describe what your concern is and make readers share it. Do you intend to correct a false notion or bad reporting? Then be sure to tell readers what setting the record straight accomplishes. Appalled by the apathy of voters, the dangers of global warming, the infringements of free speech on campus? Then explain what makes such issues matter today and why readers should pay attention.

develop a thesis
p. 336

Don't just jump into a claim: Take a few sentences or paragraphs to set up the situation. Quote a nasty politician or tell an eye-popping story or two. Get readers invested in what's to come.

Make a point or build toward one. Arguments can unfurl just as reports do, with unmistakable claims followed by reams of supporting evidence. But they can also work like crime dramas, in which the evidence in a case builds toward a compelling conclusion—your thesis perhaps. Consider the ethanol issue. You could argue straight up that this fuel causes more problems than it solves. Or you could open by wondering if ethanol really is the miracle fuel some claim it to be and then offer evidence that contradicts the media hype. In both cases, readers get the same claim and reasons. But the first approach might work better for readers already interested in environmental issues while the second might grab those who aren't by arousing their curiosity. This is your call. ○

Address counterpoints when necessary, not in a separate section. *Necessary* is when your readers start thinking to themselves, "Yeah, but what about . . . ?" Such doubts likely surface approximately where your own do—and, admit it, you have *some* misgivings about your argument. So take them on. Strategically, it rarely makes sense to consign major objections to a lengthy section near the end of a paper. That's asking for trouble. Do you really want to offer a case for the opposition just when your readers are finishing up?

On the plus side, dealing with opposing arguments can be like caffeine for your writing, sharpening your attention and reflexes. Here's Ann Hulbert, for example, eager to take on those who now argue that it's boys who are being shortchanged in schools by curriculums and modes of teaching that favor girls:

> Other complaints about boy-averse pedagogy also don't quite add up—in part because they contradict one another. Sommers blamed a touchy-feely, progressive ethos for alienating boys in the classroom; males, she argued, thrive on no-nonsense authority, accountability, clarity, and peer rivalry. But now *Newsweek* blames roughly the opposite atmosphere for boy trouble:

order ideas
p. 342

the competitive, cut-and-dried, standardized-test-obsessed (and recess-less) pedagogical emphasis of the last decade. So much speculative certainty doesn't really shed much light on the puzzle of what's deterring young men from college.

– "Will Boys Be Boys?" Slate.com, February 1, 2006

Hold your best arguments for the end.   Of course, you want strong points throughout the paper. But you need a high note early on to get readers invested and then another choral moment as you finish to send them out the door humming. If you must summarize an argument, don't let a flat recap of your main points squander an important opportunity to influence readers. End with a rhetorical flourish that reminds readers how compelling your arguments are. ○

A pithy phrase, an ironic twist, and a question to contemplate can also lock down your case. Here's Maureen Dowd, bleakly—and memorably—concluding an argument defending the job journalists have done covering the Iraq War:

Journalists die and we know who they are. We know they liked to cook and play Scrabble. But we don't know who killed them, and their killers will never be brought to justice. The enemy has no face, just a finger on a detonator.

– "Live from Baghdad: More Dying," *New York Times*, May 31, 2006

Journalists undergo training to prepare for the dangers they are likely to face in conflict zones.

shape an ending
p. 359

Choosing a style and design

Arguments vary widely in style. An unsigned editorial you write to represent the opinion of a newspaper might sound formal and serious. Composing an op-ed under your own name, you'd likely ease up on the echoing parallel clauses and allow yourself more personal pronouns. Arguing a point in an alternative newsletter, you might even slip into the lingo of its vegan or survivalist subscribers. Routine adjustments like these really matter when you need to attract and hold readers.

You should also write with sensitivity since some people reading arguments may well be wavering, defensive, or spoiling for a fight. There's no reason to distract them with fighting words if you want to offer a serious argument. Here's how political commentator Ann Coulter described a politically active group of 9/11 widows who she believed were using their status to shield their opinions of the Iraq War from criticism:

> These broads are millionaires, lionized on TV and in articles about them, reveling in their status as celebrities and stalked by grief-arazzis. I have never seen people enjoying their husbands' death so much.
>
> – *Godless: The Church of Liberalism* (2006)

Any point Coulter might make simply gets lost in her breathtaking idiom of attack.

There are many powerful and aggressive ways to frame an argument without resorting to provocative language or fallacies of argument. Following are some of those strategies. **O**

Invite readers with a strong opening.   Arguments—like advertisements—are usually discretionary reading. People can turn away the moment they grow irritated or bored. So you have to work hard to keep them invested in your ideas. You may need to open with a little surprise or drama. Try a blunt statement, an anecdote, or a striking illustration if it helps—maybe an image, too. Or consider personalizing the lead-in, giving readers a stake in the claim you are about to make. Following is a remarkable opening paragraph from an argument by Malcolm Gladwell on the wisdom of banning dogs by breed. When you finish, ask yourself whether Gladwell has earned your attention. Would you read the remainder of the piece?

read critically
p. 317

One afternoon last February, Guy Clairoux picked up his two-and-a half-year-old son, Jayden, from day care and walked him back to their house in the west end of Ottawa, Ontario. They were almost home. Jayden was straggling behind, and, as his father's back was turned, a pit bull jumped over a back-yard fence and lunged at Jayden. "The dog had his head in its mouth and started to do this shake," Clairoux's wife, JoAnn Hartley, said later. As she watched in horror, two more pit bulls jumped over the fence, joining in the assault. She and Clairoux came running, and he punched the first of the dogs in the head, until it dropped Jayden, and then he threw the boy toward his mother. Hartley fell on her son, protecting him with her body. "JoAnn!" Clairoux cried out, as all three dogs descended on his wife. "Cover your neck, cover your neck." A neighbor, sitting by her window, screamed for help. Her partner and a friend, Mario Gauthier, ran outside. A neighborhood boy grabbed his hockey stick and threw it to Gauthier. He began hitting one of the dogs over the head, until the stick broke. "They wouldn't stop," Gauthier said. "As soon as you'd stop, they'd attack again. I've never seen a dog go so crazy. They were like Tasmanian devils." The police came. The dogs were pulled away, and the Clairouxes and one of the rescuers were taken to the hospital. Five days later, the Ontario legislature banned the ownership of pit bulls. "Just as we wouldn't let a great white shark in a swimming pool," the province's attorney general, Michael Bryant, had said, "maybe we shouldn't have these animals on the civilized streets."

– "Troublemakers," *New Yorker*, February 6, 2006

Write vibrant sentences.   You can write arguments full throttle, using a complete range of rhetorical devices, from deliberate repetition and parallelism to dialogue and quotation. Metaphors, similes, and analogies fit right in too. The trick is to create sentences with a texture rich enough to keep readers hooked, yet lean enough to advance an argument. In the following three paragraphs, follow the highlighting to see how Thomas L. Friedman uses parallelism and one intriguing metaphor after another to argue in favor of immigration legislation after witnessing the diversity in a high school graduation class in Maryland. O

improve your sentences
p. 378

There is a lot to be worried about in America today: a war in Iraq that is getting worse not better, an administration whose fiscal irresponsibility we will be paying for for a long time, an education system that is not producing enough young Americans skilled in math and science, and inner cities where way too many black males are failing. We must work harder and get smarter if we want to maintain our standard of living.

But if there is one reason to still be optimistic about America it is represented by the stunning diversity of the Montgomery Blair class of 2006. America is still the world's greatest human magnet. We are not the only country that embraces diversity, but there is something about our free society and free market that still attracts people like no other. Our greatest asset is our ability to still cream off not only the first-round intellectual draft choices from around the world but the low-skilled–high-aspiring ones as well, and that is the main reason that I am not yet ready to cede the twenty-first century to China. Our Chinese will still beat their Chinese.

This influx of brainy and brawny immigrants is our oil well – one that never runs dry. It is an endless source of renewable human energy and creativity. Congress ought to stop debating gay marriage and finally give us a framework to maintain a free flow of legal immigration.

– "A Well of Smiths and Xias," *New York Times*, June 7, 2006

Ask rhetorical questions.   The danger of rhetorical questions is that they can seem stagy and readers might not answer them the way you want. But the device can be very powerful in hammering a point home. Good questions also invite readers to think about an issue in exactly the terms that a writer prefers. Here's George Will using rhetorical questions to conclude a piece on global warming.

In fact, the earth is always experiencing either warming or cooling. But suppose the scientists and their journalistic conduits, who today say they were so spectacularly wrong so recently, are now correct. Suppose the earth is warming and suppose the warming is caused by human activity. Are we sure there will be proportionate benefits from whatever climate change can be purchased at the cost of slowing economic growth and spending trillions? Are we sure the consequences of climate change – remember, a thick sheet of ice once covered the Midwest – must be bad?

Or has the science-journalism complex decided that debate about these questions, too, is "over"?

– "Let Cooler Heads Prevail," *Washington Post*, April 2, 2006

Use images and design to make a point.   If we didn't know it already (and we did), the video and photographic images from 9/11, Abu Ghraib, and Hurricane Katrina clearly prove that persuasion doesn't occur by words only. We react powerfully to what we see with our own eyes.

And yet words still play a part because most images become *focused* arguments only when accompanied by commentary—as commentators routinely prove when they put a spin on news photographs or video. And because digital technology now makes it so easy to incorporate nonverbal media into texts, whether on a page, screen, or PowerPoint slide, you should always consider how just the right image might enhance the case you want to make. And now you don't always have to start with words. A series of photographs might be shaped into a photo-essay every bit as powerful as a conventional op-ed piece.

In fact, you already have the tools on your computer to create posters, advertisements, slides, and brochures, all of which may be instruments of persuasion. **O**

Photographs of people trapped on rooftops by flooding from Hurricane Katrina became an important element of that story, and the argument that followed.

work with visuals
p. 504

Examining models

ARGUMENT FROM PERSONAL EXPERIENCE   In "Protecting What Really Matters," Shane McNamee offers a rationale for gay marriage and a good deal more. McNamee makes strong personal and emotional connections with readers by sharing portions of his life, while he assembles a logical chain of reasons for supporting his claim about gay marriage. He wrote this essay in response to an assignment in a college writing class.

McNamee 1

Shane McNamee

Professor Lavigne

Composition 12

12 December, 20--

Protecting What Really Matters

Some consider me an anomaly. As a gay man with certain conservative values, I've seen ideologues of all types distort homosexuality to advance their political agendas. Regardless of how sexual orientation is determined or defined, we should treat the subject with candor. I'll volunteer to go first.

> Establishes a trustworthy ethos.

Stereotypical gay culture doesn't suit me. I hate shopping, and you'll never see me inside a gay dance club. Hearing about such places from my gay friends creeps me out. If one craves mindless conversation or a one-night stand, he might find it there. And you're right if you think that some in the gay community regard youthful beauty more highly than traditional Christian values like chastity and committed relationships. But if your identity were criticized by defenders of traditional values from the time you hit puberty, wouldn't you yearn for alternative ideals?

> Rhetorical question leads readers to identify with McNamee's dilemma.

Gay Americans can't have their cake, much less eat it. Conservatives tell homosexuals to suppress their emotions and

91

McNamee 2

desires for a lifetime. When these bottled-up feelings explode in a burst of liberation, conservatives scold a lack of restraint. I'm all for encouraging monogamy, but many who advocate it also don't want gay marriage. With such limited options, no wonder so many gay men and women say, "The hell with you guys. You don't want me to do anything, so I'll do whatever I please."

Is homosexuality wrong? The U.S. military and the Catholic Church share similar party lines here: No — if homosexuality means nothing beyond same-sex physical attraction. But if you act on such thoughts, the plot thickens.

Military officers usually won't ask if you don't tell. They're concerned that openly gay servicemembers will hurt morale — never mind that Australia, Britain, Canada, and Israel allow openly gay servicemembers and have seen positive morale effects ("Impact"). If their subordinates seem less-than-straight and can be implicated with photos, eyewitness testimony, or a written statement from the accused, they'll likely face dishonorable discharge. I didn't like those prospects while in air force ROTC my freshman year of college. Pretending to be heterosexual at times and asexual at others proved tiresome. So I quit.

Whereas the military strictly enforces its policies, the typical Catholic Church is more relaxed. A Catholic priest, despite any ambivalence he may feel about the issue, will give you the Vatican's stance: Once you cross the line from temptation to indulgence — by acting on your homosexual desires — you commit a sin and risk going to hell. This condemnation stems from three mistakes made by those who cite the Bible passages most commonly used against

> Paragraphs about the military and Church both explore how homosexuality is tolerated so long as homosexuals deny their nature.

McNamee 3

homosexuals: mistranslation, taking a verse out of context, and reading too much into vague wording of scripture.

Though many see the Bible as the inerrant word of God, its sixty-six different books have been written by an unknown number of people throughout 1,200 years. God may have dictated to the original authors, but I doubt that God edits every translation of original scripture. Since few people know Aramaic and other relevant ancient languages, what prevents scholars from tacking their bias onto an ambiguous translation? Furthermore, we trust that the original authors were pure of heart. Saint Paul gives us room for pause.

Conservative Christians sometimes quote Paul in their attacks on homosexuality, forgetting that Jesus was mute on the subject. Modern believers should also know that Paul's values sometimes differed from Jesus'. If you admire this former persecutor of Christians, maybe you'll agree with his opinion that a woman shouldn't "teach or have authority over a man; she is to keep silent. . . ." Paul is not the only reason why we need to think more critically about the Bible.

Look at the passage that inspired the word sodomy: "Then the LORD rained upon Sodom and upon Gomorrah brimstone and fire from the LORD out of heaven. . . ." (Gen. 19:24). Many preachers interpret these lines as God punishing the Sodomites for trying to rape the angels who visit Lot. Others argue that this passage begs us to be hospitable hosts. Even if we accept the first interpretation as truth, angel-rape is a far cry from consensual homosexual relation-ships. Rape involves coercion and violence; loving relationships require free will and respect. Other infamously antigay Bible pas-sages refer to child molestation and cavorting pagans. In fact,

Uses sources to challenge religious strictures.

Offers logical reasons to question scriptural interpretations.

McNamee 4

nowhere does the Bible refer to "homosexuality." The word didn't
exist back then. Scripture that supposedly condemns same-sex
intercourse typically involves other factors: rape, prostitution, sex
with minors, etc. Homosexual relationships between consenting
adults go unmentioned.

Biblical interpretations aside, some think that homosexuals
mistake lust for love—a reasonable opinion at first glance. Most
scientists and ministers would agree that human sexuality is
tricky. Alfred Kinsey's research from the 1940s indicates that
heterosexuals act on occasional same-sex attractions ("Kinsey's").
Are these people merely confused, deviating from their prescribed
sexual destinies? Perhaps, if you accept the premise that sexual
orientation is permanently fixed.

Considering a growing scientific consensus, Christians should at
least acknowledge evidence that homosexuality has a genetic basis.
A recent study conducted by Dr. Brian Mustanski from the University
of Illinois at Chicago supports earlier scientific forays into sexual
orientation by building "on previous studies that have consistently
found evidence of genetic influence on sexual orientation" ("Is There a
Gay Gene?" 1). Mustanski scoured the human genome for genetic
material shared among hundreds of sets of brothers, both gay and
straight. He found that regions of DNA from three chromosomes were
shared by 60% of gay brothers, more than the 50% expected from
chance alone. These findings suggest that homosexuality, while not
determined solely by genetics, results from more than just social factors.

Environmental variables certainly help establish sexuality, but
if we're going to play that game, here's some personal history: (1) I

> Uses both research and personal experience to question Western attitudes toward homosexuality.

> Uses scientific evidence to argue key point.

McNamee 5

was never molested; (2) my relationship with my father has always been peachy; and (3) I rarely saw homosexuals on TV or otherwise as a youngster—not until after I already suspected that I was different from other boys. These facts disprove those who believe that homosexuality is caused by traumatic childhood experience, a distant father, or indoctrination. And just so we're clear, most geneticists now believe that human traits depend on the interaction between both our genes and our environment—trait-expressing DNA segments are triggered by environmental stimuli, including both chemical and social agents.

Yet science is only one source of authority. Practically speaking, human experience is more relevant than academic debate. If God is as great as we all hope, I think He'd want us to be happy with whomever we love. Last summer I found someone who makes me happy.

I love Jonathan Miguel Jiménez, and I'm not afraid to say it. We're from different backgrounds and are of two minds when it comes to politics. He's much more liberal than I am. Though we have our disagreements, these debates add to the joy we derive from our relationship. JJ has already taught me more about myself and about crafting a solid argument than a lifetime of personal reflection and formal education.

If openly embracing homosexuality still bothers you, forget for the moment the rainbow flags and pink triangles. Gay pride is not about being homosexual; it's about the integrity and courage it takes to be honest with yourself and your loved ones. It's about spending life with whomever you want and not worrying what the government or the neighbors think. Let's protect that truth, not some rigid view of sexual

> Risks his relationship with readers with frank declaration.

> Throughout, argument is both personal and political.

McNamee 6

Responsibility for action on gay marriage is laid on readers.

orientation or marriage. Keep gay marriage out of your church if you like, but if you value monogamy as I do, give me an alternative that doesn't involve dishonesty or a life of loneliness. Many upstanding gay citizens yearn for recognition of their loving, committed relationships. Unless you enjoy being lied to and are ready to send your gay friends and family on a Trail of Queers to Massachusetts or Canada—where gay marriage is legal—then consider letting them live as they wish.

McNamee 7

Works Cited

"Impact of Lifting the Ban: Other Agencies and Countries That Allow
    Open Service." *HRC.org.* Human Rights Campaign, 2009. Web. 5
    Mar. 2009.

"Is There a Gay Gene?" *WebMD.* WebMD, 28 Jan. 2005. Web. 23 Feb.
    2009.

"Kinsey's Heterosexual-Homosexual Rating Scale." *Kinsey Institute.*
    Kinsey Inst. for Research in Sex, Gender, and Reproduction, Mar.
    2009. Web. 10 Mar. 2009.

ARGUMENT ABOUT A PUBLIC ISSUE Writing during the run-up to the American invasion of Afghanistan, Anna Quindlen argues in "Uncle Sam and Aunt Samantha" that, should a military draft be necessary, women must be included. The piece appeared in *Newsweek* in November 2001.

Uncle Sam and Aunt Samantha

ANNA QUINDLEN

One out of every five new recruits in the United States military is female.

The Marines gave the Combat Action Ribbon for service in the Persian Gulf to twenty-three women.

Two female soldiers were killed in the bombing of the USS *Cole*.

The Selective Service registers for the draft all male citizens between the ages of eighteen and twenty-five.

What's wrong with this picture?

As Americans read and realize that the lives of most women in this country are as different from those of Afghan women as a Cunard cruise is from maximum-security lockdown, there has nonetheless been little attention paid to one persistent gender inequity in U.S. public policy. An astonishing anachronism, really: While women are represented today in virtually all fields, including the armed forces, only men are required to register for the military draft that would be used in the event of a national security crisis.

Since the nation is as close to such a crisis as it has been in more than sixty years, it's a good moment to consider how the draft wound up in this particular time warp. It's not the time warp of the Taliban, certainly, stuck in the worst part of the thirteenth century, forbidding women to attend school or hold jobs or even reveal their arms, forcing them into sex and marriage. Our own time warp is several decades old. The last time the draft was considered seriously was twenty years ago, when registration with the Selective Service was restored by Jimmy Carter after the Soviet invasion of,

> Defines a
> clear problem.

yep, Afghanistan. The president, as well as army chief of staff, asked at the time for the registration of women as well as men.

Amid a welter of arguments—women interfere with esprit decorps, women don't have the physical strength, women prisoners could be sexually assaulted, women soldiers would distract male soldiers from their mission—Congress shot down the notion of gender-blind registration. So did the Supreme Court, ruling that since women were forbidden to serve in combat positions and the purpose of the draft was to create a combat-ready force, it made sense not to register them.

But that was then, and this is now. Women have indeed served in combat positions, in the Balkans and the Middle East. More than forty thousand managed to serve in the Persian Gulf without destroying unit cohesion or failing because of upper-body strength. Some are even now taking out targets in Afghanistan from fighter jets, and apparently without any male soldier's falling prey to some predicted excess of chivalry or lust.

Talk about cognitive dissonance. All these military personnel, male and female alike, have come of age at a time when a significant level of parity was taken for granted. Yet they are supposed to accept that only males will be required to defend their country in a time of national emergency. This is insulting to men. And it is insulting to women. Caroline Forell, an expert on women's legal rights and a professor at the University of Oregon School of Law, puts it bluntly: "Failing to require this of women makes us lesser citizens."

Neither the left nor the right has been particularly inclined to consider this issue judiciously. Many feminists came from the antiwar movement and have let their distaste for the military in general and the draft in particular mute their response. In 1980 NOW released a resolution that buried support for the registration of women beneath opposition to the draft, despite the fact that the draft had been re-designed to eliminate the vexing inequities of Vietnam, when the sons of the working class served and the sons of the Ivy League did not. Conservatives, meanwhile, used an equal-opportunity draft as the linchpin of opposition to the Equal Rights Amendment, along with the terrifying specter of unisex bathrooms. (I

Two paragraphs provide background information.

Forell states what is, in effect, Quindlen's thesis.

Concedes fault on all sides.

have seen the urinal, and it is benign.) The legislative director of the right-wing group Concerned Women for America once defended the existing regulations by saying that most women "don't want to be included in the draft." All those young men who went to Canada during Vietnam and those who today register with fear and trembling in the face of the Trade Center devastation might be amazed to discover that lack of desire is an affirmative defense.

Parents face a series of unique new challenges in this more egalitarian world, not the least of which would be sending a daughter off to war. But parents all over this country are doing that right now, with daughters who enlisted; some have even expressed surprise that young women, in this day and age, are not required to register alongside their brothers and friends. While all involved in this debate over the years have invoked the assumed opposition of the people, even ten years ago more than half of all Americans polled believed women should be made eligible for the draft. Besides, this is not about comfort but about fairness. My son has to register with the Selective Service this year, and if his sister does not when she turns eighteen, it makes a mockery not only of the standards of this household but of the standards of this nation.

> "Fairness" is premise for key argument.

It is possible in Afghanistan for women to be treated like little more than fecund pack animals precisely because gender fear and ignorance and hatred have been codified and permitted to hold sway. In this country, largely because of the concerted efforts of those allied with the women's movement over a century of struggle, much of that bigotry has been beaten back, even buried. Yet in improbable places the creaky old ways surface, the ways suggesting that we women were made of finer stuff. The finer stuff was usually porcelain, decorative and on the shelf, suitable for meals and show. Happily, the finer stuff has been transmuted into the right stuff. But with rights come responsibilities, as teachers like to tell their students. This is a responsibility that should fall equally upon all, male and female alike. If the empirical evidence is considered rationally, if the decision is divested of outmoded stereotypes, that's the only possible conclusion to be reached.

> Only stereotypes prevent reasonable change in U.S. draft policy. Conclusion shows how elements of Quindlen's argument connect.

VISUAL ARGUMENT

"Vampire Energy" appeared in the January/February 2008 issue of *GOOD* magazine, an online periodical. While the image conveys a great deal of information, it also makes an explicit argument for energy conservation.

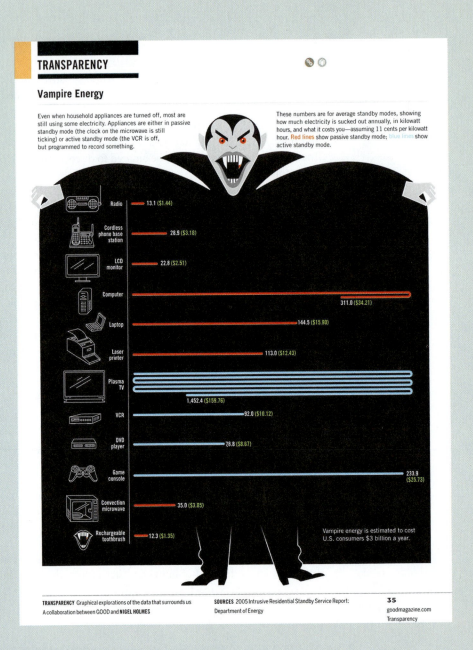

TRANSPARENCY

Vampire Energy

Even when household appliances are turned off, most are still using some electricity. Appliances are either in passive standby mode (the clock on the microwave is still ticking) or active standby mode (the VCR is off, but programmed to record something.

These numbers are for average standby modes, showing how much electricity is sucked out annually, in kilowatt hours, and what it costs you—assuming 11 cents per kilowatt hour. Red lines show passive standby mode; blue lines show active standby mode.

Radio — 13.1 ($1.44)

Cordless phone base station — 28.9 ($3.18)

LCD monitor — 22.8 ($2.51)

Computer — 311.0 ($34.21)

Laptop — 144.5 ($15.90)

Laser printer — 113.0 ($12.43)

Plasma TV — 1,452.4 ($159.76)

VCR — 92.0 ($10.12)

DVD player — 78.8 ($8.67)

Game console — 233.9 ($25.73)

Convection microwave — 35.0 ($3.85)

Rechargeable toothbrush — 12.3 ($1.35)

Vampire energy is estimated to cost U.S. consumers $3 billion a year.

TRANSPARENCY Graphical explorations of the data that surrounds us
A collaboration between GOOD and **NIGEL HOLMES**

SOURCES 2005 Intrusive Residential Standby Service Report: Department of Energy

35

goodmagazine.com
Transparency

Assignments

1. **Argument from Personal Experience:** Write an argument that draws heavily on your personal experiences but potentially affects a large segment of the public, in the manner of Shane McNamee's "Protecting What Really Matters" (p. 91). Be sure, though, that your argument also draws on a range of outside sources.

2. **Argument about a Public Issue:** As Anna Quindlen does in "Uncle Sam and Aunt Samantha" (p. 97), assemble the facts about a controversy on your campus or in your community — academic, social, political, or religious — and take a stand on the issue. Gather the necessary background information and keep abreast of day-to-day developments, following coverage of the issue in multiple sources when possible. Finally, offer a perspective of your own and defend your claim authoritatively in an essay short enough to serve as an op-ed piece in your campus or local newspaper.

3. **Visual Argument:** In "Vampire Energy," *GOOD* magazine supports an argument about energy usage by making factual information powerfully visual (p. 100). Design a visual argument of your own that not only offers a specific claim (e.g., *Drill here, drill now*) but also presents visual evidence to support or extend it.

4. **Online Argument:** If you have the technical skills, design a Web site or blog that focuses on an issue — local or national — that you believe deserves more attention. Using current sites or blogs as models, be sure your project introduces the topic, explains your purpose, provides a forum for feedback, and includes both images and links relevant to the topic and online community.

How to start

- Need a **topic**? See page 107.
- Need **criteria for your evaluation**? See page 110.
- Need to **organize your criteria and evidence**? See page 113.

4 Evaluation

makes a claim about the value of something

Evaluations—in the forms of commentary and criticism—are so much a part of our lives that you might only notice them when they are specifically assigned. The others just happen.

- On a course evaluation, you explain in detail how your physics instructor made a mystifying subject you detested relevant and clear.

- After reviewing the draft of a friend's short story, you send her an e-mail explaining why it needs a thorough reorganization and rewrite.

- You run an increasingly popular blog featuring reviews of recent Hollywood movies from your particular red-state point of view.

- You sort through two dozen brochures and Web sites trying to find a 10-megapixel digital SLR camera that would meet your semiprofessional needs and very amateur budget.

- It's late August, time once again to go ballistic when *Sports Illustrated* fails even to rank your team among the top-ten prospects for the NCAA national title in football. How can the editors be so stupid? You're more than willing to explain.

UNDERSTANDING EVALUATIONS.   It's one thing to offer an opinion, an entirely different matter to back up a claim with reasons and evidence. Only when you do will readers (or listeners) take you seriously. But you'll also have to convince them that you know *how* to evaluate a book, a social policy, even a cup of coffee by reasonable standards. It helps when you use objective standards to make judgments, counting and measuring the road to excellence. But evaluations frequently involve people debating matters of taste. Here's how to frame this kind of argument. ○

Make value judgments.   You'll either judge something as good, bad, or indifferent when you write an evaluation or challenge an opinion someone else has offered. Of course, fair judgments can be quite complex: Even movie critics who do thumbs-up-or-down routines don't offer those verdicts until after they first talk about their subjects in detail.

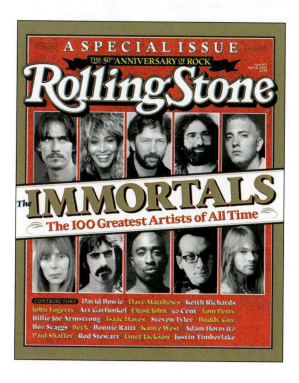

Popular magazines frequently evaluate or rank artists and celebrities, and their work. Cover photo from *Rolling Stone*, April 21, 2005. ©Rolling Stone LLC 2005. All rights reserved. Reprinted by permission.

○

understand argument
p. 68

Establish and defend criteria.   *Criteria* are the standards by which objects are measured: *A good furnace should heat a home quickly and efficiently. Successful presidents leave office with the country in better shape than when they entered.* When readers will generally agree with your criteria, you need to explain little about them. When they won't, you have to defend them. O And sometimes you'll break new ground—as happened when critics first asked, *What is good Web design?* and *Which are the best blogs?* In such cases, new criteria of evaluation had to be invented and rationalized.

Offer convincing evidence.   Evidence in the form of facts, statistics, testimony, examples, and good reasons provides the link between an evaluative claim and the criteria used to make it. If good furnaces heat homes quickly and efficiently, then you'd have to supply data to show that a product you judged faulty didn't meet those minimal standards. (It might be noisy and unreliable to boot.) Evidence will obviously vary from subject to subject, anything from hard numbers to harrowing tales of personal woe. O

Offer useful advice.   Some evaluations are just for fun: Consider all the hoopla that arguments about sports rankings generate. But most evaluations, when done right, also provide practical information—some of it offered in clever forms that make it easy for readers to find and consult. So evaluations do important work, whether they rank humidifiers, books, or candidates in a city-council race.

Here's a review of the type millions of people consult annually when they consider spending $25,000 or more to buy a new car. You'll note that the following review of a Toyota Camry Hybrid not only describes the product in detail but also attempts to match the vehicle to its likely buyers. Many different criteria of evaluation are embedded in the review, some of them relating specifically to a hybrid vehicle designed to enhance fuel economy, not driving pleasure.

develop ideas
p. 346

interview and observe
p. 412

Erik B. Johnson's review in *Automobile* magazine acknowledges the merit of the new Camry for readers considering a hybrid vehicle, offering good reasons to examine it in the showroom. But Johnson leaves readers to make the final judgment with their checkbooks.

2007 Toyota Camry Hybrid

ERIK B. JOHNSON

With fuel prices in flux and environmental concerns deepening, the seductive song of the hybrid sirens is louder than ever, despite increasing skepticism about hybrid vehicles' positive effects on wallets and the environment. Perhaps the problem is that there hasn't yet been a fuel-sipping hybrid sedan for the common family man. The current hybrid sedans are either too conspicuous (Toyota Prius), too small (Honda Civic Hybrid), or too focused on performance rather than economy (Lexus GS450h and Honda Accord Hybrid). But Toyota's latest gasoline/electric model, the Camry Hybrid, is a fastball grooved right down the Everyman's strike zone. With it, Toyota aims to bring hybrid ownership to the masses; after all, the 2007 Camry on which it is based is the successor to the best-selling car in America.

Toyota Camry Hybrid

> **Opening paragraph establishes criteria for hybrid.**

The Camry Hybrid is a comfortable and unassuming machine as long as you drive it calmly over smooth pavement, where you'll enjoy generally placid ride characteristics. But stay away from pockmarked roads, where the Hybrid's body control goes limp (likely due to the extra weight of the hybrid system), poor damping allows unwanted vibrations into the cabin, and severe bumps cause kickback through the steering wheel.

Author makes important observation: The car sounds and feels slower than it is.

One of the Hybrid's oddest attributes is the relationship between its throttle, engine speed, and engine sound. The accelerator has long travel and is desensitized to all but the most urgent stomps; when you mash the pedal, the continuously variable transmission revs the engine endlessly, making it sound not unlike a broken food processor. All of this makes the car seem unbearably sluggish, but in an extremely scientific test—OK, a drag race—the Hybrid outpulled its conventional four-cylinder twin by a hefty margin.

Over a day of driving in urban and suburban settings, the Camry Hybrid returned 37 mpg, which is close to the EPA's combined estimate of 39 mpg. (Unlike the Accord Hybrid, the Camry Hybrid will run solely on battery power for several minutes if you go easy on the gas.) But before you fill out that Sierra Club application, consider that a regular four-cylinder Camry LE with a five-speed automatic achieved 31 mpg on the same route.

Compares mileage figures to provide evidence for consumers.

It would seem almost foolish to opt for the Hybrid, if not for its compelling price. Most hybrids command a lofty premium over nonhybrid versions of the same vehicle, but at $26,480, the equipment-heavy Camry Hybrid is only about $1,500 more than a similarly outfitted four-cylinder Camry XLE. Is 6 mpg worth the additional cash? It almost doesn't matter, because the Hybrid's negatives—including its smaller trunk, due to the hybrid system's components—won't be enough to dissuade people from plunking down the extra money if they really want one. Simply put, hybrids make a lot of people feel good, and, in the end, that's just as valid a reason to buy a car as avant-garde styling or world-class handling.

Exploring purpose and topic

Most evaluations you're required to prepare for school or work come with assigned topics. But to choose an object to evaluate, follow different strategies, depending on what you hope to accomplish. ○

Evaluate a subject you know well.   This is the safest option, built on the assumption that everyone is an expert on something. Years of reading *Gourmet* magazine or playing tennis might make it natural for you to review restaurants or tennis rackets. You've accumulated not only basic facts but also lots of tactile knowledge—the sort that gives you confidence when you make a claim. So go ahead and demonstrate your expertise.

topic ◄

Evaluate a subject you need to investigate.   Perhaps you are considering graduate schools to apply to, looking for family-friendly companies to work for, or thinking about purchasing an HDTV. To make such choices, you'll need more information. So kill two birds with a single assignment: Use the school project to explore the issues you face, find the necessary facts and data, and make a case for (or against) Michigan State, Whole Foods, or Sharp.

Evaluate a subject you'd like to know more about.   How do wine connoisseurs tell one cabernet from another and rank them so confidently? How would a college football championship team from the fifties match up against more recent winning teams? Use an assignment to settle questions like these that you an d your friends may have debated late into an evening.

Keep an open mind.   Whatever your topic, you probably shouldn't begin an evaluation already knowing the outcome—hating a book before you read it or dead set against any chilies not grown in Hatch, New Mexico. Follow your criteria and data to the reasonable choice—even if it's one you don't prefer. Don't review what you can't treat fairly.

A fair evaluation requires an open mind.

find a topic
p. 308

Understanding your audience

Your job as a reviewer is made easier when you can assume readers might be interested in your opinions. Fortunately, most people consult evaluations and reviews willingly, hoping to find specific information: *Is the latest Tony Hillerman novel up to snuff? Who's the most important American architect working today? Mets or Marlins in the NL East this year?* But you'll still have to gauge the level of potential readers and make appropriate adjustments.

Write for experts.   Knowledgeable readers can be a tough audience because they bring to a subject strong, maybe inflexible, opinions. But if you know your stuff, you can take on the experts because they know their stuff too: You don't have to provide tedious background information or discuss criteria of evaluation in detail. You can use the technical vocabulary experts share and make allusions to people and concepts they'd recognize. Here's a paragraph from *Road & Track* that isn't making concessions to the general public:

> The new Variable Turbine Geometry technology is not new, having been used on diesels for years. It works by adding vanes outside the turbine that can change pitch with an electric motor. The vanes focus exhaust flow onto the turbine blades at low throttle opening, but at larger flow rates, i.e., high rpm, they open up to decrease the restriction. Porsche's breakthrough in applying this to a gasoline engine centers on the materials that are used to control thermal expansion due to the hotter exhaust gases from gasoline engines.
>
> — Shaun Bailey, "2007 Porsche 911 Turbo," June 2006

Need help thinking about your audience? See "How to Revise Your Work" on pp. 390–91.

Write for a general audience.   You have to explain more to general audiences than to specialists, clarifying your criteria of evaluation, providing background information, and defining key terms. But general readers usually are willing to learn more about a topic. Here's noted film critic Roger Ebert doing exactly that:

> *The Lake House* tells the story of a romance that spans years but involves only a few kisses. It succeeds despite being based on two paradoxes: time travel and the ability of two people to have conversations that are, under the terms established by the film, impossible. Neither one of these

problems bothered me in the slightest. Take time travel: I used to get distracted by its logical flaws and contradictory time lines. Now in my wisdom I have decided to simply accept it as a premise, no questions asked. A time-travel story works on emotional, not temporal, logic.

–rogerebert.com, June 16, 2006

Write for novices.   You have a lot of explaining to do when readers are absolutely fresh to a subject and need lots of background information. For instance, because *Consumer Reports* reviews a range of products well beyond the expertise of any individual, the editors always take care to explain how they make their judgments, whether the subject be washing machines, waffles, or Web sites. Do the same yourself. Take special care to define technical terms for your readers.

Are buffalo dangerous?   For some audiences, you have to explain *everything*.

The following, for example, is a warning attached to camera reviews at Digital Photography Review, a Web site that examines photographic equipment in detail; "If you're new to digital photography you may wish to read the Digital Photography *Glossary* before diving into this article (it may help you understand some of the terms used)." Clicking the link leads to a fully illustrated dictionary of terms meant to help amateurs understand the qualities of a good digital camera.

Finding and developing materials

Assigned to write a review, it makes sense to research your subject thoroughly, even one you think you know pretty well. Online research is easy: Do a quick Web search to see if your notions are still current in a world where opinions change rapidly. ○

For many subjects (and products especially), it's easy to discover what others have already written, particularly when a topic has a distinctive name. Just type that name followed by the word *review* into Google's search window and see what pops up. But don't merely parrot opinions you find in sources: Challenge conventional views whenever you can offer better ones. (At one time, most critics thought good poetry should rhyme—until some poets and critics argued otherwise.) Make a fresh and distinctive case of your own. To do that, focus on criteria and evidence.

▶ develop
criteria

Decide on your criteria. Get them firmly in mind, even if you're just evaluating pizza. Should the crust be hard or soft? The sauce red and spicy, or white and creamy? How thick should pizza be? How salty? And, to all these opinions—*why*?

Didn't expect the *why*? You really don't have a criterion until you attach a plausible reason to it. ○ The rationale should be clear in your own mind even if you don't expect to expound on it in the review or evaluation itself: *Great pizza comes with a soft crust that wraps each bite and topping in a floury texture that merges the contrasting flavors.* More important, any criteria you use will have to make sense to readers either on its own (*Public art should be beautiful*) or after you've explained and defended it (*Public art should be scandalous because people need to be jolted out of conformist thinking*).

Look for hard criteria. It helps when criteria are countable or observable. You'll seem objective when your criteria at least *seem* grounded in numbers. Think, for example, of how instructors set numerical standards for your performance in their courses, translating all sorts of activities, from papers to class participation, into numbers. Teachers aren't alone in deferring to numbers. Following, for example, are the criteria CNET Reviews follows for evaluating televisions, as explained on its Web site:

refine your search
p. 406

develop a thesis
p. 336

Design (30 percent of the total rating): We look at not only the overall aesthetics of the product but also its interface and included remote. An uninspiring but functional design will rate a 5. Higher scores will be given for a well-designed remote with backlit buttons, a clear onscreen navigation system, and particularly sleek cosmetics.

Features (30 percent of the total rating): The range of features is considered in determining this portion of the rating. From picture-in-picture (PIP) and 2:3 pull-down to the appropriate number of A/V inputs, we consider everything this product delivers to the consumer. A set that comes armed with a suitable number of inputs and basic features will earn a 5. Products with more inputs, individual input memories, or other extras will earn a better rating.

Performance (40 percent of the total rating): We consider picture quality to be the most important criteria for displays, so we give it the most weight. A score of 5 represents a television that can produce a serviceable picture with only a reasonable amount of adjustment. Sets with a particularly sharp picture; rich, accurate color; deep black levels; and good video processing will earn a higher score.

Argue for criteria that can't be measured.   How do you measure the success or failure of something that can't be objectively calculated—a student dance recital, Scorsese's latest film, or the new abstract sculpture just hauled onto the campus? Do some research to find out how such topics are customarily discussed. Get familiar with what sensible critics have to say about whatever you're evaluating—contemporary art, fine saddles, good teaching, TV crime dramas. If you read carefully, you'll find values and criteria deeply embedded in all your sources. O

In the following, for example, James Morris explains why he believes American television is often better than Hollywood films. Morris's criteria are highlighted.

What I admire most about these shows, and most deplore about contemporary movies, is the quality of the scripts. The TV series are devised and written by smart people who seem to be allowed to let their intelligence show. Yes, the individual and ensemble performances on several of the series are superb, but would the actors be as good as they are if they were miming the action? TV shows are designed for the small screen and cannot rely, as movies do,

read closely
p. 317

on visual and aural effects to distract audiences. If what's being said on TV isn't interesting, why bother to watch? Television is rigorous, right down to the confinement of hour or half-hour time slots, further reduced by commercials. There's no room for the narrative bloat that inflates so many Hollywood movies from their natural party-balloon size to Thanksgiving-parade dimensions.

—"My Favorite Wasteland," *Wilson Quarterly*, Autumn 2005

Stand by your values.   Make sure you define criteria that apply to more than just the individual case you are examining at the moment. Think about what makes socially conscious rap music, world-class sculpture, a great president. For instance, you may have a special fondness for Jimmy Carter, but should criteria for great presidents be measured by what they do *after* they leave office? Similarly, you might admire artists or actors who overcome great personal tragedies on their paths to stardom. But to make such heroics a *necessary* criterion for artistic achievement might look like special pleading.

Gather your evidence.   In writing an evaluation, some of your evidence will come from secondary sources, especially when assessing something like a government program or historical event. Before offering an opinion on the merit of Social Security or the wisdom of Truman's decision to drop atomic bombs to end World War II, expect to do critical reading. Weigh the evidence and arguments you find in these sources before you offer your own judgment—and then cite some of these sources for evidence and support. O

Other evidence will come from careful observation. When judging a book, a movie, a restaurant, or an art exhibit, for instance, take careful notes not only of your initial impressions but also of the details that support or explain them. When appropriate, take time to measure, weigh, photograph, and interview your subjects. If it makes sense to survey what others think about an issue (about a campus political issue, for example), keep a record of such opinions. Finally, be willing to alter your opinion when the evidence you gather in support of a hypothesis heads in a direction you hadn't expected. (See Scott Standley's "Rock the Vote: Useful Harm?" on p. 121.)

analyze claims and
evidence p. 420

Creating a structure

As with other arguments, evaluations have distinct parts that can be built into a pattern or structure.

organize ◄
criteria

Choose a simple structure when your criteria and categories are predictable. A basic review might announce a subject and make a claim, list criteria of evaluation, present evidence to show whether the subject meets those standards, and draw conclusions. Here's one version of that pattern with the criteria discussed all at once, at the opening of the piece.

> **Introduction** leading to an **evaluative claim**
>
> **Criteria of evaluation** stated and, if necessary, defended
>
> → **Subject** measured by first **criterion + evidence**
>
> → **Subject** measured by second **criterion + evidence**
>
> → **Subject** measured by additional **criteria + evidence**
>
> **Conclusion**

And here's a template with the criteria of evaluation introduced one at a time.

> **Introduction** leading to an **evaluative claim**
>
> **First criterion of evaluation** stated and, if necessary, defended
>
> → **Subject** measured by first **criterion + evidence**
>
> **Second criterion** stated/defended
>
> → **Subject** measured by second **criterion + evidence**
>
> **Additional criteria** stated/defended
>
> → **Subject** measured by additional **criteria + evidence**
>
> **Conclusion**

You might find structures this tight and predictable, for instance, in job-performance reviews at work or in consumer magazines. Once a pattern is established for measuring TVs, computers, paint sprayers, even teachers (consider those forms you fill in at the end of the term), it can be repeated for each new subject and results can be compared.

Yet what works for hardware and tech products is not quite so convincing when applied to music, books, or other subjects that are more than the sum of their parts. Imagine a film critic whose *every* review marched through the same predictable set of criteria: acting, directing, writing, set design, cinematography, and costumes. When a subject can't be reviewed via simple categories, you will need to decide which of its many possible aspects deserve attention. O

Choose a focal point.   Look for features that you and your readers will surely notice, that is, what makes you react strongly and intellectually to the subject. You could, in fact, organize an entire review around one or more shrewd insights, and many reviewers do. The trick is to make connections between key or controlling ideas and various aspects of your subject. Look carefully at Rob Sheffield's review of Green Day's *American Idiot* (p. 119) and you'll discover that what holds it together are the writer's expressions of surprise that an aging punk band can still do relevant work. Sheffield makes that point at both the beginning and the end of the evaluation:

> Tell the truth: Did anybody think Green Day would still be around in 2004? Ten years ago, when they blew up into the hot summer band of 1994, they were snotty little Berkeley, California, punk kids who sounded ready to pogo off the face of the earth in three-chord tantrums such as "Basket Case."
>   . . . Against all odds, Green Day have found a way to hit their thirties without either betraying their original spirit or falling on their faces.

Compare and contrast.   Another obvious way to organize an evaluation is to examine differences. Strengths and weaknesses stand out especially well when similar subjects are examined critically, as in the following opening paragraph of a review in the *Wall Street Journal*:

shape your work
p. 340

We've been testing this new iMac, and our verdict is that it's the gold standard of desktop PCs. To put it simply: No desktop offered by Dell or Hewlett-Packard or Sony or Gateway can match the new iMac G5's combination of power, elegance, simplicity, ease of use, built-in software, stability, and security. From setup to performing the most intense tasks, it's a pleasure to use. And, contrary to common misconceptions, this Mac is competitively priced, when compared with comparably equipped midrange Windows PCs; and it handles all common Windows files, as well as the Internet and e-mail, with aplomb.

–Walter S. Mossberg and Catherine Boehret, "A Gold Standard for PCs," November 30, 2005

To keep extended comparisons on track, the simplest structure is to evaluate one subject at a time, running through its features completely before moving on to the next. Let's say you decided to contrast economic conditions in France and Germany. Here's how such a paper might look in a scratch outline if you focused on the countries one at a time. **O**

France and Germany: An Economic Report Card

I. France
   A. Rate of growth
   B. Unemployment rate
   C. Productivity
   D. Gross national product
   E. Debt

II. Germany
   A. Rate of growth
   B. Unemployment rate
   C. Productivity
   D. Gross national product
   E. Debt

order ideas
p. 342

The disadvantage of evaluating subjects one at a time is that actual comparisons, let's say, of rates of employment in the outline above, might appear pages apart. So in some cases, you might prefer a comparison-contrast structure that looks at features point by point.

France and Germany: An Economic Report Card

   I. Rate of growth
     A. France
     B. Germany
  II. Unemployment rate
     A. France
     B. Germany
 III. Productivity
     A. France
     B. Germany
 IV. Gross national product
     A. France
     B. Germany
  V. Debt
     A. France
     B. Germany

Choosing a style and design

Depending on the aim of the review you are composing and your stance within it, evaluations can be written in any style, from high to low. ○ You should also look for opportunities to present evaluations visually.

Use a high or formal style.   Technical reviews tend to be the most formal and impersonal: They may be almost indistinguishable from reports, spelling out findings in plain, unemotional language. Such a style gives the impression of scientific objectivity, even though the work may reflect someone's agenda. For instance, here's a paragraph in formal style from the National Assessment of Educational Progress summarizing the performance of American students in science.

> At grade 8, there was no overall improvement. In 2005, 59 percent of students scored at or above the *Basic* level. An example of the knowledge and skills at the *Basic* level is being able to compare changes in heart rate during and after exercise. Twenty-nine percent performed at or above the *Proficient* level. Identifying the energy conversions that occur in an electric fan is an example of the knowledge and skills at the *Proficient* level.
>
> –*Nation's Report Card*, 2005 Science Assessment (http://nationsreportcard .gov/science_2005)

Use a middle style.   When the writer has a more direct stake in the work—as is typical in restaurant or movie reviews, for example—the style moves more decisively toward the middle. Even though a reviewer may never use *I,* you still sense a person behind the writing, making judgments and offering opinions. That's certainly the case in these two paragraphs by Clive Crook, written shortly after the death of noted economist John Kenneth Galbraith: Words, phrases, even sentence fragments that humanize the assessment are highlighted.

> Galbraith, despite the Harvard professorship, was never really an economist in the ordinary sense in the first place. In one of countless well-turned pronouncements, he said, "Economics is extremely useful as a form of employment for economists." He disdained the scientific pretensions and formal apparatus of modern economics—all that math and number

crunching—believing that it missed the point. This view did not spring from mastery of the techniques: Galbraith disdained them from the outset, which saved time.

   Friedman, in contrast, devoted his career to grinding out top-quality scholarly work, while publishing the occasional best seller as a sideline. He too was no math whiz, but he was painstakingly scientific in his methods (when engaged in scholarly research) and devoted to data. All that was rather beneath Galbraith. Brilliant, yes; productive, certainly. But he was a bureaucrat, a diplomat, a political pundit, and a popular economics writer of commanding presence more than a serious economic thinker, let alone a great one.

   —"John Kenneth Galbraith, Revisited," *National Journal*, May 15, 2006

Use a low style.   Many reviews get chummy with readers and so personal they verge on arrogance. You probably want evaluations you write for academic or work assignments to be relatively low-key in style, focused more on the subject than on you as the reviewer. But you have an enormous range of options—all the more reason to look at models of the kind of evaluation you will be preparing. For examples of highly personal reviews using an informal style, check those of products on Amazon.com.

Present evaluations visually.   Comparisons work especially well when presented via tables, charts, or graphs. O Readers see relationships that could not be explained quite as efficiently in words alone.

PET scan of two human brains.   To evaluate patients, doctors use comparison and contrast as a diagnostic tool. The brain on the left reflects normal brain activity; that on the right shows the brain activity of a schizophrenic.

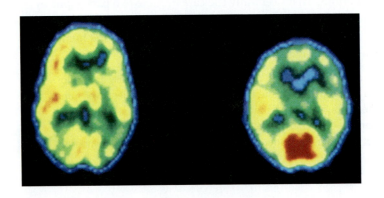

O
display data
p. 514

Examining models

MUSIC REVIEW   Rob Sheffield couldn't know how successful Green Day's CD *American Idiot* would be when he reviewed it in September 2004 for *Rolling Stone,* well before it won multiple Grammys and a huge following. But his review holds up because he examines the music in its context, recognizing weaknesses, yet admitting its unanticipated strengths. The review also demonstrates how demanding a colloquial style, with its idiosyncratic vocabulary and in-the-know allusions, can be.

Green Day: *American Idiot*

ROB SHEFFIELD

Tell the truth: Did anybody think Green Day would still be around in 2004? Ten years ago, when they blew up into the hot summer band of 1994, they were snotty little Berkeley, California, punk kids who sounded ready to pogo off the face of the earth in three-chord tantrums such as "Basket Case." Between Billie Joe Armstrong's adenoidal snarl and Tre Cool's maniac drums, Green Day seemed like a Saturday-morning-cartoon version of *The Young Ones,* three cheeky monkeys who came to raid the bar and disappear. But here they are with *American Idiot*: a fifty-seven-minute politically charged epic depicting a character named Jesus of Suburbia as he suffers through the decline and fall of the American dream. And all this from the boys who brought you *Dookie.*

   American Idiot is the kind of old-school rock opera that went out of style when Keith Moon still had a valid driver's license, in the tradition of the Who's *Tommy,* Yes's *Relayer,* or Styx's *Kilroy Was Here.* Since Green Day are punk rockers, they obviously have a specific model in mind: Hüsker Dü's 1984 *Zen Arcade,* which showed how a street-level hardcore band could play around with storytelling without diluting the primal anger of the music. On *American Idiot,* the thirteen tracks segue together,

> Provides information to locate *American Idiot* musically.

> This sentence serves as thesis. *Surprise— this music is serious.*

expanding into piano balladry and acoustic country shuffles. The big statement "Jesus of Suburbia" is a nine-minute five-part suite, with Roman-numeral chapters including "City of the Damned," "Dearly Beloved," and "Tales of Another Broken Home."

American Idiot could have been a mess; in fact, it is a mess. The plot has characters with names such as St. Jimmy and Whatsername, young rebels who end up on the "Boulevard of Broken Dreams." But the individual tunes are tough and punchy enough to work on their own. You can guess who the "American Idiot" is in the bang-up title tune, as Armstrong rages against the "subliminal mind-fuck America" of the George W. Bush era: "Welcome to a new kind of tension / All across the alien nation." Green Day have always swiped licks from the Clash, even back when they were still singing about high school shrinks and whores, so it makes sense for them to come on like Joe Strummer. The other Clash flashback is "Are We the Waiting," a grandiose ballad evoking Side Three of *London Calling*. "Wake Me Up When September Ends" is an acoustic power ballad, a sadder, more adult sequel to "Good Riddance (Time of Your Life)." Even better, there are punk ravers such as "Give Me Novocaine," "Extraordinary Girl," and "Letterbomb," which bites off a big juicy chunk of the Cheap Trick oldie "She's Tight."

Since rock operas are self-conscious and pompous beasts by definition, Green Day obligingly cram all their bad ideas into one monstrously awful track, the nine-minute "Homecoming," which sounds like the Who's "A Quick One While He's Away" without any of the funny parts. But aside from that, *Idiot* does a fine job of revving up the basic Green Day conceit, adding emotional flavor to top-shelf Armstrong songs. They don't skimp on basic tunefulness—not even in the other big nine-minute track, "Jesus of Suburbia," which packs in punk thrash, naked piano, glockenspiel, Beach Boys harmonies, and a Springsteen-style production number about a 7-Eleven parking lot where there are some mystical goings-down indeed. Against all odds, Green Day have found a way to hit their thirties without either betraying their original spirit or falling on their faces. Good Charlotte, you better be taking notes.

Claim seems paradoxical: CD is a mess, but it works.

Major weakness in the CD acknowledged.

Sheffield summarizes the accomplishments of *American Idiot*.

EVALUATION OF A PUBLIC SERVICE CAMPAIGN   Scott Standley was initially turned off by the idea that Rock the Vote—an organization dedicated to bringing more young Americans to the polls—relies on celebrities and star power to raise civic awareness. A look at actual evidence changed his mind about the group's campaign during a recent election. Standley wrote this paper in response to an assignment in a college writing class.

Standley 1

Scott Standley
Professor Cole
English Writing 02
9 May, 20--

Rock the Vote: Useful Harm?

I was planning on writing a paper that revealed the absurdities of using celebrity influence for political purposes. I was going to base my accusations in my generation's deep immersion in harmful levels of celebrity exposure. I would suggest that this toxic influence has lulled us into a sedentary, apathetic lifestyle and that campaigns like Rock the Vote only contribute to this behavior by perpetuating the importance of celebrity. My conclusion was going to be killer. Instead of encouraging political action, I was going to claim that Rock the Vote detracts from it by promulgating the very thing that creates widespread apathy: a celebrity-laden culture of unbalanced priorities and revoltingly trivial lifestyles. After formulating my perfect ending, I decided that some actual evidence would be a good idea, so I sat down and watched some of Rock the Vote's TV spots on YouTube.

What I heard on one of their commercials went something like this:

> Opening paragraph outlines plan for an essay of evaluation Standley did *not* write.

Standley 2

Script from a Rock the Vote ad is key piece of evidence for paper.

If you care about the environment, if you care about the cost of education, if you care whether there's a military draft. Politicians are passing laws that affect the air we breathe, the water we drink, who fights the war in Iraq, how much you pay for your college education, and who makes the sacrifices, the many issues that will be decided this election. Don't keep your opinions to yourself. Show you care. Vote. The most important thing I can do is the same thing you can do. Vote on November 2nd. ("Vote!")

If I had read this script prior to seeing the actual commercial, I can tell you I would have been very pleased to know that it had been broadcast on national television. Looking purely at the textual aspect of this commercial, I see a very important and legitimate attempt at getting a higher voter turnout. Of course, this is only one script from a bigger ad campaign and cannot vouch for all of Rock the Vote, but in itself, I see a message that I wish more people received. Politicians profoundly influence our lives! I would hope everyone knew that and applied that realization to their actions.

Analysis of the script causes an opinion shift.

One explanation offered for lower voting numbers among 18-25 year olds is that they don't yet fully understand how deeply government policy can influence their lives. I find this point legitimate when I recall my days of political ambivalence in high school and notice similar attitudes in younger people now. The dialogue in Rock the Vote's script directly attacks this problem of political cluelessness among youth. By simply listing some of the many political issues that heavily influence young voters, the

Standley 3

commercial, if nothing else, is at least showing why we should care who staffs our government's ranks. The only part in the script that panders to celebrity status is the line, "The most important thing I can do is the same thing you can do." Even this is mild in terms of celebrity focus, so I don't find it particularly appalling or shameful. So I consider the text of the "Rock the Vote" ad to be beneficial to anyone watching. It is a direct reminder of the connection between our vote and the behavior of our government.

Moving past the script of Rock the Vote's commercial, we come to its more controversial feature: the conveyors of the message. The cast for this commercial includes Justin Timberlake, Leonardo DiCaprio, and Samuel Jackson, three of the best-known figures in the world of pop culture. Does this casting demean the message being delivered? Do these actors somehow strip the argument of its validity? I would like to think that a good argument maintains itself regardless of its source. One could argue that these celebrities have absolutely no background or credentials in politics, and so they are illegitimate spokesmen for a political movement—but is that really even the point? If some brilliant scientist discovered a cure for a disease but used his suave and attractive assistant to explain the method to the public, would his cure be any less valuable? Clearly the scientist would be the higher authority in the matter, but letting a more appealing figure relay the message shouldn't matter if the cure works. Would Rock the Vote's political message be more legitimate if spoken by a political scientist from Harvard as opposed to Justin Timberlake? I say that it doesn't really matter: An argument's legitimacy stands regardless who delivers it. While a credible ethos is always desirable, public service announcements are designed to spread awareness. The truth is,

---

Raises second major issue of evaluation.

Key premise is: Those delivering message don't really affect its content.

Offers reasons to defend Rock the Vote's strategies.

Middle style is both personal and serious.

Standley 4

when it comes to gaining the public's attention, a famous face can be vastly more effective than an impressive résumé.

But I haven't abandoned the opinion that our celebrity-laden culture has created unbalanced priorities and trivial lifestyles. What I realized is that pinning this problem on groups like Rock the Vote doesn't make much sense. Rock the Vote is using long-established social systems and hierarchies to reach potential voters who would otherwise be unreachable. While the power celebrities wield may be a regrettable feature of our culture, I can't blame Rock the Vote for exploiting this fact. I have long been politically informed, and every day I see reasons for political action that are far stronger than endorsements from Top-40 musicians. This is why I initially reacted so vehemently to Rock the Vote. Given that, I know that plenty of young, nonvoters do need motivation and that many of them won't find it until they flip the channel to find a favorite celebrity offering compelling reasons to take the government's behavior seriously.

Standley 5

Works Cited

"Vote!" *YouTube.* Rock the Vote, 10 April 2008. Web. 18 April 2008.

MOVIE POSTERS

These posters (here and on the next page) from two film versions of the Zorro legend, *The Mark of Zorro* (1940) and *The Legend of Zorro* (2005), are not, in themselves, evaluations. But their stark differences in theme, design, and style seem to embody significant changes in cultural values over sixty-five years and are, therefore, well worth comparing and evaluating.

The Mark of Zorro (1940)

The Legend of Zorro (2005)

Assignments

1. **Cultural Evaluation:** Drawing on your expertise as a consumer of popular culture (the way Rob Sheffield does in his *Rolling Stone* review of *American Idiot*—see p. 119), explain why you admire a book, movie, television series, musical piece, artist, or performer that most people do not. For instance, you might argue that *Gilligan's Island* is as sophisticated a situation comedy as *Seinfeld*. Or, taking the opposite tack, explain why you don't share the public's enthusiasm for some widely admired artist or entertainment. Write a review strong enough to change someone's mind.

2. **Cultural Evaluation:** Assess a public figure or social movement you believe deserves serious and detailed appreciation. In other words, don't write a paper simply describing the person or group as good or bad, talented or pathetic, successful or unsuccessful. Instead, offer readers a careful evaluation of what they do and accomplish, perhaps using Scott Standley's "Rock the Vote: Useful Harm?" (see p. 121) as a model.

3. **Evaluation of Visual Texts:** Compare and evaluate two or more visual texts that you believe embody different values the way the Zorro movie posters on pages 125–26 do. You might, for example, compare political campaign videos (readily available on YouTube), book covers, product packages, or even fashions.

4. **Cultural Evaluation:** Evaluate a program or facility on your campus that you believe works especially well or is atrociously run. Imagine your audience is an administrator with the power to reward or shut down the operation.

5. **Product Review:** Choose a product that you own or use regularly, anything from a Coleman lantern to Dunkin' Donuts coffee. Limit the evaluation to one well-designed page (preferably with graphics), perhaps creating a structure that might be used to review other similar items.

How to start

- Need a **topic**? See page 134.
- Need to identify **possible causes**? See page 138.
- Need to **organize your analysis**? See page 141.

5 Causal Analysis

examines *why* or *what if* something happens

We all do causal analyses daily. Someone asks, "Why?" We reply, "Because . . ." and then offer reasons and explanations. Such a response comes naturally.

- An instructor asks for a ten-page paper examining the root causes of a major armed conflict during the twentieth century. You choose to write about the Korean War because you know almost nothing about it.

- An uncle has been diagnosed with macular degeneration. You go online to learn the causes of this eye disease and its likely consequences.

- The provost of your university has proposed to tie fee increases to the rate of inflation. You prepare a response that shows this move would damage student services and discourage the development of new programs.

- You notice that most students now walk across campus chatting on cell phones or listening to music. You wonder if this phenomenon has any relationship to a recent drop in the numbers of students joining campus clubs and activities.

UNDERSTANDING CAUSAL ANALYSIS.   From global warming to childhood obesity to high school students performing poorly on standardized tests, the daily news is full of issues framed by *why* and *what if* questions. Take childhood obesity. The public wants to know why we have a generation of overweight kids. Too many burgers? Not enough dodge ball? People worry, too, about the consequences of the trend. Will these portly children grow into obese adults? Will they develop medical problems? We're interested in such questions because they really do matter, and we're often eager to find solutions. But solid analyses of cause and effect require persistence, precision, and research. ◯ Even then, you'll often have to deal with a world that seems complicated or contradictory. Not every problem or issue can—or should—be explained simply.

Don't jump to conclusions.   It's just plain hard to say precisely which factors, past or present, are responsible for a particular event, activity, or

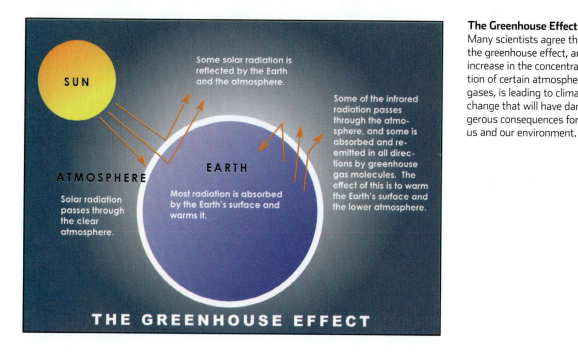

SUN

Some solar radiation is reflected by the Earth and the atmosphere.

Some of the infrared radiation passes through the atmosphere, and some is absorbed and re-emitted in all directions by greenhouse gas molecules. The effect of this is to warm the Earth's surface and the lower atmosphere.

ATMOSPHERE

EARTH

Most radiation is absorbed by the Earth's surface and warms it.

Solar radiation passes through the clear atmosphere.

THE GREENHOUSE EFFECT

The Greenhouse Effect
Many scientists agree that the greenhouse effect, an increase in the concentration of certain atmospheric gases, is leading to climate change that will have dangerous consequences for us and our environment.

◯
analyze claims and evidence p. 415

△

behavior. And it is even tougher to project how events or actions happening now might alter the future. So you shouldn't make a causal claim lightly, and you should qualify it carefully or perhaps offer your thesis tentatively. ○

Dealing with causes and effects will quickly teach you humility—even if you *don't* jump to hasty conclusions. In fact, many causal analyses begin by undercutting or correcting someone else's prior claims, dutifully researched and sensibly presented.

Appreciate the limits of causal analysis.   There are no easy answers when investigating causes and effects. The space shuttle *Columbia* burned up on reentry because a 1.67-pound piece of foam hit the wing of the 240,000-pound craft on liftoff. Who could have imagined such an unlikely sequence of events? Yet investigators had to follow the evidence relentlessly to its conclusion.

But if the aim of causal analyses is to find correct explanations, the fact remains that you'll usually have to offer answers that are merely plausible or probable. That's because causal analyses—especially outside the hard sciences—typically deal with imprecise or unpredictable forces and phenomena and sometimes require a leap of imagination.

Offer sufficient evidence for claims.   Your academic and professional analyses of cause and effect will be held to a high standard of proof— particularly in the sciences. ○ The evidence you provide may be a little looser in the popular media, where readers will entertain some anecdotal and casual examples. But even there, back up your claims with a preponderance of plausible evidence, not hearsay.

For instance, you may have an interesting theory that a successful third political party will develop in the United States to end the deadlock between Democrats and Republicans. But without supporting facts and analysis, all you have is speculation — not causal analysis.

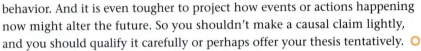

develop a thesis
p. 336

understand lab reports
p. 290

Tobias Salinger's "Unplugging Ads, Not Conversations" offers one explanation for the popularity of iPods among students and young people. Like many examinations of popular culture, this causal analysis is both speculative and argumentative and very much attuned to its audience. The piece originally appeared in the *Daily Texan*, a student newspaper at the University of Texas at Austin. As you'll see, Salinger doesn't pretend to examine the iPod phenomenon exhaustively. Instead, he wants to correct the mistaken analyses of various social commentators he mocks as "geezers."

Unplugging Ads, Not Conversations

Tobias Salinger

June 28, 2006

Comic opening raises a serious causal issue: Why don't older people understand youth?

Young people are always picking up habits that infuriate old geezers. If they're not wearing their pants so low that their damn underwear is showing, they have baseball caps on backward. If they're not growing their hair down to their waists, they're constantly fornicating. Whippersnappers are a constant source of aggravation for sensible adults.

These days, the elders have found another youth fad that gets on their nerves: iPods. Just look at college campuses, they say. Those spoiled brats strut around with their iPods in their ears like they own the whole world or something.

The geezer world is raging at this newfangled music player. George F. Will, the spokesman for perturbed yet prudent old fogeys, considers devices like the iPod a threat to our moral fabric. In a November 20 column, Will found no coincidence in the seemingly unrelated facts that two teens were caught having sex in a school auditorium and that *Desperate Housewives* can now be watched on a video iPod.

Focuses on claim made by George Will.

"The connection is this: Many people have no notion of propriety when in the presence of other people, because they are not actually in the presence of other people, even when they are in public," Will wrote.

Christine Rosen is a fellow at the Ethics and Public Policy Center, a think tank that analyzes current events using Judeo-Christian morals. In a piece on the iPod in the May 15 edition of *The NewsHour with Jim Lehrer*, she said people use devices like the iPod to shut out ideas that they don't want to hear.

"We don't have to hear or see things we haven't already programmed into our iPods or into our TiVos," Rosen said. "And so, in that sense, I think it can have a narrowing effect on what we encounter on a day-to-day basis."

In other words, we use iPods because we no longer value human interaction or manners. The music in our ears purportedly takes us into our own world, a place where nobody else matters.

I can understand these reservations. They should know, however, that iPod users are more than happy to take out their earphones when they see someone they know. We would just rather listen to our favorite music than car engines, construction vehicles, and other noise pollution.

> **Summarizes causal claim he will dispute.**

> **Refutes that claim with commonsense observation.**

Some people see a young man enjoying his music, a ball game or a favorite show. Others see an isolationist who doesn't want to engage with society or his surroundings. Is the truth somewhere in between?

Furthermore, if critics like Rosen and Will weren't so busy being annoyed with whippersnappers, they would see that gadgets like iPods and DVRs are revolutions in consumer choice. MP3 players are liberating us from the curse that is commercial radio music.

Instead of choosing between Top 40 "mix" stations that play every song you've heard way too much, "classic rock" stations that have continuous loops of Aerosmith, the Steve Miller Band, and the Eagles, and "oldies" stations that make you feel like you're wearing Depends, we get to actually choose our music, free of commercials.

The TiVo turns the same great trick on the corporate broadcast channels. The only thing we tech-savvy kids are tuning out is crappy programming and advertisements.

MP3 players are also on the cutting edge of the fastest-growing grassroots democracy anywhere: Internet piracy.

You can now easily get almost any piece of music off the Web, download it to your computer, and listen to it on your iPod. When you do this, you have effectively sidestepped the dominant means of communication and all the paradigms that go with it. No matter how hard authorities like the federal government and record companies try, it's getting easier to obtain free music and movies off the Internet. That fact should render any attempt by telecommunications companies to stop Net neutrality as unenforceable as a ban on illegal immigrants.

None of this means that the popularity of the iPod is some sort of victory against the evil empire. Products like MP3 players are just more consumer goods for our materialistic society to obsess over. But that doesn't mean that they're not helpful in changing the world we're going to inherit from the old geezers.

Offers more serious claim.

Offers evidence for his claim.

Anticipates objection and states thesis, suggesting outcome of his causal analysis.

Exploring purpose and topic

▶ topic

To find a topic for a causal analysis, begin a sentence with *why* or *what if* and then finish it, drawing on what you may already know about a trend or problem. ○

> Why are American high schools producing fewer students interested in science?
>
> Why is the occurrence of juvenile asthma spiking?
>
> Why do so few men study nursing or so few women study petroleum engineering?

There are, of course, many other ways to phrase questions about cause and effect in order to attach important conditions and qualifications.

> What if scientists figure out how to stop the human aging process—as now seems plausible within twenty years? What are the consequences for society?
>
> How likely is it that a successful third political party might develop in the United States to end the deadlock between Republicans and Democrats?

As you can see, none of these topics would just drop from a tree—like the apocryphal apple that supposedly inspired Isaac Newton to ponder gravity. They require knowledge and thinking. So look for potential cause-and-effect issues in your academic courses or professional life. Or search for them in the culture and media—though you should probably shy away from worn-out

This graph from *The Onion* (September 12, 2005) parodies causal analysis.

Reprinted with permission of THE ONION. Copyright © 2008, by ONION, INC. www.theonion.com.

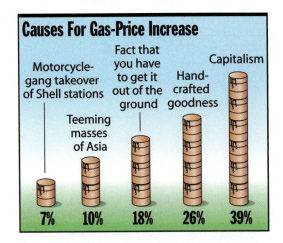

Causes For Gas-Price Increase

Motorcycle-gang takeover of Shell stations — 7%

Teeming masses of Asia — 10%

Fact that you have to get it out of the ground — 18%

Hand-crafted goodness — 26%

Capitalism — 39%

find a topic
p. 308

subjects—global warming, obesity, plagiarism—unless you can offer a fresh insight (as Salinger does with iPods, see p. 131).

Following are some approaches to finding a subject.

Look again at a subject you know well.   It may be one that has affected you personally or might in the future. Or a topic you think is ripe for rethinking because of insights you can offer. For instance, you may have experienced firsthand the effects of high-stakes testing in high school or have theories about why people your age still smoke. Offer a hypothesis.

Look for an issue new to you.   Given a choice of topics for an academic paper, choose a subject you've always wanted to know more about (for example, the Korean War). You probably won't be able to offer a thesis or hypothesis until after you've done some research, but that's the appeal of this strategy. The material is fresh and you are energized. ○

Examine a local issue.   Is there an issue you can explore or test with personal research or observation? ○ Look for recent changes and examine why these changes happened or what the consequences may be. With a community issue, talk to the people responsible or affected. Tuition raised? Admissions standards lowered? Speech code modified? Why, or what if?

Choose a subject with many dimensions.   An issue that is complicated and challenging will simply push you harder and sharpen your thinking. Don't rush to judgment; remain open-minded about contrary evidence, conflicting motives, and different points of view.

Tackle an issue that seems settled.   If you really have guts, look for a phenomenon that most people assume has been adequately explained. Tired of the way Republicans, feminists, Wall Street economists, vegans, funda-mentalists, or the women on *The View* smugly explain the way things are? Pick one sore point and offer a different—and better—causal analysis.

find a topic
p. 308

interview and observe
p. 412

Understanding your audience

Audiences for cause-and-effect analysis are diverse, but it may help to distinguish between a readership you create by drawing attention to a subject and readers who come to your work because it deals with a topic they already care about.

Create an audience.   In some situations, you must set the stage for your causal analysis by telling readers why they should be concerned by the phenomenon you intend to explore. ○ Assume they are smart enough to become engaged by a topic once they appreciate its significance—and how it might affect them. But you first have to make that case. That's exactly what the editors of the *Wall Street Journal* do in an editorial noting the sustained decrease in traffic deaths that followed a congressional decision ten years earlier to do away with a national 55-mph speed limit. (The complete editorial appears on pp. 146–48.)

Anticipate readers who might ask, *Why does this issue matter?*

This may seem noncontroversial now, but at the time the debate was shrill and filled with predictions of doom. Ralph Nader claimed that "history will never forgive Congress for this assault on the sanctity of human life." Judith Stone, president of the Advocates for Highway and Auto Safety, predicted to Katie Couric on NBC's *Today Show* that there would be "6,400 added highway fatalities a year and millions of more injuries." Federico Peña, the Clinton administration's secretary of transportation, declared: "Allowing speed limits to rise above 55 simply means that more Americans will die and be injured on our highways."

– "Safe at Any Speed," July 7, 2006

Write to an existing audience.   In many cases, you'll enter a cause-and-effect debate on topics already on the public agenda. You may intend to reaffirm what people now believe or, more controversially, ask them to rethink their positions. But in either case, you'll likely be dealing with readers as knowledgeable (and opinionated) on the subject as you are. Still, they'll lend you an ear, at least briefly, because the subject already matters to them. They may routinely pay attention to topics such as traffic safety, sustainability, the tax code, and so on. In the following opening paragraphs from a lengthy article about urban sprawl, notice how author Robert Bruegmann addresses an audience that he assumes is quite well-informed.

develop a thesis
p. 336

There is overwhelming evidence that urban sprawl has been beneficial for many people. Year after year, the vast majority of Americans respond to batteries of polls by saying that they are quite happy with where they live, whether it is a city, suburb, or elsewhere. Most objective indicators about American urban life are positive. We are more affluent than ever; home ownership is up; life spans are up; pollution is down; crime in most cities has declined. Even where sprawl has created negative consequences, it has not precipitated any crisis.

> Assumes readers understand what *urban sprawl* means.

So what explains the power of today's antisprawl crusade? How is it possible that a prominent lawyer could open a recent book with the unqualified assertion that "sprawl is America's most lethal disease"? Worse than drug use, crime, unemployment, and poverty? Why has a campaign against sprawl expanded into a major political force across America and much of the economically advanced world?

> Presumes readers know that sprawl has critics.

> Poses a question readers might entertain.

I would argue that worries about sprawl have become so vivid not because conditions are really as bad as the critics suggest but precisely because conditions are so good. During boom years, expectations can easily run far ahead of any possibility of fulfilling them. A fast-rising economy often produces a revolution of expectations. I believe these soaring expectations are responsible for many contemporary panics.

> Offers causal claim likely to engage readers.

–"How Sprawl Got a Bad Name," *American Enterprise*, June 2006

This aerial view of a housing development depicts what some people call "urban sprawl."

Finding and developing materials

Expect to do as much research for a causal analysis as for any fact-based report or argument. Even when you speculate about popular culture, as Tobias Salinger did earlier, you need to show that you have considered what others have written on the subject. ○

Be careful not to ascribe the wrong cause to an event just because two actions might have occurred close in time or have some other fragile connection. Does the economy really improve after tax cuts? Do children in fact do better in school if they have participated in Head Start programs? Exposing faulty causality in situations like these can make for powerful arguments. ○ You can avoid faulty analyses by appreciating the various kinds of genuine causal relationships outlined below.

▶ consider causes

Understand necessary causes.   A *necessary cause* is any factor that must be in place for something to occur. For example, sunlight, chlorophyll, and water are all necessary for photosynthesis to happen. Remove one of those elements from the equation and the natural process simply doesn't take place. But since none of them could cause photosynthesis on its own, they are necessary causes, but not sufficient (see *sufficient cause* below).

On a less scientific level, necessary causes are those that seem so important that we can't imagine something happening without them. You might argue, for example, that a team could not win a World Series without a specific pitcher on the roster: Remove him and the team doesn't get to the play-offs. Or you might claim that, while fanaticism doesn't itself cause terrorism, terrorism doesn't exist without fanaticism. In any such analysis, it helps to separate necessary causes from those that may be merely *contributing* (see *contributing factors* on p. 140).

Understand sufficient causes.   A *sufficient cause,* in itself, is enough to bring on a particular effect. Not being eighteen would be a sufficient cause for being arrested for drinking alcohol in the United States. But there are many other potential sufficient causes for getting arrested. In a causal argument, you might need to establish which of several possible sufficient causes is the one actually responsible for a specific event or phenomenon—assuming that a single explanation exists. A plane might have crashed

refine your search
p. 406

read critically
p. 317

because it was overloaded, ran out of fuel, had a structural failure, encountered severe wind shear, and so on.

Understand precipitating causes.   Think of a *precipitating cause* as the proverbial straw that finally breaks the camel's back. In itself, the factor may seem trivial. But it becomes the spark that sets a field gone dry for months ablaze. By refusing to give up her bus seat to a white passenger in Montgomery, Alabama, Rosa Parks triggered a civil rights movement in 1955, but she didn't actually cause it: The necessary conditions had been accumulating for generations.

Understand proximate causes.   A *proximate cause* is nearby and often easy to spot. A corporation declares bankruptcy when it can no longer meet its massive debt obligations; a minivan crashes because a front tire explodes; a student fails a course because she plagiarizes a paper. But in an analysis, getting the facts right about such proximate causes may just be your starting point as you work toward a deeper understanding of a situation. As you might guess, proximate causes may sometimes also be sufficient causes.

Understand remote causes.   A *remote cause*, as the term suggests, may act at some distance from an event but is intimately related to it. That bankrupt corporation may have defaulted on its loans because of a decade of bad management decisions; the tire exploded because it was underinflated and its tread worn; the student resorted to plagiarism *because* she ran out of time *because* she was working two jobs to pay for a Hawaiian vacation *because* she wanted a memorable spring break to impress her friends—a string of remote causes. Remote causes—which are usually contributing factors as well (see p. 140)—are what make many causal analyses challenging and interesting: Figuring them out is like detective work.

Understand reciprocal causes.   You have a *reciprocal* situation when a cause leads to an effect which, in turn, strengthens the cause. Consider how creating science internships for college women might encourage more women to become scientists who then sponsor more internships, creating

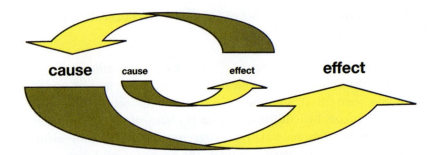

yet more female scientists. Many analyses of global warming describe reciprocal relationships, with CO_2 emissions supposedly leading to warming, which increases plant growth or alters ocean currents, which in turn releases more CO_2 or heat and so on.

Understand contributing factors.   When analyzing social or cultural issues, you'll often spend time assessing factors too general or ambiguous to be called necessary, sufficient, or even remote causes but which, nonetheless, might play a role in explaining an event. To account for an outbreak of high school violence in the late 1990s, social critics quickly identified a host of potential factors: divorce, guns, video games, goth culture, bullying, cliques, movies, psychosis, and so on. Though none of these explanations was entirely convincing, they couldn't simply be dismissed either. Many factors that might contribute to violence were (and remain) in play within the culture of American high schools.

Come to conclusions thoughtfully.   Causal analyses do often require some imagination: You are playing detective with the complexities of life and so you may need to think outside the box. But you also have to give your notions the same tough scrutiny that you would give any smart idea. Just because a causal explanation is clever or novel doesn't mean it's right.

Don't oversimplify situations or manipulate facts.   By acknowledging any weaknesses in your own analyses, you may actually enhance your credibility or lead a reader toward a better conclusion than what you've come up with. Sometimes, you may have to be content with solving only part of a problem.

Need help assessing your own work? See "How to Use the Writing Center," on pp. 328–29.

Creating a structure

Take introductions seriously. They are unusually important and often quite lengthy in causal analyses; you'll often need more than one paragraph to provide enough detail for readers to appreciate the significance of your subject. The following brief paragraph might seem like the opener of a causal essay on the failures of dog training. ○

> For thousands of years, humans have been training dogs to be hunters, herders, searchers, guards, and companions. Why are we doing so badly? The problem may lie more with our methods than with us.
>
> – Jon Katz, "Train in Vain," Slate.com, January 14, 2005

In fact, *seven* paragraphs precede this one to set up the causal claim. Those paragraphs help readers (especially dog owners) recognize a problem many will find familiar. The actual first paragraph has Katz narrating a dog-owner's dilemma.

> Sam was distressed. His West Highland terrier, aptly named Lightning, was constantly darting out of doors and dashing into busy suburban Connecticut streets. Sam owned three acres behind his house, and he was afraid to let the dog roam any of it.

By paragraph seven, Katz has offered enough similar details and situations to provoke a crisis in dogdom, a problem that leaves readers hoping for an explanation.

◀ organize ideas

> The results of this failure are everywhere: Neurotic and compulsive dog behaviors like barking, biting, chasing cars, and chewing furniture — sometimes severe enough to warrant antidepressants — are growing. Lesser training problems — an inability to sit, stop begging, come, or stay — are epidemic.

Following your introduction, you have several options for developing analyses of cause and effect.

Explain why something happened.   If you are simply offering plausible causes to explain a phenomenon, your structure will be quite simple. You'll move from an introduction that explains that phenomenon to a thesis or

shape a beginning
p. 354

hypothesis. Then you will work through your list of factors toward a conclusion. In a persuasive paper, you'd build toward the most convincing explanation supported by the best evidence.

Introduction leading to a **causal claim**

First cause explored + **reasons/evidence**

Next cause explored + **reasons/evidence** . . .

Best cause explored + **reasons/evidence**

Conclusion

Explain the consequences of a phenomenon.   A structure similar to that immediately above lends itself to exploring the effects that follow from some action, event, policy, or change in the status quo. Once again, begin with an introduction that fully describes a situation you believe will have consequences; then work through those consequences, connecting them as you need to. The conclusion could then draw out the implications of your paper.

Introduction focusing on a **change** or **cause**

First effect proposed + **reasons**

Other effect(s) proposed + **reasons** . . .

Assessment and conclusion

Suggest an alternative view of cause and effect.   A natural strategy is to open a causal analysis by refuting someone else's faulty claim and then offering your own. After all, we often think about causality when someone makes a claim we disagree with. It's a structure used in this chapter by both Tobias Salinger (p. 131) and Liza Mundy (p. 149).

Introduction questioning a **causal claim**

Reasons to doubt claim offered + **evidence**

Alternative cause(s) explored . . .

Best cause examined + **reasons/evidence**

Conclusion

Explain a chain of causes.   Quite often, causes occur simultaneously
and so in presenting them you have to make judgments about their relative
importance. But maybe just as often, you'll be describing causes that operate
in sequence: A causes B, B leads to C, C trips D, and so on. In such a case,
you might use a sequential pattern of organization, giving special attention
to the links (or transitions) in the chain. ○

Introduction suggesting a **chain** of **causes/consequences**

First link presented + **reasons/evidence**

Next link(s) presented + **reasons/evidence** . . .

Final link presented + **reasons/evidence**

Conclusion

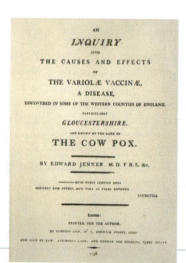

People have been writing
causal analysis for centuries. Here is the title page
of Edward Jenner's 1798
publication, *An Inquiry into
the Causes and Effects
of the Variolae Vaccinae.*
Jenner's research led to an
inoculation that pro-
tected human beings from
smallpox.

shape your
work p. 340

Choosing a style and design

When you analyze cause and effect, you'll often be offering an argument or exploring an idea for an audience you need to interest. You can do that through both style and design.

Consider a middle style.   Even causal analyses written for fairly academic audiences incline toward the middle style because of its flexibility: It can be both familiar and serious. ○ Here Robert Bruegmann, discussing the causes of urban sprawl, uses language that is simple, clear, and colloquial—and almost entirely free of technical jargon.

> When asked, most Americans declare themselves to be against sprawl, just as they say they are against pollution or the destruction of historic buildings. But the very development that one individual targets as sprawl is often another family's much-loved community. Very few people believe that they themselves live in sprawl or contribute to sprawl. Sprawl is where other people live, particularly people with less good taste. Much antisprawl activism is based on a desire to reform these other people's lives.

Adapt the style to the subject matter.   Friendly as it is, a middle style can still make demands of readers, as the following passage from an essay by Malcolm Gladwell demonstrates. To explain author Steve Johnson's theory that pop culture is making people smarter, Gladwell uses extremely intricate sentences filled with pop-culture allusions and cultural details. Yet he maintains a sense of voice too: Notice how he uses italics to signal how a word should be read. This is middle style at its complex best, making claims and proving them in a way that keeps readers interested.

> As Johnson points out, television is very different now from what it was thirty years ago. It's *harder.* A typical episode of *Starsky and Hutch,* in the 1970s, followed an essentially linear path: two characters, engaged in a single story line, moving toward a decisive conclusion. To watch an episode of *Dallas* today is to be stunned by its glacial pace – by the arduous attempts to establish social relationships, by the excruciating simplicity of the plotline, by how *obvious* it was. A single episode of *The Sopranos,* by contrast, might follow five narrative threads, involving a dozen characters who weave in and out of the plot. Modern television also

define your style
p. 366

requires the viewer to do a lot of what Johnson calls "filling in," as in a *Seinfeld* episode that subtly parodies the Kennedy assassination conspiracists, or a typical *Simpsons* episode, which may contain numerous allusions to politics or cinema or pop culture. The extraordinary amount of money now being made in the television aftermarket – DVD sales and syndication – means that the creators of television shows now have an incentive to make programming that can sustain two or three or four viewings.

– "Brain Candy," *The New Yorker*, May 16, 2005

Use appropriate supporting media.   Causal analyses have no special design features. But, like reports and arguments, they can employ charts that summarize information and graphics that illustrate ideas. *USA Today*, for instance, uses its daily "snapshots" to present causal data culled from surveys. Because causal analyses usually have distinct sections or parts (see "Creating a structure," p. 141), they do fit nicely into PowerPoint presentations. ○

A graphic like this one reflects a statistical approach to causality, polling people to find out why they do what they do.

○
work with visuals
p. 504

Examining models

EDITORIAL The editors of the *Wall Street Journal* are pleased that federal legislation no longer dictates how fast people in the states may drive. To make their point, the editors remind readers how much the predicted consequences of abolishing the national 55-mph speed limit in 1995 differed from the actual effects.

Safe at Any Speed

WITH HIGHER SPEED LIMITS, OUR HIGHWAYS HAVE BEEN GETTING SAFER

Editors of the *Wall Street Journal*

Friday, July 7, 2006 12:01 A.M.

It's another summer weekend, when millions of families pack up the minivan or SUV and hit the road. So this is also an apt moment to trumpet some good, and underreported, news: Driving on the highways is safer today than ever before.

In 2005, according to new data from the National Highway Safety Administration, the rate of injuries per mile traveled was lower than at any time since the Interstate Highway System was built fifty years ago. The fatality rate was the second lowest ever, just a tick higher than in 2004.

As a public-policy matter, this steady decline is a vindication of the repeal of the 55-miles-per-hour federal speed-limit law in 1995. That 1974 federal speed limit was arguably the most disobeyed and despised law since Prohibition. "Double nickel," as it was often called, was first adopted to save gasoline during the Arab oil embargo, though later the justification became saving lives. But to Westerners with open spaces and low traffic density, the law became a symbol of the heavy hand of the federal nanny state. To top it off, Congress would deny states their own federal highway construction dollars if they failed to comply.

In repealing the law, the newly minted Republican majority in Congress declared that states were free to impose their own limits.

> Key claim is that abolishing national speed limit made sense.

> Background information explains the 55-mph speed limit.

146

Many states immediately took up this nod to federalism by raising their limits to 70 or 75 mph. Texas just raised its speed limit again on rural highways to 80.

Analysis of effects begins here.

This may seem noncontroversial now, but at the time the debate was shrill and filled with predictions of doom. Ralph Nader claimed that "history will never forgive Congress for this assault on the sanctity of human life." Judith Stone, president of the Advocates for Highway and Auto Safety, predicted to Katie Couric on NBC's *Today Show* that there would be "6,400 added highway fatalities a year and millions of more injuries." Federico Peña, the Clinton administration's secretary of transportation, declared: "Allowing speed limits to rise above 55 simply means that more Americans will die and be injured on our highways."

Higher Speed Limits, More Safety

	1995	2005	% Decline
Highway fatality rate*	1.73	1.46	16%
Injuries*	143	90	37
Crashes*	560	375	33
Pedestrian deaths	5,584	4,674	16

*Per 100 million vehicle miles traveled
Source: National Highway Traffic Safety Administration, 2006.

We now have ten years of evidence proving that the only "assault" was on the sanctity of the truth. The nearby table shows that the death, injury, and crash rates have fallen sharply since 1995. Per mile traveled, there were about 5,000 fewer deaths and almost one million fewer injuries in 2005 than in the mid-1990s. This is all the more remarkable given that a dozen years ago Americans lacked today's distraction of driving while also talking on their cell phones.

Dire predictions are undermined by statistics.

More facts offered to prove dire predictions were wrong.

Of the thirty-one states that have raised their speed limits to more than 70 mph, twenty-nine saw a decline in the death and injury rate and only two—the Dakotas—have seen fatalities increase. Two studies, by the National Motorists Association and by the Cato Institute, have compared crash data in states that raised their speed limits with those that didn't and found no increase in deaths in the higher speed states.

Article presents positive effects of higher speed limits.

Jim Baxter, president of the National Motorists Association, says that by the early 1990s "compliance with the 55-mph law was only about 5 percent—in other words, about 95 percent of drivers were exceeding the speed limit." Now motorists can coast at these faster speeds without being on the constant lookout for radar guns, speed traps, and state troopers. Americans have also arrived at their destinations sooner, worth an estimated $30 billion a year in time saved, according to the Cato study.

Editors make an important qualification.

The tragedy is that 43,000 Americans still die on the roads every year, or about 15 times the number of U.S. combat deaths in Iraq. Car accidents remain a leading cause of death among teenagers in particular. The Interstate Highway System is nonetheless one of the greatest public works programs in American history, and the two-thirds decline in road deaths per mile traveled since the mid-1950s has been a spectacular achievement. Tough drunk-driving laws, better road technology, and such improving auto safety features as power steering and brakes are all proven life savers.

Editors conclude by offering a political implication.

We are often told, by nanny-state advocates, that such public goods as safety require a loss of liberty. In the case of speed limits and traffic deaths, that just isn't so.

EXPLORATORY ESSAY   Liza Mundy, a writer for the *Washington Post,* offers a classic kind of causal analysis—one in which readers are asked to consider a subject from an entirely different point of view. That shift in perspective illuminates her subject and raises unexpected and scary consequences.

Slate.com

Posted: Wednesday, May 3, 2006, at 10:20 AM ET
From: Liza Mundy

What's Really behind the Plunge in Teen Pregnancy?

May 3 — in case you didn't know it — was "National Day to Prevent Teen Pregnancy." In the past decade, possibly no social program has been as dramatically effective as the effort to reduce teen pregnancy, and no results so uniformly celebrated. Between 1990 and 2000, the U.S. teen pregnancy rate plummeted by 28 percent, dropping from 117 to 84 pregnancies per 1,000 women aged 15–19. Births to teenagers are also down, as are teen abortion rates. It's an achievement so profound and so heartening that left and right are eager to take credit for it, and both can probably do so. Child-health advocates generally acknowledge that liberal sex education and conservative abstinence initiatives are both to thank for the fact that fewer teenagers are ending up in school bathroom stalls sobbing over the results of a home pregnancy test.

What, though, if the drop in teen pregnancy isn't a good thing, or not entirely? What if there's a third explanation, one that has nothing to do with just-say-no campaigns or safe-sex educational posters? What if teenagers are less fertile than they used to be?

Not the girls — the boys?

It's a conversation that's taking place among a different and somewhat less vocal interest group: scientists who study human and animal reproduction. Like many scientific inquiries, this one is hotly contested and not likely to be resolved anytime soon. Still, the

Identifies a trend that needs a causal explanation.

Offers a startling hypothesis.

Poses question about causality.

Reminds readers how contentious studies of causality can be.

fact that it's going on provides a useful reminder that not every social trend is the sole result of partisan policy initiatives and think-tank-generated outreach efforts. It reminds us that a drop in something as profound as fertility, in human creatures of any age, might also have something to do with health, perhaps even the future of the species.

The great sperm-count debate began in 1992, when a group of Danish scientists published a study suggesting that sperm counts declined globally by about 1 percent a year between 1938 and 1990. This study postulated that "environmental influences," particularly widely used chemical compounds with an impact like that of the female hormone estrogen, might be contributing to a drop in fertility among males. If true, this was obviously an alarming development, particularly given that human sperm counts are already strikingly low compared to almost any other species. "Humans have the worst sperm except for gorillas and ganders of any animal on the planet," points out Sherman Silber, a high-profile urologist who attributes this in part to short-term female monogamy. Since one man's sperm rarely has to race that of another man to the finish, things like speed and volume are less important in human sperm than in other animals, permitting a certain amount of atrophy among humans.

> New causal factor is presented and explored.

The Danish study set an argument in motion. Other studies were published showing that sperm counts were staying the same; still others showed them going up. In the late 1990s, however, an American reproductive epidemiologist named Shanna Swan published work confirming the Danish findings. In a well-respected study published in *Environmental Health Perspectives,* Swan, now at the University of Rochester Medical Center, found that sperm counts are dropping by about 1.5 percent a year in the United States and 3 percent in Europe and Australia, though they do not appear to be falling in the less-developed world. This may not

> Detailed paragraphs present evidence that sperm counts are dropping.

sound like a lot, but cumulatively — like compound interest — a drop of 1 percent has a big effect. Swan showed, further, that in the United States there appears to be a regional variation in sperm counts: They tend to be lower in rural sectors and higher in cities, suggesting the possible impact of chemicals (such as pesticides) particular to one locality.

Swan is part of a group of scientists whose work suggests that environmental changes are indeed having a reproductive impact. Under the auspices of a women's health group at Stanford University and an alliance called the Collaborative on Health and the Environment, some of these scientists met in February 2005 at a retreat in Menlo Park, California, to discuss their findings. Among the evidence presented are several trends that seem to point to a subtle feminization of male babies: a worldwide rise in hypospadias, a birth defect in which the urethral opening is located on the shaft of the penis rather than at the tip; a rise in cryptorchidism, or undescended testicles; and experiments Swan has done showing that in male babies with high exposure to compounds called phthalates, something called the anogenital distance is decreasing. If you measure the distance from a baby's anus to the genitals, the distance in these males is shorter, more like that of . . . girls.

Wildlife biologists also talked about the fact that alligators living in one contaminated Florida lake were found to have small phalli and low testosterone levels, while females in the same lake had problems associated with abnormally high levels of estrogen. In 1980, the alligators' mothers had been exposed to a major pesticide dump, which, some believe, was working like an estrogen on their young, disrupting their natural hormones. A report later published by this group pointed out that similar disruptions have been found in a "wide range of species from seagulls to polar bears, seals to salmon, mollusks to frogs." As evidence that a parent's

Analysis assumes a knowledgeable, not expert, audience.

exposure to toxicants can powerfully affect the development of offspring, the example of DES, or diethylstilbestrol, was also, of course, offered. Widely given to pregnant women beginning in the late 1930s under the mistaken assumption that it would prevent miscarriage, DES left the women unaffected but profoundly affected their female fetuses, some of whom would die of cancer, others of whom would find their reproductive capacity compromised. The consensus was that the so-called chemical revolution may well be disrupting the development of reproductive organs in young males, among others. This research is controversial, certainly, but accepted enough, as a hypothesis, that it appears in developmental-biology textbooks.

> Explains what other causal studies are needed.

Tellingly, the U.S. government is also taking this conversation seriously. Together, the National Institutes of Health and the U.S. Centers for Disease Control are sponsoring a longitudinal effort to study the effect of environment on fertility. This study will track couples living in Texas and Michigan, following their efforts to become pregnant. The aim is to determine whether toxicants are affecting the reproductive potential of female and male alike.

It will be welcome information. In the United States, good statistics about infertility are strikingly hard to come by. There is no government-sponsored effort to track male fertility rates, even though male-factor problems account for half of all infertility. Even among women, who are regularly interrogated about reproductive details, it's difficult to get a good handle on developments. For years, government researchers included only married women in the category of "infertility," creating a real problem for demographers and epidemiologists looking for trends. The National Center for Health Statistics created a second category called "impaired fecundity," which includes any woman, of any marital category, who is trying to get pregnant and not having luck.

> Puts qualifications and limits on available statistics.

And the "impaired fecundity" category contains findings that may have a bearing on the are-young-men-more-infertile-than-their-fathers question. In the United States, "impaired fecundity" among women has seen, over several decades, a steady rise. And while much attention has focused on older women, the most striking rise between 1982 and 1995 took place among women under twenty-five. In that period, impaired fecundity in women under twenty-five rose by 42 percent, from 4.3 percent of women to 6.1 percent. Recently published data from 2002 show a continued rise in impaired fecundity among the youngest age cohort.

In a 1999 letter to *Family Planning Perspectives,* Swan sensibly proposed "that the role of the male be considered in this equation." If sperm counts drop each year, then the youngest men will be most acutely affected, and these will be the men who are having trouble impregnating their partners. In 2002, Danish researchers published an opinion piece in *Human Reproduction* noting that teen pregnancy rates (already much lower than in the United States) fell steadily in Denmark between 1985 and 1999. Unlike in the United States, in Denmark there have been no changes in outreach efforts to encourage responsible behavior in teens: no abstinence campaigns, no big new push for condom distribution. Wider social trends notwithstanding, they note that "it seems reasonable also to consider widespread poor semen quality among men as a potential contributing factor to low fertility rates among teenagers."

Among other things, the sperm-count debate reminds us that we should not be smug about the success of teen-pregnancy prevention efforts. We may not want today's teenagers to become pregnant now, but we certainly want them to become pregnant in the future, providing they want to be. If nothing else, the sperm-count hypothesis shows that when it comes to teenagers and sexual behavior, there's always something new to worry about.

Last paragraph warns against jumping to conclusions too quickly.

Charles Paul Freund's "The Politics of Pants," a summary of James Sullivan's book *Jeans: A Cultural History of an American Icon,* argues that consumers, not manufacturers or marketers, determine the cultural significance of products—such as jeans. In fact, Levi Strauss, the original manufacturer of blue jeans, had a hard time understanding why young people in the middle of the twentieth century adopted jeans as a symbol of freedom and protest. Maybe the pictures say it all?

The Politics of Pants

CHARLES PAUL FREUND

In the 1950s, Levi Strauss & Co. decided to update the image of its denim clothes. Until then, the company had been depending for sales on the romantic appeal of the gold rush and the rugged image of the cowboy. Hell, it was still calling its signature pants, the ones with the copper rivets, "waist overalls." It didn't want to abandon the evocative gold-rush connection, but the postwar world was filling with consumption-minded creatures called "teenagers," and it seemed time to rethink the company's pitch.

So in 1956 Levi Strauss tried an experiment, releasing a line of black denim pants it called Elvis Presley Jeans. It was the perfect endorsement. On the branding level, it was a successful marriage of an old product and its developing new character. People had long worn denim for work, or to "westernize" themselves; now a new set of customers was wearing it to identify themselves with the postwar scene of rebellious urban (and suburban) outliers. Upon the release of Elvis's 1956 hit movie *Jailhouse Rock,* writes James Sullivan in *Jeans: A Cultural History of an American Icon* (Gotham Books), "black

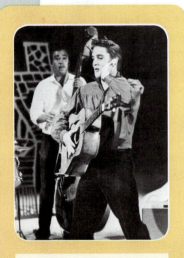

Elvis Presley made jeans hip, but he didn't like them.

Jeans were once for cowboys or actors who played them.

jeans became the rage of the season." That transition would eventually make undreamed-of profits for Levi Strauss and its many competitors.

The endorsement was wonderfully revealing from within too. Elvis actually disliked denim. To him, as to most people from real working-class backgrounds, it was just a reminder of working hard and being poor. The less denim Elvis wore, the happier he was. As for the company suits at Levi Strauss, they had no idea where their new customers would take them. The company was a lot more comfortable dealing with a safe, midcult crooner like Bing Crosby. In 1951 Levi Strauss had presented Crosby with a custom-made denim tuxedo jacket, just the kind of empty PR stunt the company bosses understood. The eroticizing Presley was unknown territory to them, and they nearly fumbled the whole bad boy connection—one that had already emerged via Presley, Brando, James Dean, and even the Beats[1]—that would help put their product on nearly every pair of hips in the Western world (and on plenty of hips everywhere else too).

---

[1]**Brando, James Dean, and even the Beats:** In the early 1950s, actors Marlon Brando and James Dean were known for their roles in disaffected-youth films such as *The Wild One* and *Rebel Without a Cause*. The "Beat Generation" of young poets came to prominence in the late 1950s and early 1960s, subsequently affecting the wider youth culture.

In fact, as Sullivan, a former critic for the *San Francisco Chronicle,* tells the story, the denim industry worked hard to undermine its own success. When jeans started making a transition from working clothes to something darker—the preferred style of the dreaded "juvenile delinquent"—the industry got worried. When school districts started promulgating antidungaree "dress codes," it panicked. Suddenly a Denim Council sprang up to persuade adults that jeans were "Right for School." Young people who wore denim, the industry group argued, were exemplary citizens who studied hard and who honored their fathers and mothers. Happily for Levi's, Wrangler, and Lee (and for Jordache, Guess, Lucky, and the wave of designers to come) nobody paid much attention to the Denim Council.

It was civil libertarians who took care of the dress codes, with a legal strategy the industry never would have dreamed of. Groups challenged the codes as, in Sullivan's words, "an imposition on freedom of expression." In fact, the industry old-timers still don't get it. Looking back on

Cool personified: James Dean, as Jett Rink in *Giant.*

the emergence of jeans wearing as an issue of "expression," one such old-timer can still tell Sullivan, "Amazing . . . Just for a pair of pants."

This series of events takes up just a few pages in one chapter of Sullivan's 303-page book. But I've focused on it because it is a stellar example of a primary market issue that many people—not only markets' critics but some of their defenders too—have failed to acknowledge. It's neither makers nor marketers who successfully attach meaning to the products they want to sell. It's the consumers who impute meaning to those products they choose to buy.

The anthropologist Grant Mc-Cracken has done a lot of scholarly work to elucidate this distinction, and the *New Yorker's* Malcolm Gladwell has been a pioneer in reporting it. His famous 1997 piece "The Coolhunt" focused on consultants who attempt to monitor "coolness" as it is attached to—and detached from—consumer goods by a hierarchy of influential buyers. Gladwell offered case studies of brands, such as Hush Puppies shoes, that had become cool (for a while, anyway) without the manufacturer or its ad people ever having a clue. Jeans conquered the world—Levi's 501s are the single most successful garment ever designed—not because of the denim industry's efforts to give them meaning but in spite of them.

How to scare parents, in the 1950s: Brando in leather and denim.

The rest of Sullivan's book is addressed to the culture, the fashion, and of course the business of jeans. The last of these threads is the most valuable, since it is probably the least known and the most revealing. Who knew, for example, that leisure suits were introduced by Lee? (And what does *that* episode say about the marketers' conception, let alone control, of a product's meaning?) Sullivan's book is as comprehensive on its subject as you are likely to want, if not more so. Jeans and Jack Kerouac.[2] Jeans and the dude ranch. Jeans and the advent of the zipper. Jeans and punk. Jeans and disco. Jeans and the indigo trade. Thousand-dollar Jeans. Collectible jeans. Even pants (not jeans) and Brigham Young,[3] who in 1830 charged that trousers with buttons in front were "fornication pants."

There's even jeans and the color blue. Sullivan has penned an ode to blueness that goes on for four pages. ("The deeper blue becomes," he quotes the artist Wassily Kandinsky as saying, "the more urgently it summons man toward the infinite.") Best of all, though, is jeans and Vladimir Nabokov,[4] despite the fact that Nabokov has nothing much to say about jeans.

Sullivan uses Nabokov inventively, quoting from his 1955 novel, *Lolita*, to demonstrate how the narrator's "refined" sensibility is transformed by a whole world of low-end culture that has become—for him—eroticized. The novel's motels and shopping strips, writes Sullivan, "are the consummate low-culture backdrops for Lolita's jeans, sneakers, and lollipops." It's not just Lolita that Nabokov's intellectual narrator has fallen for. And if you don't see what eroticized low-end culture has to do with the triumph of American jeans, then Elvis really has left the building, and you've gone with him.

---

[2]**Jack Kerouac:** "Beat" writer; his novel *On the Road* was one of the best-known works to come out of the Beat Generation.

[3]**Brigham Young:** Influential nineteenth-century leader of the Church of Jesus Christ of Latter-day Saints (better known as the Mormon Church).

[4]**Vladimir Nabokov:** Russian writer of fiction; best known for his novel *Lolita*.

1. **Opinion:** Like Tobias Salinger in "Unplugging Ads, Not Conversations" (p. 131), you've probably objected to a superficial explanation for a phenomenon you know well. It might be college faculty explaining lamely why grades are inflated or why students browse the Web during classes. Or maybe you belong to a group that has been the subject of causal analyses verging on prejudicial. If so, refute the faulty analysis of cause and effect by offering a more plausible explanation.

2. **Opinion:** Using the *Wall Street Journal*'s editorial "Safe at Any Speed" as a model (p. 146), develop a cause-and-effect analysis to suggest that some other causal prediction may have gone awry—particularly something in the public sector. Like the *WSJ* editors, be sure to explain what factors made the prediction go wrong. What changed or what consequences couldn't be easily foreseen or anticipated?

3. **Exploratory Essay:** Liza Mundy's analysis of cause and effect in "What's Really behind the Plunge in Teen Pregnancy?" (p. 149) has significant cultural and political implications. Locate a similarly challenging analysis in a national newspaper or news magazine. Then write a detailed response to the causal issues it raises, suggesting, for instance, why you find it convincing or speculating about how society might respond to its conclusions. You'll find many analyses covering topics such as the environment, terrorism, education, religion, culture, and so on.

4. **Cultural Analysis:** Like Charles Paul Freund dealing with jeans (p. 154), identify a trend you have noticed or some significant change in society or culture. It might relate to music, films, choice of majors, political preferences, and so on. Write an analysis of the phenomenon, considering either causes or potential consequences of this fashion. Then illustrate the trend with images that suggest its cultural reach or significance. Spend some time in the opening of your paper describing the trend and proving that it is real.

How to start
- Need a **topic**? See page 166.
- Need to come up with a **solution**? See page 170.
- Need to **organize your ideas**? See page 172.

6 Proposal

defines a problem & suggests a solution

Proposals are written to try to solve problems. You'll usually write a proposal to initiate an action or change. At a minimum, you hope to alter someone's thinking—even if only to recommend leaving things as they are.

- You write to your academic advisor suggesting that a service-learning experience would be a better senior project for you than writing a traditional thesis—given your talents and interests.

- Noticing the difficulty students with disabilities have navigating campus, you make a plan to enhance accessibility the keystone of your campaign for a seat on student government.

- Your major has so many requirements that most students take five or six years to graduate—adding tens of thousands of dollars to the cost of their degrees. You think it's high time for faculty to rethink the program.

- You show your banker why loaning you money to open a barbecue restaurant would make sound fiscal sense, especially since no one else in town serves decent brisket and ribs.

UNDERSTANDING PROPOSALS.   *Got an issue or a problem? Good—let's
deal with it.* That's the logic driving most proposals, both the professional
types that pursue grant money and less formal propositions that are part of
everyday life, academic or otherwise. Like causal analysis, proposal is another
form of argument. ⭕

Although grant writing shares some of the elements of informal
proposals, it is driven by rigid formulas set by foundations and government
agencies, usually covering things like budgets, personnel, evaluation,
outcomes, and so on. Informal proposals are much easier. Though they
may not bring large sums of cash your way, they're still important tools
for addressing problems. A sensible proposal can make a difference in any
situation—be it academic, personal, or political.

Following are some moves you'll need to make in framing a proposal.
Not every proposal needs to do each of these things. In a first-round pitch,

Buy Nothing Day   Imagine that you want
people to consider an economic system *not*
based on growth and exploitation of the
natural environment. How might you get
their attention? By proposing a day without
shopping to highlight the evils of capitalism
and rampant consumerism. In the United
States, Buy Nothing Day occurs on the
Friday after Thanksgiving—traditionally one
of the biggest shopping days of the year.

understand argument
p. 68

you might just test whether an idea will work at all; a more serious plan headed for public scrutiny would have to punch the ticket on more of the items.

Define a problem.   Set the stage for a proposal by describing the specific situation, problem, or opportunity in enough detail that readers *get it*: They see a compelling need for action. In many cases, a proposal needs to explain what's wrong with the status quo.

Target the proposal.   To make a difference, you have to reach people with the power to change a situation. That means first identifying such individuals (or groups) and then tailoring your proposal to their expectations. Use the Web or library, for example, to get the names and contact information of government or corporate officials. ○ When the people in power *are* the problem, go over their heads to more general audiences with clout of their own: voters, consumers, women, fellow citizens, the elderly, and so on.

Consider reasonable options.   Your proposal won't be taken seriously unless you have weighed all the workable possibilities, explaining their advantages and downsides. Only then will you be prepared to make a case for your specific ideas.

Make specific recommendations.   Explain what you propose to do about the situation or problem; don't just complain that someone else has gotten it wrong. The more detailed your solution is, the better.

Make realistic recommendations.   You need to address two related issues: *feasibility* and *implementation*. A proposal is feasible if it can be achieved with available resources and is acceptable to the parties involved. And, of course, a feasible plan still needs a plausible pathway to implementation: *First we do this; then we do this.*

plan a project
p. 400

The following proposal originally appeared in *Time* (August 21, 2005). Its author Barrett Seaman doesn't have the space to do much more than alert the general public (or, more likely, parents of college students) to the need for action to end alcohol abuse on campuses. Still, he does have a surprising suggestion to offer about dealing with bingeing — one most readers might not initially favor. More important, the brief essay does what a proposal must: It makes a plausible case and gets people talking.

How Bingeing Became the New College Sport

BARRETT SEAMAN

In the coming weeks, millions of students will begin their fall semester of college, with all the attendant rituals of campus life: freshman orientation, registering for classes, rushing by fraternities and sororities, and, in a more recent nocturnal college tradition, "pregaming" in their rooms.

Pregaming is probably unfamiliar to people who went to college before the 1990s. But it is now a common practice among eighteen-, nineteen- and twenty-year-old students who cannot legally buy or consume alcohol. It usually involves sitting in a dorm room or an off-campus apartment and drinking as much hard liquor as possible before heading out for the evening's parties. While reporting for my book *Binge*, I witnessed the hospitalization of several students for acute alcohol poisoning. Among them was a Hamilton College freshman who had consumed twenty-two shots of vodka while sitting in a dorm room with her friends. Such hospitalizations are routine on campuses across the nation. By the Thanksgiving break of the year I visited Harvard, the university's health center had admitted nearly seventy students for alcohol poisoning.

When students are hospitalized—or worse yet, die from alcohol poisoning, which happens about 300 times each year—college presidents tend to react by declaring their campuses dry or shutting down fraternity houses. But tighter enforcement of the minimum drinking age of twenty-one is not the solution. It's part of the problem.

Marginal notes:

Defines problem he intends to address: bingeing known as *pregaming*.

Proposal draws on research the author has done.

Points out that current solutions to college drinking don't work.

Over the past forty years, the United States has taken a confusing approach to the age-appropriateness of various rights, privileges, and behaviors. It used to be that twenty-one was the age that legally defined adulthood. On the heels of the student revolution of the late '60s, however, came sweeping changes: The voting age was reduced to eighteen; privacy laws were enacted that protected college students' academic, health, and disciplinary records from outsiders, including parents; and the drinking age, which had varied from state to state, was lowered to eighteen.

Then, thanks in large measure to intense lobbying by Mothers Against Drunk Driving, Congress in 1984 effectively blackmailed states into hiking the minimum drinking age to twenty-one by passing a law that tied compliance to the distribution of federal-aid highway funds—an amount that will average $690 million per state this year. There is no doubt that the law, which achieved full fifty-state compliance in 1988, saved lives, but it had the unintended consequence of creating a covert culture around alcohol as the young adult's forbidden fruit.

Drinking has been an aspect of college life since the first western universities in the fourteenth century. My friends and I drank in college in the 1960s—sometimes a lot but not so much that we had to be hospitalized. Veteran college administrators cite a sea change in campus culture that began, not without coincidence, in the 1990s. It was marked by a shift from beer to hard liquor, consumed not in large social settings, since that is now illegal, but furtively and dangerously in students' residences.

In my reporting at colleges around the country, I did not meet any presidents or deans who felt that the twenty-one-year age minimum helps their efforts to curb the abuse of alcohol on their campuses. Quite the opposite. They thought the law impeded their efforts since it takes away the ability to monitor and supervise drinking activity.

What would happen if the drinking age was rolled back to eighteen or nineteen? Initially, there would be a surge in binge drinking as young adults savored their newfound freedom. But over time, I predict, U.S. college students would settle into the saner approach to alcohol I saw on the one campus I visited where the legal drinking age is eighteen: Montreal's

---

Margin notes:

Explains factors responsible for the spike in alcohol abuse.

Points out that current law makes it harder to deal with bingeing.

Offers specific proposal tentatively, posed as question.

McGill University, which enrolls about two thousand American under-graduates a year. Many, when they first arrive, go overboard, exploiting their ability to drink legally. But by midterms, when McGill's demanding academic standards must be met, the vast majority have put drinking into its practical place among their priorities.

A culture like that is achievable at U.S. colleges if Congress can muster the fortitude to reverse a bad policy. If lawmakers want to reduce drunk driving, they should do what the Norwegians do: Throw the book at offenders no matter what their age. Meanwhile, we should let the pregamers come out of their dorm rooms so that they can learn to handle alcohol like the adults we hope and expect them to be.

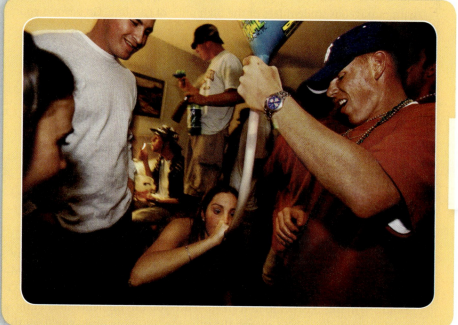

Exploring purpose and topic

Most people will agree to reasonable proposals—as long as it doesn't cost them anything. So moving audiences from *I agree* to *I'll do something about it* takes
a powerful act of persuasion. And for that reason, proposals are usually framed as arguments, requiring all the strategies used in that genre. ○

Occasionally, you'll be asked to solve a particular problem in school or on the job. Having a topic assigned makes your task a little easier, but you can bet that any problem assigned will be complex and open to multiple solutions. Otherwise, there would be no challenge to it.

When choosing your own proposal topic, keep the following standards in mind. ○

Look for a genuine issue.   Spend the first part of your project defining a problem readers will care about. You may think it's a shame no one retails Prada close to campus, but your classmates could plausibly be more concerned with outrageous student fees or the high price of gasoline. Go beyond your own concerns in settling on a problem.

Look for a challenging problem.   It helps if others have tried to fix it in the past, but failed—and for reasons you can identify. Times change, attitudes shift, technology improves: All of these can be factors that make what seemed like an insoluble problem in the past more manageable now. Choose a serious topic to which you can bring fresh perspectives.

Look for a soluble problem.   Challenges *are* good, but impossible dreams are for Broadway musicals. Parking on campus is the classic impasse—always present, always frustrating. Steer clear of problems no one has ever solved, unless you have a *really* good idea.

Look for a local issue.   It's best to leave "world peace" to celebrity activists like Bono. You can investigate a problem in your community more credibly, talking with people involved or searching local archives for material. ○
Doing so makes it easier to find an audience you can influence, including people potentially able to change the situation. It's more likely you'll get the attention of your dean of students than the secretary of state.

▶ topic

Need help deciding what to write about? See "How to Browse for Ideas" on pp. 312–13.

understand argument
p. 68

find a topic
p. 308

interview and
observe p. 412

Understanding your audience

While preparing a proposal, keep two audiences in mind—one fairly narrow and the other more broad. The first group includes people who could possibly do something about a problem; the second are general readers who could influence those in the first group by bringing the weight of public opinion down on them. And public opinion makes a difference.

Writers adjust for audience all the time in offering proposals. Grant writers especially make it a point to learn what agencies and institutions expect in applications. Quite often, it takes two or three tries to figure out how to present a winning grant submission. You won't have that luxury with most academic or political pieces, but you can certainly study models of successful proposals, noting how the writers raise an issue with readers, provide them with information and options, and then argue for a particular solution.

Write to people who can make a difference.   A personal letter you might prepare for the dean of students to protest her policies on downloading MP3 files onto university-controlled servers would likely have a respectful and perhaps legalistic tone, pointing to case law on the subject and university policies on freedom of speech. You'd also want to assure the dean of your good sense and provide her with sound reasons to consider your case.

You'd be in good company adopting such a strategy. Listen to how matter-of-factly environmentalist David R. Brower argues—in a famous proposal—that the gates of the massive Glen Canyon Dam should be opened and the waters of Lake Powell drained. Radical stuff, but his strategy was sensible. For one thing, he argued, the artificial reservoir leaked.

> One of the strongest selling points [for removing the dam] comes from the Bureau of Reclamation itself. In 1996, the bureau found that almost a million acre-feet, or 8 percent of the river's flow, disappeared between the stations recording the reservoir's inflow and outflow. Almost 600,000 acre-feet were presumed lost to evaporation. Nobody knows for sure about the rest. The bureau said some of the loss was a gain—being stored in the banks of the reservoir—but it has no idea how much of that gain it will ever get back. Some bank storage is recoverable, but all too likely the region's downward-slanting geological strata are leading some of Powell's waters

into the dark unknown. It takes only one drain to empty a bathtub, and we don't know where, when, or how the Powell tub leaks. A million acre-feet could meet the annual domestic needs of 4 million people and at today's prices are worth $435 million in the Salt Lake City area—more than a billion on my hill in Berkeley, California.

— "Let the River Run Through It," *Sierra*, March/April 1997

Rally people who represent public opinion.   Imagine you've had no response from the dean of students on the file-sharing proposal you made. Time to take the issue to the public, perhaps via an op-ed or letter sent to the student paper. Though still keeping the dean firmly in mind, you'd now also write to stir up student and community opinion. Your new piece could be more emotional than your letter and less burdened by legal points—though still citing facts and presenting solid reasons for allowing students to download music files to university computers. ○

The fact is that people often need a spur to move them—that is, some strategy that frames an issue to help them find their part in it. Again, you'd be in good company in leading an audience to your position. In 1962 when President John F. Kennedy proposed a mission to the moon, he did it in language that stirred a public reasonably skeptical about the cost and challenges of such an implausible undertaking.

OCEAN HILLS Community Meeting

Learn About the New Mall

Scheduled To Speak:

Mayor Tom Smith
Planning Comissioner Laura Tarkle
Principal Jack Snow

Followed by an open discussion and
question period

Thursday Night
7:00 PM

Andrews Middle School Auditorium
23434 Sycamore Blvd.
Ocean Hills

Proposals to very small or targeted groups can be as simple as this unadorned but clear and direct leaflet.

refine your tone
p. 374

JFK Aims High
In 1962, the president challenged Americans to go to the moon; in 2008, we were asked to pump up our tires.

There is no strife, no prejudice, no national conflict in outer space as yet. Its hazards are hostile to us all. Its conquest deserves the best of all mankind, and its opportunity for peaceful cooperation may never come again. But why, some say, the moon? Why choose this as our goal? And they may well ask why climb the highest mountain? Why, thirty-five years ago, fly the Atlantic? Why does Rice play Texas?

We choose to go to the moon. We choose to go to the moon in this decade and do the other things, not because they are easy, but because they are hard, because that goal will serve to organize and measure the best of our energies and skills, because that challenge is one that we are willing to accept, one we are unwilling to postpone, and one which we intend to win, and the others, too.

—Rice Stadium "Moon Speech," September 12, 1962

Finding and developing materials

Proposals might begin with whining and complaining (*I want my MP3s!*), but they can't stay in that mode long. Like any serious work, proposals must be grounded in solid thinking and research.

What makes them distinctive, however, is the sheer variety of strategies you might use in a single document. To write a convincing proposal, you may have to narrate, report, argue, evaluate, and explore cause and effect. A proposal can be a little like old-time TV variety shows, with one act following another, displaying a surprising range of talent. Here's how you might develop those various parts.

Define the problem. First, research the existing problem fully enough to explain it to your readers. Run through the traditional journalist's questions—*Who? What? Where? When? Why? How?*—to be sure you've got the basics of your topic down cold. When appropriate, interview experts or people involved with an issue; for instance, in college communities, the best repositories of institutional memory will usually be staff. ○

Even when you think you know the topic well, spend time locating any documents that might provide hard facts to cite for skeptical readers. For instance, if you propose to change a long-standing policy, find out when it was imposed, by whom, and for what reasons.

Examine prior solutions. If a problem is persistent, other people have certainly tried to solve it—or perhaps they caused it. In either case, do the research necessary to figure out, as best you can, what happened in these earlier efforts. But expect controversy. Your sources may provide different and contradictory accounts that you will have to sort out in a plausible narrative.

Once you know the history of an issue, shift into an evaluative mode to explain why earlier solutions or strategies did not work. ○ Provide reliable information so that readers can later make comparisons with your own proposal and appreciate its ingenuity.

The Journalist's Questions

Who?	What?
Where?	When?
Why?	How?

▶ consider solutions

interview and observe p. 412

understand evaluation p. 102

Make a proposal.   Coming up with a proposal may take all the creativity you can muster, to the point where a strong case can be made for working collaboratively when that's an option. ○ You'll benefit from the additional feedback. Be sure to write down your ideas as they emerge so you can see what exactly you are recommending. Be specific about numbers and costs.

For instance, if you propose that high school students in your district take a course in practical economics (balancing a checkbook, credit card use, etc.) to better prepare them for adult responsibilities, do the research necessary to figure out who might teach such classes and how many new instructors the school district would have to hire. Your results could preempt an implausibly expensive proposal or suggest more feasible alternatives for handling the problem that you see.

Defend the proposal.   Any ideas that threaten the status quo will surely provoke arguments. That's half the fun of offering proposals. So prove your position, using all the tools of argument available to you, from the logical and factual to the emotional. It is particularly important to anticipate objections, because readers invested in the status quo will have them in spades. Take time to define a successful solution to a problem, and point out every way your solution meets that definition. Above all, you've got to show that your idea will work.

Be prepared, too, to show that your plan is feasible—that is to say, that it can be achieved with existing or new resources. For example, you might actually solve your school's traffic problems by proposing a monorail linking the central campus to huge new parking garages. But who would pay for the multimillion-dollar system? Still, don't be put off too easily by the objection that *we can't possibly do that.* A little ingenuity goes a long way—it's part of the problem-solving process.

Figure out how to implement the proposal.   Readers will want assurances that your ideas can be implemented: Show them how. Figure out what has to happen to meet your goals: where new resources will come from, how personnel can be recruited and hired, where brochures or manuals will be printed, and so on. Provide a timetable.

collaborate
p. 314

Creating a structure

▶ organize
ideas

Proposals follow the mental processes many people go through in dealing with issues and problems, and some of these problems have more history and complications than others. ⭘ Generally, the less formal the proposal, the fewer structural elements it will have. So you should adapt the proposal paradigm below to your purposes, using it as a checklist of *possible* issues to consider in your own project.

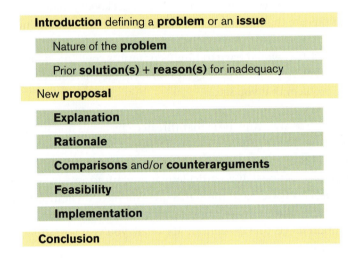

Introduction defining a **problem** or an **issue**

Nature of the **problem**

Prior **solution(s)** + **reason(s)** for inadequacy

New **proposal**

Explanation

Rationale

Comparisons and/or **counterarguments**

Feasibility

Implementation

Conclusion

You might use a similar structure when you intend to explore the effects that follow from some action, event, policy, or change in the status quo. Once again, you'd begin with an introduction that fully describes the situation you believe will have consequences; then you would work through those consequences, connecting them as necessary. Your conclusion could then draw out the implications of your paper.

shape your work
p. 340

Choosing a style and design

Proposals do come in many forms and, occasionally, they may be frivolous or comic. But whenever you suggest upending the status quo or spending someone else's money, you probably need to show a little respect and humility.

Use a formal style.   Professional proposals—especially those seeking grant money—are typically written in a formal and impersonal high style, as if the project would be jeopardized by the slightest hint of enthusiasm or personality. ○ But academic audiences are hardly less serious. So you might use a formal style in proposals you write for school when your intended readers are specific and official—a professor, a government agency, a dean.

Observe the no-nonsense tone Thao Tran adopts early in an academic essay whose title alone suggests its sober intentions: "Coping with Population Aging in the Industrialized World."

Leaders of industrialized nations and children of baby boomers must understand the consequences of population aging and minimize its economic effects. This report will recommend steps for coping with aging in the industrialized world and will assess counterarguments to those steps. With a dwindling workforce and rising elderly population, industrialized countries must take a multi-step approach to expand the workforce and support the elderly. Governments should attempt to attract immigrants, women, and elderly people into the workforce. Supporting an increasing elderly population will require reforming pension systems and raising indirect taxes. It will also require developing pronatalist policies, in which governments subsidize childrearing costs to encourage births. Many of these strategies will challenge traditional cultural notions and require a change in cultural attitudes. While change will not be easy, industrialized nations must recognize and address this trend quickly in order to reduce its effects.

> Point of view is impersonal: *This report* rather than *I*.

> Purpose of proposal is clearly explained.

> Premises and assumptions of proposal are offered in abstract language.

Use a middle style, when appropriate.   You might shift toward a middle style whenever establishing a personal relationship could help your proposal or when you need to persuade a wider, more general audience.

It is possible, too, for styles to vary within a document. Your language might be coldly efficient as you scrutinize previous failures or tick off the advantages of your specific proposal. But as you near the end of the piece,

define your style
p. 366

you decide another style would better reflect your vision for the future or your enthusiasm for an idea. Earlier in this chapter, environmentalist David R. Brower supplied an example of technical prose in explaining why draining Lake Powell would make commercial sense. Here is a far more emotional paragraph from the conclusion of his proposal:

> The sooner we begin, the sooner lost paradises will begin to recover— Cathedral in the Desert, Music Temple, Hidden Passage, Dove Canyon, Little Arch, Dungeon, and a hundred others. Glen Canyon itself can probably lose its ugly white sidewalls in two or three decades. The tapestries can reemerge, along with the desert varnish, the exiled species of plants and animals, the pictographs and other mementos of people long gone. The canyon's music will be known again, and "the sudden poetry of springs," Wallace Stegner's beautiful phrase, will be revealed again below the sculptured walls of Navajo sandstone. The phrase, "as long as the rivers shall run and the grasses grow," will regain its meaning.

Place names listed have poetic effect.

Lush details add to emotional appeal of proposal.

Final quotation summarizes mission of Brower's proposal.

Pay attention to elements of design.   Writers often incorporate images, charts, tables, graphs, and flowcharts to illustrate what is at stake in a proposal or to make comparisons easy. ○ Images also help readers visualize solutions or proposals and make those ideas attractive.

This artist's rendering of the Rose Kennedy Greenway, a plan for new public parklands in the city of Boston, helps people imagine the future — enhancing the plausibility of the proposal.

think visually
p. 500

Examining models

Michael Gurian's "Disappearing Act," which appeared in the *Washington Post*, is an example of a proposal that focuses more on defining a problem than on offering a solution. As Gurian himself notes late in his piece, not much happens until the public takes notice of an issue. "Disappearing Act" bases its arguments on both personal experience and various studies and statistics. But the tight confines of a newspaper feature preclude the documentation readers might want to follow up on for Gurian's claims.

Disappearing Act

WHERE HAVE THE MEN GONE?
NO PLACE GOOD

Michael Gurian

Sunday, December 4, 2005

In the 1990s, I taught for six years at a small liberal-arts college in Spokane, Washington. In my third year, I started noticing something that was happening right in front of me. There were more young women in my classes than young men, and on average, they were getting better grades than the guys. Many of the young men stared blankly at me as I lectured. They didn't take notes as well as the young women. They didn't seem to care as much about what I taught—literature, writing, and psychology. They were bright kids, but many of their faces said, "Sitting here, listening, staring at these words—this is not really who I am."

That was a decade ago, but just last month, I spoke with an administrator at Howard University in the District. He told me that what I observed a decade ago has become one of the "biggest agenda items" at Howard. "We are having trouble recruiting and retaining male students," he said. "We are at about a 2-to-1 ratio, women to men."

Howard is not alone. Colleges and universities across the country are grappling with the case of the mysteriously vanishing male. Where men once dominated, they now make up no more than 43 percent of students at American institutions of higher learning, according to 2003

Identifies genuine and challenging issue.

Suggests problem has long-term consequences.

175

statistics, and this downward trend shows every sign of continuing unabated. If we don't reverse it soon, we will gradually diminish the male identity, and thus the productivity and the mission, of the next generation of young men, and all the ones that follow.

The trend of females overtaking males in college was initially measured in 1978. Yet despite the well-documented disappearance of ever more young men from college campuses, we have yet to fully react to what has become a significant crisis. Largely, that is because of cultural perceptions about males and their societal role. Many times a week, a reporter or other media person will ask me: "Why should we care so much about boys when men still run everything?"

It's a fair and logical question, but what it really reflects is that our culture is still caught up in old industrial images. We still see thousands of men who succeed quite well in the professional world and in industry—men who get elected president, who own software companies, who make six figures selling cars. We see the Bill Gateses and John Robertses and George Bushes—and so we're not as concerned as we ought to be about the millions of young men who are floundering or lost.

But they're there: The young men who are working in the lowest-level (and most dangerous) jobs instead of going to college. Who are sitting in prison instead of going to college. Who are staying out of the long-term marriage pool because they have little to offer to young women. Who are remaining adolescents, wasting years of their lives playing video games for hours a day, until they're in their thirties, by which time the world has passed many of them by.

The old industrial promise—"That guy will get a decent job no matter what"—is just that, an old promise. So is the old promise that a man will be able to feed his family and find personal meaning by "following in his father's footsteps," which has vanished for millions of males who are not raised with fathers or substantial role models. The old promise that an old boys' network will always come through for "the guys" is likewise gone for many young men who have never seen and will never see such a network (though they may see a dangerous gang). Most frightening, the old promise that schools will take care of boys and educate them to succeed is also breaking down, as boys dominate the

Tries to rally audience.

Defines problem as one of class—rich vs. poor.

Explains why prior solutions do not work now.

failure statistics in our schools, starting at the elementary level and continuing through high school.

Of course, not every male has to go to college to succeed, to be a good husband, to be a good and productive man. But a dismal future lies ahead for large numbers of boys in this generation who will not go to college. Statistics show that a young man who doesn't finish school or go to college in 2005 will likely earn less than half what a college graduate earns. He'll be three times more likely to be unemployed and more likely to be homeless. He'll be more likely to get divorced, more likely to engage in violence against women, and more likely to engage in crime. He'll be more likely to develop substance-abuse problems and to be a greater burden on the economy, statistically, since men who don't attend college pay less in Social Security and other taxes, depend more on government welfare, are more likely to father children out of wedlock, and are more likely not to pay child support.

When I worked as a counselor at a federal prison, I saw these statistics up close. The young men and adult males I worked with were mainly uneducated, had been raised in families that didn't promote education, and had found little of relevance in the schools they had attended. They were passionate people, capable of great love and even possible future success. Many of them told me how much they wanted to get an education. At an intuitive level, they knew how important it was.

Whether in the prison system, in my university classes, or in the schools where I help train teachers, I have noticed a systemic problem with how we teach and mentor boys that I call "industrial schooling" and that I believe is a primary root of our sons' falling behind in school, and quite often in life.

Two hundred years ago, realizing the necessity of schooling millions of kids, we took them off the farms and out of the marketplace and put them in large industrial-size classrooms (one teacher, twenty-five to thirty kids). For many kids, this system worked—and still works. But from the beginning, there were some for whom it wasn't working very well. Initially, it was girls. It took more than 150 years to get parity for them.

Now we're seeing what's wrong with the system for millions of boys. Beginning in very early grades, the sit-still, read-your-book, raise-your-hand-quietly, don't-learn-by-doing-but-by-taking-notes classroom is a

Studies cited demonstrate seriousness of problem.

Examines complex causes of current problem.

worse fit for more boys than it is for most girls. This was always the case, but we couldn't see it one hundred years ago. We didn't have the comparative element of girls at par in classrooms. We taught a lot of our boys and girls separately. We educated children with greater emphasis on certain basic educational principles that kept a lot of boys "in line"—competitive learning was one. And our families were deeply involved in a child's education.

Now, however, the boys who don't fit the classrooms are glaringly clear. Many families are barely involved in their children's education. Girls outperform boys in nearly every academic area. Many of the old principles of education are diminished. In a classroom of thirty kids, about five boys will begin to fail in the first few years of preschool and elementary school. By fifth grade, they will be diagnosed as learning disabled, ADD/ADHD, behaviorally disordered, or "unmotivated." They will no longer do their homework (though they may say they are doing it), they will disrupt class or withdraw from it, they will find a few islands of competence (like video games or computers) and overemphasize those.

Boys have a lot of Huck Finn in them—they don't, on average, learn as well as girls by sitting still, concentrating, multitasking, listening to words. For twenty years, I have been taking brain research into homes and classrooms to show teachers, parents, and others how differently boys and girls learn. Once a person sees a PET or SPECT scan[1] of a boy's brain and a girl's brain, showing the different ways these brains learn, they understand. As one teacher put it to me, "Wow, no wonder we're having so many problems with boys."

Yet every decade the industrial classroom becomes more and more protective of the female learning style and harsher on the male, yielding statistics such as these:

The majority of National Merit scholarships, as well as college academic scholarships, go to girls and young women.

Boys and young men comprise the majority of high school dropouts, as high as 80 percent in many cities.

Boys and young men are 1½ years behind girls and young women in reading ability (this gap does not even out in high school, as some have

Solution may require different approaches tailored to boys and girls.

1. **PET or SPECT scan:** Types of brain scans showing sites and levels of brain activity.

argued; a male reading/writing gap continues into college and the workplace).

The industrial classroom is one that some boys do fine in, many boys just "hang on" in, many boys fall behind in, many boys fail in, and many boys drop out of. The boys who do fine would probably do fine in any environment, and the boys who are hanging on and getting by will probably reemerge later with some modicum of success, but the millions who fall behind and fail will generally become the statistics we saw earlier.

Grasping the mismatch between the minds of boys and the industrial classroom is only the first step in understanding the needs of our sons. Lack of fathering and male role models take a heavy toll on boys, as does lack of attachment to many family members (whether grandparents, extended families, moms, or dads). Our sons are becoming very lonely. And even more politically difficult to deal with: The boys-are-privileged-but-the-girls-are-shortchanged emphasis of the last twenty years (an emphasis that I, as a father of two daughters and an advocate of girls, have seen firsthand) has muddied the water for child development in general, pitting funding for girls against funding for boys.

We still barely see the burdens our sons are carrying as we change from an industrial culture to a postindustrial one. We want them to shut up, calm down, and become perfect intimate partners. It doesn't matter too much who boys and men are—what matters is who we think they should be. When I think back to the kind of classroom I created for my college students, I feel regret for the males who dropped out. When I think back to my time working in the prison system, I feel a deep sadness for the present and future generations of boys whom we still have time to save.

And I do think we can save them. I get hundreds of e-mails and letters every week, from parents, teachers, and others who are beginning to realize that we must do for our sons what we did for our daughters in the industrialized schooling system—realize that boys are struggling and need help. These teachers and parents are part of a social movement—a boys' movement that started, I think, about ten years ago. It's a movement that gets noticed for brief moments by the media (when Columbine happened, when Laura Bush talked about boys) and then goes underground again. It's a movement very much powered by

Margin notes:

Explains steps in implementing solution.

Middle style underscores appeal to general readers, especially parents.

Asserts feasibility of solution.

individual women—mainly mothers of sons—who say things to me like the e-mailers who wrote, "I don't know anyone who doesn't have a son struggling in school" or "I thought having a boy would be like having a girl, but when my son was born, I had to rethink things."

We all need to rethink things. We need to stop blaming, suspecting, and overly medicating our boys, as if we can change this guy into the learner we want. When we decide—as we did with our daughters—that there isn't anything inherently wrong with our sons, when we look closely at the system that boys learn in, we will discover these boys again, for all that they are. And maybe we'll see more of them in college again.

ACADEMIC PROPOSAL   Ricky Patel wrote "Mandatory HIV Testing" for a course at the University of Texas at Austin, modifying his first draft to deal with the numerous comments it generated during an in-class editing session. Patel's research-based final version reproduced here would still likely generate much discussion and disagreement. But that's often the point of a proposal.

Patel 1

Ricky Patel

Professor Rossi

Composition 1

19 April 20--

Mandatory HIV Testing

For many young adults, college is the gateway to freedom. Some use the opportunity to make new friends, others experiment with substances like alcohol and marijuana, and still others experiment with sex. Unfortunately, the decision to have sex could be the worst mistake of their lives, given the consequences to their

Patel 2

Defines problem on college campuses: continuing danger of HIV and AIDS.

health. Among the many sexually transmitted diseases, HIV remains the most feared and unforeseeable. This virus can lead to AIDS, which takes the lives of millions of individuals each year worldwide, adding new victims each day. In fact, according to the Centers for Disease Control and Prevention (CDC), "1 in 500 college students is infected with HIV." Responsible officials at colleges and universities should therefore require each incoming student, solely for the individual's benefit, to take an HIV test.

Proposal targets school officials.

Many of those who have contracted HIV simply fail to realize it. For some, it may take up to ten years before AIDS symptoms ever show—plenty of time for an individual to spread the virus to his or her many partners. Additionally, those partners who are infected could just as easily spread the disease to more victims. But if someone knows that he or she has HIV, the likelihood of continued sexual encounters is greatly reduced. According to Dr. Julie Gerberding, director of the CDC, "When people know they're positive [they have the virus], the research has shown they take steps to protect others from infection. People who don't know it continue to transmit the virus" (Smith). By requiring each prospective student to take a test for HIV as an incoming freshman, educational institutions can greatly reduce the spread of this disease in the United States. Obviously, there are those who will engage in promiscuous activity even after they know they have the virus. However, many others will realize they do not want to burden anyone else with the difficult disease.

Explains how proposal would reduce AIDS transmission among young adults.

Cites authorities to support claims and judgments.

Ignorance about AIDS remains a serious problem. According to a recent survey of a group of students performed by AVERT, a charity for AIDS victims, 38% falsely thought the HIV virus could be

Offers second reason for mandatory AIDS testing.

Patel 3

transmitted by kissing, 25% believed the virus could be transmitted by sharing a glass of wine, and 18% thought the infection could spread by touching a toilet seat ("HIV"). But education should be the most effective tool to help prevent the spread of HIV. By mandating an HIV test, schools can be more sure that their students will be better educated about the risks of AIDS and methods of prevention available for those who wish to engage in sex.

Additionally, mandatory testing of all students means no groups are targeted by the program. AIDS specialist Dr. Rochelle Walensky explains that "when [people] realized you were not asking them if they wanted an HIV test because of who they were, what they looked like, or what they came for—but that you were offering it to them because that was just a service of that clinic—then there was no stigma" (Smith). Ultimately, university-enforced HIV testing might encourage potential carriers to take the test without any fear of discrimination or assumptions. Furthermore, if HIV is detected early enough, the individual has a greater chance of getting treatment to live "a long, productive life." Research shows that early treatment is more effective than treatment after a number of years.

However, there are moral implications when dealing with the sensitive subject of required testing: Some individuals may feel that their rights are being violated. Nonetheless, there are many laws in the United States, like the Patriot Act, by which citizens give up some of their liberties to ensure the safety of all Americans. With respect to AIDS, social responsibility clearly overshadows some privacy rights. All students in the United States have a personal responsibility to get tested for HIV. The test is simply there to tell them that they should consider making wise decisions in the future

Anticipating objections, Patel suggests that mandatory testing will remove stigma.

Uses emotional style to encourage readers to accept loss of privacy.

Addresses major objection: potential violation of privacy rights.

Patel 4

and get treatment immediately if they test positive. The average cost of an HIV test is $8—a small price, roughly that of a movie ticket, for such life-changing information. How could people live with themselves if they unknowingly infected someone with HIV when such an inexpensive test might have prevented it? Surely the benefits of mandatory testing outweigh the negatives.

Unfortunately, there still isn't a cure for this disease, but through awareness and education, HIV's spread can be greatly limited. A simple, inexpensive test could save dozens of lives at each major university. Since many colleges already require student testing for hepatitis and meningitis, what harm would there be if they also required HIV testing? Every student has a responsibility to themselves and each other to get tested and get treatment.

Argues feasibility by pointing to precedents.

Patel 5

Works Cited

Centers for Disease Control and Prevention. "HIV/AIDS and College Students." *AEGiS.org.* AEGiS, 1995. Web. 20 Mar. 2009.

"HIV and AIDS in America." *AVERT.org.* AVERT, 16 Mar. 2009. Web. 24 Mar. 2009.

Smith, Stephen. "US Calls for Making HIV Testing Routine." *Boston Globe.* NY Times, 22 Sept. 2006. Web. 10 Mar. 2009.

VISUAL PROPOSAL

In "Carchitecture," artists Tyler Brett and Tony Romano challenge the values of consumerist society, and offer a proposal for making cars more earth-friendly. This piece originally appeared in *Adbusters* magazine (November/December 2004).

CARCHITECTURE

We are all forced to negotiate our way through the everyday car-inundated environment whether on foot, bicycle, or automobile. This project is really about envisioning a way to be more actively and creatively engaged in that environment. We see the potential to imagine a future whose basic structure is tied to the political and economic realities of here and now.

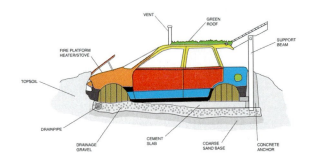

A carchitectural shelter will:

-Provide protection from the elements
-Keep the inside air warm
-Provide ventilation with minimum condensation

Carchitecture is virtually airtight, which is good and bad. Good, because it makes for a superb weatherproof shelter. Bad, because the carbon monoxide gas you produce from cooking and heating will poison you. Ventilation is imperative! Follow these plans to build a carchitectural shelter. To begin, you'll need to replace the car's internal combustion engine with a fire platform consisting of a six-inch bed of flat river stones.

Build a fire from two or three dry logs around two feet in length, allowing plenty of air to get to the fire. Dry kindling, like wood and lichen, can be found under the lower branches of trees, and will usually be dry even during the wettest seasons of the year. The opened hood (positioned 45 degrees to the existing windshield) will reflect the heat into the shelter and also serves as a wind screen. Two carchitectural shelters may be built facing one another with a fire between. When you do this you gain a great advantage. A lot of time is saved, more space is provided, and one fire will heat both shelters.

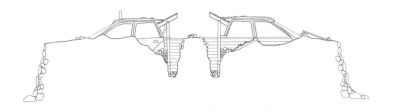

1. **Proposal for Change:** In calling for reducing the drinking age, Barrett Seaman's "How Bingeing Became the New College Sport" (p. 163) offers a solution to alcohol abuse that some might call "politically incorrect." Indeed, many politicians or school officials would likely be reluctant to support a lowered drinking age — even if it might make people more responsible. Choose an issue that you think needs as radical a rethinking as college-age drinking, and write a research-based proposal of your own. Like Seaman, be sure to offer your ideas in language cool and persuasive enough to make responsible adults at least consider them.

2. **Proposal Identifying a Problem:** Michael Gurian was prompted to write "Disappearing Act" (p. 175) after recalling the difficulties he observed young men having in school. Drawing on your own observations and experiences, identify a specific problem on your college campus or in the local community. Research the issue thoroughly, using both human resources and materials such as college manuals and policies, campus newspapers, official records, reports, and so on. Come up with a plausible approach to the problem, and then write a proposal in the form of a detailed letter directed to a person or group with the power to deal with it. Such a letter would likely have to be much shorter, however, than Gurian's article.

3. **Counterproposal:** You likely will find many proposals—such as Ricky Patel's call for mandatory AIDS testing on page 180— totally unacceptable. Identify such a proposal and write a paper in which you counter the idea with good reasons, evidence, and maybe a little humor (if appropriate), explaining why it won't work or why the solution might be worse than the problem.

4. **Visual Proposal:** The artists make a serious point with their humorous cartoon (and commentary) in "Carchitecture" (p. 184). Create a visual text of your own that offers a similarly satirical proposal.

How to start

- Need to **find a text to analyze**? See page 195.
- Need to come up with **ideas**? See page 198.
- Need to **organize your ideas**? See page 204.

7 Literary Analysis

responds critically to cultural works

Unless you're an English major, the papers you write for Literature 101 may seem as mechanical as chemistry lab reports—something done just to get a degree. But hardly a day goes by when you don't respond strongly to some cultural experience, sharing your thoughts and opinions about the books, music, and entertainment you love. It's worth learning to do this well.

- You write a paper explaining your theory that Lady Macbeth, though a tragic figure by definition, has strong comic elements in her character designed to make her appear more absurd and pathetic than evil.

- Rather than roll your eyes like your companions, you take abstract art seriously. You consider Kayla Mohammadi's painting (on p. 187), and try to explain what you see to someone who "doesn't get it."

- Having spent several seasons watching the TV series *24*, you wonder whether other programs—or maybe stage dramas or novels—have similarly experimented with the passage of time, making it so powerful a factor in telling a story.

UNDERSTANDING LITERARY ANALYSIS.   In a traditional literary analysis, you respond to a poem, novel, play, or short story. That response can be analytical, looking at theme, plot, structure, characters, genre, style, and so on. Or it can be critical, theoretical, or evaluative—locating works within their social, political, historic, and even philosophic neighborhoods. Or you might approach a literary work expressively, describing how you connect with it intellectually and emotionally. Or you can combine these approaches or imagine alternative ones—perhaps reflecting new attitudes and assumptions about media.

Other potential genres for analysis include films, TV offerings, popular music, comic books, and games. Distinctions between high and popular culture have not so much dissolved as ceased to be interesting. After all, you can say dumb things about *Hamlet* and smart things about *The Sopranos*. Moreover, every genre of artistic expression—from sonnets to opera to graphic novels—at some point struggled for respectability. What matters is

***Red Tide—Maine* by Kayla Mohammadi**   The artist explains that "the intention is not literal portrayal, but rather a visual translation. A translation based on color, value, and space."

the quality of a literary analysis and whether you help readers appreciate the novel *Pride and Prejudice* or, maybe, the video game *Valkyrie Profile 2: Silmeria*. Expect your literary or cultural analyses to do *some* of the following.

Begin with a close reading.   In an analysis, you slow the pace at which people typically operate in a 24/7 world to look deliberately and closely at a text. You might study the way individual words and images connect in a poem, how plot evolves in a novel, or how rapid editing defines the character of a movie. In short, you ponder the *calculated* choices writers and artists make in creating their work. ○

Make a claim or an observation.   Your encounter with a text will ordinarily lead to a thesis. The claim won't always be argumentative or controversial: You may be amazed at the simplicity of Wordsworth's Lucy poems or blown away by Jimi Hendrix's take on "All Along the Watchtower." But more typically, you'll make a statement or an observation that you believe is worth proving either by research or, just as often, by evidence from within the work itself.

Present works in context.   Works of art exist in our real world; that's what we like about them and why they sometimes change our lives. Your analysis can explore these relationships among texts, people, and society.

Draw on previous research.   Your response to a work need not agree with what others have written. But you should be willing to learn from previous scholarship and criticism—readily available in libraries or online. ○

Use texts for evidence.   A compelling analysis unwraps the complexities of a book, movie, poem, drama, or song, explaining it so that readers might better appreciate what they did not notice before. In short, direct them to the neat stuff. For that reason, the well-chosen quotation is the mighty tool of successful literary papers.

read closely
p. 317

plan a project
p. 400

Textual Analysis

In "Distinguishing the *Other* in Two Works by Tolstoy," Melissa Miller assembles evidence from *The Cossacks* and "A Prisoner in the Caucasus" to make one strong claim about author Leo Tolstoy's response to the ethnic peoples he describes. In a paper written for an assignment, she uses a simple comparison structure to organize numerous quotations from the two works to support her point.

Miller 1

Melissa Miller

Professor Spahr

English 112

November 23, 20--

Distinguishing the *Other* in Two Works by Tolstoy

The Cossacks and the Chechens are two very different peoples; they share neither language nor religion. The Cossacks are Russian-speaking Christians, while the Chechens speak a Caucasian language and follow Islam. Certainly, Leo Tolstoy (1828-1910) knew these facts, since he spent a significant length of time in the Caucasus. However, it is difficult to distinguish them as different peoples in Tolstoy's work. The Cossacks in Tolstoy's novel of the same name (1863) and the Chechens in his story "A Prisoner in the Caucasus" (1872) share so many cultural and ethnic features — appearance, reverence for warriors and horses, their behavior — that they appear to be the same people. As a result, their deep cultural differences all but disappear to Tolstoy and his European readers.

From Tolstoy's descriptions of the Cossacks and the Chechens, they appear identical: Both groups are dark in complexion, wear beshmets, and are wild. The Cossack men have black beards and Maryanka has black eyes (*Cossacks* 30; 55), while Dina has black hair and a face like her father's, "the dark man" ("Prisoner" 316). In

Title identifies topic and highlights key term.

Providing dates of writer's birth/death is a helpful convention.

Thesis is straightforward: Tolstoy doesn't show differences between Cossacks and Chechens.

Miller's close reading of text supports her claim.

Miller 2

addition to the black, both groups are red in countenance: Uncle Yeroshka is "cinnamon-colored" (*Cossacks* 60), Maryanka is sunburned (93), and Kazi Muhamet is always referred to as "the red Tatar" ("Prisoner" 315). Moreover, Tolstoy describes both the Cossack and the Chechen youths' clothing in terms of what they lack. For example, Maryanka wears "nothing but a pink shirt" (*Cossacks* 55), while Zhilin encounters "shaven-headed youngsters, with nothing but shirts on, and nothing on their legs" ("Prisoner" 315). Animal imagery characterizes both groups as well. When Ivan first sees Uncle Yeroshka, he gazes at the old man "as if he were some sort of strange wild beast" (*Cossacks* 62). Likewise, the old man who despises Zhilin "glares like a wolf" ("Prisoner" 327). This imagery extends to the women as well; Tolstoy implies they both carry themselves like animals instead of people. After meeting Ivan and Olyenin, Maryanka dashes away, prompting Ivan to declare her a "regular colt!" (*Cossacks* 57); similarly, upon giving Zhilin water, Dina darts away "like a wild goat" ("Prisoner" 316).

In Tolstoy's representations of both the Cossacks and the Chechens, warriors are central. In *The Cossacks,* the narrator directly states, "the chief traits" of the Cossacks' characters are "brigandage and war" (19). In "A Prisoner in the Caucasus," the same point is made, albeit more subtly. When Tolstoy relates how the Chechens dress and the layout of their homes, he sets weapons in the center of his descriptions. For example, Kazi Muhamet wears "a silk beshmet, a silver dagger in his belt, and sandals on his bare feet" and inside Zhilin's master's hut, "on the sides hung costly rugs; on the rugs were guns, pistols, and sabers, all silver-mounted. On one side a little oven was set in" ("Prisoner" 314; 317). In both of these cases, the

---

Events narrated in present tense, following conventions of literary analysis.

Quotations function as important bits of evidence.

Direct quotations are smoothly integrated into paper and carefully documented.

Miller 3

weapons—the dagger, guns, pistols, and sabers—appear among the other details; thus they are the syntactic heart of these sentences. Which, being key observations about these people's lives, it follows that war and weapons lie at the heart of this way of life.

In both cultures the people revere the horse. When Olyenin arrives in the Caucasus, he sees "two Cossacks appear on horseback . . . rhythmically swinging as their horses gallop along with brown and gray legs intermingling" (*Cossacks* 17); the brown legs belong to the horses, the gray belong to the men, as they are wearing felt boots. Thus, the first impression of these people is that they and their horses share one existence, symbolized by the unity of their legs. The same conclusion appears in "A Prisoner in the Caucasus," even though it is found in a more complicated scene. When Kazi Muhamet's brother dies, his friends and family bring him home, "dead on his saddle" (331), thus symbolizing that the unity between man and horse has been broken. After the burial, a group of Chechens holds the head of a mare while Kazi Muhamet slits its throat. He then chops it up and feeds it to the entire community at his hut. That they all participate in killing and eating the horse shows that the horse has become a part of all the Chechens in the village, thus restoring the unity that was lost.

Similarities extend to the women as well. From simple commonalities, such as wearing a solid silver half-ruble necklace, to complex behaviors, the Cossack Maryanka and the Chechen Dina are remarkably alike. They both fulfill the role of servant to the Russians who come to live with them, as it is their job to ease the Russians' thirst. Maryanka's mother tells her she must "draw [Olyenin's wine] from the opened cask" (*Cossacks* 63); likewise, Dina's father presumably tells her to bring Zhilin something to drink, since after he

Thesis supported by detailed comparison of works.

Evidence from analyzed texts carefully documented in MLA style.

Miller 4

gives her "some command," she leaves and quickly returns with "a little tin pitcher" ("Prisoner" 316). Moreover, they both disobey their traditional roles in order to have contact with the Russians. Maryanka makes special visits to Olyenin, and we know this behavior is socially unacceptable because, when Lukashka questions her, she cries, "I'll do just as I please . . . you are not my father, nor my mother . . . I'll love the one I want to love" (*Cossacks* 185). That Maryanka defies Lukashka, the husband the community has chosen for her, symbolizes her wish to go against what society has planned for her.

While Dina does not voice these convictions directly, she behaves according to their sentiment. She breaks the social norms of her village repeatedly by helping Zhilin; we know these are not activities she should be engaged in because Zhilin tells us if her family discovered she helped him, "they would flog [Dina]" ("Prisoner" 343). While it is true he bribes her into helping him some of the time, the assistance she renders while he is in the pit is entirely of her own accord. Zhilin has made no attempt to give her a gift, and yet, "a cake [falls] directly into his lap, then another, and some cherries [followed]. He looked up, and there was Dina" (342). Furthermore, a few days later, she saves his life by revealing that her father intends to kill him. Right before she tells him, he offers her some new dolls. That she responds, "I can't take them" (343) and then proceeds to disclose the danger he is in shows she is acting of her own free will.

One might argue that it is indeed simple to distinguish between the Cossacks and the Chechens in Tolstoy's work because these people have different languages and religions. While this assertion is of course true in real life, it is not so in Tolstoy's ethnographic portraits of these distinct groups of mountain men. From his

Miller 5

descriptions, the Cossacks and the Chechens seem to speak one language and practice one religion. Tolstoy repeatedly implies that the Cossacks and the Chechens do not speak Russian, but doesn't give an indication of what languages they do speak. Thus, both languages seem the same. For example, when Olyenin arrives in the village, he sees an "*arba,* or native cart" drive past (*Cossacks* 18). Foreign words the Chechens speak are also presented with italics and a definition, such as "a Tatar *salika,* a mountain-hut in the Caucasus" ("Prisoner" 314). Furthermore, it is not clear that these two groups practice different religions. Technically, the Cossacks are Christians, but we do not see them worship in Tolstoy's novel. We do, however, witness them invoking Allah, as Uncle Yeroshka teaches Olyenin that he must reply, "*Allah razi bo sun*" when someone greets him with "*koshkildui*" (*Cossacks* 61). Presumably, this is very important to the Cossacks, as Uncle Yeroshka says that it is part of "our ways" (61).

In *The Cossacks* and "A Prisoner in the Caucasus," Tolstoy strove to give us what Turgenev deemed "an incomparable picture of men and things in the Caucasus" (*Cossacks* v). Undoubtedly, Tolstoy has succeeded in providing readers with a full and varied portrait of how people in the Caucasus live and work. The problem lies in the fact that, while the Cossacks and the Chechens are two distinct populations, Tolstoy's descriptions of them are so similar that it is difficult to distinguish between the two. Thus, Tolstoy would not escape the criticism of Edward Said, who accused the West of portraying the East as one big, undifferentiated Other, instead of as the wide variety of "social, linguistic, political, and historical realities" (48) that actually comprise the East.

Prior research by Edward Said cited to bolster conclusion.

Miller 6

Works Cited

Said, Edward W. *Orientalism*. New York: Vintage, 1976. Print.

Tolstoy, Leo. *The Cossacks*. New York: Scribner's, 1899. Print.

---. "A Prisoner in the Caucasus." *Walk in the Light and Twenty-three Tales*. Maryknoll, NY: Orbis, 2003. 78. Print.

"I'm not convinced that 'Chekhov on Ice' was a good idea."

Exploring purpose and topic

find a text ◀

In most cases, you write a literary analysis to meet a course requirement, a project usually designed to improve your skills as a reader of literature and art. Such a lofty goal, however, doesn't mean you can't enjoy the project or put your own spin on it.

Your first priority is to read any assignment sheet closely to find out exactly what you are supposed to do. Underline any key words in the project description and take them seriously. Typically you will see terms such as *compare and contrast*, *classify*, *analyze*, or *interpret*. They mean different things.

Once you know your purpose in writing an analysis, you may have to choose a subject. ○ It's not unusual to have a work assigned (*Three pages on The House on Mango Street by Friday*), but more typically, you'll be able to select works to study from within a range defined by a course title or unit: British sci-fi; Puritan literature; Native American literature since 1920. Which should you choose?

Choose a text you connect with.   It makes sense to spend time writing about works that move you, perhaps by touching on an aspect of your life or identity. You may feel more confident commenting on them because of who you are and what you've experienced.

Choose a text you want to learn more about.   In the back of their minds, most people have lists of works and artists they've always wanted to read or explore. So use an assignment as an opportunity to sample one of them: *Beowulf, The Chronicles of Narnia*, or the work of William Gibson, Leslie Marmon Silko, or the Clash. Or use an assignment to venture beyond works within your comfort zone: Examine writers and artists from different cultures and with challenging points of view.

get an idea
p. 308

Choose a text that you _don't_ understand.   Most writers tend to write about works that are immediately accessible and relatively new: Why struggle with a hoary epic poem when you can just watch *The Lord of the Rings* on DVD? One obvious reason may be to figure out how works from different eras can still be powerfully connected to our own; the very strangeness of older and more difficult texts may even prompt you to ask more provocative questions. In short, you'll pay more attention to literary texts that place demands on you.

Stills from _Smoke Signals_ (1998) and _Bury My Heart at Wounded Knee_ (2007) How much do you know about Native American fiction or film? Use an assignment as an opportunity to learn more.

Understanding your audience

Unless you write book reviews or essays for a campus literary magazine, the readers of your analyses of works of art and culture are likely a professor and other students in your course. But in either situation, assume a degree of expertise among your readers. Moreover, many people will examine your literary analysis simply because they're interested—a tremendous advantage. Be sure to respect the needs of your audience.

Clearly identify the author and works you are analyzing. Seems like common sense, but this consideration is often neglected in academic papers precisely because writers assume that *the teacher must know what I'm doing.* Don't make this mistake. Also briefly recap what happens in the works you are analyzing—especially with texts not everyone has read recently. ○ Follow the model of good reviewers, who typically summarize key elements before commenting on them. Such summaries give readers their bearings at the beginning of a paper. Here's James Wood introducing a novel by Marilynne Robinson that he will be reviewing for the *New York Times*.

> *Gilead* is set in 1956 in the small town of Gilead, Iowa, and is narrated by a seventy-six-year-old pastor named John Ames, who has recently been told he has angina pectoris and believes he is facing imminent death. In this terminal spirit, he decides to write a long letter to his seven-year-old son, the fruit of a recent marriage to a much younger woman. This novel is that letter, set down in the easy, discontinuous form of a diary, mixing long and short entries, reminiscences, moral advice, and so on.

Define key terms. Many specialized and technical expressions are used in a literary analysis. Your instructor will know what an *epithet, peripeteia,* or *rondel* might be, but you may still have to define terms like these for a wider audience—your classmates, for instance. Alternatively, you can look for more accessible synonyms and expressions.

Don't aim to please professional critics. Are you tempted to imitate the style of serious academic theorists you've encountered while researching your paper? No need—your instructor probably won't expect you to write in that way, at least not until graduate school.

sum up ideas
p. 424

Finding and developing materials

▶ develop
  ideas

With an assignment in hand and works to analyze, the next step—and it's a necessary one—is to establish that you have a reliable "text" of whatever you'll be studying. In a course, a professor may assign a particular edition or literary anthology for you to use, making your job easier.

This Bedford/St. Martin's edition of *Frankenstein* provides important textual information and background. Look for texts with such material when studying classic novels, poems, and plays.

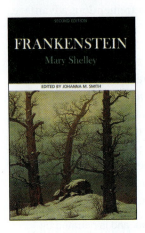

Be aware that many texts are available in multiple editions. (For instance, the novel *Frankenstein* first appeared in 1818, but the revised third edition of 1831 is the one most widely read today.) For classical works, such as the plays of Shakespeare, choose an edition from a major publisher, preferably one that includes thorough notes and perhaps some essays and criticism. When in doubt, ask your professor which texts to use. Don't just browse the library shelves.

Other kinds of media pose interesting problems as well. For instance, you may have to decide which version of a movie to study—the one seen by audiences in theaters or the "director's cut" on a DVD. Similarly, you might find multiple recordings of musical works: Look for widely respected performances. Even popular music may come in both studio (*American Idiot*) and live (*Bullet in a Bible*) versions. Then there is the question of drama: Do you read it on the page, watch a video when one is available, or see it in a theater? Perhaps you do all three. But whatever versions of a text you choose for study, be sure to identify them in your project, either in the text itself or on the Works Cited page. ○

understand citation
styles p. 435

Establishing a text is the easy part. How then do you find something specific to write about, an angle on the subject? ○ Following are some strategies and approaches.

Examine the text closely.   Guided by your assignment, begin your project by closely reading, watching, or examining the selected work(s) and taking notes. Obviously, you'll treat some works differently than others. You can read a Seamus Heaney sonnet a dozen times to absorb its nuances, but it's unlikely you'd push through Rudolfo A. Anaya's novel *Bless Me, Ultima* more than once or twice for a paper. But, in either case, you'll need a suitable way to take notes or to annotate what you're analyzing.

Honestly, you should count on a minimum of two readings or viewings of any text, the first to get familiar with the work and find a potential approach, the second and subsequent readings to confirm your thesis and to find supporting evidence for it.

Focus on the text itself.   Your earliest literature papers probably tackled basic questions about plot, character, setting, theme, and language. But these are not simple matters—just the kinds of issues that fascinate most readers. You might, for example, look for moments when the plot of the novel you're examining reinforces its theme or study how characters change in response to specific events. Even the setting of a short story or film might be worth writing about when it becomes a factor in the story: Can you imagine the film *Casablanca* taking place in any other location?

Questions about language loom large in many analyses. How does word choice work with or against the subject of a poem? Does the style of a novel reinforce its story? How does a writer create irony through dialogue? Indeed, any feature of a work might be researched and studied, from the narrators in novels to the rhyme schemes in poetry.

Focus on its meanings, themes, and interpretations.   Although finding themes or meanings in literary works seems like an occupation mostly for English majors, the tendency really is universal and irresistible. If you take any work seriously, you'll discover angles and ideas worth sharing with readers. Maybe *Seinfeld* is a modern version of *Everyman* or *O Brother,*

find a topic
p. 308

Where Art Thou? is a retelling of the *Odyssey* by Homer or maybe not. Observe carefully and open your mind to possible connections: What have you seen like this before? What patterns do you detect? What images recur in the text or what ideas are supported or undercut?

Focus on its authorship and history.   Some artists stand apart from their creations, while others cannot be separated from them. So you might explore in what ways a work reflects the life, education, and attitudes of its author. What psychological forces or religious perspectives might be detected in particular characters or themes? Is the author writing to represent his or her gender, race, ethnicity, or class? Or does the work repudiate its author's identity, class, or religion?

Similarly, consider how a text embodies the assumptions, attitudes, politics, fashions, and even technology of the times during which it was composed. A work as familiar as Jonathan Swift's "A Modest Proposal" still requires readers to know at least a *little* about Irish and English politics in the eighteenth century. How does Swift's satire open up when you learn even more about its world?

Focus on its genre.   Genres are formulas. Take a noble hero, give him a catastrophic flaw, have him make a bad choice, and then kill him off: That's tragedy—or, in the wrong hands, melodrama. With a little brainstorming, you could identify dozens of genres and subcategories: epics, sonnets, historical novels, superhero comics, grand opera, soap opera, and so on. Artists' works often fall between genres, sometimes creating new ones. Readers, too, bring clear-cut expectations to a text: Try to turn a 007 action-spy thriller into a three-hankie chick flick, and you've got trouble in River City.

You can analyze genre in various ways. For instance, track a text backward to discover its literary forebears—the works that influenced its author. Even texts that revolt against previous genres bear traces of what they have rejected. It's also possible to study the way artists combine different genres or play with or against the expectations of audiences. Needless to say, you can also explore the relationships of works within a genre. In fact, it's often a shared genre that makes comparisons interesting or provocative. For example, what do twentieth-century coming-of-age stories such as *A Separate Peace*, *The Catcher in the Rye*, and *Lord of the Flies* have in common?

Focus on its influence. Some works have an obvious impact on life or society, changing how people think or behave: *Uncle Tom's Cabin, To Kill a Mockingbird, Roots, Schindler's List.* TV shows have broadened people's notions of family; musical genres such as jazz and gospel have created and sustained entire communities.

But impact doesn't always occur on such a grand scale or express itself through social movements. Books influence other books, films other films, and so on—with not a few texts crossing genres. Who could have foreseen all the ties between comic books in the 1930s, TV shows in the 1950s, superhero films in the 1980s, and video games in the new century? And, for better or worse, books, movies, and other cultural productions influence styles, fashions, and even the way people speak. Consider *Fast Times at Ridgemont High* or *Clueless*. You may have to think outside the box, but projects that trace and study influence can shake things up.

Focus on its social connections. In recent decades, many texts have been studied for what they reveal about relationships between genders, races, ethnicities, and social classes. Works by new writers are now more widely read in schools, and hard questions asked about texts traditionally taught: What do they reveal about the treatment of women or minorities? Whose lives have been ignored in dominant texts, or how are minorities or working classes represented? What responsibility do cultural texts have for maintaining repressive political or social arrangements? These critical approaches have changed how many people view literature and art, and you can follow up on such studies and extend them to texts you think deserve more attention. Such inquiries themselves, however, are as agenda driven as other kinds of analysis and so should also be subjected to the same critical scrutiny.

Find good sources. Developing a literary paper provides you with many opportunities and choices. Fortunately, you needn't make all your decisions on your own. Ample commentary and research is available on almost any literary subject or method, both in print and online. O Your instructor and local librarians can help you focus on the best resources for your project, but the following box lists some possibilities.

O refine your search
p. 406

Literary Resources in Print

Abrams, M. H., and Geoffrey Harpham. *A Glossary of Literary Terms*. 8th ed. New York: Heinle, 2004.

Beacham, Walton, ed. *Research Guide to Biography and Criticism*. Washington, DC: Research, 1986.

Crystal, David. *The Cambridge Encyclopedia of Language*. 2nd ed. New York: Cambridge UP, 1997.

Drabble, Margaret, ed. *The Oxford Companion to English Literature*. 6th ed. Oxford: Oxford UP, 2000.

Encyclopedia of World Literature in the 20th Century. 3rd ed. Farmington Hills, MI: St. James, 1999.

Gates, Henry Louis, Jr., et al. *The Norton Anthology of African American Literature*. New York: Norton, 1997.

Gilbert, Sandra M., and Susan Gubar. *The Norton Anthology of Literature by Women: The Traditions in English*. 2nd ed. New York: Norton, 1996.

Harmon, William, and Hugh Holman. *A Handbook to Literature*. 11th ed. New York: Prentice, 2008.

Harner, James L. *Literary Research Guide: A Guide to Reference Sources for the Study of Literature in English and Related Topics*. 4th ed. New York: MLA, 2002.

Hart, James D., ed. *The Oxford Companion to American Literature*. 6th ed. New York: Oxford UP, 1995.

Howatson, M. C. *The Oxford Companion to Classical Literature*. 2nd ed. New York: Oxford UP, 1989.

Leitch, Vincent, et al. *The Norton Anthology of Theory and Criticism*. New York: Norton, 2001.

Preminger, Alex, and T. V. F. Brogan, eds. *The New Princeton Encyclopedia of Poetry and Poetics*. Princeton: Princeton UP, 1993.

Sage, Lorna. *The Cambridge Guide to Women's Writing in English*. Cambridge: Cambridge UP, 1999.

Sampson, George. *The Concise Cambridge History of English Literature*. 3rd ed. Cambridge: Cambridge UP, 1972.

Literary Resources Online

Annotated Bibliography for English Studies (ABES) (http://routledgeabes.com)

Annual Bibliography of English Language and Literature (ABELL) (http://collections.chadwyck.com/home/home_abell.jsp)

Atlantic Unbound (http://www.theatlantic.com) (for book reviews)

The Complete Works of William Shakespeare (http://thetech.mit.edu/Shakespeare)

The English Server (http://eserver.org)

A Handbook of Rhetorical Devices (http://www.virtualsalt.com/rhetoric.htm)

Images: A Journal of Film and Popular Culture (http://www.imagesjournal.com/)

Internet Public Library: Literary Criticism (http://www.ipl.org/div/litcrit/)

Literary Resources on the Net (http://andromeda.rutgers.edu/~jlynch/Lit)

Literature Resource Center (Gale Group – by library subscription)

MIT Literature Resources (http://libraries.mit.edu/guides/subjects/literature/)

MLA on the Web (http://www.mla.org)

New York Review of Books (http://www.nybooks.com/)

New York Times Book Review (http://www.nytimes.com/pages/books)

The Online Books Page (http://digital.library.upenn.edu/books)

Browne Popular Culture Library (http://www.bgsu.edu/colleges/library/pcl)

University of Virginia Library Scholar's Lab (http://www2.lib.virginia.edu/scholarslab)

Voice of the Shuttle (http://vos.ucsb.edu/index.asp)

Yahoo! Arts: Humanities: Literature (http://www.yahoo.com/Arts/Humanities/Literature)

Creating a structure

The shape of your literary analysis evolves as you learn more about your topic and decide how to treat it. Your project takes on the character of a report if you're interested in sharing information or demonstrating a case. Or it becomes an argument if your thesis veers toward a controversial position. ○ Whatever its trajectory, give attention to certain features.

▶ organize
ideas

Focus on a particular observation, claim, or point.   Always have a point firmly in mind as you draft a project, whether you work with individual literary texts or more general cultural questions. Following are some examples of claims or points that literary analyses might explore.

STUDY OF THEME

In <u>Bless Me, Ultima</u>, the youngster Antonio has to find a way to reconcile his traditional values and mystical beliefs with Ultima's prediction that he will become a "man of learning."

CONTRAST OF GENRES

The movie version of Annie Proulx's short story "Brokeback Mountain" actually improves on the original work, making it more powerful, specific, and believable.

CULTURAL ANALYSIS

One likely impact of digital technology will be to eliminate the barriers between art, entertainment, and commerce — with books becoming films, films morphing into games, and games inspiring graphic art.

Imagine a structure.   Here are three simple forms a literary analysis might take, the first developing from a thesis stated early on, the second comparing two works to make a point, and the third building toward a conclusion rather than opening with a thesis. ○

Introduction leading to a **claim**

First supporting reason + textual **evidence**

Second supporting reason + textual **evidence**

Additional supporting reasons + textual **evidence**

Conclusion

understand
argument p. 68

develop a thesis
p. 336

Introduction leading to a **claim** about Texts 1 & 2

First **supporting reason**

Evidence from Text 1

Evidence from Text 2

Next **supporting reason**

Evidence from Text 1

Evidence from Text 2

Additional **supporting reasons** . . .

Evidence from Text 1

Evidence from Text 2

Conclusion or **point**

Introduction presenting an **issue** or a **problem**

First **point** or **connection**, leading to . . .

Next **point** or **connection**, leading to . . .

Next **point** or **connection**, leading to . . .

A **summary observation** or **point**

Work on your opening.   Be certain that your introductory sections provide background for your analysis and identify what works you may be examining, and what you hope to accomplish. ○ Provide enough context so that the project stands on its own and would make sense to someone other than the instructor who assigned it.

shape a beginning
p. 354

Choosing a style and design

As the student examples in this chapter suggest, the literary analyses you write for courses will typically be serious in tone, formal in vocabulary, and, for the most part, impersonal—all markers of a formal or high style. ○ Elements of that style can be identified in this paragraph from an academic paper in which Manasi Deshpande analyzes Emily Brontë's *Wuthering Heights*. Here she explores the character of its Byronic hero, Heathcliff:

Examines Heathcliff from the perspective of a potential reader, not from her own.

Complex sentences smoothly incorporate quotations and documentation.

Related points are expressed in parallel clauses.

Vocabulary throughout is accessible, but formal. No contractions.

In witnessing Heathcliff's blatantly violent behavior, the reader is caught between sympathy for the tormented Heathcliff and shock at the intensity of his cruelty and mistreatment of others. Intent on avenging Hindley's treatment of him, Heathcliff turns his wrath toward Hareton by keeping him in such an uneducated and dependent state that young Cathy becomes "upset at the bare notion of relationship with such a clown" (193). Living first under Hindley's neglect and later under Heathcliff's wrath, Hareton escapes his situation only when Catherine befriends him and Heathcliff dies. In addition, Heathcliff marries Isabella only because Catherine wants to "'torture [him] to death for [her] amusement'" and must "'allow [him] to amuse [himself] a little in the same style'"(111). Heathcliff's sole objective in seducing and running away with Isabella is to take revenge on Catherine for abandoning him. Heathcliff's sadism is so strong that he is willing to harm innocent third parties in order to punish those who have caused his misery. He even forces young Cathy and Linton to marry by locking them in Wuthering Heights and keeping Cathy from her dying father until she has married Linton, further illustrating his willingness to torture others out of spite and vengeance.

Occasionally, you may be asked to write brief essays called *position papers*, in which you record your immediate reactions to poems, short stories, or other readings. ○ In these assignments, an instructor may expect to hear your voice and even encourage exploratory responses. Here is Cheryl Lovelady responding somewhat personally to a literary work in a proposal to revive the Broadway musical *Fiddler on the Roof*:

Question focuses paragraph. Reply suggests strong personal opinion.

How can a play set in a small, tradition-bound Jewish village during the Russian Revolution be modernized? I would argue that *Fiddler on the Roof* is actually an apt portrayal of our own time. Throughout the show, the conflicted main character, Tevye, is on the brink of pivotal decisions. Perplexed by his daughters' increasingly modern

define your style
p. 366

understand position
papers p. 260

choices, Tevye prays aloud, "Where do they think they are, America?" Tevye identifies America as a symbol of personal freedom—the antithesis of the tradition which keeps his life from being "as shaky as a fiddler on the roof." Forty years after the play's debut, America has become startlingly more like the Anatevka Tevye knows than the America he envisions. Post-9/11 America parallels Anatevka in a multitude of ways: political agendas ideologically separate the United States from most of the world; public safety and conventional wisdom are valued over individual freedoms; Americans have felt the shock of violence brought onto their own soil; minority groups are isolated or isolate themselves in closed communities; and societal taboos dictate whom people may marry.

Basic style remains serious and quite formal: Note series of roughly parallel clauses that follow colon.

A 1964 production of the musical *Fiddler on the Roof.*

Literary papers usually follow MLA documentation style. ◯ Here are some guidelines that apply specifically to literary papers.

Describe action in the present tense.   In writing literary analyses, you'll be doing plenty of summarizing and paraphrasing. In most cases, when you narrate the events in a story or poem, set the action in the present tense.

cite in MLA
p. 437

Provide dates for authors and literary works.   The first time you name authors or artists in a paper, give their dates of birth and death in parentheses. Similarly, provide a year of publication or release date for any major work you mention in your analysis.

> Joan Didion (b. 1934) is the author of *Play It as It Lays* (1970), *Slouching Towards Bethlehem* (1968), and *The Year of Magical Thinking* (2005).

Use appropriate abbreviations.   An English or rhetoric major may want to own a copy of the *MLA Handbook for Writers of Research Papers* if for nothing more than its full chapter on abbreviations common in literary papers. Some of the abbreviations appear chiefly in notes and documentation; others make it easier to refer to very familiar texts; still others identify various parts and sections of literary works.

Follow conventions for quotations.   In a literary paper, you'll be frequently citing passages from novels, short stories, and poems as well as quoting the comments of critics. All of these items need to be appropriately introduced and, if necessary, modified to fit smoothly into your sentences and paragraphs. O

Cite plays correctly.   Plays are cited by act, scene, and line number. In the past, passages from Shakespeare were routinely identified using a combination of roman and arabic numerals. But more recently, MLA recommends arabic numerals only for such references.

> **FORMER STYLE**
>
> Hamlet's final words are "The rest is silence" (*Ham.* V.ii.358).

> **CURRENT STYLE**
>
> Hamlet's final words are "The rest is silence" (*Ham.* 5.2.358).

use quotations
p. 431

Examining models

TEXTUAL ANALYSIS In "Insanity: Two Women," Kanaka Sathasivan examines a poem (Emily Dickinson's "I felt a Funeral, in My Brain") and a short story (Charlotte Perkins Gilman's "The Yellow Wallpaper") to discover a disturbing common theme in the work of these two American women writers. The essay, written in a formal academic style, uses a structure that examines the works individually, drawing comparisons in a final paragraph. Note, in particular, how Sathasivan manages the close reading of the poem by Emily Dickinson, moving through it almost line by line to draw out its themes and meanings. Here's the text of "I felt a Funeral, in my Brain."

> I felt a Funeral, in my Brain,
> And Mourners to and fro
> Kept treading – treading – till it seemed
> That Sense was breaking through –
>
> And when they all were seated,
> A Service, like a Drum –
> Kept beating – beating – till I thought
> My Mind was going numb–
>
> And then I heard them lift a Box
> And creak across my Soul
> With those same Boots of Lead, again,
> Then Space – began to toll,
>
> As all the Heavens were a Bell,
> And Being, but an Ear,
> And I, and Silence, some strange Race
> Wrecked, solitary, here –
>
> And then a Plank in Reason, broke,
> And I dropped down, and down –
> And hit a World, at every plunge,
> And Finished knowing – then –

You can find the full text of "The Yellow Wallpaper" searching online by the title. One such text is available at the University of Virginia Library Electronic Text Center: http://etext.virginia.edu/toc/modeng/public/GilYell.html.

Sathasivan 1

Kanaka Sathasivan

Dr. Glotzer

English 150

March 3, 20--

Insanity: Two Women

The societal expectations of women in the late nineteenth century served to keep women demure, submissive, and dumb. Although women's rights had begun to improve as more people rejected these stereotypes, many women remained trapped in their roles because of the pressures placed on them by men. Their suppression had deep impacts not only on their lives but also on their art as well. At a time when women writers often published under male aliases to gain respect, two of America's well-known authors, Emily Dickinson (1830-1886) and Charlotte Perkins Gilman (1860-1935), both wrote disturbing pieces describing the spiritual and mental imprisonment of women. In verse, Dickinson uses a funeral as a metaphor for the silencing of women and the insanity it subsequently causes. Gilman's prose piece "The Yellow Wallpaper" (1899) gives us a firsthand look into the mental degradation of a suppressed woman. These two works use vivid sensory images and rhythmic narration to describe sequential declines into madness.

In "I felt a Funeral, in My Brain" (first published 1896), Dickinson outlines the stages of a burial ceremony, using them as

Works to be analyzed are set in context: late nineteenth century.

Identifies authors and sets works in thematic relationship.

States thesis for the comparison.

Sathasivan 2

metaphors for a silenced woman's departure from sanity. The first verse, the arrival of Mourners, symbolizes the imposition of men and society on her mind. They are "treading" "to and fro," breaking down her thoughts and principles, until even she is convinced of their ideas (Dickinson 3, 2). The Service comes next, representing the closure—the acceptance of fate. Her "Mind was going numb" as they force her to stop thinking and begin accepting her doomed life. These first two verses use repetition at parallel points as they describe the Mourners "treading—treading" and the service like a drum is "beating—beating" (Dickinson 3, 7). The repetition emphasizes the incessant insistence of men; they try to control threatening women with such vigor and persistence that eventually even the women themselves begin to believe it and allow their minds to be silenced.

As the funeral progresses, the Mourners carry her casket from the service. Here Dickinson describes how they scar her very Soul using the "same Boots of Lead" which destroyed her mind (Dickinson 11). From the rest of the poem, one can infer that the service took place inside a church, and the act of parting from a house of God places another level of finality on the loss of her spirituality. While the figures in the poem transport her, the church's chimes begin to ring, and, as if "all the Heavens were a Bell / And Being, but an Ear," the noise consumes her (Dickinson 13). In this tremendous sound, her voice finally dissolves forever; her race with Silence has ended, "wrecked," and Silence has won (Dickinson 16). Finally, after the loss of her mind, her soul, and her voice, she loses her sanity as they lower her casket into the grave and bury her. She "hit a World, at every plunge, / And Finished knowing" (Dickinson 20). The worlds she hits represent further stages of psychosis, and

Offers close reading of Dickinson's poem.

Sathasivan 3

she plunges deeper until she hits the bottom, completely broken.

    Like Dickinson, Gilman in "The Yellow Wallpaper" also segments her character's descent into madness. The narrator of the story expresses her thoughts in a diary written while she takes a vacation for her health. Each journal entry represents another step toward insanity, and Gilman reveals the woman's psychosis with subtle hints and clues placed discreetly within the entries. These often take the form of new information about the yellow room the woman has been confined to, such as the peeled wallpaper or bite marks on the bedpost. The inconspicuous presentation of such details leads the reader to think that these artifacts have long existed, created by someone else, and only now does the narrator share them with us. "I wonder how it was done and who did it, and what they did it for," she says, speaking of a groove that follows the perimeter of the walls. Here, Gilman reuses specific words at crucial points in the narration to allude to the state of her character's mental health. In this particular example, both the narrator and the maid use the word "smooch" to describe, respectively, the groove in the wall, and yellow smudges on the narrator's clothes. This repetition indicates that she created the groove in the room, a fact affirmed at the end of the story.

    Gilman's narrator not only seems to believe other people have caused the damage she sees but also imagines a woman lives trapped within the paper, shaking the pattern in her **attempts** to escape. "I think that woman gets out in the daytime!" the narrator exclaims, recounting her memories of a woman "creeping" about the garden (Gilman 400, 401). Again, Gilman uses repetition to make associations for the reader as the narrator uses "creeping" to

---

With simple transition, turns to Gilman's short story.

Uses present tense to describe action in "The Yellow Wallpaper."

Sathasivan 4

describe her own exploits. As in the previous example, the end of the story reveals that the woman in the paper is none other than the narrator, tricked by her insanity. This connection also symbolizes the narrator's oppression. The design of the wallpaper trapping the woman represents the spiritual bars placed on the narrator by her husband and doctor, who prescribes mental rest, forbidding her from working or thinking. Even the description of the room lends itself to the image of a dungeon or cell, with "barred" windows and "rings and things in the walls" (Gilman 392). Just as the woman escapes during the daytime, so too does the narrator, giving in to her sickness and disobeying her husband by writing. Finally, like the woman in the paper breaking free, the narrator succumbs to her insanity.

    Both Dickinson's and Gilman's works explore society's influence on a woman's mental health. Like Dickinson's character, Gilman's narrator has also been compelled into silence by a man. Although she knows she is sick, her husband insists it isn't so and that she, a fragile woman, simply needs to avoid intellectual stimulation. Like a Mourner, "treading—treading," he continually assures her he knows best and that she shouldn't socialize or work. This advice, however, only leads to further degradation as her solitude allows her to indulge her mental delusions. When the narrator attempts to argue with her husband, she is silenced, losing the same race as Dickinson's character.

    In both these pieces, the characters remain mildly aware of their declining mental health, but neither tries to fight it. In Dickinson's poem, the woman passively observes her funeral, commenting objectively on her suppression and burial. Dickinson uses sound to describe every

> Draws attention to common themes and strategies in the two works.

> Notes difference in technique between authors.

Sathasivan 5

step, creating the feel of secondary sensory images—images that cannot create a picture alone and require interpretation to do so. Gilman's narrator also talks of her sickness passively, showing her decline only by describing mental fatigue. In these moments she often comments that her husband "loves [her] very dearly" and she usually accepts the advice he offers (Gilman 396). Even on those rare occasions when she disagrees, she remains submissive and allows her suppression to continue. In contrast to Dickinson, Gilman uses visual images to create this portrait, describing most of all how the narrator sees the yellow wallpaper, an approach which allows insight into the narrator's mental state.

> Concludes that writers use similar techniques to explore a common theme in two very different works.

Both Dickinson and Gilman used their writing to make profound statements about the painful lives led by many women in the nineteenth century. Through repetition, metaphor, symbolism, and sensory images, both "I felt a Funeral, in My Brain" and "The Yellow Wallpaper" describe a woman's mental breakdown, as caused by societal expectations and oppression. The poetry and prose parallel one another and together give insight into a horrific picture of insanity.

Sathasivan 6

Works Cited

Dickinson, Emily. "I felt a Funeral, in My Brain." *Concise Anthology of American Literature*. 5th ed. Ed. George McMichael. Upper Saddle River: Prentice, 2001. 1129. Print.

Gilman, Charlotte Perkins. "The Yellow Wallpaper." *The American Short Story and Its Writer, An Anthology*. Ed. Ann Charters. Boston: Bedford, 2000. 391-403. Print.

> MLA documentation style used for in-text notes and Works Cited.

Liz Miller, a columnist for the popular literary Web site Bookslut, writes about the relationship between books and movies. In "Size Doesn't Matter" (January 2006), edited slightly here for length, Miller explores a general question about film adaptations by examining how one admired short story, Annie Proulx's "Brokeback Mountain," became a celebrated and successful film. Miller nicely walks a line between the personal tone of a blog entry and the serious perspectives of film criticism.

bookslut.com

Posted: January 2006
From: Liz Miller

Size Doesn't Matter:
Brokeback Mountain

There's a real question when it comes to adaptations as to what length work adapts the best—mainly because there's no pattern to be found. Novels can lose their depth in the course of the condensing process, short stories are stretched to an airy thinness.

An Oprah Winfrey favorite is reduced to long lingering glances, filling in the space left by the passages of inner monologue. Conceptually interesting genre vignettes with weak story lines become the setup for sci-fi action spectaculars, their original resolutions tossed aside and replaced with an extra hour of fisticuffs and wry comebacks.

Recently, I've been reviewing material under consideration for film adaptation, and it's interesting to see how a small and slender book can pop with smart ideas and strong plotting and a much thicker tome will ultimately have less story than the first twenty minutes of *Hitch*. It doesn't surprise me, though, because of Annie Proulx's short story "Brokeback Mountain" and what it became with the guidance of director Ang Lee and writers Larry McMurtry and Diana Ossana. . . .

After reading the story the first time, it became clear that there was no reason why Ang Lee's adaptation shouldn't succeed, at

Raises main issue: What length of literary work adapts best to a film script?

Essay has a more personal tone and style than most academic literary analysis.

least on a script level. Proulx's brusque prose details the passing of years with brevity and elegance—each intense emotion is given just enough breath to burst with life. The rough-spoken love story of Ennis Del Mar and Jack Twist, two men ultimately kept apart by fear, takes the possibilities promised by a vast expanse of western landscape and reveals how meaningless they are if left unpursued. It's a powerful piece of work. It is also a complete and thorough treatment for a movie.

Seeing the trailer after reading the short story a few more times, I began to suspect that maybe I wasn't the only one who saw that. Every story beat and every line of dialogue of the trailer were straight from the prose, including images that would make no sense to someone who hadn't read the story, like Heath Ledger clenching two button-down shirts to his chest. It was a good omen—a good omen that didn't disappoint.

When I tell people that the entire movie fit totally into Annie Proulx's fifteen pages of prose, they honestly don't believe me. But the passing of years that Proulx so deftly skims over are broadened, enriched by elegant montages, giving the lives of the characters greater detail without feeling out of place (mainly because everything Ang Lee shoots tends to feel a little bit like a montage). And scenes glossed over in the story are given considerable screen time: A casual, after-the-fact reference to a bruise on Jack's jaw, for example, becomes an intensely physical and silent moment between the two characters, something that a few paragraphs of description might have captured, but not nearly so elegantly as the film managed.

The film, for the record, is great across the board. Directing, cinematography, music, and most especially acting. That girl from *Dawson's Creek*! That guy from *10 Things I Hate about You*! That girl from *Princess Diaries*! And all of it simple, understated: in service of the story.

One of the reasons I've read the short story more than once is that I keep finding new details that I overlooked in previous readings—

Provides synopsis of "Brokeback Mountain" to explain why original short story might work as a film.

Argues that movie trailer also provided evidence of successful adaptation.

Examines the two "texts" closely to appreciate adaptation of story to film.

Actors Heath Ledger and Jake Gyllenhaal in the movie *Brokeback Mountain.*

little asides on Proulx's part that continually add to a deeper meaning. *Brokeback Mountain* is a movie made by people who read every word of the story every single day, wringing out its potential for drama like you'd wring out a soaked washcloth. The largest additions are in Jack Twist's passing of years, filling out details unexplored by the story's reliance on the Ennis POV,[1] but of those scenes only one—in which Jack stands up to his rich and domineering father-in-law at Thanksgiving—feels at all out of place.

And the sum of all this is a small love story with an epic feel: a critical favorite, an Oscar front-runner, and the only other film of 2005 that can challenge *Sin City* for the title of Year's Most Faithful Adaptation. A two-hour movie from a fifteen-page short story, with minimal addition.

> Conclusion still has main point clearly in mind.

Sometimes, with adaptations, you sometimes get to see a dull caterpillar transform into a beautiful butterfly, but most of the time you watch a beautiful caterpillar burst from the cocoon as a dull brown moth. *Brokeback* is the rarest of species—it emerged transformed, but still recognizable. Still just as gorgeous as before.

Just a little longer.

1. *POV:* Point of view.

PHOTOGRAPHS AS LITERARY TEXTS   Photography attained its status as art in the twentieth century. Even documentary photographs not originally conceived as works of art became prized for their striking depictions of the human condition. Three artists recognized for such work are Dorothea Lange (1895–1965), Walker Evans (1903–1975), and Gordon Parks (1912–2006). During the Great Depression and subsequent years, they produced photographs for the Farm Security Administration (FSA) intended to record all aspects of American life. But their best portraits of people and places often reach beyond the immediate historical context, as the three images below and on pages 219–20 demonstrate. Note how these photographs present and frame their subjects, encouraging viewers to expand and interpret their meanings.

Dorothea Lange, "Jobless on Edge of Pea Field, Imperial Valley, California" (1937)

Walker Evans, "Burroughs Family Cabin, Hale County, Alabama" (1936)

Gordon Parks, "American Gothic" (1942)

Assignments

1. **Textual Analysis:** Study Melissa Miller's "Distinguishing the *Other* in Two Works by Tolstoy" (p. 189). Then examine how a favorite author or filmmaker treats a specific age, gender, ethnic, professional, or political group in a short story, novel, or film. Help readers see a pattern that they (or you) may not have noticed before. If it helps, examine several works by a single artist.

2. **Textual Analysis:** In "Insanity: Two Women" (p. 210) Kanaka Sathasivan does a close analysis of Emily Dickinson's "I felt a Funeral, in My Brain." Do a similar close reading of a favorite short poem. Tease out all the meanings and strategies you can uncover and show readers how the poem works. Alternatively, apply this kind of reading to song lyrics.

3. **Comparing Genres:** Choose a favorite short story and explain why a film adaptation of it would or would not be successful. See Liz Miller's "Size Doesn't Matter: *Brokeback Mountain*" (p. 215) for ideas about what to pay attention to in moving from a literary tale to a visual story.

4. **Analysis of Three Photographs:** Photographers Dorothea Lange, Walker Evans, and Gordon Parks (pp. 218–20) recorded images documenting the long-term effects of the Great Depression. In a short paper, describe the specific scenes you would photograph today if you hoped to leave as important a documentary legacy as Lange, Evans, and Parks. To make the project manageable, focus on your local community. Showcase your own images in a photoessay.

5. **Cultural Analysis:** Compare two literary works in one genre written at least a half-century apart, such as two tragedies, two sonnets, two short stories, two mystery novels. Support your claims with textual evidence.

6. **Cultural Analysis:** Examine several recent works of literature, art, or popular culture that reflect what you find to be an important trend or attitude in society. You may detect, for example, common themes in films, TV series, novels, dance, or even video games. Show how the trend crosses genres or changes how people think or behave.

How to start
- Need to **find a text to analyze**? See page 228.
- Need to come up with **ideas**? See page 230.
- Need to **organize your ideas**? See page 233.

8 Rhetorical Analysis

examines
in detail
the way
texts work

Rhetorical analyses foster the kind of close reading that makes writers better thinkers. Moreover, they're everywhere in daily life, especially in politics and law. In fact, they're hard to avoid.

- An editorial in the college paper calls for yet another fee to support a get-out-the-vote initiative on campus. You respond with an op-ed of your own, pointing out the editor's factual errors and logical inconsistencies.

- As part of a course evaluation, you argue that the assigned history textbook inappropriately endorses a particular interpretation of contemporary European history rather than just stating facts and leaving it for readers to make judgments.

- In your blog, you post a paragraph-by-paragraph refutation of a review published by the *Los Angeles Times* of your favorite band's latest CD. You point to ample textual evidence that the reviewer is neither well-informed nor objective.

- You're pretty sure global warming is the real deal, but you find yourself wishing that news reporters wouldn't blame every spring tornado and summer thunderstorm on the phenomenon.

UNDERSTANDING RHETORICAL ANALYSIS. You react to what others say or write all the time. Sometimes an advertisement, speech, or maybe a political anthem grabs you so hard that you want to take it apart to see how it works. Put those discoveries into words and you've composed a *rhetorical analysis*.

Rhetoric is the art of using language and media to achieve particular goals. A rhetorical analysis is an argument that takes a close look at the strategies of persuasion within a text; it lists and describes specific techniques

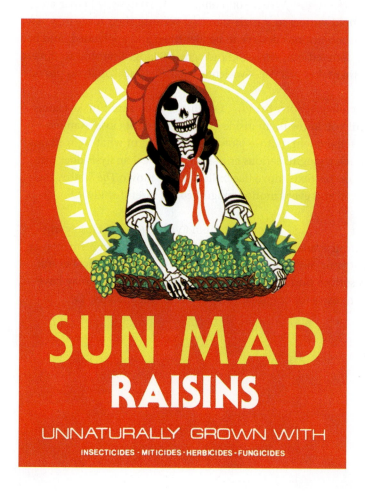

"Sun Mad Raisins"
This reworking of the familiar Sun-Maid Raisin box by artist Esther Hernandez provides plentiful material for a rhetorical analysis.
Sun Mad © 1981 Esther Hernandez.

that a writer, speaker, editor, or advertiser has employed and then assesses their effectiveness. ⭘ You can take a rhetorical analysis one step further and respond to a particular argument by offering good reasons for agreeing or disagreeing with it. Such a detailed critique of a text is sometimes called a *critical analysis.*

When you write a rhetorical analysis, you'll do the following things.

Take words seriously.   When you compose an analysis, whether admiring or critical, hold writers to a high standard because their ideas may have consequences. Good notions deserve to be identified and applauded. And bad ones should be ferreted out, exposed, and sent packing. Learning to discern one from the other takes practice—which is what rhetorical analyses provide.

Make strong claims about texts.   Of course, you cannot make claims about texts until you know them inside out. The need for close examination may seem self-evident, but we blow through most of what we read (and see) without much thought. Serious critical or rhetorical analysis does just the opposite: It makes texts move like bullets in the movie *The Matrix,* their trajectories slowed and every motion magnified for careful study. ⭘

Mine texts for evidence.   Not only should you read texts closely in preparing a rhetorical analysis: Use their words (and any other elements) as the evidence for your own claims. That's one of the goals of critical examinations of this sort: to find and cite what other readers of a text may have missed. Expect to use a lot of quotations in a rhetorical analysis. ⭘

understand argument
p. 68

read closely
p. 317

use quotations
p. 431

This polished and highly entertaining critical analysis is from the "Ad Report Card" series on Slate.com. Seth Stevenson goes after the famous Apple ad campaign comparing Macs and PCs, explaining how it misreads an important audience segment, and gets its facts wrong, too. Notice the personal point of view in this piece: Stevenson has no qualms about using his own experiences as grounds for dissing the ads. He explains exactly why.

Slate.com

Posted: Monday, June 19, 2006, at 6:29 A.M. E.T.
From: Seth Stevenson

Ad Report Card:
Mac Attack

Apple's mean-spirited new ad campaign

The Spot: *Two men stand side by side in front of a featureless, white background. "Hello, I'm a Mac," says the guy on the right (who is much younger and dressed in jeans). "And I'm a PC," says the guy on the left (who wears dorky glasses, ill-fitting khakis, and a jacket and tie). The two men discuss the many advantages of using a Mac and seem to agree that Macs are "better" than PCs.*

When I write about ads, I often face an obstacle: I'm not in the target demographic. Am I really in a position to judge whether, say, a Lexus ad is on the mark? The chances that I (driver of a 1996 Saturn with 105,000 miles on it) will buy a luxury sedan are essentially nil. Likewise, who am I to say if those adult-diaper spots are winning mindshare with senior citizens? Incontinence is a health issue that has (knock on wood) not yet hit my radar screen.

In the case of these Mac ads, however, I'm smack in the middle of the target demo. I'm a PC user, and I've often considered switching to an Apple. Thus, I feel equipped to say: These ads don't work on me. They are conceptually brilliant, beautifully

Articles in this series open by describing text to be analyzed.

Written in a middle style, colloquial and personal: *Who am I to say.*

Explains why he is qualified to assess Mac ads.

executed, and highly entertaining. But they don't make me want to buy a Mac.

Let's talk about the good news first. Directed by Phil Morrison (who also directed *Junebug*—my favorite film last year—and the recent VW ads featuring shocking car crashes), the campaign is a marvel of clarity and simplicity. No slogans. No video effects. No voice-overs. And lots of clean, white space. It's like a bath of cool mineral water when these ads come on after a string of garish, jam-packed spots for other products. (This bare-bones look is right in tune with Apple's consistently stripped-down marketing approach. To understand what makes Apple's aesthetic stand apart, check out this joke video—actually created by Microsoft employees—that envisions what might happen if Microsoft redesigned the iPod's packaging.)

My problem with these ads begins with the casting. As the Mac character, Justin Long (who was in the forgettable movie *Dodgeball* and the forgettabler TV show *Ed*) is just the sort of unshaven, hoodie-wearing, hands-in-pockets hipster we've always imagined when picturing a Mac enthusiast. He's perfect. *Too* perfect. It's like Apple is parodying its own image while also cementing it. If the idea was to reach out to new types of consumers (the kind who aren't already evangelizing for Macs), they ought to have used a different type of actor.

Meanwhile, the PC is played by John Hodgman—contributor to *The Daily Show* and *This American Life,* host of an amusing lecture series, and all-around dry-wit extraordinaire. Even as he plays the chump in these Apple spots, his humor and likability are evident. (Look at that hilariously perfect pratfall he pulls off in the spot titled "Viruses.") The ads pose a seemingly obvious question—Would you rather be the laid-back young dude or the portly old dweeb?—but I found myself consistently giving the "wrong" answer: I'd much sooner associate myself with Hodgman than with Long.

The writing may have something to do with this, too. Hodgman gets all the laugh lines! And Mr. Mac comes off as a smug little twit, who (in the spot titled "WSJ") just happens to carry around a newspaper that has a great review of himself inside. (Even Norman Mailer usually refrains from such crassness.)

The final straw, for me, is that the spots make unconvincing claims. The one titled "Network" has a funny bit where "that new digital camera from Japan" is represented by a Japanese woman in a minidress. While Hodgman has trouble talking with the woman, Long speaks Japanese and shares giggles with her because "everything just kind of works with a Mac." Now, I happen to have a digital camera from Japan, and it works just fine with my PC. It did from the moment I connected it. Similarly, the spot titled "Out of the Box" (again, a very funny visual metaphor, with Hodgman and Long crouching in cardboard boxes) suggests that new PCs require tons of attention and alteration when you first fire them up. But I bought a new ThinkPad notebook just a few months ago, and it ran on all cylinders pretty much straight out of the gate. Why insult my intelligence by telling me something that I know isn't true?

> **Earns credibility by qualifying his own argument.**

I suppose the answer is that some people don't know yet. I can see how these ads might be effective with inexperienced computer users. If you're a first-time buyer, the idea that a Mac will make your life immeasurably easier sure does sound appealing. But if you're a PC user, these ads are more likely to irritate you than convert you.

Grade: C+. As usual, Apple hopes to shift the debate away from a battle over specs and value and toward a battle we can all understand: cool kid versus nerd. But these days, aren't nerds like John Hodgman the new cool kids? And isn't smug superiority (no matter how affable and casually dressed) a bit off-putting as a brand strategy?

> **Most rhetorical analyses don't include grades, but conclusion is specific and biting.**

Exploring purpose and topic

Make a difference.   Done right, rhetorical analyses can be as important as the texts they examine. They may change readers' opinions or keep an important argument going. They may also uncover rhetorical strategies and techniques worth imitating or avoiding.

When you write an angry letter to the editor complaining about bias in the news coverage, you don't fret much about defining a purpose or topic—they are given. But when responding to a course assignment and particularly when you can choose a text to analyze rhetorically, you've got to establish the boundaries. Given a choice, select a text to analyze with the following characteristics.

▶ find a text

Choose a text you can work with.   Find a gutsy piece that makes a claim you or someone else might actually disagree with. It helps if you have a stake in the issue and already know something about it. The text should also be of a manageable length that you can explore coherently within the limits of the assignment.

Choose a text you can learn more about.   Some items won't make much sense out of context. So choose a text that you can research. ○ It will obviously help to know when it was written or published, by whom, and where it first appeared. This information is just as important for visual texts, such as posters and advertisements, as for traditional speeches or articles.

Need help deciding what to write about? See "How to Browse for Ideas" on pp. 312–13.

Choose a text with handles.   Investigate arguments that do interesting things. Maybe a speech uses lots of anecdotes or repetition to generate emotional appeals; perhaps a photoessay's commentary is more provocative than the images; or an ad arrests attention by its simplicity but is still full of cultural significance. You've got to write about the piece. Make sure it offers you interesting things to say.

Choose a text you know how to analyze.   Stick to printed texts if you aren't sure how to write about ads or films or even speeches. But don't sell yourself short. You don't need highly technical terms to describe poor logic, inept design, or offensive strategies, no matter where they appear. ○ And you can pick up the necessary vocabulary by reading models of rhetorical and critical analysis.

find a topic
p. 308

design your work
p. 517

Understanding your audience

Some published rhetorical analyses are written to ready-made audiences already inclined to agree with the authors. Riled up by an offensive editorial or a controversial ad campaign, people these days, especially on the Web, may even seek and enjoy mean-spirited, over-the-top criticism. But the rhetorical and critical analyses you write for class should be relatively restrained because you won't be able to predict how your readers might feel about the arguments you are examining. So assume that you are writing for a diverse and thoughtful audience, full of readers who prefer reflective analysis to clever put-downs. You don't have to be dull or passionless. Just avoid the easy slide into rudeness. ○

"got milk?" Advertisements in this famous series lend themselves to rhetorical analysis because they are so carefully designed for specific audiences, in this case fans of Masi Oka from the TV series *Heroes*. The character he plays on the show is able to manipulate time.

respect your readers
p. 374

Finding and developing materials

▶ ideas

Before you analyze a text of any kind, do some background research. ○ Discover what you can about its author, creator, publisher, sponsor, and so on. For example, it may be important to know that the TV commercial you want to understand better has aired only on sports networks or lifestyle programs on cable. Become familiar, too, with the contexts in which an argument occurs. If you reply to a *Wall Street Journal* editorial, know what news or events sparked that item and investigate the paper's editorial slant.

Read the piece carefully just for information first, highlighting names or allusions you don't recognize. Then look them up: There's very little you can't uncover quickly these days via a Web search. When you think you understand the basics, you are prepared to approach the text rhetorically. Pay attention to any standout aspects of the text you're analyzing—perhaps how it wins over wary readers through conciliatory language or draws on the life experiences of its author to frame its subject. ○ You might look at any of the following elements.

Consider the topic or subject matter of the text.   What is novel or striking about the topic? How well-defined is it? Could it be clearer? Is it important? Relevant? Controversial? Is the subject covered comprehensively or selectively? What is the level of detail? Does the piece make a point?

Consider the audiences of the text.   To whom is the piece addressed? How is the text adapted to its audience? Who is excluded from the audience and how can you tell? What does the text offer its audience: information, controversy, entertainment? What does it expect from its audience?

Consider its author.   What is the author's relationship to the material? Is the writer or creator personally invested or distant? Is the author an expert, a knowledgeable amateur, or something else? What does the author hope to accomplish?

Consider its medium or language.   What is the medium or genre of the text: essay, article, editorial, advertisement, book excerpt, poster, video, podcast, and so on? How well does the medium suit the subject? How might

appraise your
resources p. 415

read critically
p. 317

the material look different in another medium? What is the level of the language: formal, informal, colloquial? ○ What is the tone of the text— logical, sarcastic, humorous, angry, condescending? How do the various elements of design—such as arrangement, color, fonts, images, white space, audio, video, and so on—work in the text?

Consider its occasion.   Why was the text created? To what circumstances or situations does it respond, and what might the reactions to it be? What problems does it solve or create? What pleasure might it give? Who benefits from the text?

Consider its contexts.   What purposes do texts of this type serve? Do texts of this sort have a history? Do they serve the interests of specific groups or classes? Have they evolved over time? Does the text represent a new genre?

Consider its use of rhetorical appeals.   Persuasive texts are often ana- lyzed according to how they use three types of rhetorical appeal. Typically, a text may establish the character and credibility of its author (*ethos*); generate emotions in order to move audiences (*pathos*); and use evidence and logic to make its case (*logos*).

Ethos—the appeal to character—may be the toughest argumentative strategy to understand. Every text and argument is presented by someone or something, whether an individual, a group, or an institution. Audiences are usually influenced and swayed by writers or speakers who present themselves as knowledgeable, honest, fair-minded, and even likable. Here, for example, Susan Estrich injects herself into a column she wrote about the governor of California to reinforce her own appealing sense of fair play.

> What Schwarzenegger has accomplished in the past eight months, substantively, is remarkable. I'm a lifelong Democrat who was asked to serve on the Schwarzenegger transition team. I did. He also put together a coalition of Democrats and Republicans.
>
> –"Schwarzenegger's California Formula: Bipartisanship + Civility = Progress," *USA Today*, May 27, 2004

define your style
p. 366

Pathos—the emotional appeal—is usually easy to detect. Look for ways that a text generates strong feelings to support its points or win over readers. The strategy is legitimate so long as an emotion fits the situation and doesn't manipulate audiences. For example, columnist Peggy Noonan routinely uses emotions to make her political points.

> We fought a war to free slaves. We sent millions of white men to battle and destroyed a portion of our nation to free millions of black men. What kind of nation does this? We went to Europe, fought, died, and won, and then taxed ourselves to save our enemies with the Marshall Plan. What kind of nation does this? Soviet communism stalked the world and we were the ones who steeled ourselves and taxed ourselves to stop it. Again: What kind of nation does this?
>   Only a very great one.
>
> —"Patriots, Then and Now," *Wall Street Journal,* March 30, 2006

Logos—the appeal to reason and evidence—is most favored in academic texts. Look carefully at the claims a text offers and whether they are supported by facts, data, testimony, and good reasons. What assumptions lie beneath the argument? Ask questions about evidence too. Does it come from reliable sources or valid research? Is it up-to-date? Has it been reported accurately and fully? Has due attention been given to alternative points of view and explanations? Has enough evidence been offered to make a valid point?

Creating a structure

In a rhetorical analysis, you'll make a statement about how well the argumentative strategy of a piece works. Don't expect to come up with a thesis immediately or easily: You need to study a speech, editorial, or advertisement closely to figure out how it works and then think about its strengths and weaknesses. Draft a tentative thesis (or hypothesis) and then refine your words throughout the process of writing until they assert a claim you can prove. O

Look for a complex and interesting thesis; don't just list some rhetorical features: *This ad has some good logical arguments and uses emotions and rhetorical questions.* Why would someone want to read (or write) a paper with such an empty claim? The following yields a far more interesting rhetorical analysis:

organize ◀
ideas

> The latest government antidrug posters offer good reasons for avoiding steroids but do it in a visual style so closely resembling typical health posters that most students will just ignore them.

Develop a structure. Once you have a thesis or hypothesis, try sketching a design based on a thesis / supporting reason / evidence plan. Focus on those features of the text that illustrate the points you wish to make. You don't have to discuss every facet of the text.

Introduction leading to a **claim**

> **First supporting reason** + textual **evidence**
>
> **Second supporting reason** + textual **evidence**
>
> **Additional supporting reasons** + textual **evidence**

Conclusion

Under some circumstances, you might perform what amounts to a line-by-line or paragraph-by-paragraph deconstruction of a text. This structure—though not yet common in classrooms—shows up frequently online. Such analyses practically organize themselves, but your commentary must be smart, factually accurate, and stylish to keep readers on board.

develop a thesis
p. 336

Introduction leading to a **claim**

> **First section/paragraph** + detailed **analysis**

> **Next section/paragraph** + detailed **analysis**

> **Additional section/paragraph** + detailed **analysis**

Conclusion

In this example, political blogger Hugh Hewitt responds paragraph-by-paragraph to a letter from *New York Times* executive editor Bill Keller (June 25, 2006) justifying his newspaper's decision to reveal a top-secret antiterrorist spy program. Keller's remarks are below, followed immediately by Hewitt's critical analysis in italics.

> Most Americans seem to support extraordinary measures in defense against this extraordinary threat, but some officials who have been involved in these programs have spoken to the *Times* about their discomfort over the legality of the government's actions and over the adequacy of oversight. We believe the *Times* and others in the press have served the public interest by accurately reporting on these programs so that the public can have an informed view of them.

> *Without disclosing the officials, we cannot be certain of their rank, their rancor, and their other agendas. We only know they are willing to break the law and their oaths. Mr. Keller's refusal to acknowledge this basic problem is more evidence of the deep dishonesty of his letter. He again asserts a "public interest" that is not his to judge as against the laws passed by Congress, signed by presidents and interpreted by courts. But he doesn't argue why his judgment in this matter trumps that of the government and the people's elected representatives.*

Choosing a style and design

The style of your textual analyses will vary depending on audience, but you always face one problem that can sometimes be helped by design: making the text you are analyzing more accessible to readers.

Consider a high style.   Rhetorical and critical analyses you write in school will usually be formal and use a "high" style. ○ Your tone should be respectful, your vocabulary as technical as the material requires, and your perspective impersonal—avoiding *I* and *you.* Such a style gives the impression of objectivity and seriousness. Unless an instructor gives you more leeway, use a formal style for critical analyses.

Consider a middle style.   Oddly, rhetorical and critical analyses appearing in the public arena—rather than in the classroom—will usually be less formal and exploit the connection with readers that a middle style encourages. While still serious, such a style gives writers more options for expressing strong opinions and feelings (sometimes including anger, outrage, and contempt). In much public writing, you can detect a personal voice offering an opinion or advancing an agenda.

Make the text accessible to readers.   A special challenge in any rhetorical analysis is to help readers understand the text you are scrutinizing. At a minimum, furnish basic information about the author, title, place of publication, and date, and briefly explain the context of the work.

When possible, also attach a photocopy of the article directly to your analysis or include a link to it if you are working online. But your analysis should still be written *as if readers do not have that text in hand.* One way to achieve that clarity is to summarize and quote selectively from the text as you examine it. You can see examples of this technique in Matthew James Nance's essay on pages 236–40.

Annotate the text.   When analyzing an image or a text available in digital form, consider attaching your comments directly to the item. Do this by simply inserting a copy of the image or article directly into your project and then using the design tools of your word processor to create annotations.

This poster appears on the Web site of the Navy Environmental Health Center. Does that fact about its context change its message in any way?

define your style
p. 366

Examining models

For a class assignment on rhetorical analysis, Matthew James Nance chose as his subject the award-winning feature article "Can't Die for Trying" by journalist Laura Miller — who later would serve as mayor of Dallas. In the essay, Nance explains in detail how Miller manages to present the story of a convicted killer who wants to be executed to readers who might have contrary views about capital punishment. Nance's analysis is both technical and objective. He does an especially good job helping readers follow the argument of "Can't Die for Trying," a fairly long and complicated article.

Nance 1

Matthew James Nance

Professor Norcia

English 201

June 14 20--

A Mockery of Justice

In 1987, David Martin Long was convicted of double homicide and sentenced to death. He made no attempt to appeal this sentence, and surprisingly, did everything he could to expedite his execution. Nonetheless, due to an automatic appeals process, Long remained on Texas's Death Row for twelve years before he was finally executed. For various reasons, including investigations into whether he was mentally ill, the state of Texas had continued to postpone his execution date. In 1994, when David Long was still in the middle of his appeals process, *Dallas Observer* columnist Laura Miller took up his case in the award-winning article "Can't Die for Trying." In this article, Miller explores the enigma of a legal system in which a sociopath willing to die continues to be mired in the legal process. The article is no typical plea on behalf of a death-row inmate, and Miller manages to avoid a facile political stance on capital punishment. Instead, Miller uses an effective combination

> Sets scene carefully and provides necessary background information.

> Miller defies expectations and Nance explains why in his thesis.

236

Nance 2

of logical reasoning and emotional appeal to evoke from readers a sense of frustration at the system's absurdity.

    To show that David Martin Long's execution should be carried out as soon as possible, Miller offers a reasoned argument based on two premises: that he wants death and that he deserves it. Miller cites Long's statement from the day he was arrested: "I realize what I did was wrong. I don't belong in this society. I never have. . . . I'd wish they'd hurry up and get this over with" (5). She emphasizes that this desire has not changed, by quoting Long's correspondence from 1988, 1991, and 1992. In this way, Miller makes Long's argument seem reasoned and well thought out, not simply a temporary gesture of desperation. "Yes, there are innocent men here, retarded men, insane men, and men who just plain deserve another chance," Long wrote [State District Judge Larry] Baraka in April 1992, "But I am none of these!" (5). Miller also points out his guilty plea, and the jury's remarkably short deliberation: "The jury took only an hour to find Long guilty of capital murder — and 45 minutes to give him the death penalty" (5). Miller does not stop there, however. She gives a grisly description of the murders themselves, followed by Long's calculated behavior in the aftermath:

> He hacked away at Laura twenty-one times before going back inside where he gave Donna fourteen chops. The blind woman, who lay in bed screaming while he savaged Donna, got five chops. Long washed the hatchet, stuck it in the kitchen sink, and headed out of town in Donna's brown station wagon. (5)

Long paragraph furnishes detailed evidence for Miller's two premises.

Provides both summaries and quotations from article so that readers can follow Miller's argument.

Nance 3

Miller's juxtaposition of reasoned deliberation with the bloody narrative of the murders allows her to show that Long, in refusing to appeal, is reacting justly to his own sociopathy. Not only is it right that he die; it is also right that he does not object to his death.

In the midst of this reasoned argument, Miller expresses frustration at the bureaucratic inefficiency that is at odds with her logic. She offers a pragmatic, resource-based view of the situation:

> Of course, in the handful of instances where a person is wrongly accused . . . this [death-penalty activism] is noble, important work. But I would argue that in others — David Martin Long in particular — it is a sheer waste of taxpayer dollars. And a mockery of justice. (6)

Miller portrays the system as being practically incompatible with her brand of pragmatism. The figures involved in Long's case are painted as invisible, equivocal, or both. For instance, in spite of Long's plea, Judge Baraka was forced to appoint one of Long's attorneys to start the appeals process. "The judge didn't have a choice. Texas law requires that a death-penalty verdict be automatically appealed. . . . [This] is supposed to expedite the process. But the court sat on Long's case for four long years" (5). Miller also mentions Danny Burn, a Fort Worth lawyer in association with the Texas Resource Center, one of the "do-good . . . organizations whose sole feverish purpose is to get people off Death Row. . . . No matter how airtight the cases" (6). Burn filed on Long's behalf, though he never met Long in person. This fact underscores Miller's notion of the death-row bureaucracy as being inaccessible, and by extension, incomprehensible.

This parade of equivocal incompetence culminates in Miller's

Notice how smoothly quotations merge into Nance's sentences.

To clarify Miller's point, Nance adds phrase in brackets to quotation.

Nance 4

interview with John Blume, another activist who argued on Long's behalf. Miller paints Blume as so equivocal that he comes across as a straw man. "As a general rule," says Blume, "I tend to think most people who are telling you that are telling you something else, and that's their way of expressing it. There's something else they're depressed or upset about" (6). The article ends with Miller's rejoinder: "Well, I'd wager, Mr. Blume, that something is a lawyer like you" (6). Whereas the article up to this point has maintained a balance between reason and frustration, here, Miller seems to let gradually building frustration get the best of her. She does not adequately address whether Blume might be correct in implying that Long is insane, mentally ill, or otherwise misguided. She attempts to dismiss this idea by repeatedly pointing out Long's consistency in his stance and his own statements that he is not retarded, but her fallacy is obvious: Consistency does not imply sanity. Clearly, Miller would have benefited from citing Long's medical history and comparing his case with those of other death-row inmates, both mentally ill and well. Then her frustrated attack on Blume would seem more justified.

Miller also evokes frustration through her empathetic portrayal of Long. Although the article is essentially a plea for Long to get what he wants, this same fact prevents Miller from portraying Long sympathetically. Miller is stuck in a rhetorical bind; if her readers become sympathetic toward Long, they won't want him to die. However, the audience needs an emotional connection with Long to accept the argument on his behalf. Miller gets around this problem by abandoning sympathy altogether, portraying Long as a cold-blooded killer. The quotation "I've never seen a more cold-blooded, steel-eyed sociopath ever" (5) is set apart from

Nance makes a clear judgment about Miller's objectivity—then offers evidence for his claim.

Nance examines the way Miller deals with the problem she has portraying a cold-blooded killer to readers.

Nance 5

the text in a large font, and Miller notes that "This is a case of a really bad dude, plain and simple. . . . Use any cliché you want. It fits"(5). Miller here opts for a weak appeal; evoking from the audience the same negative emotion that Long feels. She gives voice to Long's frustration over his interminable appeals: "Long stewed. . . . Long steamed. . . . Long fumes. . . ." (6). She also points out Long's fear of himself: "I fear I'll kill again" (6). Clearly, the audience is meant to echo these feelings of frustration and fear. This may seem like a weak emotional connection with Long, but perhaps it is the best Miller could do, given that a primary goal of hers was to show that Long deserves death.

Laura Miller won the H. L. Mencken Award for this article, which raises important questions about the legal process. Part of its appeal is that it approaches capital punishment without taking a simplistic position. It can appeal to people on both sides of the capital punishment debate. The argument is logically valid, and for the most part, the emotional appeal is effective. Its deficiencies, including the weak emotional appeal for Long, are ultimately outweighed by Miller's overarching rationale, which calls for pragmatism in the face of absurdity.

Nance 6

Work Cited

Miller, Laura. "Can't Die for Trying." *Dallas Observer* 12 Jan. 1994: 5-6. Print.

ANALYSIS OF TWO FILM TRAILERS   Ryan Hailey examines the way a movie studio has adjusted a trailer for a blockbuster film to appeal to two different and equally important markets. Those markets, of course, represent the rhetorical concept of "audience."

Hailey 1

Ryan Hailey

Dr. Kinder

Writing 127

February 22, 20--

The *Die Hard* Trailer:

American Version vs. International Version

An unspoken and intangible contract between movie audiences and movie studios is made when viewers watch previews of coming attractions. Audiences know the movie studios have tailored and often manipulated the preview to appeal to the broadest possible demographic, yet the audience still uses the strength of the trailer to decide whether to see the movie. However, most people don't realize how tailored these previews are until they examine the way studios try to persuade different cultures to see the same movie. This summer, 20th Century Fox will release *Live Free or Die Hard,* or, as it is called in the rest of the world, *Die Hard 4.0.* Although both the American and international versions of the fourth trailer highlight the film's action, the two trailers are otherwise vastly different. Specifically, the American trailer is characterized by blatant American patriotic themes while the international version makes the film out to be a standard, over-the-top action movie.

"I'm doing America a favor," says a character at the start of the American trailer, presumably a villain. The screen cuts to a shot of the front lawn of the U.S. Capitol in Washington with the

> Hailey offers thesis for analysis of movie trailers.

> Hailey contrasts the way American and international trailers open.

Hailey 2

American flag waving gracefully in front. While quick shots of various characters loading weapons flash on screen, the bad guy finishes his sentence. "Is the country ready to pay for it?" So in the first twenty seconds of the American trailer, the audience knows the film takes place in the United States. American audiences are immediately given a theme they can relate to and thus are enticed to learn more about the film.

The international trailer for the fourth *Die Hard* begins with flashy graphics, reminiscent of random surveillance cameras, and this tag superimposed on top of it: "The entire world relies on technology . . . But even technology . . . can be taken hostage." The screen then flashes to a police car flying off a ramp and into a helicopter, spawning a massive and fiery explosion. This collision sets the tone for the rest of the two-minute-and-three-second trailer that's filled with no less than six explosions, seven shoot-outs, four car chases, and two fistfights. The stark contrast between these two beginnings is obvious. The American version sets the trailer up with an ambiguous question about America while the international version opens with a vague scenario that the entire international community can relate to. Hollywood movie studios usually make only a domestic (U.S.) trailer and one trailer to serve the rest of the world. This is why the international trailer has to be so broad in scope that any country could connect with its meaning, and hence the "The entire world relies on technology . . . " tagline. It's useful to note that the theme of terrorism is prevalent in both trailers since, today, everyone in the world can relate to it.

How Bruce Willis and his character John McClane are used in each trailer similarly demonstrates how the studio was trying to persuade American and international audiences differently to see

> Using middle style enables Hailey to shift between lighter details and more serious points.

> Examines second difference between trailers, focusing on the name *John McClane*.

Hailey 3

the movie. With the premiere of the original *Die Hard* in 1988, Bruce Willis was catapulted to both domestic and international stardom, becoming one of the most profitable film actors alive today. Both trailers build anticipation about who is going to be the hero in the film — and the payoff is a close-up of Bruce Willis. Since Willis is popular around the world, 20th Century Fox no doubt believes that his image will excite any moviegoer. However, the name of Bruce Willis's famous character in the *Die Hard* franchise, John McClane, is not mentioned in the international trailer, yet it *is* used in the American clip. In the international community the presence of Bruce Willis in the movie probably overshadows the fact that he's in a *Die Hard* film. But in America, John McClane has earned a special place in its pop culture as one of the greatest action characters of all time in one of the greatest action movies of all time. While *Die Hard* was a megahit worldwide, one could argue that it started a revolution in America and virtually redefined the American action movie. Americans see Bruce Willis in multiple movies every year, but it's not every day that they get to see Bruce Willis don the John McClane character. Although international audiences may see Bruce Willis as "that guy in cool action movies," the name *John McClane* doesn't immediately pull a delightful trigger in the minds of international audiences as it does for American audiences.

The most interesting distinction between the American and international trailers for the new *Die Hard* movie is the different names the film is given. In America the film will be called *Live Free or Die Hard*. Internationally, it will be called *Die Hard 4.0*. The American title is a play on "Live Free or Die," the state motto of New Hampshire. It is a slogan unique to America and, perhaps, the

Hailey examines why film has two titles.

Hailey 4

Western world. Imagine how foreign the concept of "live free or die" might be to a moviegoer in China or North Korea. While democracy may be spreading throughout the world, it is not widely accepted enough for 20th Century Fox to risk confusing potential ticket purchasers. That may be the reason for the title being changed internationally to *Die Hard 4.0,* a phrase that also reflects its technology-based plot. In contrast, the title *Live Free or Die Hard* is uncompromisingly American, aggressively asserting the American dream. It is a title that will surely appeal to many Americans. Taking advantage of the contemporary political climate, the studio is banking on the idea that Americans will come out in droves to watch John McClane kick the butts of terrorists threatening our American way of life of living free.

Since the American and international trailers for movies are shown only in their respective regions, most moviegoers never know that they are being specifically targeted and influenced into buying a ticket for the movies they see. While the movies might be exactly the same domestically as they are globally, the contents emphasized (or omitted) in promotional campaigns often have an extremely specific purpose and reflect how studios view the tastes of particular audiences. The people at 20th Century Fox clearly believe that American audiences are ready for John McClane to be their public defender against global terrorism in the movies this summer. But with the reputation of America dwindling in the international community, Fox doesn't think some moviegoers around the globe will particularly care to pay to see the United States of America be defended from terrorists. That's why the movie looks like just another action-packed, shoot-'em-up, Bruce Willis flick in the trailer that's shown everywhere but America.

ANALYSIS OF A CULTURAL TREND   Andy Newman makes an odd visual phenomenon the subject of an essay that appeared in the *New York Times*. Like many rhetorical analyses, he begins with the question *Why?*

They're Soft and Cuddly, So Why Lash Them to the Front of a Truck?

Andy Newman

November 13, 2005

A bear with a prominent grease spot on his little beige nose spends his days wedged behind the bumper guard of an ironworker's pickup in the Gowanus section of Brooklyn. A fuzzy rabbit and a clown, garroted by a bungee cord, slump from the front of a Dodge van in Park Slope. Stewie, the evil baby from *Family Guy,* scowls from the grille of a Pepperidge Farm delivery truck in Brooklyn Heights, mold occasionally sprouting from his forehead.

All are soldiers in the tattered, scattered army of the stuffed: mostly discarded toys plucked from the trash and given new if punishing lives on the prows of large motor vehicles, their fluffy white guts flapping from burst seams and going gray in the soot-stream of a thousand exhaust pipes.

Grille-mounted stuffed animals form a compelling yet little-studied aspect of the urban streetscape, a traveling gallery of baldly transgressive public art. The time has come not just to praise them but to ask the big question. Why?

That is, why do a small percentage of trucks and vans have filthy plush toys lashed to their fronts, like prisoners at the mast? Are they someone's idea of a joke? Parking aids? Talismans against summonses?

Don't expect an easy answer.

Interviews with half a dozen truckers as well as folklorists, art historians, and anthropologists revealed the grille-mounted plush toy to be a

Photo: James Estrin/© The New York Times/Redux.

product of a tangle of physical circumstance, proximate and indirect influence, ethnic tradition, occupational mindset, and Jungian[1] archetype.

Like all adornments, of course, the grille pet advertises something about its owner. The very act of decorating a truck indicates an openness on the driver's part, according to Dan DiVittorio, owner of D & N Services, a carting company in Queens, and of a garbage truck with a squishy red skull on the front.

"It has to do something with their character," said Mr. DiVittorio, twenty-seven. "I don't see anybody that wouldn't be a halfway decent person putting something on their truck."

But a truck can be aesthetically modified in a million ways: *Mom* in spiffy gold letters across the hood; mudflaps depicting top-heavy women; flames painted along the sides. Why use beat-up stuffed animals?

One prevalent theory among truckers is that chicks dig them.

Robert Marbury, an artist who photographed dozens of Manhattan bumper fauna for a project in 2000 (see urbanbeast.com/faq/strapped.html), said he had once asked a trash hauler why he had a family of three mismatched bears strapped to his rig.

"He said: 'Yo, man, I drive a garbage truck. How am I going to get the ladies to look at me?'" Mr. Marbury recalled.

---

1. Jungian: Psychiatrist Carl Jung (1875–1961) theorized that human beings' lives were lived according to innate forms, or archetypes.

Photo: Robert Stolarik/© The New York Times/Redux.

Mr. Marbury, who holds a degree in anthropology, added that the battered bear and his brethren had at least one foot in the vernacular cultures of Latin America, where the festive and the ghoulish enjoy a symbiotic relationship. Most of the drivers whose trucks he photographed were Hispanic, he said.

Monroe Denton, a lecturer in art history at the School of Visual Arts, traced the phenomenon's roots back to the figureheads that have animated bows of ships since the time of the pharaohs.

"There was some sort of heraldic device to deny the fact of this gigantic machine," he said. "You would have these humanizing forms, anthropomorphic forms—a device that both proclaims the identity of the machine and conceals it."

Whatever its origins, the grille-mounted cuddle object is found across the country. It has been spotted in Baltimore, Miami, Chicago, and other cities.

Mierle Laderman Ukeles, the artist in residence at New York City's Department of Sanitation, said that when she noticed the animals on garbagemen's trucks in the late 1970s, she "felt they were like these spirit creatures that were accompanying them on this endless journey in flux."

There are differences, though, between the dragon crowning a Viking ship—or, for that matter, the chrome bulldog guarding the hood of a Mack truck—and the scuzzy bunny bound to the bumper with rubber hose. The main one is that the grille-mounted stuffed animal is almost

Photo: David F. Gallagher/© The New York Times/Redux

always a found object—*mongo* in garbageman's parlance. And in that respect it functions as a sort of trophy.

"I always felt," Ms. Ukeles said, "with these creatures that they withdrew from the garbage and refused to let go of, that there was an act of rescue involved."

That is certainly true for Julio Hernandez, a laborer for Aspen Tree Specialists in Brooklyn.

The GMC chipper truck he rides in is graced with eleven figurines, each defective in one way or another—Hulk Hogan with both hands missing, a Frankenstein monster with a hole in his head, a nearly disintegrated black rubber rat. "People throw them out because they're broken," Mr. Hernandez, thirty-eight, said in Spanish. "They catch my attention."

A few months ago, Roberto Argueto spotted a floppy doll in the gutter near the headquarters of Sasco Construction in Brooklyn. The doll had brown pigtails, a white bonnet, and the bluest eyes. He hung her from the front wall of the flatbed of his truck with a coat hanger, and he named her Margaret.

"I like the doll," said Mr. Argueto, thirty-nine. "She's pretty."

The flatbed carries some unforgiving payloads—scaffolding, bricks, sandbags—but Mr. Argueto protects Margaret.

"When I put something back there, I try to cover her," he said.

For all the reclaimed toys that are fussed over, though, there seem to be at least as many that are mistreated: tied to grilles in positions that recall the rack and exposed to the maximum amount of road salt and mud spray.

Why do this? Whence the urge to debase an icon of innocence?

This is the true mystery of the grille-mounted stuffed animal, and it is here that the terrain gets heavily psychological and a bit murky.

Ms. Ukeles, who claims to understand sanitation workers fairly well, having shaken hands with 8,500 of them during a three-year performance project, said they identified on some level with their mascots.

"There's a transference in this," she said. "There's this soft, flesh-and-bone sanitation worker, who knows very well they could be crushed against this truck. The creature could be the sanitation worker in a very dangerous position, so the animal could be a stand-in."

(Stuffed animals, sadly, are verboten on city garbage trucks and nearly impossible to find these days; they were against department regulations even in the 1970s, but perhaps sanitation men are not the free spirits now that they were back then.)

At the same time, Ms. Ukeles said, the trucker, perhaps uncomfortable with his soft side, may feel compelled to punish it.

"Binding a soft thing to a very powerful truck—there's a kind of macho thing about that," she said.

That double identification with both victim and agent of violence may reflect the driver's frustrating position in society. Stuffed animals are found mostly on the trucks of men who perform hard, messy labor, which, despite the strength and bravery it demands, places them on the lower rungs of the ladder of occupational prestige.

The motley animal, then, can function as a badge of outsider status, a thumbed nose to the squares and suits. In that case, the cuter the mascot, the more meaningful its disintegration.

Thus, while Mr. DiVittorio, of the Queens carting company, is quite fond of the red plastic skull that adorns his garbage truck, he will never forget its predecessor, a three-foot-high stuffed Scooby-Doo.

"Scooby was great," he recalled. "He covered the whole radiator and down to the bumper. You can't even imagine how many people took pictures of him."

Life on the road took its toll. "He got junked out riding in the front of the truck," Mr. DiVittorio said. "One of his arms was starting to fall off."

Mr. DiVittorio blamed the rivet-studded wire ties that held the dog fast. "You know how," he said, "if you have cuffs on your wrists, they dig into you?"

Eventually, Mr. DiVittorio said, Scooby's time came: "He went from the front of the truck to the back. We had to throw him away."

Scooby's story lends credence to the theory of Mr. Denton, the art historian, that the grille-mounted stuffed animal draws from the same well as the "abject art" movement that flourished in the 1990s and trafficked heavily in images of filth and of distressed bodies.

"That is part of the abject," he said, "this toy that is loved to death quite literally."

The externalization of an indoor object is another abject trope, Mr. Denton said. "An important aspect of the abject is the *informe,* the lack of boundaries," he said, using the French critical theory term, "the insides oozing out."

Charlie Maixner, a steamfitter for Deacon Corporation in Jericho on Long Island, has taken the *informe* to its logical extreme.

On the dashboard of his Econoline van is an adorable and pristine white bear, a gift from his five-year-old daughter. But the bear is not for the outside world. On the grille is Mr. Hankey, salvaged from a chef's office during a kitchen renovation job.

Mr. Hankey, to the pop-culturally illiterate, appears to be a brown worm in a Santa hat. He is not. He is the carol-crooning excrement from *South Park,* where he is formally known as Mr. Hankey the Christmas Poo.

"The bear on the dashboard, that's 'I love you, Daddy,' " Mr. Maixner said. "The other one is 'Daddy, what's that?' "

For that question, Mr. Maixner has a ready answer:

"I just tell her it's Mr. Hankey."

1. **Analysis of a Text:** Browse recent news or popular-interest magazines (such as *Time, Newsweek, GQ, The New Yorker,* etc.) to locate a serious article you find especially well argued and persuasive. Like Matthew James Nance in "A Mockery of Justice" (p. 236), study the piece carefully enough to understand the techniques it uses to influence readers. Then write a rhetorical analysis in which you make and support a specific claim about the rhetorical strategies of the piece.

2. **Genre Analysis:** Using Seth Stevenson's "Ad Report Card: Mac Attack" on p. 225 as a model, write your own critical analysis of a single ad or full ad campaign you find worthy of attention. Choose a fresh campaign, one that hasn't yet received much commentary.

3. **Audience Analysis:** Find an example of a cultural text — it can be a political poster, an ad, a CD cover, a video game — that comes in different versions, depending on the audience. Then do what Ryan Hailey does in "The *Die Hard* Trailer: American Version vs. International Version" (p. 241): Write a rhetorical analysis to account for the differences.

4. **Visual Analysis:** Analyze a visual text that you find in a public space — a massive poster, a billboard along the interstate, a political mural in a train station or library. Be sure to take its physical location into account: who it reaches, who it might offend. Look to Andy Newman's "They're Soft and Cuddly, So Why Lash Them to the Front of a Truck?" (p. 245) for inspiration.

5. **Rhetorical Analysis:** Try a paragraph-by-paragraph refutation of an argument you find poorly reasoned, inadequately supported, or defective in some other way. If you are examining a visual text you can reproduce electronically, experiment with using callouts to annotate the problems as you find them.

Special
Assignments

2

Need a form you don't see here? Try "Genres," on page 2.

How to start ● **Got a test tomorrow?**
Read exam questions carefully. See page 255.

9

Essay Examination

**requires
answers
written
within a
time limit**

Essay examinations test not only your knowledge of a subject but also your ability to write about it coherently and professionally.

● For a class in nursing, you must write a short essay about the role health-care providers play in dealing with patients who have been victims of domestic abuse.

● For an examination in a literature class, you must offer a close reading of a sonnet, explicating its argument and poetic images line by line.

● For a standardized test, you must read a passage by a critic of globalization and respond to the case made and evidence presented.

● For a psychology exam, you must explore the ethical issues raised by two research articles on brain research and the nature of consciousness.

UNDERSTANDING ESSAY EXAMS.   You've probably taken enough essay exams to know that there are no magic bullets to slay this dragon, and that the best approach is to know your material well enough to make several credible points in an hour or so. You must also write—*under pressure*—coherent sentences and paragraphs. Here are some specific strategies to increase your odds of doing well.

Anticipate the types of questions you might be asked.   What happens in class—the concepts presented, the issues raised, the assignments given—is like a coming-attractions trailer for an exam. If you attend class and do the required readings, you'll figure out at least some of an instructor's habitual moves and learn something to boot. Review any sample essay exams too—they may even be available on a course Web site.

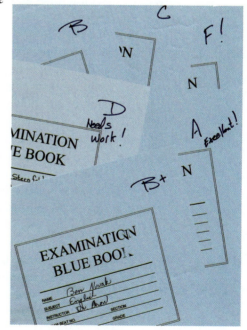

got a test
tomorrow?

Read exam questions carefully.   Underscore key words such as *divide*, *classify*, *evaluate*, *compare*, *compare and contrast*, and *analyze* and then respect the differences between these strategies. Exam questions may be short essays themselves, setting out background information or offering a passage to read before the actual query appears. Respond to that specific question and not to your own take on the preliminary materials.

Sketch out a plan for your essay(s).   The first part of the plan should deal with *time*. Read all the exam questions carefully and then estimate how many minutes to spend on each—understanding that some will take more effort than others. (Pay attention to point totals too: Focus on essay questions that count more, but don't ignore any. Five points is five points.) Allow time for planning and editing each answer. Sketch outlines and come up with a thesis for each question. ○ Then stick to your time limits.

Organize your answer strategically.   If any form of writing benefits from a pattern of development worn like an exoskeleton, it's a response to an essay question. In your first paragraph, state your main point and preview the structure of the whole essay. That way, even if you cannot finish, a reader will know where you were heading and possibly give you partial credit for incomplete work.

Offer strong evidence for your claims.   The overall structure of the essay should convey your grasp of concepts—your ability to see the big picture. Within that structure, arrange details and evidence to show your command of the subject. Use memorable examples culled from class reading to make your points: Cite important names, concepts, and dates; mention critical issues and terms; rattle off the titles of books and articles.

Come to a conclusion.   Even if you run short on time, find a moment to write a paragraph that brings your ideas together. Don't just repeat the topic sentences of your paragraphs. A reader will already have those ideas firmly in mind as he or she assesses your work. So add something new—an implication or extrapolation—to chew on.

Keep the tone serious.   Write essay examinations in a high or middle style. Avoid a personal point of view unless the question invites you to enter your opinion on a controversy. Given the press of time, you can probably get away with contractions and some standard abbreviations. But make sure the essay reads like prose, not a text message.

Don't panic.   Keep your eye on the clock, but *don't panic*. Everyone else is working under the same constraints and will be able to produce only so much prose in an hour or two. If you've prepared for the exam and start with a plan, you may find first-rate ideas materializing in the process of writing. Even if they don't, keep writing. You'll get no credit for blank pages.

develop a thesis
p. 336

Wade Lamb offered the following response to this essay question on a mid-term essay examination in a course entitled Classical to Modern Rhetoric:

> The structure of Plato's *Phaedrus* is dominated by three speeches about the lover and non-lover—one by Lysias (as read by Phaedrus) and two by Socrates. How do these speeches differ in their themes and strategies, and what point do they make about rhetoric and truth?

Lamb 1

Wade Lamb

Professor Karishky

Writing 101

September 19, 20--

　　Plato's *Phaedrus* is unique among Platonic dialogues because it takes place in a rural setting between only two characters—Socrates and the youth Phaedrus. It is, however, like Plato's *Gorgias* in that it is "based on a distinction between knowledge and belief" and focuses on some of the ways we can use rhetoric to seek the truth.

　　The first speech presented in *Phaedrus,* written by Lysias and read aloud by Phaedrus, is the simplest of the three. Composed by Lysias to demonstrate the power of rhetoric to persuade an audience, it claims perversely that it is better to have a relationship with a non-lover than with a lover.

　　Socrates responds with a speech of his own making the same point, which he composes on the spot and which he describes as "a greater lie than Lysias's." Unlike Lysias, however, Socrates begins by carefully defining his terms and organizes his speech more effectively. He does so to teach Phaedrus that in order to persuade an audience, an orator must first understand the subject and divide

Opening focuses directly on issues posed in question.

Short quotation functions as piece of evidence.

Sensibly organized around three speeches to be examined: one paragraph per speech.

Lamb 2

it into its appropriate parts. However, Socrates delivers this speech with a veil over his head because he knows that what he and Lysias have claimed about love is false.

Most important speech gets lengthiest and most detailed treatment.

The third speech—again made by Socrates—is the most important. In it, Socrates demonstrates that persuasion that leads merely to belief (not truth) damages both the orator and the audience. He likens rhetoric such as that used by Lysias to the unconcerned and harmful lust of a non-lover. Good rhetoric, on the other hand—which Socrates says is persuasion that leads to knowledge—is like the true lover who seeks to lead his beloved to transcendent truth. Socrates shows that he believes good rhetoric should ultimately be concerned with finding and teaching truth, not just with making a clever argument someone might believe, as Lysias's speech does.

Conclusion states Lamb's thesis, describing the point he believes Plato wished to make about rhetoric in *Phaedrus*.

By comparing the three speeches in the *Phaedrus,* Plato shows that he gives some value to rhetoric, but not in the form practiced by orators such as Lysias. Plato emphasizes the importance of the distinction between belief and knowledge and argues for a rhetoric that searches for and propagates the truth.

Getting the details right

Allow a few minutes near the end of the exam period to reread what you have written and insert corrections and emendations. You won't have time to fix large-scale issues: If you've confused the Spanish Armada with Torquemada, you're toast. But a quick edit may catch embarrassing gaffes or omissions. ○ When you write quickly, you probably leave out or transpose some words or simply use the wrong expression. Take a moment to edit these fixable errors. In the process, you may also amplify or repair an idea or two. Here are some other useful strategies to follow.

Use transition words and phrases. Essay examinations are the perfect place to employ such transparent transitional devices as *first, second,* and *third* or *next, even more important, nonetheless, in summary, in conclusion,* and so on. Don't be subtle: The transitions guide you as you write and help keep your instructor on track later. You will seem to be in control of your material.

Do a quick check of grammar, mechanics, and spelling. Some instructors take great offense at mechanical slips, even minor ones. At a minimum, avoid the common errors, covered in Part 9 of this book. Also be sure to spell correctly any names and concepts that you've been reviewing in preparation for the examination. ○ It's *Macbeth,* not *McBeth.*

Write legibly or print. Few people do much handwriting anymore. But most essay examinations still probably use paper or blue books. If you are out of practice or your handwriting is just flat-out illegible, print. Printing takes more time, but instructors appreciate the effort. Write in ink, as pencil can be faint and hard to read. Also consider double-spacing your essay to allow room for corrections and additions. But be careful not to spread your words too far apart. A blue book with just a few sentences per page undermines your ethos: It looks juvenile.

revise and edit
p. 386

common errors
p. 524

How to start ● **Confused?**
Read the assignment carefully. See page 262.

10 Position Paper

requires a brief critical response

A course instructor may ask you to respond to an assigned reading, lecture, film, or other activity with a position paper in which you record your reactions to the material—such as your impressions or observations. Such a paper is usually brief—often not much longer than a page or two—and due the next class session. Typically, you won't have time for more than a draft and quick revision.

- You summarize and assess the findings of a journal article studying the relationship between a full night's sleep and student success on college exams.

- You speculate about how a feminist philosopher of science, whose work you have read for a class, might react to recent developments in genetics.

- You respond to ideas raised by a panel of your classmates discussing a proposition to restore the draft or require national service.

- You offer a gut reaction to your first-ever viewing of *Triumph of the Will*, a notorious propaganda film made for Germany's National Socialist (Nazi) Party in 1935.

UNDERSTANDING POSITION PAPERS.   Instructors usually have several goals in assigning position papers: to focus your attention on a particular reading or class presentation; to measure how well you've understood course materials; to push you to connect one concept or reading with another. Because they may want you to take some risks, instructors often mark position papers less completely than full essays and grade them by different standards.

Because these assignments can be quick, low-stakes items, you might be tempted to blow them off. That would be an error. Position papers give you practice in writing about a subject and so prepare you for other papers and exams; the assignments may even preview the types of essay questions an instructor favors. Position papers also help to establish your ethos in a course, marking you as a careful reader and thinker or, perhaps, someone just along for the ride.

Use a few simple strategies to write a strong position paper.

Protesters taking a position
While some feel that security cameras ensure safety, others believe them to be an invasion of privacy.

△

 confused?

Read the assignment carefully.   Understand exactly what your instruc-tor wants: Look for key words such as *summarize, describe, classify, evaluate, compare, compare and contrast,* and *analyze* and then respect the differences between them.

Review assigned material carefully.   Consider photocopying readings so that you can annotate their margins or underscore key claims and evi-dence. Practice smart reading: Always look for conflicts, points of difference, or issues raised in class or in the public arena—what some writers call *hooks*. Then use the most provocative material to jump-start your own thinking, using whatever brainstorming techniques work best for you. ○

Mine the texts for evidence.   Identify key passages worth quoting or features worth describing in detail. ○ For instance, you may find some star-tling facts worth repeating, a claim or two you resist heartily, or pithy sum-maries of complicated issues. Anchor your position paper around such strong passages. Be sure, too, you know how to merge quoted material smoothly with your own writing.

Organize the paper sensibly.   Unless the assignment specifically states otherwise, don't write the position paper off the top of your head. Take the time to offer a thesis or to set up a comparison, an evaluation, or another structure of organization. Give a position paper the same structural integrity you would a longer and more consequential assignment.

Here's a position paper written by Heidi Rogers as an early assignment in a lower-level course on visual rhetoric. Rogers's assignment was to offer an hon-est response to director Leni Riefenstahl's infamous documentary, *Triumph of the Will,* which showcases the National Socialist Party rallies in Munich in 1934. In the film, we see the German people embracing Hitler and his Nazi regime as they consolidate their power.

○

get an idea
p. 308

○

use quotations
p. 431

Rogers 1

Heidi Rogers

Professor Wachtel

Writing 203

September 22, 20--

Triumph of the Lens

The 1935 film *Triumph of the Will*, directed by Leni Riefenstahl, masterfully shows how visuals can be a powerful form of rhetoric. In the documentary we see Adolph Hitler, recognized today as one of the greatest mass murderers in history, portrayed as a strong, loving, and inspirational leader who could be the savior of Germany. However, as I was watching this film I was taken aback. I am supposed to hate this man, detest him for his brutal crimes against humanity, and yet I found myself drawn to him, liking him, even smiling as he greeted his fellow Germans on the streets of Munich. How did this filmmaker accomplish this, drawing viewers in and giving them such pride in their leader?

Riefenstahl's technique was to layer selected visuals to create the different emotions she wanted her audience to feel toward Hitler and his regime. Her first step was to introduce locations and natural images that were peaceful and soothing. Next, she would insert images of the German people themselves: children playing and laughing, women cheering and blowing kisses to Hitler, men in uniform proudly united under the Nazi flag. The next step was to weave in images of Hitler himself among these German people, so that even when he wasn't smiling or evoking any emotions at all, it would seem as if he were conveying the happiness, pride, or strength drawn from the images edited around him. The final piece of the puzzle was to put Hitler front and center, usually giving a

Offers a thesis to explain how film makes Hitler attractive.

To explain how film works, describes pattern she sees in Riefenstahl's editing technique.

Rogers 2

rousing speech that would inspire his audience and make him seem larger than life.

Provides extended example to support claim about how *Triumph of the Will* was edited.

A good example of this technique came during the youth rally sequence. First, Riefenstahl presents peaceful images of the area around the Munich stadium, including beautiful trees with the sun streaming between the branches. We then see the vastness of the city stadium, designed by Hitler himself. Then we watch thousands of young boys and girls smiling and cheering in the stands. These masses erupt when Hitler enters the arena and Riefenstahl artfully juxtaposes images of him, usually with a cold, emotionless face, with enthusiastic youth looking up to him as if he were a god. Hitler then delivers an intoxicating speech about the future of Germany and the greatness that the people will achieve under his leadership. The crowd goes wild as he leaves the stage and we see an audience filled with awe and purpose.

Explores implications of claim—that clever editing enabled Riefenstahl to reach many audiences.

What Riefenstahl did in *Triumph of the Will* is a common technique in film editing. When you have to reach a massive audience, you want to cover all of your bases and appeal to all of them at once. Therefore, the more kinds of *ethos*, *pathos*, and *logos* you can layer onto a piece of film, the better your chances will be of convincing the greatest number of people of your cause. As hard as this is to admit, if I had lived in a devastated 1935 Germany and I saw this film, I might have wanted this guy to lead my country too.

Triumph of the Will features numerous imposing shots of crowds cheering for Hitler.

Getting the details right

Edit the final version.   The assignment may seem informal, but edit and proofread your text carefully before you turn it in. ⭘ Think of a position paper as a trial run for a longer paper in your course. As such, it should follow the conventions of any given field or major. Even when an instructor seems casual about the assignment, don't ease up.

Identify key terms and concepts and use them correctly and often.   The instructor may be checking to see how carefully you read a book or article. So, in your paper, make a point of referring to the new concepts or terms you've encountered in your reading, as Rogers does with *ethos*, *pathos*, and *logos* in the annotated essay.

Treat your sources appropriately.   Either identify them by author and title within the paper or list them at the end of the paper in the correct documentation form (e.g., MLA or APA). Make sure quotations are set up accurately, properly introduced, and documented. Offer page numbers for any direct quotations you use. ⭘

Spell names and concepts correctly.   You lose credibility immediately if you misspell technical terms or proper nouns that appear throughout the course readings. In literary papers especially, get characters' names and book titles right.

Respond to your colleagues' work.   Position papers are often posted to electronic discussion boards to jumpstart conversations about ideas or readings. So take the opportunity to reply substantively to what your classmates have written. Don't just say "I agree" or "You've got to be kidding!" Add good reasons and evidence to your remarks. Remember, too, that your instructor may review these comments, looking for evidence of serious engagement with the course material.

revise and edit
p. 386

understand citation
styles p. 435

How to start → ● **Want to get the reader's attention?**
Choose a sensible subject line. See page 270.

E-mail

communicates electronically

E-mail has quickly become the preferred method for most business (and personal) communication because it is quick, efficient, easy to archive, and easy to search.

- You write to the coordinator of the writing center to apply for a job as a tutor, courtesy copying the message to a professor who has agreed to serve as a reference.

- You send an e-mail to several administrators in which you complain about campus fire safety when you discover there are no smoke alarms in the student lounge.

- You send an e-mail to classmates in a writing class, looking for someone to collaborate on a Web project.

- You e-mail the entire College of Liberal Arts faculty to invite them to attend a student production of Chekhov's *Uncle Vanya*.

UNDERSTANDING E-MAIL.   E-mail is now so common and informal that writers take it for granted, forgetting that e-mail can become important documentation when transacting business. Though usually composed quickly, e-mails have a long shelf life once they're archived. They can also spread well beyond their original audiences. Remember too that e-mails can be printed and filed as hard copy.

You probably know how to handle personal e-mails well enough. But you may not be as savvy about the more specialized messages you send to organizations, businesses, professors, groups of classmates, and so on. The following strategies will help.

Explain your purpose clearly and logically.   Use both the subject line and first paragraph of an e-mail to explain your reason for writing: Be specific about names, titles, dates, places, and so on, especially when your message opens a discussion. Write your message so that it will still make sense a year or more later, specifying references and pronouns (*we, it, them*). ○

Tell readers what you want them to do.   Lay out a clear agenda for accomplishing one task: Ask for a document, a response, or a reply by a specific date. If you have several requests to make of a single person or group, consider writing separate e-mails. It's easier to track short, single-purpose e-mails than to deal with complex documents requiring several different actions.

Write for intended and unintended audiences.   The specific audience in the "To" line is usually the only audience for your message. But e-mail is more public than traditional surface mail, easily duplicated and sent to whole networks of recipients with just a click. So compose your business e-mails as if they *might* be read by everyone in a unit or even published in a local paper. Assume that nothing in business e-mail is private.

Minimize the clutter.   When e-mails run through a series of replies, they grow so thick with headers, copied messages, and

○

common errors
p. 524

signatures that any new message can be hard to find. Make the latest message stand out, perhaps separating it slightly from the headers and transmission data.

Keep your messages brief.   Lengthy blocks of e-mail prose without paragraph breaks irritate readers. Indeed, meandering or chatty e-mails in business situations can make a writer seem disorganized and out of control. Try to limit your e-mail messages to what fits on a single screen. If you can't, use headings, spacing, and color to create visual pauses. **O**

Distribute your messages sensibly.   Send a copy of an e-mail to anyone directly involved in the message, as well as to those who might need to be informed. For example, if filing a grade complaint with an instructor, you may also copy the chair of his or her academic department or the dean of students. But don't let the copy (Cc) and blind copy (Bcc) lines in the e-mail header tempt you to send messages outside the essential audience.

Here's a fairly informal e-mail announcing a weekend trip, written to members of a department. Despite the relaxed event it describes, the e-mail still provides clear and direct information, gets to the point quickly, and offers an agenda for action.

To: DRW Faculty
From: John Ruszkiewicz
Subject: Annual Big Bend Trip
Cc: Alumni in Rhetoric
Bcc:
Attachments:

Dear Colleagues –

The Division of Rhetoric and Writing's eighth annual Big Bend trip is scheduled for October 8–11, 2008, at Big Bend National Park in West Texas. If you are considering making the trip this year, please let me know by e-mail and I will put you on the mailing list.

Clear, specific subject line makes message easy to find and search: Key search term would be "Big Bend."

Business letters use colon after greeting, but e-mails are often less formal.

Opening paragraph explains point of e-mail and what colleagues should do.

design your work
p. 517

You should know that the trip is neither an official DRW event, nor highly organized—just a group of colleagues enjoying the best natural environment Texas has to offer for a few days. If you've been to Big Bend, you know what to expect. If you haven't, see <http://www.nps.gov/bibe/home.htm>.

Second paragraph provides background information for readers who haven't been on trip before—including helpful Web link.

The weather at Big Bend in October is usually splendid. I say "usually" because we had heavy rains a few years ago and an ice storm in 2000. But such precipitation is rare: It is a desert park.

Tone is professional, but casual, and language is tight and correct. No emoticons.

In the past, most people have camped at the campground, which is first come, first serve. Lodging may be available in the park itself, but rooms are hard to get throughout the fall season. Also available are hotels in nearby Study Butte, Terlingua, and Lajitas.

I'll contact those interested in the trip in a few weeks. We can begin then to plan sharing rides and equipment. And please let other friends of the DRW know about the trip.

Final paragraph outlines subsequent actions, letting readers know what to expect.

Best,
JR

John Ruszkiewicz, Professor
The University of Texas at Austin
Department of Rhetoric and Writing
Austin, TX
Phone: (512) 555-1234
Fax: (512) 555-5678
ruszkiewicz@mail.utexas.edu

Signature is complete, opening various routes for communication.

Getting the details right

Because most people receive e-mail messages frequently, make any you send easy to process.

▶ want to get the reader's attention?

Choose a sensible subject line.   The subject line should clearly identify the topic and include helpful keywords that might later be searched. If your e-mail is specifically about a grading policy, your student loan, or mold in your gym locker, make sure a word you'll recall afterward—like *policy, loan,* or *mold*—gets in the subject line. In professional e-mails, subjects such as *A question, Hi!* or *Meeting* are useless.

Arrange your text clearly.   You can do almost as much visually in e-mail as you can in a word-processing program, including choosing fonts, inserting lines, and adding color, images, and videos. But you shouldn't do more than you need. A simple block style with spaces between single-spaced paragraphs works well enough for most messages. If a lengthy e-mail breaks into natural divisions, use boldfaced headings. You might even highlight key information with a readable color (dark blue or red, *not* yellow or lime green).

Check the recipient list before you hit send.   Routinely double-check all the recipient fields—especially when you're replying to a message. The original writer may have copied the message widely: Do you want to send your reply to that entire group or just to the original writer?

Include an appropriate signature.   Professional e-mail of any kind should include a signature that identifies you and provides contact information readers need. Your e-mail address alone may not be clear enough to identify who you are, especially if you are writing to your instructor.

But be careful: You may not want to provide readers with a *home* phone number or address since you don't know precisely who may see your e-mail. When you send e-mail, the recipient can reach you simply by replying.

Use standard grammar.   Professional e-mails should be almost as pol-ished as business letters: At least give readers the courtesy of a quick review to catch humiliating gaffes or misspellings. ○ Emoticons and smiley faces have also largely disappeared from serious communications.

Have a sensible e-mail address.   You might enjoy communicating with friends as HorribleHagar or DaisyGirl, but such an e-mail signature will undermine your credibility with a professor or potential employer. Save the oddball name for a private e-mail account.

Don't be a pain.   You just add to the daily clutter if you send unnecessary replies to e-mails—a pointless *thanks* or *Yes!* or *WooHoo!* Just as bad is CCing everyone on a list when you've received a query that needs to go to one person only: For example, when someone trying to arrange a meeting asks members of a group for available times and those members carbon copy their replies to all other members.

revise and edit
p. 386

How to start

- **Want to get a response?**
  Explain your purpose clearly and logically.
  See page 273.

12 Business Letter

communicates formally

The formal business letter remains an important instrument for sending information in professional situations. Though business letters can be transmitted electronically these days, legal letters or decisions about admissions to schools or programs often still arrive on paper, complete with a real signature.

- Responding to an internship opportunity at Boeing, you outline your engineering credentials for the position in a cover letter and attach your résumé.

- You send a brief letter to the director of admissions of a law school, graciously declining your acceptance into the program.

- You send a letter of complaint to an auto company, documenting the list of problems you've had with your SUV and indicating your intention to seek redress under your state's "lemon law."

- You write to a management company to accept the terms of a lease, enclosing a check for the security deposit on your future apartment.

UNDERSTANDING BUSINESS LETTERS.   As you would expect, business letters are generally formal in structure and tone, and follow a number of specific conventions, designed to make the document a suitable record or to support additional communication. Yet the principles for composing a business or job letter are not much different from those for a business e-mail. ○

Explain your purpose clearly and logically.   Don't assume a reader will understand why you are writing. Use the first paragraph to announce your concern and explain your purpose, anticipating familiar *who, what, where, when, how,* and *why* questions. Be specific about names, titles, dates, and places. If you're applying for a job, scholarship, or admission to a program, name the specific position or item. Remember that your letter is a record that may have a long life in a file cabinet. Write your document so that it will make sense later.

want to get a ◀ response?

Tell your readers what you want them to do.   Don't leave them guessing about how they should respond to your message. Lay out a clear agenda for accomplishing one task: Apply for a job, request information, or make an inquiry or complaint. Don't hesitate to ask for a reply, even by a specific date when that is necessary.

Write for your audience.   Quite often, you won't know the people to whom you are sending a business letter. So you have to construct your letter considering how an executive, an employer, an admissions officer, or a manager of complaints might be most effectively persuaded. Courtesy and goodwill go a long way—though you may have to be firm and impersonal in some situations. Avoid phony emotions or tributes.

An application or cover letter poses special challenges. You need to present your work and credentials in the best possible light without seeming full of yourself. Be succinct and specific, letting achievements speak mostly for themselves—though you

JOBS! JOBS! JOBS!

○

understand e-mail
p. 266

can explain details that a reader might not appreciate. Focus on recent events and credentials and explain what skills and strengths you bring to the job. Speak in your own voice, clipped slightly by a formal style. ○

Keep the letter focused and brief.   Like e-mails, business letters become hard to read when they extend beyond a page or two. A busy administrator or employee prefers a concise message, handsomely laid out on good stationery. Even a job-application letter should be relatively short, highlighting just your strongest credentials: Leave it to the accompanying résumé or dossier to flesh out the details.

Use a conventional form.   All business letters should include your address (called the *return address*), the date of the message, the address of the person to whom you are writing (called the *inside address*), a formal salutation or greeting, a closing, a signature in ink (when possible), and information about copies or enclosures.

Both *block format* and *modified-block format* are acceptable in business communication. In block forms, all elements are aligned against the left-hand margin (with the exception of the letterhead address at the top). In modified-block form, the return address, date, closing, and signature are aligned with the center of the page. In both cases, paragraphs in the body of the letter are set as single-spaced blocks of type, their first lines not indented, and with an extra line space between paragraphs.

In indented form (not shown), the elements of the letter are arranged as in modified-block form, but the first lines of body paragraphs are indented five spaces, with no line spaces between the single-spaced paragraphs.

Distribute copies of your letter sensibly.   Copy anyone involved in a message, as well as anyone who might have a legitimate interest in your action. For example, in filing a product complaint with a company, you may also want to send your letter to the state office of consumer affairs. Copies are noted and listed at the bottom of the letter, introduced by the abbreviation *Cc* (for *courtesy copy*).

Following are two business letters: the first is a concise letter of complaint, while the second is a more detailed letter from a student applying for a scholarship.

define your style
p. 366

John Humbert
95 Primrose Lane
Columbus, OH 43209

September 12, 2008

Home Design Magazine
3652 Delmar Drive
Prince, NY 10012

Dear *Home Design* Magazine:

I am a subscriber to your magazine, but I never received my
July 2008 or August 2008 issues. When my subscription
expires later this year, please extend it two more months at no
charge to make up for this error. Originally, my last issue
would have been the March 2009 magazine. Since I have
missed two issues and since my subscription was paid in full
almost a year ago, please send me the April and May 2009
Home Design at no additional charge.

Thank you for your attention.

Sincerely,

J. Humbert

John Humbert

Letterhead is preprinted
stationery carrying the
return address of the writer
or institution. It may also
include a corporate logo.

Allow two or three spaces
between the date and ad-
dress.

Allow one line space above
and below the salutation. A
colon follows the greeting.

The letter is in block form,
with all major elements
aligned with the left
margin.

In modified-block form, return address, date, closing, and signature are centered.

1001 Harold Circle #10
Austin, TX 78712
June 28, 2008

Mr. Josh Greenwood
ABC Corporate Advisors, Inc.
9034 Brae Rd., Suite 1111
Austin, TX 78731

Dear Mr. Greenwood:

Opening paragraph clearly states thesis of letter: Nancy Linn wants this job.

Rita Weeks, a prelaw advisor at the University of Texas at Austin, e-mailed me about an internship opportunity at your firm. Working at ABC Corporate Advisors sounds like an excellent chance for me to further my interests in finance and corporate law. I would like to apply for the position.

Letter highlights key accomplishments succinctly and specifically.

This past year, I worked as a clerical intern at GTBS, an estate-planning law firm. Creating financial spreadsheets, copying and filing documents, running errands, and answering phones have taught me how to serve the needs of an office of professionals and clients. I am ready to apply what I have learned at GTBS to a job that more closely relates to my career goals: becoming a certified financial and/or valuation analyst and corporate lawyer.

Candidate repeatedly explains how internship fits career goals.

As vice president and financial director of the Honors Business Association at UT-Austin, I used my skills as a writer and speaker to obtain funding for this student organization. By e-mailing and speaking with corporate recruiters, I raised $5,500 from Microsoft, ExxonMobil, Deloitte, and other companies. I also secured $2,400 from the University Co-op through written proposals.

Additional contact information provided.

Please call (210-555-0000) or e-mail me at NLINN@abcd.com to schedule an interview. Thank you for considering me as a potential intern. I look forward to meeting you.

Sincerely,
Nancy Linn

Enclosure: Résumé
CC: Rita Weeks

Courtesy copy of letter sent to advisor mentioned in first paragraph; can be contacted as reference.

Getting the details right

Perhaps the most important detail in a business letter is keeping the format you use consistent and correct. Be sure to print your letter on good quality paper or letterhead and to send it in a proper business envelope, one large enough to accommodate a page $8\frac{1}{2}$ inches wide.

Use consistent margins and spacing.   Generally, 1-inch margins all around work well, but you can use larger margins (up to $1\frac{1}{2}$ inches) when your message is short. The top margin can also be adjusted if you want to balance the letter on the page, though the body need not be centered.

Finesse the greeting.   Write to a particular person at a firm or institution. Address them as *Mr.* or *Ms.*—unless you actually know that a woman prefers *Mrs.* You may also address people by their full names: *Dear Margaret Hitchens.* When you don't have a name, fall back on *Dear Sir or Madam* or *To Whom It May Concern,* though these forms of address (especially *madam*) seem increasingly dated. When it doesn't sound absurd, you can address the institution or entity: *Dear Exxon* or *Dear IRS*—again, not a preferred form.

Spell everything right.   Be scrupulous about the grammar and mechanics too—especially in a job-application letter. Until you get an interview, that piece of paper represents you to a potential client or employer. Would you hire someone who misspelled your company's name or made noticeable errors? ○

Photocopy the letter as a record.   An important business letter needs a paper copy, even when you have an electronic version archived: The photocopied signature may mean something.

Don't forget the promised enclosures.   A résumé should routinely accompany a job-application letter. ○

Fold the letter correctly and send it in a suitable envelope.
Business letters always go on $8\frac{1}{2}$ x 11 inch paper sent in standard business envelopes, generally $4\frac{1}{8}$ x $9\frac{1}{2}$ inches. Fold the letter in three sections, trying to put the creases through white space in the letter so that the body of the message remains readable.

common errors
p. 524

understand résumés
p. 278

How to start   ● **Want to get a job?**
Design pages that are easy to read. See page 281.

Résumé

records
professional
achievements

A one-page résumé usually accompanies any letter of application you send for a position or job. The résumé gathers and organizes details about your experiences at school, on the job, and in the community. For some types of career, you may recap years of work and achievements in a longer, but similarly organized, document called a CV (curriculum vitae).

● For a part-time position at a local day-care center, you prepare a résumé that chronicles your relevant experience.

● For an application to graduate school, you prepare a résumé that gives first priority to your accomplishments as a dean's list dual major in government and English.

● You modify your résumé slightly to highlight your internships with several law firms because you are applying for a paralegal clerk position at Baker Botts LLP.

● For a campus service scholarship, you tweak your résumé to emphasize activities more likely to interest college administrators than potential employees.

UNDERSTANDING RÉSUMÉS.   The point of a résumé is to provide a quick, easy-to-scan summary of your accomplishments to someone interested in hiring you professionally. The document must be readable at a glance, meticulously accurate, and reasonably handsome. Think of it this way: A résumé is your one- or two-page chance to make a memorable first impression.

Contrary to what you may think, there's no standard form for résumés, but they do usually contain some mix of the following information:

- Basic contact data: your name, address, phone number, and e-mail address

- Educational attainments (college and above): degrees earned, where and when

- Work experience: job title, company, dates of employment, with a brief list of the skills you used in specific jobs (such as customer service, sales, software programs, language proficiencies, and so on)

A strong résumé can be your ticket to the job or position you want.

● Other accomplishments: extracurricular activities, community service, volunteer work, honors, awards, and so on. These may be broken into sub-categories.

Depending on the situation, you might also include the following elements:

● A brief statement of your career goals

● A list of people willing to serve as references (with their contact information)

You can add additional categories to your résumé, too, whenever they might improve your chances at a job. The résumé you'll compile as your career evolves, for instance, may eventually include items such as administrative appointments, committee service, awards, patents, publications, lectures, participation in business organizations, community service, and so on. But keep the document brief. Ordinarily, a first résumé shouldn't exceed one page—though it may have to run longer if you are asked to provide references.

Résumés, which often resemble outlines without the numbers or letters, vary enormously in design. You have to decide on everything from fonts and headings to alignments and paper. You can choose to pay companies to fashion your résumé or buy special software to produce these documents. But your word processor has all the power you need to create a competent résumé on your own. Here's some advice.

Gather the necessary information.   You'll have to assemble this career data sooner or later. It's much simpler if you start in college and gradually build a full résumé over the years.

Don't guess or rely on memory for résumé information: Take the time necessary to get the data right. Verify your job titles and your months or years of employment; identify your major as it is named in your college catalog; make an accurate list of your achievements and activities without embellishing them. Don't turn an afternoon at a sandlot into "coaching high-school baseball." Focus on attainments during your college years and beyond. Grade- and high-school achievements don't mean much, unless you're LeBron James.

Decide on appropriate categories.   In most cases, right out of college, you'll use the résumé categories noted above. But you may vary their order and emphasis, depending on the job or career you pursue. In the past, one expensively printed résumé served all occasions; today you can—and should—tailor your electronically crafted résumé to individual job searches.

Arrange the information within categories in reverse chronological order.   The most recent attainments come first in each of your categories. If such a list threatens to bury your most significant items, you have several options: Cut the lesser achievements from the list, break out special achievements in some consistent way, or highlight those special achievements in your cover letter.

Design pages that are easy to read.   Basic design principles aren't rocket science: Headings and key information should stand out and individual items should be clearly separated. The pages should look substantive but not cluttered. White space makes any document friendly, but too much in a résumé can suggest a lack of achievement. O

In general, treat the résumé as a conservative document. This is not the time to experiment with fonts and flash or curlicues. Don't include a photograph either, even a good one.

want to ◀
get a job?

Proofread every line in the résumé several times.   Careful editing isn't a "detail" when it comes to résumés: It can be the whole ball game. When employers have more job candidates than they can handle, they may look for reasons to dismiss weak cases. Misspelled words, poor design of headings and text, and incomplete or confusing chronology are the kinds of mistakes that can terminate your job quest. O

The following résumé, by Andrea Palladino, is arranged in reverse chronological order. Palladino uses a simple design that aligns the major headings and dates in a column down the left-hand margin and indents the detailed accomplishments to separate them, making them highly readable.

Applying for a job
need not be as dreary
as it once was—
or as sexist.

design your work
p. 517

common errors
p. 524

Contact information centered at top of page for quick reference. If necessary, give both school and permanent addresses.

Optional "career objective" functions like thesis.

Alignments further emphasize headings and dates.

Ample, but not excessive, white space enhances readability.

Andrea Palladino
600 Oak St.
Austin, TX 78705
(281) 555-1234

CAREER OBJECTIVE   Soon-to-be college graduate seeking full-time position that allows for regular interpersonal communication and continued professional growth.

EDUCATION
8/02–5/06   University of Texas at Austin – Psychology, B.A.

EXPERIENCE
3/04–Present   Writing Consultant
University of Texas at Austin Undergraduate Writing Center – Austin, TX
Tutor students at various stages of the writing process. Work with a variety of assignments. Attend professional development workshops.

5/04–Present   Child Care Provider
CoCare Children's Services – Austin, TX
Care for infants through children age ten, including children with physical and mental disabilities. Change diapers, give food and comfort, engage children in stimulating play, and clean/disinfect toys after childcare. Work on standby and substitute for coworkers when needed.

5/03–12/04   Salesperson/Stockperson
Eloise's Collectibles – Katy, TX
Unpacked new shipments, prepared outgoing shipments, and kept inventory. Interacted with customers and performed the duties of a cashier.

ACCOMPLISHMENTS
2003–Present   College Scholar for 3 yrs. – acknowledgment of in-residence GPA of at least 3.50

10/05–Present   Big Brothers Big Sisters of Central Texas

Fall 2003   University of Texas at Austin Children's Research Lab – Research Assistant

Getting the details right

With its fussy dates, headings, columns, and margins, a résumé is all about the details. Fortunately, it is brief enough to make a thorough going-over easy. Here are some important considerations.

Don't leave unexplained gaps in your education or work career.
Readers will wonder about blanks in your history (Are you a spy? slacker? felon?) and so may dismiss your application in favor of candidates whose career chronology raises no red flags. Simply account for any long periods (a year or so) you may have spent wandering the capitals of Europe or flipping burgers. Do so either in the résumé or in the job-application letter—especially if the experiences contributed to your skills. O

Be consistent.   Keep the headings and alignments the same through-out the document. Express all dates in the same form: For example, if you abbreviate months and seasons, do so everywhere. Use hyphens between dates.

Protect your personal data.   You don't have to volunteer information about your race, gender, age, or sexual orientation on a job application or résumé. Neither should you provide financial data, Social Security or credit card numbers, or other information you don't want in the public domain and that is not pertinent to your job search. However, you do need to be accurate and honest about the relevant job information: Any disparity about what you state on a résumé and your actual accomplishments may be a firing offense down the road.

Consider having your résumés designed and printed professionally.
You may save time by letting someone else design and print your document, especially if you aren't particularly computer savvy. If you do produce your own résumé, be sure to print it on high-quality paper. Ordinary typing paper won't cut it.

understand business
letters p. 272

How to start   ● **Feeling lost?**
Gather your material. See page 286.

14 Personal Statement

explains a person's experiences and goals

Preparing a short personal statement has become almost a ritual among people applying for admission to college, professional school, or graduate school, or for jobs, promotions, scholarships, internships, and even elective office.

- An application for an internship asks for an essay in which you explain how your career goals will contribute to a more tolerant and diverse society.

- All candidates for the student government offices you're interested in must file a personal statement explaining their positions. Your statement, limited to 300 words, will be printed in the campus newspaper and posted online.

- You dust off the personal statement you wrote to apply to college to see what portions you can use in an essay required for admission to upper-division courses in the College of Communication.

UNDERSTANDING PERSONAL STATEMENTS. Institutions that ask for personal statements are rarely interested in who you are. Rather, they want to see whether you can *represent* yourself as a person with whom they might want to be affiliated. That may seem harsh, but consider the personal statements you have already written. At best, they are a slice of your life—the verbal equivalent of you in full-dress mode.

If you want a sense of what a school, business, or other institution expects in the essays they request from applicants, read whatever passes for that group's statement of mission or core values. If the words sound a little stiff, inflated, and unrealistic, you've got it—except that you shouldn't actually sound as pretentious as an institution. A little blood has to flow through the veins of your personal statement, just not so much that someone in an office gets nervous about your emotional pitch.

Hitting the right balance between displaying overwhelming competence and admitting human foibles in a personal statement is tough. Here's some advice for composing a successful essay.

Present yourself in your personal statement the same way you would in an interview: confident, professional, and pleasant.

Read the essay prompt carefully. Essay topics are often deliberately open-ended to give you some freedom in pursuing a topic, but only answer the question actually posed, not one you'd prefer to deal with. Ideally, the question will focus on a specific aspect of your work or education; try to write about this even if the question is more general.

Be realistic about your audience. Your personal statements are read by strangers. That's scary, but you can usually count on them to be reasonable people, and well-disposed to give you a fair hearing. They measure you against other applicants—not unreachable standards of perfection.

▶ feeling lost?

Gather your material.   In most cases, a personal statement is part of an application package that may already include an application letter or résumé. If that's the case, don't waste your essay repeating what's already on record elsewhere. Instead, look for incidents and anecdotes in your life that bring your résumé lines to life. Talk about the experiences that prepared you for the work you want to do or, perhaps, determined the direction of your life. If the prompt encourages personal reminiscences (e.g., *the person who influenced you the most*), think hard about how to convey those experiences concretely to a perfect stranger.

Decide on a focus or theme.   Personal statements are short, so decide how to make best use of a reader's time. Don't ramble about your opinions or educational career. Instead, choose a theme that builds on the strongest aspects of your application. If you're driven by a passion for research, arrange the elements of your life to illustrate this. If your best work is extracurricular, explain in a scholarship application how your commitment to people and activities makes you a more estimable student. You may find it odd to turn your life into a thesis statement, but you need to make a clear point about yourself in any personal essay.

Organize the piece conventionally.   Many personal statements take a narrative form, though they may also borrow some elements of reports and even proposals. Whatever structures you adopt for the essay, pay attention to the introduction, conclusion, and transitions: You cannot risk readers getting confused or lost. ⭘

Try a high or middle style.   You don't want to be breezy or casual in an essay for law school or medical school, but a *personal* statement does invite a human voice. So a style that marries the correctness and formal vocabulary of a high style with the occasional untailored feel of the middle style might be perfect for many personal statements.

The Academic Service Partnership Foundation asked candidates for an internship to prepare an essay addressing a series of questions. The prompt and one response to it follows.

connect ideas
p. 350

ASPF NATIONAL INTERNSHIP PROGRAM

Please submit a 250–500 word typed essay answering the following three questions:

1. Why do you want an internship with the ASPF?
2. What do you hope to accomplish in your academic and professional career goals?
3. What are your strengths and skills, and how would you use these in your internship?

Specific questions limit reply, but also help to organize it.

Michael Villaverde

April 14, 2008

The opportunity to work within a health-related government agency alongside top-notch professionals initially attracted me to the Academic Service Partnership Foundation (ASPF) National Internship Program. I was excited after reading about the program's success and its extensive network of alumni. Participating in the ASPF's internship program would enable me to augment the health-services research skills I've gained through work at the VERDICT Research Center in San Antonio and the M. D. Anderson Cancer Center in Houston. This ASPF internship could also give me the chance to gain experience in health policy and administration.

I support the ASPF's mission to foster closer relations between formal education and public service and believe that I could contribute to this mission. If selected as an ASPF intern, I will become an active alumnus of the program. I would love to do my part by advising younger students and recruiting future ASPF interns. Most importantly, I make it a point to improve the operations of programs from which I benefit. Any opportunities provided to me by the ASPF will be repaid in kind.

Opening sentence states writer's thesis or intent; First two paragraphs address first question.

Essay uses first person (*I, me*) but is fairly formal in tone and vocabulary, between high and middle style.

Personal note slips through in enthusiasm author shows for internship opportunity.

This statement transitions smoothly into second issue raised in prompt.

Formidable and *specific* goals speak for themselves in straightforward language.

Another transition introduces third issue raised by prompt.

Qualifications offered are numerous and detailed.

Special interest/concern is noted, likely to impress reviewers of statement.

Final sentence affirms enthusiasm for technical internship.

Other strengths I bring to the ASPF's National Internship Program are my broad educational background and dedication. My undergraduate studies will culminate in two honors degrees (finance and liberal arts) with additional pre-med coursework. Afterward, I wish to enroll in a combined M.D./Ph.D. program in health-services research. Following my formal education, I will devote my career to seeing patients in a primary-care setting, researching health-care issues as a university faculty member, teaching bioethics, and developing public policy at a health-related government agency.

The coursework at my undergraduate institution has provided me with basic laboratory and computer experience, but my strengths lie in oral and written communication. Comparing digital and film-screen mammography equipment for a project at M.D. Anderson honed my technical-writing skills and comprehension of statistical analysis. Qualitative analysis methods I learned at VERDICT while evaluating strategies used by the Veterans Health Administration in implementing clinical practice guidelines will be a significant resource to any prospective employer. By the end of this semester, I will also possess basic knowledge of Statistical Package for the Social Sciences (SPSS) software.

During my internship I would like to research one of the following topics: health-care finance, health policy, or ethnic disparities in access to quality health-care. I have read much about the Medicare Prescription Drug, Improvement, and Modernization Act of 2003 and would especially enjoy studying the implications of this legislation. I would learn a great deal from working with officials responsible for the operation and strategic planning of a program like Medicare (or a nonprofit hospital system). The greater the prospects for multiple responsibilities, the more excited I will be to show up to work each day.

Getting the details right

As with résumés, there's no room for errors or slips in personal statements. ○ They are a test of your writing skills, plain and simple, and so you need to get the spelling, mechanics, and usage right. In addition, consider the following advice.

Don't get too artsy.   A striking image or two may work well in the statement, as may the occasional metaphor or simile. But don't build your essay around a running theme, an extended analogy, or a pop-culture allusion that a reader might dismiss as hokey or simply not get. If a phrase or feature stands out too noticeably, change it, even though *you* may like it.

Use commonsense.   You probably already have the good grace not to offend gender, racial, religious, and ethnic groups in your personal statements. You should also take the time to read your essay from the point of view of people from less protected groups who may take umbrage at your dismissal of *old folks*, *fundamentalists*, or even Republicans. You don't know who may be reading your essay.

Write the essay yourself.   It's the ethical thing to do. If you don't, and you're caught, you're toast. You might ask someone to review your statement or take a draft to a writing center for a consultation. ○ This review or consult by a parent or English-major roommate should not purge your *self* from the essay. Remember, too, that wherever you arrive, you'll need to write at the level you display in the statement that got you there.

common errors
p. 524

peer review
p. 392

How to start ▶ ● **First time writing a lab report?**
Look at model reports. See page 292.

15 Lab Report

records a scientific experiment

In most courses in the natural or social sciences, you are expected to learn how to describe experiments systematically and report information accurately. It goes with the territory. The vehicle for such work is the familiar lab report.

- For a physics course, you describe an experiment that uses a series of collisions to demonstrate the conservation of energy.

- In an organic chemistry lab, you try to produce chemical luminescence and report your results.

- For a psychology class, you describe the results of an experiment you created to determine whether students taking examinations benefit from a good night's sleep the night before the test.

UNDERSTANDING LAB REPORTS.   Formal scientific papers published in academic journals have conventional features designed to convey information to readers professionally interested in the results of studies and experiments. The key elements of such a scientific paper are the following:

- Descriptive title clearly describing the content of the paper

- Introduction explaining the purpose of the study or experiment and reviewing previous work on the subject (called a literature review)

- Description of materials and methods, explaining the factual and procedural details of the experiment

- Results section, tabulating and reporting the data

- Discussion of the results, interpreting the data

- References list or bibliography, documenting articles and books cited in the paper

- Abstract (not always required) condensing a summary of the main points in your report

For details about composing full scientific papers, consult the handbooks used in your particular field (and recommended by your instructor), such as *The CSE Manual for Authors, Editors, and Publishers* (7th edition, 2006), or the *Publication Manual of the American Psychological Association* (5th edition, 2001).

Lab reports borrow many of the features of the scientific papers published in academic journals, but are generally much shorter and tailored to specific situations. Typically, you prepare lab reports to describe the results of experiments you're assigned to perform in science courses. But you may also write lab reports to document original research done with colleagues or professors.

Follow instructions to the letter.   In a course with a lab, you typically receive precise instructions on how to compile a lab notebook or prepare and submit reports. Read these guidelines carefully and ask the instructor or teaching assistant questions about any specifications you do not understand. Each section of a lab report provides a specific kind of information that helps a reader understand and, possibly, repeat a procedure or an experiment.

▶ first time writing a lab report?

Look at model reports.   Lab report requirements may vary not only from subject to subject but also from course to course. So ask the instructor whether sample reports might be available for a particular lab section. If so, study them closely. The best way to understand what your work should look like is to see a successful model.

Be efficient.   If an abstract is required, keep it brief. Use charts, tables, and graphs (as required) to report information and then don't repeat that data elsewhere. Keep your reporting of results separate from the discussion and commentary.

Edit the final version.   In a lab report, editing means not only proofreading your language but also reviewing the structure of equations or formulas, assessing the clarity of methods or procedures sections, and checking any numbers, calculations, equations, or formulas. ○ Be sure to label all sections and items accurately, numbering any figures, tables, and charts. Use these numbers to refer to these items in the body of your report.

Following is a lab report produced for a course in organic chemistry. It follows a structure defined in a full page of instructions. Some sections—such as "Main Reactions and Mechanisms"—are clearly tied to the specific subject matter of the chemistry class. Other sections—such as "Data and Results"—would be found in lab reports in many disciplines.

Like any lab report, this one is mostly business. But there are informal moments ("Did it glow? Yes!"), probably reflecting the fact that the writer had already gained a sense of what was acceptable in this course: This was the seventh of more than a dozen required reports.

revise and edit
p. 386

Sandra Ramos

3/22/20--

Synthesis of Luminol

CH 210C Syllabus, Supplement I.

INTRODUCTION

The purpose of this lab is to synthesize a chemiluminescent product

and observe chemiluminescence.

MAIN REACTIONS AND MECHANISMS

a.

Luciferin   Decarboxyketoluciferin

b.

3- Nitrophthalic Acid   Hydrazine   5- Nitrophthalhydrazide   Luminol

Almost all lab reports use headings for their structure. "Introduction" functions as thesis.

"Materials and Methods" section starts here. (Assignment instructions specified different language for these headings.)

Ramos 2

c.

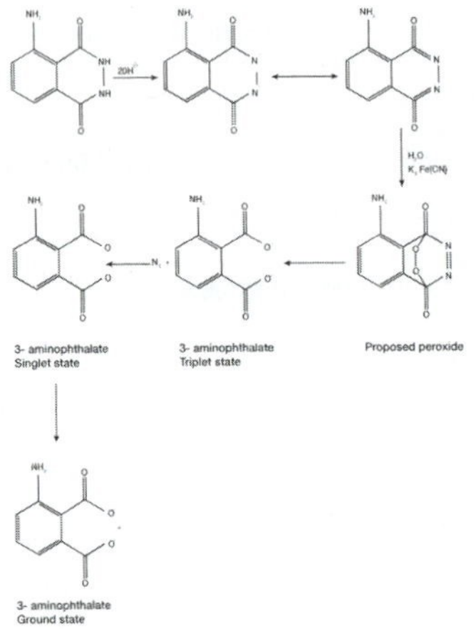

3- aminophthalate
Singlet state

3- aminophthalate
Triplet state

Proposed peroxide

3- aminophthalate
Ground state

TABLE OF REACTANTS AND PRODUCTS

Included 3-nitrophthalic acid, hydrazine solution, triethylene glycol,
NaOH, sodium hydrosulfite dihydrate, acetic acid, luminol,
potassium ferricyanide, hydrogen peroxide

SYNOPSIS OF PROCEDURE

APPARATUS:

5 ml conical vial, hot plate, heating block, spin vane, Hirsch funnel,
250 ml Erlenmeyer flask, and thermometer

SYNTHESIS OF LUMINOL:

1. Heated 5 ml vial containing 200 mg 3-nitrophthalic acid and 0.4
   ml aq 8% hydrazine sol'n until solid dissolved.

Abbreviations are not followed by periods.

Ramos 3

2. Once dissolved, add 0.6 ml triethylene glycol and clamped vial in vertical position. Added spin vane and inserted thermometer into vial.

3. Brought sol'n to vigorous boil to boil away excess water. During this time, temperature should be around 110°C.

4. Once water boiled off, temperature rose to 215°C in a 3–4 minute period. Maintained the 215–220°C temperature for 2 minutes.

5. Removed the vial and cooled it to 100°C. While cooling, placed 10 ml water in Erlenmeyer flask and heated to boiling.

6. Once sample cooled to 100°C, added 3 ml boiling water.

7. Collected yellow crystals by vacuum filtration using a Hirsch funnel.

8. Transferred solid back to vial and added 1 ml of 3.0 M NaOH and stirred with a stirring rod until the solid was dissolved. Then added 0.6 g of fresh sodium hydrosulfite dihydrate to the deep brown-red solution.

9. Heated solution slightly under boiling for 5 minutes, taking care not to cause bumping. Then added 0.4 ml acetic acid.

10. Cooled tube in beaker of cool water, and collected solid luminol by vacuum filtration using Hirsch funnel.

LIGHT-PRODUCING REACTION:

1. Combined two samples of luminol. Dissolved them in 2 ml of 3 M NaOH and 18 ml water (sol'n A).

2. Next, prepared a sol'n of 4 ml 3% aqueous potassium ferricyanide, 4 ml 3% H_2O_2 and 32 ml H_2O (sol'n B).

3. Now, diluted 5 ml sol'n A with 35 ml water. In a dark place, poured diluted sol'n and sol'n B simultaneously into an Erlenmeyer flask. Swirled flask; looking for blue-green light.

Standard notation is used to describe chemical reactions.

Ramos 4

Data sections are rarely
this simple. Most would
require tables, charts, etc.

DATA AND RESULTS

Did it glow?   Yes!

DISCUSSION AND CONCLUSION

When a chemical reaction generates light, chemiluminescence has
occurred. The product of such a reaction is in an excited electronic
state and emits a photon. One example of chemiluminescence is the
luciferase-catalyzed reaction of luciferin with molecular oxygen in
the male firefly. Chemiluminescence occurring through biochemical
processes is also called bioluminescence.

Luminol is synthesized through two steps. 4-nitrophthalic acid
and hydrazine react to produce 5-nitrophthalhydrazide, which is
reduced by sodium dithionite to form luminol. In alkaline solution,
luminol emits blue-green light when mixed with H_2O_2 and potassium
ferricyanide.

Although the mechanism of this reaction isn't fully understood,
chemists believe that a peroxide decays to form 3-diaminophthalate
in an excited triplet state (two unpaired electrons with the same
spin). Slowly, the 3-diaminophthalate converts to a singlet state (two
unpaired electrons now have different spins), which then decays to
the ground state, emitting light through fluorescence. In contrast,
phosphorescence occurs in reactions where a triplet state emits
photons while converting to a singlet state.

Blue-green light glowed for a fraction of a second when I mixed
solutions A and B. This indicates that I successfully synthesized enough
luminol to run the chemiluminescent reaction. Only a small amount of
dissolved luminol was required, so a high yield was not necessary.

Getting the details right

Even the conventions of scientists vary, so it helps to know what sorts of issues may come up in preparing a lab report for a given course. Again, ask questions when you aren't sure what conventions to follow.

Keep the lab report impersonal.   Keep yourself and any lab partners out of the work. In fact, most instructors will *require* that you use the third person and passive voice throughout: *The beaker was heated* rather than *We heated the beaker*. Though some instructors do allow the use of first-person pronouns in undergraduate work—preferring the clarity of active sentences—always check before using *I* or *we*. O

Keep the style clear.   Written for knowledgeable readers, lab reports needn't apologize for using technical terms, jargon, and scientific notation. However, sentences still need to be coherent and grammatical in structure and free of clutter. Avoid contractions, however, as well as any trendy or slang terms.

Follow the conventions.   Learn the rules as they apply in particular fields. In general, however, you should italicize scientific names expressed in Latin, write out formulas and equations on separate lines, use only metric quantities and measures, use standard abbreviations, and narrate the materials and methods section in the past tense.

Label charts, tables, and graphs carefully.   Any data you present graphically should make sense at a glance if your design is sensible and the labels are thorough and accurate. Don't leave readers wondering what the numbers in a column represent or what the scale of a drawing might be. O

Document the report correctly.   Most lab reports won't require documentation or a list of references. But a scientific paper will. Determine the documentation style manual used in the subject area and follow its guidelines closely. O

define your style
p. 366

display data
p. 514

understand citation
styles p. 435

How to start   ● **Adapting material?**
Organize your presentation. See page 299.

16 Oral Report

presents information to a live audience

For an oral report, you must not only research a subject and organize information but also find ways to convey your points powerfully and sometimes graphically to an audience listening and watching rather than reading.

- For a government class, you use your technical expertise and a series of slides to explain why you believe electronic voting equipment is far from secure.

- For a psychology exam, you use presentation software to review the results of an experiment you and several colleagues designed to test which types of music were most conducive to studying for examinations.

- For a group of middle-school children, you and three colleagues from a college drama club use lots of props to demonstrate how you stage a full Shakespeare production every spring.

- Prepping a crowd for a protest march, you use a bullhorn and a little humor to review the very serious ground rules for staging a peaceful demonstration on the grounds of the state capitol.

UNDERSTANDING ORAL REPORTS. Oral reports can be deceptive. To watch someone give an effective three-minute talk, you may assume they spent less time preparing it than they would a ten-page paper. But be warned: Oral presentations require all the research, analysis, and drafting of any other type of assignment, and then some. After all the background work is done, the material needs to be distilled into its most important points and sold to an audience. Here is some advice for preparing effective oral reports.

Know your stuff. Having a strong grasp of your subject will make your presentation more effective. Knowledge brings you confidence that will ease your anxieties about speaking in public. You'll appear believable and persuasive to an audience. And you'll feel more comfortable improvising and taking questions.

What's more, even the best-prepared reports can run into problems. Equipment may fail or perhaps you won't be able to find your note cards. But if you are in command of your subject, you'll survive.

Organize your presentation. If your report is based on material you've already written, reduce it to an outline, memorize the key points (or put them on a card), and then practice speaking to each point. If it helps, connect each point to one or two strong examples listeners will later remember. Make the report seem spontaneous, but plan every detail.

adapting
material?

The process is similar for an oral report built from scratch. First, study your subject. Then list the points you want to cover and arrange them in a way that will make sense to listeners—choosing a pattern of organization that fits your topic. Either note cards or the outlining tools that you'll find in programs like Word or PowerPoint are ideal for exploring options for arranging your talk.

Once into your subject, tell your audience briefly what you intend to cover and in what order. Then, throughout the report at critical transition points, tell the audience where you are by simply explaining what comes next: *The second issue I want to discuss. . . . ; Now that we've examined the phenomenon,*

The best equipment can't save a poorly prepared report.

order ideas
p. 342

let's look at its consequences. ○ Don't be shy about stating your main points this directly or worry about repetition. In an oral report, strategic repetition is your friend.

Finally, signal your conclusion when you get there and end the report shortly thereafter, as promised. If you're taking questions after your presentations, follow up with *Any questions?*

Adapt your material to the time available.   Don't worry about running out of things to say if you know your subject: Few speakers have that problem once they get rolling. But be realistic about how much material you can cover within the assigned limit, especially if you have to answer questions at the end. Tie your key ideas to fixed points on a clock. Know where you need to be at a quarter, half, and three-quarters of the way through the available time.

Practice your presentation.   Complete several dry runs for an oral report. Each session will increase your confidence and alert you to problems you can then steer around. You'll know immediately where the report works and where to make adjustments. Whenever possible, have one or more friends or colleagues watch you practice and give you feedback on how to improve.

Practice sessions are needed, too, to time the presentation. Speak any material aloud *exactly* as you intend to deliver it and go through all the motions, especially if you have accompanying media such as slides or video clips. If you practice only in your head, you will greatly underestimate the duration of the report.

If your presentation is collaborative, choreograph the report with the full group, agreeing on the introductions, handoffs, and interactions with the audience. Who runs the slide projector? Who distributes the handouts and when? Who handles the question-and-answer session? Details like these seem minor until they are mishandled on game day.

connect ideas
p. 350

At least one run-through should, if possible, occur at the actual location for the report. You'll feel far more comfortable during the presentation if you've stood on the stage, handled the microphone and podium, found places to plug in the media equipment, and heard your voice from the front of the room, even if it is a classroom you've been sitting in all term.

The PowerPoint presentation on this page was created by Terri Sagastume, a resident of a small Florida town who opposes a proposed real-estate development, Edenlawn Estates on property near his home. J&M Investments, the real-estate developer that recently purchased the property, hopes to create a new multistory condominium complex, known as Edenlawn Estates, in place of the property's existing single-family homes. Sagastume's goal is to inform the public of the damage such a development would do to the surrounding area, and he is trying to convince his audience to sign a petition, which he will present to the local government in an effort to shut the project down.

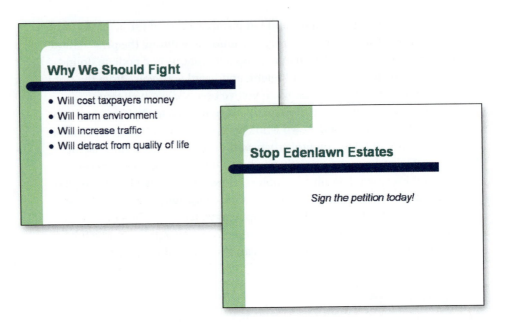

The slides themselves are extremely simple and brief: They are merely the bullet points that Sagastume uses to ground his presentation.

With the first slide as his backdrop, Sagastume provides a preview of his speech in three broad sections. First, he explains to his audience that the real-estate developer—a Miami-based conglomerate with no personal ties to the area—wants to change the existing building codes and zoning laws in order to maximize profits. Second, he reminds his audience of the reason those codes and laws are there, and that much could be lost if exceptions are made. And finally, he convinces his audience that, together, they can fight the big developer and win.

create slides
p. 510

Getting the details right

An oral report, whether onstage, in school, or at work, is a performance. You aren't just reading information aloud; you're working an audience in a more physical way.

Fortunately, as a speaker you have some advantages. You stand front and center in the room, possibly with a microphone to amplify your voice and a PowerPoint slide presentation to illustrate your points. And, for about thirty seconds, you'll probably have the automatic goodwill of an audience. After that, you've got to earn every minute of their continued attention. Here's how to do it.

Stay connected to your listeners.   Once the oral presentation begins, consult your notes as you need them, but spend most of your report looking at the crowd. Make eye contact with individuals and sweep the room. Watch their reactions. When it's clear you've made a point, move on. If you see puzzled looks, explain more. No speaker charms everyone, so don't let a random yawn or frown throw you. But if the whole crowd starts to snooze, you *are* the problem. Connect or lose 'em.

Be sure to speak *to* your listeners, not to a text or notes. If you look downward too often, you lose eye contact and your voice may be muffled, even with a microphone. Print your notes in a font and type size large enough to read easily from a distance so that you can look up without worrying about losing your place.

Use your voice.   Speak clearly and deliberately, and be sure people in back can hear you. Nervous speakers unconsciously accelerate until they're racing to their conclusions, and their voices will sometimes be higher-pitched than usual. If you get skittish, take a deep breath and smile. You'll calm down a bit and be better able to continue.

If in rehearsal you find yourself punctuating every few words in your sentences with *uh, um, ok, like,* or *you know,* you've got a problem that you'll want to fix. Try recording your presentations to discover any annoying repetitions. Then make a conscious effort to eliminate them, continuing to record your speech to gauge your progress. You won't eliminate *you know* overnight, but it can be done.

△

Use your body.   If the room is large and a fixed microphone doesn't confine you, try moving around on the stage to reach more of the audience. Use gestures too. They are a natural part of public speaking, especially for arguments and personal narratives.

If you are stuck behind a podium, you can still use your voice, posture, and gestures to keep listeners engaged. If the occasion and your paper are very academic, at least look steady onstage. Don't rock as you read.

Dress for the occasion too. A little spit and polish earns you the goodwill of most audiences. Your classmates may razz you about the tie or skirt, but it just proves they're paying attention. And that's a good thing.

Use humor.   In longer reports to less familiar groups, consider easing into your material with an anecdote that connects you, your subject, and your listeners. Self-deprecating humor sometimes helps. And don't forget to introduce yourself if there is no one to perform that task. (Short, in-class presentations won't need much, if any, warm-up material.)

Use appropriate props.   There's nothing wrong with a report that relies on the spoken word alone. Still, audiences appreciate supporting material, including flip charts that summarize key points; handouts that duplicate passages, texts, or data germane to the presentation; visual or audio samplings; and so on. All such materials, clearly labeled and handsomely reproduced, should also be genuinely relevant to the report. Resist the temptation to show something just because it's cool.

reference

Ideas

3

Need help organizing or drafting? See page 334.

17 Brainstorming

find a topic/
get an idea

A great deal of thinking occurs at the beginning of a project or assignment. How exactly will you fill ten or twenty pages with your thoughts on Incan architecture, the life cycle of dung beetles, or what you did last summer? What hasn't already been written about religion in America, cattle in Africa, or the cultural hegemony of iTunes? What do you do when you find yourself clueless or stuck or just overwhelmed by the possibilities—or lack thereof? Simple answer: Brainstorm.

Put a notion on the table and see where it goes—and what you might do with it or learn about it. Toy with an idea like a kitten with a catnip mouse. Push yourself to think through, around, over, and under a proposition. Dare to be politically incorrect or, alternatively, so conventional that your good behavior might scare even your elders.

But don't think of brainstorming as disordered and muddled. Consider the metaphor itself: Storms are awesomely organized events. They generate power by physical processes so complex that we're just beginning to understand them. Similarly, a first-rate brainstorming session spins ideas from the most complex chemistry in our bodies, the tumult of the human brain.

Naturally, you'll match brainstorming techniques to the type of writing you hope to produce. Beginning a personal tale about a trip to Wrigley Field, you might make a list of sensory details to jog your memory—the smell of hot dogs, the catcalls of fans, the green

Chalkboards, flip charts, and even sticky notes can help you rapidly record your ideas.

grass of the outfield. But for an assigned report on DNA fingerprinting, your brainstorming might itemize things you still must learn about the subject: what DNA fingerprinting is, how it is done, when it can be used, how reliable it is, and so on.

Find routines that support thinking.   Use whatever brainstorming techniques get you invested in a project. Jogging, swimming, knitting, or sipping brew at the coffeehouse may be your stimulus of choice. Such routine activities keep the body occupied, allowing insights to mature. Your thoughts do need to be captured and recorded, either in notes or, perhaps, voice memos.

One warning: Brainstorming activities of this kind can become simple procrastination. That comfortable chair in Starbucks might evolve into a spot too social for much thinking or writing. Recognize when your productivity has been compromised and change tactics.

Ideas won't keep; something must be done about them.

—Alfred North Whitehead

Build lists.   Brainstorm to list potential topics or, if you already have a subject, to explore the major points you might cover. Add all items that come to mind: If you're too picky or detailed at the start, you defeat the power of brainstorming—in which one idea, written on paper or on a screen, suggests another, then another. Even grocery lists work this way.

Lists work especially well when you already know something about a subject. For instance, preparing a letter to the editor in defense of collegiate sports, you can first inventory the arguments you've heard from friends or have made yourself. Then list the counterarguments you come up with as well. Write down everything that bubbles up, both reasonable and off-the-wall. Finally, winnow out the better items based on their quality or plausibility, and arrange them tentatively, perhaps pairing arguments and counterarguments. Even when you don't know much about a potential topic, assemble a list of basic questions that might lead to greater knowledge, to stimulate your ideas and thinking.

Map your ideas.   If you find a list too static as a prompt for writing, another way may be to explore the relationships between your ideas *visually*. Some writers use logic trees to represent their thinking, starting with a single general concept and breaking it into smaller and smaller parts. You can find examples of "tree diagrams" from many fields by using a search engine to investigate a keyword and then clicking the Image option.

Try freewriting.   Freewriting is a brainstorming technique of nonstop composing designed to loosen the bonds we sometimes use to clamp down on our own thinking. Typically, freewriting sessions begin slowly, with disconnected phrases and words. Suddenly, there's a spark and words stream onto the paper—but slow or fast you must still keep writing. The moment you settle back in your chair, you break the circuit that makes freewriting work. By forcing yourself to write, you push yourself to think and, perhaps, to discover what really matters in a subject.

Like other brainstorming techniques, freewriting works best when you already have some knowledge of your subject. You might freewrite successfully about standardized testing or working at fast-food restaurants if you've experienced both; you'll stumble trying to freewrite on subjects you know next to nothing about, maybe thermodynamics, ergonomics, or the career of Maria Callas. Freewriting tends to work best for personal narratives, personal statements, arguments, and proposals, and less well for reports and technical projects.

Although freewriting comes in many forms, the basic formula is simple.

STAGE ONE

- Start with a blank screen or sheet of paper.
- Put your subject or title at the top of the page.
- Write on that subject nonstop for ten minutes.
- Don't stop typing or lift your pen from the paper during that time.
- Write nonsense if you must, but keep writing.

STAGE TWO

- Stop at ten minutes and review what you have written.
- Underscore or highlight the most intriguing idea, phrase, or sentence.
- Put the highlighted idea at the top of a new screen or sheet.
- Freewrite for another ten minutes on the new, more focused topic.

Use memory prompts.   When writing personal narratives, institutional histories, or even résumés, you might trigger ideas with photographs, year-books, diaries, or personal memorabilia. An image from a vacation may bring events worth writing about flooding back to you. Even checkbooks or credit card statements may help you reconstruct past events or see patterns in your life worth exploring in writing.

Search online for your ideas.   You can get lots of ideas simply by exploring most topics online through keywords. Indeed, determining those initial keywords and then following up with new terms you discover while browsing is a potent form of brainstorming in itself.

A photo album is a great place to look for writing ideas, because we tend to document meaningful moments.

Uncle Bob, who's a cop, complains about the *"CSI effect."* What is that?

Wikipedia isn't an academic source, but it gives me a new term: *"CSI* syndrome."

Web   Images   Video   News   Maps   Gmail   mor

Google   csi effect

Web

1 **CSI Effect** - Wikipedia, the free encycloped
The **"CSI Effect"** (sometimes referred to as the **"CSI**
phenomenon of popular television shows such as the
en.wikipedia.org/wiki/**CSI**_Effect - 45k - Cached - Sim

2 USATODAY.com - **'CSI effect'** has juries wa
Like viewers across the nation, folks in Galveston, T
crime-scene investigators. Jury consultant Robert Hi
www.usatoday.com/news/nation/2004-08-05-**csi-effe**

3 **"CSI' Effect"** Is Mixed Blessing for Real Cri
Popular television shows like **CSI**: Crime Scene Inve
in forensics. So what is the job of a crime-scene inve
news.nationalgeographic.com/news/2004/09/0923_04
Cached - Similar pages

The **CSI effect**: On TV, it's all slam-dunk ev

Your continued donations keep Wikipedia running!

| article | discussion | edit this page | history |

CSI Effect

From Wikipedia, the free encyclopedia

The **"CSI Effect"** (sometimes referred to as the **"CSI syndrome"**) i
phenomenon of popular television shows such as the *CSI* franchise
jury members' real-world expectations of forensic science, especia
and DNA testing.[1] Much of these concerns stem from the "drama
writers of forensic science television--glamorizing the field, overstat
techniques, and exaggerating the abilities of forensic science.[2] Th
the way many trials are presented today, in that prosecutors are pr
forensic evidence in court.[3][4]

Contents [hide]

1 Manifestations of the CSI Effect
   1.1 Influence on jurors
   1.2 Influence on the criminal mind
   1.3 Influence on forensic science training programs
2 See also
3 References

Manifestations of the CSI Effect

Influence on jurors

Although speculation as to the validity of the *CSI* effect abounds,[5]

WIKIPEDIA
The Free Encyclopedia

navigation
- Main Page
- Contents
- Featured content
- Current events
- Random article

interaction
- About Wikipedia
- Community portal
- Recent changes
- Contact Wikipedia
- Donate to Wikipedia
- Help

search

[Go] [Search]

toolbox
- What links here
- Related changes

Consider the source.

It looks like lawyers and juries are affected—and juries think trials should be like *CSI* episodes.

A *"mixed* blessing"? I hadn't thought of the *"CSI* effect" as a positive thing—I wonder what they mean by that.

USA TODAY

Classifieds: cars.com | careerbuilder.com | Marketplace

Home
News
Travel
Money
Sports
Life
Tech
Weather
Search

powered by YAHOO! GO

Wash/Politics
Washington home
Washington briefs
Government guide
Health&Behavior
H&B home
Medical resources
Health information
Opinion
Opinion home
Columnists
Cartoons
More News
Top news briefs
Nation briefs
World briefs

Nation

• E-MAIL THIS • PRINT THIS • SAVE THIS • MOST POPULAR • S

Posted 8/5/2004 1:05 AM   Updated 8/5/2004 1:06 AM

'CSI effect' has juries wanting more evidence

By Richard Willing, USA TODAY

Like viewers across the nation, folks in Galveston, Texas, watch a lot of TV shows about crime-scene investigators. Jury consultant Robert Hirschhorn couldn't be happier about that.

CSI: Miami characters sort through evidence. It seems the crime show franchise has given jurors an incomplete picture of forensics. CBS

USA TODAY, August 5, 2004. Reprinted with permission.

NATIONAL GEOGRAPH

REPORTING YOUR WORLD DA

MAIN   ANIMAL NEWS   ANCIENT WORLD   ENVIRONMENT NEWS   CULTURES NEWS

"'CSI' Effect" Is Mixed Blessing for Real Crime Labs

Stefan Lovgren
for National Geographic News
September 23, 2004

A few months ago, a crime scene investigator from the Los Angeles County Sheriff's Department was dusting for fingerprints at the scene of a residential burglary. The victim of the crime was not impressed, however. "That's not the way they do it on television," she told the investigator.

Capt. Chris Beattie, who heads the L.A. County's Scientific Services Bureau—or "the crime lab"—calls it the "*CSI* effect." The popularity of television shows like *CSI: Crime Scene Investigation* and *Forensic Files,* he says, has turned millions of viewers into real-life science sleuths.

🖨 Printer Friendly
✉ Email to s

The phenomenon has reached into both classrooms and courtrooms. Universities have seen a dramatic increase in applications to

2

Determine who has something at stake.

3

Question claims.

18 Brainstorming with Others

collaborate

You've probably seen films or TV series that mock groupthink in corporations—wherein cowering yes-men and -women gather around a table to rubber-stamp the dumb ideas of a domineering CEO. Real group brainstorming is just the opposite. It encourages a freewheeling discovery and sharing of ideas among people with a stake in the outcome.

Group brainstorming comes in several varieties. The notorious college dorm-room bull session is a famous example, though with obvious defects. Such boozy late-night talk is likely to be frank,

open-ended, wide-ranging, and passionate. But it typically doesn't lead any-where or produce an agenda for action.

In academic or professional situations, formal brainstorming within a group requires specific strategies to produce solid results.

Choose a leader.   Leaders should be strong enough to keep discussions moving, cordial enough to encourage everyone to participate, and modest enough to draw out a range of opinions without pursuing agendas of their own. The leader probably shouldn't be the person with the most power in the group—not the CEO, chair of the department, or president of the student government. In fact, in serious brainstorming sessions, an outsider or trained facilitator might be the best choice.

Begin with a goal and set an agenda.   Most groups don't brainstorm for the pleasure of it. Some need or concern brings participants to the table—for instance, an assignment that requires a committee's response or, maybe, decision-making for a project that's more work than one person can handle. The leader should get the group to agree on a goal and a simple agenda. Even if that goal is open-ended, it will help keep discussions on track. And both the goal and agenda can be written on a board or flip chart to keep the group on-message. Without an agenda, brainstorming activity can dissolve into a bull session.

As the session evolves, a leader should help the group understand what it is accomplishing by stating and restating positions as they develop from discussion, posing important questions, and recording ideas as they emerge.

Set time limits.   Groups are most productive when working against reasonable time restraints. Given open-ended sessions (such as those dorm-room all-nighters), nothing productive may ever occur. But with only an hour or two for brainstorming, a group serious about its work will focus mightily. Time restraints also give a leader leverage to stifle the chatterers.

Encourage everyone to participate.   A leader or facilitator can call on the quiet types, but other participants can help too just by asking a col-league, "What do you think?" In a group setting, a reluctant participant's first contribution is usually the toughest, but it's worth any prodding: The silent observer in a group may come up with the sharpest insight.

Avoid premature criticism.   Leaders and participants alike need to encourage outside-the-box thinking and avoid a tendency to cut off contributions at the knees. No sneering, guffawing, or eye-rolling—even when ideas *are* stupid. Early on, get every scheme, suggestion, and proposal on the blackboard or flip chart. Criticism and commentary can come later.

It might even help to open the session with everyone freewriting on a key idea for five or ten minutes as a warmup, then reading their best ideas aloud. **O**

Test all ideas.   Sometimes, a group agrees too readily when a sudden good idea gains momentum. Such a notion should be challenged hard—even if it means someone has to play devil's advocate, that is, raise arguments or objections just to test the leading idea or claim. Even good ideas need to have their mettle proved.

Keep good records.   Many brainstorming sessions fail not because the ideas didn't emerge, but because no one bothered to catch them. Someone competent should take notes detailed enough to make sense a month later, when memories start to fade. Here again a flip chart may be useful, since points written on it don't get erased. The facilitator should follow up on the session by seeing that the notes get organized, written up, and promptly distributed to the group.

Agree on an end product.   Effective brainstorming sessions should lead to action of some kind or, at least, a clear agenda for further discussion. Keeping an eye on the clock, the leader of the group should wind up general discussion early enough to push the group toward conclusions and plans for action. Not every brainstorming session reaches its goals, but participants will want closure on their work.

get an idea
p. 308

Smart Reading 19

We get antsy when our written work gets criticized (or even edited) because ideas we put on a page or screen emerge from our own thinking—writing is *us*. Granted, our words rarely express *exactly* who we are, or what we've been imagining, but such distinctions get lost quickly when someone points to our work and says, "That's stupid" or "What nonsense!" The criticism cuts deep; it feels personal.

Challenges to a writer's assumptions, strategies, or evidence are part of the give-and-take of academic and professional life. You'll survive criticism and controversy if your work has integrity. But you'll have no defense at all if your writing is found thoughtless or careless when, in fact, *it is*.

Fortunately the surest way to avoid embarrassing criticism is also the best way to come up with fine ideas and impressive writing: *reading*. Reading can deepen your impressions of a subject, enrich your understanding, sharpen your critical acumen, and introduce you to alternative views. Reading also places you within a community of writers who have thought about a subject.

Of course, not all reading serves the same purposes.

- You pack a romance novel for pleasure reading on the beach.

- You consult stock market quotes or baseball box scores because you need info *now*.

read critically/read closely

- You check out a dozen scholarly books to do research for a paper.

- You read an old diary or memoir to imagine what life was like in the past.

- You thumb a graphic novel to move into a different reality.

Yet any of these reading experiences, as well as thousands of others, might lead to ideas for projects.

You've probably been thoroughly schooled in basic techniques of critical reading: Survey the table of contents; preread to get a sense of the whole; look up terms or concepts you don't know; and so on. It's good advice, especially for difficult scholarly or professional texts. Following is advice for using reading to boost your college-level writing.

Read to deepen what you already know.　Whatever your interests or experiences in life, you're not alone. Others have explored similar paths and probably written about them. Reading such work may give you confidence to bring your own thoughts to public attention. Whether your passion is tintype photography, skateboarding, or film fashions of the 1930s, you'll find excellent books on the subjects by browsing library catalogs or even just checking Amazon.com. O

For example, if you have worked at a fast-food franchise and know what goes on there, you might find a book like Eric Schlosser's *Fast Food Nation: The Dark Side of the All-American Meal* engrossing. You'll be drawn in because your experience makes you an informed critic. You can agree and disagree intelligently with Schlosser and, perhaps, see how his arguments might be extended or amended. At a minimum, you'll walk away from the book knowing even more about the fast-food industry and knowing the titles of dozens of additional sources, should you want to learn more.

Read above your level of knowledge.　It's comfortable to connect with people online who share your interests, but you'll often be chatting with people who don't know much more than you do. To find new ideas, push your reading to a higher and more demanding level. Spend some time with

refine your search
p. 406

books and articles you can't blow right through. You'll know you are there when you find yourself looking up names, adding terms to your vocabulary, and feeling humbled at what you still need to learn about a subject. That's when thinking occurs and ideas germinate.

Don't get in a rut.   It's easy to shut down intellectually by always foraging in the same topics—like baby boomers who haven't moved on from Dylan and the Beatles. But most of us now have access to technologies that connect us to endless paths of information. So why, especially when you're young, restrict your life to superficial topics of immediate current interest: sports, celebrities, fashion, music, or politics?

But even these topics can take on texture if you examine them critically. The car guy who tricks out Civics or Lancers might start wondering about the economics of motor sports or the auto industry. A fan of contemporary music might suddenly wonder how genres like punk or hip-hop developed and what inspired the artists who created them. The information is out there and worth pursuing.

Be curious.   You'll never be at a loss for ideas if you learn to read the world critically. *Critically* does not mean finding fault with everything but rather letting nothing you experience breeze by without scrutiny. You can *read* the architecture of your dorm room, the latest trends in women's politics, the changing menu options in local restaurants, and ponder their meanings. Why are there so few men in liberal-arts courses? What topics does your campus newspaper studiously avoid and why? How have your friends changed now that most come equipped with earbuds and cell phones? The world you inhabit is a text to be read and reread.

Read for claims, reasons, and evidence.   Browsing online has made many of us superficial readers. For serious texts, forget speed-reading and slow down. Read more systematically and analytically. ○ Begin by identifying the claims writers make and the reasons they make them. Then examine the assumptions they work from and the evidence they present.

If you don't have the time to read, you don't have the time or tools to write.
—Stephen King

understand argument
p. 68

Claims are the passages in a text where a writer makes an assertion, offers an argument, or presents a hypothesis, for which the writer will provide evidence.

Using a cell phone while driving is dangerous.

Playing video games can improve intelligence.

Some assertions early in a work may seem to state a thesis or goal for a project, but that's only one type of claim. Sentences that assert or advance a writer's ideas about a topic may occur just about anywhere in an article, report, or book. So look for claims in the topic sentences of paragraphs, in transitional sentences, or in summary materials at the end of sections or the entire work. (The exception may be formal scientific writing, in which the hypothesis, results, and discussion will occur in specific sections of an article.) O

Most major claims in a text are accompanied by supporting *reasons* either in the same sentence or in adjoining material. These reasons may be announced by expressions such as *because, if, to,* and *so.* Or look for more elaborate connective phrases that similarly imply a causal or logical link. The statement of a reason provides a rationale or a condition for accepting a claim.

Using a cell phone while driving is dangerous *because* distractions are a proven cause of auto accidents.

Playing video games can improve intelligence *if* they teach young gamers to make logical decisions quickly.

Supporting all important claims and reasons are *assumptions* or *premises.* In oral arguments when people say *I understand where you're coming from,* they signal that they get your assumptions. You want similar clarity when reading serious reports and arguments yourself, especially when claims are controversial or argumentative. Premises and assumptions are the values upon which writers and researchers base their work. They can be specific or general, conventional or highly controversial, such as the following.

We should discourage behaviors that contribute to accidents.

Improving intelligence is a desirable goal.

understand lab reports
p. 290

The physical world is organized by coherent and predictable principles.

Freedom is better than tyranny.

Developing the environment is better than preserving it.

Writers typically assume that they share basic premises with at least some of their readers. Or they take time to explain and defend their assumptions. As you read a serious work, try to locate or put into your own words its key assumptions—either stated outright in source material or, much more often, merely implied.

Finally, as you read, be sure that all major claims and assumptions are supported by *evidence* to confirm them. A claim without evidence attached is just that—a barefaced assertion no better than a child's "Oh yeah?" You should review evidence skeptically, always judging whether it is sufficient, complete, reliable, and unbiased. Does the source offer enough evidence to make a convincing case? Has the author done original research and drawn on respectable sources or, instead, relied on evidence that seems flimsy or anecdotal? These are questions to ask routinely and single-mindedly.

Read to expose logical fallacies.   Reasonable texts by honest writers have nothing to hide. They name names, identify sources, and generate appropriate emotions. They acknowledge weakness in their arguments and concede readily when the opposition has a point. Look for these qualities in the texts you read and use as sources.

However, be alert for the opposite strategy, often expressed through various logical fallacies. *Fallacies* are rhetorical moves that corrupt solid reasoning—the verbal equivalent of sleight of hand. When you read a text, look for the following devices and remain aware that they can undermine the credibility of a text.

- **Appeals to false authority.** Be suspicious of writers who may not actually have the knowledge, authority, or credentials to deal with their subjects: *I'm not a doctor, but I play one on television.*

- **Dogmatism.** Writers fall back on dogmatism whenever they want to give the impression, usually false, that they control the party line on an issue and know what all the correct answers are. The tip-off for dogmatism can be the phrase *No serious person would disagree.* . . .

● **Ad hominem attacks.** Writers sometimes attempt to bolster their own credentials or authority by attacking the character of their opponents when character isn't an issue in the argument. They may even resort to name-calling or character assassination.

● **Either/or choices.** When complex issues are reduced to simple choices, look closer. Be deeply suspicious whenever you encounter some version of this collocation: *Either we . . . or we will surely.* . . . Also, writers reducing complicated issues to black-and-white will typically present one side as completely wrong.

"Either you left the TV on downstairs or we have whales again."

- **Scare tactics.** An argument that makes its appeal chiefly by raising fears—usually of the unknown—is automatically suspect. Examine such a claim carefully to see whether its warnings are backed by facts and good reasons. If not, point out the deficiency or don't cite the source.

- **Sentimental appeals.** Maybe it's fair for the Humane Society to decorate its pleas for cash with pictures of puppies, but you can see how the tactic might be abused. Be wary, too, of language that pushes buttons the same way, *oohing* and *aahing* readers out of their best judgment.

- **Hasty generalizations.** It is remarkably tempting to draw conclusions from one or two examples or instances, particularly when they are dramatic and fit the writer's preconceived notions. Ask questions whenever a writer seems too eager to make his or her point based on scant evidence.

- **Faulty causality.** Just because two events or phenomena occur close together in time doesn't mean that one caused the other. (The Tigers didn't start hitting *because* you put on the lucky boxers.) People are fond of leaping to such easy conclusions, but causal situations involving issues of science, health, politics, and culture are almost always too complicated to explain simply. Review closely any texts that push readers to make quick judgments. ○

© The New Yorker Collection 2006 Ariel Molvig from cartoonbank.com. All Rights Reserved.

understand causal
analysis p. 128

- **Equivocations and evasions.** *Equivocations* are lies that look like truths; *evasions* simply avoid the truth entirely. You'll find the statements of politicians and bureaucracies filled with such interesting uses of language: "It depends on what the meaning of the word *is* is." When you find these kinds of examples, take them apart to figure out what's really being said—or not said.

- **Straw men.** *Straw men* are easy or habitual targets that a writer aims at to win an argument. Often the issue in such an attack has long been defused or discredited: for example, welfare recipients driving Cadillacs; immigrants taking jobs from hard-working citizens; the rich not paying a fair share of taxes. Writers who resort to straw-man arguments may not have much else in their arsenals.

- **Slippery-slope arguments.** Take one wrong step off the righteous path and you'll slide all the way down the hill: That's the warning that a slippery-slope argument makes. They aren't always inaccurate, but be wary, particularly when the imagined chain of events begins to sound plausible. Will buying an SUV really doom the planet? Maybe not.

- **Bandwagon appeals.** People who want to be in on the latest trend or fad are easy targets, and advertisers know it. But be alert for feeding frenzies in the media or public arena too. When a writer suggests that it's time to stop debate and jump aboard the bandwagon, push back.

- **Faulty analogies.** Similes and analogies are worth applauding when they illuminate ideas or make them comprehensible or memorable. But analogies deserve more scrutiny when they have serious implications. Calling a military action either "another Vietnam" or a "crusade" might raise serious issues, as does comparing one's opponents to "Commies" or Nazis. Be skeptical of writers who use such tactics.

Experts 20

Forget about *expert* as an intimidating word. When you need help with your writing, you should consult knowledgeable people who either know more about your subject than you do or more about how to handle the project. Admittedly, those answers may come from different people, but that's not a problem: The more people you talk to, the better.

Knowledgeable people can get you on track quickly, confirming the merit of your topic ideas, cutting through issues irrelevant to your work, and directing you to the best sources.

ask for help

Talk with your instructor.   Don't be timid. Instructors hold office hours to answer your questions, especially about assignments. Save yourself time and, perhaps, much grief by getting feedback early on your ideas and topic. It's better to learn immediately that your thesis is hopeless, before you compose a first draft.

Just as important, your instructor might help you see aspects of a topic you hadn't noticed or direct you to indispensable sources. Don't try to write a paper only to please instructors, but you'd be foolish to ignore their counsel.

Take your ideas to the writing center.   Many student writers think the only time to use a campus writing center is when their teacher returns a draft on life support. Most writing center tutors prefer not to be seen as emergency room personnel. So they are eager to help at the start of a project, when you're still developing ideas and thinking about strategies. Tutors may not be experts on your subject, but they have seen enough bad papers to offer sensible advice for focusing a topic, shaping a thesis, or adapting a subject to an audience. ○ They also recognize when you're so clueless that you need to talk with your instructor pronto.

Find local experts.   Don't consult an expert for information you could find easily yourself in the library or online: Save human contacts for when you need serious help on a major writing project—a senior thesis, an important story for a campus periodical, a public presentation on a controversial subject. But then do take advantage of the human resources you have. Campuses are thick with knowledgeable people and that doesn't just include faculty in their various disciplines. Staff and administrative personnel at your school can advise you on everything from trends in college admissions to local crime statistics.

Look to the local community for expertise and advice as well. Is there a paper to be written about declining audiences for feature films? You couldn't call Steven Spielberg and get through, but you could chat with a few local theater owners or managers to learn what they think about the business. Their perceptions might change the direction of your project.

Check with librarians.   Campus librarians have lots of experience helping writers find information, steering you toward fertile topics and away from ideas that may not have much intellectual standing. They can't be as specific or directive as, for example, your instructor, but they have just as firm a grasp on the resources available for a project and what sorts of topic ideas the library's resources will and will not support.

Chat with peers.   Peers aren't really experts, but an honest classroom conversation among fellow students can be an eye-opening experience. You'll likely see a wide spectrum of opinions (if the discussion is frank) and even be surprised by objections to your ideas that you hadn't anticipated.

develop a thesis
p. 336

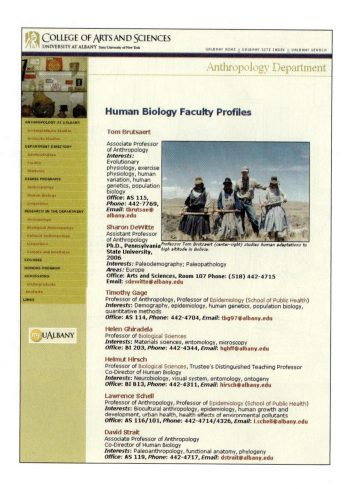

Colleges and universities often provide lists of faculty and staff with special expertise in their fields.

Peers often have a surprising range of knowledge and, if the group is diverse, your friends will bring a breadth of life experiences to the conversation. You might be eager to champion advances in medical technology, but someone from a community where hospitals can't afford high-tech gear might add a wrinkle to your thinking.

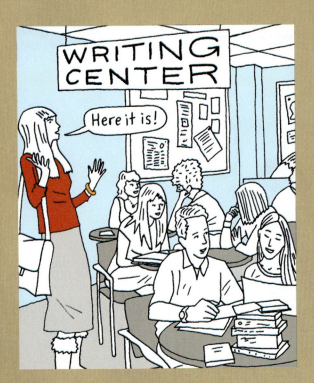

1 Bring materials with you, including the assignment, previous drafts or outlines, comments from your instructor if you have any, a pen, and a notebook.

2 Be actively involved during the session, and arrive with specific goals in mind. Your tutor may ask questions about your writing process and your paper. Be prepared to think about and respond to your tutor's suggestions.

3 Keep revising. While the tutor may be able to help you with some aspects of your writing, you are ultimately responsible for the finished paper—and your grade.

21 Writer's Block

tackle
hard stuff

Waiting until the last minute to write a paper hasn't been defined as a medical problem yet. But give it time. Already a condition called *executive dysfunction* describes the inability of some children and adults to plan, organize, pace, and complete tasks. No doubt we've all experienced some of its symptoms, describing the state as *procrastination* when it comes to doing the laundry and *writer's block* when it applies to finishing papers on time.

Getting writing done isn't hard because the process is painful, but rather because it is so fragile and vulnerable to ridiculous excuses and distractions. Who hasn't vacuumed a floor or washed a car rather than composing a paragraph? Writing also comes with no guarantees, no necessary connection between labor put in and satisfactory pages churned out. Like baseball, writing is a game without time limits. When a paper isn't going well, you can stretch into fruitless twelfth and thirteenth innings with no end in sight. And if you do finish, readers may not like what you have done—even when you know the work is solid, based on honest reading, observation, and research. Such concerns are enough to give anyone writer's block.

So what do you do when you'd rather crack walnuts with your teeth than write a term paper?

Break the project into parts.   Getting started is usually the hard part for writers simply because the project taken as a whole seems overwhelming. Even a simple one-page position paper can ruin a whole weekend, and a term paper—with its multiple drafts, abstract, notes, bibliography, tables, and graphs—stretches beyond the pale.

But what if, instead of thinking about how much time and energy the whole project will take, you divide it into manageable stages? Then you can do the work in chunks and celebrate the success that comes from completing each part. That position paper might be broken down into two, maybe three, more convenient stages: doing the assigned reading; brainstorming the paper; writing the page required. The same procedure makes a research paper less intimidating: You have more parts to manage, but you also have a strategy to finish them.

Set manageable goals.   Unless you are very disciplined, writing projects absorb all the time available to them. Worse, you'll likely expend more energy fretting than working. To gain control, set reasonable goals for completing the project and stick to them. In other words, don't dedicate a whole Saturday to preparing your résumé or working up a lab report; instead, commit yourself to the full and uninterrupted two hours the task will really take if you sit down and concentrate.

If you have trouble estimating how much time a project may take, consider that it is better to set a goal than to face an open-ended commitment. That's one good reason both teachers and publishers set deadlines.

Create a calendar.   For complicated assignments that extend over weeks or even months, create a calendar or timeline and stick with it. ◯ First break the task into parts and estimate how much time each stage of the paper or other project will take. Knowing your own work habits, you can draw on past experience with similar assignments to construct a levelheaded plan. You'll feel better once you've got a road map leading to completion.

Don't draw up so elaborate a schedule that you build in failure by trying to manage too many events. Assume that some stages, especially research

> Inspiration is wonderful when it happens, but the writer must develop an approach for the rest of the time. . . . The wait is simply too long.

— Leonard Bernstein

plan a project
p. 400

or drafting, may take more time than you originally expect. But do stick to your schedule, even if it means starting a draft with research still remaining or cutting off the drafting process to allow time for thorough revision.

Limit distractions.   Put yourself in a place that encourages writing and minimizes any temptations that might pull you away from your work. Schedule a specific time for writing and give it priority over all other activities, from paying your bills to feeding the dog. (On second thought, feed that dog to stop the barking.) Shut down your e-mail accounts, turn off the cell phone, shuffle from Green Day to R. Carlos Nakai on the iPod, start writing, and don't stop for an hour.

Do the parts you like first.   Movies aren't filmed in sequence and papers don't have to be written that way either. Compose those parts of a project that interest you most or feel ready to go. Then later you can work on the transitions to make the paper feel seamless, the way an editor cuts disparate scenes into a coherent film. Once you have portions of it already composed you'll be more inclined to continue working on a paper: The project suddenly seems manageable.

Write a zero draft.   When you really are blocked, try a zero draft—that is, a version of the paper composed in one sitting, virtually nonstop. The process may resemble freewriting, but this time you aren't trawling for ideas. You're ready to write, having done the necessary brainstorming, reading, and research. You might even have a thesis and an outline. What you lack is the confidence to turn this preparation into coherent sentences. So turn off your inhibitions by writing relentlessly, without pausing to reread and review your stuff. Keep at it for several hours if need be. Imagine you're writing an essay exam. ○

The draft you produce won't be elegant (though you might surprise yourself), and some spots might be rough indeed. But keep pushing until you've finished a full draft, from introduction to conclusion. When you're done, put this version aside, delaying any revision for a few hours or even days. Then, instead of facing an empty tablet or screen, you have full pages of prose to work with.

Reward yourself.   People respond remarkably well to incentives, so promise yourself some prize correlated to the writing task you face. Finishing a position paper is probably worth a personal-size pizza. A term paper might earn you dinner and a movie. A dissertation is worth a used Honda Civic.

understand essay
exams p. 254

Shaping & Drafting

part four

4

Need help developing your ideas? See page 346.   /   Need style help? See page 366.

22 Thesis

develop a thesis

A *thesis* is a statement in which a writer affirms or defends the specific idea that will focus or organize a paper. Typically, the thesis appears in an opening paragraph or section, but it may also emerge as the paper unfolds. In some cases, it may not be stated in classic form until the very conclusion. A thesis can be complex enough to require several sentences to explain, or a single sentence might suffice. But a thesis will be in the writing somewhere.

Offering a thesis is a move as necessary and, eventually, as instinctive to a writer as stepping on a clutch before shifting is to drivers. No thesis, no forward motion.

How do you write and frame a thesis? Consider the following advice.

Write a complete sentence.   Phrases can identify topic areas, even intriguing ones, but they don't make the assertions or claims that provoke thinking and require support. Sentences do. ○ None of the following phrases comes close to providing direction for a paper.

> Polygamy in the United States
>
> Reasons for global warming
>
> Economist Steven D. Levitt's controversial theory about declining crime rates

common errors
p. 524

Make a significant claim or assertion. *Significant* here means that the notion provokes discussion or inquiry. Give readers substance or controversy—in other words, a reason to spend time with your writing.

> Until communities recognize that polygamy still exists in parts of the United States, girls and young women will be exploited by the practice.

> Global warming won't stop until industrial nations either lower their standards of living or acknowledge the inevitability of nuclear power.

Write a declarative sentence, not a question. Questions may focus attention, but they are not assertions. So, while you might use a question to introduce a topic, don't rely on it to state your claim. A humdrum question acting as a thesis can provoke simplistic responses. There's always the danger, too, that in offering your thesis as a question, you invite strong reactions from readers—and not the ones you want. But introduce an idea as a statement and you gain more control. One exception to this guideline: Provocative questions can often help structure personal and exploratory writing.

Expect your thesis to mature. Your initial thesis will likely grow more complicated as you learn more about your subject. That's natural. But even at the outset, resist the notion that a thesis is simply a statement that breaks a subject into three parts. Conventional theses too often read like shopping lists, with few connections between the ideas presented. Just putting the claims in such a statement into a relationship often makes for a more compelling thesis. The items in olive type do that job in the second example below.

ORIGINAL THESIS

Crime in the United States has declined because more people are in prison, the population is growing older, and DNA testing has made it harder to get away with murder.

REVISED THESIS

It is much more likely that crime in the United States has declined because more people are in prison than because the population is growing older or DNA testing has made it harder to get away with murder.

Introduce a thesis early in a project.   This sound guideline is especially relevant for academic term papers. Instructors will usually want to know up front what the point of a paper will be, especially in reports and some arguments. Whether phrased as a single sentence or several, a thesis typically follows an introductory paragraph or two. Here's the thesis (highlighted in yellow) of Andrew Kleinfeld and Judith Kleinfeld's essay "Go Ahead, Call Us Cowboys," bringing up the rear of an opening paragraph that explains the context for their claim.

> Everywhere, Americans are called *cowboys*. On foreign tongues, the reference to America's Western rural laborers is an insult. Cowboys, we are told, plundered the earth, arrogantly rode roughshod over neighbors, and were addicted to mindless violence. So some of us hang our heads in shame. We shouldn't. The cowboy is in fact our Homeric hero, an archetype that sticks because there's truth in it.

Or state a thesis late in a project.   In high school, you may have heard that the thesis statement is *always* the last sentence in the first paragraph. That may be so in conventional five-paragraph essays, but you'll rarely be asked to follow so predictable a pattern in college or elsewhere.

In fact, it is not unusual, especially in some arguments, for a paper to build toward a thesis—and that statement may not appear until the final paragraph or sentence. ○ Such a strategy makes sense when a claim might not be convincing or rhetorically effective if stated baldly at the opening of the piece. Bret Stephens uses this strategy in an essay entitled "Just Like Stalingrad" to debunk frequent comparisons between President George W. Bush and either Hitler or Stalin. Stephens's real concern turns out to be not these exaggerated comparisons themselves but rather what happens to language when it is abused by sloppy writers. The final two paragraphs of his essay summarize this case and, arguably, lead up to a thesis in the very last sentence of the essay—more rhetorically convincing there because it comes as something of a surprise.

> Care for language is more than a concern for purity. When one describes President Bush as a fascist, what words remain for real fascists? When one describes Fallujah as Stalingrad-like, how can we express, in the words that remain to the language, what Stalingrad was like?

understand arguments
p. 68

George Orwell wrote that the English language "becomes ugly and inaccurate because our thoughts are foolish, but the slovenliness of our language makes it easier for us to have foolish thoughts." In taking care with language, we take care of ourselves.

—*Wall Street Journal*, June 23, 2004

Write a thesis to fit your audience and purpose.

Almost everything you write will have a purpose and a point (see following table), but not every piece will have a formal thesis. In professional and scientific writing, readers want to know your claim immediately. For persuasive and exploratory writing, you might prefer to keep readers intrigued or have them track the path of your thinking, and delay the thesis until later.

Type of Assignment	Thesis or Point
Narrative	Usually implied, not stated. (See thesis example on p. 8.)
Report	Thesis usually previews material or explains its purpose. (See thesis example on p. 60.)
Argument	Thesis makes an explicit and arguable claim. (See thesis example on p. 73.)
Evaluation	Thesis makes an explicit claim of value based on criteria of evaluation. (See thesis example on p. 105.)
Causal analysis	Thesis asserts or denies a causal relationship, based on an analysis of evidence. (See thesis example on p. 131.)
Proposal	Thesis offers a proposal for action. (See thesis example on p. 165.)
Literary analysis	Thesis explains the point of the analysis. (See thesis example on p. 189.)
Rhetorical analysis	Thesis explains the point of the analysis. (See thesis example on p. 236.)
Essay examination	Thesis previews the entire answer, like a mini-outline. (See thesis example on p. 258.)
Position paper	Thesis makes specific assertion about reading or issue raised in class. (See thesis example on p. 263.)
E-mail	Subject line may function as thesis or title. (See thesis example on p. 268.)
Business letter	Thesis states the intention for writing. (See thesis example on p. 276.)
Résumé	"Career objective" may function as a thesis. (See thesis example on p. 282.)
Personal statement	May state an explicit purpose or thesis or lead readers to inferences about qualifications. (See thesis example on p. 287.)
Lab report	Thesis describes purpose of experiment. (See thesis example on p. 293.)
Oral report	Introduction or preview slide describes purpose. (See thesis example on p. 301–02.)

23 Organization

shape your work

To describe the organization of their projects, writers often use metaphors or other figures of speech. They visualize the elements of their work linked by chains, frames, patterns, or even skeletons. Such structural concepts help writers keep their emerging ideas on track, giving them shape and consistency. Effective organization also makes life easier for readers who come fresh to any paper or project, wondering how its words and ideas will fit together.

In Parts 1 and 2, you'll find specific suggestions for structuring a wide variety of writing genres. Following is some general advice about organizing your work.

Examine model documents. Many types of writing are highly conventional—which simply means that they follow predictable patterns and formulas. So study the structure of several examples of any genre you're expected to compose. Some structural devices are immediately obvious, such as headings or introductory and concluding sections. But look for more subtle moves too—for example, many editorials first describe a problem, then blame someone for it, and finally make a comment or offer a comparison. Working with models of a genre will point your project in the right direction.

Sketch out a plan or sequence. Even if you are brainstorming, starting with a rough plan helps give a project direction and purpose. A scratch (or informal) outline or similar device puts your initial ideas on paper, suggests relationships between them (sequence, similarity, difference), and perhaps suggests obvious flaws or omissions. ○ Just as important, creating a structure makes a writing project suddenly seem more doable because you've broken a complex task into smaller, more manageable parts.

Visualize structure when appropriate.   Technology can make it easier to organize your project. Consider how deftly you can move the slides in a PowerPoint project until you find the most effective order. Pen and paper can work just as well for visualizing the relationships between elements in a project, whether they are separate events on a flowchart, divergent features in a comparison/contrast piece, or the administrative structure of a complex organization. Seeing these items at a glance can quickly suggest ways of organizing everything from a paper to a Web site.

Provide clear steps or signals for readers.   Just because you know how the parts of your paper or project fit together, don't assume readers will. You have to give them cues—which come in various forms, including titles, headings, captions, and especially transitional words and phrases. For example, in a narrative you might include transitional words to mark the passage of time (*next, then, before, afterward*). Or if you organize a project according to a principle of magnitude, readers need signals that clearly show a change from *best* to *worst*; *cheapest* to *most expensive*; *most common species* to *endangered*. And if you are writing to inform or report, you may also rely heavily on visuals to help make your point. ○

Deliver on your commitments.   This is a basic principle of organization. If, for example, you promise in an introductory paragraph to offer three reasons in support of a claim, you need to offer three clearly identifiable reasons in that paper or readers will feel that they missed something. But commitments are broader than that: Narratives ordinarily lead somewhere, perhaps to a climax; editorials offer opinions; proposals offer and defend new ideas; evaluations make judgments. You can depart from these structural expectations, but you should do so knowing what readers expect and anticipating how they might react to your straying from the formula.

Your ideas won't march in rows like these ants, so you'll need a plan for your work.

order ideas
p. 342

work with visuals
p. 504

24 Outlines

Outlines are supposed to make writing easier, not harder, as they help you put ideas in manageable form. And you'll feel more confident when you begin with a plan. The trick is to start simple and let outlines evolve to fit your needs.

order ideas

Begin with scratch outlines.   Many writers prefer working first with scratch, or informal, outlines—the verbal equivalent of the clever mechanical idea hurriedly sketched on a cocktail napkin. In fact, the analogy is especially apt because good ideas often do evolve from simple, sometimes crude, notions that begin to make sense only when seen on paper. Both the Internet and the structure of the DNA molecule began with the visual equivalents of scratch outlines.

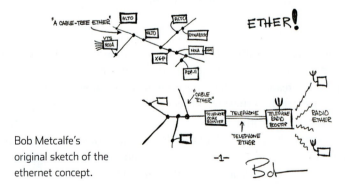

Bob Metcalfe's original sketch of the ethernet concept.

List key ideas.   Write down your preliminary thoughts so you can see what they are exactly, eliminating any that obviously overlap. Keep these notes brief but specific, using words and phrases rather than complete sentences. Your initial scratch outline will likely resemble a mildly edited brainstorming list, like the one that follows.

Fuel-efficient vehicles

Hybrids
Electric cars haven't worked well
Europeans prefer diesels
Strengths and weaknesses
Costs might be high
Mechanically reliable?

Once you have ideas, begin applying the three principles that make outlining such a powerful tool of organization: *relationship*, *subordination*, and *sequence*.

Look for relationships.   Examine the initial items on your list and try grouping *like* with *like*—or look for opposites and contrasts. Experiment with various arrangements or clusters. In the brief sketch outline above, for example, you might decide that the items fall into two distinct categories. The three types of fuel-efficient cars are obviously related, while the remaining items represent aspects of these vehicles.

Hybrids	Strengths
Electric cars	Weaknesses
Diesels	Costs
	Reliability

Subordinate ideas.   Some ideas belong not only grouped with others but also under them—that is to say, they belong to a smaller subset within a larger set. Outlines are built on this principle of subordination or hierarchy: You are systematically dividing a subject into topics and subtopics.

For instance, looking again at those simple groupings of fuel-efficient vehicles, you could argue that *cost* and *reliability* are items that fit better under either *strengths* or *weaknesses*. They are aspects of these larger categories. So you remove them from the outline for the moment.

You might notice, too, that your notes so far suggest a comparison/contrast structure for your project. (See "Compare and contrast" on p. 114 of Chapter 4, "Evaluation.") Deciding to replace *strengths* and *weaknesses* with the slightly more aggressive terms *advantages* and *disadvantages*, you sketch out a rather more complex outline.

> <u>Fuel-efficient vehicles</u>
> Advantages
>   Hybrids
>   Electric cars
>   Diesels
> Disadvantages
>   Hybrids
>   Electric cars
>   Diesels

Decide on a sequence.   Now that you've moved from an initial list of ideas to a basic design, consider in which order to present the material. You might arrange the items chronologically or by magnitude. Or your order may be determined rhetorically—by how you want readers to respond.

Let's say you drive a Prius and have done enough research to believe that hybrids represent the best option for saving on fuel costs. So you arrange the paper to end on that note, understanding that readers are most likely to remember what they read last. Reading the end of your paper, the audience will focus on the advantages of gas-electric hybrid vehicles.

> A. Disadvantages of fuel-efficient vehicles
>   1. Electrics
>   2. Diesels
>   3. Gas-electric hybrids
> B. Advantages of fuel-efficient vehicles
>   1. Electrics
>   2. Diesels
>   3. Gas-electric hybrids

Move up to a formal outline.   You may be required to submit a formal outline with your final paper. By adhering to the following outline conventions, you can ferret out weaknesses in your thinking. ○

- Align the headings at every level (see example).

- Present at least two items at every heading level (I, A, and 1). If you can't find a second item to match the first in a new level of heads, perhaps the new level isn't needed.

- Present all items (except the thesis) as complete and parallel statements (not questions), properly punctuated.

- Place a topic sentence above the outline, underlined or italicized. That topic sentence sitting atop the project may keep you from wandering off-subject.

Thesis: <u>Though all fuel-efficient vehicles have technological strengths and weaknesses, hybrids currently represent the best option for drivers today.</u>

I. Currently available fuel-efficient vehicles have different technological problems.
    A. Electric vehicles lack versatility.
        1. Their batteries limit them to city use, preferably in flat regions.
        2. Their electric batteries are heavy, expensive, and slow to charge.
    B. Diesel vehicles can be truck-like.
        1. Their emissions are laden with harmful particulates.
        2. They smoke when cold.
        3. Their fuel is smelly and toxic.
    C. Gas-electric hybrids are technologically risky.
        1. They are expensive.
        2. Their dual propulsion systems (gas and electric) are complex.
II. Fuel-efficient vehicles have significant strengths.
    A. Electric vehicles are simple and civilized machines.
        1. They emit no measurable pollution where they are used.
        2. Their motors are almost silent and free of vibration.
    B. Diesels are robust vehicles suitable for all road conditions.
        1. Their engines are based on well-proven and robust technology.
        2. They use fuel efficiently.
    C. Gas-electric hybrids combine advantages of other fuel-efficient vehicles.
        1. They work like electric vehicles in the city.
        2. They are as strong as diesels on the highway.
        3. They combine well-proven electric and internal-combustion technologies.

develop a thesis
p. 336

25 Paragraphs

**develop
ideas**

Paragraphs are a practical invention, created to make long continuous blocks of writing easier to read by dividing them up. Because they give writers a physical way to shape ideas and transmit them to readers, paragraphs are a powerful tool. You've heard many rules and definitions over the years, but the fact is that paragraphs exist to help you develop and structure your ideas, not the other way around. Here are some helpful ways to think about them.

Make sure paragraphs lead somewhere.   Sometimes you'll use an explicit topic sentence to state your point and introduce a claim that the rest of your paragraph will develop. ○ But, just as often, you may wait until the concluding sentences to make your point, or you may weave a key idea into the fabric of the entire paragraph (as in the first paragraph of the example below). Whatever your strategy, all paragraphs should do significant work: introduce a subject, move a narrative forward, offer a new argument or claim, provide support for a claim already made, contradict another point, amplify an idea, furnish more examples, even bring discussion to an end. It has to do *something* that readers see as purposeful and connected to what comes before and after.

For instance, reviewing the third album of the rock band Coldplay, music critic Jon Pareles leads his readers through an opening paragraph demanding enough to try any rocker's patience. Where's he going with this? But then he delivers his

346

develop a thesis
p. 336

deathblow in a second, much shorter, paragraph. Suddenly, you have no doubt where Pareles stands—and probably want to read the entire review, even if you like the band.

> There's nothing wrong with self-pity. As a spur to songwriting, it's right up there with lust, anger, and greed, and probably better than the remaining deadly sins. There's nothing wrong, either, with striving for musical grandeur, using every bit of skill and studio illusion to create a sound large enough to get lost in. Male sensitivity, a quality that's under siege in a pop culture full of unrepentant bullying and machismo, shouldn't be dismissed out of hand, no matter how risible it can be in practice. And building a sound on the lessons of past bands is virtually unavoidable.
>
> But put them all together and they add up to Coldplay, the most insufferable band of the decade.
>
> —"The Case Against Coldplay," *New York Times*, June 5, 2005

Develop ideas adequately.   Instructors who insist that paragraphs run a minimum number of sentences (say 6–10) are usually just tired of students who don't back up claims with details and evidence. ○ In fact, most writers don't count sentences when they build paragraphs. Instead, they develop a sense for paragraph length, matching the swell of their ideas to the habits of their intended readers.

Consider the following paragraph, which describes the last moments of the final Apollo moon mission in December 1972. The paragraph might be reduced to a single sentence: *All that remained of the 363-foot Saturn V Apollo 17 launch vehicle was a 9-foot capsule recovered in the ocean.* But what would be lost? The pleasure of the full paragraph resides in the details the writer assembles to support the final sentence, which contains his point.

> A powerful Sikorsky Sea King helicopter, already hovering nearby as they [the *Apollo 17* crew] hit the water, retrieved the astronauts and brought them to the carrier, where the spacecraft was recovered shortly later. The recovery crew saw not a gleaming instrument of exotic perfection, but a blasted, torn, and ragged survivor, its titanic strength utterly exhausted, a husk now a shell. The capsule they hauled out of the ocean was all that remained of the *Apollo 17* Saturn V. The journey had spent, incinerated, smashed, or blistered into atoms every other part of the colossal, 363-foot white rocket, leaving only this burnt and brutalized 9-foot capsule. A great

understand argument
p. 68

△

shining army had set out over the horizon, and a lone squadron had returned, savaged beyond recognition, collapsing into the arms of its rescuers, dead. Such was the price of reaching for another world.

—David West Reynolds, *Apollo: The Epic Journey to the Moon*

Organize paragraphs logically.   It would be surprising if paragraphs didn't borrow structural strategies used by full essays: thesis and support, sequence, and division. But ideas drive the shape of paragraphs, not patterns of organization. Most writers don't pause to wonder whether their next paragraph should follow a narrative or cause-effect plan. They just write it, making sure it makes a point and offers sufficient evidence to keep readers engaged.

In fact, individual paragraphs in any longer piece can be organized many different ways. And because paragraphs are relatively short, you usually see their patterns unfold right before your eyes. Following are some paragraphs from an essay by Jon Katz entitled "Do Dogs Think?" Each uses the structure Katz needs at that given moment.

Narrative paragraph describes changes in Blue's behavior.

Blue, Heather's normally affectionate and obedient Rottweiler, began tearing up the house shortly after Heather went back to work as an accountant after several years at home. The contents of the trash cans were strewn all over the house. A favorite comforter was destroyed. Then Blue began peeing all over Heather's expensive new living-room carpet and systematically ripped through cables and electrical wires.

Katz uses *causal* pattern to explore Blue's behavioral problem.

Lots of dogs get nervous when they don't know what's expected of them, and when they get anxious, they can also grow restless. Blue hadn't had to occupy time alone before. Dogs can get unnerved by this. They bark, chew, scratch, destroy. Getting yelled at and punished later doesn't help: The dog probably knows it's doing something wrong, but it has no idea what. Since there's nobody around to correct behaviors when the dog is alone, how could the dog know which behavior is the problem? Which action was wrong?

Paragraph uses simple *statement-proof* structure.

I don't believe that dogs act out of spite or that they can plot retribution, though countless dog owners swear otherwise. To punish or deceive requires the perpetrator to understand that his victim or object has a particular point of view and to consciously work to manipulate or thwart it. That requires mental processes dogs don't have.

Why will Clementine come instantly if she's looking at me, but not if she's sniffing deer droppings? Is it because she's being stubborn or, as many people tell me, going through "adolescence"? Or because, when following her keen predatory instincts, she simply doesn't hear me? Should my response be to tug at her leash or yell? Maybe I should be sure we've established eye contact before I give her a command, or better yet, offer a liver treat as an alternative to whatever's distracting her. But how do I establish eye contact when her nose is buried? Can I cluck or bark? Use a whistle or hoot like an owl?

I've found that coughing, of all things, fascinates her, catches her attention, and makes her head swivel, after which she responds. If you walk with us, you will hear me clearing my throat repeatedly. What can I say? It works. She looks at me, comes to me, gets rewarded.

—Slate.com, October 6, 2005

These two paragraphs follow *problem-solution* structure common in *proposal* arguments.

Design paragraphs for readability. Paragraph breaks work best when they coincide with shifts or breaks within the writing itself. Readers understand that your thoughts have moved in some different direction. But paragraphs are often at the mercy of a text's physical environment as well. When you read a news items on the Web, the short paragraphs used in these single-column stories look fine. But hit the "print this article" link and the text suddenly sprawls across the screen, becoming difficult to read.

The point? You can manipulate the length and shape of paragraphs to suit the environment in which your words will appear.

Use paragraphs to manage transitions. Paragraphs often provide direction in a paper. An opening paragraph can be used to set the scene in a narrative or to preview the content in a report. ⭕ You might occasionally use very brief paragraphs—sometimes just a sentence or two long—to punctuate a piece by drawing attention to a turn in your thinking or offering a strong judgment. You've likely seen paragraphs that consist of nothing more than an indignant "Nonsense!" or a sarcastic "Nuts" or "Go figure." There's a risk in penning a paragraph with so much attitude, but it's an option when the occasion calls for it. In longer papers, you might need full transitional paragraphs to summarize what has already been covered or to point the project in new directions.

shape a beginning
p. 354

26 Transitions

connect ideas

What exactly makes words, sentences, and ideas flow from paragraph to paragraph as fluidly as Tour de France champion Lance Armstrong cycling through the French Alps? *Transitional words and phrases,* many writers would reply—thinking of words such as *and, but, however, neither . . . nor, first . . . second . . . third*, and so on. Placed where readers need them, these connecting words make a paper read smoothly. But they are only part of the story.

Almost any successful piece of writing is held together by more devices than most writers can consciously juggle. Fortunately, a few of the devices—such as connections between pronouns and their referents—almost take care of themselves. Here are some guidelines for making smooth transitions between ideas in paragraphs and sections of your writing.

Common Transitions

Connection or Consequence	Contrast	Correlation	Sequence or Time	Indication
and	but	if . . . then	first . . . second	this
or	yet	either . . . or	and then	that
so	however	from . . . to	initially	there
therefore	nevertheless		subsequently	for instance
moreover	on the contrary		before	for example
consequently	despite		after	in this case
hence	still		until	
	although		next	
			in conclusion	

Use appropriate transitional words and phrases.   There's nothing complicated or arcane about them: You'll recognize every word in any list of transitions. But be aware that they have different functions and uses, with subtle differences even between words as close in meaning as *but* and *yet*.

Transitional words are often found at the beginnings of sentences and paragraphs, simply because that's the place where readers expect a little guidance. There are no rules, per se, for positioning transitions—though they can be set off from the rest of the sentence with commas.

Use the right word or phrase to show time or sequence.   Readers often need specific words or phrases to help keep events in order. Such expressions can simply mark off stages: *first, second, third*. Or they might help readers keep track of more complicated passages of time.

Use sentence structure to connect ideas.   When you build sentences with similar structures, readers will infer that the ideas in them are related. Devices you can use to make this kind of linkage include *parallelism* and *repetition*.

In the following example, the final paragraph in Catherine Crier's *The Case Against Lawyers*, you can see both strategies at work. Though its structure is more elaborate than you would ordinarily use, the paragraph brings a lengthy book to a rousing conclusion. Parallel items are highlighted.

> Despite the horror, September 11 was an amazing example of the best we can be. It was not rules or regulations that made us great that day. It certainly wasn't lawyers or lawsuits. It was just an emotion and feeling of unity that gave us strength in the face of such tragedy. It is time to do more than fly the flag. We must understand and proclaim American principles that have given life to hopes and dreams around the world. We must actively rescue our liberties from those who would tyrannize us. Finally, we must restore the rule of law to its proper place as our safeguard in a government created of and by and for the American people.

Pay attention to nouns and pronouns.   Understated transitions in a piece can occur between pronouns and their antecedents, but make sure the relationships between the nouns and pronouns are clear. ○ And, fortunately, readers usually don't mind encountering a pronoun over and over—except maybe *I*. Note how effortlessly Adam Nicolson moves between *George Abbot, he,* and *man* in the following paragraph from *God's Secretaries* (2003), in which the writer describes one of the men responsible for the King James translation of the Bible:

> George Abbot was perhaps the ugliest of them all, a morose, intemperate man, whose portraits exude a sullen rage. Even in death, he was portrayed on his tomb in Holy Trinity, Guilford, as a man of immense weight, with heavy, wrinkled brow and coldly open, staring eyes. He looks like a bruiser, a man of such conviction and seriousness that anyone would think twice about crossing him. What was it that made George Abbot so angry?

Use synonyms.   Simply by repeating a noun from sentence to sentence, you make an obvious and logical connection within a paper—whether you are naming an object, an idea, or a person. To avoid monotony, vary terms you have to use frequently. But don't strain with archaic or inappropriate synonyms which will distract the reader.

common errors
p. 524

Note the sensible variants on the word *trailer* in the following paragraph.

Hype and hysteria have always been a part of movie advertising, but the frenzy of film trailers today follows a visual style first introduced by music videos in the 1980s. The quick cut is everything, accompanied by a deafening soundtrack. Next time you go to a film, study the three or four previews that precede the main feature. How are these teasers constructed? What are their common features? What emotions or reactions do they raise in you? What might trailers say about the expectations of audiences today?

Use physical devices for transitions.   You know all the ways movies manage transitions between scenes, from quick cuts to various kinds of dissolves. Writing has fewer visual techniques to mark transitions, but they are important. Titles and headings in lab reports, for instance, let your reader know precisely when you are moving from "Method" to "Results" to "Discussion." ○ In books, you'll encounter chapter breaks as well as divisions within chapters, sometimes marked by asterisks or perhaps a blank space. Seeing these markers, readers expect that the narration is changing in some way. Even the numbers in a list or shaded boxes in a magazine can be effective transitional devices, moving readers from one place to another.

Read a draft aloud to locate weak transitions.   The best way to test your transitions in a paper or project may be to listen to yourself. As you read, mark every point in the paper where you pause, stumble, or find yourself adding a transitional word or phrase not in the original text. Record even the smallest bobble because tiny slips have a way of cascading into bigger problems.

understand lab reports
p. 290

27 Introductions

shape a beginning

An introduction has to grab and hold a reader's attention, but that's not all. It also must introduce a topic, a writer, and a purpose. Like the music over a film's opening credits, an introduction tells readers what to expect. Any doubts about where the following opening lines are heading?

> Use this package to figure and pay your estimated tax. If you are not required to make estimated tax payments for 2005, you can discard this package.
>
> — Form 1040-ES/V (OCR) Estimated Tax for Individuals, Department of the Treasury, Internal Revenue Service

> The shell game that political professionals play with the campaign laws has taken an encouraging hit in the House. Enough Democrats joined Republicans to pass a bill to plug the egregious soft-money loophole used in 2004 to flood the presidential campaign with hundreds of millions of dollars in attack ads and voter drives.
>
> — "Political Animal Bites Fat Cat," Editorial, *New York Times*, April 8, 2006

Of course, you will want to write introductions that fit your projects. In some cases a single line may be enough—as in an e-mail request for information. ○ A paragraph can provide all the push you need to get a short paper rolling. In a senior thesis or

understand e-mail
p. 266

book, a preface or an entire chapter can set the stage for your project. Realize, too, that in longer projects, you'll write what amounts to an introduction for every new section or major division.

What should your introductory paragraphs accomplish? Following are some options.

Announce your project.   In academic papers, introductions typically declare a subject directly and indicate how it will be developed. Quite often, an introductory paragraph or section leads directly to a thesis statement or a hypothesis. ○ This is a pattern you can use in many situations.

> In her novel *Wuthering Heights* (1847), Emily Brontë presents the story of the families of Wuthering Heights and Thrushcross Grange through the seemingly impartial perspective of Nelly Dean, a servant who grows up with the families. Upon closer inspection, however, it becomes apparent that Nelly acts as much more than a bystander in the tragic events taking place around her. In her status as an outsider with influence over the families, Nelly strikingly resembles the Byronic hero Heathcliff and competes with him for power. Although the author depicts Heathcliff as the more overt gothic hero, Brontë allows the reader to infer from Nelly's story her true character and role in the family. The author draws a parallel between Nelly Dean and Heathcliff in their relationships to the Earnshaw family, in their similar roles as tortured heroes, and in their competition for power within their adoptive families.

Paper opens by identifying its general topic or theme.

Detailed thesis states what paper will prove.

—Manasi Deshpande, "Servant and Stranger: Nelly and Heathcliff in *Wuthering Heights*"

Preview your project.   Sometimes you'll have to use an introductory section to set up the material to follow, helping readers to understand why an issue deserves their attention. You might, for example, present an anecdote, describe a trend, or point to some change or development readers may not have noticed. Then you can explore its significance or implications. In the following example, Gabriela Montell, a writer for *The Chronicle of Higher*

develop a thesis
p. 336

Education, first describes a research study to then explain why she is interested in whether looks matter for college professors.

News article opens by getting readers interested in research study.

Researchers identified and study described in sufficient, but limited, detail.

Professors aren't known for fussing about their looks, but the results of a new study suggest they may have to if they want better teaching evaluations.

Daniel Hamermesh, a professor of economics at the University of Texas at Austin, and Amy Parker, one of his students, found that attractive professors consistently outscore their less comely colleagues by a significant margin on student evaluations of teaching. The findings, they say, raise serious questions about the use of student evaluations as a valid measure of teaching quality.

In their study, Mr. Hamermesh and Ms. Parker asked students to look at photographs of ninety-four professors and rate their beauty. Then they compared those ratings to the average student evaluation scores for the courses taught by those professors. The two found that the professors who had been rated among the most beautiful scored a point higher than those rated least beautiful (that's a substantial difference, since student evaluations don't generally vary by much).

Full story will examine implications of study for educators.

While it's not news that beauty trumps brains in many quarters, you would think that the ivory tower would be relatively exempt from such shallowness.

—"Do Good Looks Equal Good Evaluations?" October 15, 2003

Provide background information.   Decide what your readers need to know about a subject and then fill in the blanks. Provide too little background information on a subject and readers may find the remainder of the project confusing. Supply too much context and you lose readers quickly: They may assume that the paper has nothing new to offer them or may simply grow impatient.

And yet, even when readers know a subject well, you still need, especially in academic papers, to answer basic questions about the project or topic—*who, what, where, when, how,* and *why.* Name names in your introduction, offer accurate titles, furnish dates, and explain what your subject is. Imagine readers from just slightly outside your target audience who might not instantly recall, for instance, that Shakespeare wrote a play titled *Henry V* or that Hurricane Katrina struck New Orleans on August 29, 2005.

Catch the attention of readers.   Offer your readers a reason to enter a text. You can invite them any number of ways—with a compelling incident or amusing story, with a recitation of surprising or intriguing facts, with a dramatic question, with a provocative description or quotation.

For visual texts like a brochure or poster, a cover, masthead, or headline can lead readers inside the project. Naturally, any opening has to be in synch with the material that follows—not outrageously emotional if the argument is sober; not lighthearted and comic if the paper has a serious theme. It is hard to imagine a reader even modestly interested in history not being caught by the opening paragraph of Barbara Tuchman's *The First Salute* (1998):

> White puffs of gun smoke over a turquoise sea followed by the boom of cannon rose from an unassuming fort on the diminutive Dutch island of St. Eustatius in the West Indies on November 16, 1776. The guns of Fort Orange on St. Eustatius were returning the ritual salute on entering a foreign port of an American vessel, the *Andrew Doria*, as she came up the roadstead, flying at her mast the red-and-white-striped flag of the Continental Congress. In its responding salute the small voice of St. Eustatius was the first officially to greet the largest event of the century—the entry into the society of nations of a new Atlantic state destined to change the direction of history.

Set a tone.   Introductory material sends readers all sorts of signals, some of them almost subliminal. Make noticeable errors in grammar and usage in an opening section and you immediately lose credibility with your readers.

More typically, though, readers use your opening material to determine whether they belong to the audience you are addressing. A paper opening with highly technical language indicates that the territory is open to specialists only, while a more personal or colloquial style signals a broader audience. O

Follow any required formulas.   Many genres of writing specify how you may enter a subject. This is especially the case for technical material (lab reports, research articles, scholarly essays) and highly conventional genres

refine your tone
p. 374

such as business letters, job-application letters, and even e-mail. Quite often, these conventions are simple: A business letter opens with a formal salutation; a job letter announces that you are applying for a specific announced position. You cannot ignore these details without raising eyebrows and doubts. To get such introductions right, review models of the genre and follow them.

Write an introduction when you're ready.   The opening of a project— especially of longer efforts such as research papers and theses—can be notoriously difficult to compose. If you are blocked at the outset of a project, plunge directly into the body of the paper and see where things go. You can even write the opening section last. No one will know.

Similarly, if you write your introduction first, review it when you come to the end of the paper—and revise as necessary. ○ Sometimes, the promises you made at the beginning aren't the same ones you delivered on. When that's the case, recast the opening to reflect the paper's new content or revise the body of the paper to conform to important commitments made in the introduction.

revise and edit
p. 386

Conclusions 28

Composing introductions carries all the trepidations of asking for a first date. So conclusions should be much easier, right? By the time you write it, you've established a relationship with readers, provided necessary background, laid down arguments, and discussed important issues. All that remains is the verbal equivalent of a good-night kiss. . . . Okay, maybe conclusions aren't that simple.

Like introductions, conclusions serve different purposes and audiences. A brief e-mail or memo may need no more sign-off than a simple closing: *regards*, *best*, *later*. A senior thesis, however, could require a whole chapter to wrap things up. Here are some of the options when writing conclusions.

Summarize your points, then connect them.   In reports and arguments, use the concluding section to recap what you've covered and tie your major points together. Following is the systematic conclusion of a college report on a childhood developmental disorder, Cri Du Chat Syndrome (CDCS). Note that this summary paragraph also leads where many other scientific and scholarly articles do: to a call for additional research.

> Though research on CDCS remains far from abundant, existing studies prescribe early and ongoing intervention by a team of specialists, including speech-language pathologists, physical and occupational therapists, various medical and

shape an
ending

Major point

Major point

educational professionals, and parents. Such intervention has been shown to allow individuals with CDCS to live happy, long, and full lives. The research, however, indicates that the syndrome affects all aspects of a child's development and should therefore be taken quite seriously. Most children require numerous medical interventions, including surgery (especially to correct heart defects), feeding tubes, body braces, and repeated treatment of infections. Currently, the best attempts are being made to help young children with CDCS reach developmental milestones earlier, communicate effectively, and function as independently as possible. However, as the authors of the aforementioned studies suggest, much more research is needed to clarify the causes of varying degrees of disability, to identify effective and innovative treatments/interventions (especially in the area of education), and to individualize intervention plans.

Conclusion ties together main points made in paper, using transitional words and phrases.

—Marissa Dahlstrom, "Developmental Disorders: Cri Du Chat Syndrome"

Reveal your point.   In some writing, including many arguments, you may not want to reveal your key point until the very end, following a full presentation of claims and evidence. ○ The paper unfurls a bit like a mystery, keeping readers eager to discover your point. You don't open with a thesis, nor do you tip your hand completely until the conclusion.

Here, for example, are the concluding paragraphs of an article in which Andrew Sullivan has been guiding readers through a city he argues has grown more self-absorbed and alienated because of technologies like the Internet and iPod. In his conclusion, Sullivan raises important questions that lead toward his chief belief that we need to turn outward again to enrich our lives.

We become masters of our own interests [thanks to technology], more connected to people like us over the Internet, more instantly in touch with anything we want, need, or think we want and think we need. Ever tried a Stairmaster in silence? But what are we missing? That hilarious shard of an overheard conversation that stays with you all day; the child whose chatter on the pavement takes you back to your early memories; birdsong; weather; accents; the laughter of others. And those thoughts that come not by filling your head with selected diversion, but by allowing your mind to wander aimlessly through the regular background noise of human and mechanical life.

Details give argument power: Plugged in, we're missing a lot.

understand argument
p. 68

External stimulation can crowd out the interior mind. Even the boredom that we flee has its uses. We are forced to find our own means to overcome it.

And so we enrich our life from within, rather than from white wires. It's hard to give up, though, isn't it?

Not so long ago I was on a trip and realized I had left my iPod behind. Panic. But then something else. I noticed the rhythms of others again, the sound of the airplane, the opinions of the taxi driver, the small social cues that had been obscured before. I noticed how others related to each other. And I felt just a little bit connected again and a little more aware.

Try it. There's a world out there. And it has a soundtrack all its own.

— "Society Is Dead: We Have Retreated into the iWorld"

> Sullivan anticipates readers' objections and acknowledges his own weakness.

> Final anecdote drives home key point.

> Three short concluding sentences punctuate the essay.

Finish dramatically.   Arguments, personal narratives, and many other kinds of writing often call for conclusions that will influence readers and maybe change their opinions. Since final paragraphs are what many readers remember, it makes sense that they be powerfully written. Here's the conclusion of a lengthy personal essay by Shane McNamee that leads up to a poignant political appeal. (To read the entire essay, see Chapter 3, p. 91.)

Forget for the moment the rainbow flags and pink triangles. Gay pride is not about being homosexual; it's about the integrity and courage it takes to be honest with yourself and your loved ones. It's about spending life with whomever you want and not worrying what the government or the neighbors think. Let's protect that truth, not some rigid view of sexual orientation or marriage. Keep gay marriage out of your church if you like, but if you value monogamy as I do, give me an alternative that doesn't involve dishonesty or a life of loneliness. Many upstanding gay citizens yearn for recognition of their loving, committed relationships. Unless you enjoy being lied to and are ready to send your gay friends and family on a Trail of Queers to Massachusetts or Canada — where gay marriage is legal — then consider letting them live as they wish.

— "Protecting What Really Matters"

> Deliberate repetition focuses readers on serious point.

> Conclusion makes direct appeal to readers, addressed as *you.*

> Final sentence appeals emotionally through both images and language.

29 Titles

name your
work

Titles may not strike you as an important aspect of organization, but they can be. Of course, a proper title tells readers what a paper is about, but it can play a role during the writing process and make a document easier to locate later. Titles *can* be provocative, but more often their goal is to let readers know what they're about to read or see.

Use titles to focus documents. A too-broad title early on in a project can determine whether you have identified a workable subject. If all you have is "Sea Battles in World War II" or "Children in America," do more reading and research. If no title comes to mind, you don't have a subject. ○ You're still exploring ideas.

Titles for academic papers need only be descriptive. Consider these items culled at random from one issue of the *Stanford Undergraduate Research Journal* (Spring 2005). As you might expect, scientific papers aimed at a knowledgeable audience of specialists have highly technical titles. Titles in the social sciences and liberal arts are slightly less intimidating, but just as focused on providing information about their subjects. And a few papers do have titles designed, perhaps, to simply attract attention.

> "Hydrogenation Energies and Vibration Frequencies of Hydrogenated Carbon Nanotubes: Exploring Possibilities for Hydrogen Storage"
>
> — Ashok Kumar

develop a thesis
p. 336

"Married Women and AIDS Vulnerability"

—Jenny Tolan

"Druze and Jews"

—Adi Greif

Create searchable titles.   For academic or professional papers, a title should make sense standing on its own and out of context. That way if the paper winds up in someone's bibliography or in an online database, readers know what your subject is. Your title should also include keywords by which it might be searched in a database or online.

"Rethinking the Threat of Domestic Terrorism"

If you must be clever or allusive, follow the cute title with a colon and an explanatory subtitle.

"Out, Damn'd Spot!': Images of Conscience and Remorse in Shakespeare's *Macbeth*"

"Out, Damn'd Spot: Housebreaking Your Puppy"

Avoid whimsical or suggestive titles.   A bad title will haunt you like a silly screen name. At this point you may not worry about publication, but documents take on a life of their own when uploaded to the Web or listed on a résumé. Any document posted where the public can search for it online needs a levelheaded title, especially when you approach the job market.

Capitalize and punctuate titles carefully.   The guidelines for capitalizing titles vary between disciplines. See Chapters 44 and 45 for the MLA and APA guidelines, or consult the style manual for your discipline.

Your titles should avoid all caps, boldface, underscoring, and italics (except for titles within titles; see *Macbeth* above). For Web sites, newsletters, PowerPoint presentations, and so on, you can be bolder graphically. O

Titles tell readers what to expect.

design your work
p. 517

Style

part five

5

Need help with revising and editing? See page 384. / Need help with common errors? See page 524.

30 High, Middle, and Low Style

define your style / refine your tone

We all have an ear for the way words work in sentences and paragraphs, for the distinctive melding of voice, tone, rhythm, and texture some call *style*. You might not be able to explain exactly why one paragraph sparkles and another is flat as day-old soda, but you know when writing feels energetic, precise, and clear or stodgy, lifeless, and plodding. Choices you make about sentence type, sentence length, vocabulary, pronouns, and punctuation *do* create distinctive verbal styles—which may or may not fit particular types of writing. ○

   In fact, there are as many styles of writing as of dress. In most cases, language that is clear, active, and economical will do the job. But even such an essential style has variations. Since the time of the ancient Greeks, writers have imagined a "high" or formal style at one end of a scale and a "low" or colloquial style at the other, bracketing a just-right porridge in the middle. Style is more complex than that, but keeping the full range in mind reveals some of your options.

High, middle, and low styles of weddings: formal and traditional, less formal, and totally informal.

improve your sentences
p. 378

Use high style for formal, scientific, and scholarly writing. You will find high style in professional journals, scholarly books, legal briefs, formal addresses, many editorials, some types of technical writing, and some wedding invitations. Use it yourself when a lot is at stake—in a scholarship application, for example, or a job letter, term paper, or thesis. High style is signaled by some combination of the following features—all of which can vary.

- Serious or professional subjects
- Knowledgeable or professional audiences
- Dominant third-person (*he, she, it, they*) or impersonal point of view
- Relatively complex and self-consciously patterned sentences (that display *parallelism, balance, repetition*), often in the passive voice
- Professional vocabulary, often abstract and technical
- No contractions, colloquial expressions, or nonstandard forms
- Conventional grammar and punctuation; standard document design
- Formal documentation, when required, often with notes and a bibliography

Following is an example from a scholarly journal. The article uses a formal scientific style, appropriate when an expert in a field is writing for an audience of his or her peers.

Temperament is a construct closely related to personality. In human research, temperament has been defined by some researchers as the inherited, early appearing tendencies that continue throughout life and serve as the foundation for personality (A. H. Buss, 1995; Goldsmith et al., 1987). Although this definition is not adopted uniformly by human researchers (McCrae et al., 2000), animal researchers agree even less about how to define temperament (Budaev, 2000). In some cases, the word *temperament* appears to be used purely to avoid using the word *personality*, which some animal researchers associate with anthropomorphism. Thus, to ensure that my review captured all potentially relevant reports, I searched for studies that examined either personality or temperament.

–Sam D. Gosling, "From Mice to Men: What Can We Learn About Personality from Animal Research?" *Psychological Bulletin*

> Technical term introduced and defined.

> Sources documented.

> Perspective generally impersonal—though *I* is used.

The *New York Times* editorial below also uses a formal style. This is common when dealing with serious political or social issues.

Tone of first paragraph is sober and direct.

Haiti, founded two centuries ago by ex-slaves who fought to regain their freedom, has again become a hub of human trafficking.

Today, tens of thousands of Haitian children live lives of modern-day bondage. Under the system known as *restavek,* a Creole word meaning "stay with," these children work for wealthier families in exchange for education and shelter. They frequently end up cruelly overworked, physically or sexually abused, and without access to education.

Key term is defined.

Vocabulary is fairly abstract.

The most effective way to root out this deeply oppressive but deeply ingrained system would be to attack the conditions that sustain it — chiefly, impoverished, environmentally unsustainable agriculture and a severe shortage of rural schools.

This is an area in which America can and should help. Washington has been quick to respond to political turmoil in Haiti, with its accompanying fears of uncontrollable refugee flows. But the frenzied flurries of international crisis management that follow typically leave no lasting results.

Borrows technical language of diplomacy and government.

A wiser, more promising alternative would be to help create long-term economic options by improving access to schools and creating sustainable agriculture. Meanwhile, the United States should work with nongovernmental organizations to battle the resigned acceptance by many Haitians of the restavek system. They could, for example, help local radio stations broadcast programs of open dialogue about how damaging the system is, and include restavek survivors or human-rights experts.

Voice throughout is that of a serious institution, not an individual.

The primary responsibility for eliminating the restavek system lies with the Haitian people and their government. After years of political crisis, there is a new democratically elected government. Eradicating the restavek system should be one of its top priorities, combining law enforcement efforts with attacks on the root social and economic causes.

Tone of final paragraph is more emotional than rest of editorial.

The former slaves who won Haiti's freedom two hundred years ago dreamed of something better for their children than restavek bondage. The time is overdue for helping those dreams become reality.

—"The Lost Children of Haiti," *New York Times*

Use middle style for personal, argumentative, and some academic writing.   This style, perhaps the most common, falls between the extremes. It is the language of journalism, popular books and magazines, professional memos and nonscientific reports, instructional guides and manuals, and most commercial Web sites. Use this style in position papers, letters to the editor, personal statements, and business e-mails and memos—even in some business and professional work, once you are comfortable with the people to whom you are writing. Middle style doesn't so much claim features of its own as walk a path between formal and everyday language. It may combine some of the following characteristics:

- Full range of topics, from serious to humorous
- General audiences
- Range of perspectives, including first (*I*) and second (*you*) person points of view
- More often a human rather than an institutional voice
- Sentences in active voice varied in complexity and length
- General vocabulary, more specific than abstract, with concrete nouns and action verbs and with unfamiliar terms or concepts defined
- Informal expressions, some dialogue, slang, and contractions
- Conventional grammar and reasonably correct formats
- Informal documentation, usually without notes

In the following article for the online magazine *Slate* Joel Waldfogel, a professor of business and public policy, explains recent research in his field to a general audience—people who are not experts in either business or public policy.

It is well-documented that short people earn less money than tall people do. To be clear, pay does not vary lockstep by height. If your friend is taller than you are, then it's nearly a coin toss whether she earns more. But if you compare two large groups of people who are similar in every respect but

Readers addressed familiarly as "you" and example offered to clarify principle of causality.

height, the average pay for the taller group will be higher. Each additional inch of height adds roughly 2 percent to average annual earnings, for both men and women. So, if the average heights of our hypothetical groups were 6 feet and 5 feet 7 inches, the average pay difference between them would be 10 percent.

But why? One possibility is height discrimination in favor of the tall. A second involves adolescence. A few years ago, Nicola Persico and Andrew Postlewaite of the University of Pennsylvania and Dan Silverman of the University of Michigan discovered that adult earnings are more sharply related to height at age sixteen than to adult height – suggesting, scarily, that the high-school social order determined the adult economic order. For boys at least, height at sixteen affects things like social and athletic success – scoring chicks and baskets or, as the authors put it, "participation in clubs and athletics." And maybe those things affect later earning power.

That wasn't likely to make short people feel good, but the latest explanation is worse. In a new study, Anne Case and Christina Paxson, both of Princeton University, find that tall people earn more, on average, because they're smarter, on average. Yikes.

– Joel Waldfogel, "Short End," Slate.com

Transition between paragraphs reads like spoken English: easy and natural.

Sources cited, but not documented.

Highlights difference between his informality and high style of scholars.

Surprisingly colloquial term punctuates paragraph.

Next, in this excerpt from an article that appeared in the popular magazine *Psychology Today,* Ellen McGrath uses a conversational middle style to present scientific information to a general audience.

Families often inherit a negative thinking style that carries the germ of depression. Typically it is a legacy passed from one generation to the next, a pattern of pessimism invoked to protect loved ones from disappointment or stress. But in fact, negative thinking patterns do just the opposite, eroding the mental health of all exposed.

When Dad consistently expresses his disappointment in Josh for bringing home a B minus in chemistry although all the other grades are As, he is exhibiting a kind of cognitive distortion that children learn to deploy

Vocabulary is sophisticated but not technical.

Familiar example (fictional son is even named) illustrates technical term: cognitive distortion.

on themselves — a mental filtering that screens out positive experience from consideration.

> Or perhaps the father envisions catastrophe, seeing such grades as foreclosing the possibility of a top college, thus dooming his son's future. It is their repetition over time that gives these events power to shape a person's belief system.
>
> — Ellen McGrath, "Is Depression Contagious?" *Psychology Today*

Phrase following dash offers further clarification helpful to educated, but nonexpert, readers.

Use a low style for personal, informal, and even playful writing.

Don't think of "low" here in a negative sense: A colloquial or informal style is fine on occasions when you want or need to sound more at ease and open. Low style can be right for your personal e-mails and instant messaging, of course, as well as in many blogs, advertisements, magazines trying to be hip, personal narratives, and in humor writing. Low style has many of the following features.

- Everyday or off-the-wall subjects, often humorous or parodic
- In-group or specialized readers
- Highly personal and idiosyncratic points of view; lots of *I, me, you, us,* and dialogue
- Shorter sentences and irregular constructions, especially fragments
- Vocabulary from pop culture and the street — idiomatic, allusive, and obscure to outsiders
- Colloquial expressions resembling speech
- Unconventional grammar and mechanics and alternative formats
- No systematic acknowledgment of sources

△

Note the relaxed style this former college instructor uses in her blog.

TUESDAY, JANUARY 03, 2006

Dumpster diving

Stuff and *kids* immediately signal casual tone—as does sentence fragment.

Stuff I've found in or near the dumpsters after the college kids move out of our apartment complex between semesters:

- Brand new HP printer, all cords still attached
- Tall oak computer-printer stand on wheels
- Blank computer discs and CD-ROMs
- China tea set
- Funky 1950s plates and saucers, left in a box beside the garbage bin
- Unopened bottle of semi-expensive champagne (still in my fridge)
- Nearly full bottles of expensive shampoos and conditioners
- Leather camera bag
- Replacement car antenna, still in unopened package
- Framed movie posters

Highly personal parenthetical remark—and slangy *fridge*.

One of my students told me about one of the rare perks of being a resident assistant in the dorm. She really made out bigtime with stuff left behind. One girl moved out and left all the dresser drawers loaded with clothes (and not by accident . . . she just didn't want to pack the stuff). Lots of students abandon bicycles, stereos, VCRs, TVs, sofas, and futons. Best days for scavenging are during final exams and right after.

"Really made out bigtime" is deliberately low, echoing student chatter.

Pause marked by ellipsis.

Article omitted at beginning of sentence makes advice seem casual.

The very serious story told in the *9/11 Commission Report* was retold in *The 9/11 Report: A Graphic Adaptation.* Creators Sid Jacobson and Ernie Colón use the colloquial visual style of a comic book to make the formidable data and conclusions of a government report accessible to a wider audience.

Panels combine verbal and visual elements to tell story.

Political figures become characters in drama.

Sounds (*Shoom!*) are represented visually—as in superhero tales.

Real images (the photograph on the left) are sometimes juxtaposed with cartoon panels as part of collage.

31 Inclusive and Culturally Sensitive Style

respect your
readers

Writers in school or business today need to remember how small and tightly connected the world has become and how readily people may be offended. When you compose any document electronically (including a Word file), it may sail quickly around the Web. You can't make every reader in this potential audience happy, but you can at least write respectfully, accurately, and, yes, honestly. Language that is both inclusive and culturally sensitive can and should have these qualities.

Avoid expressions that stereotype genders. Largely purged from contemporary English usage are job titles that suggest that they are occupied exclusively by men or women. Gone are *poetess* and *stewardess*, *policeman* and *congressman*, *postman* and *woman scientist*. When referring to professions, even those still dominated by one gender or another, avoid using a gendered pronoun.

Don't strain sense to be politically correct. *Nun* and *NFL quarterback* are still gendered, as are *witch* and *warlock*—and *surrogate mother*. Here are some easy solutions.

STEREOTYPED	The postman came up the walk.
INCLUSIVE	The letter carrier came up the walk.
STEREOTYPED	Amongst all her other tasks, a nurse must also stay up-to-date on her medical education.
INCLUSIVE	Amongst all their other tasks, nurses must also stay up-to-date on their medical education.

Outdated Terms	Alternatives
postman	letter carrier, postal worker
mankind	humankind, people, humans
congressman	congressional representative
chairman	chair
policeman	police officer
stewardess	flight attendant
actress, poetess	actor, poet
fireman	firefighter

Avoid expressions that stereotype races, ethnic groups, or religious groups.   Deliberate racial slurs these days tend to be rare in professional writing. But it is still not unusual to find well-meaning writers noting how "hard-working," "articulate," "athletic," "well-groomed," or "ambitious" members of minority and religious groups are. The praise rings hollow because it draws on old and brutal stereotypes. You have an obligation to learn the history and nature of such ethnic caricatures and grow beyond them. It's part of your education, no matter what group or groups you belong to.

Refer to people and groups by the expressions used in serious publications, understanding that almost all racial and ethnic terms are contested: *African American, black* (or *Black*), *Negro, people of color, Asian American, Hispanic, Mexican American, Cuban American, Native American, Indian, Inuit, Anglo, white* (or *White*). Even the ancient group of American Indians once called Anasazi now go by the more culturally and historically accurate Native Puebloans. While shifts of this sort may seem fussy or politically correct to some, it costs little to address people as they prefer, acknowledging both their humanity and our differences.

Be aware, too, that being part of an ethnic or racial group usually gives you license to say things about the group not open to outsiders. Chris Rock and Margaret Cho can joke about topics Jay Leno can't touch, using epithets that would cost the *Tonight Show* host his job. In academic and professional settings, show similar discretion in your language—though not in your treatment of serious subjects. Sensitivities of language should not become an excuse for avoiding open debate, nor a weapon to chill it. In the table below are suggestions for inclusive, culturally sensitive terms.

Outdated Terms	Alternatives
Eskimo	Inuit
Oriental	Asian American (better to specify country of origin)
Hispanic	Specify: Mexican, Cuban, Nicaraguan, and so on
Negro (acceptable to some)	African American, black
colored	people of color
a gay, the gays	gay, lesbian, gays and lesbians
cancer victim	person who has had cancer
boys, girls (to refer to adults)	men, women
woman doctor	doctor
male nurse	nurse

Treat all people with respect.   This policy makes sense in all writing. Some slights may not be intended—against the elderly, for example. But writing that someone drives *like an old woman* manages to offend two groups. In other cases, you might mistakenly think that most readers share your prejudices or narrow vision when describing members of campus groups, religious groups, the military, gays and lesbians, athletes, and so on. You know the derogatory terms and references well enough and you should avoid them if for no other reason than the golden rule. Everyone is a member of some group that has at one time or another been mocked or stereotyped. So writing that is respectful will itself be treated with respect.

Avoid sensational language.   It happens every semester. One or more students asks the instructor whether it's okay to use four-letter words in their papers. Some instructors tolerate expletives in personal narratives, but it is difficult to make a case for them in academic reports, research papers, or position papers unless they are part of quoted material—as they may be in writing about contemporary literature or song lyrics.

Certain kinds of writing do effectively push the limits of their audience or, rather, appreciate that their readers might occasionally enjoy seeing a subject justly skewered by a few well-chosen words. You'll see this gleeful meanness in book, movie, or music reviews, for example. ⭘ Following is the opening paragraph of a film review written by a critic taking her scalpel to the movie version of teen-author Christopher Paolini's novel *Eragon*. Note that, for the most part, the writer avoids offensive language, but she doesn't mince words either.

> *Eragon* is what happens when misguided studio executives option a novel written by a teenager (Christopher Paolini) with a head full of Anne McCaffrey and Ursula K. Le Guin. Not full enough, however; this boy-and-his-dragon fantasy set in a land bristling with Tolkienesque nomenclature and earnest British actors is as lacking in fresh ideas as Tim Allen's manager. Even the scaly star, a Delft-blue beastie whose tint suggests either royal lineage or hypothermia, seems unsure of her motivation.
>
> –Jeanette Catsoulis, "A Boy and His Dragon," *New York Times*

⭘ understand evaluation
p. 102

32

Vigorous, Clear, Economical Style

improve your
sentences

Ordinarily, tips and tricks don't do much to enhance your skills as a writer. But a few guidelines, applied sensibly, can improve your sentences and paragraphs noticeably—and upgrade your credibility as a writer. You sound more professional and confident when every word and phrase pulls its weight.

Always consider the big picture in applying the following tips: Work with whole pages and paragraphs, not just individual sentences. Remember, too, that these are guidelines, not rules. Ignore them when your good sense suggests a better alternative.

Use strong, concrete subjects and objects.   Scholar Richard Lanham famously advised writers troubled by tangled sentences to ask, "Who is kicking who?" That's a memorable way of suggesting that readers shouldn't have to puzzle over what they read.

Lower the level of generality to add interest. Nouns should be as specific as possible so that sentences create images for readers.

ABSTRACT	SPECIFIC
bird	roadrunner
cactus	prickly pear
animal	coyote

Most readers can more readily imagine *students* than *constituencies*; they can picture a *school*, not an *academic institution*. A wordy sentence can seem almost hopeless until you start translating phrases like "current fiscal pressures" into everyday English.

WORDY   **All of the separate constituencies at this academic institution** must be invited to participate in the decision making process **under the current fiscal pressures we face.**

BETTER   **Faculty, students, and staff at this school** must all have a say **during this current budget crunch.**

Don't use words too big for the subject. Don't say "infinitely" when you mean "very," otherwise you'll have no word left when you want to talk about something really infinite.
—C. S. Lewis

Avoid clumsy noun phrases.

It's too easy to build massive noun phrases that sound impressive but give readers fits, especially as they accumulate over an entire page. You can spot such phrases by various markers:

- Strings of prepositional phrases
- Verbs turned into nouns via endings such as *-ation* (*implement* becomes *implementation*)
- Lots of articles (*the*, *a*)
- Lots of heavily modified verbals

Such expressions are not always inaccurate or wrong, just tedious. They make your reader work hard for no reason. They are remarkably easy to pare down once you notice them.

WORDY   **members of the student body** at Arizona State

BETTER   **students** at Arizona State

WORDY   **the manufacturing of** products **made up of** steel

BETTER   **making** steel products

WORDY   **the prioritization of decisions for policies** of the student government

BETTER   the student government's **priorities**

Avoid sentences with long windups.

Get to the point quickly. The more stuff you pile up ahead of the main verb, the more readers have to remember. Most people today prefer sentences that defer their lengthy modifying phrases and clauses until after the main verb. This sentence from the Internal Revenue Service Web site piles up too many prepositional phrases before the verb. It's easy to fix.

ORIGINAL   A new scam e-mail that appears to be a solicitation from the IRS and the U.S. government for charitable contributions to victims of the recent Southern California wildfires has been making the rounds.

REVISED   A new scam e-mail making the rounds asks for charitable contributions to victims of the recent Southern California wildfires. It appears to be from the IRS and the U.S. government, but it is not legitimate.

Use action verbs when possible.   Verbs get as tangled up as nouns if you lose track of the action. Cut through the clutter.

WORDY VERB PHRASE   We must **make a decision** soon.

BETTER   We must **decide** soon.

WORDY VERB PHRASE   Students **are reliant** on credit cards.

BETTER   Students **rely** on credit cards.

WORDY VERB PHRASE   Engineers **proceeded to reinforce** the levee.

BETTER   Engineers **reinforced** the levee.

Avoid strings of prepositional phrases.   Prepositional phrases consist of a preposition and its object, which may take modifiers: *under* the spreading chestnut tree; *between* you and me; *in* the line *of* duty. You can't write without prepositional phrases. But use more than two or, rarely, three, in a row and they drain the energy from your sentences. Try moving the prepositions or turning them into more compact modifiers. Sometimes you can alter the verb to eliminate a preposition, or it might be necessary to revise the sentence even more substantially.

TOO MANY PHRASES   We stood **in line at the observatory on the top of a hill in the mountains** to look **in a huge telescope at the moons of Saturn.**

BETTER   We **lined up at the mountaintop observatory** to view Saturn's moons **through a huge telescope.**

Don't repeat key words close together.   You can often improve the style of a passage just by making sure you haven't used a particular word or phrase too often or in too close proximity—unless you repeat it deliberately for effect (*government of the people, by the people, for the people*). When you edit to fix unintentional repetition, the resulting variety will make your sentences sound fresher.

This is a guideline to apply sensibly: Sometimes to be clear, especially in technical writing, you must repeat key nouns and verbs sentence after sentence.

> The New Horizons payload is incredibly power efficient, with the instruments collectively drawing only about 28 watts. The payload consists of three optical instruments, two plasma instruments, a dust sensor, and a radio science receiver/radiometer.
>
> —NASA, "New Horizons Spacecraft Ready for Flight"

Avoid doublings.   In speech, we tend to repeat ourselves or say things two or three different ways to be sure listeners get the point. Such repetitions are natural, even appreciated. But in writing, the habit of doubling can be irritating. And it is very much a habit, backed by a long literary tradition comfortable with pairings such as *home and hearth, friend and colleague, tried and true, clean and sober, neat and tidy,* and so on.

Often, writers will add an extra noun or two to be sure they have covered the bases: *colleges and universities; books and articles; ideas and opinions.* There may be good reasons for a second (or third) item. But not infrequently, the doubling is just extra baggage that slows down the train. Leave it at the station.

Turn clauses into more direct modifiers.   If you are fond of *that, which,* and *who* clauses, be sure you need them. You can sometimes save a word or two by pulling the modifiers out of the clause and moving them ahead of the words they embellish. Or you may be able to tighten a sentence just by cutting *that, which,* or *who.*

WORDY   Our coach, who is nationally renowned, expected a raise.
BETTER   Our nationally renowned coach expected a raise.

WORDY	Our coach, **who is nationally renowned and already rich,** still expected a raise.
BETTER	Our coach, **nationally renowned and already rich,** still expected a raise.

Cut introductory expressions such as *it is* and *there is/are* when you can.

Such expressions, called *expletives,* are just part of the way we say some things: *It is going to rain today; There is a tide in the affairs of men.* Cut them to save a few words, though, and you sound like Yoda: *Rain it will today*. But don't let an expletive substitute for a clearer expression.

WORDY	**It is** necessary that we reform the housing policies.
BETTER	**We** need to reform the housing policies.

WORDY	**There were** many incentives offered by the company to its sales force.
BETTER	**The company** offered its sales force many incentives.

Vary your sentence lengths and structures.

Sentences, like music, have rhythm. If all your sentences run about the same length or rarely vary from a predictable subject–verb–object pattern, readers grow bored without even knowing why. Every so often, surprise readers with a really short statement. Or begin with a longer-than-usual introductory phrase. Or try compound subjects or verbs, or attach a series of parallel modifiers to the verb or object. Or let a sentence roll toward a grand conclusion, as in the example below.

> [Carl] Newman is a singing encyclopedia of pop power. He has identified, cultured, and cloned the most buoyant elements of his favorite Squeeze, Raspberries, Supertramp, and Sparks records, and he's pretty pathological about making sure there's something unpredictable and catchy happening in a New Pornographers song every couple of seconds—a stereo flurry of *oooh*s, an extra beat or two bubbling up unexpectedly.
>
> — Douglas Wolk, "Something to Talk About," *Spin*

Listen to what you have written.

Read everything that matters aloud at least once. Then fix the words or phrases that cause you to pause or stumble. This is a great way to find problem spots. If you can't follow your own writing, a reader won't be able to either. Better yet, persuade a friend or roommate to read your draft to you and take notes.

Cut a first draft by 25 percent—or more.   If you tend to be wordy, try to cut your first drafts by at least one-quarter. Put all your thoughts down on the page when drafting a paper. But when editing, cut every unnecessary expression. Think of it as a competition. However, don't eliminate any important ideas and facts. If possible, ask an honest friend to read your work and point out where you might tighten your language.

> I believe more in the scissors than I do in the pencil.

—Truman Capote

If you ~~are aware that you~~ tend to ~~say more than you need to in your writing,~~ *be wordy,*

~~then get in the habit of~~ try~~ing~~ to cut ~~the~~ first drafts ~~that you have written~~ by *your*

at least one-quarter. ~~There may be good reasons for you to~~ put all your

thoughts ~~and ideas~~ down on the page when ~~you are in the process of~~

drafting a paper ~~or project~~. But when ~~you are in the process of~~ editing, ~~you~~

~~should be sure to~~ cut every unnecessary ~~word that is not needed or~~ *expression.*

~~necessary. You may find it advantageous to~~ think of it as a competition ~~or a~~ *T* *.*

~~game. In making your cuts, it is important that you~~ don't eliminate any *However,*

important ideas ~~that may be essential or~~ facts ~~that may be important.~~ If ~~you~~ *and* *.*

~~find it~~ possible, ~~you might consider~~ ask~~ing~~ an honest friend ~~whom you trust~~

to read your ~~writing~~ and ~~ask them to~~ point out ~~those places in your writing~~ *work*

where you might ~~make~~ your language ~~tighter.~~ *tighten* *.*

Revising & Editing

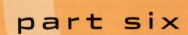

part six

Need style help? See page 364. / Need help with common errors? See page 524.

33 Revising Your Own Work

How much time should you spend revising a draft? Decide this based on the importance of the document and the time available to complete it. A job-application letter, résumé, or term paper had better be perfect. But you shouldn't send even an e-mail without a quick review, if only to make certain you're sending it to the right people and that your tone is appropriate. Errors might not bother you, but don't assume that other readers are just as easygoing. Given a choice, a well-edited piece always trumps sloppy work.

How you revise your work is a different matter. Some people edit line-by-line, perfecting every sentence before moving to the next. Others write whole drafts quickly and then revise, and others combine these methods.

In most cases, it makes sense to draft a project fairly quickly and then edit it. Why? Because revising is hierarchical: Some issues matter more to your work than others. You might spend hours on a draft, getting each comma right and deleting every word not pulling its weight. But then you read the whole thing and you get that sinking feeling: The paper doesn't meet the assignment or is aimed at the wrong audience. So you trash paragraph after carefully edited paragraph and reorganize many of your ideas. Maybe you even start from scratch.

Wouldn't it have been better to discover those big problems early on, before you put in so many hours getting every comma right? With major projects, consider revising and editing sequentially, starting with the big issues like content and organization. Think of *revising* as making sweeping changes, and *editing* as finessing the details.

Revise to see the big picture.   When you revise, be willing to overhaul your whole project. Of course, you'll need a draft first and it should be a real one with actual words on the page, not just good intentions. With media projects such as a Web site, you might work with a site plan and page designs. **O** But nothing beats a prototype to test a project. Revisions at this top level may require wholesale rewrites of the paper, even starting over. Whatever it takes.

- **Does the project meet the assignment?** You really can get so wrapped up in a paper that you forget the original assignment. If you received an assignment sheet, go back and measure your draft by its requirements. If it asks for a report and you have argued, prepare for major revisions. Review, too, any requirements set for length or use of sources.

- **Does the project reach its intended audience?** Who will read your paper? Is your tone and the level of vocabulary right for these people? What kinds of sources have you used? You'll have to revise heavily if your project won't work for the assigned or intended audience.

- **Does the project do justice to its subject?** This is a tough question to address and you may want to get another reader's input. It might also help to review a successful model of the assignment before you revise your paper. Look for such work in magazines, newspapers, and textbooks. Or ask your instructor or a writing-center staff member to suggest examples. How well does yours compare? Be certain you treat your subject intelligently and thoroughly and have included all the parts required. (These requirements obviously vary from assignment to assignment.) If you find some sections of the paper wanting, admit it, and fix the problem.

design your work
p. 517

Edit to make the paper flow.   There are different opinions as to what *flow* means when applied to writing, but it's a good thing. Once you are confident that you've met the major requirements of an assignment, check how well you have coordinated all these elements. Editing to improve flow takes time and can produce substantial changes in a paper. It's the stage that gets skipped in more hurried forms of communication.

- **Does the organization work for the reader?** You may understand how a project fits together, but is that structure clear to readers? If your paper needs a thesis, does it have one that readers can identify readily and will find challenging? Do your paragraphs develop coherent points? Pay particular attention to the opening sentences in those paragraphs: They must both connect to what you just wrote and preview the upcoming material.

- **Does the paper have smooth and frequent transitions?** Transitional words and phrases support the overall organization. They are road signs to help keep readers on track. Make sure transitions appear not only at the beginning of paragraphs but also throughout the project. To navigate media projects, readers need other devices, from the captions and boxes on brochures to headings and links on Web sites. O

- **Is the paper readable?** Once you've got the basics in place, especially a sound organization, you can tinker to your heart's content with the language, varying sentence structures, choosing words to achieve the level of style you want, and paring away clumsy verbiage (almost rhymes with *garbage*). Review the chapters on style and apply those suggestions to the paper at this stage.

Edit to get the details right.   Most people are perfectionists when it comes to things that matter to them, but have a hard time understanding the obsessions of others. In preparing your paper, you may wonder who cares whether a page number is in the right place, a figure is correctly captioned, or a title is italicized. You'd be surprised.

connect ideas
p. 350

When editing a paper, nothing clears your mind as much as putting a draft aside for a few days and then looking at it with fresh eyes. You will be amazed at all the changes you will want to make. But you have to plan ahead to take advantage of this unsurpassed editing technique. Wait until the last minute to complete a project and you lose that opportunity.

- **Is the format correct right down to the details?** Many academic and professional projects follow templates from which you cannot vary. In fact, you may be expected to learn these requirements as a condition for entering a profession or major. So if you are asked to prepare a paper in Modern Language Association (MLA) or American Psychological Association (APA) style, for instance, invest the few minutes it takes to get details right for titles, margins, headings, and page number formats. ◯ Give similar attention to the formats for lab reports, e-mails, Web sites, and so on. You'll look like a pro if you do.

- **Are the grammar and mechanics right?** Word-processing programs offer a surprising amount of help in these areas. But use this assistance only as a first line of defense, not as a replacement for carefully reread-ing every word yourself. Even then, you still have to pay close atten-tion to errors you make habitually. You know what they are. ◯

- **Is the spelling correct?** Spell-checkers pick up some obvious gaffes but may not be any help with proper nouns or other special items—such as your professor's last name. They also don't catch correctly spelled words that simply aren't the ones you meant to use: *the* instead of *then*, *a* instead of *an*, and so on.

understand citation styles
p. 435

common errors
p. 524

1 Put the paper aside for a few days (or at least a few hours) before revising.

2 Print out the paper, clear space on your desk, and read with fresh eyes. Does the paper respond to the assignment? Will it make sense to readers?

3 Read your paper aloud to yourself, your roommate, your goldfish—anyone who will listen. Mark the parts that confuse you or your audience.

34 Peer Editing

Many people get nervous when asked to play editor, though such requests come all the time: "Read this for me?" Either they don't want to offend a colleague with their criticisms, or they have doubts about their own competence. These are predictable reactions, but you need to get beyond them.

Your job in peer editing drafts is not to criticize writers, but to help them. And you will accomplish that best by approaching any draft honestly, from the perspective of a typical reader. You may not know all the finer points of grammar, but you will know if a paper is boring, confusing, or unconvincing. Writers need this perspective. So you really do have the expertise to give a classmate feedback about issues that require immediate attention.

And yet most peer editors in college or professional situations edit minimally. They focus on tiny matters, such as misspellings or commas, and ignore arguments that completely lack evidence or paragraphs dull enough to kill small mammals. Frankly, spelling and punctuation errors are just easy to circle. It's much tougher to suggest that whole pages need to be reworked or that a writer should do more research. But there's nothing kind about ignoring these deeper issues when a writer's grade or career may be on the line. So what do you do?

First, before you edit any project, agree on the ground rules for making comments. It is very easy to annotate electronic drafts since you won't have to touch or change the original file. But writers may be more protective of paper copies of their work. It's better to leave any comments on a photocopy, making sure your handwriting is legible and your remarks signed or initialed.

Peer edit the same way you revise your own work.   As suggested in Chapter 33, pay attention to global issues first. ○ Examine the purpose, audience, and subject matter of the project before dealing with its sentence structure, grammar, or mechanics. Deal with these major issues in a thoughtful and supportive written comment at the end of the paper. Use marginal comments and proofreading symbols (see p. 394) to highlight mechanical problems. But don't correct these items. Leave it to the writer to figure out what is wrong.

Be specific in identifying problems or opportunities.   For instance, it doesn't help a writer to read "organization is confusing." Instead, point to places in the draft that went off track. If one sentence or paragraph exemplifies a particular problem—or strength—highlight it in some fashion and mention it in the final comment. Nothing helps a writer less than vague complaints or cheerleading: *You did a real good job though I'm not sure you supported your thesis.* It's far better to write something like the following: *Your thesis on the opening page is clear and challenging, but by the second page, you seem to have forgotten what you are trying to prove. The paragraphs there don't seem tied to the original claim, nor do I find enough evidence to support the points you do make. Restructure these opening pages.* Too tough? Not at all. The editor takes the paper seriously enough to explain why it's not working.

Offer suggestions for improvement.   You soften criticism when you follow it up with reasonable suggestions or strategies for revision. It's fine, too, to direct writers to resources they might use, from more authoritative sources to better software. Avoid the tendency, however, to revise the paper for your colleague or to redesign it to suit your own interests and opinions.

> No passion in the world is equal to the passion to alter someone else's draft.

—H. G. Wells

revise and edit
p. 386

Praise what is genuinely good in the paper.   An editor can easily overlook what's working well in a paper, and yet a writer needs that information as much as any pertinent criticism. Find something good to say, too, even about a paper that mostly doesn't work. You'll encourage the writer who may be facing some lengthy revisions. But don't make an issue of it. Writers will know immediately if you are scraping bottom to find something worthy of praise.

Use proofreading symbols.   Proofreading marks may seem fussy or impersonal, but they can be a useful way of quickly highlighting some basic errors or omissions. Here are some you might want to remember and use when editing a paper draft.

sp	Word misspelled (not a standard mark, but useful)
✗	Check for error here (not a standard mark)
ϒ	Delete marked item
⌒	Close up space
⋀	Insert word or phrase
⋏	Insert comma
❝ ❞	Insert quotation marks
≡	Capitalize
⊙	Insert period
∩∪	Transpose or reverse the items marked
¶	Begin new paragraph
#	Insert or open up space
(ital)	Italicize word or phrase

how

It is amazing much of our day-to-day lives now depend on increasingly

SP seemless kinds of communication, our cell phones talking to our PDAs,

drawing e-mails from the air, sharing texts with each other, down loading

images, and taking pictures. Our communications now seem infinitely

layered a real life *Alice in Wonderland* experience Messages don't begin

or end somewhere; they are part of a magical stream of information that

extends the reach of human intelligence, to make us all connected to

anything we want.

Keep comments tactful.   Treat another writer's work the way you'd like to have your own efforts treated. Slips in writing can be embarrassing enough without an editor making sport of them.

How to... *Insert a comment in a Word document*

Using an earlier version of Microsoft Word? See bedfordstmartins.com/howtowrite.

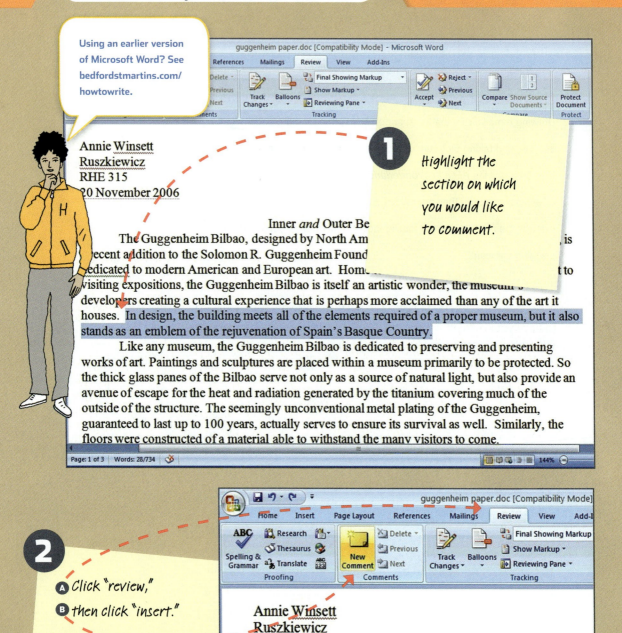

1 Highlight the section on which you would like to comment.

2

Ⓐ Click "review,"

Ⓑ then click "insert."

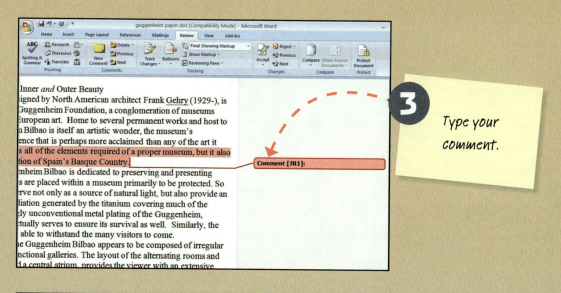

3 Type your comment.

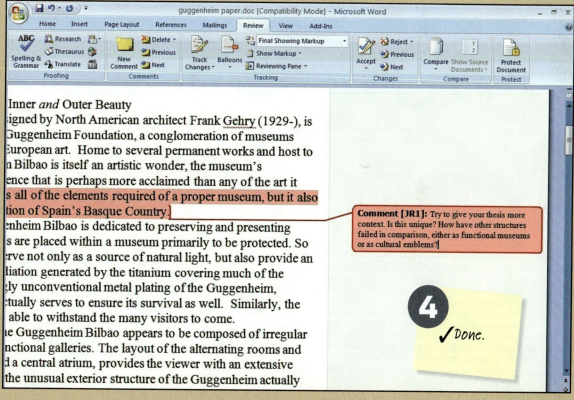

4 ✓ Done.

Research & Sources

part seven

7

35 Beginning Your Research

plan a project

Research can be part of any major writing project. Creative writers spend hours in a library gathering data about historical periods or contemporary events. Authors of reports conduct surveys and studies to confirm what they believe about a topic. And people engaged in arguments (ideally, at least) consult dozens of professional sources to be sure their claims are accurate and fully supported. O

When doing research, you uncover what is already known about a topic. For humanities courses, this involves examining a wide range of books, articles, and Web sources. In the social and natural sciences, you may also perform experiments or do field research to create and share new knowledge about a topic.

So where do you begin your research project and how do you keep from being swamped by the sheer weight of information available? You need smart research strategies.

Know your assignment.   Begin by reviewing the assignment sheet for a term paper or research project, when one is provided, and be sure you understand the kinds of research the paper requires. For a one-page position paper related to a class discussion, you might use only the reference section of the library and your textbook. An argument about current events will likely send you to newspapers, magazines, and various Web sites, while a full-length term paper is researched by seeking out academic books

400

understand argument
p. 68

and journals. (For details and advice on a wide variety of assignments, refer to Parts One and Two.)

Come up with a plan.   Research takes time. You have to find sources, read them, record your findings, and then write about them. Most research projects also require formal documentation and some type of formal presentation, either as a research paper or, perhaps, an oral report. This stuff cannot be scammed the night before. You can avoid chaos by preparing a calendar that links specific tasks to specific dates. Simply creating the schedule (and you should keep it *simple*) might even jump-start your actual research. At a minimum, record important due dates in your day planner. Here's a basic schedule for a research paper with three deadlines.

Research is formalized curiosity. It is poking and prying with a purpose.

—*Zora Neale Hurston*

Schedule: Research Paper

February 19: Topic Proposal Due
___ *Explore and select a topic*
___ *Do preliminary library research*
___ *Define a thesis or hypothesis*
___ *Prepare an annotated bibliography*

March 26: First draft due
___ *Read, summarize, and paraphrase sources*
___ *Organize the paper*

April 16: Final draft due
___ *Get peer feedback on draft*
___ *Revise the project*
___ *Check documentation*
___ *Edit the project*

Find a manageable topic.   Keep in mind that any topic and thesis for a research project should present you with a reasonable problem to solve.

(For ample advice on finding and developing topics, see Part Three.) Look for an idea or a question you can explore sensibly within the scope of the assignment and the allotted time, and with the resources available to you.

When asked to submit a ten- or twenty-page term paper, some writers panic, thinking they need a topic broad or general enough to fill up all these blank pages. But the opposite is true. You will have more success finding useful sources if you break off small but intriguing parts of much larger subjects.

> *not* Military Aircraft, *but* The Development of Jet Fighters in World War II
>
> *not* The History of Punk Rock, *but* The Influence of 1970s Punk Rock on Nirvana
>
> *not* Developmental Disorders in Children, *but* Cri Du Chat Syndrome

Read broadly at first in order to find a general subject to then narrow down to a topic. Then brainstorm this topic to come up with focused questions you might ask in your preliminary research. By the end of this early stage of the research process, your goal is to have turned a topic idea or phrase into a claim at least one full sentence long. ○

In the natural and social sciences, topics sometimes evolve from research problems already on the table in various fields. Presented with this research agenda in a course, you then ordinarily begin with a "review of the literature" to determine what others have published on this issue in the major journals. Then create an experiment in which your research question—offered as a claim called a *hypothesis*—either confirms the direction of ongoing work in the field or perhaps advances or changes it. In basic science courses, get plenty of advice from your instructor about framing sensible research questions and hypotheses.

Seek professional help.   During your preliminary research phase, you'll quickly discover that not all sources are equal. ○ They differ in purpose, method, media, audience, and credibility. Until you get your legs as a re-searcher, never hesitate to ask questions about research tools and strategies: Get recommendations about the best available journals, books, and authors from teachers and reference librarians. Ask them which publishers, institu-

develop a thesis
p. 336

find reliable sources
p. 415

tions, and experts carry the most intellectual authority in their fields. If your topic is highly specialized, plan to spend additional time tracking down sources outside of your own library.

Distinguish between *primary* and *secondary* sources.   This basic distinction is worth keeping in mind as you approach a new subject and project: A *primary source* is a document that provides an eyewitness account of an event or phenomenon; a *secondary source* is a step or two removed, an article or book that interprets or reports on events and phenomena described in primary sources. The famous Zapruder film of the John F. Kennedy assassination in Dallas (November 22, 1963) is a memorable primary historical document; the many books or articles that draw on the film to comment on the assassination are secondary sources. Both types of sources are useful to you as a researcher.

Use primary sources when doing research that breaks new ground. Primary sources represent raw data—letters, journals, newspaper accounts, official documents, laws, court opinions, statistics, research reports, audio and video recordings, and so on. Working with primary materials, you generate your own ideas about a subject, free of anyone else's opinions or explanations. Or you can review the actual evidence others have used to make prior claims and arguments, perhaps reinterpreting their findings or bringing a new perspective to the subject.

Web sites featuring government resources, such as Thomas or FedStats, and corporate annual reports provide primary material for analysis.

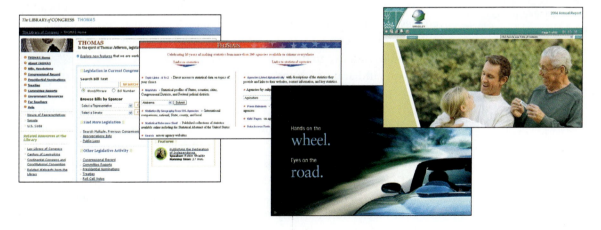

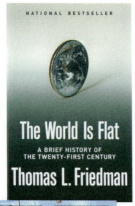

Reprinted by permission from Macmillan Publishers Ltd.: NATURE, © January 2008.

Books and magazines often provide secondary, not primary, information.

Use secondary sources to learn what others have discovered or said about a subject. In many fields, you spend most of your time reviewing secondary materials, especially when researching areas of knowledge new to you. Secondary sources include scholarly books and articles, encyclopedias, magazine pieces, and many Web sites. In academic assignments, you may find yourself moving easily between different kinds of materials, first reading a primary text like *Hamlet* and then reading various commentaries on it.

Record every source you examine.   Most writers and researchers download or photocopy sources rather than examine original copies in a library and take notes. However you plan on working, *you must* accurately record every source you encounter right from the start, gathering the following information:

- Authors, editors, translators, sponsors (of Web sites) or other major contributors
- Titles, subtitles, edition numbers, volumes
- Publication information, including places of publication and publishers (for books); titles of magazines and journals, volume and page numbers; dates of publication and access (the latter for online materials)
- Page numbers, URLs, electronic pathways, or other locators

You'll need these details later to document your sources.

It might seem obsessive to collect basic bibliographic data on books and articles you know you are unlikely to use. But when you expect to spend weeks or months on an assignment, log all material you examine so that later you won't have to backtrack, wondering "Did I miss this source?" A log also comes in handy if you need to revisit a source later in your research.

Prepare a topic proposal.   Your instructor may request a topic proposal. Typically, this includes a topic idea, a draft thesis or hypothesis, potential sources, your intended approach, and a list of potential problems.

Remember that such proposals are written to get feedback about your project's feasibility, and that even a good idea raises questions. Following is a sample proposal for a short project directed chiefly to peers invited to respond via electronic discussion board.

Eades 1

Micah Eades

Professor Kurtz

English 201

March 20, 20--

Causal Analysis Proposal: Awkward Atmospheres

People don't like going to the doctor's office. You wait in an office room decorated from the 1980s reading *Highlights* or last year's *Field & Stream* and listen to patients in the next room talking about the details of their proctology exam. Since I am planning a future as a primary care physician, I don't want people to dread coming to see me.

My paper will propose that patient dissatisfaction with visits to their physicians may not be due entirely to fear of upcoming medical examinations but rather to the unwelcoming atmosphere of most waiting and treatment rooms. More specifically, I will examine the negative effect that noise, poor interior design, and unsympathetic staff attitudes may have on patient comfort. I will propose that these factors have a much larger impact on patient well-being than previously expected. Additionally, I will propose possible remedies and ways to change these negative perceptions.

My biggest problem may be finding concrete evidence for my claims. For evidence, I do intend to cite the relatively few clinical studies that have been conducted on patient satisfaction and atmosphere. My audience will be a tough crowd: doctors who have neither an awareness of the problems I describe nor much desire to improve the ambience of their offices.

Marginal notes:

Opening paragraph offers rationale for subject choice.

Title indicates that proposal responds to specific assignment.

Describes planned content and structure of paper.

Has done enough research to know that literature on subject is not extensive.

Paper will be directed to specific audience.

36

Finding Print and Online Sources

When beginning an academic research project, whether a brief report or a full term paper or thesis, you'll likely turn to three resources: local and school libraries, informational databases and indexes, and the Internet.

At the library are books, journals, and newspapers and other printed materials in a collection overseen by librarians to preserve information and support research. Often, the help of these librarians is necessary to locate and evaluate sources.

refine your
search

Also at a library or among its online resources are databases and indexes with electronic access to abstracts or full-text versions of up-to-date research materials in professional journals, magazines, and newspaper archives. Your library or school purchases licenses to allow you to use these password-protected resources—services such as EBSCOhost, InfoTrac, and LexisNexis.

And, of course, you can find endless streams of information with your computer simply by exploring the Web, using search engines such as Google and Yahoo! to locate data. Information on the Web varies hugely in quality, but covers just about every subject imaginable.

Whether working in a physical library, within a library catalog or an electronic database, or at home on your computer, you need to know how to use the full capacity of research tools designed to search large bodies of information.

Learn to navigate the library catalog.   All but the smallest or most specialized libraries now organize their collections electronically. Be sure you know how the electronic catalog works: It tells you if the library has an item you need, where it is on the shelves, and whether it has been checked out. You can search for most items by author, title, subject, keywords, and even call number.

Pay special attention to the terms or keywords by which an item you've located in an electronic catalog has been indexed: You can then use those terms to search for similar materials, an important way of generating leads on a topic.

In addition to author, title, and publication information, the full entry for an item in a library catalog will include subject headings. These terms may suggest additional avenues of research.

Locate research guides.   Another excellent option for starting an academic project is to use research sites prepared by libraries or universities to help researchers working in specific fields. Check to see whether your institution has developed such materials. Or simply search the phrase "library research guides" on Google. Such sites identify resources both within and outside of academic institutions, and may also give you suggestions for topic ideas or research areas. Use these guides carefully, since they may contain links to sites that libraries and schools cannot vouch for entirely. The charts on pages 408 and 411 will help you find databases for your subject.

You will probably begin your search with one or more multidisciplinary databases such as *LexisNexis Academic*, *Academic OneFile*, or *Academic Search Premier*. These resources cover a wide range of materials, including newspapers, respected magazines, and some professional journals. Most libraries subscribe to one or more such information services, and these can be searched using keywords.

But for more in-depth work, focus on the databases within your specific discipline. There are, in fact, hundreds of such databases and tools, far too many to list here. Look for databases that present current materials at a level you can understand: Some online resources may be too specific or technical for your project. When working with a database for the first time, review

Research Guides and Databases	
Institution	**Subject Guides at**
Columbia University Library	www.columbia.edu/cu/lweb/eresources
New York Public Library	www.nypl.org/research/electronic/subject.cfm
The Ohio State University	library.osu.edu/sites/thegateway
Stanford University	http://library.stanford.edu/research_help/res_quick_start
University of Chicago	www.lib.uchicago.edu/e/su
The University of Texas at Austin	www.lib.utexas.edu/subject
University of Virginia	www.lib.virginia.edu/resguide.html
Yale University Library	www.library.yale.edu/guides
Electronic Books	www.lib.utexas.edu/books/etext.html
Infomine	http://infomine.ucr.edu
The Internet Public Library	www.ipl.org
Librarians' Internet Index	http://lii.org
Library of Congress Research Centers	http://lcweb.loc.gov/rr/research-centers.html

the Help section or page to find the most efficient way to conduct your searches. Librarians, too, can offer professional advice on refining your search techniques.

Identify the best reference tools for your needs.   For encyclopedias, almanacs, historical records, maps, and so on, head to the reference section of your library and ask the librarian to direct you to the appropriate items.

Quite often, for instance, you'll need to trace the biographical facts of important people—dates of birth, countries of origin, schools attended, career paths, and so on. For current newsmakers, you might find enough fairly reliable data from a Google or Yahoo! search or a Wikipedia entry. But to get the most accurate information on historical figures, consult more authoritative library tools such as the *Oxford Dictionary of National Biography* (focusing on the United Kingdom) or the *Dictionary of American Biography.* The British work is available in an up-to-date online version. Libraries also have more specialized biographical resources, both in print and online.

When you need information from old newspapers, you'll need more ingenuity. Libraries don't store newspapers, so local and selected national papers will be available only on microfilm. Just as limiting, few older papers are indexed. So, unless you know the approximate date of an event, you may have a tough time finding a story in the microfilmed copies of newspapers. Fortunately, both the *New York Times* and *Wall Street Journal* are indexed and available on microfilm in most major libraries. You'll also find older magazines on microfilm. These may be indexed (up to 1982) in print bibliographies such as *Readers' Guide to Periodical Literature.* Ask a librarian for help.

When your library doesn't have the material you need, ask the librarian if it's possible to acquire the material from another facility through interlibrary loan. The loan process may take time, but if you plan ahead, you can get any reasonable item.

Use online sources intelligently.   Browsing the Web daily to check the sports scores and surf your favorite blogs and Web sites is a completely different matter than using the Web for research. Thanks to exhaustive search engines like Google and Yahoo!, you can find facts on just about any subject—often too much information. And the quality of the results you turn up in a Web search will be uneven. Hits are returned by popularity, not reliability.

Improve your online research the same way you navigate a library's academic databases: Study the Help screens that accompany the Web browser. Most offer advanced search options to help you turn up fewer and more pertinent materials.

But you also need to exercise care with Web sources. Be certain you know who is responsible for the material (for instance, a government agency, a congressional office, a news service, a corporation), who is posting it, who is the author of the material or sponsor of the Web site, what the date of

Google's Help screen
provides tips on how to
search the Internet.

publication is, and so on. ○ A site's information is often skewed by those who pay its bills or run it; it can also be outdated, if no one regularly updates the site.

Keep current with Web developments, too. Web companies such as Google are making more books and journal articles both searchable and available through their sites. Although these and other projects to broaden access to scholarly information do raise questions about copyright and the ownership of intellectual property, you should certainly take time to explore the tools as they become available.

For instance, a tool such as Google Scholar will direct you to academic sources and scholarly papers on a subject—exactly the kind of material you would want to use in a term paper or report. As an experiment, you might compare the hits you get on a topic with a regular Google search with those that turn up when you select the Scholar option. You'll quickly notice that the Scholar items are more serious and technical—and also more difficult to access. In some cases, you may see only an abstract of a journal article or the first page of the item. Yet the sources you locate may be worth a trip to the library to retrieve in their entirely.

find reliable sources
p. 415

Resources to Consult When Conducting Research

Source	What It Provides	Usefulness in Academic Research	Where to Find It
Scholarly Books	Fully documented and detailed primary research and analyses by scholars	Highly useful, if not too high-level or technical	Library, Google Scholar
Scholarly Journals	Carefully documented primary research by scientists and scholars	Highly useful, if not too high-level or technical	Library, databases
Newspapers	Accounts of current events	Useful as starting point	Library, microfilm, databases (LexisNexis), Internet
Magazines	Wide topic range, usually based on secondary research; written for popular audience	Useful if magazine has serious reputation	Libraries, newsstands, databases (EBSCOhost, InfoTrac), Internet
Encyclopedias (General or Discipline-Specific)	Brief articles	Useful as a starting point	Libraries, Internet
Wikipedia	Open-source encyclopedia: entries written/edited by online contributors	Not considered reliable for academic projects	Internet: www.wikipedia.org
Special Collections	Materials such as maps, paintings, artifacts, etc.	Highly useful for specialized projects	Libraries, museums; images available via Internet
Government, Academic, or Organization Web Sites	Vast data compilations of varying quality, some of it reviewed	Highly useful	Internet sites with URLs ending in: *.gov*, *.edu*, or *.org*
Commercial Web Sites	Information on many subjects; quality varies	Useful if possible biases are known	Internet sites
Blogs	Controlled, often highly partisan discussions of specialized topics	Useful when affiliated with reputable sources such as newspapers	Internet
Personal Web Sites	Often idiosyncratic information	Rarely useful; content varies widely	Internet

37 Doing Field Research

While most research you do will be built on the work of others—that is, their books, articles, and fact-finding—you can strike out on your own in many situations. For instance, you might interview people with experiences or information related to the subject you're exploring. O Or support a claim by carefully observing and recording how people actually behave or think.

interview and observe

Interview people with unique knowledge of your subject. When considering whether an interview makes sense for your project, ask yourself the important question, What do I expect to learn from the interviewee? If the information you seek is readily available online or in print, don't waste everyone's time going through with an interview. If, on the other hand, this person provides a unique perspective on your topic, a personal interview may make an excellent contribution to your research.

Written interviews, whether by e-mail or letter, allow you to keep questions and answers focused and provide a written record of your interviewee's exact words. But spoken interviews, both in person and on the phone, allow in-depth discussion of a topic, and may lead to more memorable quotes or deeper insights. Be flexible in setting up the type of interview most convenient for your subject. For interviews, keep the following suggestions in mind:

ask for help
p. 325

- Request an interview formally by phone, confirming it with a follow-up e-mail.

- Give your subjects a compelling reason for meeting or corresponding with you, briefly explaining your research project and why their knowledge or experience is essential to your work.

- Let potential interviewees know how you chose them as subjects. If possible, provide a personal reference—a professor or administrator who can vouch for you.

- Prepare a set of smart and relevant interview questions to encourage your subject to elaborate.

- Start the interview by thanking the interviewee for his or her time and providing a brief reminder of your research project.

- Keep a written record of material you wish to quote. If necessary, confirm the exact wording with your interviewee.

- End the interview by again expressing your thanks.

- Follow up on the interview with a thank-you note or e-mail and, if the interviewee's contributions were substantial, send him or her a copy of the research paper.

- In your paper, give full credit to any people interviewed by properly documenting the information they provided. ○

If you conduct your interview in writing, request a response by a certain date—one or two weeks is reasonable for ten questions. Refer to Chapter 11 for e-mail etiquette and Chapter 12 for guidelines on writing business letters.

For telephone interviews, call from a place with good reception, and where you will not be interrupted. Your cell phone should be fully charged or plugged in.

For an interview conducted in person, arrive at the predetermined meeting place on time and dressed professionally. If you wish to tape-record the interview, be sure to ask permission first.

Make careful and verifiable observations.   In writing both reports and arguments, especially those addressed to a local community, you might find yourself lacking sufficient data to move your claims beyond mere opinion.

understand citation
styles p. 435

The point of systematic observation is to provide a clear, reliable, and verifiable way of studying a narrowly defined activity or phenomenon.

To argue, for example, that open meeting rooms in the student union are not used efficiently, you could construct a systematic observation of these facilities, showing exactly how many student groups use them on what basis over a given period of time. This kind of real evidence carries more weight than opinion because your readers can study exactly how you conducted your observations and accept or challenge your results.

Some situations can't be counted or measured as readily as the one described above. If, for example, you wanted to compare the various meeting rooms to determine whether rooms with windows facilitated more productive discussions than those without, your observations would need to be more qualitative. For example, to record whether meeting participants appeared alert or distracted, you might describe the tone of their voices and the general mood of the room. Numbers should figure in this observation as well; for instance, you could track how many people participated in the discussion or the number of tasks accomplished during the meeting.

To avoid bias in their observations, many researchers use double-column notebooks. In one column, they record the physical details of their observation as objectively as possible—descriptions, sounds, countable data, weather, time, circumstances, activity, and so on. In the second column, they record their interpretations and commentaries on the data.

In addition to careful and objective note-taking techniques, devices such as cameras, video recorders, and tape recorders provide reliable backup evidence about an event. Also, having more than one witness observe a situation can help verify your findings.

A double-column note-book entry

OBSERVABLE DATA	COMMENTARY
9/12/07	
2 P.M.	
Meeting of Entertainment Committee	
Room MUB210 (no windows)	
91 degrees outside	
Air conditioning broken	Heat and lack of a/c probably making
People appear quiet, tired, hot	everyone miserable.

Evaluating Sources

38

In Chapter 36, you were steered in the direction of the best possible print and online sources for your research. But the fact is, all sources, no mater how prestigious, have strengths and weaknesses, biases and limitations. Even the most well-intentioned librarians have their own preferences and prejudices, too. So evaluating sources is simply a routine and unavoidable part of any research process. Here are some strategies to use when making your own judgments about potential sources.

find reliable sources

Preview source materials for their key features and strategies.

Give any source a quick once-over, looking for clues to its aim, content, and structure. Begin with the title and subtitle, taking seriously its key terms and qualifiers. A good title tells what a piece is—and is not—about. For many scholarly articles, the subtitle (which typically follows a colon) describes the substance of the argument.

Then scan the introduction (in a book) or abstract (in an article). From these, you should be able to quickly grasp what the source will cover, its methods, and what the author hopes to prove or accomplish.

Pay attention to the table of contents in a book or the headings in an article, using them to grasp the overall structure of the work or to find specific information. Briefly review charts, tables, and illustrations, too, to discover what they offer, and look up a key term or subject in the index.

If the work appears promising, read its final section or chapter. Knowing how the source concludes gives considerable insight into its possible usefulness for you during your actual research. Finally, look over the bibliography. The list of sources indicates how thorough the author has been and, not incidentally, points you to other sources you might want to consult.

Check who published or produced the source.   In general, books published by presses associated with colleges and universities (Harvard, Oxford, Stanford, etc.) are reputable sources for college papers. So are articles from professional journals described as *refereed* or *peer-reviewed*. These terms are used for journals in which the articles have been impartially reviewed by panels of experts prior to publication.

You can also usually rely on material from reputable commercial publishers and from established institutions and agencies. The *New York Times, Newsweek,* CNN, Random House, and the U.S. government make their share of mistakes, of course, but are generally considered to be more reliable than personal Web sites or blogs.

Check who wrote the work.   Ordinarily, you should cite authorities on your topic. Look for authors who are mentioned frequently and favorably within a field or whose works appear regularly in notes or bibliographies. Get familiar with these names.

The Web makes it possible to review the careers of many authors whom you might not recognize. Perform a Google search for their names to confirm that they are professional experts or reputable journalists. Avoid citing authors working too far beyond their areas of professional expertise. Celebrities especially like to cross boundaries, sometimes mistaking their passion for an issue for genuine mastery of the subject.

You can learn a lot about a
source by previewing a few
basic elements.

Available online at www.sciencedirect.com

SCIENCE @ DIRECT®

ACADEMIC
PRESS

Journal of Research in Personality 36 (2002) 607–614

JOURNAL OF
RESEARCH IN
PERSONALITY

www.academicpress.com

Brief report

Are we barking up the right tree?
Evaluating a comparative approach
to personality

Playful title nonetheless fits:
Article is about animals.

Samuel D. Gosling * and Simine Vazire

Department of Psychology, University of Texas, Austin, TX, USA

Abstract

Animal studies can enrich the field of human personality psychology by addressing questions that are difficult or impossible to address with human studies
alone. However, the benefits of a comparative approach to personality cannot be
reaped until the tenability of the personality construct has been established in animals. Using criteria established in the wake of the person–situation debate (Kenrick & Funder, 1988), the authors evaluate the status of personality traits in
animals. The animal literature provides strong evidence that personality does exist
in animals. That is, personality ratings of animals: (a) show strong levels of inte-
robserver agreement, (b) show evidence of validity in terms of predicting behaviors and real-world outcomes, and (c) do not merely reflect the implicit theories of
observers projected onto animals. Although much work remains to be done,
the preliminary groundwork has been laid for a comparative approach to personality.
© 2002 Elsevier Science (USA). All rights reserved.

Abstract previews entire
article.

Introduction

Personality characteristics have been examined in a broad range of non-
human species including chimpanzees, rhesus monkeys, ferrets, hyenas, rats,

Headings throughout signal
this is a research article.

* Corresponding author. Fax: 1-512- 471-5935.
   E-mail address: gosling@psy.utexas.edu (S.D. Gosling).

0092-6566/02/$ - see front matter © 2002 Elsevier Science (USA). All rights reserved.
PII: S0092-6566(02)00511-1

sheep, rhinoceros, hedgehogs, zebra finches, garter snakes, guppies, and oc-topuses (for a full review, see Gosling, 2001). Such research is important be-cause animal studies can be used to tackle questions that are difficult or impossible to address with human studies alone. By reaping the benefits of animal research, a comparative approach to personality can enrich the field of human personality psychology, providing unique opportunities to examine the biological, genetic, and environmental bases of personality, and to study personality development, personality-health links, and person-ality perception. However, all of these benefits hinge on the tenability of the personality construct in non-human animals. Thus, the purpose of the pres-ent paper is to address a key question in the animal domain: is personality real? That is, do personality traits reflect real properties of individuals or are they fictions in the minds of perceivers?

Thirty years ago, the question of the reality of personality occupied the attention of human-personality researchers, so our evaluation of the com-parative approach to personality draws on the lessons learned in the hu-man domain. Mischel's (1968) influential critique of research on human personality was the first of a series of direct challenges to the assumptions that personality exists and predicts meaningful real-world behaviors. Based on a review of the personality literature, Mischel (1968) pointed to the lack of evidence that individuals' behaviors are consistent across situations (Mi-schel & Peake, 1982). Over the next two decades, personality researchers garnered substantial empirical evidence to counter the critiques of person-ality. In an important article, Kenrick and Funder (1988) carefully ana-lyzed the various arguments that had been leveled against personality and summarized the theoretical and empirical work refuting these argu-ments.

The recent appearance of studies of animal personality has elicited re-newed debate about the status of personality traits. Gosling, Lilienfeld, and Marino (in press) proposed that the conditions put forward by Kenrick and Funder (1988) to evaluate the idea of human personality can be mobi-lized in the service of evaluating the idea of animal personality. Gosling et al. (in press) used these criteria to evaluate research on personality in non-human primates. In the present paper, we extend their analysis to the broad-er field of comparative psychology, considering research on nonhuman animals from several species and taxa. Kenrick and Funder's paper delin-eates three major criteria that must be met to establish the existence of per-sonality traits: (1) assessments by independent observers must agree with one another; (2) these assessments must predict behaviors and real-world outcomes; and (3) observer ratings must be shown to reflect genuine attri-butes of the individuals rated, not merely the observers' implicit theories about how personality traits covary. Drawing on evidence from the animal-behavior literature, we evaluate whether these three criteria have been met with respect to animal personality.

Point of this brief study is defined at end of opening paragraph.

This page reviews literature on studies of animal per-sonality.

Consider the audience for a source.   What passes for adequate information in the general marketplace of ideas may not cut it when you're doing academic research. Many widely read books and articles that popularize a subject—such as global warming or problems with health care—may, in fact, be based on more technical scholarly books and articles. For academic projects, rely primarily on those scholarly works themselves, even if you were inspired to choose a subject by reading respectable nonfiction. Glossy magazines shouldn't play a role in your research either, though the lines can get blurry. *People, Oprah,* probably *Rolling Stone,* or *Spin* might be important in writing about popular culture or music, but not for much else.

Establish how current a source is.   Scholarly work doesn't come with an expiration date, but you should base your research on the latest information. For fields in which research builds on previous work, the date of publication may even be highlighted by its system of documentation. Copyright pages, on the back of the title page, list the date of publication.

Check the source's documentation.   All serious scholarly and scientific research is documented. Claims are based on solid evidence backed up by formal notes, data packed into charts and tables, and there will be a bibliography at the end.

In a news story, journalists may establish the credibility of their information by naming their sources or, at a minimum, attributing their findings to reliable unnamed sources—and usually more than one. The authors of serious magazine pieces don't use footnotes and bibliographies either, but they too credit their major sources somewhere in the work. No serious claim should be left hanging.

For your own academic projects, avoid authors and sources with undocumented assertions. Sometimes you have to trust authors when they are writing about personal experiences or working as field reporters, but let readers know when your claims are based on uncorroborated personal accounts.

Orlando Bloom at a conference on the environment: He may contribute his two cents to campaigns combating global warming, but don't cite him in research papers.

Critical Reading and Note-Taking Strategies

analyze claims and evidence / take notes

Once you locate trustworthy sources, review them to identify the best ideas and most convincing evidence for your project. During this process of careful and critical reading, you annotate, summarize, and paraphrase your sources, in effect creating the notes you need to compose your paper.

Read sources critically to identify *claims, assumptions, and evidence.* Read important sources closely enough to understand not only what they say but also how they reached their conclusions or compiled their data. In a sense, you have to become an expert on the sources you cite, to locate and analyze claims, assumptions, and evidence in a text. ○

Annotate a source to understand it. Begin by noting and highlighting specific claims, themes, or thesis statements a writer offers early in a text. Then pay attention to the way these ideas recur within the work, especially near the conclusion. At a minimum, decide whether a writer has made reasonable claims, developed them consistently, and delivered on promised evidence. In the example that follows, claims and reasons are highlighted in yellow.

Finding and annotating the assumptions in a source can be *much* trickier. Highlight any assumptions stated outright in the source. They will be rare. More often, you have to infer the writer's assumptions, put them in your own words, and perhaps record

understand rhetorical
analysis p. 222

them in marginal notes. Identifying controversial or debatable assumptions is particularly important. For instance, if a writer makes the claim that *America needs tighter border security to prevent terrorist attacks*, you draw the inference that the writer believes that terrorism is caused by people crossing inadequately patrolled borders. Is that assumption accurate? Should the writer explain or defend it? Raise such questions. The one key assumption in the example below is highlighted in orange.

At the same time, look for evidence the authors use to support their claims, which usually make up the bulk of the academic materials you read. So highlight only the key items of supporting evidence—especially facts or testimony you intend to cite in your project. Make sure no crucial point goes unsupported. In the following example, key evidence is highlighted in blue.

Finally, your marginal annotations should record your own reactions and responses to a text, and represent your assessment of or objections to particular ideas or research claims. To be certain you don't later mistake your comments for observations *from* the source, use first person or pose questions as you respond. Use personal annotations, too, to draw connections to other source materials you have read. In the following example, personal reactions appear on the left.

Sanity 101

Parents of adolescents usually strive for an aura of calm and reason. But just two words can trigger irrational behavior in parent and child alike: "college admissions."

CLAIM AND REASON: Fear of college admissions procedures is key point in editorial.

It's not an unreasonable response, actually, given the list of exasperating questions facing parents seeking to maximize their children's prospects: Do I tutor my child to boost college admissions test scores? Do I rely on the school admissions counselor or hire a private adviser? Do I hire a professional editor to shape my child's college essay?

EVIDENCE: Specific concerns support initial claim. They are the issues troubling parents most.

CLAIM

EVIDENCE

READER'S REACTION:
Why don't colleges realize
how unfair their admissions
policies might be to poorer
applicants?

The price tags behind those decisions drive up the angst. A testing tutor "guaranteeing" a 200-point score boost on the SAT admissions test will charge roughly $2,400. Hiring a private college counselor can cost from $1,300 to $10,000. And hiring an essay editor can cost between $60 and $1,800. Wealthy suburbs are particularly lucrative for the college prep industry. Less affluent families are left with even greater reason to fret: Their children face an unfair disadvantage.

Now, private employers are stepping in to help out.

CLAIM

EVIDENCE

In a front-page article on Tuesday, *USA TODAY*'s education reporter Mary Beth Marklein revealed a range of counseling packages that companies are offering parents of college applicants, from brown-bag discussion lunches to Web-based programs that manage the entire admissions process.

It's thoughtful of the employers, but it shouldn't be necessary.

READER'S REACTION:
Might there be a parallel
here to out-of-control sports
programs? Why are schools
so poorly administered?

EVIDENCE

Thanks to overanxious parents, aggressive college admissions officials and hustling college prep entrepreneurs, the admissions system has spun out of control. And the colleges have done little to restore sanity.

CLAIM:
This assertion, midway
through editorial, may in
fact be its thesis.

Take just one example, the "early decision" process in which seniors apply to a college by November 1 and promise to attend if admitted.

Early decision induces students to cram demanding courses into their junior year so they will appear on the application record. That makes an already stressful year for students and parents even more so. Plus, students must commit to a college long before they are ready. The real advantages of early decision go to colleges, which gain more control over their student mix and rise in national rankings by raising their acceptance rates.

Parents and students can combat the stress factor by keeping a few key facts in mind. While it's true that the very top colleges are ruthlessly selective—both Harvard and Yale accept slightly less than 10 percent of applicants—most colleges are barely selective. Of the 1,400 four-year colleges in the United States, only about 100 are very selective, and they aren't right for every student. Among the other 1,300, an acceptance rate of about 85 percent is more the norm.

And the best part of all: Many of those 1,300 colleges are more interested in educating your child than burnishing their rankings on lists of the "top" institutions. So the next time you hear the words "college admissions," don't instantly open your wallet. First, take a deep breath.

—Editorial/Opinion, *USA Today,* January 19, 2006

CLAIM AND REASON:
Parents are worrying too much.

EVIDENCE:
Statistics offer reasons not to fear college admissions procedures.

ASSUMPTION:
Change "are" to "should be" and you have the assumption underlying this entire argument.

40 Summarizing Sources

Once you determine that an article, book, or other text deserves closer scrutiny and you have read it critically—with an eye toward using its insights and data in your own project—you're ready to put the ideas you've discovered into your own words. In effect, your brief summaries or fuller paraphrases will be the notes for composing your paper. ○

sum up ideas

Use a summary to recap what a writer has said.   Look carefully for the main point and build your summary on it, making sure that this statement *does* accurately reflect the content of the source. ○ Be certain that the summary is *entirely* in your own words. Include the author and title of the work, too, so you can easily cite it later. Following is one summary of the *USA Today* editorial reprinted in Chapter 39 (p. 421), with all the required citation information:

> In "Sanity 101," the editors of *USA Today* (January 19, 2006) criticize current college admission practices, which, they argue, make students and parents alike fear that getting into an appropriate school is harder than it really is.
>
> Source: "Sanity 101." Editorial. *USA Today* 19 Jan. 2006: 10A. Print.

restate ideas
p. 428

develop a thesis
p. 336

Be sure your summary is accurate and complete.   Even when a source makes several points, moves in contradictory directions, or offers a complex conclusion, your job is simply to describe what the material does. Don't embellish the material or blur the distinction between the source's words and yours. Include all bibliographical information (title, author, and date) from the source. The following summary of "Sanity 101" shows what can go wrong if you are not careful.

According to *USA Today*, ==most students get into the colleges they want.== But admission into most colleges is so tough that many parents blow a fortune on tutors and counselors so that their kids can win early admission. But the paper's advice to parents is ==don't instantly open your wallet. First, take a deep breath.==

> Omits title/source. Opening claim is not in editorial.
>
> Editorial actually makes opposite point.
>
> Summary improperly uses source's exact words. Might lead to inadvertent plagiarism later on.

Use a summary to record your take on a source.   In addition to reporting the contents of the material accurately, note also how the source might (or might not) contribute to your paper. Make sure that your comments won't be confused with claims made in the summarized article itself. Following are two acceptable sample summaries for "Sanity 101."

In "Sanity 101" *USA Today* (January 19, 2006) describes the efforts of college applicants and parents to deal with the progressively more competitive admissions policies of elite institutions. The editorial claims that most schools, however, are far less selective. The article includes a reference to another *USA Today* piece by Mary Beth Markelin on the support some companies offer employees to assist them with college admissions issues.

Source: "Sanity 101." Editorial. *USA Today* 19 Jan. 2006: 10A. Print.

In an editorial (January 19, 2006) entitled "Sanity 101," *USA Today* counsels parents against worrying too much about hyper-competitive current college admission practices. In reality only a small percentage of schools are highly selective about admissions. The editorial doesn't provide the schools' side of the issue.

Source: "Sanity 101." Editorial. *USA Today* 19 Jan. 2006: 10A. Print.

Use summaries to prepare an annotated bibliography.   An annotated bibliography is your alphabetical list of research materials, followed by a summary and evaluation of each item. Instructors may ask you to prepare an annotated bibliography early in a research project—sometimes even as part of the topic proposal—to be sure you're on track, reading good sources, and getting the most out of them. Or you may have to attach an annotated bibliography to the final version of a project, enabling your teacher to determine at a glance how well you've researched your subject.

An entry in an annotated bibliography typically has three, sometimes four, parts:

1.   Full citation of the work in correct form ○

2.   Summary of the work

3.   Assessment of the work

4.   Explanation of the role the item may play in your research (when the annotated bibliography is part of a topic proposal or prospectus)

Following are three items from an annotated bibliography offered as part of a topic proposal on the cultural impact of the iPod.

Full bibliographical citation in MLA style.

Summary of Stephenson's argument.

Potential role source might play in paper.

Stephenson, Seth. "You and Your Shadow." *Slate.com* 2 Mar. 2004. Web. 3 Mar. 2007. This article from *Slate*'s "Ad Report Card" series argues that the original iPod ads featuring silhouetted dancers may alienate viewers by suggesting that the product is cooler than the people who buy it. Stephenson explains why some people may resent the advertisements. The piece may be useful for explaining early reactions to the iPod as a cultural phenomenon.

Sullivan, Andrew. "Society Is Dead: We Have Retreated into the iWorld." *Sunday Times* 20 Feb. 2005. Web. 27 Feb. 2007. In this opinion piece, Sullivan examines how people in cities use iPods to isolate themselves from their surroundings. The author makes a highly personal, but plausible case for turning off the machines. The column demonstrates how quickly the iPod influenced society and culture.

Evaluation of Sullivan's opinion piece.

understand citation
styles p. 435

Walker, Rob. "The Guts of a New Machine." *New York Times Magazine* 30 Nov. 2003. *OneFile*. Web. 1 Mar. 2007. This lengthy report describes in detail how Apple developed the concept and technology of the iPod. Walker not only provides a detailed early look at the product but the article also shows how badly Apple's competitors underestimated its market strength.

Citation demonstrates how to cite an article from a database; in this case, *OneFile*.

Prepare a summary to provide a useful record of a source.   After reading a research source, you may decide that all you need is a brief description of it—the gist of it—recorded either on a card or in an electronic file (with complete bibliographic data). Such a summary establishes that you have, in fact, seen and reviewed the source, which can be no small comfort when developing longer projects. After you've examined dozens and dozens of sources, it's quite easy to forget what exactly you've already read.

Paraphrasing Sources

Paraphrasing provides more complete records of the sources you examine than do summaries. Like a summary, a paraphrase includes a recap of a source's main point, but it also traces the claims leading up to its conclusion. Paraphrase materials you expect to use extensively in a project, both to record what these sources contain and to understand them well enough to put their key ideas into your own words.

restate ideas

Identify the claims and structure of the source.   Determine the main points made by a source, and determine how the work organizes information to support its claims. Be certain your paraphrase follows the same structure as your source. For example, your paraphrase will likely be sequentially arranged when a work has a story to tell; arranged by topic when you're dealing with reported information; or logically structured when you take notes from arguments or editorials.

Track the source faithfully.   A paraphrase should follow the reasoning of the source, moving through it economically but remaining faithful to its organization, tone, and, to some extent, style. In effect, you are preparing an abstract of the material, complete and readable in itself. ○ So take compact and sensible notes, adapting the paraphrase to your needs—understanding that some materials will be more valuable to your project than others.

understand lab reports
p. 290

Record key pieces of evidence.   Thanks to photocopies and downloaded files, you don't usually have to copy data laboriously into your notes—and you probably shouldn't. (The chances of error greatly multiply whenever you copy information by hand.) But be certain that your paraphrase does record all key evidence, facts, and supporting reasons for major claims. Key evidence proves a point or seals the deal. Also, keep track of page numbers for the important data so you can cite this material directly from your notes.

Be certain your notes are entirely in your own words.   If you borrow the language of sources as you paraphrase them, you'll likely slip into plagiarism when you compose your paper. Deliberately or not, you could find yourself copying phrases or sentences from the sources into your project.

When you are confident that you've paraphrased sources correctly, never borrowing their language, you then may safely transfer those notes directly into your project—giving the original writers due credit. In effect, you've begun to compose your own paper whenever you write competent paraphrases.

Following is a paraphrase of "Sanity 101," the complete, fully annotated text of which appears in Chapter 39 (see p. 421). Compare the paraphrase here to the summaries of the article that appear in Chapter 40 (see p. 424).

> In an editorial entitled "Sanity 101" (January 19, 2006), the editors of *USA Today* worry that many fearful parents are resorting to costly measures to help assure their child's college admission, some hiring private counselors and tutors that poorer families can't afford. Companies now even offer college admission assistance as part of employees' job packages. Colleges themselves are to blame for the hysteria, in part because of "early admission" practices that benefit them more than students. But parents and students should consider the facts. Only a handful of colleges are truly selective; most have acceptance rates near 85 percent. In addition, most schools care more about students than about their own rankings.

Avoid misleading or inaccurate paraphrasing.   Your notes on sources won't be worth much if your paraphrases distort the content of the material you read. Don't rearrange the information, give it a spin you might prefer, or offer your own opinions on a subject. Make it evident whenever your comments focus just on particular sections or chapters of a source, rather than on the entire piece. That way, you won't misread your notes months later and give readers a wrong impression about an article or book. Following is a paraphrase of "Sanity 101" that gets almost everything wrong.

Opening sentences follow and language of editorial too closely, and also distort structure of editorial.

Parents of teens usually try to be reasonable the editors of *USA Today* complained on January 19, 2006. But the words "college admission" can make both child and parent irrational. The response is not unreasonable given all the irritating questions facing parents seeking to improve their children's prospects. But the fact is that just a few colleges are highly selective. Most of the four-year schools in the country have acceptance rates of 85 percent. So high school students and parents should just chill and not blow their wallets on extra expenses. Rely on the school admissions counselor; don't hire a private advisor or professional editor to shape your child's college essay. A testing tutor might charge $2,400; a private college counselor can cost from $1,300 to $10,000. This is unfair to poorer families too, especially when companies start offering special admissions services to their employees. As always, the colleges are to blame with their pushy "early admissions" programs which make them look good in rankings but just screw their students.

Paraphrase shifts tone, becoming much more colloquial than editorial.

Paraphrase borrows words and phrases too freely from original.

Paraphrase offers opinion on subject, its criticism of colleges going beyond original editorial.

Integrating Sources into Your Work

When you integrate sources effectively into your work, you give readers information they need to identify paraphrased or quoted items and to understand how they may have been edited for clarity or accuracy.

Signal the introduction of all borrowed material, whether summarized, paraphrased, or quoted directly. Readers always need to be able to distinguish between your ideas and those you've borrowed from other authors. So you must provide a signal whenever source material is introduced. Think of it as framing this material to set it off from your own words. Framing also enables you to offer an explanation or context for borrowed material, giving it the weight and power you believe it should have.

Often, all that's required for a frame is a brief signal phrase that identifies the author, title, or source you are drawing on.

> President Clinton explained at a press conference that ". . .
>
> According to a report in *Scientific American*, . . .
>
> . . ." said the former CEO of General Electric, arguing that ". . .
>
> In *Blink*, Malcolm Gladwell makes some odd claims. For example, he . . .

At other times you'll need a few words or a complete sentence or more to incorporate borrowed material into a paper. Readers

avoid
plagiarism /
use quotations

MLA and APA Style
The examples in this section follow MLA (Modern Language Association) style, covered in Chapter 44. For information on APA (American Psychological Association) style, see Chapter 45.

should never be in doubt about your use of a source. Your frame can introduce, interrupt, follow, or even surround the words or ideas taken from sources, but be sure that your signal phrases are grammatical and lead naturally into the material.

Select an appropriate "verb of attribution" to frame borrowed material.   Note that source material is often introduced or framed by a "verb of attribution" or "signal verb." These verbs influence what readers think of borrowed ideas or quoted material.

Use more neutral signal verbs in reports and descriptive or even biased terms in arguments. Note that, by MLA convention, verbs of attribution are usually in the present tense when talking about current work or ideas. (In APA, these verbs are generally in the past or present perfect tense.)

Verbs of Attribution		
Neutral	**Descriptive**	**Biased**
adds	acknowledges	admits
explains	argues	charges
finds	asserts	concedes
notes	believes	confuses
offers	claims	derides
observes	confirms	disputes
says	disagrees	evades
shows	responds	insists
states	reveals	pretends
writes	suggests	smears

Use ellipsis marks [. . .] to shorten a lengthy quotation.   When quoting a source in your paper, it's not necessary to use every word or sentence, so long as the cuts you make don't distort the meaning of the original material. An ellipsis mark, formed from three spaced periods, shows where words, phrases, full sentences, or more have been removed from a quotation. The mark doesn't replace punctuation within a sentence. Thus you might see a period or a comma immediately followed by the ellipsis mark.

ORIGINAL PASSAGE

Although gift giving has been a pillar of Hopi society, trade has also flourished in Hopi towns since prehistory, with a network that extended from the Great Plains to the Pacific Coast, and from the Great Basin, centered on present-day Nevada and Utah, to the Valley of Mexico. Manufactured goods, raw materials, and gems drove the trade, supplemented by exotic items such as parrots. The Hopis were producers as well, manufacturing large quantities of cotton cloth and ceramics for the trade. To this day, interhousehold trade and barter, especially for items of traditional manufacture for ceremonial use (such as basketry, bows, cloth, moccasins, pottery, and rattles), remain vigorous.

– Peter M. Whiteley, "Ties That Bind: Hopi Gift Culture and Its First Encounter with the United States," *Natural History,* Nov. 2004, p. 26

Highlighting shows words to be deleted when passage is quoted.

PASSAGE WITH ELLIPSES

Whiteley has characterized the practice this way:

Although gift giving has been a pillar of Hopi society, trade has also flourished in Hopi towns since prehistory. . . . Manufactured goods, raw materials, and gems drove the trade, supplemented by exotic items such as parrots. The Hopis were producers as well, manufacturing large quantities of cotton cloth and ceramics for the trade. To this day, inter-household trade and barter, especially for items of traditional manufacture for ceremonial use, . . . remain vigorous. (26)

Ellipses show where words have been deleted.

Use brackets [ ] to insert explanatory material into a quotation.   By convention, readers understand that the bracketed words are not part of the original material.

Writing in the *London Review of Books* (January 26, 2006), John Lancaster describes the fears of publishers: "At the moment Google says they have no intention of providing access to this content [scanned books still under copyright]; but why should anybody believe them?"

Use ellipsis marks, brackets, and other devices to make quoted materials suit the grammar of your sentences.   Sometimes, the structure of sentences you want to quote won't quite match the grammar, tense, or perspectives of your own surrounding prose. If necessary, cut up a quoted passage to slip appropriate sections into your own sentences, adding bracketed changes or explanations to smooth the transition.

ORIGINAL PASSAGE

Words to be quoted are highlighted.

Among Chandler's most charming sights are the business-casual dads joining their wives and kids for lunch in the mall food court. The food isn't the point, let alone whether it's from Subway or Dairy Queen. The restaurants merely provide the props and setting for the family time. When those kids grow up, they'll remember the food court as happily as an older generation recalls the diners and motels of Route 66—not because of the businesses' innate appeal but because of the memories they evoke.

—Virginia Postrel, "In Defense of Chain Stores," *Atlantic Monthly*, December 2006

MATERIAL AS QUOTED

Words quoted from source are highlighted.

People who dislike chain stores should ponder the small-town America that cultural critic Virginia Postrel describes, one where "business-casual dads [join] their wives and kids for lunch in the mall food court," a place which future generations of kids will remember "as happily as an older generation recalls the motels and diners of Route 66."

Use [sic] to signal an obvious error in quoted material.   You don't want readers to blame a mistake on you, and yet you are obligated to reproduce a quotation exactly—including blunders in the original. You can highlight an error by putting *sic* (the Latin word for "thus") in brackets immediately following the mistake. The device says, in effect, that this is the way you found it.

Senator Kennedy took Supreme Court nominee Samuel Alito to task for his record: "In an era when America is still too divided by race and riches, Judge Alioto [sic] has not written one single opinion on the merits in favor of a person of color alleging race discrimination on the job."

Documenting Sources

43

Required to document your research paper? It seems simple: Just list your sources and note where and how you use them. But the practice can be intimidating. For one thing, you have to follow rules for everything from capitalizing titles to captioning images. For another, documentation systems differ between fields. What worked for a Shakespeare paper won't transfer to your psychology class research project. Bummer. What do you need to do?

understand citation styles

Understand the point of documentation. Documentation systems differ to serve the writers and researchers who use them. Modern Language Association (MLA) documentation, which you probably know from composition and literature classes, highlights author names and books and article titles, and assumes that writers will be quoting a lot—as literature scholars do. American Psychological Association (APA) documentation, gospel in psychology and social sciences, focuses on publication dates because scholars in these fields value the latest research. Council of Science Editors (CSE) documentation, used in the hard sciences, provides predictably detailed advice for handling formulas and numbers.

So systems of documentation aren't arbitrary. Their rules simply anticipate problems researchers face when dealing with sources.

Understand what you accomplish through documentation. First, you clearly identify your sources. In a world awash with information, readers really do need to have reliable author, title, and publication information.

By identifying your sources, you provide evidence for your claims. You also certify the quality of your research, and receive due credit for your labor. A shrewd reader or instructor can tell a lot from your bibliography alone.

Finally, when you document a paper, you encourage readers to follow up on your work. When you've done a good job on a paper, serious readers will want to know more. Both your citations and your bibliography enable them to take the next step in the research.

Style Guides Used in Various Disciplines

Field or Discipline	Documentation and Style Guides
Anthropology	*Chicago Manual of Style* (15th ed., 2003)
Biology	*Scientific Style and Format: The CSE Manual for Authors, Editors, and Publishers* (7th ed., 2006)
Business and management	*The Business Style Handbook: An A-to-Z Guide for Writing on the Job* (2002)
Chemistry	*The ACS Style Guide: Effective Communication of Scientific Information* (3rd ed., 2006)
Earth sciences	*Geowriting: A Guide to Writing, Editing, and Printing in Earth Science* (5th ed., 1995)
Engineering	Varies by area; *IEEE Standards Style Manual* (2007) (online)
Federal government	*United States Government Printing Office Manual* (29th ed., 2000)
History	*Chicago Manual of Style* (15th ed., 2003)
Humanities	*MLA Handbook for Writers of Research Papers* (6th ed., 2003)
Journalism	*The AP Stylebook and Briefing on Media Law* (2008); *UPI Stylebook and Guide to Newswriting* (4th ed., 2004)
Law	*The Bluebook: A Uniform System of Citation* (18th ed., 2005)
Mathematics	*A Manual for Authors of Mathematical Papers* (8th ed., 1990)
Music	*Writing about Music: An Introductory Guide* (3rd ed., 2001)
Nursing	*Writing for Publication in Nursing* (2001)
Political science	*The Style Manual for Political Science* (2006)
Psychology	*Publication Manual of the American Psychological Association* (5th ed., 2001)
Sociology	*ASA Style Guide* (2nd ed., 1998)

MLA Documentation and Format

44

The style of the Modern Language Association (MLA) is used in many humanities disciplines. For complete details about MLA style, consult the *MLA Handbook for Writers of Research Papers* (2009). The basic details for documenting sources and formatting research papers in MLA style are presented below.

Document sources according to convention. When you use sources in a research paper, you are required to cite the source, letting readers know that the information has been borrowed from somewhere else, and showing them how to find the original material if they would like to study it further. An MLA-style citation includes two parts: a brief in-text citation and a more detailed works cited entry to be included in a list at of the end of your paper.

cite in MLA

In-text citations must include the author's name as well as the number of the page where the borrowed material can be found. The author's name (shaded in orange) is generally included in the signal phrase that introduces the passage, and the page number (shaded in yellow) is included in parentheses after the borrowed text.

> Frazier points out that the Wetherill-sponsored expedition to explore Chaco Canyon was roundly criticized (43).

Alternatively, the author's name can be included in parentheses along with the page number.

The Wetherill-sponsored expedition to explore Chaco Canyon was roundly criticized (Frazier 43).

At the end of the paper, in the works cited list, a more detailed citation includes the author's name as well as the title (shaded in beige) and publication information about the source (shaded in blue).

Frazier, Kendrick. *People of Chaco: A Canyon and Its Culture.* Rev. ed. New York: Norton, 1999. Print.

Both in-text citations and works cited entries can vary greatly depending on the type of source cited (book, periodical, Web site, etc.). The following pages give specific examples of how to cite a wide range of sources in MLA style.

Directory of MLA In-Text Citations

1. Author named in signal phrase 434
2. Author named in parentheses 439
3. With block quotations 439
4. Two or three authors 440
5. Four or more authors 440
6. Group, corporate, or government author 440
7. Two or more works by the same author 440
8. Authors with same last name 441
9. Unidentified author 441
10. Multivolume work 441
11. Work in an anthology 441
12. Entry in a reference book 442
13. Literary work 442
14. Sacred work 443
15. Entire work 443
16. Secondary source 443
17. No page numbers 443
18. Multiple sources in the same citation 444

MLA in-text citation

1. Author Named in Signal Phrase

Include the author's name in the signal phrase that introduces the borrowed material. Follow the borrowed material with the page number of the source in parentheses. Note that the period comes after the parentheses. For a source without an author, see item 9; for a source without a page number, see item 17.

> According to Seabrook, "astronomy was a vital and practical form of knowledge" for the ancient Greeks (98).

2. Author Named in Parentheses

Follow the borrowed material with the author and page number of the source in parentheses, and end with a period. For a source without an author, see item 9; for a source without a page number, see item 17.

> For the ancient Greeks, "astronomy was a vital and practical form of knowledge" (Seabrook 98).

Note: Most of the examples below follow the style of item 1, but naming the author in parentheses (as shown in item 2) is also acceptable.

3. With Block Quotations

For quotations of four or more lines, MLA requires that you set off the borrowed material as indented text. Include the author's name in the introductory text (or in the parentheses at the end). End the block quotation with the page number(s) in parentheses, *after* the end punctuation of the quoted material.

> Jake Page, writing in *American History*, underscores the significance of the well-organized Pueblo revolt:

> > Although their victory proved temporary, in the history of Indian-white relations in North America the Pueblo Indians were the only Native Americans to successfully oust European invaders from their territory. . . . Apart from the Pueblos, only the Seminoles were able to retain some of their homeland for any length of time, by waging war from the swamps of the Florida Everglades. (36)

4. Two or Three Authors

If your source has two or three authors, include all of their names in either the signal phrase or parentheses.

> Muhlheim and Heusser assert that the story "analyzes how crucially our actions are shaped by the society . . . in which we live" (29).

> According to some experts, "Children fear adult attempts to fix their social lives" (Thompson, Grace, and Cohen 8).

5. Four or More Authors

If your source has four or more authors, list the first author's name followed by "et al." (meaning "and others") in the signal phrase or parentheses.

> Hansen et al. estimate that the amount of fish caught and sold illegally worldwide is between 10% and 30% (974).

6. Group, Corporate, or Government Author

Treat the name of the group, corporation, or government agency just as you would any other author, including the name in either the signal phrase or the parentheses.

> The United States Environmental Protection Agency states that if a public water supply contains dangerous amounts of lead, the municipality is required to educate the public about the problems associated with lead in drinking water (3).

7. Two or More Works by the Same Author

If your paper includes two or more works by the same author, add a brief version of the works' titles (shaded in green) in parentheses to help readers locate the right source.

> Mills suggests that new assessments of older archaeological work, not new discoveries in the field, are revising the history of Chaco Canyon ("Recent Research" 66). She argues, for example, that new analysis of public spaces can teach us about the ritual of feasting in the Puebloan Southwest (Mills, "Performing the Feast" 211).

8. Authors with Same Last Name

If your paper includes two or more sources whose authors have the same last name, include a first initial with the last name in either the signal phrase or the parentheses.

> According to T. Smith, "as much as 60 percent of the computers sold in India are unbranded and made by local assemblers at about a third of the price of overseas brands" (12).

9. Unidentified Author

If the author of your work is unknown, include a brief title of the work in parentheses.

> The amount of protein that tilapia provides when eaten exceeds the amount that it consumes when alive, making it a sustainable fish ("Dream Fish" 26).

10. Multivolume Work

If you cite material from more than one volume of a multivolume work, include in the parentheses the volume number followed by a colon before the page number. (See also item 11, on p. 452, for including multivolume works in your works cited list.)

> Odekon defines *access-to-enterprise zones* as "geographic areas in which taxes and government regulations are lowered or eliminated as a way to stimulate business activity and create jobs" (1: 2).

11. Work in an Anthology

Include the author of the work in the signal phrase or parentheses. There is no need to refer to the editor of the anthology in the in-text citation; this and other details will be included in the works cited list at the end of your paper.

> Vonnegut suggests that *Hamlet* is considered such a masterpiece because "Shakespeare told us the truth, and [writers] so rarely tell us the truth" (354).

12. Entry in a Reference Book

In the signal phrase, include the author of the entry you are referring to, if there is one. In the parentheses, include the title of the entry and the page number(s) on which the entry appears.

> Willis points out that, at 1,250 feet tall and built in just over one year, the Empire State Building was a record-breaking feat of engineering ("Empire State Building" 375-76).

For reference entries with no author (such as dictionaries), simply include the name of the article in quotation marks along with the page reference in parentheses.

> *Black* is defined as a color "producing or reflecting comparatively little light and having no predominant hue" ("Black" 143).

13. Literary Work

Include as much information as possible to help readers locate your borrowed material. For classic novels, which are available in many editions, include the page number, followed by a semicolon, and additional information such as book ("bk."), volume ("vol."), or chapter ("ch.") numbers.

> At the climax of Brontë's *Jane Eyre,* Jane fears that her wedding is doomed, and her description of the chestnut tree that has been struck by lightning is ominous: "it stood up, black and riven: the trunk, split down the center, gaped ghastly" (274; vol. 2, ch. 25).

For classic poems and plays, include division numbers such as act, scene, and line numbers; do not include page numbers. Separate all numbers with periods. Use arabic (1, 2, 3, etc.) numerals instead of roman (I, II, III, etc.) unless your instructor prefers otherwise.

> In Homer's epic poem *The Iliad,* Agamemnon admits that he has been wrong to fight with Achilles, but he blames Zeus, whom he says "has given me bitterness, who drives me into unprofitable abuse and quarrels" (2.375-76).

14. Sacred Work

Instead of page numbers, include book, chapter, and verse numbers when citing material from sacred texts.

> Jesus' association with the sun is undeniable in this familiar passage from the Bible: "I am the light of the world. Whoever follows me will not walk in darkness, but will have the light of life" (John 8.12).

15. Entire Work

When referring to an entire work, there is no need to include page numbers in parentheses; simply include the author's name(s) in the signal phrase.

> Boyer and Nissenbaum argue that the witchcraft trials persisted because of the unique social and political environment that existed in Salem in 1692.

16. Secondary Source

To cite a source you found within another source, include the name of the original author in the signal phrase. In the parentheses, include the term "qtd. in" and give the author of the source where you found the quote, along with the page number. Note that your works cited entry for this material will be listed under the secondary source name (Pollan) rather than the original writer (Howard).

> Writing in 1943, Howard asserted that "artificial manures lead inevitably to artificial nutrition, artificial food, artificial animals, and finally to artificial men and women" (qtd. in Pollan 148).

17. No Page Numbers

If the work you are citing has no page numbers, include only the author's name (or the brief title, if there is no author) for your in-text citation.

> Gorman reported that in early 2007, hunger-striking enemy combatants at Guantanamo Bay were strapped down and force-fed with tubes inserted through their noses.

18. Multiple Sources in the Same Citation

If one statement in your paper can be attributed to multiple sources, alphabetically list all the authors with page numbers, separated by semicolons.

> Most historians agree that the Puritan religion played a significant role in the hysteria surrounding the Salem witchcraft trials (Karlsen 14; Norton 22; Reis 145).

Directory of MLA Works Cited Entries

AUTHOR INFORMATION

1. Single author 447
2. Two or three authors 447
3. Four or more authors 447
4. Corporate author 447
5. Unidentified author 448
6. Multiple works by the same author 448

BOOKS

7. Book: basic format 448
8. Author and editor 449
9. Edited collection 449
10. Work in an anthology or collection 449
11. Multivolume work 452
12. Part of a series 452
13. Republished book 452
14. Later edition 453
15. Sacred work 453
16. Translation 453
17. Article in a reference book 454
18. Introduction, preface, foreword, or afterword 454
19. Title within a title 454

PERIODICALS

20. Article in a scholarly journal 454
21. Article in a scholarly journal with no volume number 455
22. Magazine article 455
23. Newspaper article 455
24. Editorial 458
25. Letter to the editor 458
26. Unsigned article 458
27. Review 458

ELECTRONIC SOURCES

28. Short work from a Web site 459
29. Entire Web site 459
30. Entire Weblog 459
31. Entry in a Weblog 459
32. Online book 460

General Guidelines for MLA Works Cited Entries

AUTHOR NAMES

- Authors listed at the start of an entry should be listed last name first and should end with a period.
- Subsequent author names, or the names of authors or editors listed in the middle of the entry, should be listed first name first.

DATES

- Dates should be formatted day month year: 27 May 2007.
- Use abbreviations for all months except for May, June, and July, which are short enough to spell out: Jan., Feb., Mar., Apr., Aug., Sept., Oct., Nov., Dec. (Note that months should always be spelled out in the text of your paper.)

TITLES

- Titles of long works—such as books, plays, periodicals, entire Web sites, and films—should be italicized. (Underlining is an acceptable alternative to italics, but note that whichever format you choose, you should be consistent throughout your paper.)
- Titles of short works—such as essays, articles, poems, and songs—should be placed in quotation marks.

PUBLICATION INFORMATION

- For familiar cities such as New York, San Francisco, and London, include only the city name.
- For less familiar places, include postal abbreviations for states, and, if necessary, foreign states and countries ("Newton, MA").
- Abbreviate familiar words such as *University* ("U") and *Press* ("P") in the publisher's name. Leave out terms such as *Inc.* and *Corp.*
- Include the medium of publication for each entry (Print, Web, DVD, Radio, etc.).

MLA works cited entries

AUTHOR INFORMATION

1. Single Author

Author's Last Name, First Name. *Book Title*. Publication City: Publisher, Year of Publication. Medium.

Will, George. *Men at Work: The Craft of Baseball*. New York: Macmillan, 1990. Print.

2. Two or Three Authors

List the authors in the order shown on the title page.

First Author's Last Name, First Name, and Second Author's First and Last Name. *Book Title*. Publication City: Publisher, Year of Publication. Medium.

Mortenson, Greg, and David Oliver Relin. *Three Cups of Tea: One Man's Mission to Promote Peace . . . One School at a Time*. New York: Penguin, 2007. Print.

Clark, Ricky, George W. Knepper, and Ellice Ronsheim. *Quilts in Community: Ohio's Traditions*. Nashville: Rutledge, 1991. Print.

3. Four or More Authors

When a source has four or more authors, list only the name of the first author (last name first), followed by a comma and the Latin term *et al.* (meaning "and others").

First Author's Last Name, First Name, et al. *Book Title*. Publication City: Publisher, Year of Publication. Medium.

Roark, James L., et al. *The American Promise: A History of the United States*. 4th ed. Boston: Bedford, 2009. Print.

4. Corporate Author

If a group or corporation rather than a person appears to be the author, include that name as the work's author in your list of works cited.

Name of Corporation. *Book Title*. Publication City: Publisher, Year of Publication. Medium.

> Congressional Quarterly. *Presidential Elections: 1789-2004.* Washington: CQ, 2005. Print.

5. Unidentified Author

If the author of a work is unknown, begin the works cited entry with the title of the work.

Note that in the example given, "The New York Times" is not italicized because it is a title within a title (see item 19).

> *Book Title.* Publication City: Publisher, Year of Publication. Medium.

> The New York Times *Guide to Essential Knowledge: A Desk Reference for the Curious Mind.* New York: St. Martin's, 2004. Print.

6. Multiple Works by the Same Author

To cite two or more works by the same author in your list of works cited, organize the works alphabetically by title (ignoring introductory articles such as *The* and *A*). Include the author's name only for the first entry; for subsequent entries, type three hyphens followed by a period in place of the author's name.

> Author's Last Name, First Name. *Title of Work.* Publication City: Publisher, Year of Publication. Medium.

> ---. *Title of Work.* Publication City: Publisher, Year of Publication. Medium.

> Friedman, Thomas L. *The Lexus and the Olive Tree: Understanding Globalization.* New York: Farrar, 1999. Print.

> ---. *The World Is Flat: A Brief History of the Twenty-First Century.* New York: Farrar, 2005. Print.

BOOKS

7. Book: Basic Format

The example here is the basic format for a book with one author. For author variations, see items 1–6. For more information on the treatment of authors, dates, titles, and publication information, see the box on page 446. After listing the author's name, include the title (and subtitle, if any) of the book, italicized. Next give the publication city, publisher's name, and year. End with the medium of publication.

Author. *Book Title: Book Subtitle.* Publication City: Publisher, Publication Year. Medium.

Mah, Adeline Yen. *Falling Leaves: The True Story of an Unwanted Chinese Daughter*. New York: Wiley, 1997. Print.

8. Author and Editor

Include the author's name first if you are referring to the text itself. If, however, you are citing material written by the editor, include the editor's name first, followed by a comma and *ed.*

Author's Last Name, First Name. *Book Title*. Year of Original Publication. Ed. First and Last Name of Editor. Publication City: Publisher, Year of Publication. Medium.

Editor's Last Name, First Name, ed. *Book Title*. Year of Original Publication. By Author's First Name Last Name. Publication City: Publisher, Year of Publication. Medium.

Dickens, Charles. *Great Expectations*. 1861. Ed. Janice Carlisle. Boston: Bedford, 1996. Print.

Carlisle, Janice., ed. *Great Expectations*. 1861. By Charles Dickens. Boston: Bedford, 1996. Print.

9. Edited Collection

Last Name, First Name of Editor, ed. *Book Title.* Publication City: Publisher, Year of Publication. Medium.

Abbott, Megan, ed. *A Hell of a Woman: An Anthology of Female Noir*. Houston: Busted Flush, 2007. Print.

10. Work in an Anthology or a Collection

Author Last Name, First Name. "Title of Work." *Book Title.* Ed. First and Last Name of Editor. Publication City: Publisher, Year of Publication. Page Numbers of Work. Medium.

How to...
Cite from a book (MLA)

BOOK COVER

TITLE PAGE

Turn the page to find the copyright page.

FIGHTING FOR AIR

THE BATTLE TO CONTROL AMERICA'S MEDIA

ERIC KLINENBERG

FIGHTING FOR AIR
THE BATTLE TO CONTROL AMERICA'S MEDIA

ERIC KLINENBERG

METROPOLITAN BOOKS
Henry Holt and Company   New York

1 author

2 book title

3 city of publication and publisher

COPYRIGHT PAGE

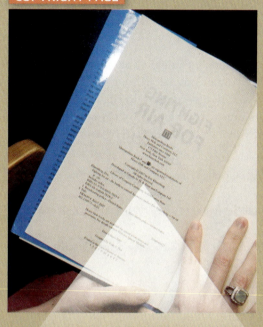

Copyright © 2007 by Eric Klinenberg

4 year and medium of publication

QUOTED PAGE

33

5 page number

MLA in-text citation

Some politicians might fear that "the industry's influence determines the fate of policy proposals, political campaigns, and, in turn, their own careers" (Klinenberg 33).

1 **1** **5** **2**

MLA works cited entry

Klinenberg, Eric. *Fighting for Air: The Battle to Control America's Media.*

New York: Metropolitan, 2007. Print.

3 **4**

Okpewho, Isidore. "The Cousins of Uncle Remus." *The Black Columbiad: Defining Moments in African American Literature and Culture*. Ed. Werner Sollors and Maria Diedrich. Cambridge: Harvard UP, 1994. 15-27. Print.

11. Multivolume Work

To cite one volume of a multivolume work, include the volume number after the title. Note that by including the volume number in your list of works cited, you do not need to list it in your in-text citation. To cite two or more volumes, include the number of volumes after the title. In this case, you would need to include the specific volume number in each of your in-text citations for this source.

Author or Editor. *Title of Work*. Vol. Number. Publication City: Publisher, Year of Publication. Medium.

Odekon, Mehmet, ed. *Encyclopedia of World Poverty*. Vol. 2. Thousand Oaks, CA: Sage, 2006. Print.

Author or Editor. *Title of Work*. Number of Vols. Publication City: Publisher, Year of Publication. Medium.

Odekon, Mehmet, ed. *Encyclopedia of World Poverty*. 3 vols. Thousand Oaks, CA: Sage, 2006. Print.

12. Part of a Series

Include the series title from the title page and number (if any) after the title of the book.

Author or Editor. *Title of Work*. Title and Number of Series. Publication City: Publisher, Year of Publication. Medium.

Dixon, Kelly J. *Boomtown Saloons: Archaeology and History in Virginia City*. *Wilbur S. Shepperson Ser. in Nevada Hist*. Reno: U of Nevada P, 2005. Print.

13. Republished Book

If the book you are citing was previously published, include the original publication date after the title. If the new publication includes additional text, such as an introduction, include that, along with the name of its author, before the current publication information.

Author Last Name, First Name. *Title of Work.* Original Year of Publication. New Material Author First Name Last Name. Publication City: Publisher, Year of Publication. Medium.

Twain, Mark. *Life on the Mississippi.* 1883. Introd. Justin Kaplan. New York: Penguin, 2001. Print.

14. Later Edition

Include the edition number as a numeral with letters (*2nd, 3rd, 4th,* etc.) followed by *ed.* after the book's title. If the edition is listed on the title page as *Revised,* without a number, include *Rev. ed.* after the title of the book.

Author(s). *Title of Work.* Number ed. Publication City: Publisher, Year of Publication. Medium.

Hartt, Frederick, and David G. Wilkins. *History of Italian Renaissance Art: Painting, Sculpture, Architecture.* 4th ed. New York: Abrams, 2006. Print.

15. Sacred Work

Include the title of the work as it is shown on the title page. If there is an editor or a translator listed, include the name after the title with either *Ed.* or *Trans.*

Title of Work. Editor or Translator. Publication City: Publisher, Year of Publication. Medium.

The New American Bible. New York: Catholic Book Publishing, 1987. Print.

The Qu'ran: A New Translation. Trans. M. A. S. Abdel Haleem. New York: Oxford UP, 2004. Print.

16. Translation

Original Author Last Name, First Name. *Title of Work.* Trans. First Name Last Name. Publication City: Publisher, Year of Publication. Medium.

Fasce, Ferdinando. *An American Family: The Great War and Corporate Culture in America.* Trans. Ian Harvey. Columbus: Ohio State UP, 2002. Print.

17. Article in a Reference Book

If there is no article author, begin with the title of the article.

> Last Name, First Name of Article Author. "Title of Article." *Book Title.*
>   Publication City: Publisher, Year of Publication. Medium.

> Lutzger, Michael A. "Peace Movements." *The Encyclopedia of New York
>   City*. New Haven: Yale UP, 1995. Print.

> "The History of the National Anthem." *The World Almanac and Book of
>   Facts 2004*. New York: World Almanac, 2004. Print.

18. Introduction, Preface, Foreword, or Afterword

> Last Name, First Name of Book Part Author. Name of Book Part. *Book Title.*
>   Book Author or Editor. Publication City: Publisher, Year of Publication.
>   page numbers. Medium.

> Groening, Matt. Introduction. *Best American Nonrequired Reading 2006*. Ed.
>   Dave Eggers. Boston: Houghton, 2006. xi-xvii. Print.

19. Title within a Title

If a book's title includes the title of another long work (play, book, or
periodical) within it, do not italicize the internal title.

> Last Name, First Name of Author. *Book Title* Title within Title. Publication City:
>   Publisher, Year of Publication. Medium.

> Norris, Margot. *A Companion to James Joyce's* Ulysses. Boston: Bedford,
>   1998. Print.

PERIODICALS

20. Article in a Scholarly Journal

List the author(s) first, then include the article title, the journal title (in
italics), the volume number, the issue number, the publication year, the
page numbers, and the publication medium.

Author(s). "Title of Article." *Title of Journal* Volume Number. Issue Number (Year of Publication): page numbers. Medium.

Burt, Stephen, et al. "Does Poetry Have a Social Function?" *Poetry* 189.4 (2007): 297-309. Print.

21. Article in a Scholarly Journal with no Volume Number

Follow the format for scholarly journals (as shown in item 20), but list only the issue number before the year of publication.

Author(s). "Title of Article." *Title of Journal* Issue Number (Year of Publication): page numbers. Medium.

Lee, Christopher. "Enacting the Asian Canadian." *Canadian Literature* 199 (2008): 6-27. Print.

22. Magazine Article

Include the date of publication rather than volume and issue numbers. (See abbreviation rules in the box on p. 446.) If page numbers are not consecutive, add "+" after the initial page.

Author(s). "Title of Article." *Title of Magazine* Date of Publication: page numbers. Medium.

Fredenburg, Peter. "Mekong Harvests: Balancing Shrimp and Rice Farming in Vietnam." *World and I* Mar. 2002: 204+. Print.

23. Newspaper Article

If a specific edition is listed on the newspaper's masthead, such as *Late Edition* or *National Edition*, include an abbreviation of this after the date.

Author(s). "Title of Article." *Title of Newspaper* Date of Publication: page numbers. Medium.

Smith, Stephen. "Taunting May Affect Health of Obese Youths." *Boston Globe* 11 July 2007: A1+. Print.

Author(s). "Title of Article." *Title of Newspaper* Date of Publication, spec. ed.: page numbers. Medium.

Rohde, David. "Taliban Push Poppy Production to a Record Again." *New York Times* 26 Aug. 2007, natl. ed.: 3. Print.

MAGAZINE COVER

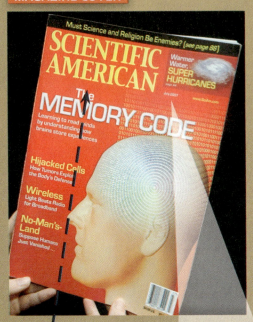

ARTICLE

1 magazine title

2 publication date

3 author

4 article title

58

5 page number of quoted passage

52

6 first and last pages of article

59

7 medium of publication

MLA
in-text
citation

Analysis of one research team's recent findings "reinforces the idea that the brain is not simply a device that records every detail of a particular event" (Tsien 58).

3 **6**

MLA
works cited
entry

3 **4** **1** **2** **6** **7**

Tsien, Joe Z. "The Memory Code." *Scientific American* July 2007: 52-59. Print.

If a paper numbers each section individually, without attaching letters to the page numbers (as on p. 455), include the section number in your citation.

Author(s). "Title of Article." *Title of Newspaper* Date of Publication, sec. Section Number: page numbers. Medium.

Bowley, Graham. "Keeping Up with the Windsors." *New York Times* 15 July 2007, sec. 3: 1+. Print.

24. Editorial

For a newspaper editorial, do not include an author, but do include the word *Editorial*, followed by a period, after the title of the article.

"Title of Article." Editorial. *Title of Newspaper* Date of Publication: page number(s). Medium.

"Living on Iraq Time." Editorial. *New York Times* 28 May 2007: A15. Print.

25. Letter to the Editor

Last Name, First Name of Letter Writer. Letter. *Title of Newspaper* Date of Publication: page number. Medium.

Zita, Ken. Letter. *Financial Times* 16 Aug. 2006: 8. Print.

26. Unsigned Article

"Title of Article." *Title of Newspaper* Date of Publication: page number. Medium.

"Justice Probes Lenders." *Washington Post* 26 July 2007: DO2. Print.

27. Review

Add *Rev. of* before the title of the work being reviewed.

Review Author. "Title of Review." Rev. of *Title of Work Being Reviewed*, by Author of Work Being Reviewed. *Title of Publication in Which Review Appears.* Volume.Issue (Year of Publication): page numbers. Medium.

Levin, Yuval. "Diagnosis and Cure." Rev. of *Sick: The Untold Story of America's Health-Care Crisis and the People Who Pay the Price*, by Jonathan Cohn. *Commentary* 124.1 (2007): 80-82. Print.

ELECTRONIC SOURCES

28. Short Work from a Web Site

Last Name, First Name of Short Work Author. "Title of Short Work." *Title of Web Site.* Name of Sponsoring Organization, Date of Publication or Most Recent Update. Medium. Date of Access.

McFee, Gord. "Why 'Revisionism' Isn't." *The Holocaust History Project.* Holocaust Hist. Project.15 May 1999. Web. 10 Sept. 2007.

29. Entire Web Site

Last Name, First Name of Short Work Author. *Title of Web Site.* Name of Sponsoring Organization, Date of Publication or Most Recent Update. Medium. Date of Access.

Myers, Robert, et al. *Exploring the Environment.* Wheeling Jesuit U, 28 Apr. 2005. Web. 12 Sept. 2007.

30. Entire Weblog

Include any of the following elements that are available. If there is no publisher or sponsoring organization, use the abbreviation "N.p."

Last Name, First Name of Weblog's Author. *Title of Weblog.* Name of Sponsoring Organization (if any), Date of Most Recent Post. Medium. Date of Access.

Sellers, Heather. *Word after Word.* N.p., 21 Jun. 2008. Web. 24 Jun. 2008.

31. Entry in a Weblog

Last Name, First Name of Entry's Author. "Title of Weblog Entry." *Title of Weblog.* Name of Sponsoring Organization (if any), Date of Entry. Medium. Date of Access.

Sellers, Heather. "East Coast." *Word after Word.* N.p., 7 Nov. 2007. Web. 30 Jan. 2008.

32. Online Book

Last Name, First Name of Book Author. *Title of Book.* Book Publication City: Book Publisher, Book Publication Year. *Title of Web Site.* Medium. Date of Access.

Riis, Jacob. *How the Other Half Lives.* New York: Scribner's, 1890. *Bartleby. com: Great Books Online.* Web. 6 Nov. 2007.

33. Work from a Library Subscription Service (such as InfoTrac or FirstSearch)

Follow the format for periodical articles as shown in items 20–27, above. If page numbers are not available, use the abbreviation "n. pag." End the citation with the database name (in italics), the publication medium ("Web"), and date of access.

Author(s) of Article. "Title of Article." *Title of Periodical.* Volume Number.Issue Number (Year of Publication): page numbers. *Name of Database.* Medium. Date of Access.

Cotugna, Nancy, and Connie Vickery. "Educating Early Childhood Teachers about Nutrition: A Collaborative Venture." *Childhood Education* 83.4 (2007): 194-98. *Academic OneFile.* Web. 10 July 2007.

34. Work from an Online Periodical

Follow the format for periodical articles as shown in items 20–27, above, listing the Web site name, in italics, as the periodical title. For articles in scholarly journals, include page numbers (or the abbreviation "n. pag." if page numbers are unavailable). End the citation with the publication medium ("Web") and the date of access.

Author(s) of Journal Article. "Title of Article." *Title of Online Journal* Volume Number.Issue Number (Year of Publication): page numbers (or "n. pag."). Medium. Date of Access.

Arora, Vibha, and Justin Scott-Coe. "Fieldwork and Interdisciplinary Research." *Reconstruction* 9.1 (2009): n. pag. Web. 13 Apr. 2009.

For articles appearing in online magazines and newspapers, list the publisher's name after the online periodical title. Page numbers are not required for nonscholarly articles published online.

Author(s) of Magazine or Newspaper Article. "Title of Article." *Title of Online Periodical.* Periodical Publisher, Publication Date. Medium. Date of Access.

Gogoi, Pallavi. "The Trouble with Business Ethics." *BusinessWeek.* McGraw, 25 June 2007. Web. 3 Oct. 2007.

35. Online Posting

Author of Post. "Title (or Subject) of Post." *Title of Message Board.* Date of Post. Medium. Date of Access.

Winkleman, Tallulah. "Reducing Your Food Miles." *Farm Folk City Folk Bulletin*, 13 July 2007. Web. 10 Sept. 2007.

36. E-mail

E-mail Author Last Name, First Name. "Subject of E-mail." Message to the author (or Name of Recipient). Date Sent. Medium.

Gingrich, Newt. "Drill here. Drill now." Message to the author. 20 May 2008. E-mail.

37. CD-ROM

Last Name, First Name of CD-ROM author (if any). *Title of CD-ROM.* Publication City: Publisher, Publication Year. Medium.

History through Art: The Twentieth Century. San Jose: Fogware, 2001. CD-ROM.

38. Podcast

For downloaded podcasts, include the file type, such as "MP3," as the medium. If the file type is unknown, use the term "Digital file."

"Title of Podcast." Name and Function of Pertinent Individual(s). *Title of Web Site.* Name of Sponsoring Organization, Date of Publication. Medium.

"Capping Pollution at the Source." Prod. Lester Graham. *The Environment Report.* Nature Conservancy, 31 July 2006. MP3.

For podcasts that were listened to directly from the host Web site, list "Web" as the medium and include an access date at the end.

39. Entry in a Wiki

Wiki content is continually edited by its users, so there is no author to cite.

"Title of Entry." *Title of Wiki.* Name of Sponsoring Organization, Date of Publication or Most Recent Update. Medium. Date of Access.

"Emo." *Wikipedia.* Wikimedia Foundation, 24 June 2008. Web. 2 Feb. 2009.

How to...
Cite from a Web site (MLA)

1 Web site title

2 Sponsor of site

3 article title

4 publication date

5 author

6 Medium of Publication

7 date of access

Tuesday, July 22, 2008

MLA in-text citation

The Secretary General of Amnesty International argues that "the right question is not whether the human rights situation today is better or worse than last year. It is whether one should be more hopeful or less that this country will turn a corner on human rights" (Khan).

5
3
5
1

Khan, Irene. "Ending the Downward Spiral in Bangladesh." *Amnesty*

2
4
6
7

International. Amnesty Intl., 23 Jan. 2008. Web. 22 July 2008.

MLA works cited entry

1 author   **2** article title   **3** volume and issue number

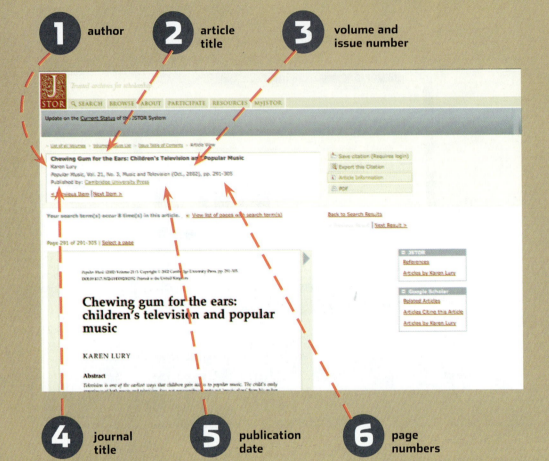

4 journal title   **5** publication date   **6** page numbers

7 database name

8 Medium of Publication

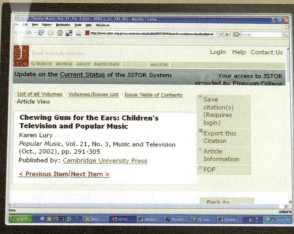

9 date of access

Tuesday, July 22, 2008

MLA in-text citation

Children accept even nonsensical lyrics as legitimate musical expression, and one researcher calls their tolerance "a mode of engagement carried productively into the adult's experience of popular songs" (Lury 300).

①   ② ① ⑥

Lury, Karen. "Chewing Gum for the Ears: Children's Television and

① ④ ③ ⑤ ⑥ ⑦ ⑧

MLA works cited entry

Popular Music." *Popular Music* 21.3 (2002): 291-305. *JSTOR.* Web.

⑨

22 July 2008.

OTHER

40. Dissertation

For unpublished dissertations, put the title in quotation marks.

> Author Last Name, First Name. "Dissertation Title." Diss. Name of University, Year. Medium.

Mooney, John Alfonso. "Shadows of Dominion: White Men and Power in
  Slavery, War, and the New South." Diss. U of Virginia, 2007. Print.

If the dissertation is published as a book, italicize the title and include the publication information.

> Author Last Name, First Name. *Dissertation Title*. Diss. Name of University, Year. Publication City: Publisher, Publication Year, Medium.

Beetham, Christopher A. *Echoes of Scripture in the Letter of Paul to the
  Colossians*. Diss. Wheaton Coll. Graduate School, 2005. Boston: Brill,
  2008, Print.

41. Published Conference Proceedings

List the editor(s) name(s), followed by *ed.* or *eds.* and italicize the title of the proceedings. Before the conference information, add *Proc. of* and follow with the conference title, dates, and location.

> Editor Names, eds. *Title of Proceedings*. Proc. of Conference Title, Conference Date, Conference Location. Publication City: Publisher, Year. Medium.

Westfahl, G., and George Slusser, eds. *Nursery Realms: Children in the World
  of Science Fiction, Fantasy, and Horror*. Proc. of J. Lloyd Eaton Conf. on
  Science Fiction and Fantasy Lit., Jan. 1999, U of California, Riverside.
  Athens: U of Georgia P, 1999. Print.

42. Government Document

Begin by listing the government (usually a country or state) that issued the document, and then list the specific department or agency. Most U.S. government documents are published by the Washington-based Government Printing Office (GPO).

Government. Department or Agency. *Title of Document.* Publication City:
    Publisher, Date of Publication. Medium.

United States. Dept. of Labor. *Summary Data from the Consumer Price Index
    News Release.* Washington, DC: GPO, Oct. 2006. Print.

43. Pamphlet

Pamphlet Title. Publication City: Publisher, Year of Publication. Medium.

50 Ways to Be Water Smart. West Palm Beach: South Florida Water
    Management Dist., 2006. Print.

44. Letter (Personal and Published)

For personal letters that you received, give the name of the letter writer
followed by the description "Letter to the author." For publication medium,
list *TS* ("typescript") for typed letters or *MS* ("manuscript") for handwritten
letters. For E-mail, see item 36.

Last Name, First Name of Letter Writer. Letter to the author. Date of Letter.
    Medium.

Nader, Ralph. Letter to the author. 15 Oct. 2007. TS.

For published letters, list the letter writer as well as the recipient.

Last Name, First Name of Letter Writer. Letter to First Name Last Name. Date
    of Letter. *Title of Book.* Ed. Name of Editor. Publication City: Publisher,
    Year. Medium.

Lincoln, Abraham. Letter to T. J. Pickett. 16 Apr. 1859. *Wit & Wisdom of
    Abraham Lincoln: As Reflected in His Letters and Speeches.* Ed. H. Jack
    Lang. Mechanicsburg, PA: Stackpole, 2006. Print.

45. Legal Source

List the names of laws or acts, followed by the Public Law number and the
date. Also give the Statutes at Large cataloging number and the medium.
For other legal sources, refer to *The Bluebook: A Uniform System of Citation,*
18th ed. (Cambridge: Harvard Law Review Assn., 2005).

Title of Law. Pub. L. number. Date of Enactment. Stat. number. Medium.

No Child Left Behind Act of 2001. Pub. L. 107-110. 8 Jan. 2002. Stat. 1425. Print.

46. Lecture or Public Address

For the medium, describe the type of speech (*Reading*, *Address*, *Lecture*, etc.).

Speaker Last Name, First Name. "Title of Speech." Name of Sponsoring
  Institution. Location of Speech. Date of Speech. Medium.

Wallace, David Foster. "Kenyon Commencement Speech." Kenyon Coll.,
  Gambier, OH. 21 May 2005. Address.

47. Interview

For published or broadcast interviews, give the title (if any), followed by the
publication or broadcast information for the source that aired or published
the interview. If there is no title, use *Interview* followed by a period.

Name of Person Interviewed. "Title of Interview." *Book, Periodical, Web Site, or
  Program Title.* Publication or Broadcast Information (see specific entry for
  guidance). Medium.

Rushdie, Salman. "Humanism and the Territory of Novelists." *Humanist* 67.4
  (2007): 19-21. Print.

Roth, Philip. Interview. *Fresh Air*. Natl. Public Radio. WQCS, Fort Pierce, FL.
  18 May 2006. Radio.

For interviews that you conduct yourself, include the name of the
interviewee, interview type (personal, e-mail, telephone, etc.), and date.

Dean, Howard. E-mail interview. 12 Oct. 2007.

48. Television or Radio Program

If you access an archived show online, include the access date after the
medium.

"Episode title." *Program Title.* Series Title. Network. Local Channel's Call
  Letters, City (if any). Air Date. Medium.

"Ella Fitzgerald." *American Masters*. PBS. WGBH, Boston. 18 July 2007.
  Television.

"Past Deals Come Back to Haunt UAW." *Marketplace Morning Report*. Amer.
  Public Media. 29 June 2007. Web. 2 Nov. 2007.

49. Film or Video Recording

If you accessed the film via videocassette or DVD, include the distributor name and release date.

> *Film Title.* Dir. Director First Name Last Name. Original Release Date. Distributor, Release Date of Recording. Medium.

> *Rear Window.* Dir. Alfred Hitchcock. 1954. Universal, 2001. DVD.

To highlight a particular individual's performance or contribution, begin with that person's name, followed by a descriptive label (for example, "perf." or "chor.").

> Stewart, James, perf. *Rear Window.* Dir. Alfred Hitchcock. 1954. Universal, 2001. DVD.

50. Sound Recording

> Performer or Band Name. "Title of Song." *Title of Album.* Record Label, Year. Medium.

> Thomas, Irma. "Time Is on My Side." *Live: Simply the Best.* Rounder, 1991. CD.

51. Musical Composition

Long works such as operas, ballets, and named symphonies should be italicized. Additional information, such as key or movement, may be added at the end.

> Composer Name. *Title of Long Work.* Medium.

> Mozart, Wolfgang Amadeus. *Le nozze di Figaro.* CD.

> Beethoven, Ludwig van. Sonata no. 16 in G major, op. 31. LP.

52. Live Performance

> *Performance Title.* By Author Name. Dir. Director Name. Perf. Performer Name(s). Theater or Venue Name, City. Date of Performance. Medium.

> *Frost/Nixon.* By Peter Morgan. Dir. Michael Grandage. Perf. Frank Langella and Michael Sheen. Bernard B. Jacobs Theater, New York. 17 Aug. 2007. Performance.

53. Work of Art

Artist Last Name, First Name.   *Title of Artwork.*   Date. Institution, City.

Sargent, John Singer. *The Daughters of Edward Darley Boit*. 1882. Museum of
Fine Arts, Boston.

A publication medium is required only for reproduced works, such as in
books or online. For works accessed on the Web, include an access date.

Kapoor, Anish. *Ishi's Light*. 2003. Tate Mod., London. *Tate Online*. Web.
4 Oct. 2007.

54. Map or Chart

Title of Map. Map.   Publication City: Publisher Name, Year. Medium.

Northwest Territories and Yukon Territory. Map. Vancouver: Intl. Travel
Maps, 1998. Print.

If you accessed the map online, include an access date.

Cambodia. Map. *Google Maps*. 2009. 15 April 2009. Web.

55. Cartoon or Comic Strip

Artist Last Name, First Name.   "Cartoon Title (if given)." Cartoon. *Title of
Periodical.*   Date: page number.   Medium.

Chast, Roz. "National Everything Awareness Day." Cartoon. *New Yorker*
3 Sept. 2007: 107. Print.

56. Advertisement

Product Name.   Advertisement. *Title of Periodical*   Date: page number(s).
Medium.

Louis Vuitton. Advertisement. *New York Times* 22 July 2007, sec. 9: 8-9.
Print.

Format an MLA paper correctly.   You can now find software to format your academic papers in MLA style, but the key alignments for such documents are usually simple enough for you to manage on your own. (For this entire sample student paper using MLA style, see pp. 189–94.)

- Set up a header on the right-hand side of each page, one-half inch from the top. The header should include your last name and the page number.

- In the upper left on the first—or title—page, include your name, the instructor's name, the course title and/or number, and the date.

- Center the title above the first line of text.

- Use one-inch margins on all sides of the paper.

- Double-space the entire paper (including your name and course information, the title, and any block quotations).

- Indent paragraphs one-half inch.

- Use block quotations for quoted material of four or more lines. Indent block quotations one inch from the left margin.

- Do not include a separate title page unless your instructor requires one.

- When you document using MLA style, you'll need to create an alphabetically arranged Works Cited page at the end of the paper so that readers have a convenient list of all the books, articles, and other data you have used.

Miller 1

Student's name, instructor's name, course title, and date appear in upper-left corner.

Melissa Miller

Professor Spahr

English 112

November 23, 20--

Distinguishing the *Other* in Two Works by Tolstoy

Center title.

The Cossacks and the Chechens are two very different peoples; they share neither language nor religion. The Cossacks are Russian-speaking Christians, while the Chechens speak a Caucasian language and follow Islam. Certainly, Leo Tolstoy (1828-1910) knew these facts, since he spent a significant length of time in the Caucasus. However, it is difficult to distinguish them as different peoples in Tolstoy's work. The Cossacks in Tolstoy's novel of the same name (1863) and the Chechens in his story "A Prisoner in the Caucasus" (1872) share so many cultural and ethnic features — appearance, reverence for warriors and horses, their behavior — that they appear to be the same people. As a result, their deep cultural differences all but disappear to Tolstoy and his European readers.

1-inch margin on all sides of page.

Double-space all elements on title page.

From Tolstoy's descriptions of the Cossacks and the Chechens, they appear identical: Both groups are dark in complexion, wear beshmets, and are wild. The Cossack men have black beards and Maryanka has black eyes (*Cossacks* 30, 55), while Dina has black hair and a face like her father's, "the dark man" ("Prisoner" 316). In addition to the black, both groups are red in countenance: Uncle Yeroshka is "cinnamon-colored" (*Cossacks* 60), Maryanka is sunburned (93), and Kazi Muhamet is always referred to as "the red Tatar" ("Prisoner" 315). Moreover, Tolstoy describes both the Cossack and the Chechen youths' clothing in terms of what they

Half-inch indent for new paragraph.

Source and page number appear in parentheses.

Miller 6

Works Cited

Said, Edward W. *Orientalism*. New York: Vintage, 1976. Print.

Tolstoy, Leo. *The Cossacks*. New York: Scribner's, 1899. Print.

---. "A Prisoner in the Caucasus." *Walk in the Light and Twenty-
    three Tales*. Maryknoll, NY: Orbis, 2003. 78. Print.

"Works Cited" centered at top of page.

Entire page is double-spaced: no extra spaces between entries.

Begins on separate page.

Entries arranged alphabetically.

Second and subsequent lines of entries indent five spaces or one-half inch.

45 APA Documentation and Format

APA (American Psychological Association) style is used in many social science disciplines. For full details about APA style and documentation, consult the *Publication Manual of the American Psychological Association*, Fifth ed. (2001). The basic details for documenting sources and formatting research papers in APA style are presented below.

cite in APA

Document sources according to convention.   When you use sources in a research paper, you are required to cite the source, letting readers know that the information has been borrowed from somewhere else and showing them how to find the original material if they would like to study it further. Like MLA style, APA includes two parts: a brief in-text citation and a more detailed reference entry.

In-text citations should include the author's name, the year the material was published, and the page number(s) that the borrowed material can be found on. The author's name and year of publication are generally included in a signal phrase that introduces the passage, and the page number is included in parentheses after the borrowed text. Note that for APA style, the verb in the signal phrase should be in the past tense (*reported*, as in the example on p. 475) or present perfect tense (*has reported*).

Millman (2007) reported that college students around the country are participating in Harry Potter discussion groups, sports activities, and even courses for college credit (p. A4).

Alternatively, the author's name and year can be included in parentheses with the page number.

College students around the country are participating in Harry Potter discussion groups, sports activities, and even courses for college credit (Millman, 2007, p. A4).

The list of references at the end of the paper contains more detailed citations that repeat the author's name and publication year and include the title and additional publication information about the source. Inclusive page numbers are included for periodical articles and parts of books.

Millman, S. (2007). Generation hex. *The Chronicle of Higher Education, 53*(46), A4.

Both in-text citations and reference entries can vary greatly depending on the type of source cited (book, periodical, Web site, etc.). The following pages give specific examples of how to cite a wide range of sources in APA style.

Directory of APA In-Text Citations

1. Author named in signal phrase 477
2. Author named in parentheses 477
3. With block quotations 477
4. Two authors 477
5. Three to five authors 478
6. Six or more authors 478
7. Group, corporate, or government author 478
8. Two or more works by the same author 479
9. Authors with the same last name 479
10. Unknown author 479
11. Personal communication 479
12. Electronic source 480
13. Musical recording 480
14. Secondary source 480
15. Multiple sources in same citation 480

△

General Guidelines for In-Text Citations in APA Style

AUTHOR NAMES

- Give last names only, unless two authors have the same last name (see item 9 on p. 479) or if the source is a personal communication (see item 11 on p. 479). In these cases, include the first initial before the last name ("J. Smith").

DATES

- Give only the year in the in-text citation. The one exception to this rule is personal communications, which should include a full date (see item 11 on p. 479).

- Months and days for periodical publications should not be given with the year in in-text citations; this information will be provided as needed in the reference entry at the end of your paper.

- If you have two or more works by the same author in the same year, see item 8 on page 479.

- If you can't locate a date for your source, include the abbreviation "n.d." (for "no date") in place of the date in parentheses.

TITLES

- Titles of works generally do not need to be given in in-text citations. Exceptions include works with no author and two or more works by the same author. See items 8 and 10 on page 479 for details.

PAGE NUMBERS

- Include whenever possible in parentheses after borrowed material. Put "p." (or "pp.") before the page number(s).

- When you have a range of pages, list the full first and last page numbers (for example, "311-324"). If the borrowed material isn't printed on consecutive pages list all the pages it appears on (for example, "A1, A4-A6").

- If page numbers are not available, use section names and/or paragraph (written as "para.") numbers when available to help a reader locate a specific quotation. See items 7 and 12 on pages 478 and 480 for examples.

APA in-text citation

1. Author Named in Signal Phrase

Doyle (2005) asserted that "[a]lthough some immigrants are a burden on the welfare system, as a group they pay far more in taxes than they receive in government benefits, such as public education and social services" (p. 25).

2. Author Named in Parentheses

"Although some immigrants are a burden on the welfare system, as a group they pay far more in taxes than they receive in government benefits, such as public education and social services" (Doyle, 2005, p. 25).

3. With Block Quotations

For excerpts of forty or more words, indent the quoted material one-half inch and include the page number at the end of the quotation after the end punctuation.

Pollan (2006) suggested that the prized marbled meat that results from feeding corn to cattle (ruminants) may not be good for us:

> Yet this corn-fed meat is demonstrably less healthy for us, since it contains more saturated fat and less omega-3 fatty acids than the meat of animals fed grass. A growing body of research suggests that many of the health problems associated with eating beef are really problems with corn-fed beef. . . . In the same way ruminants are ill adapted to eating corn, humans in turn may be poorly adapted to eating ruminants that eat corn. (p. 75)

4. Two Authors

Note that if you name the authors in the parentheses, connect them with an ampersand (&).

Sharpe and Young (2005) reported that new understandings about tooth development, along with advances in stem-cell technology, have brought researchers closer to the possibility of producing replacement teeth from human tissue (p. 36).

New understandings about tooth development, along with advances in stem-cell technology, have brought researchers closer to the possibility of producing replacement teeth from human tissue (Sharpe & Young, 2005, p. 36).

5. Three to Five Authors

The first time you cite a source with three to five authors, list all their names in either the signal phrase or parentheses. If you cite the same source again in your paper, use just the first name followed by *et al.*

Swain, Scahill, Lombroso, King, and Leckman (2007) pointed out that "[a]lthough no ideal treatment for tics has been established, randomized clinical trials have clarified the short-term benefits of a number of agents" (p. 947).

Swain et al. (2007) claimed that "[m]any tics are often under partial voluntary control, evidenced by patients' capacity to suppress them for brief periods of time" (p. 948).

6. Six or More Authors

List the first name only, followed by "et al."

Grossoehme et al. (2007) examined the disparity between the number of pediatricians who claim that religion and spirituality are important factors in treating patients and those who actually use religion and spirituality in their practice (p. 968).

7. Group, Corporate, or Government Author

The resolution called on the United States to ban all forms of torture in interrogation procedures (American Psychological Association [APA], 2007, para. 1). It also reasserted "the organization's absolute opposition to all forms of torture and abuse, regardless of circumstance" (APA, 2007, para. 5).

8. Two or More Works by the Same Author

To see reference list entries for these sources, see item 6 on page 484.

> Shermer (2005a) has reported that false acupuncture (in placebo experi-
> ments) is as effective as true acupuncture (p. 30).

> Shermer (2005b) has observed that psychics rely on vague and flatter-
> ing statements, such as "You are wise in the ways of the world, a wisdom
> gained through hard experience rather than book learning," to earn the
> trust of their clients (p. 6).

9. Authors with the Same Last Name

> M. Dunn (2003) argued that, in fact, the opposite may be true (p. 5).

10. Unknown Author

If the author is listed as Anonymous, treat this term as the author in your
citation.

> Tilapia provides more protein when eaten than it consumes when alive,
> making it a sustainable fish ("Dream Fish," 2007, 26).

> The book *Go Ask Alice* (Anonymous, 1971) portrayed the fictional life of a
> teenager who is destroyed by her addiction to drugs.

11. Personal Communication

If you cite personal letters or e-mails or your own interviews for your research paper, cite these as personal communication in your in-text citation,
including the author of the material (with first initial), the term *personal communication*, and the date. Personal communications should not be included
in your reference list.

> One instructor has argued that it is important to "make peer review a lot
> more than a proofreading/grammar/mechanics exercise" (J. Bone, personal
> communication, July 27, 2007).

To include the author of a personal communication in the signal phrase,
use the following format:

> J. Bone (personal communication, July 27, 2007) has argued that it is important to "make peer review a lot more than a proofreading/grammar/mechanics exercise."

12. Electronic Source

If page numbers are not given, use section names or paragraph numbers to help your readers track down the source.

> A recent report showed that, in 2006, "59 percent of KIPP fifth graders outperformed their local districts in reading, and 74 percent did so in mathematics" ("Charter Schools/Choice," 2007, para. 4).

13. Musical Recording

> In a somewhat ironic twist, Mick Jagger sings backup on the song "You're So Vain" (Simon, 1972, track 3).

14. Secondary Source

Include the name of the original author in the signal phrase. In the parentheses, add *as cited in,* and give the author of the quoted material along with the date and page number. Note that your end-of-paper reference entry for this material will be listed under the secondary source name (Pollan) rather than the original writer (Howard).

> Writing in 1943, Howard asserted that "artificial manures lead inevitably to artificial nutrition, artificial food, artificial animals, and finally to artificial men and women" (as cited in Pollan, 2006, p. 148).

15. Multiple Sources in Same Citation

If one statement in your paper can be attributed to multiple sources, alphabetically list all the authors with dates, separated by semicolons.

> Most historians agree that the Puritan religion played a significant role in the hysteria surrounding the Salem witchcraft trials (Karlsen, 1998; Norton, 2002; Reis, 1997).

Directory of APA Reference Entries

General Guidelines for Reference Entries in APA Style

AUTHOR NAMES

- When an author's name appears *before* the title of the work, list it by last name followed by a comma and first initial followed by a period. (Middle initials may also be included.)
- If an author, editor, or other name is listed *after* the title, then the initial(s) precede the last name (see examples on pp. 485–486).
- When multiple authors are listed, their names should be separated by commas, and an ampersand (&) should precede the final author.

DATES

- For scholarly journals, include only the year (2007).
- For monthly magazines, include the year followed by a comma and the month (2007, May).
- For newspapers and weekly magazines, include the year, followed by a comma and the month and the day (2007, May 27).
- Access dates for electronic documents use the month-day-year format: "Retrieved May 27, 2007."
- Months should not be abbreviated.
- If a date is not available, use "n.d." (for "no date") in parentheses.

TITLES

- Titles of periodicals should be italicized, and all major words capitalized (*Psychology Today*; *Journal of Archaeological Research*).
- Titles of books, Web sites, and other nonperiodical long works should be italicized. Capitalize the first word of the title (and subtitle, if any) and proper nouns only (*Legacy of ashes: The history of the CIA*).
- For short works such as essays, articles, and chapters capitalize the first word of the title (and subtitle, if any) and proper nouns only (The black sites: A rare look inside the CIA's secret interrogation program).

PAGE NUMBERS

- Reference entries for periodical articles and sections of books should include the range of pages: 245-257. For material in parentheses, include the abbreviation *p.* or *pp.* before the page numbers (pp. A4-A5).
- If the pages are not continuous, list all the pages separated by commas: 245, 249, 301-306.

APA reference entries

AUTHOR INFORMATION

1. One Author

Chopra, A. (2007). *King of Bollywood: Shah Rukh Khan and the seductive world of Indian cinema*. New York: Warner Books.

2. Two Authors

Johnson, M. E., & Vickers, C. (2005). *Threading the generations: A Mississippi family's quilt legacy*. Jackson: University Press of Mississippi.

3. Three or More Authors

For seven or more authors, use the abbreviation *et al.* (meaning "and others") after the sixth author's name and initials.

Thompson, M., Grace, C. O., & Cohen, L. J. (2001). *Best friends, worst enemies: Understanding the social lives of children*. New York: Ballantine Books.

Gahagan, S., Sharpe, T. T., Brimacombe, M., Fry-Johnson, Y., Levine, R., Mengel, M., et al. (2007). Pediatricians' knowledge, training, and experience in the care of children with fetal alcohol syndrome. *Journal of the American Academy of Child and Adolescent Psychiatry, 46*(4), 456.

4. Group, Corporate, or Government Author

In many cases, the group name is the same as the publisher. Instead of repeating the group name, use the term *Author* for the publisher's name.

Society for the Protection of the Rights of the Child. (2003). *The state of Pakistan's children 2002*. Islamabad: Author.

5. Unidentified Author

If the author is listed on the work as "Anonymous," list that in your reference entry, alphabetizing accordingly. Otherwise, start with and alphabetize by title.

Dream fish. (2007, July/August). *Eating Well, 6*, 26-30.

Anonymous. (1971). *Go ask Alice*. New York: Simon & Schuster.

6. Multiple Works by the Same Author

Shermer, M. (2003). I knew you would say that [Review of the book *Intuition: Its powers and perils*]. *Skeptic, 10*(1), 92-94.

Shermer, M. (2005a, August). Full of holes: The curious case of acupuncture. *Scientific American, 293*(2), 30.

Shermer, M. (2005b). *Science friction*. New York: Henry Holt.

BOOKS

7. Book: Basic Format

Author. (Publication Year). *Book title: Book subtitle*. Publication City: Publisher.

Mah, A. Y. (1997). *Falling leaves: The true story of an unwanted Chinese daughter*. New York: John Wiley & Sons.

8. Author and Editor

Author. (Publication Year). *Book title: Book subtitle* (Editor's Initial(s). Editor's Last Name, Ed.). Publication City: Publisher.

Faulkner, W. (2004). *Essays, speeches, and public letters* (J. B. Meriwether, Ed.). New York: Modern Library.

9. Work in an Anthology or a Collection

Begin with the author and date of the short work and include the title as you would a periodical title (no quotations and minimal capitalization). Then list *In* and the editor's first initial and last name followed by *Ed.* in parentheses. Next give the anthology title and page numbers in parentheses. End with the publication information. If an anthology has two editors, connect them with an ampersand (&) and use *Eds.* For six or more editors, use *et al.*

Author. (Publication Year). Title of short work. In Editor's First Initial. Editor's Last Name (Ed.), *Title of anthology* (pp. page numbers). Publication City: Publisher.

Plimpton, G. (2002). Final twist of the drama. In N. Dawidoff (Ed.), *Baseball: A literary anthology* (pp. 457-475). New York: Library of America.

For three to five editors, connect them with commas and an ampersand.

J. Smith, L. Hoey, & R. Burns (Eds.)

J. Smith et al. (Eds.)

10. Edited Collection

Editor. (Ed.). (Publication Year). *Book title: Book subtitle.* Publication City: Publisher.

Danquah, M. N. (Ed.). (2000). *Becoming American: Personal essays by first generation immigrant women.* New York: Hyperion.

11. Multivolume Work

Author(s) or Editor(s). (Year of Publication). *Book title: Book subtitle* (Vols. volume numbers). Publication City: Publisher.

Lindahl, C., MacNamara, J., & Lindow, J. (Eds.). (2000). *Medieval folklore: An encyclopedia of myths, legends, tales, beliefs, and customs* (Vols. 1-2). Santa Barbara: ABC-CLIO.

12. Later Edition

In parentheses include the edition type (such as *Rev.* for "Revised" or *Abr.* for "Abridged") or number (*2nd, 3rd, 4th,* etc.) as shown on the title page, along with the abbreviation *ed.* after the book title.

Author Name. (Publication Year). *Book title* (Edition Type or Number ed.). Publication City: Publisher.

Handlin, D. P. (2004). *American architecture* (2nd ed.). London: Thames and Hudson.

13. Translation

List the translator's initial, last name, and *Trans.* in parentheses after the title. After the publication information, list *Original work published* and year in parentheses. Note that the period is omitted after the final parenthesis.

> Author Name. (Publication Year of Translation). *Book title* (Translator Initial(s). Last Name, Trans.). Publication City: Publisher. (Original work published Year)

> Camus, A. (1988). *The stranger* (M. Ward, Trans.). New York: Knopf. (Original work published 1942)

14. Article in a Reference Book

> Article Author. (Publication Year). Article title. In Initial(s). Last Name of Editor (Ed.), *Reference book title* (pp. page numbers). Publication City: Publisher.

> Schwartz, J. (1995). Brownstones. In K. T. Jackson (Ed.), *Encyclopedia of New York City* (pp. 162-163). New Haven: Yale University Press.

If a reference book entry has no author, begin with the title of the article.

> Article title. (Publication Year). In *Book title.* Publication City: Publisher.

> The history of the national anthem. (2004). In *The world almanac and book of facts 2004.* New York: World Almanac Books.

PERIODICALS

15. Article in a Journal Paginated by Volume

> Author Name(s). (Publication Year). Title of article. *Title of Journal, Volume Number,* page numbers.

> Harwood, J. (2004). Relational, role, and social identity as expressed in grandparents' personal Web sites. *Communication Studies, 55,* 300-318.

16. Article in a Journal Paginated by Issue

> Author Name(s). (Publication Year). Title of article. *Title of Journal, Volume Number*(Issue Number), page numbers.

Clancy, S., & Simpson, L. (2002). Literacy learning for indigenous students: Setting a research agenda. *Australian Journal of Language and Literacy, 25*(2), 47-64.

17. Magazine Article

Author Name(s). (Publication Year, Month). Title of article. *Title of Magazine, Volume Number,* page number(s).

Murrel, J. (2007, July). In the year of the storm: The topography of resurrection in New Orleans. *Harper's Magazine, 315,* 35-52.

18. Newspaper Article

Author Name(s). (Publication Year, Month Day). Title of article. Title of *Newspaper,* p. page number.

Dempsey, J. (2007, August 26). Germans ease curbs on skilled labor from Eastern Europe. *The New York Times,* p. 8.

19. Letter to the Editor

Include *Letter to the editor* in brackets after the letter title (if any) and before the period.

Author Name. (Publication Year, Month Day). Title of letter [Letter to the editor]. *Title of Newspaper,* p. page number.

Miller, E. D. (2007, August 29). It is the sworn duty of law officers to uphold the law [Letter to the editor]. *The Stuart News,* p. A6.

20. Review

After the review title (if any), include in brackets *Review of* and the medium of the work being reviewed (book, film, CD, etc.) before the name of the work.

Author Name. (Publication Year, Month Day). Title of review [Review of the book *Book title*]. *Title of Periodical, volume number,* page number.

Adams, L. (2007, July 15). The way west [Review of the book *Shadow of the Silk Road*]. *The New York Times Book Review, 1,* 10.

ELECTRONIC SOURCES

Below are additional listings for specific electronically based sources.

21. Article Retrieved from a Database

> Hansen, J. E. (2006). Can we still avoid dangerous human-made climate change? *Social Research, 73*(2), 949-971. Retrieved October 15, 2007, from Academic OneFile database.

22. Online Article with Print Version

> Rosenfield, D., Manuel, D. G., & Alter, D. A. (2007). The Smoking Regulatory Index: A new way to measure public health performance. *Canadian Medical Association Journal, 174*(10), 1403-1404. Retrieved from http://www.cmaj.ca/cgi/content/full/174/10/1403

23. Article in Internet-Only Periodical

Note that there is no period after the URL.

> Clark-Flory, T. (2007, August 31). Do we teach children to fear men? *Salon.com.* Retrieved November 23, 2007, from http://www.salon.com/mwt/broadsheet/2007/08/31/men/index.html

24. Multipage Web Site

If the Web site is part of a university program, mention this before the URL, and follow with a colon. Do not add a period at the end of the entry.

> Web Site Author or Sponsor. (Year of Most Recent Update). *Title of Web site.* Retrieved date from URL

> Annie E. Casey Foundation. (2007). *Kids count.* Retrieved September 9, 2007, from http://www.aecf.org/MajorInitiatives/KIDSCOUNT.aspx

> Hartmann, D., Gerteis, J., & Edgell, P. (2007). *American Mosaic Project.* Retrieved August 31, 2007, from University of Minnesota, Department of Sociology Web site: http://www.soc.umn.edu/research/amp/

25. Part of a Web Site

Short Work Author. (Year of Most Recent Update). Title of short work. *Title of Web site.* Retrieved date from URL

Taylor, W., Jr. (2005, November 16). A time to be thankful. *The Hopi Tribe Web site.* Retrieved January 27, 2006, from http://www.hopi.nsn.us/ view_article.asp?id=116&cat=3

26. Online Posting

Author of Post. (Year, Month Day of post). Title of post [Msg message number]. Message posted to URL

Winkleman, T. (2007, July 13). Reducing your food miles [Msg 220]. Message posted to http://tech.groups.yahoo.com/group/ FFCFBulletin/message/220

27. Computer Software

If the software has an author or editor, the reference begins with that.

Title of software [Computer software]. (Publication Year). Publication City: Publisher.

History through art: The twentieth century [Computer software]. (2001). San Jose: Fogware.

28. Entry in a Weblog

Sellers, H. (2008, June 21). Re: East Coast. Message posted to

http://heathersellers.com/blog/index.php

29. Podcast

Graham, L. (Producer). (2006, July 31). Capping pollution at the source. *The Environment Report.* Podcast retrieved from http:// www.environmentreport.org/story.php3?story_id=3102

30. Entry in a Wiki

Article title. Date retrieved, from [name of] wiki: <URL>.

Emo. (n.d.). Retrieved June 24, 2008, from Wikipedia: http:// en.wikipedia.org/wiki/Emo

How to...
Cite from a database (APA)

1 author

2 publication year

3 page number

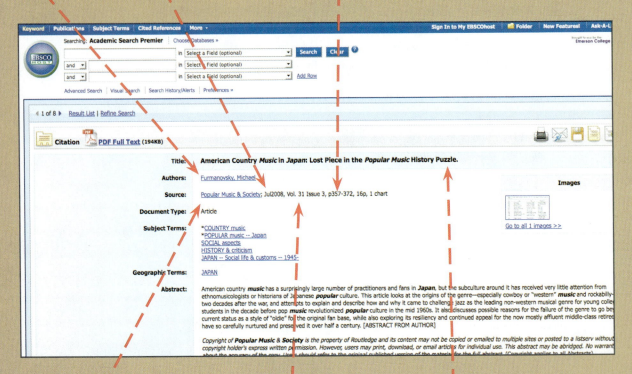

4 journal title

5 volume and issue number

6 article title

Scroll down to find more information.

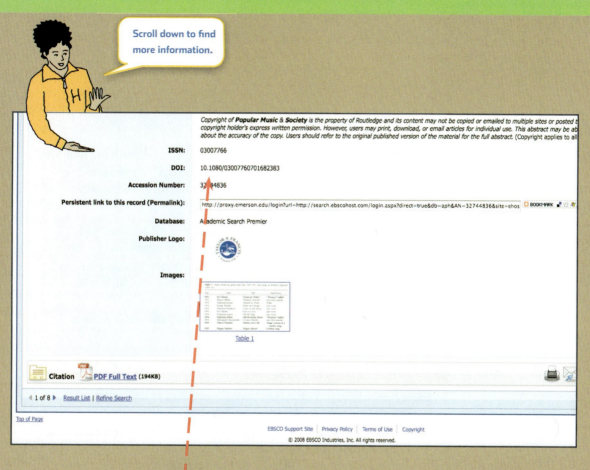

Copyright of **Popular Music** & **Society** is the property of Routledge and its content may not be copied or emailed to multiple sites or posted t copyright holder's express written permission. However, users may print, download, or email articles for individual use. This abstract may be ab about the accuracy of the copy. Users should refer to the original published version of the material for the full abstract. (Copyright applies to all

ISSN:	03007766
DOI:	10.1080/03007760701682383
Accession Number:	32744836
Persistent link to this record (Permalink):	http://proxy.emerson.edu/login?url=http://search.ebscohost.com/login.aspx?direct=true&db=aph&AN=32744836&site=ehos
Database:	Academic Search Premier
Publisher Logo:	
Images:	Table 1

Citation   PDF Full Text (194KB)

◀ 1 of 8 ▶ Result List | Refine Search

Top of Page

7   **DOI (Digital Object Identifier)**

APA in-text citation

① **②**
Furmanovsky (2008) has shown that many of the first Japanese country musicians aimed for "a meticulous and highly stylized cowboy image with cowboy outfits ordered from the U.S." (p. 362). **③**

APA references list entry

① **②** **⑥**
Furmanovsky, M. (2008). American country music in Japan: Lost piece

④
in the popular music history puzzle. *Popular Music & Society,*
⑤ **③** **⑦**
31(3), 357-372. doi:10.1080/03007760701682383

OTHER

31. Group, Corporate, or Government Document

List the group or agency as the author, and include any identifying numbers. Many federal agencies' works are published by the U.S. Government Printing Office. If the group is also the publisher, use the word *Author* rather than repeating the group name at the end of the entry.

> Name of Group, Corporation, or Government Agency. (Publication Year). *Title of document* (Identifying number, if any). Publication City: Publisher.

U.S. Department of Health and Human Services. (1995). *Disability among older persons: United States and Canada* (HE 20.6209:5/8). Washington, DC: U.S. Government Printing Office.

Florida Department of Elder Affairs. (2006). *Making choices: A guide to end-of-life planning.* Tallahassee: Author.

32. Published Conference Proceedings

> Editor Names. (Eds.). (Publication Year). *Proceedings of the Conference Name: Book title.* Publication City: Publisher.

Bourguignon, F., Pleskovic, B., & Van Der Gaag, J. (Eds.). (2006). *Proceedings of the Annual World Bank Conference on Development Economics 2006: Securing development in an unstable world.* Washington, DC: World Bank.

33. Dissertation Abstract

For dissertations abstracted in *Dissertation Abstracts International,* include the author's name, date, and dissertation title. Then include volume, issue, and page number. If you access the dissertation from an electronic database, include the database name and any identifying number. If you retrieve the abstract from a university, include the words *Doctoral dissertation*, the university name, and the date of the dissertation.

Author. (Year of Publication). Title of dissertation. *Dissertation Abstracts International, Volume Number*(Issue Number), page number.

Berger, M. A. (2000). The impact of organized sports participation on self-esteem in middle school children. *Dissertation Abstracts International, 60*(11), 5762B.

Berger, M. A. (2000). The impact of organized sports participation on self-esteem in middle school children. Retrieved from ProQuest Digital Dissertations. (730241441)

Berger, M. A. (2000). The impact of organized sports participation on self-esteem in middle school children (Doctoral dissertation, Pace University, 1999). *Dissertation Abstracts International, 60*(11), 5762B.

34. Film

Names of Writer(s), Producer(s), Director(s). (Release year). *Film title* [Motion picture]. Country of Origin: Movie Studio.

Haggis, P. (Writer/Director/Producer), & Moresco, B. (Writer/Producer). (2004). *Crash* [Motion picture]. United States: Lions Gate Films.

35. Television Program

Writer Last Names, Initials. (Writers), & Director Last Name, Initial. (Director). (Year of Release). Title of episode [Television series episode]. In Producer Initials. Last Name (Producer), *Title of series.* City: Broadcast Company.

Hochman, G., & Collins, M. (Writers), & Wolfinger, K. (Director). (2004). Ancient refuge in the Holy Land [Television series episode]. In P. S. Apsell (Producer), *NOVA*. Boston: WGBH.

36. Musical Recording

Writer. (Copyright Year). Title of song [Recorded by Artist Name]. On *Album title* [Recording medium]. City of Recording: Record Label. (Recording Year).

Cornell, C. (1991). Rusty cage [Recorded by J. Cash]. On *Unchained* [CD]. Burbank, CA: American Recordings. (1994).

Format an APA paper correctly.   Below are a list of guidelines to help you prepare a manuscript using APA style.

- Set up a header on the right-hand side of each page (including the title page, if your instructor requests same), one-half inch from the top. The header should state a brief title of your paper and the page number.

- Margins should be set at one inch on all sides of the paper.

- Check with your instructor to see if a title page is preferred. The title page should include the title of your paper, your name, the course title, your instructor's name, and the date. If included, the title page should be considered page number 1.

- If you include an abstract for your paper, put it on a separate page, immediately following the title page.

- All lines of text (including the title page, abstract, block quotations, and the list of references) should be double-spaced.

- Indent first lines of paragraphs one-half inch or five spaces.

- Use block quotations for quoted material of four or more lines. Indent block quotations one inch from the left margin.

- When you document a paper using APA style, you'll need to create an alphabetically arranged References page at the end of the project so that readers have a convenient list of all the books, articles, and other data you have used in the paper or project.

Cri Du Chat Syndrome i

Developmental Disorders:

Cri Du Chat Syndrome

Marissa Dahlstrom

Course Title

Instructor's Name

Date

Short title and page number. Lowercase roman numerals are used on title page and abstract page.

Full title centered in middle of page.

Writer's name, course name, instructor's name, and date are all centered.

Cri Du Chat Syndrome 1

Developmental Disorders: Cri Du Chat Syndrome

Developmental disorders pose a serious threat to young children.
However, early detection, treatment, and intervention often allow a
child to lead a fulfilling life. To detect a problem at the beginning of
life, medical professionals and caregivers must recognize normal
development as well as potential warning signs. Research provides
this knowledge. In most cases, research also allows for accurate
diagnosis and effective intervention. Such is the case with Cri Du
Chat Syndrome (CDCS), also commonly known as Cat Cry Syndrome,
5p-Syndrome, and 5p-Minus Syndrome.

Cri Du Chat Syndrome, a fairly rare genetic disorder first
identified in 1963 by Dr. Jerome Lejeune, affects between one in
fifteen thousand to one in fifty thousand live births (Campbell,
Carlin, Justen, & Baird, 2004). The syndrome is caused by partial
deletion of chromosome number 5, specifically the portion labeled as
5p; hence the alternative name for the disorder (Five P-Minus
Society). While the exact cause of the deletion is unknown, it is likely
that "the majority of cases are due to spontaneous loss . . . during
development of an egg or sperm. A minority of cases result from one
parent carrying a rearrangement of chromosome 5 called a
translocation" (Sondheimer, 2005). The deletion leads to many
different symptoms and outcomes. Perhaps the most noted
characteristic of children affected by this syndrome--a high-pitched
cry resembling the mewing of a cat--explains Lejeune's choice of the
name *Cri Du Chat* Syndrome. Pediatric nurse Mary Kugler writes
that the cry is caused by "problems with the larynx and nervous
system" (2006). Other symptoms, characteristics, and complications
resulting from the chromosomal abnormality include, but are not

---

Margin notes:

Full title, centered.

Short title and page number. Arabic numerals used for page numbers on text pages.

The authors' names and publication date appear in parentheses.

A signal phrase including author's name introduces quotation, so only date appears in parentheses.

References

Campbell, D., Carlin M., Justen, J., III, & Baird, S. (2004). Cri-du-chat syndrome: A topical overview. Retrieved from http://www.fivepminus.org/online.htm

Denny, M., Marchand-Martella, N., Martella, R., Reilly, J. R., & Reilly, J. F. (2000, November). Using parent-delivered graduated guidance to teach functional living skills to a child with cri du chat syndrome. *Education & Treatment of Children, 23*(4), 441.

Five P-Minus Society. (n.d.). *About 5P-syndrome*. Retrieved from http://www.fivepminus.org/about.htm

Kugler, M. (2006). Cri-du-chat syndrome: Distinctive kitten-like cry in infancy. Retrieved from http://rarediseases.about.com/cs/criduchatsynd/a/010704.htm

McClean, P. (1997). Genomic analysis: *In situ* hybridization. Retrieved from http://www.ndsu.nodak.edu/instruct/mcclean/plsc431/genomic/genomic2.htm

Sarimski, K. (2003, February). Early play behavior in children with 5p-syndrome. *Journal of Intellectual Disability Research, 47*(2), 113-120.

Sondheimer, N. (2005). Cri du chat syndrome. In *MedlinePlus medical encyclopedia*. Retrieved from http://www.nlm.nih.gov/medlineplus/ency/article/001593.htm

Media & Design

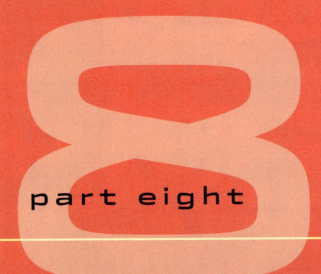

part eight

46 Understanding Images

Most of us realize how powerful images can be, particularly when they perfectly capture a moment or make an argument that words alone struggle to express. The famous "Blue Marble" shot of the Earth taken by *Apollo 17* in 1972 is one such image—conveying both the wonder and fragility of our planet hanging in space.

More recently, the numerous still and video shots of human suffering following Hurricane Katrina galvanized a nation and altered the political landscape (for an example, see p. 90).

But media need not be spectacular or inimitable to effectively communicate ideas. We routinely use images of all kinds, from simple photographs to CT scans of human organs, to organize and present information. Consider how the average campus map easily directs users to the buildings and services they need, relying on nothing more than drawings, colors, symbols, and various legends or keys—all important communication devices.

When enhanced by sound and action, images become complex multimedia experiences. A sports fan can watch virtual baseball and football games on ESPN.com, thanks to an interface that mimics the actions and sounds on the remote playing field.

Images relate different kinds of experiences and achieve a variety of results: The riveting and emotional photograph clinches an argument, as does the cool-headed and clear chart's display of data. Following are a few strategies to keep in mind when designing and using images, to reach readers effectively and powerfully.

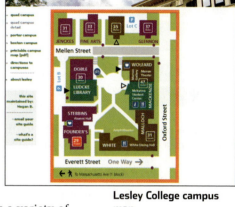

Lesley College campus map

Design an image showing a sequence.

Like a narrative, an image can show information in stages or steps. ○ The sequence might be alphabetical, chronological, or by degree or magnitude (for example, greater to lesser, cheap to expensive)—whatever works for the material. ○ However, the arrangement of data should be self-evident to readers, whether in a chart, Web page, or map. They should never have to guess how the material works or what the sequence illustrates. The American Red Cross, for example, depicts its history on its Web museum through a visual timeline. The reader simply clicks on any of the scrolling panels for more information about a specific period.

Visual timeline from the Web site of the American Red Cross

understand narrative
p. 4

shape your work
p. 340

**Seating plan for the
Santa Fe Opera House.**

Design an image displaying differences.   Many types of images use
boundaries of various kinds—lines, boxes, columns, contrasting colors,
and so on—to highlight divisions. A simple seating guide to an auditorium
mimics its floor plan to guide you to your box. An online weather map
shows the entire country marked off into states, counties, climatic regions,
and so on.

   Color-coding is often added to such images to convey even further
information. The colors in that seating guide tell you that there is a price
difference between the loge and the mezzanine sections; on a weather map,
colors indicate temperatures or storm fronts.

Design an image demonstrating a process.   Sometimes processes are
easier to understand if they are broken down into components and displayed
visually. In a flowchart, a reader follows a series of distinct steps, often
making one or more choices along the way, in order to reach a conclusion.

   Even complex cause-and-effect relationships can be displayed visually,
either as static images or more elaborate animations. ◦ For example, *USA
Today*—one of the leaders in innovative information design—uses an animated sequence online to show how cat-dander allergies can occur and be
overcome. The graphic allows readers to pick several options and then "play"
the item to see the results. Note that the image explains to readers where to
start and what to do.

This *USA Today* interactive
graphic enables readers to
see how scientists are learning to shut down allergic
reactions.

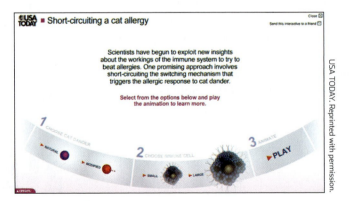

USA TODAY. Reprinted with permission.

understand causal
analysis p. 128

Design an image showing how information is related.   Quite often, information needs to be presented in diagrams that show hierarchies and other relationships. A family tree illustrates the genealogical connections among a person's ancestors. A site map displays the main pages and sub-pages of a Web site. An organizational chart (or "org chart," as it is commonly called) lets readers know who reports to whom within an organization.

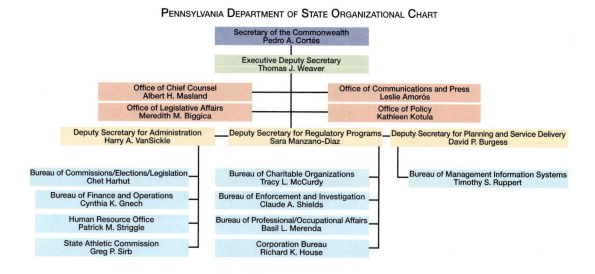

PENNSYLVANIA DEPARTMENT OF STATE ORGANIZATIONAL CHART

Design an image displaying three dimensions.   Many images, particularly in the fields of science and engineering, attempt to convey three-dimensional information in two dimensions, enabling viewers to understand how objects work, how parts mesh, or how the natural world functions. Consider how cutaway drawings enable viewers to see relationships that would be very difficult to explain in words alone.

Using Images

Use images in various academic papers and projects to help illustrate a topic or argue a point. ⭕ The images may be embedded in a paper or other print document, appear on a Web page, or become part of a multimedia project. In order to use images sensibly and effectively in your work, consider the following guidelines.

Have a good reason for using every image.   A photograph or clip should do what words cannot. For instance, a verbal description of the unique style of a Frank Gehry or Santiago Calatrava building probably wouldn't do justice to the subject. Readers should benefit from seeing a photograph in your text—which is exactly why Annie Winsett includes the photograph of the Guggenheim Bilbao in her report on page 60. On the other hand,

think visually
p. 500

what would be gained from downloading images of the president or secretary of state into a report for a government class: Who doesn't already know what they look like? Using unnecessary images contributes to *clutter*, the visual equivalent of wordiness. O

Download and save images.   Most images on the Web can be saved on your computer simply by control clicking (or right clicking) on them. You can also purchase whole libraries of clip art and stock photography, which you can then use without worrying about copyright infringement. If you are working with a digital camera, download your own images onto your computer, where you can edit them and import them into various documents.

To import an image into a Word or PowerPoint document, select Picture (or another option) from the Insert menu, find the appropriate image file, and click on it. Alternatively, you can copy an online image directly from its source (by right clicking or control clicking) and paste it into your document. If you choose this method, be *extremely careful* to document the source site; obtain permission if necessary. O

Keep careful tabs on the images you collect for your project. Create a dedicated folder on your desktop or other memorable place on your hard drive, and save each image with a new name that will remind you exactly where it came from. Keeping a printed record of images, with more detailed background about copyright and source information, will be a great time-saver later, when you are putting your project or paper together.

Use digital images of an appropriate size.   Even if you have limited knowledge of image file formats (such as JPG, GIF, or TIFF), you probably understand that digital files come in varying sizes. The size of a digital-image file is directly related to the quality, or resolution, of the image. Attach a few high resolution photos to an e-mail, and you'll quickly clog the recipient's mailbox.

For most Web pages and online documents, compressed or lower resolution images will be acceptable. On the other hand, if you intend to print an image—in a paper or brochure, for example—use the highest

At this size, the image downloaded from the Web is clear enough. But it would become distorted if you tried to enlarge it, because its resolution is too low.

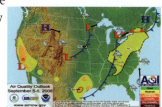

improve your sentences
p. 378

understand citation
styles p. 435

resolution image (the greatest number of pixels) available to assure maximum sharpness and quality.

Use tools to crop and improve an image.   Even the simplest image-editing software enables you to adjust the tint, contrast, saturation, and sharpness of your digital photographs. For instance, heightening the contrast of a PowerPoint image so that it projects better. Or adjusting the tint in a portrait to get the green out of skin tones. More sophisticated programs such as iPhoto, Photoshop, or Photo Editor allow you to do even more. Don't, however, tinker with the settings on professional photographs, even if you have permission to use them. Unless you have purchased the images from a stock photography library, they belong to someone else.

Use the cropping tool to select just the portion of an image you need for your project. Be aware, though, that when you enlarge a section of a larger digital image, it loses sharpness. And never crop an image in a way that distorts its meaning.

Improving a Photo Using Photo Editor   Image-editing software offers numerous options for enhancing picture files. Look for them on palettes, toolbars, or dropdown menus.

Caption an image correctly.   When using images in an academic paper, number, label, and caption them. Captions provide context for readers, so they know why they're looking at the image. MLA and APA styles have different guidelines for captioning images and referring to them in the text, so consult the relevant guidebook before writing your captions. In general, however, captions should include the source of the image and any copyright and publication information. The photo below has not been previously published, but note we still had to ask the photographer for permission to reprint.

Respect copyrights.   The images you find, whether online or in print, are someone else's property. You cannot use them for commercial purposes—Web sites, brochures, posters, magazine articles, and so on—without permission.

Fig. 1. The Floating Market in Phuket, Thailand. (Courtesy Sid Darion.)

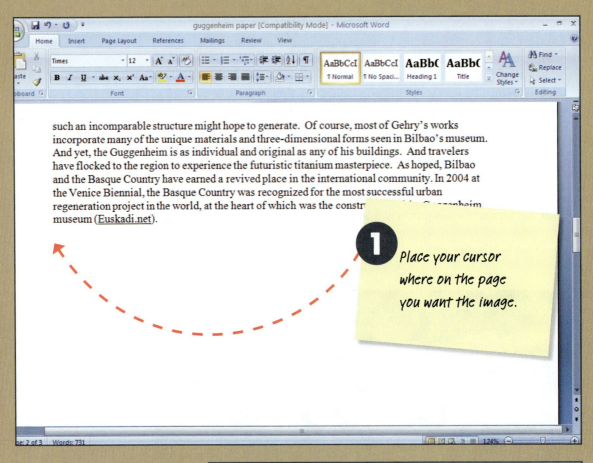

such an incomparable structure might hope to generate. Of course, most of Gehry's works incorporate many of the unique materials and three-dimensional forms seen in Bilbao's museum. And yet, the Guggenheim is as individual and original as any of his buildings. And travelers have flocked to the region to experience the futuristic titanium masterpiece. As hoped, Bilbao and the Basque Country have earned a revived place in the international community. In 2004 at the Venice Biennial, the Basque Country was recognized for the most successful urban regeneration project in the world, at the heart of which was the constr... ...Guggenheim museum (Euskadi.net).

1 Place your cursor where on the page you want the image.

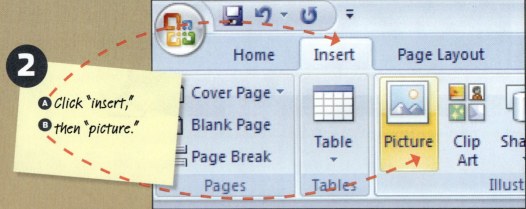

2

A Click "insert,"
B then "picture."

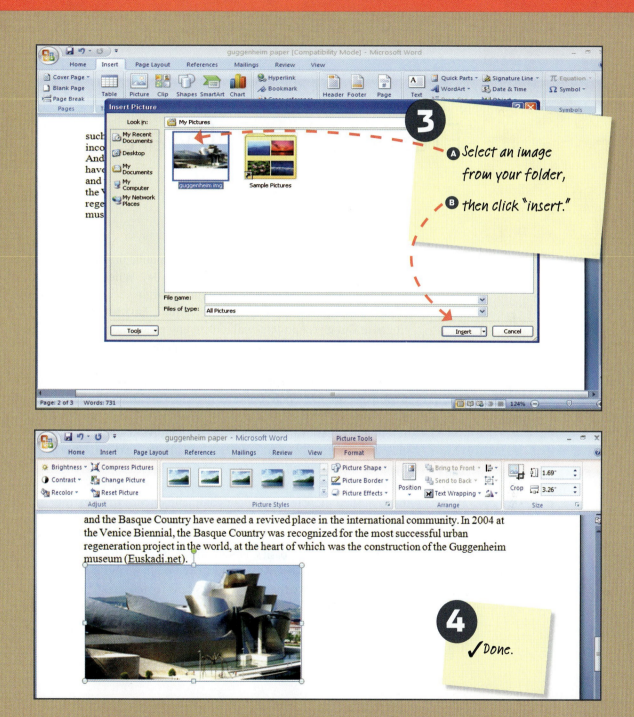

48 Presentation Software

PowerPoint is the dominant software used in public presentations, perhaps as often as tens of millions of times a day. When asked to do an oral report, most people automatically begin with Power-Point or a comparable product such as Keynote. Easy to use, these programs can give a professional look to any presentation. For an example of a PowerPoint presentation, see page 301 in Chapter 16 on oral reports.

create slides

With presentation software, you create a sequence of slides to accompany an oral report, building the slides yourself or picking them from a gallery of ready-made designs and color schemes that fit different occasions. You can also choose individual layouts for slides to accommodate text only, text and photos, text and charts, images only, and so on.

Once created, the slides can be edited and rearranged. Set up the final slide show to run at your command or click through the slides yourself, with the transitions accompanied by various sound effects and animations.

Those are just the basics. Presentation software offers so many bells and whistles that novices tend to overdo it, allowing the software to dominate the report. Here's how to make PowerPoint or Keynote work for you.

For presentations, PowerPoint offers both design templates (left) and individual slide layouts (right).

Be certain you need presentation software.   A short talk that makes only one or two points probably works better if viewers focus on you, not on a screen. Use presentation software to keep audiences on track through more complicated material, to highlight major issues or points, or to display images viewers really need to see. A little humor or eye candy is fine once in a while, but don't expect audiences to be impressed by glitz. What matters is the content of the report. O

Use slides to introduce points, not cover them.   If you find yourself reading your slides, you've put too much material on them. And you'll bore your audience to distraction. Put material on-screen that audiences need to see: main points, charts, and images directly relevant to the report. It's fine, too, for a slide to outline your presentation at the beginning and to summarize your points at the end. In fact, it's helpful to have a slide that obviously signals a conclusion.

Use a simple and consistent design.   Select one of the design templates provided or create a design of your own that fits your subject. A consistent design scheme will unify your report and minimize distractions. O

For academic presentations, choose simple designs and fonts. Make the text size large enough for viewers at the back of the room to read easily. For reasons of legibility, avoid elegant, playful, or eccentric fonts, including

understand oral reports p. 298

design your work p. 517

Make your slides readable

❖ Avoid fonts so fancy that they are hard to read.

❖ Avoid eccentric or cursive fonts.

❖ Don't crowd your slide with more words than you need.

❖ Don't put everything you expect to say on a slide because readers will be bored.

❖ **Boldface for emphasis, but rarely!**

❖ Be sure to show enough contrast between words and background.

Make your slides readable

❖ Use readable fonts.

❖ Avoid eccentric or cursive fonts.

❖ Don't crowd your slides.

❖ Maintain contrast between font and background.

those that resemble handwriting or Old English styles. And don't use more than one or two fonts within the presentation. Use boldface very selectively for emphasis. If you have to boldface a font to make it visible at a distance, simply find a thicker font. Italics are fine for occasional use, but in some fonts they are hard to read at a distance.

Check, too, that you have plenty of contrast between words and background on a screen so that your points don't fade away. For academic reports, keep colors sober and compatible. Avoid dark backgrounds and bright fonts. Look for an opportunity to preview your slides in the room where they'll be presented, and under the actual lighting conditions. Be familiar with the slideshow equipment.

Keep transitions between slides simple.   PowerPoint offers numerous options for transitions between slides, many of them animated and accompanied by sound effects. Simple transitions such as *dissolve* and *appear* are restrained enough for academic reports. But many of the other choices are better suited to cartoons and rock videos. Browse these special effects to get them out of your system. Then avoid them unless you have a compelling reason to use one. For example, *camera* nicely mimics the sound of a shutter closing. When you are presenting just one or two special photographs, the transition can work nicely and won't seem gimmicky.

Edit your slides ruthlessly.   Errors in spelling and punctuation never look good. But when projected in living color on a screen in front of an audience, they are just plain embarrassing and destroy your credibility. Make sure to review and proofread your work for careless mistakes. O

proofread
p. 386

49 Charts, Tables, and Graphs

display data

Just as images and photographs are often the media of choice for conveying visual information, charts, graphs, and tables are usually your best bet for displaying numerical and statistical data.

In programs like Word and PowerPoint, you can create charts with the various tools on the drawing toolbar. A spreadsheet application such as Excel automatically creates charts and graphs for you once you input your information. Excel charts can then be inserted into Word or PowerPoint as needed.

Use tables to present statistical data. Tables consist of horizontal rows and vertical columns into which you drop data.

Often the most effective way to describe, explore, and summarize a set of numbers—even a very large set—is to look at pictures of those numbers.
—Edward R. Tufte

Table A. Expectation of life by age, race, and sex: United States, 2002
[Race categories are consistent with the 1977 Office of Management and Budget guidelines]

Age	All races			White			Black		
	Total	Male	Female	Total	Male	Female	Total	Male	Female
0	77.3	74.5	79.9	77.7	75.1	80.3	72.3	68.8	75.6
1	76.8	74.1	79.4	77.2	74.6	79.7	72.4	68.8	75.6
5	72.9	70.2	75.4	73.3	70.7	75.8	68.5	65.0	71.7
10	67.9	65.3	70.5	68.3	65.7	70.8	63.6	60.1	66.8
15	63.0	60.3	65.5	63.4	60.8	65.9	58.7	55.2	61.8
20	58.2	55.6	60.7	58.6	56.1	61.0	53.9	50.5	57.0
25	53.5	51.0	55.8	53.8	51.4	56.1	49.3	46.0	52.1
30	48.7	46.3	51.0	49.0	46.7	51.2	44.7	41.6	47.4
35	44.0	41.6	46.1	44.3	42.0	46.4	40.1	37.1	42.7
40	39.3	37.0	41.4	39.6	37.4	41.6	35.6	32.8	38.1
45	34.8	32.6	36.7	35.0	32.9	36.9	31.3	28.5	33.7
50	30.3	28.3	32.2	30.5	28.5	32.4	27.3	24.6	29.5
55	26.1	24.1	27.7	26.2	24.3	27.9	23.4	21.0	25.4
60	22.0	20.2	23.5	22.1	20.3	23.6	19.9	17.6	21.6
65	18.2	16.6	19.5	18.2	16.6	19.5	16.6	14.6	18.0
70	14.7	13.2	15.8	14.7	13.3	15.8	13.5	11.8	14.7
75	11.5	10.3	12.4	11.5	10.3	12.3	10.9	9.5	11.7
80	8.8	7.8	9.4	8.7	7.7	9.3	8.6	7.5	9.2
85	6.5	5.7	6.9	6.4	5.7	6.8	6.6	5.8	7.0
90	4.8	4.2	5.0	4.7	4.1	4.9	5.1	4.5	5.3
95	3.6	3.2	3.7	3.4	3.0	3.5	3.9	3.6	4.0
100	2.7	2.5	2.8	2.4	2.3	2.5	3.0	2.9	3.0

Table

514

They are ideal for organizing lots of information without actually interpreting it. A table may show trends and suggest comparisons, but readers must find them on their own—one of the pleasures of reading tables.

You can make tables using a word processing program, either drawing them yourself or via an automatic function in which you specify the number of columns and rows you will need and select a design template. Some of the ready-made designs use color and even 3-D effects to highlight information. But good tables can be very plain. In fact, many of the tables on federal government Web sites, though packed with information, are dirt simple and yet very clear.

Use graphs to plot relationships within sets of data.

Graphs highlight relationships you choose to draw out of data by plotting one significant variable against another. Column and bar graphs emphasize comparisons; if well designed, they enable readers to grasp relationships that would otherwise take many words to explain.

Line graphs are more dynamic, plotting changes in variables, often over a period of time, so that readers can see both relationships and trends. Line graphs often are used to show the heart of many political and social arguments: for example, changes in employment, average world temperatures, or stock prices.

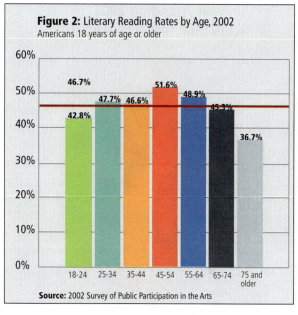

Figure 2: Literary Reading Rates by Age, 2002
Americans 18 years of age or older

Source: 2002 Survey of Public Participation in the Arts

Bar Chart

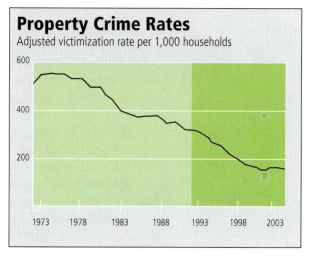

Property Crime Rates
Adjusted victimization rate per 1,000 households

Line Graph

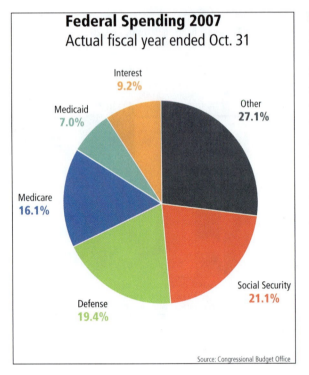

Federal Spending 2007
Actual fiscal year ended Oct. 31

Interest
9.2%

Medicaid
7.0%

Other
27.1%

Medicare
16.1%

Defense
19.4%

Social Security
21.1%

Source: Congressional Budget Office

Pie Chart

Use pie charts to display proportions.

Pie charts show how groups within a larger whole stand in relationship to one another. For instance, you might use a pie chart to show the relative size of major ethnic groups (white, Hispanic, black, Asian) within the total U.S. population. Keep in mind that the segments in a pie chart should always total 100 percent. To finish this ethnic pie, you would need to include a segment called "Other" to account for groups not represented in the major categories.

Pie-chart sections can be cut only so thin before they begin to lose clarity. If you wanted to use a pie chart to depict all the specific religious groups in the United States, you'd find yourself with hundreds of slivers readers couldn't possibly distinguish. Better to transfer the data to a table, which would handle each creed in a separate row.

Use maps to depict varying types of information.

A plain old atlas or road map delivers an immense amount of information, from the location of cities and mountains to the distances between them. But many other kinds of data can be laid atop geographic boundaries. Consider how hikers use a topographical map that shows elevations and trails. Maps are also helpful in displaying social and political data.

Label all charts and graphs.

In an academic paper, label and number all charts, graphs, and tables. Include publication information for any chart or graph you reproduce from another source.

APA style has its own detailed guidelines for constructing and labeling tables and charts. Be sure to use the *Publication Manual of the American Psychological Association,* Fifth Edition, when preparing graphics for a major paper in APA style.

Designing Print and Online Documents

Much advice about good visual design is common sense: You could guess that the design of most academic and professional documents should be balanced, consistent, and uncluttered. But it is not always simple to translate abstract principles into practice. Nor are any visual qualities absolute. A balanced and consistent design is exactly what you want for government documents and research reports, but to create newsletters or brochures, you need more visual snap. As always, purpose and audience determine what works.

design your work

Keep page designs simple and uncluttered.   Simple doesn't mean a design should be simplistic, only that you shouldn't try to do more on a page than it (or your design skills) can handle. You want readers to find information they need, navigate your document without missteps, and perceive the structure of your project. Key information should stand out. If you keep the basic design uncomplicated, you can present lots of information without a page feeling cluttered.

Consider, for example, how cleverly Anthro Technology Furniture uses design cues as simple as *Step 1*, *Step 2*, and *Step 3* to guide consumers on a Web page through the complex process of configuring a workstation. A reader simply moves left to right across a page making specific choices. They don't feel overwhelmed by the options, even though the material is detailed.

517

Understand the special elements of Web design.   A Web page, especially a home page, works differently than a printed page. It must not only present information (often through both words and images) but also interact with readers, directing them, for example, to links of various kinds. Some of the links may lead to material deeper within a site while others may take readers to external locations or initiate actions (such as starting an audio or video clip or printing a page). The challenge is to create (or adapt) design elements that help readers use the page resources intuitively.

Horizontal header guides reader across page.

Configuring the piece of furniture is broken into four easy steps.

Thumbnail images depict wide range of possible accessories.

Special box keeps track of consumer's decisions.

Keep the design logical and consistent.   Readers need to be able to grasp the logic of a design quickly and then see those principles operating in design elements throughout a document—especially on Web sites, in Power-Point presentations, and in long papers.

Look to successful Web sites for models of logical and consistent design. Many sites build their pages around distinct horizontal and vertical columns that help readers locate information. A main menu generally appears near the top of the page, more detailed navigational links are usually found in a narrow side column, and featured stories often appear in wide columns in the center. To separate columns as well as individual items, the site designers use headlines, horizontal rules, images, or some combination of these devices. Handled well, pages are easy to navigate and thick with information, yet somehow seem uncluttered.

NASA home page

NASA's page has consistent horizontal orientation. The eye moves left to right to explore major options. Horizontal sections also break page into visually coherent and manageable segments.

One large photograph and many thumbnail images, all carefully aligned, help to organize information and make it appealing.

Full screen (not reproduced here) offers more than sixty links or options.

Keep the design balanced. Think of balance as a dynamic term—what you hope to achieve *overall* in a design. You probably don't want many pages that, if split down the middle, would show mirror images. Strive for active page designs, in which, for example, a large photograph on one side of a page is countered on the other by blocks of print and maybe several smaller images. The overall effect required is balance, even though the individual page elements may all differ in size and shape.

You can see basic design principles at work on the front pages of most newspapers, where editors try to come up with a look that gives impact to the news. They have many elements to work with, including their paper's masthead, headlines of varying size, photographs and images, columns of copy, screened boxes, and much more. The pages of a newspaper can teach you a lot about design.

Use templates sensibly. If you have the time and talent to design all of your own documents, that's terrific. But for many projects, you could do worse than to begin with the templates offered by many software products. The Project Gallery in Microsoft software, for example, helps you create business letters, brochures, PowerPoint presentations, and more. It sets up a generic document, placing its margins, aligning key elements and graphics, and offering an array of customizations. No two projects based on the same template need look alike.

If you resist borrowing such materials from software, not wanting yet another part of your life packaged by corporate types, know that it is tough to design documents from scratch. Even if you intend to design an item yourself, consider examining a template to figure out how to assemble a complex document. Take what you learn from the model and then strike out on your own.

Front page of the *San Francisco Chronicle*, May 11, 2008

Colorful column of boxes and photos previews paper content.

Large photo on fold (with secondary photo and pull quote below) provides lead-in for a feature.

For variety, column width changes for feature story.

On slow news days without big headlines, masthead dominates front page.

Below masthead, candidate photo (in shaded box) separates two visually balanced stories on politics.

Print-heavy right-hand column helps balance many images on page.

Coordinate your colors.   Your mother was right: Pay attention to colors and patterns when you dress and when you design color documents. To learn elementary principles of color coordination, try searching "*color* wheel" on the Web, but recognize that the subject is both complicated and more art than science. As an amateur, keep your design work simple.

For academic papers, the text is black and the background is white. You may use one additional color for headings, but make it a highly readable choice. Avoid flashy or gaudy tints, such as reverse lime green and bright purple. For Web sites and other projects, keep background colors pale, if you use them at all, and maintain adequate contrast between text and background.

Use headings if needed.   Readers really appreciate headings. In academic work, they should be descriptive more than clever. If you have prepared a good scratch or topic outline, the major points may provide you with headings almost ready-made. O Like items in an outline, headings at the same level should be roughly parallel in style. O

A short paper (3–5 pages) doesn't require much more than a title. For longer papers (10–20 pages), it's possible to use top-level items from your outline as headings. For some projects, especially in the sciences, you must use the headings you're given. This is especially true for lab reports and scientific articles, and you shouldn't vary from the template. For an example of a report with headings, see pages 56–60 in Chapter 2.

Choose appropriate fonts.   There are likely dozens or even hundreds of fonts to work with on your computer, but, as with most other design elements, simple is generally best. Here is some basic information to help you choose the best font for your needs.

Serif fonts, such as Century, show thin flares and embellishments (called serifs; circled in the illustration on p. 523) at the tops and bottoms of their letters and characters. These fonts have a traditional look: Note the newspaper masthead on page 521. In contrast, *sans serif* fonts, such as Helvetica, lack the decorations of serif fonts. They are smoother and more contemporary-looking. For an example, see the article headlines on page 521.

O

order ideas
p. 342

O

common errors
p. 524

Century

Helvetica

Century, a serif font

Helvetica, a sans serif font

Serif fonts are more readable than sans serif, for extended passages of writing, such as papers. A sans serif font heading often contrasts well for a document using serif-font text. Some designers prefer sans serif fonts for Web sites and PowerPoint presentations, especially for headings and smaller items.

Display and decorative fonts are designed to attract attention. Avoid them for academic and professional writing, but you may want to explore their use when creating posters, brochures, or special PowerPoint presentations. Beyond the few words of a heading, display fonts are hard to read: Never use them for extended passages of writing.

For typical academic projects, all text, headings, and other elements—including the title—are set in one font size, either 10 or 12 point. In professional or business projects, such as résumés, newsletters, or PowerPoint slides, you'll need to vary type sizes to distinguish headings, captions, and headlines from other elements. Examine your pages carefully in the draft stage to see that there is a balance between the larger and smaller fonts. The impact of a résumé in particular can be diluted by headings that overwhelm the career data. Be careful, too, with smaller sizes. Some fonts look crowded (and strain eyesight) as they dip below 10 points.

Boldfaced items stand out clearly on a page but only if they are rare. Too many boldfaced headings too close together (or too much highlighting) and your page looks heavy and cluttered. Don't use boldface as the regular text throughout your project. If you want an emphatic font, find one that looks that way in its regular form.

Common Errors

part nine

51 Capitalization

Spring or
spring?

You know to capitalize most proper nouns (and the proper adjectives formed from them), book and movie titles, the first words of sentences, and so on. In principle, the guidelines can seem straightforward, but the fact is you make many judgment calls when capitalizing, some of which will require a dictionary (ask your instructor if he or she can advise you on a good one). Here are just a few of the special cases that can complicate your editing.

Capitalize the names of ethnic, religious, and political groups.   The names of these groups are considered proper nouns. Nonspecific groups are lowercase.

South Korean	Mexican American	American Indians
Buddhists	Presbyterians	Muslims
Green Party	Republicans	
the Quincy City Council		the city council

Capitalize modifiers formed from proper nouns.   In some cases, such as "french fry," the expressions have become so common that the adjective does not need to be capitalized. When in doubt, consult a dictionary.

PROPER NOUN	PROPER NOUN USED AS MODIFIER
French	French thought
Navajo	Navajo rug
Jew	Jewish lore
American	American history

Capitalize all words in titles except prepositions, articles, or conjunctions.

This is the basic rule for the titles of books, movies, long poems, and so on.

Dickens and the Dream of Cinema

All Quiet on the Western Front

The variations and exceptions to this general rule, however, are numerous. MLA style specifies that the first and last words in titles always be capitalized, including any articles or prepositions.

The Guide to National Parks of the Southwest

To the Lighthouse

Such Stuff as Dreams Are Made Of

APA style doesn't make that qualification, but does specify that all words longer than four letters be capitalized in titles—even prepositions.

A Walk Among the Tombstones

Sleeping Through the Night and Other Lies

In all major styles, any word following a colon (or, much rarer, a dash) in a title is capitalized, even an article or preposition:

Bob Dylan: In His Own Words

2001: A Space Odyssey

Finally, note that in APA style *documentation*—that is, within the notes and on the References page, titles are capitalized differently. Only the first word in most titles, any proper nouns or adjectives, and any words following a colon are capitalized. All other words are in lowercase:

Bat predation and the evolution of frog vocalizations in the neotropics

Human aging: Usual and successful

Take care with compass points, directions, and specific geographical areas.   Points of the compass and simple directions are not capitalized when referring to general locations.

north	southwest
northern Ohio	eastern Canada
southern exposure	western horizons

But these same terms *are* capitalized when they refer to specific regions that are geographically, culturally, or politically significant (keep that dictionary handy!). Such terms are often preceded by the definite article, *the*.

the West	the Old South
the Third Coast	Southern California
Middle Eastern politics	the Western allies

Understand academic conventions.   Academic degrees are not capitalized, except when abbreviated.

bachelor of arts	doctor of medicine
M.A.	Ph.D.

Specific course titles are capitalized, but they are lowercase when used as general subjects. Exception: Languages are always capitalized when referring to academic subjects.

Art History 101	Civil Engineering
an art history course	an English literature paper

Capitalize months, days, holidays, and historical periods.   But not the seasons.

January	winter
Monday	fall
Halloween	autumn
the Renaissance	

Apostrophes

Like gnats, apostrophes are small and irritating. They have two major functions: to signal that a noun is possessive and to indicate where letters have been left out in contractions.

Use apostrophes to form the possessive. The basic rules for forming the possessive aren't complicated: For singular nouns, add *'s* to the end of the word:

> the wolf**'s** lair
>
> the woman**'s** portfolio
>
> IBM**'s** profits
>
> Bush**'s** foreign policy

it's or *its*?

Some possessives, while correct, look or sound awkward. In these cases, try an alternative:

ORIGINAL	REVISED
the class**'s** photo	the class photo; the photo of the class
Bright Eyes**'s** latest single	the latest single by Bright Eyes
in Kansas**'s** budget	in the Kansas budget; in the budget of Kansas

For plural nouns that do not end in *s*, also add *'s* to the end of the word:

> men**'s** shoes   the mice**'s** cages   the geese**'s** nemesis

△

For plural nouns that do end in *s*, add an apostrophe after that terminal *s*:

the wolves' pups

the Bushes' foreign policies

three senators' votes

Use apostrophes in contractions.   An apostrophe in a contraction takes the place of missing letters. Edit carefully, keeping in mind that a spell checker doesn't help you with such blunders. It only catches words that make no sense without apostrophes, such as *dont* or *Ive*.

ORIGINAL	**Its** a shame that **its** come to this.
REVISED	**It's** (It is) a shame that **it's** (it has) come to this.
ORIGINAL	**Whose** got the list of **whose** going on the trip?
REVISED	**Who's** (Who has) got the list of **who's** (who is) going on the trip?

Don't use apostrophes with possessive pronouns.   The following possessives do not take apostrophes: *its, whose, his, hers, ours, yours,* and *theirs*.

ORIGINAL	We shot the tower at **it's** best angle.
REVISED	We shot the tower at **its** best angle.
ORIGINAL	The book is **her's,** not his.
REVISED	The book is **hers,** not his.
ORIGINAL	**Their's** may be an Oscar-winning film, but **our's** is still better.
REVISED	**Theirs** may be an Oscar-winning film, but **ours** is still better.

There is, inevitably, an exception. Indefinite pronouns such as *everybody, anybody, nobody,* and so on show possession via *'s*.

The film was **everybody's** favorite.

Why it was so successful is **anybody's** guess.

Commas

The comma has more uses than any other punctuation mark—uses which can often seem complex. Below are some of the most common comma situations in academic writing.

Use a comma and a coordinating conjunction to separate two independent clauses.

Independent clauses can stand on their own as a sentence. To join two of them, you need two things: a coordinating conjunction and a comma.

> Fiona's car broke down. She had to walk two miles to the train station.

> Fiona's car broke down, so she had to walk two miles to the train station.

There are several key points to remember here. Be sure you truly have two independent clauses, and not just a compound subject or verb. Also, make certain to include both a comma and a coordinating conjunction (*and, but, for, nor, or, so, yet*). Leaving out the coordinating conjunction creates an error known as a comma splice (see p. 534).

Use a comma after an introductory word group.

Introductory word groups are descriptive phrases or clauses that open a sentence. Separate these introductions from the main part of the sentence with a comma.

need to connect ideas?

Within two years of getting a degree in journalism, Nobuko was writing for the *New York Times*.

For very brief introductory phrases, the comma may be omitted, but it is not wrong to leave it in.

After college I plan to join the Peace Corps.

After college, I plan to join the Peace Corps.

Use commas with transitional words and phrases.   Transitional expressions such as *however* and *for example* should be set off from a sentence with a pair of commas.

These fans can be among the first, however, to clamor for a new stadium to boost their favorite franchise.

If a transitional word or phrase opens a sentence, it should be followed by a comma.

Moreover, studies have shown that trans fats can lower the amount of good cholesterol found in the body.

Put commas around nonrestrictive (that is, nonessential) elements.   You'll know when a word or phrase is functioning as a nonrestrictive modifier if you can remove it from the sentence without destroying the overall meaning of the sentence.

Cicero, ancient Rome's greatest orator and lawyer, was a self-made man.

Cicero was a self-made man.

The second sentence is less informative, but still functions. See also the guideline below, "Do not use commas to set off restrictive elements."

Use commas to separate items in a series.   Commas are necessary when you have three or more items in a series.

American highways were once ruled by powerful muscle cars such as Mustangs, GTOs, and Camaros.

Do not use commas to separate compound verbs.   Don't confuse
a true compound sentence (with two independent clauses) with a sentence
that has two verbs.

ORIGINAL   They rumbled through city streets, and smoked down drag strips.

REVISED   They rumbled through city streets and smoked down drag strips.

They rumbled through city streets is an independent clause, but *and smoked
down drag strips* is not, because it doesn't have a subject. To join the two
verbs, use *and* with no comma. The only exception to this rule is if you have
three or more verbs, which should be treated as items in a series and separated with commas.

Muscle cars guzzled gasoline, polluted incessantly, and drove parents crazy.

Do not use a comma between subject and verb.   Perhaps it's obvious
why such commas don't work when you try one in a short sentence.

Keeping focused, can be difficult.

When a subject gets long and complicated, you might be more tempted to
insert the comma, but it would still be both unnecessary and wrong.

Keeping focused on driving while simultaneously trying to operate a cell phone,
can be difficult.

Do not use commas to set off restrictive elements.   Phrases you
cannot remove from a sentence without significantly altering meaning are
called restrictive or essential. They are modifiers that provide information
needed to understand the subject.

The canyon that John Wesley Powell explored in 1869 has been inhabited by
Native Americans for thousands of years.

The Native Puebloans who built Tusayan Pueblo around 1185 abandoned it
within a century.

Delete the highlighted phrases in the above examples, and you are left with
sentences that are vague or confusing.

54 Comma Splices, Run-ons, and Fragments

need a complete sentence?

The sentence errors marked most often in college writing are comma splices, run-ons, and fragments.

Identify comma splices and run-ons. A *comma splice* occurs when only a comma is used to join two independent clauses (an independent clause contains a complete subject and verb).

Identify a comma splice simply by reading the clauses on either side of a doubtful comma. If *both* clauses stand on their own as sentences (with their own subjects and verbs), it's a comma splice.

COMMA SPLICE   Officials at many elementary schools are trying to reduce childhood obesity on their campuses, research suggests that few of their strategies will work.

A *run-on* sentence is similar to a comma splice, but it doesn't even include the comma to let readers take a break between independent clauses. The clauses knock together, confusing readers.

RUN-ON SENTENCE   Officials at many elementary schools are trying to reduce childhood obesity on their campuses research suggests that few of their strategies will work.

Fix comma splices and run-ons. To fix comma splices and run-ons, you can include a comma and a coordinating conjunction after the first independent clause to join it with the second clause.

Officials at many elementary schools are trying to reduce childhood obesity on their campuses, **but** research shows that few of their strategies will work.

Or you can use a semicolon to join the two clauses.

Officials at many elementary schools are trying to reduce childhood obesity on their campuses; research shows that few of their strategies will work.

Less frequently, colons or dashes may be used if the second clause summarizes or illustrates the main point of the first clause.

Some schools have taken extreme measures: They have banned cookies, snacks, and other high-calorie foods from their vending machines.

Along with the semicolon (or colon or dash), you may wish to add a transitional word or phrase (such as *however* or *in fact*). If you do so, set off the transitional word or phrase with commas. O

Officials at many elementary schools are trying to reduce childhood obesity on their campuses; research, **however,** shows that few of their strategies will work.

Other schools emphasize a need for more exercise—**in fact,** some have even gone so far as to reinstate recess.

You can also rewrite the sentence to make one of the clauses subordinate. Using a subordinating conjunction, revise so that one of the clauses in the sentence can no longer stand as a sentence on its own.

Although officials at many elementary schools are trying to reduce childhood obesity on their campuses, research shows that few of their strategies will work.

Or use end punctuation to create two independent sentences.

Officials at many elementary schools are trying to reduce childhood obesity on their campuses. Research shows that few of their strategies will work.

Identify sentence fragments.   A sentence fragment is a word group that lacks a subject, verb, or possibly both. As such, it is not a complete sentence and is not appropriate for most academic and professional writing.

FRAGMENT   Climatologists see much physical evidence of global warming. **Especially in the receding of glaciers around the world.**

Common Coordinating Conjunctions

and	or
but	so
for	yet
nor	

Common Subordinating Conjunctions

after	once
although	since
as	that
because	though
before	unless
except	until
if	when

connect ideas
p. 350

Fix sentence fragments in your work.   You have two options for fixing sentence fragments. Attach the fragment to a nearby sentence:

COMPLETE SENTENCE   Climatologists see much physical evidence of global warming, especially in the receding of glaciers around the world.

Turn the fragment into its own sentence:

COMPLETE SENTENCE   Climatologists see much physical evidence of global warming. They are especially concerned by the receding of glaciers around the world.

Watch for fragments in the following situations.   Often a fragment will follow a complete sentence and start with a subordinating conjunction.

FRAGMENT   Global warming seems to be the product of human activity. Though some scientists believe sun cycles may explain the changing climate.

COMPLETE SENTENCE   Global warming seems to be the product of human activity, though some scientists believe sun cycles may explain the changing climate.

Participles (such as *breaking, seeking, finding*) and infinitives (such as *to break, to seek, to find*) can also lead you into fragments.

FRAGMENT   Of course, many people welcome the warmer weather. Confounding scientists who fear governments will not act until climate change becomes irreversible.

COMPLETE SENTENCE   Of course, many people welcome the warmer weather. Their attitude confounds scientists who fear governments will not act until climate change becomes irreversible.

Use deliberate fragments only in appropriate situations.   Use deliberate fragments, such as the following colloquial expressions or clichés, in informal or popular writing only after considering your audience and purpose.

In your dreams.   Excellent.   Not on your life.

Subject / Verb Agreement

55

Verbs take many forms to express changing tenses, moods, and voices. To avoid common errors in choosing the correct verb form, follow these guidelines.

Be sure the verb agrees with its real subject. It's tempting to link a verb to the nouns closest to it (in olive below) instead of the subject, but that's a mistake.

none are or
none is?

ORIGINAL	Liftport, one of several private **companies** working on space ladder technologies, **anticipate** a working prototype by 2018.
REVISED	Liftport, one of several private companies working on space ladder technologies, **anticipates** a working prototype by 2018.
ORIGINAL	**Bottles** of water sold at the grocery store usually **costs** as much as gasoline.
REVISED	**Bottles** of water sold at the grocery store usually **cost** as much as gasoline.

Some indefinite pronouns are exceptions to this rule. See the chart on page 538.

In most cases, treat multiple subjects joined by *and* as plural. But when a subject with *and* clearly expresses a single notion, that subject is singular.

Hip-hop, rock, and country are dominant forms of popular music today.

537

Blues and folk have their fans too.

Peanut butter and jelly is the sandwich of choice in our house.

Rock and roll often **strikes** a political chord.

When singular subjects are followed by expressions such as *along with*, *together with*, or *as well as*, the subjects may feel plural, but technically they remain singular.

ORIGINAL   **Mariah Carey**, along with Gwen Stefani, Kanye West, and Green Day, **were competing** for "Record of the Year."

REVISED   **Mariah Carey**, along with Gwen Stefani, Kanye West, and Green Day, **was competing** for "Record of the Year."

If the corrected version sounds awkward, try revising the sentence.

REVISED   **Mariah Carey**, Gwen Stefani, Kanye West, and Green Day **were** all **competing** for "Record of the Year."

Indefinite Pronouns

Singular	Plural	Variable
anybody	both	all
anyone	few	any
anything	many	more
each	others	most
everybody	several	none
everyone		some
everything		
nobody		
no one		
nothing		
one		
somebody		
someone		
something		

When compound subjects are linked by *either . . . or* or *neither . . . nor*, make the verb agree with the nearer part of the subject.
Knowing this rule will make you one person among a thousand.

> Neither my sisters nor my **mother is** a fan of Kanye West.

When possible, put the plural part of the subject closer to the verb to make it sound less awkward.

> Neither my mother nor my **sisters are** fans of Kanye West.

Confirm whether an indefinite pronoun is singular, plural, or variable.   Most indefinite pronouns are singular, but consult the chart on page 538 to double-check.

> **Everybody complains** about politics, but **nobody does** much about it.
>
> **Each** of the women **expects** a promotion.
>
> **Something needs** to be done about the budget crisis.

A few indefinite pronouns are obviously plural: *both, few, many, others, several*.

> **Many complain** about politics, but **few do** much about it.

And some indefinite pronouns shift in number, depending on the prepositional phrases that modify them.

> **All** of the votes **are** in the ballot box.
>
> **All** of the fruit **is** spoiled.
>
> **Most** of the rules **are** less complicated.
>
> **Most** of the globe **is** covered by oceans.
>
> **None** of the rules **makes** sense.
>
> On the Security Council, **none** but the Russians **favor** the resolution.

Be consistent with collective nouns.   Many of these words describing a group can be treated as either singular or plural: *band, class, jury, choir, group, committee.*

> The jury seems to resent the lawyer's playing to its emotions.
>
> The jury seem to resent the lawyer's playing to their emotions.
>
> The band was unhappy with its CD.
>
> The band were unhappy with their CD.

A basic principle is to be consistent throughout a passage. If *the band* is singular the first time you mention it, keep it that way for the remainder of the project. Be sensible too. If a sentence sounds odd to your ear, modify it:

AWKWARD   The band were unhappy with their CD.

BETTER   The members of the band were unhappy with their CD.

Irregular Verbs

Verbs are considered regular if they form the past and past participle—which you use to form various tenses—simply by adding *–d* or *–ed* to the base of the verb. Below are several regular verbs.

Base form	Past tense	Past participle
smile	smiled	smiled
accept	accepted	accepted
manage	managed	managed

lie or *lay?*

Unfortunately, the most common verbs in English are irregular. The chart on page 542 lists some of them. When in doubt about the proper form of a verb, check a dictionary.

Base form	Past tense	Past participle
be	was, were	been
become	became	become
break	broke	broken
buy	bought	bought
choose	chose	chosen
come	came	come
dive	dived, dove	dived
do	did	done
drink	drank	drunk
drive	drove	driven
eat	ate	eaten
get	got	gotten
give	gave	given
go	went	gone
have	had	had
lay (to put or place)	laid	laid
lie (to recline)	lay	lain
ride	rode	ridden
ring	rang, rung	rung
rise	rose	risen
see	saw	seen
set	set	set
shine	shone, shined	shone, shined
sing	sang, sung	sung
sink	sank, sunk	sunk
speak	spoke	spoken
swear	swore	sworn
throw	threw	thrown
wake	woke, waked	woken, waked
write	wrote	written

Pronoun / Antecedent Agreement

You already know that pronouns take the place of nouns. Antecedents are the words pronouns refer to. Since pronouns in their many forms stand in for nouns, they also share some of the same markers, such as gender and number.

SINGULAR / FEMININE — The **nun** merely smiled because **she** had taken a vow of silence.

SINGULAR / MASCULINE — The **NASCAR champion** complained that **he** got little media attention.

SINGULAR / NEUTER — The **jury** seemed to take **itself** too seriously.

PLURAL — The **members of the jury** seemed to take **themselves** too seriously.

PLURAL — **They** seemed awfully subdued for **pro athletes.**

PLURAL — The **bridge and groom** wrote **their** own ditzy vows.

PLURAL — **Many** in the terminal resented searches of **their** luggage.

The basic rule for managing pronouns and antecedents couldn't be simpler: Make sure pronouns you select have the same number and gender as the words they stand for.

ORIGINAL — When a **student** spends too much time on sorority activities, **they** may suffer academically.

their or *his or hers?*

543

REVISED   When a **student** spends too much time on sorority activities, **she** may suffer academically.

As always, though, there are confusing cases and numerous exceptions. Following are the common problems.

Check the number of indefinite pronouns.

Some of the most common singular indefinite pronouns—especially *anybody, everybody, everyone*—may seem plural, but they should be treated as singular. (For the complete list of indefinite pronouns, see the chart on p. 538 in Chapter 55.)

ORIGINAL   Has **everybody** completed **their** assignment by now?

REVISED   Has **everybody** completed **his or her** assignment by now?

If using *his or her* sounds awkward, revise the sentence.

Have **all students** completed **their** assignments by now?

Correct sexist pronoun usage.

Using *his* alone (instead of *his or her*) to refer to an indefinite pronoun is considered sexist unless it clearly refers only to males. ○

Treat collective nouns consistently.

Collective nouns—such as *team, herd, congregation, mob,* and so on—can be treated as either singular or plural.

The **legion** marched until **it** reached **its** camp in Gaul.

The **legion** marched until **they** reached **their** camp in Gaul.

Just be consistent and sensible in your usage. Treat a collective noun the same way, as either singular or plural, throughout a paper or project. And don't hesitate to modify a sentence when even a correct usage sounds awkward.

AWKWARD   The **team** smiled as **it** received **its** championship jerseys.

BETTER   **Members of the team** smiled as **they** received **their** championship jerseys.

respect your readers
p. 374

Pronoun Reference

A pronoun should refer back clearly to a noun or pronoun (its *antecedent*), usually the one nearest to it that matches it in number and, when necessary, gender.

> **Consumers** will buy a **Rolex** because **they** covet **its** snob appeal.
>
> **Nancy Pelosi** spoke instead of **Harry Reid** because **she** had more interest in the legislation than **he** did.

If connections between pronouns and antecedents wobble within a single sentence or longer passage, readers will struggle. Following are three common problems you should avoid.

sure what *it* means?

Clarify confusing pronoun antecedents.   Revise sentences in which readers will find themselves wondering *who is doing what to whom*. Multiple revisions are usually possible, depending on how the confusing sentence could be interpreted.

CONFUSING	The **batter** collided with the **first baseman**, but **he** wasn't injured.
BETTER	The batter collided with the **first baseman, who** wasn't injured.
BETTER	The **batter** wasn't injured by **his** collision with the first baseman.

Make sure a pronoun has a plausible antecedent.   Sometimes the problem is that the antecedent doesn't actually exist—it is only implied. In these cases, either insert an antecedent or replace the pronoun with a noun.

CONFUSING   Grandmother had hip-replacement surgery two months ago, and it is already fully healed.

In the above sentence, the implied antecedent for *it* is *hip,* but the noun *hip* isn't in the sentence (*hip-replacement* is an adjective describing *surgery*).

BETTER   Grandmother had **her hip** replaced two months ago, and **it** is already fully healed.

BETTER   Grandmother had hip-replacement surgery two months ago, and **her hip** is already fully healed.

Don't leave the antecedent of *this, that,* or *which* deliberately vague.   In the following example, a humble *this* is asked to shoulder the burden of a writer who hasn't quite figured out how to pull together all the ideas raised in the preceding sentence. What exactly might the antecedent for *this* be? It doesn't exist. To fix the problem, the writer needs to replace *this* with a more thoughtful analysis.

> The university staff is underpaid, the labs are short on equipment, and campus maintenance is neglected. Moreover, we need two or three new parking garages to make up for the lots lost because of recent construction projects. Yet students cannot be expected to shoulder additional costs because tuition and fees are high already. **This** is a problem that must be solved.

> REVISED FINAL SENTENCE
>
> **How to fund both academic departments and infrastructure needs without increasing students' financial outlay** is a problem that must be solved.

Pronoun Case  59

In spoken English, you hear it when you run into a problem with pronoun case.

> "Let's just keep this matter between **you** and . . . *ummmm* . . . **me**."

> "To **who** . . . I mean, uh . . . **whom** does this letter go?"

> "Hector is more of a people person than **her** . . . than **she is**."

Like nouns, pronouns can be subjects, objects, or possessives, and their forms vary to show which case they express in a sentence. Unfortunately, determining case is the problem. Here are some strategies for dealing with these common situations.

I or *me? who* or *whom?*

Subjective pronouns	Objective pronouns	Possessive pronouns
I	me	my, mine
you	you	your, yours
he, she, it	him, her, it	his, her, hers, its
we	us	our, ours
they	them	their, theirs
who	whom	whose

Use the subjective case for pronouns that are subjects.

When pronouns are the only subject in a clause, they rarely cause a problem. But double the subject, and there's trouble.

Sara and . . . **me** . . . , or is it Sara and **I** wrote the report?

To make the right choice, try answering the question for one subject at a time. You quickly recognize that *Sara* wrote the report, and *I* did the same thing. So one possible revision is:

Sara and I wrote the report.

Or, you can recast the sentence to avoid the difficulty in the first place.

We wrote the report.

Use the objective case for pronouns that are objects.   Again, choosing one objective pronoun is generally obvious, but with two objects, the choice is less clear. How do you decide what to do in the following sentence?

The corporate attorney will represent both Geoff and **I** . . . Geoff and **me**?

Again, deal with one object at a time. Since the attorney will represent *me*, and will also represent *Geoff*, a possible revision is:

The corporate attorney will represent **Geoff and me**.

Or, to be more concise:

The corporate attorney will represent **us**.

Use *whom* when appropriate.   One simple pronoun choice brings many writers to their knees: *who* or *whom*. The rule, however, is the same as for other pronouns: Use the subjective case (*who*) for subjects and the objective case (*whom*) for objects. In some cases, the choice is obvious.

ORIGINAL   **Whom** wrote the report?

REVISED   **Who** wrote the report?

ORIGINAL   By **who** was the report written?

REVISED   By **whom** was the report written?

But this choice becomes tricky when you're dealing with subordinate clauses.

ORIGINAL   The shelter needs help from **whomever** can volunteer three hours per week.

The previous above example may sound right because *whomever* immediately follows the preposition *from*. But, because the pronoun is the subject of a subordinate clause, it needs to be in the subjective case.

REVISED   The shelter needs help from whoever can volunteer three hours per week.

Finish comparisons to determine the right case.   Many times when writers make comparisons, they leave out some understood information.

I've always thought John was more talented than Paul.

(I've always thought John was more talented than Paul *was*.)

But leaving this information out can lead to confusion when it comes to choosing the correct pronoun case. Try the sentence, adding *him*.

ORIGINAL   I've always thought John was more talented than him.

I've always thought John was more talented than him *was*.

REVISED   I've always thought John was more talented than he.

If it sounds strange to use the correct pronoun, complete the sentence.

REVISED   I've always thought John was more talented than he was.

Don't be misled by an appositive.   An *appositive* is a word or phrase that amplifies or renames a noun or pronoun. In the example below, *Americans* is the appositive. First, try reading the sentence without it.

ORIGINAL   Us Americans must defend our civil rights.

We must defend our civil rights.

REVISED   We Americans must defend our civil rights.

When the pronoun is contained within the appositive, it follows the case of the word or words it renames.

SUBJECTIVE   The bloggers who were still in the running, Lucy, Cali, and I, wrote all night trying to outdo each other.

OBJECTIVE   The site was dominated by the bloggers who were still in the running, Lucy, Cali, and me.

60 Misplaced and Dangling Modifiers

are your descriptions clear?

In general, modifiers need to be close and obviously connected to the words they modify. When they aren't, readers may become confused—or amused.

Position modifiers close to the words they modify.

MISPLACED	Tiered like a wedding cake, Mrs. DeLeon unveiled her model for the parade float.

Mrs. DeLeon is not tiered like a wedding cake; the model for the parade float is.

REVISED	Mrs. DeLeon unveiled her model for the parade float, which was tiered like a wedding cake.

Place adverbs such as *only, almost, especially,* and *even* carefully.
If these modifiers are placed improperly, their purpose can be vague or ambiguous.

VAGUE	The speaker almost angered everyone in the room.
CLEARER	The speaker angered almost everyone in the room.

AMBIGUOUS	Joan only drove a stick shift.
CLEARER	Only Joan drove a stick shift.
CLEARER	Joan drove only a stick shift.

Don't allow a modifier to dangle.   A modifying word or phrase at the beginning of a sentence should be followed immediately by the subject it modifies. When it doesn't, the modifier is said to dangle.

DANGLING   **After picking me up at the airport,** San Francisco was introduced to me by my future business partner.

San Francisco didn't pick me up at the airport; my future business partner did. So *my future business partner* needs to be the subject of the sentence.

REVISED   **After picking me up at the airport,** my future business partner introduced me to San Francisco.

61 Parallelism

When items in sentences follow similar patterns of language, they are described as parallel. Parallel structure makes your writing easier to read and understand.

When possible, make compound items parallel.   Don't confuse your readers by requiring them to untangle subjects, verbs, modifiers, or other items that could easily be parallel:

making a
list?

NOT PARALLEL	Becoming a lawyer and to write a novel are Leslie's goals.
PARALLEL	Becoming a lawyer and writing a novel are Leslie's goals.
NOT PARALLEL	The university will demolish its old stadium and bricks from it are being sold.
PARALLEL	The university will demolish its old stadium and sell the bricks.
NOT PARALLEL	The TV anchor reported the story thoroughly and with compassion.
PARALLEL	The TV anchor reported the story thoroughly and compassionately.

Keep items in a series parallel.   A series should consist of all nouns, all adjectives, all verbs, and so on.

NOT PARALLEL	She was a fine new teacher—eager, very patient, and **gets her work done.**
PARALLEL	She was a fine new teacher—eager, very patient, and **conscientious.**
NOT PARALLEL	We expected **to rehabilitate** the historic property, **break even** on the investment, and **to earn** the goodwill of the community.
PARALLEL	We expected **to rehabilitate** the historic property, **to break even** on the investment, and **to earn** the good will of the community.
PARALLEL	We expected to **rehabilitate** the historic property, **break even** on the investment, and **earn** the goodwill of the community.

Keep headings and lists parallel.   If you use headings to break up the text of a document, use a similar language pattern and design for all of them. It may help to type the headings out separately from the text to make sure you are keeping them parallel. Items in a printed list should be parallel as well.

reader

Readings

part ten

Need help with critical reading? See page 317. / Need help analyzing claims and evidence? See page 420.

62 Narrative: Readings

LITERACY NARRATIVE   David Sedaris has published five best-selling books of humorous personal essays and frequently appears on the National Public Radio program *This American Life*. This essay, from his collection *Me Talk Pretty One Day* (2000), examines Sedaris's difficulties learning French and profiles his bumpy relationship with a tough teacher. This essay can be considered a literacy narrative—a personal essay that explores how we acquire language and communication skills, and how these experiences shape us as people.

DAVID SEDARIS

Me Talk Pretty One Day

At the age of forty-one, I am returning to school and have to think of myself as what my French textbook calls "a true debutant." After paying my tuition, I was issued a student ID, which allows me a discounted entry fee at movie theaters, puppet shows, and Festyland, a far-flung amusement park that advertises with billboards picturing a cartoon stegosaurus sitting in a canoe and eating what appears to be a ham sandwich.

I've moved to Paris with hopes of learning the language. My school is an easy ten-minute walk from my apartment, and on the first day of class I arrived early, watching as the returning students greeted one another in the school lobby. Vacations were recounted, and questions were raised concerning mutual friends with names like Kang and Vlatnya. Regardless of their nationalities, everyone spoke in what sounded to me like excellent French. Some accents were better than others, but the students exhibited an ease and confidence I found intimidating. As an added discomfort, they were all young, attractive, and well dressed, causing me to feel not unlike Pa Kettle trapped backstage after a fashion show.

The first day of class was nerve-racking because I knew I'd be expected to perform. That's the way they do it here—it's everybody into the language pool, sink or swim. The teacher marched in, deeply tanned from a recent vacation, and proceeded to rattle off a series of administrative announcements. I've spent quite a few summers in Normandy, and I took a monthlong French class before leaving New York. I'm not completely in the dark, yet I understood only half of what this woman was saying.

"If you have not *meimslsxp* or *lgpdmurct* by this time, then you should not be in this room. Has everyone *apzkiubjxow*? Everyone? Good, we shall begin." She spread out her lesson plan and sighed, saying, "All right, then, who knows the alphabet?"

It was startling because (a) I hadn't been asked that question in a while and (b) I realized, while laughing, that I myself did *not* know the alphabet. They're the same letters, but in France they're pronounced differently. I know the shape of the alphabet but had no idea what it actually sounded like.

"Ahh." The teacher went to the board and sketched the letter *a*. "Do we have anyone in the room whose first name commences with an *ahh?*"

Two Polish Annas raised their hands, and the teacher instructed them to present themselves by stating their names, nationalities, occupations, and a brief list of things they liked and disliked in this world. The first Anna hailed from an industrial town outside of Warsaw and had front teeth the size of tombstones. She worked as a seamstress, enjoyed quiet times with friends, and hated the mosquito.

"Oh, really," the teacher said. "How very interesting. I thought that everyone loved the mosquito, but here, in front of all the world, you claim to detest him. How is it that we've been blessed with someone as unique and original as you? Tell us, please."

The seamstress did not understand what was being said but knew that this was an occasion for shame. Her rabbity mouth huffed for breath, and she stared down at her lap as though the appropriate comeback were stitched somewhere alongside the zipper of her slacks.

The second Anna learned from the first and claimed to love sunshine and detest lies. It sounded like a translation of one of those Playmate of the Month data sheets, the answers always written in the same loopy handwriting. "Turn-ons: Mom's famous five-alarm chili! Turnoffs: insecurity and guys who come on too strong!!!!"

The two Polish Annas surely had clear notions of what they loved and hated, but like the rest of us, they were limited in terms of vocabulary, and this made them appear less than sophisticated. The teacher forged on, and we learned that Carlos, the Argentine bandonion player, loved wine, music, and, in his words, "making sex with the womens of the world." Next came a beautiful young Yugoslav who identified herself as an optimist, saying that she loved everything that life had to offer.

The teacher licked her lips, revealing a hint of the saucebox we would later come to know. She crouched low for her attack, placed her hands on the young woman's desk, and leaned close, saying, "Oh yeah? And do you love your little war?"

While the optimist struggled to defend herself, I scrambled to think of an answer to what had obviously become a trick question. How often is one asked what he loves in this world? More to the point, how often is one asked and then publicly ridiculed for his answer? I recalled my mother, flushed with wine, pounding the tabletop late one night, saying, "Love? I love a good steak cooked rare. I love my cat, and I love . . ." My sisters and I leaned forward, waiting to hear our names. "Tums," our mother said. "I love Tums."

The teacher killed some time accusing the Yugoslavian girl of masterminding a program of genocide, and I jotted frantic notes in the margins of my pad. While I can honestly say that I love leafing through medical textbooks devoted to severe dermatological conditions, the hobby is beyond the reach of my French vocabulary, and acting it out would only have invited controversy.

When called upon, I delivered an effortless list of things that I detest: blood sausage, intestinal pâtés, brain pudding. I'd learned these words the hard way. Having given it some thought, I then declared my love for IBM typewriters, the French word for *bruise,* and my electric floor waxer. It was a short list, but still I managed to mispronounce *IBM* and assign the wrong gender to both the floor waxer and the typewriter. The teacher's reaction led me to believe that these mistakes were capital crimes in the country of France.

"Were you always this *palicmkrexis?*" she asked. "Even a *fiuscrzsa ticiwelmun* knows that a typewriter is feminine."

I absorbed as much of her abuse as I could understand, thinking—but not saying—that I find it ridiculous to assign a gender to an inanimate object incapable of disrobing and making an occasional fool of itself. Why refer to crack pipe or Good Sir Dishrag when these things could never live up to all that their sex implied?

The teacher proceeded to belittle everyone from German Eva, who hated laziness, to Japanese Yukari, who loved paintbrushes and soap. Italian, Thai, Dutch, Korean, and Chinese—we all left class foolishly believing that the worst was over. She'd shaken us up a little, but surely that was just an act designed to weed out the deadweight. We didn't know it then, but the coming months would teach us what it was like to spend time in the presence of a wild animal, something completely unpredictable. Her temperament was not based on a series of good and bad days but, rather, good and bad moments. We soon learned to dodge chalk and protect our heads and stomachs whenever she approached us with a question. She hadn't yet punched anyone, but it seemed wise to protect ourselves against the inevitable.

Though we were forbidden to speak anything but French, the teacher would occasionally use us to practice any of her five fluent languages.

"I hate you," she said to me one afternoon. Her English was flawless. "I really, really hate you." Call me sensitive, but I couldn't help but take it personally.

After being singled out as a lazy *kfdtinvfm,* I took to spending four hours a night on my homework, putting in even more time whenever we were assigned an essay. I suppose I could have gotten by with less, but I was determined to create some sort of identity for myself: David the hard worker, David the cut-up. We'd have one of those "complete this sentence" exercises, and I'd fool with the thing for hours, invariably settling on something like "A quick run around the lake? I'd love to! Just give me a moment while I strap on my wooden leg." The teacher, through word and action, conveyed the message that if this was my idea of an identity, she wanted nothing to do with it.

My fear and discomfort crept beyond the borders of the classroom and accompanied me out onto the wide boulevards. Stopping for a coffee, asking directions, depositing money in my bank account: these things were out of the question, as they involved having to speak. Before beginning school, there'd been no shutting me up, but now I was convinced that everything I said was wrong. When the phone rang, I ignored it. If someone asked me a question, I pretended to be deaf. I knew my fear was getting the best of me when I started wondering why they don't sell cuts of meat in vending machines.

My only comfort was the knowledge that I was not alone. Huddled in the hallways and making the most of our pathetic French, my fellow students and I engaged in the sort of conversation commonly overheard in refugee camps.

"Sometime me cry alone at night."

"That be common for I, also, but be more strong, you. Much work and someday you talk pretty. People start love you soon. Maybe tomorrow, okay."

Unlike the French class I had taken in New York, here there was no sense of competition. When the teacher poked a shy Korean in the eyelid with a freshly sharpened pencil, we took no comfort in the fact that, unlike Hyeyoon Cho, we all knew the irregular past tense of the verb *to defeat*. In all fairness, the teacher hadn't meant to stab the girl, but neither did she spend much time apologizing, saying only, "Well, you should have been *vkkdyo* more *kdeynfulh*."

Over time it became impossible to believe that any of us would ever improve. Fall arrived and it rained every day, meaning we would now be scolded for the water dripping from our coats and umbrellas. It was mid-October when the teacher singled me out, saying, "Every day spent with you is like having a cesarean section."

△

And it struck me that, for the first time since arriving in France, I could understand every word that someone was saying.

Understanding doesn't mean that you can suddenly speak the language. Far from it. It's a small step, nothing more, yet its rewards are intoxicating and deceptive. The teacher continued her diatribe and I settled back, bathing in the subtle beauty of each new curse and insult.

"You exhaust me with your foolishness and reward my efforts with nothing but pain, do you understand me?"

The world opened up, and it was with great joy that I responded, "I know the thing that you speak exact now. Talk me more, you, plus, please, plus."

Reading the Genre

1. This is a literacy narrative about the acquisition of a second language. Who is the villain in this story? Who are the villains and heroes in your own literacy histories, and why? (For auother example of a literacy narrative, see Richard Rodriguez's essay "Strange Tools," on pp. 20–25.)

2. How does David Sedaris use both English and a garbled form of French in this story for comedic effect? How are the two languages used to reveal his confusion, his failures, and his triumphs? (See "Compare and contrast," p. 114.)

3. Does this story end happily? Do literacy narratives have to have a happy ending? Do they have to have an epiphany? (For a definition of *epiphany*, see p. 14.)

4. Stories about schooling and education often reveal quite a bit about the group dynamic within a classroom. How does Sedaris represent the mood within this environment? How does he depict his fellow students and their collective feelings and shared experiences? (See "Develop major characters," p. 19.)

5. **WRITING:** Think about your own experiences learning a second language or dialect (a dialect can be thought of as the common vocabulary, grammar, and speech patterns of a group of people). What was it like being an outsider? Think about your struggles and successes in expressing yourself. What conclusions can you draw about the process of learning a new language or dialect?

GRAPHIC NOVEL EXCERPT Lynda Barry writes the weekly comic strip *Ernie Pook's Comeek,* found in many alternative weekly newspapers or at www.marlysmagazine.com. Barry's work is often funny but serious, sad but optimistic. When she writes about herself, as she does in these excerpts from the book *One! Hundred! Demons!* (2002), she is very honest about her own past. She currently teaches a popular writing workshop called "Writing the Unthinkable." Barry has written fifteen books; her most recent book is *What It Is* (2008).

Lost and Found

Lynda Barry

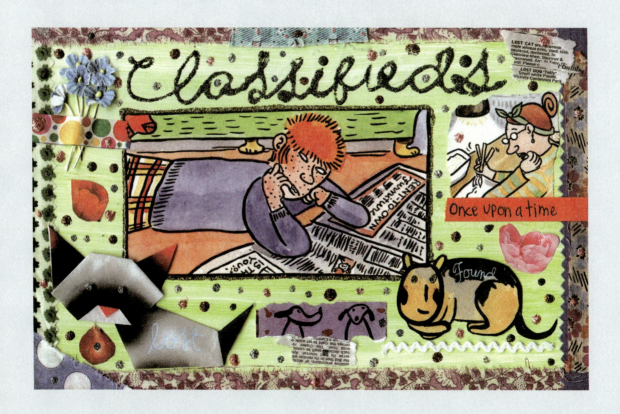

AFTER I LEARNED TO READ, I LOVED GETTING HOME FROM SCHOOL AND WAITING FOR THE AFTERNOON PAPER. WE DIDN'T HAVE BOOKS IN THE HOUSE, BUT THE PAPER GAVE ME PLENTY TO WORK WITH.

THE FIRST SECTION I TURNED TO WAS THE CLASSIFIEDS. I ALWAYS READ THE "LOST AND FOUND" ADS, TRYING TO MEMORIZE DESCRIPTIONS OF DOGS AND CATS WHO WERE OUT THERE ALONE AND SCARED.

2 YR OLD M BRN+WHT CHIHUAHUA MIX. RD COLLAR. ANS TO "HENRY." REWARD.

"JINGLES" LOST 10/2. F GRAY TABBY. BLIND RT EYE NEEDS MEDICATION.

POOR JINGLES.

EACH QUARTER-INCH AD WAS LIKE A CHAPTER IN A BOOK. I'D IMAGINE THE WHOLE STORY: THE FREAKED-OUT PEOPLE, THE FREAKED-OUT ANIMALS, AND ME, ALWAYS COMING TO THE RESCUE AND NEVER ACCEPTING THE REWARD.

NO, KEEP THE FIVE HUNDRED DOLLARS, SIR. ALL I CARE ABOUT IS THAT HENRY IS HOME.

PLEASE, MA'AM, WHAT MY NAME IS DOESN'T MATTER. AND NEITHER DOES THE TEN THOUSAND DOLLARS. ALL THAT MATTERS IS JINGLES.

LIKE MOST WRITERS, I LOVED TO READ WHEN I WAS LITTLE, BUT UNTIL RECENTLY, I NEVER REALLY THOUGHT ABOUT SOME OF THE THINGS I ENJOYED READING MOST. THE CLASSIFIED ADS FASCINATED ME.

CRYPT IN MAUSOLEUM. PRIME LOC. EYE-LEVEL. BEST OFFER. EVENINGS.

SZ. 12 WEDDING DRESS. NEVER WORN. MUST SACRIFICE.

FILL DIRT, VERY CLEAN.

PARTY PIANIST. MY PIANO OR YOURS.

THEY GAVE ME SO MANY WEIRD BLANKS TO FILL IN. LIKE WHO WAS SELLING THEIR CRYPT? I ONLY KNEW THE WORD FROM HORROR MOVIES. ZOMBIES AND VAMPIRES CAME OUT OF THEM. THE AD SAID "EVENINGS." IT SEEMED LIKE SUCH AN OBVIOUS TRICK.

DING DONG.
WHO IS IT?
UH, I'M HERE ABOUT THE CRYPT?
AAHHHH!!

SAME WITH THE WEDDING DRESS AD. WHO ELSE WAS GOING TO CALL ABOUT IT EXCEPT A MAIDEN? IT SAID "MUST SACRIFICE." WHO ELSE GOT SACRIFICED BUT MAIDENS? THE POLICE WOULD BE BAFFLED BY HOW MAIDENS KEPT DISAPPEARING.

HELLO?
YES?
YOU'VE GOT TO BE KIDDING.
OK.
NOT ANOTHER MAIDEN!
I'M AFRAID SO.
DANG!

WHEN I CAME FORWARD WITH THE SOLUTION TO THESE CRIMES, AT FIRST NO ONE WOULD BELIEVE ME. I EXPECTED THAT. I WATCHED A LOT OF MOVIES. NO ONE EVER BELIEVES KIDS AT FIRST. YOU HAVE TO WAIT UNTIL ALMOST THE END. YOU HAVE TO WAIT 'TIL YOUR LIFE IS IN DANGER.

CALLING ALL CARS! THAT KID WAS RIGHT ABOUT THE WANT ADS!

BUT NOW THE CRYPT-VAMPIRE AND THE WEDDING DRESS-ZOMBIE HAVE HER IN THEIR CLUTCHES! WE WERE SO STUPID! REPEAT! VERY STUPID!

MOSTLY I DIED IN MY CLAS-SIFIED STORIES. EVEN THEN I LOVED TRAGIC ENDINGS. PEO-PLE WOULD BE CRYING SO HARD. THEY'D COVER MY COFFIN WITH FILL DIRT, VERY CLEAN. THE PARTY PIANIST WOULD PLAY.

CHERISH IS THE WORD I USE TO DIS-CRI-IBE...

WHEN I READ ABOUT WRITER'S LIVES, THERE ARE USUALLY STORIES ABOUT WRITING FROM THE TIME THEY WERE LITTLE. I NEVER WROTE ANYTHING UN-TIL I WAS A TEENAGER, AND THEN IT WAS ONLY A DIARY THAT SAID THE SAME THING OVER AND OVER.

I thought Bill liked me but turns out he doesn't. I'm so depressed about Bill. He didn't call me. I can't stop thinking about Bill.

WRITERS TALK ABOUT ALL THE BOOKS THEY LOVED WHEN THEY WERE CHILDREN. CLASSIC STORIES I NEVER READ, BUT I LIED ABOUT BECAUSE I WAS SCARED IT WAS PROOF I WASN'T REALLY A WRITER.

AND WIND IN THE WILLOWS? AMAZING.

"THE LION, THE WITCH AND THE WARDROBE?

INCREDIBLE. SAME WITH "WATERHEAD DOWN"

YOU MEAN "WATERSHIP".

UH, YEAH.

AH, YES.

SUPER DRAMATICALLY EDUCATED. KNOWS ABOUT "STORY STRUC-TURE" AND "ARC" AND "PLOT POINTS"

JIVE-ASS FAKER WHO CAN'T SPELL AND HAS NO IDEA WHAT "STORY STRUCTURE" EVEN MEANS

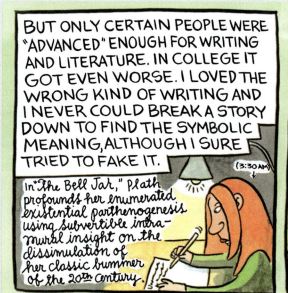

BUT ONLY CERTAIN PEOPLE WERE "ADVANCED" ENOUGH FOR WRITING AND LITERATURE. IN COLLEGE IT GOT EVEN WORSE. I LOVED THE WRONG KIND OF WRITING AND I NEVER COULD BREAK A STORY DOWN TO FIND THE SYMBOLIC MEANING, ALTHOUGH I SURE TRIED TO FAKE IT.

(3:30 AM)

In "The Bell Jar," Plath profounds her enumerated existential parthenogenesis using subvertible intra-mural insight on the dissimulation of her classic bummer of the 20th century.

MY TROUBLE ENDED WHEN I STARTED MAKING COMIC-STRIPS. IT'S NOT SOMETHING A PERSON HAS TO BE VERY "ADVANCED" TO DO. AT LEAST NOT IN THE MINDS OF LITERARY TYPES.

SO YOU'RE A CARTOONIST! HOW ADORABLE!

POLITICAL?

NO.

HUMOROUS?

KINDA.

WE'RE BOTH WRITERS.

SAY, MAYBE WE COULD COLLABORATE! WE WRITE IT AND YOU DRAW IT! HOW FUN!

NOBODY FEELS THE NEED TO PROVIDE DEEP CRITICAL IN-SIGHT TO SOMETHING WRITTEN BY HAND. MOSTLY THEY KEEP IT AS SHORT AS A WANT AD. THE WORST I GET IS, "TOO MANY WORDS. NOT FUNNY. DON'T GET THE JOKE." I CAN LIVE WITH THAT.

GALS, EVER FELT SO intimidated by the IDEA OF writing THAT you've never even given it a try? Think writing is only FOR "writers"? Sure is common!

ESPECIALLY BECAUSE I'M SURE THAT THE NINE-YEAR-OLD VERSION OF ME WHO MADE UP ALL THOSE "CLASSI-FIED STORIES" WOULD THINK THAT THIS ONE HAD A VERY HAPPY ENDING.

(and YES, Gals- the first thing I read in the paper is still the "lost and found")

LOST. SOMEWHERE AROUND PUBERTY. ABILITY TO MAKE UP STORIES. HAPPINESS DEPENDS ON IT. PLEASE WRITE.

Reading the Genre

1. Even though this essay is in comic form, it is also a literacy narrative. "Lost and Found" addresses literacy directly, discussing the author's early reading experiences. As a literacy narrative, what does "Lost and Found" teach us about the author's approach to reading and writing? (For another example of a literacy narrative, see Richard Rodriguez's essay "Strange Tools," on pp. 20–25.)

2. Unlike many other comic authors, Lynda Barry provides descriptions for some of her pictures. Why do you think she does this, and how do these descriptions contribute to the essay?

3. How is Barry's artistic and storytelling style different from that of Marjane Satrapi in the excerpt from *Persepolis* (see pp. 31–38)?

4. If Barry had presented her story without images, do you think your response to it would be different? How do comics present information, and why might a writer or artist choose this medium? (See Chapter 30, "High, Middle, and Low Style," p. 366.)

5. **WRITING:** This essay comes from the book *One! Hundred! Demons!* The concept for the book comes from an ancient Japanese painting exercise asking the artist to paint about the things that have worried her or that she has struggled with. As she began painting and writing about her demons, Barry explains that "at first the demons freaked me, but then I started to love watching them come out of my paintbrush." Try drawing or writing about memories from your own past as a student. What have you struggled with as a student? In writing about these memories, have you also come to better understand them?

REFLECTION   Ntozake Shange has published several books of essays and poetry, and her play *For Colored Girls . . .* (1975) won several drama awards, including an Obie. The following essay comes from her book *If I Can Cook/You Know God Can* (1999), which is a memoir, a history of African cooking around the world, a tribute to black cuisine, and a collection of recipes, all blended together.

NTOZAKE SHANGE

What Is It We Really Harvestin' Here?

We got a sayin', "The blacker the berry, the sweeter the juice," which is usually meant as a compliment. To my mind, it also refers to the delectable treats we as a people harvested for our owners and for our own selves all these many years, slave or free. In fact, we knew something about the land, sensuality, rhythm, and ourselves that has continued to elude our captors—puttin' aside all our treasures in the basement of the British Museum, or the Met, for that matter. What am I talkin' about? A different approach to the force of gravity, to our bodies, and what we produce: a reverence for the efforts of the group and the intimate couple. Harvesttime and Christmas were prime occasions for courtin'. A famine, a drought, a flood, or Lent do not serve as inspiration for couplin', you see.

The Juba, a dance of courtin' known in slave quarters of North America and the Caribbean, is a phenomenon that stayed with us through the jitterbug, the wobble, the butterfly, as a means of courtin' that's apparently very colored, and very "African." In fact we still have it and we've never been so "integrated"—the *Soul Train* dancers aren't all black anymore, but the dynamic certainly is. A visitor to Cuba in Lynne Fauley Emery's *Dance Horizon Book* described the Juba as a series of challenges.

> A woman advances and commencing a slow dance, made up of shuffling of the feet and various contortions of the body, thus challenges a rival from among the men. One of these, bolder than the rest, after a while steps out, and the two then

strive which shall tire the other; the woman performing many feats which the man attempts to rival, often excelling them, amid the shouts of the rest. A woman will sometimes drive two or three successive beaux from the ring, yielding her place at length to some impatient belle.

John Henry went up against a locomotive, but decades before we simply were up against ourselves and the elements. And so we are performers in the fields, in the kitchens, by kilns, and for one another. Sterling Stuckey points out, in *Slave Culture*, however, that by 1794 "it was illegal to allow slaves to dance and drink on the premises . . . without the written consent of their owners," the exceptions being Christmas and the burials, which are communal experiences. And what shall we plant and harvest, so that we might "hab big times duh fus hahves, and duh fus ting wut growed we take tuh duh church so as ebrybody could hab a pieces ub it. We pray over it and shout. Wen we hab a dance, we use tuh shout in a rinig. We ain't have wutyuh call a propuh dance tuday."

Say we've gone about our owners' business. Planted and harvested his crop of sugarcane, remembering that the "ration of slaves/sugar was ten times that of slaves/tobacco and slaves/cotton." That to plant a sugar crop we have to dig a pit three feet square and a few inches deep into which one young plant is set. Then, of course, the thing has to grow. A mature sugarcane plant is three to nine feet tall. That's got to be cut at exactly the right point. Then we've got to crush it, boil it, refine it, from thick black syrup to fine white sugar, to make sure, as they say in Virginia, that we "got the niggah out." Now it's time to tend to our own gardens. Let's grow some sweet potatoes to "keep the niggah alive."

Sweet Potatoes

Like everything else, we have to start with something. Now we need a small piece of potato with at least one of those scraggly roots hanging about for this native Central American tuber. This vegetable will stand more heat than almost any other grown in the United

States. It does not take to cool weather, and any kind of frost early or seasonal will kill the leaves, and if your soil gets cold the tubers themselves will not look very good. Get your soil ready at least two weeks before planting, weeding, turning, and generally disrupting the congealed and solid mass we refer to as dirt, so that your hands and the tubers may move easily through the soil, as will water and other nutrients.

Once the soil is free of winter, two weeks after the last frost, plant the potato slips in 6-to-12-inch ridges, 3 to 4.5 feet apart. Separate the plants by 9 to 12 inches. If we space the plants more than that, our tubers may be grand, but way too big to make good use of in the kitchen. We should harvest our sweet potatoes when the tubers are not quite ripe, but of good size, or we can wait until the vines turn yellow. Don't handle our potatoes too roughly, which could lead to bruising and decay. If a frost comes upon us unexpectedly, take those potatoes out the ground right away. Our potatoes will show marked improvement during storage, which allows the starch in them to turn to sugar. Nevertheless, let them lie out in the open for 2 to 3 hours to fully dry. Then move them to a moist and warm storage space. The growing time for our crop'll vary from 95 to 125 days.

The easiest thing to do with a sweet potato is to bake it. In its skin. I coat the thing with olive oil, or butter in a pinch. Wrap it in some aluminum foil, set it in the oven at 400 degrees. Wait till I hear sizzling, anywhere from 45 minutes to an hour after, in a very hot oven. I can eat it with my supper at that point or I can let it cool off for later. (One of the sexiest dates I ever went on was to the movies to see El Mariachi. My date brought along chilled baked sweet potatoes and ginger beer. Much nicer than canola-sprayed "buttered" popcorn with too-syrupy Coca-Cola, wouldn't you say?)

Mustard Greens

No, they are not the same as collards. We could say they, with their frilly edges and sinuous shapes, have more character, are more flirtatious, than collards. This green can be planted in the spring or the fall, so long as the soil is workable (not cold). It's not a hot weather plant, preferring short days and temperate climates. We can use the same techniques for *mustard greens that we use for lettuce. Sowing the seeds in rows 12 to 18 inches apart, seedlings 4 to 8 inches apart. These plants should get lots of fertilizer to end up tender, lots of water, too. They should be harvested before they are fully mature. Now, you've got to be alert, because mustard greens grow fast, 25 to 40 days from the time you set them in the soil to harvest. When it comes time to reap what you've sown, gather the outer leaves when they are 3 to 4 inches long, tender enough; let the inner leaves then develop more or wait till it's hot and harvest the whole plant.*

Now we cook the mustard greens just like the collards, or we don't have to cook it at all. This vegetable is fine in salads or on sandwiches and soups. If you shy away from pungent tastes, mix these greens with some collards, kale, or beet greens. That should take some of the kick out of them. I still like my peppers and vinegar, though. If we go back, pre-Columbus, the Caribs did, too. According to Spanish travelers, the Caribs, who fancied vegetables, added strong peppers called aji-aji to just about everything. We can still find aji-aji on some sauces from Spanish-speaking countries if we read the labels carefully. Like "La Morena." So appropriate.

Watermelon

The watermelon is an integral part of our actual life as much as it is a feature of our stereotypical lives in the movies, posters, racial jokes, toys, and early American portraits of the "happy darky." We could just as easily been eatin' watermelon in D. W. Griffith's Birth of a Nation as chicken legs. The implications are the same. Like the watermelon, we were a throwback to "African" prehistory, which isn't too off, since Lucy, the oldest Homo sapiens currently known, is from Africa, too.

But I remember being instructed not to order watermelon in restaurants or to eat watermelon in any public places because it makes white people think poorly of us. They already did that, so I don't see what the watermelon was going to precipitate. Europeans brought watermelon with them from Africa anyway. In Massachusetts by 1629 it was recorded as "abounding." In my rebelliousness as a child, I got so angry about the status of the watermelon, I tried to grow some in the flower box on our front porch in Missouri. My harvest was minimal to say the least.

Here's how you can really grow you some watermelon. They like summer heat, particularly sultry, damp nights. If we can grow watermelons, we can grow ourselves almost any other kind of melon. The treatment is the same. Now, these need some space, if we're looking for a refrigerator-sized melon or one ranging from 25 to 30 pounds. Let them have a foot between plants in between rows 4 to 6 feet apart. They need a lot of fertilizer, especially if the soil is heavy and doesn't drain well. When the runners (vines) are a foot to a foot and a half long, fertilize again about 8 inches from the plant itself. Put some more fertilizer when the first melons appear. Watermelons come in different varieties, but I'm telling you about the red kind. I have no primal response to a golden or blanched-fleshed melon. Once your melons set on the vines and start to really take up some space, be sure not to forget to water the vines during the ripening process.

When is your watermelon ripe? You can't tell by thumping it nor by the curly tail at the point where the melon is still on the vine. The best way to know if your melon is ready is by looking at the bottom. The center turns from a light yellow to deep amber. Your melon'll have a powdery or mushy tasteless sorta taste if you let it ripen too long.

Surely you've seen enough pictures or been to enough picnics to know how to eat a watermelon, so I won't insult you with that information. However, there is a fractious continuing debate about whether to sprinkle sugar or salt on your watermelon slice. I am not going to take sides in this matter.

Some of us were carried to the New World specifically because we knew 'bout certain crops, knew 'bout the groomin' and harvestin' of rice, for instance.

> Plantation owners were perfectly aware of the superiority . . . of African slaves from rice country. Littlefield [a journalist] writes that "as early as 1700 ships from Carolina were reported in the Gambia River." . . . In a letter dated 1756, Henry Laurens, a Charleston merchant, wrote, "The slaves from the River Gambia are prefer'd to all others with us save the Gold Coast." The previous year he had

written: "Gold Coast or Gambias are best; next to them the Windward Coast are prefer'd to Angolas."

These bits of information throw an entirely different, more dignified light on "colored" cuisine for me. Particularly since I was raised on rice and my mother's people on both sides are indefatigable Carolinians, South, to be exact, South Carolinians. To some, our "phrenologically immature brains" didn't have consequence until our mastery of the cultivation of "cargo," "patna," "joponica," and finally Carolina rice, "small-grained, rather long and wiry, and remarkably white," was transferred to the books and records of our owners. Nevertheless, our penchant for rice was not dampened by its relationship to our bondage. Whether through force or will, we held on to our rice-eatin' heritage. I repeat, I was raised on rice. If I was Joe Williams, insteada singin' "Every day, every day, I sing the blues," I'd be sayin', "Oh, every day, almost any kinda way, I get my rice."

My poor mother, Eloise, Ellie, for short, made the mistake of marrying a man who was raised by a woman from Canada. So every day, he wanted a potato, some kinda potato, mashed, boiled, baked, scalloped, fried, just a potato. Yet my mother was raising a sixth generation of Carolinians, which meant we had to eat some kinda rice. Thus, Ellie was busy fixing potato for one and rice for all the rest every day, until I finally learnt how to do one or the other and gave her a break. I asked Ellie Williams how her mother, Viola, went about preparing the rice for her "chirren"—a low-country linguistic lapse referring to offspring like me. Anyway, this is what Mama said.

Mama's Rice

"We'd buy some rice in a brown paper bag (this is in the Bronx). Soak it in a bit of water. Rinse it off and cook it the same way we do now." "How is that, Ma?" I asked. "Well, you boil a certain amount of water. Let it boil good. Add your rice and let it boil till tender. Stirring every so often because you want the water to evaporate. You lift your pot. You can

tell if your rice is okay because there's no water there. Then you fluff it with a fork. You want every kind, extra, extra, what you call it. No ordinary olive oil will do.

"Heat this up. Just a little bit of it. You don't want no greasy rice, do you? Heat this until, oh, it is so hot that the smoke is coming quick. Throw in 3 to 4 cloves garlic, maybe 1 cup chopped onion too, I forgot. Let that sizzle and soften with 1/2 cup each cilantro, pimiento, and everything. But don't let this get burned, no. So add your 4 cups water and 2 cups rice. Turn up the heat some more till there's a great boiling of rice, water, seasonings. The whole thing. Then leave it alone for a while with the cover on so all the rice cooks even. Now, when you check and see there's only a small bit of water left in the bottom of the pot, stir it all up. Turn the heat up again and wait. When there's no water left at all, at all. Just watch the steam coming up. Of course you should have a good pegau by now, but the whole pot of your rice should be delicioso, *ready even for my table. If you do as I say."*

For North Americans, a pot with burnt rice on the bottom is a scary concept. But all over the Caribbean, it's a different story entirely. In order to avoid making *asopao*—a rice moist and heavy with the sofrito or tomato-achiote mixture, almost like a thick soup where the rice becomes one mass instead of standing, each grain on its own—it is necessary to let the rice on the bottom of the pot get a crustlike bottom, assuring that all moisture has evaporated. My poor North American mother, Ellie, chastises me frequently for "ruining" good rice with all this spice. Then I remind her that outside North America we Africans were left to cook in ways that reminded us of our mother's cooking, not Jane Austen's characters. The rice tastes different, too. But sometimes I cheat and simply use Goya's Sazón—after all, I'm a modern woman. I shouldn't say that too loudly, though. Mathilde can hear all the way from her front porch any blasphemous notion I have about good cooking. No, it is her good cooking that I am to learn. I think it is more than appropriate that we know something about some of the crops that led to most of us African descendants of the Diaspora, being here, to eat anything at all.

But rather than end on a sour note, I am thinking of my classes with the great Brazilian dancer, choreographer, and teacher Mercedes Baptista at the now-legendary Clark Center. We learned a harvest dance, for these are many, but the movements of this celebratory ritual were lyrical and delicate, far from the tortured recounts of Euro-Americans to our "jigaboo" gatherings; no gyrations, repetitive shuffling that held no interest. Indeed, the simple movement of the arms, which we worked on for days until we got it, resembled a tropical port de bras worthy of any ballerina. Our hip movements, ever so subtle, with four switches to the left, then four to the right, all the while turning and covering space. The head leaning in the direction of the hips, the arms moving against it, till the next hip demanded counterpoint.

A healthy respect for the land, for what we produce for the blessing of a harvest, begot dances of communal joy. On New Year's Eve in the late fifties, we danced the Madison; today it's a burning rendition of "the Electric Slide." Eighty-year-olds jammin' with toddlers after the weddin' toast. No, we haven't changed so much.

Reading the Genre

1. Shange structures her essay around food. How does her borrowing from the genre of the recipe shape this narrative?

2. How would you describe the author's relationship with her readers? How does she develop this relationship with her audience? (See "Understanding your audience," p. 10.)

3. This essay is an example of *autoethnography*, a type of writing in which the author examines his or her own culture from the inside and then steps outside of the experience and looks at it critically. In this essay, Shange describes and examines details of the daily life of her culture and then comments on their cultural significance. What do we learn about Shange's culture from her examination of food?

4. What is the importance of Shange's use of the pronoun *we* throughout the essay? (See Chapter 30, "High, Middle, and Low Style," p. 366.)

5. **WRITING:** Choose one important dish that has been passed along in your family or your culture. Then do some research: Ask the cooks you know to tell you more about the dish; try to find out a bit about the history of its ingredients and their cultural significance; compare this recipe to versions of the dish in other cultures. You might use Internet resources such as www.foodtimeline .com. Finally, reflect on what you've learned and write about it. What does the cultural history of what you eat say about who you are?

MEMOIR   Poet and novelist Naomi Shihab Nye has written or edited more than twenty books and has won dozens of awards for her writing. Nye's mother is American and her father is Palestinian, and much of her writing is focused on helping people understand the similarities and differences between Middle Eastern and American cultures, and specifically on dispelling stereotypes about the Middle East.

NAOMI SHIHAB NYE

Mint Snowball

My great-grandfather on my mother's side ran a drugstore in a small town in central Illinois. He sold pills and rubbing alcohol from behind the big cash register and creamy ice cream from the soda fountain. My mother remembers the counter's long polished sweep, its shining face. She twirled on the stools. Dreamy fans. Wide summer afternoons. Clink of nickels in anybody's hand. He sold milkshakes, cherry cokes, old fashioned sandwiches. What did an old fashioned sandwich look like? Dark wooden shelves. Silver spigots on chocolate dispensers.

My great-grandfather had one specialty: a Mint Snowball which he invented. Some people drove all the way in from Decatur just to taste it. First he stirred fresh mint leaves with sugar and secret ingredients in a small pot on the stove for a very long time. He concocted a flamboyant elixir of mint. Its scent clung to his fingers even after he washed his hands. Then he shaved ice into tiny particles and served it mounded in a glass dish. Permeated with mint syrup. Scoops of rich vanilla ice cream to each side. My mother took a bite of minty ice and ice cream mixed together. The Mint Snowball tasted like winter. She closed her eyes to see the Swiss village my great-grandfather's parents came from. Snow frosting the roofs. Glistening, dangling spokes of ice.

Before my great-grandfather died, he sold the recipe for the mint syrup to someone in town for one hundred dollars. This hurt my grandfather's feelings. My grandfather thought he should have inherited it to carry on the tradition. As far as the family knew, the person who bought the recipe never used it. At least not in public. My mother had watched my grandfather make the syrup so often she thought she could replicate it. But what did he have in those little unmarked bottles? She experimented. Once she came close. She wrote down what she did. Now she has lost the paper.

Perhaps the clue to my entire personality connects to the lost Mint Snowball. I have always felt out-of-step with my environment, disjointed in the modern world. The crisp flush of cities makes me weep. Strip centers, Poodle grooming and Take-out Thai. I am angry over lost department stores, wistful for something I have never tasted or seen.

Although I know how to do everything one needs to know—change airplanes, find my exit off the interstate, charge gas, send a fax—there is something missing. Perhaps the stoop of my great-grandfather over the pan, the slow patient swish of his spoon. The spin of my mother on the high stool with her whole life in front of her, something fine and fragrant still to happen. When I breathe a handful of mint, even pathetic sprigs from my sunbaked Texas earth, I close my eyes. Little chips of ice on the tongue, their cool slide down. Can we follow the long river of the word "refreshment" back to its spring? Is there another land for me? Can I find any lasting solace in the color green?

Reading the Genre

1. Nye uses sentence fragments in this essay. Examine these incomplete sentences, particularly in the first two paragraphs of the essay. How is the content of each of these shorter sentences similar, and how does this work within the essay? (See Chapter 30, "High, Middle, and Low Style," p. 366.)

2. This narrative is divided into two parts. How would you describe the perspective, or point of view, in the first half and in the second? What can the author do in the second half that she can't in the first? Why? (See Chapter 26, "Transitions," p. 350, and Chapter 29, "Titles," p. 362.)

3. In order to evoke the look and feel of the drugstore, and the taste and experience of eating the mint snowball, Nye creates images with her words. Try to sketch a few of these images, or find images online, to illustrate the story with pictures. In your opinion, which of these images is most powerful?

4. **WRITING:** Consider the work history of your own family: What kind of work do your parents do, and what kind of work did their parents do? What kind of work does your extended family do? Are there specific skills or lessons, or even ways of looking at the world, that have been passed down in your family because of the sort of work your family has done? Write a short personal reflection on this topic.

5. **WRITING:** Visit a local business and interview the owner about the history of this business. Then, write a short narrative that tells the story of the business—how it began, what it specializes in, what makes it unique, how it has changed over the years, and so on.

MEMOIR   Ira Sukrungruang, a Thai American writer, is a teacher of creative nonfiction and the coeditor of *What Are You Looking At? The First Fat Fiction Anthology* (2003) and *Scoot Over, Skinny: The Fat Nonfiction Anthology* (2005). This story comes from the online journal *Brevity* (www.creativenonfiction .org/brevity), which collects very short creative nonfiction.

Brevity

Posted: Fall 2005
From: Ira Sukrungruang

Chop Suey

My mother was a champion bowler in Thailand. This was not what I knew of her. I knew only her expectations of me to be the perfect Thai boy. I knew her distaste for blonde American women she feared would seduce her son. I knew her distrust of the world she found herself in, a world of white faces and mackerel in a can. There were many things I didn't know about my mother when I was ten. She was what she was supposed to be. My mother.

At El-Mar Bowling Alley, I wanted to show her what I could do with the pins. I had bowled once before, at Dan Braun's birthday party. There, I had rolled the ball off the bumpers, knocking the pins over in a thunderous crash. I liked the sound of a bowling alley. I felt in control of the weather, the rumble of the ball on the wood floor like the coming of a storm, and the hollow explosion of the pins, distant lightning. At the bowling alley, men swore and smoked and drank.

My mother wore a light pink polo, jeans, and a golf visor. She put on a lot of powder to cover up the acne she got at 50. She poured Vapex, a strong smelling vapor rub, into her handkerchief, and covered her nose, complaining of the haze of smoke that floated over the lanes. My mother was the only woman in the place. We were the only non-white patrons.

I told her to watch me. I told her I was good. I set up, took sloppy and uneven steps, and lobbed my orange ball onto the lane with a loud thud. This time there were no bumpers. My ball veered straight for the gutter.

My mother said to try again. I did, and for the next nine frames, not one ball hit one pin. Embarrassed, I sat next to her. I put my head on her shoulder. She patted it for a while and said bowling wasn't an easy game.

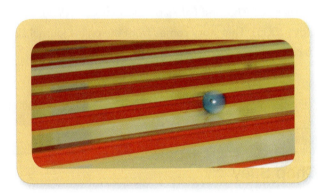

My mother rose from her chair and said she wanted to try. She changed her shoes. She picked a ball from the rack, one splattered with colors. When she was ready, she lined herself up to the pins, the ball at eye level. In five concise steps, she brought the ball back, dipped her knees, and released it smoothly, as if her hand was an extension of the floor. The ball started on the right side of the lane and curled into the center. Strike.

She bowled again and knocked down more pins. She told me about her nearly perfect game, how in Thailand she was unbeatable.

I listened, amazed that my mother could bowl a 200, that she was good at something beyond what mothers were supposed to be good at, like cooking and punishing and sewing. I clapped. I said she should stop being a mother and become a bowler.

As she changed her shoes, a man with dark hair and a mustache approached our lane. In one hand he had a cigarette and a beer. He kept looking back at his buddies a few lanes over, all huddling and whispering. I stood beside my mother, wary of any stranger. My mother's smile disappeared. She rose off the chair.

"Hi," said the man.

My mother nodded.

"My friends over there," he pointed behind him, "well, we would like to thank you." His mustache twitched.

My mother pulled me closer to her leg, hugging her purse to her chest.

He began to talk slower, over-enunciating his words, repeating again. "We . . . would . . . like . . . to . . . thank . . ."

I tugged on my mother's arm, but she stood frozen.

". . . you . . . for . . . making . . . a . . . good . . . chop . . . suey. You people make good food."

The man looked back again, toasted his beer at his friends, laughing smoke from his lips.

My mother grabbed my hand and took one step toward the man. In that instant, I saw in her face the same resolve she had when she spanked, the same resolve when she scolded. In that instant, I thought my mother was going to hit the man. And for a moment, I thought the man saw the same thing in her eyes, and his smile disappeared from his face. Quickly, she smiled—too bright, too large—and said, "You're welcome."

Reading the Genre

1. This story begins as a pleasant memory of the author's youth but ends with a difficult and awkward encounter. This development comes as a surprise to readers, just as it did to Sukrungruang and his mother. When the story ends, what emotions are you left with as a reader? What would you have wanted to do if you had been in the bowling alley that day? (See Chapter 28, "Conclusions," p. 359.)

2. At the end of this story, in the dialogue between Sukrungruang's mother and the man with "dark hair and a mustache," Sukrungruang uses ellipses to insert pauses in the discussion. What effect do these pauses have on the story and on you as a reader? (See "Use dialogue," p. 18.)

3. It's not easy to realistically describe action in a personal narrative, but using just a few details, Sukrungruang does a good job of capturing the act of throwing a bowling ball. Reread his descriptions of his own bad bowling and his mother's excellent bowling. Try to identify the adjectives and adverbs that he uses, as well as the metaphors. (See "Use figures of speech," p. 17.)

4. **WRITING:** The events Sukrungruang recounts in this story reveal a turning point in his life, a moment when he learns something important. Can you identify the turning points in your life when you discovered important things that you hadn't known before? Choose one of these moments and do some personal writing about this event.

REFLECTION   Amy Johnson Frykholm, a professor of religion, literature, and cultural studies at Colorado Mountain College, is the author of *Rapture Culture: Left Behind in Evangelical America* (2004). This article was published in the online journal *www.identitytheory.com*, which publishes socially conscious literary nonfiction. Here, Frykholm reflects on the experience of working in a soup kitchen.

Identitytheory.com

Posted: December 19, 2006
From: Amy Johnson Frykholm

Enough

Empty boxes. Banana boxes, frozen entrée boxes, Healthy Start cereal crates, waxed produce boxes. The bread boxes, usually full and available for the taking, are also empty. They are piled waist high and haphazard just to the left of the entrance to the church, remnants from a week's worth of meals, now abandoned and awaiting a free pair of hands to take them to recycling.

On the counter of the narrow, galley-style kitchen, I find four more boxes full of slightly rotting produce. I dig through softening tomatoes, spotted zucchini, and wrinkling eggplant. My brain begins to search for a formula for the day's meal. Cauliflower plus cream plus broth equals soup. Eggplant suggests ratatouille, or perhaps curry. In the refrigerator I find four cooked turkey breasts and a dozen bags of prepackaged salad. How, I wonder, does this amount to lunch for sixty people who come hungry for so much more than food? I sort out onions, cauliflower, green beans, tomatoes, and eggplant and stack them in piles on the counter. I set potatoes for peeling in a colander in the sink.

At the window from the hallway, Janice stands with her oxygen tank.

"Whatcha cooking?"

"Well," I say. "Looks like we'll have soup."

"What's in them boxes?" She peers in to the boxes I start to carry into the hallway.

"Rotten tomatoes," I say over my shoulder.

I set the counter with cutting boards and knives. Volunteers and slightly sullen community service workers have started to arrive. I set T. J. next to the soup burner so that he can cut directly into the pot. I get Mary de-boning turkey and put Cindy in the children's room on salad detail so that her two year old can watch Barney while she chops. I start to chop onions while my mind quickly calculates: one steam table pan—green beans; two—soup; three—turkey casserole; four—vegetable curry. We need one more. This isn't enough. The kitchen hums with sounds of chatter, chopping knives, and clanking pans. Dan takes over the sink beginning to accumulate stacks of used bowls and knives and pots. Potatoes are dropped into a pan of steaming water. Turkey is layered with corn, tomatoes, rice, and cheese. I no longer know whose hands are mine. By midmorning, the counter is slick with vegetable peelings, turkey bones, and plastic wrappers.

Elaine, another cook at this soup kitchen, had a dream that she was cooking a turkey in the roasting pan, and it turned into a ham. "That'll never be enough," she thought, panicking in her sleep. I once dreamed that I was making soup, but no matter how much I made the pot was empty every time I looked in. I wonder if these dreams of scarcity are about feeding those who come to the community meal or if they are about feeding something that hungers in us.

At 11:30, the fifth steam table pan of mashed potatoes is dropped into its slot. The lids are lifted. People have begun to stream in the doorway, coming in from a frosty morning. There is Richard with his stooped back and careful shuffle. Tom, Nate, Michael, and Chris come in before classes at the local college. Brian and Johnny are just off shift. Cassie and Lara come with their children. Troll, at this hour, is still sober. Janice is first in line. They fill their plates and find metal chairs at the long tables of the warm dining room. A woman comes in, but rather than heading into the dining room with the others, she stands in the doorway, looking. I don't notice her at first. There is still much to do: the counter needs to be cleared, dirty pots and bowls stacked, the sink filled with soap and hot water. She doesn't speak English. I take quick birdlike glances around the room, thinking about balance and flow, about portion size and numbers.

The woman gestures at the hallway where we usually have boxes of bread. "Pan?" she asks tentatively. "Hoy, no hay," I say. But then I remember a package of waffles in the freezer. I ask her to wait. There is a box next to the kitchen that is full of produce. I hand her the waffles and gesture to the box full of heads of lettuce, droopy green onions, and radishes, Cindy's leftovers from salad making and other remnants from the day's cooking. "Lechuga," I say before returning to the dining room to see if we are running low on forks.

A few minutes later, Mary catches my arm. "There's a woman in the hallway walking off with a whole box of produce," she says. I look. The woman has taken my gesture at heads of lettuce as a full invitation. She has loaded up our remainders—the cucumbers, lettuce, and peppers—into her box with the frozen waffles.

A whole box? Is there enough for tomorrow? The question catches in my throat. The woman hesitates. She sees that *las gringas* are talking about her. I hesitate too, and then hold up my hand to tell her it is OK. "Esta bien," I say. "Esta bien."

Only a few diners are left finishing their meal. We carry the remains back into the small kitchen—a scrape of casserole, the watery broth at the bottom of a vegetable pan, a few sad lettuce leaves, a gooey brownie. We wash dishes, the grey soapy water making tiny waves up to our elbows. Each steam table pan is scrubbed shiny. Each ceramic plate returned to a stack in the dining room. Each table cloth wiped free of smears and crumbs. In a rhythm of time and tide, the dining room empties and turns quiet. When everything is clean, I walk toward the door, hand lotion slicking my hands under my gloves and pass the heap of boxes, now topped off with a bag of plastic recycling, cake containers streaked with frosting, and several more pieces of implacable cardboard.

The stoop is dusted with snow. I take one last bag of trash to the dumpster. Every meal leaves me with a restless question I cannot ever finally answer. As I heave the trash into the metal dumpster and walk home along the snowy street, I do not know if I can trust it, this demanding abundance, this hunger in me. I wonder what is enough.

Reading the Genre

1. Why is it important for the reader to understand what the soup kitchen looks like? How does the author convey this scene to the reader? (See "Develop the setting," p. 19.)

2. How does Frykholm use lists of ingredients, kitchen supplies, and utensils in the narrative? Why does she divide things into categories? How does the reader feel about all these *things* that she must juggle?

3. The author's sense of order and organization are important in this story. How are the human characters in the story contrasted with all the ingredients? Is the author dealing primarily with people, with produce, or with something else?

4. Consider the language barrier between Frykholm and the Spanish-speaking woman. Most narratives are about coming to an understanding or learning a lesson. What effect does this narrative have on the reader when we see so much misunderstanding and confusion?

5. **WRITING:** Think about a time in your life when you were misunderstood. Try to remember how your specific language, manner, tone, or actions were misinterpreted. Create a graphic narrative that shows how this misunderstanding occurred. If you don't feel like drawing, find pictures from magazines or online sources to help you represent this misunderstanding. Then, write about how this misunderstanding occurred. (See "Use images," p. 15, and Chapter 46, "Understanding Images," p. 500.)

MEMOIR   Rob Sheffield, a former editor and columnist for *Rolling Stone,* currently writes for *Blender* magazine. Renée Crist, his first wife and the muse for the following essay (and book of the same title), passed away in 1997. You can read excerpts from his book *Love Is a Mix Tape* (2007) and listen to the music he refers to in this essay at www.randomhouse.com/crown/mixtape or at www.myspace.com/loveisamixtapethebook. You can also see one of Sheffield's music reviews (of Green Day's *American Idiot*) on page 119.

ROB SHEFFIELD

Rumblefish

A SIDE ONE DATE / TIME	**B** SIDE TWO DATE / TIME
Pavement: "Shoot the Singer"	R.E.M.: "Man on the Moon"
The Smiths: "Cemetry Gates"	10,000 Maniacs: "Candy Everybody Wants"
Belly: "Feed the Tree"	
Sloan: "Sugar Tune"	Royal Trux: "Sometimes"
L7: "Shove"	Bettie Serveert: "Palomine"
Lois: "Bonds in Seconds"	Morrissey: "We Hate It When Our Friends Become Successful"
Grenadine: "In a World Without Heroes"	
The Pooh Sticks: "Sugar Baby"	Mary Chapin Carpenter: "Passionate Kisses"
The Chills: "Part Past Part Fiction"	
Whitney Houston: "I'm Every Woman"	Pavement: "Texas Never Whispers"
L7: "Packin' A Rod"	Boy George: "The Crying Game"
	Belly: "Slow Dog"

The playback: late night, Brooklyn, a pot of coffee, and a chair by the window. I'm listening to a mix tape from 1993. Nobody can hear it but me. The neighbors are asleep. The skater kids who sit on my front steps, drink beer, and blast Polish hip-hop—they're gone for the night. The diner next door is closed, but the air is still full of borscht and kielbasa. This is where I live now. A different town, a different apartment, a different year.

This mix tape is just another piece of useless junk that Renée left behind. A category that I guess tonight includes me.

I should have gone to sleep hours ago. Instead, I was rummaging through old boxes, looking for some random paperwork, and I found this tape with her curly scribble on the label. She never played this one for me. She didn't write down the songs, so I have no idea what's in store. But I can already tell it's going to be a late night. It always is. I pop *Rumblefish* into my Panasonic RXC36 boombox on the kitchen counter, pour some more coffee, and let the music have its way with me. It's a date. Just me and Renée and some tunes she picked out.

All these tunes remind me of her now. It's like that old song, "88 Lines About 44 Women." Except it's 8,844 lines about one woman. We've done this before. We get together sometimes, in the dark, share a few songs. It's the closest we'll get to hearing each other's voices tonight.

The first song: Pavement's "Shoot the Singer." Just a sad California boy, plucking his guitar and singing about a girl he likes. They were Renée's favorite band. She used to say, "There's a lot of room in my dress for these boys."

Renée called this tape *Rumblefish*. I don't know why. She recorded it over a promo cassette by some band called Drunken Boat, who obviously didn't make a big impression, because she stuck her own label over their name, put Scotch tape over the punch holes, and made her own mix. She dated it "Ides o' March 1993." She also wrote this inspirational credo on the label:

> "You know what I'm doing—Just follow along!"
> —Jennie Garth

Ah, the old Jennie Garth workout video, *Body in Progress*. Some nights you go to the mall with your squeeze, you're both a little wasted, and you come home with a Jennie

Garth workout video. That's probably buried in one of these boxes, too. Neither of us ever threw anything away. We made a lot of mix tapes while we were together. Tapes for making out, tapes for dancing, tapes for falling asleep. Tapes for doing the dishes, for walking the dog. I kept them all. I have them piled up on my bookshelves, spilling out of my kitchen cabinets, scattered all over the bedroom floor. I don't even have pots or pans in my kitchen, just that old boombox on the counter, next to the sink. So many tapes.

I met Renée in Charlottesville, Virginia, when we were both twenty-three. When the bartender at the Eastern Standard put on a tape, Big Star's *Radio City*, she was the only other person in the room who perked up. So we drank bourbon and talked about music. We traded stories about the bands we liked, shows we'd seen. Renée loved the Replacements and Alex Chilton and the Meat Puppets. So did I.

I loved the Smiths. Renée hated the Smiths.

The second song on the tape is "Cemetry Gates" by The Smiths.

The first night we met, I told her the same thing I've told every single girl I've ever had a crush on: "I'll make you a tape!" Except this time, with this girl, it worked. When we were planning our wedding a year later, she said that instead of stepping on a glass at the end of the ceremony, she wanted to step on a cassette case, since that's what she'd been doing ever since she met me.

Falling in love with Renée was not the kind of thing you walk away from in one piece. I had no chance. She put a hitch in my git-along. She would wake up in the middle of the night and say things like "What if Bad Bad Leroy Brown was a girl?" or "Why don't they have commercials for salt like they do for milk?" Then she would fall back to sleep, while I would lie awake and give thanks for this alien creature beside whom I rested.

Renée was a real cool hell-raising Appalachian punk-rock girl. Her favorite song was the Rolling Stones' "Let's Spend the Night Together." Her favorite album was

Pavement's *Slanted and Enchanted*. She rooted for the Atlanta Braves and sewed her own silver vinyl pants. She knew which kind of screwdriver was which. She baked pies, but not very often. She could rap Roxanne Shante's "Go on Girl" all the way through. She called Eudora Welty "Miss Eudora." She had an MFA in fiction and never got any stories published, but she kept writing them anyway. She bought too many shoes and dyed her hair red. Her voice was full of the frazzle and crackle of music.

Renée was a country girl, three months older than me. She was born on November 21, 1965, the same day as Björk, in the Metropolitan Mobile Home Park in Northcross, Georgia. She grew up in southwest Virginia, with her parents, Buddy and Nadine, and her little sister. When she was three, Buddy was transferred to the defense plant in Pulaski County, and so her folks spent a summer building a house there. Renée used to sit in the backyard, feeding grass to the horses next door through the fence. She had glasses, curly brown hair, and a beagle named Snoopy. She went to Fairlawn Baptist Church and Pulaski High School and Hollins College. She got full-immersion baptized in Claytor Lake. The first record she ever owned was KC & the Sunshine Band's "Get Down Tonight." KC was her first love. I was her last.

I was a shy, skinny, Irish Catholic geek from Boston. I'd never met anybody like Renée before. I moved to Charlottesville for grad school, my plans all set: go down South, get my degree, then haul ass to the next town. The South was a scary new world. The first time I saw a possum in my driveway, I shook a bony fist at the sky and cursed this godforsaken rustic hellhole. I'm twenty-three! Life is passing me by! My ancestors spent centuries in the hills of County Kerry, waist-deep in sheep shit, getting shot at by English soldiers, and my grandparents crossed the ocean in coffin ships to come to America, just so I could get possum rabies?

Renée had never set foot north of Washington, D.C. For her, Charlottesville was the big bad city. She couldn't believe her eyes, just because there were *sidewalks* everywhere. Her ancestors were Appalachians from the hills of West Virginia; both of her grandfathers were coal miners. We had nothing in common, except we both loved music. It was the first connection we had, and we depended on it to keep us together. We did a lot of work to meet in the middle. Music brought us together. So now music was stuck with us.

I was lucky I got to be her guy for a while.

I remember this song. L7, punk-rock girls from L.A., the "Shove" single on Sub Pop. Renée did a Spin *cover story on them, right after she made this tape. She'd never seen California before. The girls in the band took her shopping and picked out some jeans for her.*

When we were married we lived in Charlottesville, in a moldy basement dump that flooded every time it rained. We often drove her creaky 1978 Chrysler LeBaron through the mountains, kicking around junk shops, looking for vinyl records and finding buried treasures on scratched-up 45s for a quarter a pop. She drove me up to the Meadow Muffin on Route 11, outside Stuart's Draft, for the finest banana milkshakes on the planet. Every afternoon, I picked Renée up from work. By night we'd head to Tokyo Rose, the local sushi bar, where bands played in the basement. We went to hear every band that came to town, whether we liked them or not. If we'd waited around for famous, successful, important bands to play Charlottesville, we would have been waiting a long time. Charlottesville was a small town; we had to make our own fun. Renée would primp for the shows, sew herself a new skirt. We knew we would see all of our friends there, including all the rock boys Renée had crushes on. The bassist—always the bassist. I'm six-five, so I would hang in the back with the other tall rock dudes and lean against the wall. Renée was five-two, and she definitely wasn't the type of gal to hang in the back, so she'd dart up front and run around and wag her tail. She made a scene. She would dive right into the crowd and let me just linger behind her, basking in her glow. Any band that was in town, Renée would invite them to crash at our place, even though there wasn't even enough room for us.

Belly? Aaaargh! Renée! Why are you doing this to me? This band blows homeless goats. I can't believe she liked this song enough to tape it.

I get sentimental over the music of the '90s. Deplorable, really. But I love it all. As far as I'm concerned, the '90s was the best era for music ever, even the stuff that I loathed at the time, even the stuff that gave me stomach cramps. Every note from those years is charged with life for me now. For instance, I hated Pearl Jam at the time. I thought they were pompous blowhards. Now, whenever a Pearl Jam song comes on the car radio, I find myself pounding my fist on the dashboard, screaming, "Pearl JAM! Pearl JAM! Now *this* is rock and roll! Jeremy's SPO-ken! But he's still al-LIIIIIIVE!"

I don't recall making the decision to love Pearl Jam. Hating them was a lot more fun.

1991. The year punk broke. The palindrome year. In the *Planet of the Apes* movies, it was the year of the ape revolution, but I'll settle for the 1991 we got. This was the year we got married. We knew it would be a big deal, and it was. The next few years were a rush. It was a glorious time for pop culture, the decade of Nirvana and Lollapalooza and *Clueless* and *My So-Called Life* and *Sassy* and *Pulp Fiction* and Greg Maddux and Garth Brooks and Green Day and Drew and Dre and Snoop and *Wayne's World*. It was the decade Johnny Depp got his *Winona Forever* tattoo, the decade Beavis and Butthead got butt-shaped tattoos on their butts. It was the decade of Kurt Cobain and Shania Twain and Taylor Dayne and Brandy Chastain. The boundaries of American culture were exploding, and music was leading the way.

There was a song Renée and I made up in the car, singing along with the radio.

Out on the road today, I saw a Sub Pop sticker on a Subaru.
A little voice inside my head said, yuppies smell teen spirit too.
I thought I knew what love was, but I was blind.
Those days are gone forever, whatever, never mind.

At the end of the working day, we rubbed each other's feet and sang Pavement songs to each other, and we knew every word was true. . . . I rubbed Lubriderm into her pantyhose burns. The Reagan-Bush nightmare was coming to an end, so close we could taste it. Nirvana was all over the radio. Corporate rock was dead. On *90210*, Dylan and Kelly were making out on the beach to "Damn, I Wish I Was Your Lover." We were young and in love and the world was changing.

When we weren't being students or working lame jobs, we were rock critics, freelancing for the *Village Voice* and *Spin* and *Option*. Our friends in other towns had fanzines, so we wrote for them, too. We were DJs on our local independent radio station, WTJU. Bands that would have been too weird, too feminist, too rough for the mainstream a year earlier suddenly *were* the mainstream, making their noise in public. Our subcultural secrets were out there, in the world, where they belonged. After work, Renée and I would cruise by Plan 9 Records and flip through the vinyl 45s. There was always something new we *had* to hear. We wrote as fast as we could, but still there was more great music out there than we had time to write about. Sometimes we got checks in the mail for writing, so we bought more records. Renée would hunker down over her typewriter and play the same Bratmobile single for hours, flipping it over every two and a half minutes, singing along. . . . Everything was changing, that was obvious. The world was so full of music, it seemed we could never run out. 'Twas bliss in that dawn to be alive, but to be young and overworked and underexposed and stuck in a nowhere town was very heaven. It was our time, the first one we had to ourselves.

It was a smashing time, and then it ended, because that's what times do.

Whitney Houston, "I'm Every Woman." Mmmmm. Whitney was so rad back then. What the hell happened?

Renée left a big mess behind: tapes, records, shoes, sewing patterns, piles of fabric she was planning to turn into skirts and handbags. Fashion mags and rock fanzines she was in the middle of reading. Novels jammed with bookmarks. Drafts of stories all over her desk. Pictures she'd ripped from magazines and taped up on the walls— Nirvana, PJ Harvey, John Travolta, Drew Barrymore, Shalom Harlow, Mo Vaughn. A framed photo of the 1975 Red Sox. A big clay Mexican sun god she brought back from doing the L7 story in L.A. A stuffed pumpkin head from—well, no idea. Nutty things she sewed for herself, mod minidresses from fabric she found with little snow peas or Marilyn Monroe faces all over. She was in the middle of everything, living her big, messy, epic life, and none of us who loved her will ever catch up with her.

Renée loved to *do* things. That was mysterious to me, since I was more comfortable talking about things and never doing them. She liked passion. She liked adventure. I cowered from passion and talked myself out of adventure. Before I met her, I was just another hermit wolfboy, scared of life, hiding in my room with my records and my fanzines. One of Renée's friends asked her, "Does your boyfriend wear glasses?" She said, "No, he wears a Walkman." I was a wallflower who planned to stay that way, who never imagined anybody else to be. Suddenly, I got all tangled up in this girl's noisy, juicy, sparkly life. Without her, I didn't want to do anything, except keep being good at Renée. You know the story about Colonel Tom Parker, after Elvis died? The Colonel said, "Hell, I'll keep right on managing him." That's how I felt. Every tree in the woods, every car that passed me on the road, every song on the radio, all seemed to be Gloria Grahame at the end of *The Big Heat*, asking the same question: "What was your wife like?" It was the only conversation I was interested in.

Our friend Suzle told me her sister didn't understand—she always thought Suzle had one friend named "Robin Renée." How did Robin Renée turn into Rob and Renée, two different people?

The whole world got cheated out of Renée. I got cheated less than anybody, since I got more of her than anybody. But still, I wanted more of her. I wanted to be her guy forever and ever. I always pictured us growing old together, like William Holden and Ernest Borgnine in *The Wild Bunch,* side by side in our sleeping bags, drinking coffee and planning the next payroll heist. We only got five years. On our fifth anniversary, we drove out to Afton Mountain and checked into a motel. We got righteously wasted and blasted David Bowie's "Five Years" over and over. It's a song about how the world is going to end in five years, which forces everybody to seize the freedom to do whatever they want, to act out their craziest desires and devour the moment and not even think about the future.

"Five years!" we screamed in unison. "That's *aaaoooowwwlll* we got!"

It *was* all we got. That was a good night. There were a lot of good nights. We got more of those than we had any right to expect, five years' worth, but I wanted more, anyway.

Another L7 song, "Packin' a Rod." It's a cover of an old L.A. hardcore punk anthem— Renée could have told you who did the original version, but I can't. And already we're at the end of side one. Eject. Flip it.

It's too late to sleep anyway. The coffee's gone cold, so I just heat up another pot. Tonight, I feel like my whole body is made out of memories. I'm a mix tape, a cassette that's been rewound so many times you can hear the fingerprints smudged on the tape.

Press play.

First song, side two: R.E.M.'s "Man on the Moon." Did Renée ever make a mix tape without R.E.M.? A whole generation of southern girls, raised on the promise of Michael Stipe.

I now get scared of forgetting anything about Renée, even the tiniest detail, even the bands on this tape I can't stand—if she touched them, I want to hear her fingerprints. Sometimes, I wake up in the middle of the night, my heart pounding, trying to remember: What was Renée's shoe size? What color were her eyes? What was her birthday, her grandparents' first names, that Willie Nelson song we heard on the radio in Atlanta? The memory comes back, hours or days later. It always comes back. But in the moment, I panic. I'm positive it's gone for good. I'm shaking from that sensation now, trying to remember some of this music. Nothing connects to the moment like music. I count on the music to bring me back—or, more precisely, to bring her forward.

There are some songs on this tape that nobody else on the planet remembers. I guarantee it. Like the Grenadine song "In a World Without Heroes." Grenadine wasn't even a real band—just a goofball side project. As far as we were concerned, though, this was easily the finest pseudo-Bowie limp-wristed fuzz-guitar indie-boy girl-worship ballad of 1992. We never convinced anyone else to agree. Not even our so-called friends would lie to us about this one.

Nobody ever liked it except me and Renée, and now she's gone, which means nobody remembers it. Not even the guy who wrote it. I know that for a fact, because Mark Robinson played a solo show at Tokyo Rose a few years later. When he asked for requests, we screamed for "In a World Without Heroes." He just stared and shook his head. A few songs later, with a little more liquid courage in us, we screamed for it again. He stopped asking for requests. So it's official: *nobody* likes this song.

A song nobody likes is a sad thing. But a love song nobody likes is hardly a thing at all.

Mary Chapin Carpenter. A big country-radio hit at the time. Wasn't she the one who wore leg-warmers?

The country singers understand. It's always that one song that gets you. You can hide, but the song comes to find you. Country singers are always twanging about that number on the jukebox they can't stand to hear you play, the one with the memories. If you're George Jones, it's 4-0-3-3. If you're Olivia Newton-John, it's B-17. If you're Johnny Paycheck, you can't stop yourself from going back to the bar where they play that song over and over, where they have a whole jukebox full of those songs. Johnny Paycheck called it "The Meanest Jukebox in Town."

Gangsters understand, too. In the old gangster movies, you're always running away to a new town, somewhere they won't know your mug shot. You can bury the dirty deeds of your past. Except the song follows you. In *Detour*, it's "I Can't Believe You're in Love with Me." The killer hears it on the truck-stop jukebox, and he realizes there's no escape from the girl. In *Gilda*, it's "Put the Blame on Mame." In *Dark Passage*, it's "Too Marvelous for Words." Barbara Stanwyck in *Clash by Night*, she's so cool and tough and unflappable, until she goes to a bar and gets jumped by a song on the jukebox, "I Hear a Rhapsody." She starts to ramble about a husband who died, and a small town where she used to sell sheet music. She's not so tough now. You can't get away from the meanest jukebox in town.

Pavement again. "Texas Never Whispers." One of our favorites. The tape creaks a little. I know it must be getting near the end.

I've been playing *Rumblefish* all night. By now, I know all the tunes. I'm writing down their titles, so I won't forget. I'm still staring out the window, but the sun won't rise for another couple of hours. The city lights are blinking through the trees of McCarren Park. The house across the street has a stuffed wooden owl whose head spins around every fifteen minutes, which is extremely annoying. The city is full of adventure, just a couple of subway stops away. But I'm not going anywhere.

We met on September 17,1989. We got married on July 13, 1991. We were married for five years and ten months. Renée died on May 11, 1997, very suddenly and unexpectedly, at home with me, of a pulmonary embolism. She was thirty-one. She's buried in Pulaski County, Virginia, on the side of a hill, next to the Wal-Mart.

As soon as Side Two cuts off, right in the middle of a terrible Belly song, I sit there and wait for the final *ca-chunka*. Then I flip the tape and press play again. The first song is Pavement's "Shoot the Singer," which I just heard an hour ago. I have some unfinished business with these tunes. I'm going to be up for a while. Renée's not done with me yet.

Reading the Genre

1. This essay is organized around the songs on a mix tape that the author's late wife had created. How does he comment on each of the songs? How do the song descriptions structure the narrative, allow the author to tell stories, or explain his relationship with his wife? (See Chapter 23, "Organization," p. 340.)

2. This narrative also has an *elegiac* tone—it is written in loving remembrance. What mood does this create for the reader? Can you find a passage that is particularly successful in conveying this mood?

3. This is a personal, reflective narrative. But most importantly, it is a memoir about a relationship. What does Sheffield reveal about himself, what does he reveal about Renée, and what does he reveal about the two of them together? What difficulties does an author face in writing about an intimate relationship?

4. Sheffield creates his own genre of narrative in this essay, by structuring the piece around the songs on his late wife's mix tape. Each song title then becomes a heading, a physical device that makes a transition between sections. (See Chapter 26, "Transitions," p. 350.) In this way, the essay relies on our understanding of the genre of the mix tape itself. What are the qualities and characteristics of a good mix tape (or mix CD, or playlist)? Can a good essay have the same qualities or characteristics as a good music mix?

5. **WRITING:** Create a list of songs that, together and in a particular order, say something about an important time in your life. Title the mix and provide a brief description of the importance of each song. Use quotations from the lyrics of each song to provide examples of the song's meaning to you. Alternatively, you might look through a box of old letters or photographs or reread your e-mail correspondence with someone you've lost touch with, and then write about these materials. (See "Finding and developing materials," p. 12.)

63

Report:
Readings

INFORMATIVE REPORT   Stephanie Armour writes about housing, jobs, and the economy for *USA Today*. This article appeared in February 2009, as the nation was in the middle of a serious economic downturn.

More Families Move in Together During Housing Crisis

Stephanie Armour

Love isn't all that's keeping family together today. The bruising housing market is, too.

Last year, Kanessa Tixe's dad had just finished building a three-family house when he lost his superintendent job in February. He wasn't sure how to make the $5,000-a-month mortgage on the new house in Queens, New York.

So Tixe and her siblings decided to help out in an unusual way: They moved in. In December, her father moved into the first floor; her stepsister and husband moved into the second floor; and her stepbrother and Tixe took the third floor. The entire family has become roommates, banding together to pay rent and help their dad with the mortgage until he finds long-term tenants.

"We're still living there now. Times are rough," says Tixe, 26, a publicist. "It's been very beneficial that we're all together. My stepbrother and I have a wonderful relationship now. We eat together for dinner, and I've become closer to my dad, too. This is an important time for family to help, the way the housing market is going. Our story is a testament to how families should come together to help with a mortgage."

The weak economy—which has brought surging foreclosures, sinking property values, vanishing home equity and mounting job losses—is playing a major role in family dynamics, pulling relatives under the same roof to pool their resources and aid relatives who've lost their homes.

Siblings are moving in with one another to help pay the mortgage. Adult children who've lost homes to foreclosure are moving back home with Mom and Dad. Even spouses in the throes of divorce are putting off separating, living together in awkward cold wars because they can't sell their houses.

That's in large part because those losing homes often have nowhere else to go. Many live paycheck to paycheck: Nearly 61% of local and state homeless coalitions are seeing an increase in homelessness since the foreclosure crisis began in 2007, according to an April 2008 study by the National Coalition for the Homeless. Only 5% said they hadn't seen an increase. The survey found that more than 76% of homeowners and renters who must move because of foreclosures are staying with family and friends.

Many are affected. Foreclosure filings surpassed 3 million in 2008, according to a recent report by RealtyTrac. The report also shows that one in 54 homes received at least one foreclosure filing during the year.

"If you have someone you love, and they're in need, and they come to you and say, 'Can I stay with you awhile?'—of course, you'll say, 'Yes.' But there are risks," says Debra Yergen, author of *Creating Job Security Resource Guide.* "Maybe they have pets, maybe they go out to eat, and that causes friction. There are all kinds of family dynamics. That's not to say it's not worth it, but you have to think it through so that no one feels taken advantage of."

All Ages Losing Homes

More families are living with relatives, based on the most recent statistics available. Nearly 3.5 million brothers or sisters are living in a sibling's house, according to 2007 Census Data, up from 3 million in 2000. And 3.6 million parents live with their adult children, up from 2.3 million. About 6.7 million householders live with other relatives, such as aunts or cousins,

compared with 4.8 million in 2000. That year, the housing market was beginning its boom stretch, which lasted until late 2005.

Some demographic groups are feeling the effects more than others, including younger first-time home buyers who purchased during the housing boom and older Americans hit by job losses and foreclosures who have less time to recover their financial footing. For example:

Seniors. Older Americans who are losing their homes often lack the financial resources to buy another property. At the same time, adult children who had been helping pay for assisted living or other living arrangements for elderly parents are opting to bring their parents into their own homes because they can no longer afford the costs.

"With the financial crunch, many adult children caregivers are having to bring Mom and Dad into their own home instead of the many other options," says Barbara McVicker, author of *Stuck in the Middle: Shared Stories and Tips for Caregiving Your Elderly Parents.* "Money is driving most of the decisions."

Homeowners 50 and older have been significantly affected by the mortgage crisis, according to a 2008 analysis by the AARP. More than 684,000 homeowners 50 and over were delinquent, were in foreclosure, or lost their homes during the six months ended December 2007.

And some family members say they're living with a senior parent because they can't afford a home on their own.

Young adults.   Younger buyers made up a large share of those who bought property during the housing boom. About 40% of home buyers in 2004–05 were first-time buyers, according to the National Association of Realtors.

These buyers are also most likely now to owe more on their homes than they are worth, according to a Moody's Economy .com report on so-called underwater mortgages. Because they are unable to sell their homes, many are trapped in mortgages they can't afford—either because of adjustable-rate mortgages resetting to higher payments or because of recent job losses. So when foreclosures loom, these younger buyers can't just sell to get out of a bind. Instead, a larger number are going through the foreclosure and then moving back in with their parents.

"Many first-time home buyers bought homes they really couldn't afford using some of the riskier loan products (adjustable-rate loans with low teaser rates and 100% financing)," says Rick Sharga, senior vice president of RealtyTrac, in an e-mail. "These homes . . . were still very much overpriced, and the combination of increased mortgage payments and depreciating home values has hit this group of buyers exceptionally hard."

And it's not just twentysomethings anymore: Even middle-age people are moving back in with their parents after a foreclosure.

Colt Phipps, 40, of Scottsdale, Arizona, worked in the mortgage industry until his business failed because of the housing crisis. His home, which was worth nearly $1 million, was foreclosed upon. So Phipps and his fiancée moved in with his parents, going from their 5,000-square-foot house to a 1,400-square-foot house. He also brought his two Shar-Pei dogs along and does what he can to pay rent to help his parents with the mortgage. He is still looking for work, and his fiancée, formerly a loan processor, is now working at Home Depot.

"It's actually brought us closer together," Phipps says. "It's close quarters, but we have weekly meetings to discuss things like budget. We help out with what we can. You learn about what's important, what's really valuable. Things are not real value. It's family and the people you're around."

Divorcing couples.   While hard times can often strain marriages, the housing downturn may be curbing divorces. The American Academy of Matrimonial Lawyers also says it's seeing divorce rates fall.

Overall, 37% of members said they see a decrease in divorce cases, according to a November report. Members responded that they typically see a drop in the number of divorce cases during national economic downturns, while only 19% cited an increase during these challenging times.

That's partly because couples used to be able to divorce and easily sell their homes. But with home sales so anemic, couples are reluctantly staying together until the housing market turns around.

"It takes months and months to sell a home. . . . They can't afford another residence," says Michael Gora, a divorce lawyer in Boca Raton, Florida. "I've had consultations where people even back off of divorce because they realize the desperate financial straits they're in."

The housing market is drawing some families together, but challenges include lifestyle differences, generational differences, depression, money squabbles, and other issues when relatives huddle together for economic relief, says Nicholas Aretakis, a career coach and author of *No More Ramen: The 20-Something's Real World Survival Guide.*

Moving in with relatives can be "demoralizing, humbling, dehumanizing—but a lot of people don't have a lot of choice," Aretakis says.

"You lose that sense of independence, privacy, and self-esteem," he says. "You lose somewhat of your identity."

Reading the Genre

1. This article begins with what journalists call a *lead*—a sentence or phrase that catches the reader's attention: "Love isn't all that's keeping family together today. The bruising housing market is, too." How does this lead create a tone for the article?

2. Armour focuses on the Tixe family to explore the trend she is reporting on. Why do you think she chooses this family? What if she had chosen a different family, for example one from a lower economic bracket? (See "Finding and developing your materials," p. 48.)

3. List the sources that Armour uses for this report, and examine the information that each source provides. How does she show her reader that these sources are reliable? (See "Find reliable sources," p. 42, and "Base reports on the best available sources," p. 48.)

4. **WRITING:** Armour focuses on how the housing crisis has affected the heads-of-household—the people who actually own the homes in question. Think about others who are affected by this crisis, but have not been recognized by Armour: young children, those who might traditionally rent rooms or apartments, even family pets. Investigate the ways that the housing crisis has affected one of these groups, based on research that you conduct yourself.

INFORMATIVE REPORT   Sharon Begley is the science columnist for the *Wall Street Journal* and the author of *Train Your Mind, Change Your Brain: How a New Science Reveals Our Extraordinary Potential to Transform Ourselves* (2007). She also maintains a blog for the *Newsweek* Web site (www.blog.newsweek .com/blogs/labnotes). In this article, first published in *Newsweek*, Begley takes a unique stance. Instead of reporting on global warming and measures to halt it, she focuses on the ways our society has prepared itself to adapt to and live with climate change.

Learning to Love Climate "Adaptation"

It's too late to stop global warming. Now we have to figure out how to survive it.

SHARON BEGLEY

Two words: airport runways. As scientists and policy types figure out what changes will be necessary to cope with global warming, it's obvious that massive sea walls will be required to hold back rising oceans, that enormous new reservoirs will be needed to cope with the alternating droughts and deluges that many regions will suffer, and that a crash program to develop heat- and drought-resistant crops would be a good idea if people are to keep eating. But it's the less-obvious yet no-less-necessary adaptations to climate change that are likely to wreak havoc. So, runways: hotter air, which we'll have more of in a greenhouse world, is less-dense air (hence, hot air rises). In less-dense air, says Bernoulli's principle, for planes to gain lift and stay aloft they need to take off faster. Ergo, airport runways will need to be longer to give planes the requisite ground speed before they're wheels up. Will someone please tell O'Hare?

It's such a polite, unthreatening word: *adapt*. The kind of thing you do as you roll with the punches or keep a stiff upper lip, modifying your behavior to a new situation. But as it will be used in 2008, *adaptation* is a euphemism for widespread, expensive changes that will be needed to cope with climate change. Although some adaptations will be modest and low tech, such as cities' establishing cooling centers to shelter residents during heat waves, others will require such herculean efforts and be so costly that we'll look back on the era beginning in 1988, when credible warnings of climate change reached critical mass, and wonder why we were so stupid as to blow the chance to keep global warming to nothing more extreme than a few more mild days in March.

According to the Intergovernmental Panel on Climate Change (which just picked up its Nobel Peace Prize), we are in for a minimum of 90 more years of warming no matter how many Hummers are junked in favor of Priuses. The reason is both atmospheric (greenhouse gases such as carbon dioxide remain aloft for about a century) and political (the world can't seem to summon the will to reduce greenhouse emissions). We are now at 385 parts per million of carbon dioxide, and there is no way, short of an asteroid impact that sends the world economy back to the Stone Age, to avoid reaching 450 ppm by midcentury, says Jay Gulledge of the Pew Center on Global Climate Change. Unfortunately, the effects of even 385 ppm are worse than forecast. More Arctic sea ice is melting, for instance, and global sea levels are rising faster. "Climate change is with us now, and the rates and impacts are greater than predicted," says Pew's Vicki Arroyo. "We have no choice but to talk about adaptation."

The required adaptations will be much more profound than turning up the air conditioning a notch come summertime. Melting glaciers will trigger "glacier lake outburst floods," warns the IPCC; if you have a child wondering which field to enter, dam engineering and building look like excellent bets. Permafrost is melting, so villages and roads in the (once) frozen north that are built on it will have to be relocated. Sea-level rise is inundating the wetlands and mangrove swamps that once absorbed storm surges; sea-wall design and construction will also be a growth industry, at least in areas that can afford it. For the tens of millions of Bangladeshis and other impoverished people living in coastal regions that will be underwater, inland areas can "adapt" by making room for unprecedented waves of environmental refugees. In a warmer world, the atmosphere holds more moisture. When moist air collides with Arctic air, freezing rain will fall, as it did in the nation's midsection in December, leaving tens of thousands of people without power for more than a week. Let's hope some smart utility engineers are figuring out how to build power lines that don't snap when they've got hundreds of pounds of ice on them.

Already some cities (New York, Seattle) and states (California, Alaska, Maryland, Oregon, Washington) have adaptation plans. Alaska is figuring out how to protect or relocate villages at risk from wave surges or flooding. California is beefing up its firefighting capacity because, in a greenhouse world, more forest fires will rage; it has also proposed desalinization plants for when seawater must substitute for rain that never fell and snowpack that never accumulated. Other locales are requiring new bridges to be built above anticipated storm surges (as for existing bridges, good luck) and developing heat-wave early-warning systems so they can ramp up cooling centers and get the word out to at-risk populations such as the elderly. They are vulnerable for both biological reasons (old bodies have trouble keeping cool) and social ones (they resist leaving their homes).

A trickle of money is beginning to fund such efforts. In August the Rockefeller Foundation announced a $70 million program on "climate-change resilience" to help the developing world in particular cope with what's coming. A climate bill in Congress would take some of the money raised from auctioning off permits to emit carbon dioxide and use it to fund adaptation research and programs (though other proposals would give the permits to industry gratis). Of course, if we do as competent a job adapting to climate change as we've done preventing it, too-short runways will be the least of our problems.

Reading the Genre

1. Reread the first and last sentences of this article. How does Begley grab your attention in the beginning and then drive home her point at the end? How important are these lines to an essay of this length, or to any report? (See Chapter 27, "Introductions," p. 354, and Chapter 28, "Conclusions," p. 359.)

2. What is the tone of this essay? How does the tone make this essay persuasive?

3. Look up the definitions of the terms *irony* and *hyperbole*. Then find lines in Begley's article that are particularly ironic or hyperbolic. How does irony or hyperbole work in a report? (See Chapter 30, "High, Middle, and Low Style," p. 366.)

4. What is the key word in this essay, and how does the author analyze it? How is this word a euphemism—a word or phrase that masks its own real meaning?

5. **WRITING:** Choose a popular euphemism that functions as doublespeak—language constructed to disguise its actual meaning. Example terms might be *right-sized, collateral damage, smart bomb, pre-owned,* or *job flexibility.* Perform a Google News search and report on the most recent and common uses of this euphemism. Then analyze how this term is used and what the use of this term reveals or conceals.

DESCRIPTIVE REPORT   Kelefa Sanneh is a staff writer for the *New Yorker* and a former music critic for the *New York Times*. In 2004, he introduced the term *rockism* to describe the snobbery of many music fans who worship "authentic" rock music and believe that rap music is somehow less sophisticated. In this article, he defends the virtues of New Orleans hip-hop and suggests that we should not be too quick to judge any form of music. He also blends his overview of the musical lineage of New Orleans with an awareness of the social and cultural history of the city, particularly after Hurricane Katrina.

KELEFA SANNEH

New Orleans Hip-Hop Is the Home of Gangsta Gumbo

For thousands of people—we'll probably never know exactly how many—Hurricane Katrina was the end. But for listeners across the country, that not-quite-natural disaster also marked the beginning of a party that hasn't ended yet. Ever since those awful days last year, the country has been celebrating the rich musical heritage of New Orleans.

There was a blitz of benefit concerts, including "From the Big Apple to the Big Easy," a pair of shows held simultaneously at Madison Square Garden and Radio City Music Hall last September. A New Orleans jam session closed the show at the Grammy Awards in February. There have been scads of well-intentioned compilations, including *Our New Orleans: A Benefit Album for the Gulf Coast* (Nonesuch), *Hurricane Relief: Come Together Now* (Concord), and *Higher Ground Hurricane Relief Benefit Concert* (Blue Note), a live album recorded at the Jazz at Lincoln Center Benefit. At the Rock and Roll Hall of Fame induction ceremony last month, a video segment paid tribute to New Orleans music through the years, from Louis Armstrong to the Neville Brothers; there was also the inevitable New Orleans jam session.

But one thing all these tributes have in common is that they all ignored the thrilling—and wildly popular—sound of New Orleans hip-hop, the music that has been the city's true soundtrack through the last few decades.

Rap music remains by far New Orleans's most popular musical export. Lil' Wayne, Master P, Juvenile, Mannie Fresh, B. G., Mystikal, and many other pioneers have sold millions of albums, and they have helped make their city an indispensable part of the hip-hop world. Unlike all the other musicians celebrated at post-Katrina tributes, these ones still show up on the pop charts, often near the top. (Juvenile's most recent album made its debut at No. 1, last month.) Yet when tourists and journalists descend upon the city next weekend, for the New Orleans Jazz and Heritage Festival, they'll find only one local rapper on the schedule: Juvenile, who is to appear on the Congo Square Louisiana Rebirth Stage at 6 p.m. Saturday.

Maybe New Orleans rappers don't mind being left out. No doubt most of them prefer popularity—and its rewards—to respect. But why should they have to choose?

Hip-hop was long considered unfit for polite society. And yet the extraordinary snubbing of New Orleans hip-hop comes at a time when the genre is gaining institutional validation. The Smithsonian Institution's National Museum of American History recently announced plans for a hip-hop exhibit. The Rock and Roll Hall of Fame and Museum exhibited "Roots, Rhyme, and Rage: The Hip-Hop Story" in 1999. Colleges and universities around the country are offering conferences and courses devoted to hip-hop history. At the same time that hip-hop is being written out of the history of New Orleans, it's being written into the history of America. Could that possibly be a coincidence?

The story of New Orleans hip-hop begins in earnest with what is known as bounce music: festive beats, exuberant chants, and simple lyrics that ruled local nightclubs and breezeway parties in the late 1980s and early '90s. The future hip-hop star Juvenile got his start in the bounce-music scene. But like many New Orleans musicians before him, Juvenile found out that having a citywide hit wasn't quite the same as having a nationwide hit.

By the mid-'90s, Southern hip-hop was starting to explode, and so some New Orleans entrepreneurs figured out ways to go national. Master P, a world-class hustler and less-than-world-class rapper from the city's rough Calliope projects, founded a label called No Limit, and used it to popularize a distinctively New Orleans–ish form of hard-boiled hip-hop. For a time Master P was one of pop music's most successful moguls. (He made the cover of *Fortune*, and he never let anyone forget it.)

Master P's crosstown rivals were the Williams brothers, proprietors of Cash Money Records, which eventually replaced No Limit as the city's dominant brand name. Cash Money signed up the hometown hero Juvenile (who was raised in the Magnolia projects), as well as the city's greatest hip-hop producer, Mannie Fresh. Working with a great group of rappers including Lil' Wayne and B. G., Fresh perfected an exuberant electronic sound; he did as much as anyone to pull the musical legacy of New Orleans into the twenty-first century. You could hear brass bands in the synthesizers, drum lines in the rattling beats, Mardi Gras Indians in the sing-song lyrics. (If you're wondering where to start, try Juvenile's head-spinning 1998 blockbuster, *400 Degreez*, which has sold 4.7 million copies.)

Like most musical stories, this one doesn't really have a happy ending—or any ending at all. Master P's empire dissolved, which explains why you might recently have seen him on *Dancing With the Stars*. Mystikal, one of the city's best and weird-est rappers, split with No Limit in 2000, and he's currently serving a jail sentence for sexual battery and tax evasion. Juvenile, B. G., and Mannie Fresh have all left Cash Money, though Lil' Wayne remains.

Then came Katrina. Not all of the city's stars were living in New Orleans when the storm hit, but all lost houses or cars or—at the very least—a hometown. Lil' Wayne moved his mother to Miami; Mannie Fresh set up shop in Los Angeles; B. G. is living in Detroit.

But the music never stopped. Juvenile's "Reality Check" (UTP/Atlantic), released last month, was the fastest-selling CD of his career; for the defiant first single, "Get

Ya Hustle On," he filmed a video in the devastated Lower Ninth Ward. B. G. recently released a strong new album, *The Heart of tha Streetz Vol. 2 (I Am What I Am)* (Koch); it was strong enough, in fact, to earn him a new record contract with Atlantic. In "Move Around," the album's first single, Mannie Fresh sings (sort of) the cheerful refrain: "I'm from the ghetto, homey / I was raised on bread and baloney / You can't come around here, 'cause you're phony."

And then there's Lil' Wayne, who last fall released *Tha Carter 2* (Cash Money/ Universal), perhaps the finest album of his career (it has sold about 900,000 copies so far). In his slick lyrics and raspy voice, you can hear a city's swagger and desperation:

> All I have in this world is a pistol and a promise
> A fistful of dollars
> A list full of problems
> I'll address 'em like P.O. Boxes
> Yeah, I'm from New Orleans, the Creole cockpit
> We so out of it
> Zero tolerance
> Gangsta gumbo—I'll serve 'em a pot of it

All right, so this isn't the stuff that feel-good tributes are made of. Despite the topical video, "Get Ya Hustle On" is a mishmash of political commentary and drug-dealer rhymes. (The song included the well-known couplet, "Everybody tryna get that check from FEMA / So he can go and score him some co-ca-een-uh.") And much of the music portrays New Orleans as a place full of violence and decadence: expensive teeth, cheap women, "choppers" (machine guns) everywhere. If you're trying to celebrate the old, festive, tourist-friendly New Orleans, maybe these aren't the locals you want.

Furthermore, much of the post-Katrina effort has focused on "saving" and "preserving" the city's musical heritage. Clearly top-selling rappers don't need charity. In fact, many have been quietly helping, through gifts to fellow residents and hip-hop charities like David Banner's Heal the Hood Foundation.

But it's worth remembering that many New Orleans hip-hop pioneers—from DJ Jimi to the influential group U.N.L.V.—aren't exactly millionaires. And for that matter, many rappers aren't nearly as rich as they claim. In any case, glowing recollections aren't the only way to pay tribute to the city. The story of Katrina is in large part a story of poverty and neglect; it's no coincidence that many of the rappers come from the same neighborhoods that still haven't been cleaned up. Surely the lyrics to a Juvenile song aren't nearly as shocking as those images most of us saw on television.

The language of preservationism sometimes conceals its own biases. If all the dying traditions are valuable, does that also mean all the valuable traditions are dying? If a genre doesn't need saving, does that also mean it's not worth saving? If New Orleans rappers seem less lovable than, say, Mardi Gras Indians or veteran soul singers, might it be because they're less needy? Cultural philanthropy is drawn to musical pioneers—especially African-American ones—who are old, poor, and humble. What do you do when the pioneers are young, rich, and cocky instead?

Believe it or not, that question brings us back to the Smithsonian, which has come to praise hip-hop. Or to bury it. Or both. The genre is over thirty years old by now, and while its early stars now seem unimpeachable (does anyone have a bad word to say about Grandmaster Flash or Run-DMC?), its current stars seem more impeachable than ever. From 50 Cent to Young Jeezy to, well, Juvenile, hip-hop might be even more controversial now than it was in the '80s; hip-hop culture has been blamed for everything from lousy schools to sexism to the riots in France. In a weird way, that might help account for the newfound respectability of the old school. To an older listener who's aghast at crack rap, the relatively innocent rhymes of Run-DMC don't seem so bad. If the new generation didn't seem so harmful, its predecessors might not seem harmless enough for the national archives.

Maybe the New Orleans hip-hop scene—"gangsta gumbo"—just hasn't been around long enough to make the history books. But that will change, as the rappers start seeming less like harbingers of an ominous future and more like relics of a colorful past. New Orleans hip-hop will endure not just because the music is so thrilling, but also because the rappers vividly evoke a city that is, for worse and (let's not forget) for better, never going to be the same.

After all, long before his name was affixed to an airport, Louis Armstrong, too, seemed manifestly unfit for polite society. Back when he recorded "Muggles," an ode to marijuana, he was a symbol of the so-called "jazz intoxication" that was corrupting an earlier generation the way hip-hop is corrupting this one.

A quarter-century from now, when the social problems that Juvenile and others so discomfitingly rap about have become one more strand of the city's official history, they may find themselves honored in just the kinds of musical tributes and cultural museums that currently shut them out. By then, their careers will probably have cooled off. They'll be less influential, less popular, less controversial; not coincidentally, they'll have a less visceral connection to the youth of New Orleans. And finally, their music—and maybe also their recording studios, their custom jewelry, their promotional posters—will seem to be worth saving. Perhaps, like so many other pop-music traditions, "gangsta gumbo" is a dish best preserved cold.

△

Reading the Genre

1. Sanneh focuses on timing in this report. How does he frame the current moment in New Orleans music by referring to the past and the future? (See "Review what is already known about a subject," p. 45.)

2. Look at how Sanneh defines various musical genres and subgenres. List all the genres and subgenres, and try to connect them. Do you think that Sanneh defines each genre well enough? How else might you define a musical genre to give your audience more information?

3. How does Sanneh explicitly link his story to Hurricane Katrina? Why doesn't this article focus on Hurricane Katrina more?

4. While this article at times honors, defends, and praises New Orleans, how does Sanneh resist making this, in his own words, a "feel-good tribute" or a story with a "happy ending"? Why does he do so? Do you think he makes the right choices as a report writer? (See "Understanding your audience," p. 47, and Chapter 30, "High, Middle, and Low Style," p. 366.)

5. **WRITING:** Choose a city you know well—maybe your hometown or a favorite place you've visited. Look at what this city has produced. Examples include cultural products, such as music or art, or more material products, such as cars or famous blueberry pies. In the style of Sanneh's essay, present a report that helps describe your city by examining its products. Your essay doesn't have to be a tribute or have a happy ending. But it should give the reader a sense of past, present, and future, as well as a picture of this place and its people.

VISUAL REPORT   Sid Jacobson and Ernie Colón have been making comics together for more than forty years, starting their collaboration at Harvey Comics, where they drew popular strips such as *Richie Rich* and *Casper the Friendly Ghost*. The following excerpt comes from their graphic adaptation of the original *9/11 Commission Report*, which was created by a group of ten distinguished lawyers, academics, and politicians and released in 2004. Here is the official definition of that commission and its duties:

> The National Commission on Terrorist Attacks Upon the United States, an independent, bipartisan commission created by congressional legislation and the signature of President George W. Bush in late 2002, is chartered to prepare a full and complete account of the circumstances surrounding the September 11, 2001, terrorist attacks, including preparedness for and the immediate response to the attacks. The Commission is also mandated to provide recommendations designed to guard against future attacks.

In a *Slate* magazine interview about *The 9/11 Report: A Graphic Adaptation*, Ernie Colón admitted that he had been trying to read the full, 585-page *9/11 Commission Report* and found it confusing. So he suggested to his friend Sid Jacobson that they take the report on as a project, and try to illustrate it, because they are "in the business of clarifying things." As you read this report, think about the ways that the illustrators clarify things, and also think about the mandate of the original group of commissioners. How do Jacobson and Colón build on the work of the commission?

From *The 9/11 Report: A Graphic Adaptation*

Sid Jacobson and Ernie Colón

Improvising a Homeland Defense

ON 9/11, THE DEFENSE OF THE UNITED STATES AIRSPACE
DEPENDED ON CLOSE INTERACTION BETWEEN THE FAA
(FEDERAL AVIATION ADMINISTRATION) AND NORAD
(NORTH AMERICAN AEROSPACE DEFENSE COMMAND).

THE FAA WAS MANDATED BY LAW TO REGULATE THE SAFETY
AND SECURITY OF CIVIL AVIATION, WHICH BASICALLY MEANT
MAINTAINING A SAFE DISTANCE BETWEEN AIRBORNE AIRCRAFT.

THERE ARE 22 AIR TRAFFIC CONTROL CENTERS, AND A
SYSTEM COMMAND CENTER IN HERNDON, VIRGINIA.
ON 9/11, THE FOUR HIJACKED AIRCRAFT WERE
MONITORED MAINLY BY THE CENTERS IN BOSTON,
NEW YORK, CLEVELAND, AND INDIANAPOLIS.
EACH CENTER KNEW PART OF WHAT WAS GOING ON,
BUT WHAT ONE KNEW WAS NOT NECESSARILY
KNOWN BY THE OTHERS.

NORAD, A BINATIONAL COMMAND
BETWEEN THE UNITED STATES
AND CANADA, WAS ESTABLISHED IN 1958 TO
DEFEND AND, ORIGINALLY, PROTECT THE
CONTINENT AGAINST SOVIET BOMBERS.
BY THE 1990S, OTHER INTERNAL AND
EXTERNAL THREATS WERE IDENTIFIED,
BUT NORAD WAS SCALED DOWN.
BY 9/11, ITS ONETIME 26 ALERT
SITES HAD BEEN REDUCED TO 7. TWO
WERE PART OF NEADS. THE PROTOCOLS FOR
FAA AND NORAD COLLABORATION REQUIRED
MULTIPLE LEVELS OF NOTIFICATION
AND APPROVAL; THEY WERE
UNSUITED IN EVERY RESPECT FOR
WHAT HAPPENED ON 9/11.

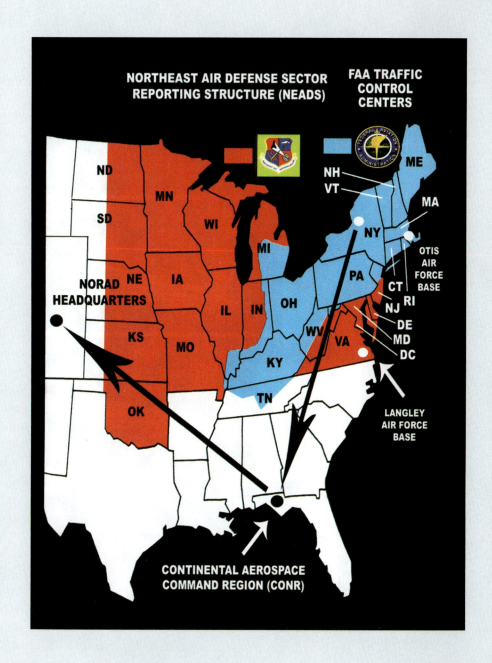

NORTHEAST AIR DEFENSE SECTOR REPORTING STRUCTURE (NEADS)

FAA TRAFFIC CONTROL CENTERS

ND

MN

SD

WI

MI

NORAD HEADQUARTERS

NE

IA

IL

IN

OH

PA

NY

ME

NH

VT

MA

OTIS AIR FORCE BASE

CT

RI

NJ

DE

MD

DC

KS

MO

KY

WV

VA

OK

TN

LANGLEY AIR FORCE BASE

CONTINENTAL AEROSPACE COMMAND REGION (CONR)

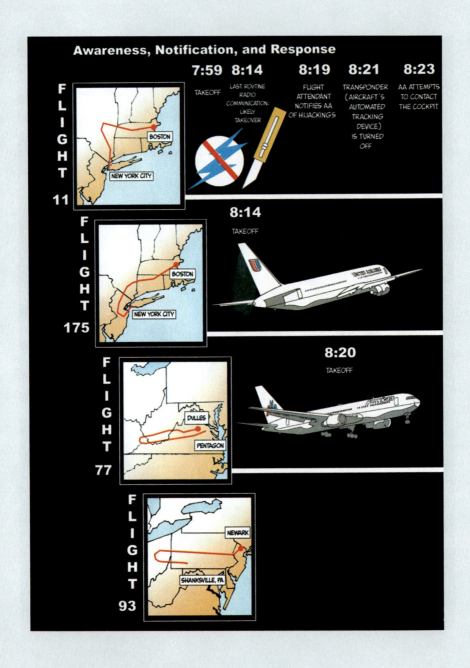

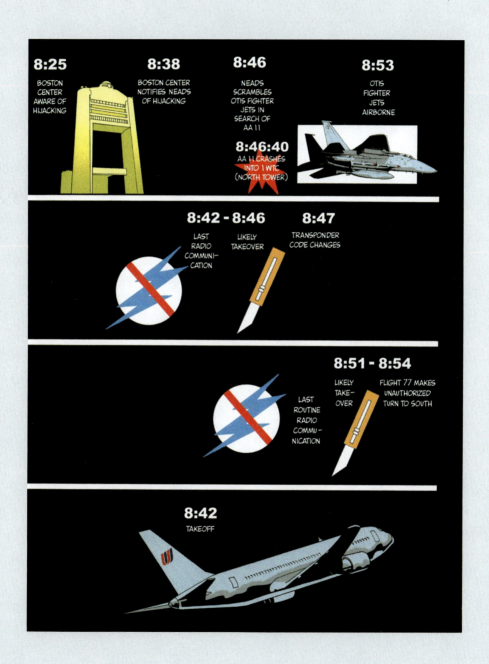

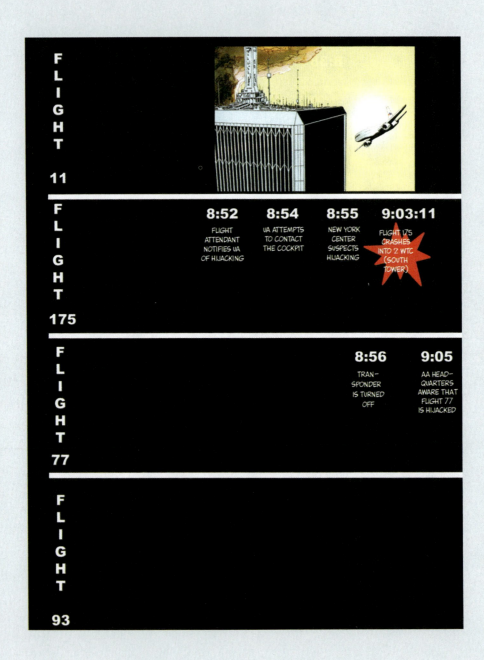

9:16

AA HEADQUARTERS AWARE THAT FLIGHT 11 HAS CRASHED INTO WTC

9:21

BOSTON CENTER ADVISES NEADS THAT AA 11 IS AIRBORNE, HEADING FOR WASHINGTON

9:24

NEADS SCRAMBLES LANGLEY FIGHTER JETS IN SEARCH OF AA 11

9:15

NEW YORK CENTER ADVISES NEADS THAT UA 175 WAS THE SECOND AIRCRAFT THAT CRASHED INTO WTC

9:20

UA HEAD-QUARTERS AWARE THAT FLIGHT 175 HAD CRASHED INTO WTC

9:25

HERNDON COMMAND CENTER ORDERS NATION-WIDE GROUND STOP

9:24

FLIGHT 93 RECEIVES WARNING FROM UA ABOUT THREAT OF POSSIBLE COCKPIT INTRUSION

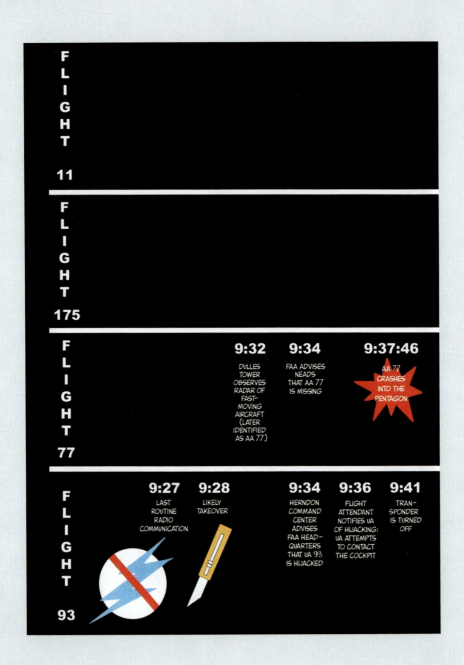

FLIGHT 11

FLIGHT 175

FLIGHT 77

9:32 DULLES TOWER OBSERVES RADAR OF FAST-MOVING AIRCRAFT (LATER IDENTIFIED AS AA 77)

9:34 FAA ADVISES NEADS THAT AA 77 IS MISSING

9:37:46 AA 77 CRASHES INTO THE PENTAGON

FLIGHT 93

9:27 LAST ROUTINE RADIO COMMUNICATION

9:28 LIKELY TAKEOVER

9:34 HERNDON COMMAND CENTER ADVISES FAA HEAD-QUARTERS THAT UA 93 IS HIJACKED

9:36 FLIGHT ATTENDANT NOTIFIES UA OF HIJACKING; UA ATTEMPTS TO CONTACT THE COCKPIT

9:41 TRAN-SPONDER IS TURNED OFF

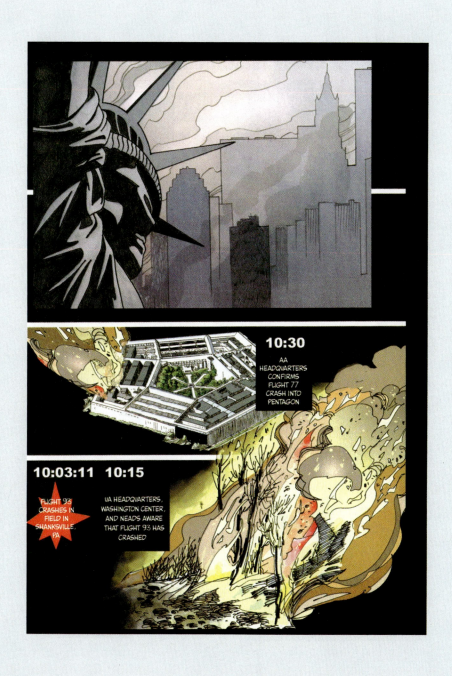

Some of the Commission's Conclusions

ALTHOUGH THE COMMAND CENTER LEARNED FLIGHT 77 WAS MISSING, NEITHER IT NOR THE FAA HEADQUARTERS ISSUED AN ALL POINTS BULLETIN TO SURROUNDING CENTERS TO SEARCH FOR PRIMARY RADAR TARGETS. AMERICAN 77 TRAVELED UNDETECTED FOR 36 MINUTES HEADING DUE EAST FOR WASHINGTON, DC.

UNITED'S FIRST DECISIVE ACTION DID NOT COME UNTIL 9:19, WHEN FLIGHT DISPATCHER ED BALLINGER BEGAN TRANSMITTING WARNINGS TO HIS SIXTEEN TRANSCONTINENTAL FLIGHTS.

WHEN AMERICAN 11 STRUCK THE WORLD TRADE CENTER AT 8:46, NO ONE IN THE WHITE HOUSE OR TRAVELING WITH THE PRESIDENT KNEW THAT IT HAD BEEN HIJACKED. WHILE THAT INFORMATION CIRCULATED WITHIN THE FAA, WE FOUND NO EVIDENCE THAT THE HIJACKING WAS REPORTED TO ANY OTHER AGENCY IN WASHINGTON BEFORE 8:46.

THE AIRLINES FACED AN ESCALATING NUMBER OF CONFLICTING AND ERRONEOUS REPORTS OF OTHER FLIGHTS AS WELL AS A LACK OF VITAL INFORMATION FROM THE FAA ABOUT THE HIJACKED FLIGHTS.

WE FOUND NO EVIDENCE THAT AMERICAN AIRLINES SENT ANY COCKPIT WARNINGS TO ITS AIRCRAFT ON 9/11.

FAA AND **NORAD** WERE UNPREPARED FOR THE TYPE OF ATTACKS LAUNCHED AGAINST THE UNITED STATES ON SEPTEMBER 11, 2001.

BOSTON CENTER DID NOT FOLLOW PROTOCOL IN SEEKING MILITARY ASSISTANCE THROUGH THE PRESCRIBED CHAIN OF COMMAND.

AS IT TURNED OUT, THE **NEADS** AIR DEFENDERS HAD NINE MINUTES' NOTICE ON THE FIRST HIJACKED PLANE AND NO ADVANCE NOTICE ON THE SECOND, THE THIRD, OR THE FOURTH.

NOT UNTIL 9:05 DID BOSTON CENTER CONFIRM FOR BOTH **FAA** AND **NORAD** THAT HIJACKERS ABOARD AMERICAN FLIGHT 11 SAID, "WE HAVE SOME PLANES."

THE CONFLICT DID NOT BEGIN ON 9/11. IT HAD BEEN PUBLICLY DECLARED YEARS EARLIER, MOST NOTABLY IN A DECLARATION FAXED EARLY IN 1998 TO AN ARABIC-LANGUAGE NEWSPAPER IN LONDON BY THE FOLLOWERS OF A SAUDI EXILE GATHERED IN ONE OF THE MOST REMOTE AND IMPOVERISHED COUNTRIES ON EARTH.

Reading the Genre

1. What different forms or genres do Jacobson and Colón use to report on this tragic sequence of events? What are the benefits of using these different forms or genres?

2. How do you think the authors of the original *9/11 Commission Report* gathered their information? What forms of research is the graphic report based on?

3. Look at the ways that this report uses *ethos, pathos,* and *logos.* (See "Consider its use of rhetorical appeals," p. 231.) Find individual images that illustrate each of the appeals. Which picture best exemplifies *pathos*? Which image uses *logos* most effectively? Which image seems to capture the *ethos* of the authors?

4. This graphic adaptation translated a very long printed document into a much shorter visual format. How do the words quoted from the printed document and the images work together? Look at the timeline on pages 626–31, and think about how the creators minimized the writing and maximized the visual elements. In particular, how did the creators emphasize the passing of time and the movement of the planes?

5. **WRITING:**   Though the event is still very prominent in our minds, we are now many years removed from September 11, 2001. Reread the commission's conclusions on page 635, and think about the ways we have responded to and acted on the findings of the *Report*. Prepare a short general report on the ways that we have responded to threats to public security in the United States since 2001.

INFORMATIVE REPORT Deb Aronson is a writer and editor who has published in a wide variety of print and online publications. She writes profiles, features, and essays about science, education, business, family, and, in her own words, "interesting people doing unusual things."

The Nurture of Nature

DEB ARONSON

What if there existed a simple object found in everyday life that could relieve stress and anxiety, promote healing, and increase powers of concentration? It appears likely that such "magic bullets" do exist, and that they come in the forms of trees or shrubs or even philodendrons. Just as plants lift their leaves to the sky, they likewise lift our spirits—helping us de-stress, recover faster, concentrate better, and control impulsive behavior.

Of course, who hasn't felt better after tending their tomato plants or walking in the park? But a growing body of scientific studies suggests even passive contact, like glimpsing nature from the window of a speeding car or looking at a picture of nature, can be as therapeutic as physically being in the midst of it. The bottom line: Nature can provide nurture—for the young, old, healthy, and sick. It can nurture those in a car, a hospital, a dorm room, and even a prison.

Why does nature have this kind of power?

"We have two kinds of attention," says Andrea Faber Taylor, an environmental psychologist and postdoctoral research associate at the University of Illinois, Urbana-Champaign. "Directed attention, which we use when driving or doing our taxes, for example, is effortful and gets tired. When directed attention is fatigued, we feel trashed and it's hard to make good decisions and to inhibit one's impulses."

Faber Taylor says the best way to restore directed attention is by giving it a rest and relying on our second type of attention.

"Involuntary attention is what we use when we stop thinking in an effortful way, like when we watch a fire or meditate," she says. "Looking at nature is soothing and undemanding of our attention. This uses our involuntary attention, enabling directed attention to rest and recover."

Roger Ulrich and his colleagues at Texas A&M University found, for example, that commuters driving along scenic roads recovered more quickly from stressful driving conditions than those who commuted along highways full of billboards, buildings, and parking lots. Beyond that immediate benefit, Ulrich discovered something he called "inoculation" effect: Drivers who had taken the scenic route responded more calmly to stressful situations later on.

Ulrich also looked at patients recovering from gall bladder surgery. He found that those patients who had a view of trees from their hospital bed needed fewer painkillers and had a shorter hospital stay than those whose bedside view was a brick wall.

So, with all our efforts to alleviate stress in our lives—from aerobics and deep breathing to yoga and Zoloft—maybe the key to improved well-being is as simple as a garden. It doesn't even have to be a big garden; even a little bit of green seems to make a big impact. Other studies suggest that having a plant in the room or looking at a picture of nature conveys similar benefits. After viewing a picture of a tree, subjects' physiological measures of stress—increased pulse rate, sweat, and electrical activity under the skin—dropped dramatically within seconds.

"It used to be that we looked at cataclysmic events as stressors, like divorce or loss of a job," says Kathleen Wolf, a research faculty member at the College of Forest Resources, University of Washington. "But now we are seeing that our daily lives have constant small stressors and the cumulative effect is really significant. Consequently, even small, incremental contacts with nature in our daily lives are beneficial."

In a University of Illinois, Urbana-Champaign, study, researchers looked at children living in Chicago's Robert Taylor Homes housing project. In this study, all children were in the same socio-economic bracket; they were all African-American; the layout of their apartments was virtually identical; families were randomly assigned to their apartments; and everyone in the study lived on the second, third, or fourth floors, the most optimal levels for viewing nature. The only difference in the living units was that in some cases the original trees and grass had survived and in others the area outside the complex had been paved.

Girls who could see nature from their windows were better able to concentrate, delay gratification, and control impulsive behavior as measured in standard psychological tests. These behaviors help children resist peer pressure, sexual pressure, or other challenging situations, making them better able to avoid juvenile delinquency and teenage pregnancy.

"Our theory was that public housing is a very fatiguing environment," says Andrea Faber Taylor, lead investigator of the study. "We were wondering if certain settings were more restful than others. It turns out that small amounts of greenery seem to make a big difference. You don't have to be living in Sherwood forests to enjoy nature's benefits."

These studies suggest that our environment can nurture our spirits—even from afar and even without any conscious effort on our part—and that we are all better served with more green spaces rather than fewer. By creating more green spaces, particularly in urban areas, we could minimize or at least buffer the stresses of everyday life and the long-term costs in mental and physical health associated with stress. Now that's a magic bullet.

The jury is still out concerning whether all humans respond so positively to nature or if it varies from culture to culture. Still, one thing is certain: When the naturalist John Burroughs said, "I go to nature to be soothed and healed and to have my senses put in order," he had the right idea.

Reading the Genre

1. Aronson takes a simple question, finds a general answer (which becomes her thesis), and then gathers the most recent research available to support this answer. What is her thesis? (See Chapter 22, "Thesis," p. 336.)

2. How does Aronson's research support this thesis? Create a list of her major sources, and then list the ways that these sources support her thesis. (See Chapter 20, "Experts," p. 325.)

3. Create a skeleton outline for this essay. How does the structure of Aronson's essay make it accessible and easy to read? How does it help readers follow her argument? (See Chapter 24, "Outlines," p. 342.)

4. If Aronson is right, that nature does nurture, then what problems do we face as a society? How does Aronson allude to these problems, and how might we extend the arguments in her essay to better address these problems?

5. **WRITING:** Create a thesis statement that challenges Aronson's thesis. Do some research to try to support this new thesis.

Argument:
Readings

PROFILE   As a writer and editor for *Time* magazine, Nancy Gibbs has written hundreds of feature articles. This essay profiles the athlete and amputee Oscar Pistorius, his quest to compete in the 2008 Beijing Olympics, and the ethical issues raised by his success as a sprinter. Pistorius is sponsored by the prosthetic company Ossur. Learn more about this company and the other athletes it sponsors on its Web site (www.ossur.com), and find videos of Pistorius's races on YouTube.

Cool Running

NANCY GIBBS

It was only a matter of time before the challenge of Oscar Pistorius would run headlong into our cherished notions of what's equal, what's fair, and what's the difference between the two.

Democracy presumes that we're all created equal; competition proves we are not, or else every race would end in a tie. We talk about a level playing field because it's the least we can do in the face of nature's injustice. Some people are born strong or stretchy, or with a tungsten will. But Pistorius's advantage comes from what nature left out and technology replaced: his body ends at the knees, and from there to the ground it's a moral puzzle.

Born in South Africa without major bones in his legs and feet, he had his lower legs amputated before he was a year old. As he grew up, so did the science of prosthetics. Now twenty-one, Pistorius runs on carbon-fiber blades known as Cheetahs. He won gold in the 200 meter at the Athens Paralympics in 2004, breaking 22 seconds; but now his eye is on the Olympics in Beijing. It was up to the world body that governs track and field, the International Association of Athletics Federations (IAAF), to determine whether using Cheetahs is cheating.

A runner's stride is not perfectly efficient. Ankles waste energy—much more, it turns out, than Pistorius's J-shaped blades. He can run just as fast using less oxygen than his competitors (one describes the sound Pistorius makes as like being chased by a giant pair of scissors). On January 14, following the findings of the researcher who evaluated him, the IAAF disqualified Pistorius from Olympic competition. He is expected to appeal, arguing that the science of advantage is not that simple. Tom Hanks is interested in his life story. No matter what happens next, Pistorius is changing the nature of the games we play.

Our intuition tells us there's a difference between innate advantages and acquired ones. A swimmer born with webbed hands might have an edge, but a swimmer who had skin grafts to turn feet into flippers would pose a problem. Elite sport is unkind to the human body; high school linemen bulk up to an extent that may help the team but wreck their knees. What about the tall girl who wants her doctor to prescribe human growth hormone because her coach said three more inches of height would guarantee her that volleyball scholarship: Unfair, or just unwise? Where exactly is the boundary between dedication and deformity?

Imagine if Pistorius's blades made him exactly as biomechanically efficient as a normal runner. What should be the baseline: Normal for the average man? Or for the average Olympian? Cyclist Lance Armstrong was born with a heart

Oscar Pistorius, the South African Paralympic runner.

and lungs that can make a mountain feel flat; he also trained harder than anyone on the planet. Where's the unfair advantage? George Eyser's wooden leg didn't stop him from winning six Olympic gymnastics medals, including in the parallel bars. But that was 1904; legs have improved since then.

The questions are worth asking because in them lies not just the future of our sports but of ourselves. Why should nature be allowed to play favorites but not parents? Science will soon deliver unto us all sorts of novel ways of redesigning our offspring or re-engineering ourselves that test what we mean by human. The fight over doping in baseball will seem quaint one day when players can dope not with drugs but with genes. Already there is black-market interest in therapies developed to treat muscular dystrophy but which could potentially be used to build superstrong athletes.

But there is no honor in shortcuts. Today's dopers are like Rosie Ruiz's winning the marathon in 1980—because she took the subway. Are Pistorius's blades the equivalent of his attaching wheels to his running shoes? "We end up with these subtle, fascinating debates about what the meaning of competition is, and endless debate over where to draw the line," says Tom Murray, president of the Hastings Center, a bioethics think tank. "Don't underestimate how difficult it will be to evaluate all the technologies that are likely to filter into sport."

We honor heroes—in sports as in life—for grace and guts as well as natural gifts. When something comes easily, it's easy not to work at it, like the bright kid who coasts through class: talent taps persistence on the shoulder, says, You're not needed here. But put the two together, Tiger Woods's easy power and ferocious discipline—and he makes history. There's some sweet irony in the fact that before Pistorius came along, there was no need for the rules that now ban him. Only when the disabled runner challenged the able-bodied ones did officials institute a rule against springs and wheels and any artificial aids to running. That's a testimony to technology, but it is also a tribute to the sheer nerve and fierce will that got him to the starting line in the first place.

Reading the Genre

1. Gibbs frequently refers to values in this essay—shared "intuition"; our "honor"; "democracy" and "equality." What impact do these references have? Do you agree with her that most of society shares these values, or does Gibbs just *hope* that we all share these values? (See "Examine your core assumptions," p. 76.)

2. How does Gibbs address her audience? Why do you think she avoids speaking in the first person? (See Chapter 30, "High, Middle, and Low Style," p. 366.)

3. Gibbs poses several hypothetical situations in her essay. Look at each of these situations. How does exploring "what if" scenarios help us better evaluate the real questions raised by Oscar Pistorius's desire to compete in the 2008 Olympics?

4. How does Gibbs represent Oscar Pistorius himself? Do you get a feeling for who he is as a person? How does Gibbs describe his appearance, and how does she tell his story? What might Gibbs do differently in writing about Pistorius?

5. **WRITING:** In a short essay, evaluate the ways that, as in athletics, successful students might have dedication and a work ethic, as well as natural gifts, and perhaps also technological or pharmacological advantages. Where should the line be drawn in our quest for success in school?

ARGUMENT FOR CHANGE   Emily Bazelon is a senior editor at the online magazine *Slate*, where she writes about legal affairs. She takes part in a weekly *Slate* podcast called "The Gabfest," talking about current political issues with colleagues David Plotz and John Dickerson. Bazelon has also written for *The Atlantic, Mother Jones,* and *The Yale Law Journal*. In this essay, Bazelon examines an age-old domestic issue: spanking.

Slate.com

Posted: Thursday, Jan. 25, 2007, at 6:16 PM ET
From: Emily Bazelon

Hitting Bottom: Why America Should Outlaw Spanking

Sally Lieber, the California assemblywoman who proposed a ban on spanking last week, must be sorry she ever opened her mouth. Before Lieber could introduce her bill, a poll showed that only 23 percent of respondents supported it. Some pediatricians disparaged the idea of outlawing spanking, and her fellow politicians called her crazy. Anyone with the slightest libertarian streak seems to believe that outlawing corporal punishment is silly. More government intrusion, and for what—to spare kids a few swats? Or, if you're pro-spanking, a spanking ban represents a sinister effort to take a crucial disciplinary tool out of the hands of good mothers and fathers—and to encourage the sort of permissive parenting that turns kids ratty and rotten.

Why, though, are we so eager to retain the right to hit our kids? Lieber's ban would apply only to children under the age of 4. Little kids may be the most infuriating; they are also the most vulnerable. And if you think that most spanking takes place in a fit of temper—and that banning it would gradually lead more parents to restrain themselves—then the idea of a hard-and-fast rule against it starts to seem not so ridiculous.

The purpose of Lieber's proposal isn't to send parents to jail, or children to foster care, because of a firm smack. Rather, it would make it easier for prosecutors to bring charges for instances of corporal punishment that they think are tantamount to child abuse. Currently, California law (and the law of other states) allows for spanking that is reasonable, age-appropriate, and does not carry a risk of serious injury. That forces judges to referee what's reasonable and what's not. How do they tell? Often, they may resort to looking for signs of injury. If a smack leaves a bruise or causes a fracture, it's illegal. If not, bombs away. In other words, allowing for "reasonable" spanking gives parents a lot of leeway to cause pain.

Who should we worry about more: The well-intentioned parent who smacks a child's bottom and gets hauled off to court, or the kid who keeps getting pounded because the cops can't find a bruise? A U.N. report on violence against children argues that "The de minimis principle—that the law does not concern itself with trivial matters" will keep minor assaults on children out of court, just as it does almost all minor assaults between adults. The U.N. Committee on the Rights of the Child has been urging countries to ban corporal punishment since 1996. The idea is that by making it illegal to hit your kids, countries will make hurting them socially unacceptable.

The United Nations has a lot of converting to do in this part of the world. Its report cites a survey showing that 84 percent of Americans believe that it's "sometimes necessary to discipline a child with a good hard spanking." On this front, we are in the company of the Koreans, 90 percent of whom reported thinking that corporal punishment is "necessary." On the other side of the spanking map are 19 countries that have banned spanking and three others that have partially banned it.

The grandmother of the bunch is Sweden, which passed a law against corporal punishment in 1979. The effects of that ban are cited by advocates on both sides of the spanking debate. Parents almost universally used corporal punishment on Swedish children born in the 1950s; the numbers dropped to 14 percent for kids born in the late 1980s, and only 8 percent of parents reported physically punishing their kids in 2000. Plus, only one child in Sweden died as the result of physical abuse by a parent between 1980 and 1996. Those statistics suggest that making spanking illegal contributes to making it less prevalent and also to making kids safer. On the other hand, reports to police of child abuse soared in the decades after the spanking ban, as did the incidence of juvenile violence. Did reports rise because frustrated, spanking-barred parents lashed out against their kids in other ways, or because the law made people more aware of child abuse? The latter is what occurred in the United States when reports of abuse spiked following the enactment of child-protective laws in the 1970s. Is the rise in kids beating on each other evidence of undisciplined, unruly child mobs, or the result of other unrelated forces? The data don't tell us, so take your pick.

A similar split exists in the American social-science literature. In a 2000 article in the *Clinical Child and Family Psychology Review,* Dr. Robert Larzelere (who approves of spanking if it's "conditional" and not abusive) reviewed 38 studies and found that spanking posed no harm to kids under the age of 7, and reduced misbehavior when deployed alongside milder punishments like scolding and timeouts. By contrast, a 2002 article in *Psychology Bulletin* by Dr. Elizabeth Gershoff (not a spanking fan) reviewed 88 studies and found an association between corporal punishment and a higher level of childhood aggression and a greater risk of physical abuse.

This is the sort of research impasse that leaves advocates free to argue what they will—and parents without much guidance. But one study stands out: An effort by University of California at Berkeley psychologist Diana Baumrind to tease out the effects of occasional spanking compared to frequent spanking and no spanking at all. Baumrind tracked about 100 white, middle-class families in the East Bay area of northern California from 1968 to 1980. The children who were hit frequently were more likely to be maladjusted. The ones who were occasionally spanked had slightly higher misbehavior scores than those who were not spanked at all. But this difference largely disappeared when Baumrind accounted for the children's poor behavior at a younger age. In other words, the kids who acted out as toddlers and preschoolers were more likely to act out later, whether they were spanked occasionally or never. Lots of spanking was bad for kids. A little didn't seem to matter.

Baumrind concluded that it is "*reliance* on physical punishment, not whether it is used at all, that is associated with harm to the child." The italics are mine. While Baumrind's evidence undercuts the abolitionist position, it doesn't justify spanking as a regular punishment. In addition, Baumrind draws a telling distinction between "impulsive and reactive" spanking and punishments that require "some restraint and forethought." In my experience as a very occasional (once or twice) spanker, impulsivity was what hitting my kid was all about. I know that I'm supposed to spank my sons more in sorrow than in anger. But does that really describe most parents, especially occasional spankers, when they raise their hand to their children? More often, I think, we strike kids when we're mad—enraged, in fact. Baumrind's findings suggest that occasional spankers don't need to worry about this much. I hope she's right. But her numbers are small: Only three children in her study weren't spanked at all. That's a tiny control group.

Baumrind argues that if the social-science research doesn't support an outright ban on spanking, then we shouldn't fight over the occasional spank, because it diverts attention from the larger problems of serious abuse and neglect. "Professional advice that categorically rejects any and all use of a disciplinary practice favored and considered functional by parents is more likely to alienate than educate them," she argues. The extremely negative reaction to Lieber's proposed ban is her best proof.

It's always difficult and awkward—and arguably misguided—to use the law as a tool for changing attitudes. In the case of corporal punishment, though, I'm not sure we'd be crazy to try. A hard-and-fast rule like Sweden's would infuriate and frustrate some perfectly loving parents. It would also make it easier for police and prosecutors to go after the really bad ones. The state would have more power over parents. But then parents have near infinite amounts of power over their kids.

Reading the Genre

1. How does Bazelon look at the many arguments against a ban on spanking? How does she address these arguments with her own refutations and arguments for a ban? Do you think that she fairly considers counterarguments? (See "Find counterarguments," p. 82.)

2. Who are the key stakeholders in this debate—that is, whom does spanking directly affect, and who should care most about it? Make a list of people involved in this debate, and rank them according to the impact that spanking has on their lives. How does Bazelon address these different stakeholders in the essay? Does she pay attention to the right people? How could identifying the stakeholders in an issue influence your own argumentative writing?

3. Bazelon uses hard evidence and other forms of research to support her arguments. Make an outline of her use of research: What kinds of research does she cite, what authority does it have, and how exactly does she use it to support her own claims? (See "Assemble your hard evidence," p. 81; Chapter 38, "Evaluating Sources," p. 415; and Chapter 42, "Integrating Sources into Your Work," p. 431.)

4. **WRITING:** Many people find it easy to criticize or second-guess parents. Write a short argument paper that makes a few suggestions to parents about how to best raise children. Keep in mind that your audience of parents might not want your advice, so write accordingly, considering possible counterarguments.

ARGUMENT FOR CHANGE   Clive Thompson writes on science, technology, and culture for the *New York Times Magazine,* and for *Wired* (where the following article first appeared). Thompson also maintains the blog Collision Detection (www.collisiondetection.net), which he says "collects bits of offbeat research" and gets nearly ten thousand readers a day.

Wired.com

Posted: October 23, 2007
From: Clive Thompson

Why Science Will Triumph Only When *Theory* Becomes *Law*

Creationists and intelligent-design boosters have a guerrilla tactic to undermine textbooks that don't jibe with their beliefs. They slap a sticker on the cover that reads, EVOLUTION IS A THEORY, NOT A FACT, REGARDING THE ORIGIN OF LIVING THINGS.

This is the central argument of evolution deniers: Evolution is an unproven "theory." For science-savvy people, this is an incredibly annoying ploy. While it's true that scientists refer to evolution as a *theory,* in science the word *theory* means an explanation of how the world works that has stood up to repeated, rigorous testing. It's hardly a term of disparagement.

But for most people, *theory* means a haphazard guess you've pulled out of your, uh, hat. It's an insult, really, a glib way to dismiss a point of view: "Ah, well, that's just your theory." Scientists use *theory* in one specific way, the public another—and opponents of evolution have expertly exploited this disconnect.

Turns out, the real culture war in science isn't about science at all—it's about language. And to fight this war, we need to change the way we talk about scientific knowledge.

Scientists are already pondering this. Last summer, physicist Helen Quinn sparked a lively debate among her colleagues with an essay for *Physics Today* arguing that scientists are too tentative when they discuss scientific knowledge. They're an inherently cautious bunch, she points out. Even when they're 99 percent certain of a theory, they know there's always the chance that a new discovery could overturn or modify it.

So when scientists talk about well-established bodies of knowledge—particularly in areas like evolution or relativity—they hedge their bets. They say they "believe" something to be true, as in, "We believe that the Jurassic period was characterized by humid tropical weather."

This deliberately nuanced language gets horribly misunderstood and often twisted in public discourse. When the average person hears phrases like "scientists believe," they read it as, "Scientists can't really prove this stuff, but they take it on faith." ("That's just what you believe" is another nifty way to dismiss someone out of hand.)

Of course, antievolution crusaders have figured out that language is the ammunition of culture wars. That's why they use those stickers. They take the intellectual strengths of scientific language—its precision, its carefulness—and wield them as weapons against science itself.

The defense against this: a revamped scientific lexicon. If the antievolutionists insist on exploiting the public's misunderstanding of words like *theory* and *believe*, then we shouldn't fight it. "We need to be a bit less cautious in public when we're talking about scientific conclusions that are generally agreed upon," Quinn says.

What does she suggest? For truly solid-gold, well-established science, let's stop using the word *theory* entirely. Instead, let's revive much more venerable language and refer to such knowledge as "law." As with Newton's law of gravity, people intuitively understand that a law is a rule that holds true and must be obeyed. The word *law* conveys precisely the same sense of authority with the public as *theory* does with scientists, but without the linguistic baggage.

Evolution is supersolid. We even base the vaccine industry on it: When we troop into the doctor's office each winter to get a flu shot—an inoculation against the latest evolved strains of the disease—we're treating evolution as a law. So why not just say "the law of evolution"?

Best of all, it performs a neat bit of linguistic jujitsu. If someone says, "I don't believe in the theory of evolution," they may sound fairly reasonable. But if someone announces, "I don't believe in the law of evolution," they sound insane. It's tantamount to saying, "I don't believe in the law of gravity."

It's time to realize that we're simply never going to school enough of the public in the precise scientific meaning of particular words. We're never going to fully communicate what's beautiful and noble about scientific caution and rigor. Public discourse is inevitably political, so we need to talk about science in a way that wins the political battle—in no uncertain terms.

At least, that's my theory.

Reading the Genre

1. This argument focuses on defining terms, as many arguments do. What are the key words here? How are they redefined in this article?

2. Who is Thompson's audience for this argument? To whom exactly is he referring when he speaks about the "public"? About "scientists"? About "we"? (See "Understanding your audience," p. 77.)

3. When Thompson writes that "science will triumph," what does he want science to triumph over?

4. What types of readers might be offended by this article? How does Thompson speak to these readers? (See Chapter 31, "Inclusive and Culturally Sensitive Style," p. 374.)

5. **WRITING:** How might a scientist argue against Thompson? Write a short defense of *theory*, imagining all the reasons why a scientist might want to defend this term, the scientific method behind it, and the philosophy behind this method. If it helps, imagine that you are an elementary school science teacher, explaining the idea of scientific theory to your students.

ANALYSIS OF CULTURAL VALUE   Poranee Natadecha-Sponsel teaches environmental philosophy, sociology, and religion at Chaminade University of Honolulu, Hawaii, where she focuses on the interconnect-
edness of religion and the environment, or "spiritual ecology." In this essay, Natadecha-Sponsel reflects
on her experiences as a newcomer to American culture.

PORANEE NATADECHA-SPONSEL

The Young, the Rich, and the Famous: Individualism as an American Cultural Value

"Hi, how are you?" "Fine, thank you, and you?" These are greetings that everybody in America hears and says every day—salutations that come ready-made and
packaged just like a hamburger and fries. There is no real expectation for any special
information in response to these greetings. Do not, under any circumstances, take up
anyone's time by responding in depth to the programmed query. What or how you
may feel at the moment is of little, if any, importance. Thai people would immediately
perceive that our concerned American friends are truly interested in our welfare, and
this concern would require polite reciprocation by spelling out the details of our current
condition. We become very disappointed when we have had enough experience in
the United States to learn that we have bored, amused, or even frightened many of
our American acquaintances by taking the greeting "How are you?" so literally. We
were reacting like Thais, but in the American context where salutations have a different meaning, our detailed reactions were inappropriate. In Thai society, a greeting
among acquaintances usually requests specific information about the other person's
condition, such as "Where are you going?" or "Have you eaten?"

    One of the American contexts in which this greeting is most confusing and
ambiguous is at the hospital or clinic. In these sterile and ritualistic settings, I have

always been uncertain exactly how to answer when the doctor or nurse asks "How are you?" If I deliver a packaged answer of "Fine," I wonder if I am telling a lie. After all, I am there in the first place precisely because I am not so fine. Finally, after debating for some time, I asked one nurse how she expected a patient to answer the query "How are you?" But after asking this question, I then wondered if it was rude to do so. However, she looked relieved after I explained to her that people from different cultures have different ways to greet other people and that for me to be asked how I am in the hospital results in awkwardness. Do I simply answer, "Fine, thank you," or do I reveal in accurate detail how I really feel at the moment? My suspicion was verified when the nurse declared that "How are you?" was really no more than a polite greeting and that she didn't expect any answer more elaborate than simply "Fine." However, she told me that some patients do answer her by describing every last ache and pain from which they are suffering.

A significant question that comes to mind is whether the verbal pattern of greetings reflects any social relationship in American culture. The apparently warm and sincere greeting may initially suggest interest in the person, yet the intention and expectations are, to me, quite superficial. For example, most often the person greets you quickly and then walks by to attend to other business without even waiting for your response! This type of greeting is just like a package of American fast food! The person eats the food quickly without enjoying the taste. The convenience is like many other American accoutrements of living such as cars, household appliances, efficient telephones, or simple, systematic, and predictable arrangements of groceries in the supermarket. However, usually when this greeting is delivered, it seems to lack a personal touch and genuine feeling. It is little more than ritualized behavior.

I have noticed that most Americans keep to themselves even at social gatherings. Conversation may revolve around many topics, but little, if anything, is revealed about oneself. Without talking much about oneself and not knowing much about others, social relations seem to remain at an abbreviated superficial level.

How could one know a person without knowing something about him or her? How much does one need to know about a person to really know that person?

After living in this culture for more than a decade, I have learned that there are many topics that should not be mentioned in conversations with American acquaintances or even close friends. One's personal life and one's income are considered to be very private and even taboo topics. Unlike my Thai culture, Americans do not show interest or curiosity by asking such personal questions, especially when one just meets the individual for the first time. Many times I have been embarrassed by my Thai acquaintances who recently arrived at the University of Hawaii and the East-West Center. For instance, one day I was walking on campus with an American friend when we met another Thai woman to whom I had been introduced a few days earlier. The Thai woman came to write her doctoral dissertation at the East-West Center where the American woman worked, so I introduced them to each other. The American woman greeted my Thai companion in Thai language, which so impressed her that she felt immediately at ease. At once, she asked the American woman numerous personal questions such as, How long did you live in Thailand? Why were you there? How long were you married to the Thai man? Why did you divorce him? How long have you been divorced? Are you going to marry a Thai again or an American? How long have you been working here? How much do you earn? The American was stunned. However, she was very patient and more or less answered all those questions as succinctly as she could. I was so uncomfortable that I had to interrupt whenever I could to get her out of the awkward situation in which she had been forced into talking about things she considered personal. For people in Thai society, such questions would be appropriate and not considered too personal, let alone taboo.

The way Americans value their individual privacy continues to impress me. Americans seem to be open and yet there is a contradiction because they are also aloof and secretive. This is reflected in many of their behavior patterns. By Thai standards, the relationship between friends in American society seems to be somewhat superficial. Many Thai students, as well as other Asians, have felt that they could not find genuine friendship with Americans. For example, I met many American classmates who were very helpful and friendly while we were in the same class. We went out, exchanged phone calls, and did the same things as would good friends in Thailand. But those activities stopped suddenly when the semester ended.

Privacy as a component of the American cultural value of individualism is nurtured in the home as children grow up. From birth they are given their own individual, private space, a bedroom separate from that of their parents. American children are taught to become progressively independent, both emotionally and economically, from their family. They learn to help themselves at an early age. In comparison, in Thailand, when parents bring a new baby home from the hospital, it shares the parents' bedroom for two to three years and then shares another bedroom with older siblings of the same sex. Most Thai children do not have their own private room until they finish high school, and some do not have their own room until another sibling moves out, usually when the sibling gets married. In Thailand, there are strong bonds within the extended family. Older siblings regularly help their parents to care for younger ones. In this and other ways, the Thai family emphasizes the interdependence of its members.

I was accustomed to helping Thai babies who fell down to stand up again. Thus, in America when I saw babies fall, it was natural for me to try to help them back on their feet. Once at a summer camp for East-West Center participants, one of the supervisors brought his wife and their ten-month-old son with him. The baby was so cute that many students were playing with him. At one point he was trying to walk and fell, so all the Asian students, males and females, rushed to help him up. Although the father and mother were nearby, they paid no attention to their fallen and crying baby. However, as the students were trying to help and comfort him, the parents told them to leave him alone; he would be all right on his own. The baby did get up and stopped crying without any assistance. Independence is yet another component of the American value of individualism.

Individualism is even reflected in the way Americans prepare, serve, and consume food. In a typical American meal, each person has a separate plate and is not supposed to share or taste food from other people's plates. My Thai friends and I are used to eating Thai style, in which you share food from a big serving dish in the middle of the table. Each person dishes a small amount from the serving dish onto his or her plate and finishes this portion before going on with the next portion of the same or a different serving dish. With the Thai pattern of eating, you regularly reach out to the serving dishes throughout the meal. But this way of eating is not considered appropriate in comparison to the common American practice where each person eats separately from his or her individual plate.

One time my American host, a divorcée who lived alone, invited a Thai girlfriend and myself to an American dinner at her home. When we were reaching out and eating a small portion of one thing at a time in Thai style, we were told to dish everything we wanted onto our plates at one time and that it was not considered polite to reach across the table. The proper American way was to have each kind of food piled up on your plate at once. If we were to eat in the same manner in Thailand, eyebrows would have been raised at the way we piled up food on our plates, and we would have been considered to be eating like pigs, greedy and inconsiderate of others who shared the meal at the table.

Individualism as a pivotal value in American culture is reflected in many other ways. Material wealth is not only a prime status marker in American society but also a guarantee and celebration of individualism—wealth allows the freedom to do almost anything, although usually within the limits of law. The pursuit of material wealth through individual achievement is instilled in Americans from the youngest age. For example, I was surprised to see an affluent American couple, who own a large ranch house and two BMW cars, send their nine-year-old son to deliver newspapers. He has to get up very early each morning to deliver the papers, even on Sunday! During summer vacation, the boy earns additional money by helping in his parents' gift shop from 10 A.M. to 5 P.M. His thirteen-year-old sister often earns money by babysitting, even at night.

In Thailand, only children from poorer families work to earn money to help the household. Middle- and high-income parents do not encourage their children to work until after they have finished their education. They provide economic support in order to free their children to concentrate on and excel in their studies. Beyond the regular schooling, families who can afford it pay for special tutoring as well as training in music, dance, or sports. However, children in low- and middle-income families help their parents with household chores and the care of younger children.

Many American children have been encouraged to get paid for their help around the house. They rarely get any gifts free of obligations. They even have to be good to get Santa's gifts at Christmas! As they grow up, they are conditioned to earn things they want; they learn that "there is no such thing as a free lunch." From an early age, children are taught to become progressively independent economically from their parents. Also, most young people are encouraged to leave home at college age to be on their own. From my viewpoint as a Thai, it seems that American family ties and closeness are not as strong as in Asian families whose children depend on family financial support until joining the work force after college age. Thereafter, it is the children's turn to help support their parents financially.

Modern American society and economy emphasize individualism in other ways. The nuclear family is more common than the extended family, and newlyweds usually establish their own independent household rather than initially living with either the husband's or the wife's parents. Parents and children appear to be close only when the children are very young. Most American parents seem to "lose" their children by the teenage years. They don't seem to belong to each other as closely as do Thai families. Even though I have seen more explicit affectionate expression among American family members than among Asian ones, the close interpersonal spirit seems to be lacking. Grandparents have relatively little to do with the grandchildren on any regular basis, in contrast to the extended family, which is more common in Thailand. The family and society seem to be graded by age to the point that grandparents, parents, and children are separated by generational subcultures that are evidently alienated from one another. Each group "does its own thing." Help and support are usually limited to whatever does not interfere with one's own life. In America, the locus of responsibility is more on the individual than on the family.

In one case I know of, a financially affluent grandmother with Alzheimer's disease is taken care of twenty-four hours a day by hired help in her own home. Her daughter visits and relieves the helper occasionally. The mature granddaughter, who has her own family, rarely visits. Yet they all live in the same neighborhood. However, each lives in a different house, and each is very independent. Although the mother worries about the grandmother, she cannot do much. Her husband also needs her, and she divides her time between him, her daughters and their children, and the grandmother. When the mother needs to go on a trip with her husband, a second hired attendant is required to care for the grandmother temporarily. When I asked why the granddaughter doesn't temporarily care for the grandmother, the reply was that she has her own life, and it would not be fair for the granddaughter to take care of the grandmother, even for a short period of time. Yet I wonder if it is fair for the grandmother to be left out. It seems to me that the value of individualism and its associated independence account for these apparent gaps in family ties and support.

In contrast to American society, in Thailand older parents with a long-term illness are asked to move in with their children and grandchildren if they are not already living with them. The children and grandchildren take turns attending to the grandparent, sometimes with help from live-in maids. Living together in the same house reinforces moral support among the generations within an extended family. The older generation is respected because of the previous economic, social, and moral support for their children and grandchildren. Family relations provide one of the most important contexts for being a "morally good person," which is traditionally the principal concern in the Buddhist society of Thailand.

In America, being young, rich, and/or famous allows one greater freedom and independence and thus promotes the American value of individualism. This is reflected in the mass appeal of major annual television events like the Super Bowl and the Academy Awards. The goal of superachievement is also seen in more mundane ways. For example, many parents encourage their children to take special courses and to work hard to excel in sports as a shortcut to becoming rich and famous. I know one mother who has taken her two sons to tennis classes and tournaments since the boys were six years old, hoping that at least one of them will be a future tennis star like Ivan Lendl. Other parents focus their children on acting, dancing, or musical talent. The children have to devote much time and hard work as well as sacrifice the ordinary activities of youth in order to develop and perform their natural talents and skills in prestigious programs. But those who excel in the sports and entertainment industries can become rich and famous, even at an early age, as for example Madonna, Tom Cruise, and Michael Jackson. Television and other media publicize these celebrities and thereby reinforce the American value of individualism, including personal achievement and financial success.

Although the American cultural values of individualism and the aspiration to become rich and famous have had some influence in Thailand, there is also cultural and religious resistance to these values. Strong social bonds, particularly within the extended family, and the hierarchical structure of the kingdom run counter to individualism. Also, youth gain social recognition through their academic achievement. From the perspective of Theravada Buddhism, which strongly influences Thai culture, aspiring to be rich and famous would be an illustration of greed, and those who have achieved wealth and fame do not celebrate it publicly as much as in American society. Being a good, moral person is paramount, and ideally Buddhists emphasize restraint and moderation.

Beyond talent and skill in the sports and entertainment industries, there are many other ways that young Americans can pursue wealth. Investment is one route. One American friend who is only a sophomore in college has already invested heavily in the stock market to start accumulating wealth. She is just one example of the 1980s trend for youth to be more concerned with their individual finances than with social, political, and environmental issues. With less attention paid to public issues, the expression of individualism seems to be magnified through emphasis on lucrative careers, financial investment, and material consumption—the "Yuppie" phenomenon. This includes new trends in dress, eating, housing (condominiums), and cars (expensive European imports). Likewise, there appears to be less of a long-term commitment to marriage. More young couples are living together without either marriage or plans for future marriage. When such couples decide to get married, prenuptial agreements are made to protect their assets. Traditional values of marriage, family, and sharing appear to be on the decline.

Individualism as one of the dominant values in American culture is expressed in many ways. This value probably stems from the history of the society as a frontier colony of immigrants in search of a better life with independence, freedom, and the opportunity for advancement through personal achievement. However, in the beliefs and customs of any culture there are some disadvantages as well as advantages. Although Thais may admire the achievements and material wealth of American society, there are costs, especially in the value of individualism and associated social phenomena.

Reading the Genre

1. Natadecha-Sponsel, who is originally from Thailand, has lived in the United States for thirty years. What does she notice about America that people who have always lived in America might not notice? How does she get her readers to look more closely at American culture? (See "Understanding your audience," p. 77, and Chapter 31, "Inclusive and Culturally Sensitive Style," p. 374.)

2. How does the author set up her comparison of the United States and other cultures? Does she have an opinion about which culture is better? Is her purpose to help us choose which culture is best? (See "Compare and contrast," p. 114.)

3. Consider what this essay has to offer to both an American reader and a non-American reader. How does Natadecha-Sponsel speak to both audiences?

4. How does Natadecha-Sponsel define the term *individualism*? Consider how she provides examples that illustrate what *individualism* means in America. How does each example help the reader understand what American individualism looks like to her? How does she connect these examples? (See Chapter 26, "Transitions," p. 350.)

5. **WRITING:** Create a "beginner's guide" to culture at your college or university. What would a new student (perhaps a foreign student) have to know to understand the cultural values at your school? Try to write about major cultural values—the big things that students believe in or assume to be inherently true—rather than cultural practices (like partying or studying). Which values would a new student find strange? Why?

ARGUMENT ABOUT A PUBLIC ISSUE　　Naomi Klein, a Canadian journalist, has written several books, including the international best seller *No Logo: Taking Aim at the Brand Bullies* (2000), which became a key text in the antiglobalization movement. The following essay, first published in *The Nation,* explains the thesis of her most recent book, *The Shock Doctrine: The Rise of Disaster Capitalism* (2007): that humanitarian relief, like the military industry, is now governed by the priorities of private profit, not by the priority of people's well-being. A quick search on YouTube will locate a short film based on the book, codirected by Klein and Oscar-nominated director Alfonso Cuarón.

Pay to Be Saved

THE FUTURE OF DISASTER RESPONSE

Naomi Klein

The Red Cross has just announced a new disaster-response partnership with Wal-Mart. When the next hurricane hits, it will be a co-production of Big Aid and Big Box.

This, apparently, is the lesson learned from the government's calamitous response to Hurricane Katrina: Businesses do disaster better.

"It's all going to be private enterprise before it's over," Billy Wagner, emergency management chief for the Florida Keys, currently under hurricane watch for Tropical Storm Ernesto, said in April. "They've got the expertise. They've got the resources."

But before this new consensus goes any further, perhaps it's time to take a look at where the privatization of disaster began, and where it will inevitably lead.

The first step was the government's abdication of its core responsibility to protect the population from disasters. Under the Bush administration, whole sectors of the government, most notably the Department of Homeland Security, have been turned into glorified temp agencies, with essential functions contracted out to private companies. The theory is that entrepreneurs, driven by the profit motive, are always more efficient (please suspend hysterical laughter).

We saw the results in New Orleans one year ago: Washington was frighteningly weak and inept, in part because its emergency management experts had fled to the private sector and its technology and infrastructure had become positively retro. At least by comparison, the private sector looked modern and competent (a *New York*

Times columnist even suggested handing FEMA over to Wal-Mart).

But the honeymoon doesn't last long. "Where has all the money gone?" ask desperate people from Baghdad to New Orleans, from Kabul to tsunami-struck Sri Lanka. One place a great deal of it has gone is into major capital expenditures for these private contractors. Largely under the public radar, billions of taxpayer dollars have been spent on the construction of a privatized disaster-response infrastructure: the Shaw Group's new state-of-the-art Baton Rouge headquarters, Bechtel's battalions of earthmoving equipment, Blackwater USA's 6,000-acre campus in North Carolina (complete with paramilitary training camp and 6,000-foot runway). I call it the Disaster Capitalism Complex. Whatever you might need in a serious crunch, these contractors can provide it: generators, water tanks, cots, port-a-potties, mobile homes, communications systems, helicopters, medicine, men with guns.

This state-within-a-state has been built almost exclusively with money from public contracts, including the training of its staff (overwhelmingly former civil servants, politicians, and soldiers). Yet it is all privately owned; taxpayers have absolutely no control over it or claim to it. So far, that reality hasn't sunk in because when these companies are getting their bills paid by government contracts, the Disaster Capitalism Complex provides its services to the public free of charge.

But here's the catch: The U.S. government is going broke, in no small part thanks to this kind of loony spending. The national debt is $8-trillion; the federal budget deficit is at least $260-billion. That means that sooner rather than later, the contracts are going to dry up. And no one knows this better than the companies themselves. Ralph Sheridan, chief executive of Good Harbor Partners, one of hundreds of new counter-terrorism companies, explains that "expenditures by governments are episodic and come in bubbles." Insiders call it the "homeland security bubble."

When it bursts, firms such as Bechtel, Fluor, and Blackwater will lose their primary revenue stream. They will still have all their high-tech gear giving them the ability to respond to disasters—while the government will have let that precious skill whither away—but now they will rent back the tax-funded infrastructure at whatever price they choose.

Here's a snapshot of what could be in store in the not-too-distant future: helicopter rides off of rooftops in flooded cities ($5,000 a pop, $7,000 for families, pets included), bottled water and "meals ready to eat" ($50 per person, steep, but that's supply and demand), and a cot in a shelter with a portable shower (show us your biometric ID—developed on a lucrative Homeland Security contract—and we'll track you down later with the bill. Don't worry, we have ways: spying has been outsourced too).

The model, of course, is the U.S. healthcare system, in which the wealthy can access best-in-class treatment in spa-like environments while 46-million Americans lack health insurance. As emergency-response, the model is already at work in the global AIDS pandemic: private-sector prowess helped produce lifesaving drugs (with heavy public subsidies), then set prices so high that the vast majority of the world's infected cannot afford treatment.

If that is the corporate world's track record on slow-motion disasters, why should we expect different values to govern fast-moving disasters, like hurricanes or even terrorist attacks? It's worth remembering that as Israeli bombs pummeled Lebanon not so long ago, the U.S. government initially tried to charge its citizens for the cost of their own evacuations. And of course anyone without a Western passport in Lebanon had no hope of rescue.

One year ago, New Orleans's working-class and poor citizens were stranded on their rooftops waiting for help that never came, while those who could pay their way escaped to safety. The country's political leaders claim it was all some terrible mistake, a breakdown in communication that is being fixed. Their solution is to go even further down the catastrophic road of "private-sector solutions."

Unless a radical change of course is demanded, New Orleans will prove to be a glimpse of a dystopic future, a future of disaster apartheid in which the wealthy are saved and everyone else is left behind.

Reading the Genre

1. This essay originally appeared on the opinion page of the *Los Angeles Times*. Opinion sections of newspapers contain several short arguments about current issues like this one every day. How do you think that this length restriction shapes the style, tone, and form of argumentation in this essay?

2. How does Klein use short phrases to describe complex issues and to get her point across? How does she use both phrases of her own invention and phrases coined by others? How do these phrases work in the essay? (See Chapter 30, "High, Middle, and Low Style," p. 366.)

3. This essay presents a vision of the not-so-distant future. How does Klein get and hold our attention? How much of her argument seems like exaggeration, and how much seems logical and real? Does she find a balance between the reality and the nightmare?

4. Consider the timing of this argument. Now that the disastrous events she recounts (including Hurricane Katrina) are further back in the past, do our reactions to her rhetoric change? Should they?

5. **WRITING:** Buy a local newspaper, and find an opinion article that interests you. Then do a Google News or Lexis/Nexis search on the issue discussed in the article, and read a few of the most recent articles on this issue in other newspapers published in the area, across the country, or around the world. Now that you know more about the issue, write a letter to the editor in response to the article. You can agree or disagree with the author, but try to model the form and tone of the letter on similar letters from the opinion pages of your local paper. (See "Consider its use of rhetorical appeals," p. 231.)

ARGUMENT ABOUT THE MEDIA　　Douglas Kellner, a key proponent of "critical media literacy," teaches philosophy at the Graduate School of Education and Information Studies at the University of California, Los Angeles, and has written or cowritten many books. In this essay, Kellner critically examines the career and the media image of Michael Jordan. The questions he asks can be transferred to analyses of other sports and entertainment stars, in order to better understand the contradictions of anyone's media image.

DOUGLAS KELLNER

Contradictions of Michael Jordan

Over the now wide span of a spectacular career, the media figure of Michael Jordan has accumulated highly contradictory representations and effects. Although he was a symbol of making it in the corporate United States, his success record has been patchy since his 1999 retirement, and he has become tarnished with the scandals and negative portrayals of excessive greed, competitiveness, predatory sexuality, and hypocrisy. Earlier, Jordan had embodied the contradictions of capitalist globalization as he was tainted with the negative images with which corporations to whom he had sold himself were fouled, such as Nike's exploitative labor practices, as well as embodying positive images of corporate power and success.

Now Jordan is fated to live out not only the contradictions of corporate global capitalism, but his own moral contradictions and conflicts. In a sense, these contradictions, as well as his array of successes and failures, make Jordan more remarkable, more human, and in many ways a more engaging and more compelling media spectacle. Michael Jordan the all-American mythology was always something of a fraud and an ideological gloss over the seamy side of corporate business, the sports/entertainment colossus, and the inevitable imperfections of a mortal human being. As a bearer of complexity and contradiction, however, Jordan presents the drama of a human life that could evolve in any number of directions, ranging from yet further unforeseen success and greatness to moral abjection and failure.

Although Jordan's contradictions and tensions were somewhat suppressed by his ideological halo, to some extent Jordan always was his own contradictions. The representations of his magical athletic body and his presentation of the body in advertising combined the well-behaved corporate black athlete and endorser with a sexy, powerful, and potentially threatening masculine image. Michael Jordan's combination of athletic prowess and his association with fashion, cologne, and the good life always made him a potential transgressor of bourgeois middle-class family values and propriety. Although Jordan's family values images articulated well with the conservative ethos of the Reagan–Bush I era (1980–92), there was always an aura of threatening sexuality and masculinity in Jordan, who was a potentially transgressive figure.

Moreover, in an era of media spectacle, avaricious and competitive media machines are eager to exploit every scandal and weakness of its stars and celebrities, even those such as Michael Jordan who have provided so much to so many. It is an irony of media spectacle, however, that what appears as scandal and transgression can augment the power and wealth of the bearer of such negativity. Dennis Rodman built a career on his bad-boy image, and Bill Clinton's popularity seemed to go up with every new revelation of scandal and transgression. . . .

Reading Jordan Critically

Jordan thus seems fated to live out the cultural contradictions of contemporary U.S. capitalism and his own personal conflicts, embodying a multifarious mixture of images and mythologies. Since Jordan's spectacle is open and ongoing, and could yield future surprises, critical interrogation of the Jordan effect and of how the media constructs and the public appropriates and lives out the Michael Jordan spectacle emerges as an important challenge for critical cultural studies.

To begin, it could be argued that Jordan represents an overvaluation of sports in contemporary U.S. and indeed global culture. Although it is positive for members of the underclass to have role models and aspirations to better themselves, it is not clear that sports can provide a means to success for any but a few. A revealing 1991 documentary, *Michael Jordan's Playground,* features a fantasy about a young African American boy who, like Michael Jordan, had been cut from his school basketball team. Jordan appears to tell the boy not to give up, to apply himself, and to struggle to make it. The rest of the story interweaves the young boy's hard work with images of Jordan's heroic basketball accomplishments, providing at once a morality tale for youth and a self-glorification of Michael Jordan as role model and teacher of youth as well as basketball deity.

The 1994 Nike-financed PLAY program, in which Jordan participated, provided images of antithesis between gangs and sports, urging youth to choose the latter. But this is arguably a false antithesis, and there are surely other choices for inner-city and poor youth, such as education, learning computer skills, or training for a profession. The 1995 documentary *Hoop Dreams* brilliantly documented the failed hopes and illusory dreams of ghetto youth making it in college basketball and the NBA. For most would-be stars, it is a false hope to dream of fame and athletic glory, thus it is not clear that Jordan's "Be like Mike" is going to be of much real use to youth. Moreover, the widespread limitation of figures from the black spectacle to sports and entertainment might also contribute to the stereotype, as Mercer (1994) suggests, that blacks are all brawn and no brain, or merely spectacular bodies and not substantive persons. Yet some criticism of Jordan as a basketball player has also circulated. Amidst the accolades after his announced retirement, some negative evaluations emerged of his style and influence on the game. Stating baldly, "I hate Michael Jordan," Jonathan Chait wrote:

> Whenever I declare this in public, I am met with stammering disbelief, as if I had expressed my desire to rape nuns. But I have my reasons. First, he has helped to change the culture of sports from one emphasizing teamwork to one emphasizing

individualism. The NBA has contributed to this by promoting superstars ("Come see Charles Barkley take on Hakeem Olajuwan!"), but Jordan buys into it, too. Once he referred to his teammates as his "supporting cast," and in last year's finals he yelled at a teammate for taking a shot in the clutch moments that he, Jordan, should have taken—after his teammate made the shot. The result is a generation of basketball players who don't know or care how to play as a team.

(*Slate,* January 19, 1999)

Chait also complained that Jordan was "the beneficiary of extremely favorable officiating," and that "Jordan has been so spoiled and pampered by his special treatment that he expects a trip to the foul line every time an opponent gets near him, and he whines if he doesn't get it. . . . The prevailing ethic in American sports used to be teamwork, fair play, and rooting for the underdog. Michael Jordan has inverted this ethic."[1]

Others noted that Jordan was so competitive and obsessed with winning that he was downright "predatory"; as teammate Luc Longley put it, "Opposing player Danny Ainge described Jordan as destroying one opponent like 'an assassin who comes to kill you and then cut your heart out.' Jordan, 'skilled at verbal blood sport,' is hard on teammates and harder still, even merciless, in baiting and belittling his nemesis [Chicago Bulls manager], Jerry Krause" (Novak 1999: X3).

Thus, it is important to read the spectacle of Michael Jordan critically for its multifarious social and political meanings, as well as the wealth of meanings generated

---

[1] David Halberstam in his study *Playing for Keeps: Michael Jordan and the World He Made* (1999: 57ff.) notes how the University of North Carolina's basketball team, on which Jordan had his start, embodied the team ethic of playing for the group, while sacrificing individual ambition and showboating, exactly the model that the emergence of superstar icons, such as Jordan, eventually reversed. Chicago sportswriter Sam Smith (1992; 1995) wrote two extremely engaging books about Jordan and the Chicago Bulls which provide demythologizing descriptions of Jordan as highly competitive, often nasty to teammates, and a less than stellar human being. Jordan reportedly called Smith an "asshole" after the first book and never spoke to him again.

by Jordan as sports and race spectacle, and the complexity of his life. Jordan's obsession with wealth, highlighted in Spike Lee's nickname for Jordan ("Money"), circulates capitalist values and ideals, promoting the commercialization of sports and greed, which many claim has despoiled the noble terrain of athletics. Jordan is the prototypical overachiever, pushing to win at all costs with his eyes on all the possible prizes of the rewards of competition and winning. Yet, so far, Jordan has not assumed the political responsibilities taken on by other athletic idols of his race, such as Paul Robeson, Jessie Owens, Joe Louis, Jackie Robinson, or Muhammad Ali.[2] As Touré put it:

> Any cause he might have championed—from something as morally simple as supporting the candidacy of fellow North Carolinian Harvey Gantt, who lost two close Senate races against Satan's cousin, Jesse Helms, to any stand against any sort of American injustice—would have been taken seriously because it was endorsed by Jordan. Yet as careful as he has been at vacuuming every possible penny into his pocket . . . he has been equally diligent about leaving every bit of political potential on the table. Couldn't the world's greatest endorser have sold us something besides shoes?
>
> (*Village Voice*, January 27–February 5, 1999)

Jordan has generally symbolized the decline of politics and replacement of all social values by monetary ones, which has characterized the past couple of decades in which he became a major media spectacle of our era.[3] Such issues are relevant in assessing the Jordan effect because superstar celebrities such as Michael Jordan mobilize desire into specific role models, ideals of behavior and values. They produce an active fantasy life whereby individuals dream that they can "be like Mike,"

---

[2] For a probing comparison of Paul Robeson and Michael Jordan, see Harrison in Andrews (2001).
[3] On the decline of politics in the contemporary era, see Boggs (2000).

to cite the mantra of the Gatorade commercial, and emulate their idol's behavior and values. Thus, part of the "Jordan effect" is the creation of role models, cultural ideals, values, and modes of behavior. Consequently, critical scrutiny of what sort of values and behavior the Jordan spectacle promotes is relevant to assessing its cultural significance.

In the more somber and serious cultural milieu in the United States after the September 11 terrorist attacks, questions arise as to whether so much celebrity and adulation should be invested in sports figures, who themselves are ever more subject to commercialization and commodification, of which Michael Jordan serves as the model. . . .

Understanding how media culture works and generates social meanings and ideologies requires a critical media literacy, which empowers individuals and undermines the mesmerizing and manipulative aspects of the media spectacle (Kellner 1995, 1998). Critical cultural studies are thus necessary to help demystify media culture and produce insights into contemporary society and culture. Reflection on the Jordan–Nike nexus reminds us that media culture is one of the sites of construction of the sports/entertainment colossus and of the icons of contemporary society. Media culture is also the stage on which social conflicts unfold and social reality is constructed, so that the ways in which the dynamics of gender, race, class, nation, and dominant values are played out is crucial for the construction of individuals and society in contemporary culture. Since Michael Jordan embodies the crucial dynamics of media culture, it is important to understand how the Jordan spectacle functions, its manifold and contradictory effects, and the ways in which the Jordan sports/entertainment spectacle embodies social meanings and circulates multiple Jordan effects. As the Michael Jordan adventure is not yet over, his figure remains a source of fascination that should evoke evaluative enquiry by critical cultural studies and social theory.

References

Boggs, C. (2000). *The End of Politics: Corporate Power and the Decline of the Public Sphere.* NY: Guilford Press.

Halberstam, David (1999). *Playing for Keeps: Michael Jordan and the World He Made.* NY: Random House.

Harrison, C. Keith. "From Paul Robeson to Althea Gibson to Michael Jordan: Images of Race Relations and Sport." In David Andrews, *Michael Jordan, Inc.* NY: SUNY Press.

Kellner, Douglas (1995). *Media Culture.* London and New York: Routledge.

Mercer, Kobena (1994). *Welcome to the Jungle: New Positions in Black Cultural Studies.* London and New York: Routledge.

Novak, Robert (1999). "Riding the Air," *Washington Post,* January 31, 1999: X3.

Reading the Genre

1. This essay focuses on contradictions. How does Kellner balance criticism of Michael Jordan against the general admiration that most people seem to have for him? Does the author's balancing of pros and cons provide a model for how you might write an argument for or against a position? (See "Compare and contrast," p. 114.)

2. Kellner critiques documentaries and television commercials featuring Michael Jordan. How does the prominence of Jordan's image compare with how little we hear him speak? If all that we have are *images* of a person, how do we make assumptions about his or her character?

3. This article uses high academic style. Choose some of the key statements in this article and "translate" them into a simpler and more straightforward style. How does this change the essay? (See Chapter 30, "High, Middle, and Low Style," p. 366.)

4. Who is the audience for this essay? How do you think the audience could be broadened? (See "Understanding your audience," p. 77.)

5. **WRITING:** As mentioned in question 2, Kellner critiques images of Jordan, looking at several classic Jordan advertisements. Look at more recent television commercials, featuring Jordan, and see if Kellner's critique still applies. Create your own analysis of these new Jordan ads, citing Kellner's analysis of the classic ads. The old and new commercials should be accessible through YouTube.

65

Evaluation: Readings

PROCESS ANALYSIS   Sasha Frere-Jones is the pop music critic for the *New Yorker,* where this essay originally appeared. He maintains a blog on the *New Yorker* site (www.newyorker.com/online/blogs/ sashafrerejones) and also collects his photographs, writing, and music at www.sashafrerejones.com. This essay examines the emerging industry behind ringtone sales and evaluates the musical integrity of ringtones.

Ring My Bell

The Expensive Pleasures of the Ringtone

SASHA FRERE-JONES

In 1997, your cell phone could make two kinds of sounds. It could "ring"—our anachronistic word for the electronic trill that phones produce when you receive a call—or it could play a single-line melody, like "Für Elise." If you've ever heard a cell phone bleep out Beethoven without the harmony, you'll understand that this wasn't much of a choice. At about this time, Nokia, the Finnish cell-phone company, introduced "smart messaging," a protocol that allowed people to send text messages to one another over their phones, and Vesa-Matti Paananen, a Finnish computer programmer, realized that it would work equally well for transmitting bits of songs. Paananen developed software called Harmonium that enabled people to program their cell phones to make musically complex sequences— melodies with rudimentary harmonic and rhythmic accompaniment—that they could forward to friends using smart messaging.

Those familiar with Linux, the freely available, open-source operating system developed by Linus Torvalds, another Finnish programmer, will not be shocked to learn that Paananen, in a nationally consistent fit of altruism, put Harmonium on the Internet for anyone to download, thus passing up a shot at becoming a billionaire. Companies called aggregators, which collect and distribute digital content, capitalized on Paananen's innovation, using his software to create what is today known as the polyphonic ringtone: a small packet of code that plays the phone as if it were a music box, producing a synthesized approximation of a song that often sounds less like the original it emulates than a gremlin making merry inside a video game. Recently, the polyphonic ringtone acquired a competitor. Called a master tone, or true tone, it is a compressed snippet of actual recorded song, and emanates from the cell-phone handset as if from a tiny radio.

Ringtones of either variety cost about two dollars and are typically no more than twenty-five seconds long. Nevertheless, according to Consect, a marketing and consulting firm in Manhattan, ringtones generated four billion dollars in sales around the world in 2004. The United States accounted for only three hundred million of these dollars, although Consect predicts that the figure will double this year. Fabrice Grinda, the CEO of Zingy, a company in New York that sells ringtones and cell-phone games, told me that in parts of Asia ringtones now outsell some types of CDs. "In 2004, the Korean ringtone market was three hundred and fifty million dollars, while the CD market for singles was just two hundred and fifty million," Grinda said.

But America is catching up. Anyone who watches MTV has probably seen ads for a company called Jamster.com, which sells polyphonic ringtones as well as cruder, monophonic versions for older handsets. For a small fee (about six dollars a month), you can buy ringtones from Jamster by entering numerical codes on your phone's keypad. This method is popular in Europe and is generally faster than the standard American approach: using your phone's Web browser to scroll through pages of song titles. Most companies allow you to sample a tone before you buy it, but not all ringtones are compatible with all cell phones, so don't get too excited if your favorite band is offering ringtones on its Web site. The song snippets may work only on that old phone you gave away to your nephew.

Consect reports that fifty-six percent of the ringtones bought in the United States during the first half of 2004 were hip-hop, and Mark Freiser, Consect's CEO, says that the vast majority of ringtone users are under the age of thirty. Teens like to assign different ringtones to different callers: something classical for Mom, an old hip-hop song for the roommate, a more recent track for the new boy in town. Since teens are fond of both hip-hop and cell phones, and have more friends than parents, it's no wonder that hip-hop ringtones rule. Of course, what's available to customers determines what they'll buy. Marketers in the mobile-media industry call these purchases "preferences." And they are right: ringtones, like the screen savers and plastic face plates that you can use to customize your phone, constitute a form of self-expression, though what you choose to tell the world about yourself is limited by a finite library of images and sounds.

A kid I met on the subway told me that his mother doesn't like his new 50 Cent ringtone, "Candy Shop," not because it features explicitly sexual rhymes but because it's not as cool as "In Da Club," a previous 50 Cent ringtone, which received *Billboard's* first Ringtone of the Year award, in 2004. A karate teacher in his thirties told me that he spends ten dollars a month on ringtones, and currently has about twenty, most of them polyphonic renditions of Led Zeppelin songs. An architect in her mid-thirties said, "I spent three days of productive work time listening to polyphonic ringtone versions of speed metal, trying to find exactly the ringtone that expressed my personality with enough irony and enough coolness that I could live with it going off ten times a day. In a quiet room, in a meeting, this phone's gonna go off—what are they going to hear?"

The ringtone also teaches us how songs work. Which clip best exemplifies a song? Did the ringtone's maker select the right bit? Do you even need to hear the singing? Perhaps the part of the song that arouses our lizard brain is the instrumental opening. It may be stranger and more sublime to hear a polyphonic impression of George Michael's voice than to listen to the real thing one more time. If a song can survive being transposed from live instruments to a cell-phone microchip, it must have musically hardy DNA. Many recent hip-hop songs make terrific ringtones because they already sound like ringtones. The polyphonic and master-tone versions of "Goodies," by Ciara, for example, are nearly identical. Ringtones, it turns out, are inherently pop: musical expression distilled to one urgent, representative hook. As ringtones become part of our environment, they could push pop music toward new levels of concision, repetition, and catchiness.

I spent more than a year sampling polyphonics, but felt stymied by the master tone, which has been trumpeted as superior because it is taken from the original recording. The first master tones I downloaded on my cell phone sounded terrible, like a transistor radio turned up to ten and stuffed inside a sock. I missed my primitive polyphonic tootles. When I finally upgraded to a newer phone, the master tones suddenly made sense. The sock was off and the radio was hi-fi. I felt the way I imagine someone who had a color TV in 1954 must have felt. I was hearing actual music, and I chose Kelis's "Milkshake" as my ringtone, guessing that the song might not be audible above the clangor of the streets but knowing that the alliance would be brief and that I'd soon be switching.

In the United States, master tones can be played only on phones available for the last year and a half, yet they already account for nearly fifty percent of ringtone sales. Musical genres that suffered as polyphonics—sonically thick guitar rock, country, and jazz—can now challenge the hip-hop hegemony. Record labels, convinced that they have lost millions of dollars in CD sales to MP3 file-swapping, have been especially attentive to ringtones, and they love master tones. Polyphonic ringtones are essentially cover versions of songs: aggregators must pay royalties to the publisher, who then pays the songwriter. But master tones are compressed versions of original recordings, which means that record labels—the entities that typically own recordings—are entitled to collect a fee, too.

That fee can be considerable: record labels get twenty-five percent of every master-tone sale (though they must pass along a portion of their take to the performer and the publisher). "It's an unbelievable mess," Les Watkins, the vice-president of Music Reports, Inc., a music-licensing and accounting firm, said. "A lot of these aggregator companies were very early players, essentially beholden to the major record labels and the music publishers to get the rights they needed. And, in this country, the music business is a very mature and consolidated business—somewhat collusive, in fact. The aggregators accepted rates and terms that they really didn't have to accept, and agreed to license the music in such a way that they're overpaying by a tremendous multiple."

This arrangement is unlikely to last. There are now Web-based companies, like Xingtone, for example, that will convert songs from your collection into master tones. Or you can do it yourself: some new cell-phone models can be connected to a computer by a data cable, allowing you to create master tones from MP3 files at home. However it is done, transferring music that you own to your phone is legal under copyright law.

Technically adept fans may thrill at the prospect of being able to make master tones for free. But the demise of the polyphonic will be a minor, and poignant, loss for music. The advent of film sound gave us the infinite blessing of composers like Ennio Morricone and Bernard Herrmann, but it took away the perfect trinity of the oncoming train, the imperilled heroine, and the trembling upper register of an upright piano. Next time you hear your favorite song playing in full verisimilitude from someone's pants, give a moment's thought to the lowly, twinkling polyphonic. Transitional stages of technology often have their own imperfect charms, memorable in ways that no one could have predicted. Polyphonic-ringtone nostalgia is approximately six months away.

Reading the Genre

1. Because the author is evaluating a relatively new technology, he needs to explain how the technology itself works. How does he do so? Are his explanations accessible and understandable? Could the explanations be improved? (See "Understanding your audience," p. 108.)

2. This essay is both a process analysis (looking at *how* ringtones work) and a cultural evaluation. In what ways does Frere-Jones think that ringtones are an expression of culture?

3. This evaluation also focuses on a cultural moment. In what ways should writing about trends (especially technological trends) pay attention to timing? How might an essay on this topic be different in two years? In ten?

4. Frere-Jones makes assertions about the varying function of ring tones and the motivations people have for using them. How important is it to consider function and motivation for any electronic medium—such as e-mail, instant messaging, Facebook, and so on? Do different people have different uses for the same technologies, and different reasons for using them?

5. **WRITING:** Part of the thesis of Frere-Jones's evaluation is that this technology will soon change significantly. In this way, this evaluation is also an argument that predicts what will happen to ringtones in the future. Write an evaluation of a technology that you use every day, but base your evaluation not on what this technology does now, but on what it might be capable of doing in the future.

FILM REVIEW   Stephanie Zacharek is the senior movie critic for Salon.com, where this review first appeared. She writes about film and music for *Entertainment Weekly*, the *Los Angeles Times*, and Salon.com. She has also written theater and book reviews for *New York* magazine and *Rolling Stone*.

Salon.com

Posted: July 10, 2007
From: Stephanie Zacharek

Harry Potter and the Order of the Phoenix

The worst thing you can do when facing the latest installment in the Harry Potter movie franchise is to yearn for the same kind of sturdy poetry J. K. Rowling has given us in the books they're based on. Which isn't to say that we haven't sometimes gotten it: Alfonso Cuarón's dreamily naturalistic 2004 *Harry Potter and the Prisoner of Azkaban* and Mike Newell's moody pastoral 2005 *Harry Potter and the Goblet of Fire* were better movies than we could have hoped for, pictures that easily captured the spirit of the books they were based on. They made the first two pictures in the series, *Harry Potter and the Sorcerer's Stone* and *Harry Potter and the Chamber of Secrets,* both of which were occasionally earnest but mostly dizzy and garish—and both directed by Chris Columbus—seem like distant, easily erased memories.

The fifth movie, David Yates's *Harry Potter and the Order of the Phoenix,* may present the trickiest case of all: This is a gangly, confusing sprawl, and yet there are enough patches of beauty scattered throughout that it's impossible to reject it wholesale. Watching the thing, I couldn't help feeling a pang of sympathy for Yates and his screenwriter, Michael Goldenberg: *Harry Potter and the Order of the Phoenix,* at nearly 900 pages, is the longest of Rowling's books, and streamlining its pleasurably meandering, Dickensian quality couldn't have been easy. Structurally, the picture is jerky and episodic, a jumble of events connected by tenuous threads; after seeing it, those who haven't read the book might be inspired to do so, just so they can be sure of what really happened.

But whatever the overarching problems with *The Order of the Phoenix* may be, many of its scenes are beautifully directed. Yates may be one of those directors who—for now, at least—is better suited to working on a small scale rather than undertaking a massive fantasy epic, especially one with such high expectations attached to it. His previous credits include the 2005 HBO movie *The Girl in the Café,* a quiet, thoughtful little picture starring Bill Nighy and Kelly Macdonald, and Yates brings a similarly delicate touch to this picture as well. Even the movie's grand climax—an operatic, unnerving sequence—includes some lovely special effects that could be viewed as a visual meditation on the nature of glass, and of the universe.

As *The Order of the Phoenix* begins, Harry has endured yet another dreadful summer at the home of his guardians, the Dursleys (once again played by Fiona Shaw and Richard Griffiths). As always, he's counting the days until he can return to Hogwarts—this will be his fifth year. But this summer has been particularly difficult: He hasn't heard from his closest friends, Ron Weasley (Rupert Grint) and Hermione Granger (Emma Watson), and the sting of that is intensified by the fact that at the end of the previous school year, he'd survived a horrifying confrontation with Lord Voldemort (Ralph Fiennes), which resulted in the death of a fellow student. Harry is sullen and dejected; he feels he deserves more sympathy than he's getting.

Worse yet, just before the school year is to begin, Harry is hauled into court for practicing magic in the Muggle world: As a defensive measure, he'd summoned his patronus (a powerful and protective spirit creature, particular to each witch or wizard) to dispatch a pack of Dementors who'd threatened to suck the spirit from his fat, lazy cousin Dudley (Harry Melling). The Minister of Magic, Cornelius Fudge (Robert Hardy), wants to see Harry expelled; he also refuses to believe that the long-exiled Voldemort is really set to return. Dumbledore (Michael Gambon) comes to Harry's defense but is also strangely distant with him, which further increases Harry's feelings of confusion and isolation.

Harry does get back into Hogwarts, but that early stumbling block is only the beginning of his trials. The biggest danger comes in the form of a beaming, nonsense-spouting little fireplug dressed in a series of pink bouclé Queen Mum–style outfits: The new Defense Against the Dark Arts teacher, Dolores Umbridge (Imelda Staunton), not only refuses to provide her charges with usable, practical information, which inherently puts them in danger; she has also been installed to keep Harry in line, and to curb his outspokenness. To that end, she drags him into detention, during which he must scratch out on a piece of paper, with an inkless pen, the line "I will not tell lies." The words appear not on the paper, but etched into his skin, his own blood seeping through the curlicued, cursive wounds of his own careful penmanship.

Harry Potter and the Goblet of Fire riffed on the bittersweetness of leaving childhood behind; *Harry Potter and the Order of the Phoenix* is a punk shout, a reflection of teenage rebellion and frustration. The finest moments of *The Order of the Phoenix* are the ones in

A still from *Harry Potter and the Order of the Phoenix*.

which Harry and his friends and fellow students band together to help *themselves*—to reject the complacent ideals of the establishment, as they're reflected in the mincing, insidious Dolores Umbridge, and to jump-start their own world—their own adult lives—by harnessing the energy and idealism of youth. Yates grasps the countercultural vibe of Rowling's book, and, as she does, he makes sure it feels modern and vital instead of like some musty fantasy imitation of Woodstock. Led by Harry, the students gather surreptitiously to try to summon their own patronuses—or should that be *patroni?*—and after many false starts, some of them do. One of the most wonderful new characters, a nearly translucent white-haired waif named Luna Lovegood (she's played, with eerie sure-footedness, by Evanna Lynch), delights when a prancing rabbit, made of sparks of light, leaps from her wand. The sequence is beautifully shaped, dazzling and alive.

Yates clearly has a knack for working with actors: He stages Harry's first kiss (the girl is Cho, played by Katie Leung, whom Harry has long had a crush on) very delicately, and without a whiff of sentimentality. Later, Yates brings that same casual touch to a scene in which Harry tries to describe the kiss to Ron and Hermione, only to find that words can't touch it. Hermione attempts to explain the rush of emotions that Cho must have felt—all intensified by the fact that her boyfriend, Cedric, was killed the previous year—while Ron listens, slack-jawed, and replies, in a moment that captures perfectly the cluelessness of young males of the species, "One person couldn't feel all that!"

The young actors here are by now so comfortable in their roles that they could practically sleepwalk through them. Thankfully, they don't: One of the pleasures of the Harry Potter movies, as uneven as they've been, is that of watching Radcliffe, Watson, and Grint grow up, both as people and as actors. One problem inherent in the series is that characters we came to love in the earlier books and movies must recede to make way for the new ones. That means Gary Oldman's Sirius Black appears in only a few scenes here, but once again, he's wonderful. (With his curly locks and velvet officer's coat, he looks like a denizen of Glastonbury, circa 1971.)

And Staunton's Umbridge, with her smug little smile and matronly deportment, is frighteningly perfect. The movie's costume and production design serve her well, too: In her sensible, square-heeled shoes and pink Welsh capes circa 1975, she's the essence of dowdy propriety. And in one of the movie's wittiest visual touches, her office walls are covered with dozens of porcelain plates, each adorned with a purring, mewing, wriggling, soft-focus kitten—a marvelous bit of shorthand for the cozy oppressiveness of cutesy decor.

There's plenty to look at in *Harry Potter and the Order of the Phoenix,* and while this isn't the prettiest Harry Potter movie, cinematographer Slawomir Idziak always prevents it from appearing overdone or gaudy. (Idziak shot Ridley Scott's *Black Hawk Down* and also collaborated with the late Krzysztof Kieslowski on nearly a dozen films.) The most frustrating thing about the picture is that in packing so much information and so many events into a very tight framework, Yates and Goldenberg lose the flow of the story. The picture desperately needs some fluidity. Even so, *The Order of the Phoenix* is an honorable movie, one that struggles to stay true to Rowling's intention and her tone. As a whole, it may not be as lyrical as we fans of Rowling's books might wish. But Yates at least gives us poetry in individual stanzas. And sometimes, just a few good lines are enough to carry you through a poem.

Reading the Genre

1. What are the challenges of writing a review of a film from a famous series like the Harry Potter movies, when there have been hundreds of other reviews written, when many readers already know the films and have formed opinions of them, and when each previous movie in the series has also been heavily reviewed? In what ways would this sort of review be *easier* to write?

2. What are the challenges of writing a review of a movie based on a famous book? In what ways might this review be *easier* to write because there is also a popular book? (See "Compare and Contrast," p. 114.)

3. A book reviewer discusses the author of the book, but who is responsible for a finished film? Making a movie is a complex collaboration among the screenwriter, director, cinematographer, and actors, as well as the author of the book, if the screenplay is an adaptation. How does Zacharek address this collaboration? How would you divide up who gets credit (or blame) for different aspects of a film?

4. **WRITING:** There are many online reviews of the Harry Potter movies. (See Chapter 36, "Finding Print and Online Sources," p. 406.) In a small group, look at reviews for two or more of these movies. Summarize the key points reviewers make about each film, and then create a chart tracing the changes in critical response between the movies. (See Chapter 40, "Summarizing Sources," p. 424.) Try to track any changes in how the films are received and reviewed, rather than changes in plot or character development. Individually or as a group, write a review of the entire franchise of Harry Potter movies, discussing how the movies have been received and reviewed since the first film in 2001.

TELEVISION REVIEW   David Bianculli, a frequent contributor to the National Public Radio radio show *Fresh Air*, served as the television critic for the *New York Daily News* for many years. He is the author of *Teleliteracy: Taking Television Seriously* (2000) and *The Dictionary of Teleliteracy* (1995), and maintains his own online magazine, *TVWorthWatching.com*. In this essay, Bianculli evaluates the humor of comedian Stephen Colbert and appraises his campaign to run for president in 2008.

Comedy Rambo

A GLADIATOR OF MOCKERY, STEPHEN COLBERT IS DISMANTLING AMERICAN SOCIETY FROM THE INSIDE

David Bianculli

Misunderestimate Stephen Colbert at your peril. Just because he is an unassuming, bespectacled physical specimen whose business cards may read "TV comedian" is no reason to dismiss him as a lightweight funnyman. Since the very night he launched his own series on Comedy Central in 2005, Colbert has thrown some vicious elbows, and demonstrated a bravura that dares his enemies to, in paraphrasing his ironic hero George W. Bush, bring it on.

As both a humorist and a political and media commentator, Colbert is a stealth bomber. A gladiator of mockery. A comedy Rambo. He's the most dangerous satirist out there right now, and neither the writers' strike nor his failure to get on the presidential-primary ballot in his native state of South Carolina will stall his advance for long.

In fact, Colbert has reached such revered status at this juncture that even in a period of relative inactivity—*not* doing a show, *not* running for president—people are talking about him, wondering about him, and waiting for his next move. He's the Al Gore of Comedy Central: even if he can't or won't run for office, he is nevertheless building anticipation. (Can a Nobel Prize be far off?)

And, like Gore, he knows it. The question is, now that he knows he has the public's attention and the media transfixed, where will he strike next? Or is not striking, and laying back, the smarter play? Colbert is nothing if not smart, and that's why you have to watch him—even if, at least right now on TV, you *can't*.

He's dangerous not only because his wit is so sharp, but because, in a clearly defined Red State–Blue State landscape,

he unpredictably cuts both ways. When he broke his wrist in July before a show taping, Colbert turned it into a satiric opportunity by starting a campaign against "wrist violence." He started wearing and distributing what he called a "WristStrong bracelet," a red plastic oval similar to—and gently poking fun at—Lance Armstrong's cancer-fighting yellow LiveStrong bracelets and the breast-cancer-awareness pink bracelets. He got Katie Couric of CBS and Brian Williams of NBC to wear one, then generated a comic mini-scandal when ABC's Charles Gibson *wouldn't*.

Poking fun at cancer awareness and liberal charities? Who *is* this guy? But then, after spending months collecting signatures on his cast—not only those of Couric and Williams, but of Bill O'Reilly, Tim Russert, Nancy Pelosi, and others—Colbert auctioned it on eBay in September. It sold for $17,200, and the proceeds went to returning war veterans.

He attacked Barry Manilow for winning the Emmy in a category in which Colbert was competing, then had him on *The Colbert Report* to sing a peace-pipe duet. He attacked Willie Nelson for having a rival flavor of Ben & Jerry's ice cream, then challenged him to a taste-off. Attack, then embrace—the strategy seems playful, even harmless, especially when the targets are cute-and-cuddly pop-culture figures. But other times, when he's embracing, he's really attacking—as when he visited *The O'Reilly Factor* or stood behind a podium to address the Washington press corps.

And it's in the political arena that he's made his most bruising forays—his latest broadside coming in the form of that ultimately unsuccessful run for the presidency of the United States. It was the briefest of campaigns: he announced his candidacy on the October 16 edition of *The Colbert Report* and was thwarted November 1, when he was denied a spot on the official South Carolina ballot. But for those two weeks, the attention given to Colbert—by a bored press corps, to be sure—more than proved one of the points he surely set out to make.

When Colbert announced his intention to run for president as both a Republican and a Democrat, Russert devoted a dozen or so minutes of NBC's *Meet the Press* to an interview with the wannabe candidate. Russert didn't come off well in that encounter, but Colbert, a Second City improv vet, did. Colbert explained, quite nakedly, that he didn't want to *be* president of the United States. He just wanted to *run* for it.

"There's a difference," he told Russert. Comprehending that difference—and I'm not convinced Russert did—is the key to understanding whom, what, why, and how Colbert is attacking with his insidious and seditious comedy.

Cultural Fifth Columnist

The Colbert Report, spun off from *The Daily Show with Jon Stewart* in October 2005, hit the ground running with perfect pitch, and perfect pitches. So much so that, in the first installment of Colbert's new show's signature bit, The WØRD, he coined a slippery concept called "truthiness." That ended up being voted Merriam-Webster's number-one word of the year—not bad for the first effort out of the gate. And it was also indicative of the range of targets that Colbert would put in his sights, everything from the language we use every day to the vapidity and self-congratulatory air of pundit-based news shows (and pundits).

The program itself, from the very start, has utilized a three-pronged attack.

First, there is the "Stephen Colbert" persona, a pompous know-it-all—opinion-it-all, actually, would be closer, since facts rarely get in the way—styled quite obviously, and hilariously, on Fox News Channel personality and pundit O'Reilly.

Second, there's the show's visual look, again emulating *The O'Reilly Factor,* from the dumbed-down graphics (host on the left, talking points on the right) to the flag-colored, flagrantly "patriotic" set. This manages to skewer O'Reilly specifically while also poking fun at almost every political talk show on television.

Third, there's the way in which Colbert, in character, dispenses his opinions and interacts with his guests. Conservatives suspect he mocks them, but come on his show or invite him into their lairs anyway—partly because they covet the young and loyal audience he attracts, and partly because they like some of what he says, even if they're almost certain he's delivering it satirically. Liberals come on his show because they're certain he's one of them—until, many times, he deflates *them*, just as skillfully and gleefully.

"Keep your friends close and your enemies closer," goes the advice in *The Godfather*. Colbert advances that a step by adding, in essence, ". . . and never let them know which is which."

Jon Stewart, Colbert's mentor and chief benefactor in this "fake news," question-all-sides approach, blazed the trail that Colbert now follows: build a loyal consistency via a sarcastic, intelligent TV show. Leverage your popularity by expanding your reach, but not to cinema (the usual platform—often an elephant's graveyard—for ambitious TV shows looking for spin-offs), rather to the book world (a thinking-person's medium). Use your TV platform to attract some newsmakers and blitzkrieg others. And when other TV hosts, hungry for a taste of your savvy young audience, invite you on their shows, only appear on the ones you like least—and then attack, and make them look foolish on their home court.

Stewart did it with *America (The Book)*, a fake textbook banned by Wal-Mart, by deconstructing politics and media on his *Daily Show*, and by eviscerating Tucker Carlson on CNN's *Crossfire*. A few years later, and Colbert, like Stewart, has his own nightly TV platform, a best-selling book—his *I Am America (And So Can You!)* just topped the *New York Times* nonfiction best-seller list for the fourth straight week—and his own colorful history of toying with targets, like a wolf in sheep's clothing, then pouncing.

Colbert's first infamous triumph in this regard came at the 2006 White House Correspondents' Dinner, with President Bush and the First Lady on the dais.

"To sit here at the same table with my hero, George W. Bush . . . somebody pinch me," Colbert told the crowd. Then, explaining that a pinch might not be enough to wake him from his dream, Colbert alluded to Vice-President Dick Cheney's recent hunting mishap by asking, "Somebody shoot me in the face." That was just for starters.

Colbert then took aim, as if brandishing a bazooka of his own, at the president, members of his cabinet, other branches of government, and, just as ruthlessly, the press corps itself. In the room that night, Colbert was met with a lot of stares and silence—but he wasn't playing to these smug inside-the-beltway news veterans. He was playing to a wider audience, the one that, like him, suspected that Washington reporters had gotten too cozy and self-satisfied, and deserved to be ridiculed, if not scolded, for their part in lowering the level of national political discourse. He reached that audience very effectively: just the clip of President Bush's isolated-camera reactions as Colbert spoke has been viewed on YouTube more than one million times.

Colbert has utilized this stealth-attack approach time and again. He's a sort of cultural fifth columnist, attacking venerated aspects of American society from the inside. He'll tackle things for laughs, sure, because that's what comedians do. But he also makes larger points about the absurdity of our blind devotion to processes and products, from the Electoral College to Wikipedia. Instead of just delivering a rant about the questionable veracity of the entries on the communal Web reference Wikipedia, Colbert used part of one show to demonstrate a devastating stunt, actually logging onto the free encyclopedia and knowingly adding incorrect information, while urging his viewers to do the same. The topic: elephants. The claim: their population had tripled in three months. The result: more than 20 articles appended with false information before Wikipedia shut down the prank.

The point, however, had been made, and Colbert had a new WØRD to coin: an agreed-upon concept of truth, known as "Wikiality."

Similarly, Colbert managed to go on O'Reilly's show, and have O'Reilly guest on his, and come out as the clear winner both times. O'Reilly made the same mistake, as host, that Russert did this past month on *Meet the Press*—trying to be mock funny, and a good sport, while still playing the role of tough inquisitor. The non-issue issue that both O'Reilly on Fox and Russert on NBC thus tried to zero in on with Colbert was the affected, later-in-life appropriation of the pronunciation Coal-BEAR as his last name. (He was born Stephen Colbert, with the last syllable of his last name rhyming with "dirt.")

And thus, both O'Reilly and Russert looked silly, huffing and puffing at a straw target that refused to be blown away. Instead, they proved the point Colbert most wanted to hammer home—that just as he was "playing" Stephen Colbert the pontificating TV host, they were playing their roles, as well. And by surrendering valuable television time to Colbert, they were playing it somewhat irresponsibly.

And in playing the irrepressibly obsequious grasshopper to O'Reilly's (unknowing) master, Colbert makes it awfully difficult for O'Reilly to hit back. "You know what I hate about people who criticize you?" Colbert asked O'Reilly one night on *The O'Reilly Factor*. "They criticize what you say, but they never give you credit for how *loud* you say it, or how *long* you say it."

Door-to-Door Mockery

Colbert can, and does, bait liberals just as often, and just as boldly. When Jane Fonda and Gloria Steinem visited *The Colbert Report* to promote a new radio-talk network for women, Colbert ushered them to a cooking set, where they could continue to chat—while making and baking a pie. The name of the segment? "Cooking with Feminists." He even wore a "Kiss the Cook" apron—though Fonda got the better of him, finally, by taking the apron's advice to heart and kissing him, which left him smiling and uncharacteristically speechless. Fonda, sensing a weakness, explored and exploited it upon her next *Colbert Report* visit, immediately crossing from her side of the table to pounce on Colbert (as a good cougar would) and spend the entire interview on his lap, kissing and nuzzling him into near incoherence. Score one for the feminists, and for the validity of that old 1960s strategy, "Make love, not war." (All that and more, by the way, is available on the new *Best of The Colbert Report* DVD from Comedy Central.)

Colbert isn't often flustered, however. Whether he's eviscerating congresspersons—and their constituencies—in his ongoing 435-part series Better Know a District (most famous victim: Democratic Florida congressman Robert Wexler, whom Colbert jokingly corralled into saying, "I enjoy cocaine because it's a fun thing to do") or announcing his on-its-face ludicrous run for the presidency, Colbert usually is entertaining with one hand and slapping his chosen subject with the other.

He's not deterred easily, either. Running for president of the United States is hard enough, especially when you aren't allowed on the ballot of the one state to which you applied—and harder still when your very pulpit, a post-prime-time cable TV show, is stopped cold by a Hollywood writers' strike. Yet at each step, Colbert got his laughs, and made his points.

The night Colbert announced his candidacy on his own show, he lampooned the pompous ritual politicians often undergo by preceding his announcement to "run" with the revelation that, "after nearly 15 minutes of soul-searching, I have heard the call."

After South Carolina rebuffed his efforts to get on the official ballot, Colbert sent out an official statement in lieu of granting interviews: "I am shocked and saddened by the South Carolina Democratic Executive Council's 13-to-3 vote to keep me off their presidential-primary ballot," he said. "Although I lost by the slimmest margin in presidential election history—only 10 votes—I have chosen not to put the country through another agonizing Supreme Court battle. It is time for this nation to heal."

Then, shrewdly folding the effect of that day's strike announcement into his narrative, Colbert added: "I want to say to my supporters, This is not over.

"While I may accept the decision of the Council, the fight goes on! The dream endures! . . . And I am going off the air until I can talk about this without weeping."

The very next day, out giving a speech but no longer doing his TV show, Colbert told the crowd, "I'm looking into the legality of mocking the candidates door to door."

While so much of what Colbert says is intentionally outrageous, his stated goal of "mocking the candidates" is very close to the truth. Mocking them while simultaneously mocking the media circus that surrounds, anoints, and destroys them. Colbert, by wanting to run for president (*run,* not *be*), sought to lampoon the process, mingle with actual voters and fellow nominees, and use humor as a weapon to deliver some serious messages and warnings about our politics and our politicians. When the writers' strike is over, even without getting on a single ballot, Colbert is likely to pick up the gauntlet somehow. It's too funny—and too serious—not to. Expect him to resurface, with a campaign that relies only on write-in votes, the old Pat Paulsen way.

And if this next election year doesn't work out, there's always 2028. Just ask Will Rogers.

"The thing that stopped our party," Rogers wrote in 1928, in his final *Life* magazine column about his playful Anti-Bunk Party run for the presidency, "is that we are a hundred years ahead of our times. . . .

"In the year 2028," he continued, "the acceptance speeches will read: 'I pledge myself, if elected, to appoint a Committee to look into the condition of the farmer, to keep the tariff so that it will protect the most voters, and absolutely pledge myself to take the question of Prohibition right out of politics.'"

All these years later, there's a certain amount of truthiness to that. There's a certain amount of Will Rogers in Colbert, and a big chunk of Paulsen, too. In 1968's *Pat Paulsen for President* special, a politician introducing Paulsen told the crowd, "Will Rogers never met a man he didn't like. Pat Paulsen never met a *woman* he didn't like."

And Stephen Colbert, it seems, never met a person he couldn't skewer.

In one of his last *Colbert Report* shows before the strike, Colbert introduced a fellow dark-horse candidate—chess grandmaster Garry Kasparov, running an opposition campaign for president of Russia—by announcing, "Finally! Someone *else* who sees the world in black and white!"

It's a good chess joke—but as an accurate description of the way the real Colbert sees things, and operates, it's not even close. Shades of gray, and moving behind enemy lines—that's where the fun is. And in that game, Colbert is a grandmaster himself, always thinking several moves ahead, and always poised to attack.

Reading the Genre

1. Bianculli uses several metaphors to describe Colbert and his show. List these metaphors, and then try to explain how each metaphor adds to your understanding of this performer and his work. In an evaluation, what do metaphors accomplish that concrete observations cannot? (See "Use figures of speech," p. 17.)

2. In rhetoric, the act of counting off your main points is called enumeration. How does Bianculli use this strategy, and to what effect? (See Chapter 23, "Organization," p. 340.)

3. Examine the image that accompanies the article, and consider how it drives home the Rambo metaphor. How does this image help establish a tone? Think about how some other metaphors might be extended through the creation of images. (See Chapter 46, "Understanding Images," p. 500.)

4. Evaluating or analyzing humor is generally considered difficult. How does Bianculli succeed or fail in revealing exactly how and why people find Colbert funny? How does Bianculli succeed or fail in arguing about what the humor accomplishes beyond just getting laughs?

5. **WRITING:** Choose a favorite cultural figure—an actor, musician, artist, or writer—and write a short essay supporting the case that this person should be president. Evaluate his or her work from this unique political perspective. Why should this person be president, based on his or her gifts and talents, and perhaps despite his or her limitations?

CULTURAL EVALUATION   Michael Pollan is a writer for the *New York Times Magazine* and a professor of journalism at the University of California, Berkeley. This essay comes from Pollan's book *The Omnivore's Dilemma: A Natural History of Four Meals*, named one of the ten best books of 2006 by the *New York Times* and the *Washington Post*. He has written three other critically acclaimed books, including his most recent, *In Defense of Food: An Eater's Manifesto* (2008). In this essay, Pollan writes about the environmental impact of our eating habits.

MICHAEL POLLAN

My Organic Industrial Meal

My shopping foray to Whole Foods yielded all the ingredients for a comforting winter Sunday night dinner: roast chicken (Rosie) with roasted vegetables (yellow potatoes, purple kale, and red winter squash from Cal-Organics), steamed asparagus, and a spring mix salad from Earthbound Farm. Dessert would be even simpler: organic ice cream from Stonyfield Farm topped with organic blackberries from Mexico.

On a hunch it probably wasn't quite ready for prime time (or at least for my wife), I served the Cascadian Farm organic TV dinner I'd bought myself for lunch, right in its microwaveable plastic bowl. Five minutes on high and it was good to go. Peeling back the polyethylene film covering the dish, I felt a little like a flight attendant serving meals, and indeed the entrée looked and tasted very much like airline food. The chunks of white meat chicken had been striped nicely with grill marks and impregnated with a salty marinade that gave the meat that slightly abstract chicken taste processed chicken often has, no doubt owing to the "natural chicken flavor" mentioned on the box's list of ingredients. The chicken chunks and allied vegetables (soft carrots, peas, green beans, and corn) were "blanketed in a creamy rosemary dill sauce"—a creaminess that had evidently been achieved synthetically, since no dairy products appeared among the ingredients. I'm betting it's the xanthan gum (or maybe the carrageenan?) that bears responsibility for the sauce's unfortunate viscosity. To be fair, one shouldn't compare an organic TV dinner to real food but to a conventional TV dinner, and by that standard (or at least my recollection of it) Cascadian Farm has nothing to be ashamed of, especially considering that an organic food scientist must work with only a tiny fraction of the synthetic preservatives, emulsifiers, and flavor agents available to his colleagues at Swanson or Kraft.

Rosie and her consort of fresh vegetables fared much better at dinner, if I don't mind saying so myself. I roasted the bird in a pan surrounded by the potatoes and chunks of winter squash. After removing the chicken from the oven, I spread the crinkled leaves of kale on a cookie sheet, sprinkled them with olive oil and salt, and slid them into the hot oven to roast. After ten minutes or so, the kale was nicely crisped and the chicken was ready to carve.

All but one of the vegetables I served that night bore the label of Cal-Organic Farms, which, along with Earthbound, dominates the organic produce section in the supermarket. Cal-Organic is a big grower of organic vegetables in the San Joaquin Valley. As part of the consolidation of the organic industry, the company was acquired by Grimmway Farms, which already enjoyed a virtual monopoly in organic carrots. Unlike Earthbound, neither Grimmway or Cal-Organic has ever been part of the organic movement. Both companies were started by conventional growers looking for a more profitable niche and worried that the state might ban certain key pesticides. "I'm not necessarily a fan of organic," a spokesman for Grimmway recently told an interviewer. "Right now I don't see that conventional farming does harm. Whether we stay with organic for the long haul depends on profitability." Philosophy, in other words, has nothing to do with it.

The combined company now controls seventeen thousand acres across California, enough land that it can, like Earthbound, rotate production up and down the West Coast (and south into Mexico) in order to ensure a twelve-month national supply

What does the label "organic" really mean?

of fresh organic produce, just as California's conventional growers have done for decades. It wasn't many years ago that organic produce had only a spotty presence in the supermarket, especially during the winter months. Today, thanks in large part to Grimmway and Earthbound, you can find pretty much everything, all year round.

Including asparagus in January, I discovered. This was the one vegetable I prepared that wasn't grown by Cal-Organic or Earthbound; it had been grown in Argentina and imported by a small San Francisco distributor. My plan had been a cozy winter dinner, but I couldn't resist the bundles of fresh asparagus on sale at Whole Foods, even though it set me back six dollars a pound. I had never tasted organic South American asparagus in January, and felt my foray into the organic empire demanded that I do. What better way to test the outer limits of the word "organic" than by dining on a springtime delicacy that had been grown according to organic rules on a farm six thousand miles (and two seasons) away, picked, packed, and chilled on Monday, flown by jet to Los Angeles Tuesday, trucked north to a Whole Foods regional distribution center, then put on sale in Berkeley by Thursday, to be steamed, by me, Sunday night?

The ethical implications of buying such a product are almost too numerous and knotty to sort out: There's the expense, there's the prodigious amounts of energy involved, the defiance of seasonality, and the whole question of whether the best soils in South America should be devoted to growing food for affluent and overfed North Americans. And yet you can also make a good argument that my purchase of organic asparagus from Argentina generates foreign exchange for a country desperately in need of it, and supports a level of care for that country's land—farming without pesticides or chemical fertilizer—it might not otherwise receive. Clearly my bunch of asparagus had delivered me deep into the thicket of trade-offs that a global organic marketplace entails.

Okay, but how did it taste?

My jet-setting Argentine asparagus tasted like damp cardboard. After the first spear or two no one touched it. Perhaps if it had been sweeter and tenderer we would have finished it, but I suspect the fact that asparagus was out of place in a winter supper made it even less appetizing. Asparagus is one of a dwindling number of foods still firmly linked in our minds to the seasonal calendar.

All the other vegetables and greens were much tastier—really good, in fact. Whether they would have been quite so sweet and bright after a cross-country truck ride is doubtful, though the Earthbound greens, in their polyethylene bag, stayed crisp right up to the expiration date, a full eighteen days after leaving the field—no small technological feat. The inert gases, scrupulous cold chain, and space-age plastic bag (which allows the leaves to respire just enough) account for much of this longevity, but some of it, as the Goodmans had explained to me, owes to the fact that the greens were grown organically. Since they're not pumped up on synthetic nitrogen, the cells of these slower-growing leaves develop thicker walls and take up less water, making them more durable.

And, I'm convinced, tastier, too. When I visited Greenways Organic, which grows both conventional and organic tomatoes, I learned that the organic ones consistently earn higher Brix scores (a measure of sugars) than the same varieties grown conventionally. More sugars means less water and more flavor. It stands to reason the same would hold true for other organic vegetables: slower growth, thicker cell walls, and less water should produce more concentrated flavors. That at least has always been my impression, though in the end freshness probably affects flavor even more than growing method.

To serve such a scrupulously organic meal begs an unavoidable question: Is organic food better? Is it worth the extra cost? My Whole Foods dinner certainly wasn't cheap, considering I made it from scratch: Rosie cost $15 ($2.99 a pound), the vegetables another $12 (thanks to that six-buck bunch of asparagus), and the dessert $7 (including $3 for a six-ounce box of blackberries). Thirty-four dollars to feed a family of three at home. (Though we did make a second meal from the leftovers.) Whether organic is better and worth it are certainly fair, straightforward questions, but the answers, I've discovered, are anything but simple.

Better for what? is the all-important corollary to that question. If the answer is "taste," then the answer is, as I've suggested, very likely, at least in the case of produce—but not necessarily. Freshly picked conventional produce is bound to taste better than organic produce that's been riding the interstates in a truck for three days. Meat is a harder call. Rosie was a tasty bird, yet, truth be told, not quite as tasty as Rocky, her bigger nonorganic brother. That's probably because Rocky is an older chicken, and older chickens generally have more flavor. The fact that the corn and soybeans in Rosie's diet were grown without chemicals probably doesn't change the taste of her meat. Though it should be said that Rocky and Rosie both taste more like chicken than mass-market birds fed on a diet of antibiotics and animal by-products, which makes for mushier and blander meat. What's in an animal's feed naturally affects how it will taste, though whether that feed is organic or not probably makes no difference.

Better for what? If the answer is "for my health," the answer, again, is probably—but not automatically. I happen to believe the organic dinner I served my family is healthier than a meal of the same foods conventionally produced, but I'd be hard-pressed to prove it scientifically. What I could prove, with the help of a mass spectrometer, is that it contained little or no pesticide residue—the traces of the carcinogens, neurotoxins, and endocrine disruptors now routinely found in conventional produce and meat. What I probably can't prove is that the low levels of these toxins present in these foods will make us sick—give us cancer, say, or interfere with my son's neurological or sexual development. But that does not mean those poisons are *not* making us sick: Remarkably little research has been done to assess the effects of regular exposure to the levels of organophosphate pesticide or growth hormone that the government deems "tolerable" in our foods. (One problem with these official tolerances is that they don't adequately account for children's exposure to pesticides, which, because of children's size and eating habits, is much greater than adults'.) Given what we do know about exposure to endocrine disruptors, the biological impact of which depends less on dose than timing, minimizing a child's exposure to these chemicals seems like a prudent idea. I very much like the fact that the milk in the ice cream I served came from cows that did not receive injections of growth hormone to boost their productivity, or that the corn those cows are fed, like the corn that feeds Rosie, contains no residues of atrazine, the herbicide commonly sprayed on American cornfields. Exposure to vanishingly small amounts

(0.1 part per billion) of this herbicide has been shown to turn normal male frogs into hermaphrodites. Frogs are not boys, of course. So I can wait for that science to be done, or for our government to ban atrazine (as European governments have done), or I can act now on the presumption that food from which this chemical is absent is better for my son's health than food that contains it.

Of course, the healthfulness of a food is not simply a question of its toxicity; we have also to consider its nutritional quality. Is there any reason to think my Whole Foods meal is any more nutritious than the same meal prepared with conventionally grown ingredients?

Over the years there have been sporadic efforts to demonstrate the nutritional superiority of organic produce, but most have foundered on the difficulty of isolating the great many variables that can affect the nutritional quality of a carrot or a potato—climate, soils, geography, freshness, farming practices, genetics, and so on. Back in the fifties, when the USDA routinely compared the nutritional quality of produce from region to region, it found striking differences: carrots grown in the deep soils of Michigan, for example, commonly had more vitamins than carrots grown in the thin, sandy soils of Florida. Naturally this information discomfited the carrot growers of Florida, which probably explains why the USDA no longer conducts this sort of research. Nowadays U.S. agricultural policy, like the Declaration of Independence, is founded on the principle that all carrots are created equal, even though there's good reason to believe this isn't really true. But in an agricultural system dedicated to quantity rather than quality, the fiction that all foods are created equal is essential. This is why, in inaugurating the federal organic program in 2000, the secretary of agriculture went out of his way to say that organic food is no better than conventional food. "The organic label is a marketing tool," Secretary Glickman said. "It is not a statement about food safety. Nor is 'organic' a value judgment about nutrition or quality."

Some intriguing recent research suggests otherwise. A study by University of California–Davis researchers published in the *Journal of Agriculture and Food Chemistry* in 2003 described an experiment in which identical varieties of corn, strawberries, and blackberries grown in neighboring plots using different methods (including organically and conventionally) were compared for levels of vitamins and polyphenols. Polyphenols are a group of secondary metabolites manufactured by plants that we've recently learned play an important role in human health and nutrition. Many are potent antioxidants; some play a role in preventing or fighting cancer; others exhibit antimicrobial properties. The Davis researchers found that organic and otherwise sustainably grown fruits and vegetables contained significantly higher levels of both ascorbic acid (vitamin C) and a wide range of polyphenols.

The recent discovery of these secondary metabolites in plants has brought our understanding of the biological and chemical complexity of foods to a deeper level of refinement; history suggests we haven't gotten anywhere near the bottom of this question, either. The first level was reached early in the nineteenth century with the identification of the macronutrients—protein, carbohydrate, and fat. Having isolated these compounds, chemists thought they'd unlocked the key to human nutrition. Yet some people (such as sailors) living on diets rich in macronutrients nevertheless got sick. The mystery was solved when scientists discovered the major vitamins—a second key to human nutrition. Now it's the polyphenols in plants that we're learning play a critical role in keeping us healthy. (And which might explain why diets heavy in processed food fortified with vitamins still aren't as nutritious as fresh foods.) You wonder what else is going on in these plants, what other undiscovered qualities in them we've evolved to depend on.

In many ways the mysteries of nutrition at the eating end of the food chain closely mirror the mysteries of fertility at the growing end: The two realms are like wildernesses that we keep convincing ourselves our chemistry has mapped, at least until the next level of complexity comes into view. Curiously, Justus von Liebig, the nineteenth-century German chemist with the spectacularly ironic surname, bears responsibility for science's overly reductive understanding of both ends of the food chain. It was Liebig, you'll recall, who thought he had found the chemical key to soil fertility with the discovery of NPK, and it was the same Liebig who thought he had found the key to human nutrition when he identified the macronutrients in food. Liebig wasn't wrong on either count, yet in both instances he made the fatal mistake of thinking that what we knew about nourishing plants and people was all we needed to know to keep them healthy. It's a mistake we'll probably keep repeating until we develop a deeper respect for the complexity of food and soil and, perhaps, the links between the two.

But back to the polyphenols, which may hint at the nature of that link. Why in the world should organically grown blackberries or corn contain significantly more of these compounds? The authors of the Davis study haven't settled the question, but they offer two suggestive theories. The reason plants produce these compounds in the first place is to defend themselves against pests and diseases; the more pressure from pathogens, the more polyphenols a plant will produce. These compounds, then, are the products of natural selection and, more specifically, the coevolutionary relationship between plants and the species that prey on them. Who would have guessed that humans evolved to profit from a diet of these plant pesticides? Or that we would invent an agriculture that then deprived us of them? The Davis authors hypothesize that plants being defended by man-made pesticides don't need to work as hard to make their own polyphenol pesticides. Coddled by us and our chemicals, the plants see no reason to invest their resources in mounting a strong defense. (Sort of like European nations during the cold war.)

A second explanation (one that subsequent research seems to support) may be that the radically simplified soils in which chemically fertilized plants grow don't supply all the raw ingredients needed to synthesize these compounds, leaving the plants more vulnerable to attack, as we know conventionally grown plants tend to be. NPK might be sufficient for plant growth yet still might not give a plant every-thing it needs to manufacture ascorbic acid or lycopene or resveratrol in quantity. As it happens, many of the polyphenols (and especially a subset called the flavonols) contribute to the characteristic taste of a fruit or vegetable. Qualities we can't yet identify in soil may contribute qualities we've only just begun to identify in our foods and our bodies.

Reading the Davis study I couldn't help thinking about the early proponents of organic agriculture, people like Sir Albert Howard and J. I. Rodale, who would have been cheered, if unsurprised, by the findings. Both men were ridiculed for their unscientific conviction that a reductive approach to soil fertility—the NPK mentality—would diminish the nutritional quality of the food grown in it and, in turn, the health of the people who lived on that food. All carrots are *not* created equal, they believed; how we grow it, the soil we grow it in, what we feed that soil all contribute qualities to a carrot, qualities that may yet escape the explanatory net of our chemistry. Sooner or later the soil scientists and nutritionists will catch up to Sir Howard, heed his admonition that we begin "treating the whole problem of health in soil, plant, animal, and man as one great subject."

So it happens that these organic blackberries perched on this mound of vanilla ice cream, having been grown in a complexly fertile soil and forced to fight their own fights against pests and disease, are in some quantifiable way more nutritious than conventional blackberries. This would probably not come as earthshaking news to Albert Howard or J. I. Rodale or any number of organic farmers, but at least now it is a claim for which we can supply a scientific citation: *J. Agric. Food. Chem.* vol. 51, no. 5, 2003. (Several other such studies have appeared since.)

Obviously there is much more to be learned about the relationship of soil to plant, animals, and health, and it would be a mistake to lean too heavily on any one study. It would also be a mistake to assume that the word *organic* on a label automati-cally signifies healthfulness, especially when that label appears on heavily processed and long-distance foods that have probably had much of their nutritional value, not to mention flavor, beaten out of them long before they arrive on our tables.

The *better for what?* question about my organic meal can of course be answered in a much less selfish way: Is it better for the environment? Better for the farmers who grew it? Better for the public health? For the taxpayer? The answer to all three questions is an (almost) unqualified yes. To grow the plants and animals that made up my meal, no pesticides found their way into any farmworker's bloodstream, no nitrogen runoff or growth hormones seeped into the watershed, no soils were poisoned, no antibiotics were squandered, no subsidy checks were written. If the high price of my all-organic meal is weighed against the comparatively low price it exacted from the larger world, as it should be, it begins to look, at least in karmic terms, like a real bargain.

And yet, and yet . . . an industrial organic meal such as mine does leave deep footprints on our world. The lot of the workers who harvested the vegetables and gathered up Rosie for slaughter is not appreciably different from that of those on nonorganic factory farms. The chickens lived only marginally better lives than their conventional counterparts; in the end a CAFO [confined animal feeding operation] is a CAFO, whether the food served in it is organic or not. As for the cows that produced the milk in our ice cream, they may well have spent time outdoors in an actual pasture (Stonyfield Farm buys most—though not all—of its milk from small dairy farmers), but the organic label guarantees no such thing. And while the organic farms I visited don't receive direct government payments, they do receive other subsidies from taxpayers, notably subsidized water and electricity in California. The two-hundred-thousand-square-foot refrigerated processing plant where my salad was washed pays half as much for its electricity as it would were Earthbound not classified as a "farm enterprise."

But perhaps most discouraging of all, my industrial organic meal is nearly as drenched in fossil fuel as its conventional counterpart. Asparagus traveling in a 747 from Argentina; blackberries trucked up from Mexico; a salad chilled to thirty-six degrees from the moment it was picked in Arizona (where Earthbound moves its entire operation every winter) to the moment I walk it out the doors of my Whole Foods. The food industry burns nearly a fifth of all the petroleum consumed in the United States (about as much as automobiles do). Today it takes between seven and ten calories of fossil fuel energy to deliver one calorie of food energy to an American plate. And while it is true that organic farmers don't spread fertilizers made from natural gas or spray pesticides made from petroleum, industrial organic farmers often wind up burning more diesel fuel than their conventional counterparts: in trucking bulky loads of compost across the countryside and weeding their fields, a particularly energy-intensive process involving extra irrigation (to germinate the weeds before planting) and extra cultivation. All told, growing food organically uses about a third less fossil fuel than growing it conventionally, according to David Pimental, though that savings disappears if the compost is not produced on site or nearby.

Yet growing the food is the least of it: only a fifth of the total energy used to feed us is consumed on the farm; the rest is spent processing the food and moving it around. At least in terms of the fuel burned to get it from the farm to my table, there's little reason to think my Cascadian Farm TV dinner or Earthbound Farm spring mix salad is any more sustainable than a conventional TV dinner or salad would have been.

Well, at least we didn't eat it in the car.

So is an industrial organic food chain finally a contradiction in terms? It's hard to escape the conclusion that it is. Of course it is possible to live with contradictions, at least for a time, and sometimes it is necessary or worthwhile. But we ought at least face up to the cost of our compromises. The inspiration for organic was to find a way to feed ourselves more in keeping with the logic of nature, to build a food system that looked more like an ecosystem that would draw its fertility and energy from the sun. To feed ourselves otherwise was "unsustainable," a word that's been so abused we're apt to forget what it very specifically means: *Sooner or later it must collapse.* To a remarkable extent, farmers succeeded in creating the new food chain on their farms; the trouble began when they encountered the expectations of the supermarket. As in so many other realms, nature's logic has proven no match for the logic of capitalism, one in which cheap energy has always been a given. And so, today, the organic food industry finds itself in a most unexpected, uncomfortable, and, yes, unsustainable position: floating on a sinking sea of petroleum.

Reading the Genre

1. Reread Pollan's descriptions of the taste of food. How does this language contrast with that used to describe the food's preparation? To what effect? What impact does this language have on the audience? (See Chapter 30, "High, Middle, and Low Style," p. 366.)

2. What question does Pollan repeat throughout the essay, and how does this help him structure his writing? (See Chapter 22, "Thesis," p. 336.) How does the repetition of this question reveal that he is evaluating more than just the taste of the food?

3. How does Pollan persuade the reader to consider broader criteria than just taste when making food choices?

4. How does Pollan use science not just to evaluate the environmental impact of food production but also to evaluate the taste of food? How do the evaluations based on science differ from those based on more subjective criteria?

5. **WRITING:** Create a food map. Choose ingredients for a small meal, and then research where your food has come from. If you can find company names, do some Internet research. Find out what you can about how and where some of the key ingredients in your meal were produced. Use what you know to ground an evaluation of your meal in the facts about its production. (See Chapter 36, "Finding Print and Online Sources," p. 406.)

PRODUCT REVIEW   Novelist and mystery writer Ayelet Waldman has also published essays in several prominent magazines, and her audio essays have aired on National Public Radio. Her latest book is *Bad Mother: A Chronicle of Maternal Crimes, Minor Calamities, and Occasional Moments of Grace* (2009).

Tool: Krups FDE3-12 Universal Grill and Panini Maker

AYELET WALDMAN

Features:

- Non-stick grill plates
- Insulated cool-touch handle
- Safety-locking latch for storage
- On/off indicator light
- Ready indicator light
- Floating hinge system

One senses intuitively that all food items can be improved by being hermetically sealed between two slices of good bread, but final proof has awaited the development by top scientists of the Krups FDE3-12 Universal Grill and Panini Maker. Any food. All food. Cheese, obviously. Eggs. Steak. Marmalade. Hot dogs. Noodles. All the contents of one's fridge, it turns out, should be subjected, under strict German conditions, to the searing and sealing heat of the Krups FDE3-12 Universal Grill and Panini Maker. Hitherto uninteresting, even inedible substances, once stamped into a sheath of golden-crusted, white-fleshed Italian loaf, are instantly transformed into delicacies. A jar of ancient cornichon? Slice thin, cover with mustard, and gently press down on the insulated cool-touch handle.

A word about that handle. It is *very* cool. Cold, even, especially when compared to the metal top of the Krups FDE3-12 Universal Grill and Panini Maker. I know this, unfortunately, because I casually leaned my elbow on the metal lid, momentarily forgetting the remarkable conductive properties of stainless steel. The burn was bright red, but did not blister, most likely because I immediately ran it under cold water—this being, incidentally, the only way to deal with a kitchen burn. Ice is less than useful, and butter is an old wives' tale of a remedy that is more harmful than helpful.

To work the Krups FDE3-12 Universal Grill and Panini Maker, one places the items on the gridded non-stick grill plates, grasps the cool handle in one's two hands, and closes the lid, pressing down with a firmness dictated by one's preference. Does one like one's panini thin, the bread nearly unrecognizable as such, or does one prefer a thicker, more sandwich-like panino?

Either way, there is a rare delicacy to bread that has undergone transformation in this magic chamber. It acquires a luster that has nothing to do with the melted butter that an experienced paninista learns to apply with a generous hand. I know this because I made a series of no-butter panini, and the bread was just as shiny and crisp. It must be an inherent action of the process of heat-sealing that lends that alabaster sheen. When one's teeth crack through the polished surface of the bread and sink into the tart, salty pool of gorgonzola, the scraps of lemon frittata, the black olive pesto, one experiences a moment of gastronomic transcendence worth a considerable amount of scrubbing and scraping.

Except that its brilliant design absolves one from any such labor. A single swipe with a paper towel over the stealth-bomber–gray non-stick grill plates, and the machine is clean and ready to reconfigure the atoms of the next humble pile of cold cuts and vegetables.

I had planned, for the purposes of this piece, to heat-seal non-food items in the Krups FDE3-12 Universal Grill and Panini Maker. I considered placing small figurines of Disney characters in a Ziploc bag between the non-stick grill plates to see if a vacuum seal would result. I imagined the potential ironing possibilities, and the sophistication of a pair of linen pants imprinted with a Panini grid. I could not, however, bring myself to sully its perfection. It is far too precious, and came to me via a generous friend who took pity on my children— forced, when their father is on the road, to eat a steady diet of take-out food and breakfast cereal for dinner. Now, when my eldest son wails, in a tone of five- year-old despair, "Can't we just eat something *American* for once?!," I can pull out the Krups FDE3-12 Universal Grill and Panini Maker and whip up a Croque Monsieur or a Pizza Romana. It's all grilled cheese to him.

Reading the Genre

1. Who might buy this product? How does Waldman address this consumer? Does she also address people who might not usually be in the market for a panini maker? Does she address this expanded market successfully? (See "Establish and defend criteria," p. 104, and "Decide on your criteria," p. 110.)

2. What is the style of writing in this evaluation? Does the style of writing suit the product being reviewed? Does the style of writing suit the potential audience for a review of this product? (See Chapter 30, "High, Middle, and Low Style," p. 366.)

3. Waldman begins the review by listing important product details. How does this help the reader? How does she address these details in the review, and how do they provide a structure for the essay? (See "Understanding your audience," p. 108.)

4. How does Waldman show us how the product works, and how does she walk us through the process of using the product? How important is it that we see this process? How important is this sort of "test-driving" to any evaluation of a product?

5. **WRITING:** What is the most used and valued product in your kitchen (at home or at school): a microwave, a toaster oven, a blender? Write a process paper that walks your reader through the process of creating something tasty using this tool. Try, as Waldman does, to use descriptive language that fully represents the process of making and eating this food but that also allows readers to reproduce this item themselves—to know how to use the kitchen tool and put the ingredients together. (See "Consider a simple sequence," p. 14.)

TELEVISION REVIEW   Carrie Brownstein, the guitarist and vocalist in the influential Portland band Sleater-Kinney, now writes the blog Monitor Mix (www.npr.org/blogs/monitormix) for National Public Radio and appears on radio and television as a music critic. In her words, Monitor Mix features "writing and musings on music, but since music is often terrible, the blog also delves into topics such as film, books, dogs, and television."

NPR.org

Posted: September 22, 2008, at 3:22 PM ET
From: Carrie Brownstein

So I Thought I Could Dance

I'm about to admit something embarrassing. Last night, I went with my family to see a live performance of the reality television show *So You Think You Can Dance.* They're fans of the program, and I love my family, so I went. No, I don't watch the show—I've never even seen it—but I'm not above reality television. For evidence of this, feel free to go back and read my post about *The Bachelor,* one of my more contentious entries, wherein people expressed major disappointment that I am not immune to, um, America.

So, while some of you were suffering through what sounds like a horrible Emmy broadcast, I was living inside of a television world and witnessing the mindset of the television viewer.

For those of you who don't know, *So You Think You Can Dance* (which from here on out will be known as *SYTYCD*) is a reality TV program wherein dancers from all genres come together and perform choreographed material in front of a live audience. Hip-hop dancers must learn to cha cha cha, ballroom dancers find their way into a breakdance routine, and modern dancers learn to do something other than float, flutter, and hug themselves. The dancers pair up and things get sexy. Or "sexy."

Portland was the second stop on the *SYTYCD* Season 4 tour. The performance took place at the Rose Garden, our giant sports stadium, which will also host an upcoming Celine Dion concert, as well as the Ice Capades. The first thing I noticed once we got to our seats was that, even though this was a live event, we were still essentially going to be watching TV. Like, the whole time. A Jumbotron provided the audience with season highlights, interviews with the cast members, and a Brady Bunch–esque segment with questions like "Which dancer likes to put ketchup and

A still from a first-season episode of the television show *So You Think You Can Dance.*

ranch dressing on everything?" In case you were wondering, the answer to that one was a dancer named Comfort.

No surprise here, but the entire show has been branded. Each dancer has his or her own look and personality. There's the wacky one, the intense one, the crybaby, the "this show saved me from my crappy life" guy, and so on. And when the dancers introduced the performances, they each came out in *SYTYCD* gear, of which there were copious amounts. And it was all for sale! There was even an intermission that seemed less about giving the dancers a rest and more about giving us a chance to go and purchase some of those souvenirs. I took the opportunity to buy a $4 bottle of water.

And, finally, there was the dancing itself. I really wanted it to be exciting. Some of these people don't just *think* they can dance; they really *can* dance. But, sadly, each piece was designed for our short, pitiful attention spans, which apparently give us about 45 seconds. All of the performances were culled from the TV show. The emcees would say, "Remember when Kate and Joshua did their piece that involved a bed?" The audience would scream. "Well, here it is!" More screams. And then Kate and Joshua would dance on a bed in a piece that was supposed to be about breaking up but made me feel about as emotional as I do about picking up dog poop. Most of the choreography told stories about love, as if all romance were merely an extension of a 14-year-old girl's imagination. The dances hinted at sex and flirtation, heartache and manipulation, but through a Disney-fied lens; magic, and magically sterile. The strangest moment—here is the music part, music-blogger purists!—came when one of the couples danced to the Mirah song "The Garden."

You'd think the live *SYTYCD* show would be an opportunity to prove that reality TV is sort of based in reality—that, in real life, the dancing is *better* than it is on TV. But when I looked at the stage from our swanky floor seats and then peeked at the Jumbotron, the dancing really did look more exciting on the Jumbotron. Somehow, even, more believable.

Most of my disappointment came from wanting to be part of something that seems surprisingly popular, to experience people enjoying an art form as unlikely as dance. In my naive hopes, I imagined more people buying season ballet tickets and checking out local dance troupes. Instead, however, I was reminded that what *SYTYCD* popularizes is not dance, but television, and bad television at that.

On the way out, I saw a guy whom I felt summed up the whole night. Wearing baggy gray sweatpants and carrying a program for the show in one arm, he had managed to stuff a 16-ounce paper cup of Coke into his right pants pocket. The straw hung out, dripping little bits of brown soda onto the floor. Other people's sense of satisfaction is a sadly beautiful thing.

Reading the Genre

1. In describing her blog, Brownstein admits that she is a bit of a "cynic and curmudgeon." She is obviously not a fan of the television show she examines in this review. What are the benefits of not liking the work you are evaluating? What are the drawbacks? (See "Decide on your criteria," p. 110.)

2. Brownstein writes about a reality television show. In what ways does she comment on this "reality"? What seems most real and most fake, and why does this matter?

3. Increasingly, television shows are, in Brownstein's words, a "television world" that has been fully "branded." The event that Brownstein attends is unique in that it centers on watching television, but it also renders the full "television world" and puts the "brand" right in the viewer's face. If a television screen is at the center of this experience, how would you describe or define all of the other things surrounding this screen, and what do they add to the show? What do these things demand of the audience? What does the audience get from this "world"?

4. Reread question 3. Consider the idea that a television show also has a variety of other products, performances, and texts surrounding it, making it a "brand" and extending it into a "television world." Choose another heavily marketed show, such as *American Idol* or *Hannah Montana*, and create a chart with a television at the center. Draw lines out from the television to connect to the other entities that spin out of the show, promote it, brand it, and make it a "world." (See Chapter 46, "Understanding Images," p. 500.) How do these things all structure the experience of the show?

5. **WRITING:** Watch an entire episode of a popular reality television show—preferably a show you aren't a fan of or don't already know well. Pay close attention to the show, as well as the commercials and the "world" around the show (product placement, tie-ins, promotions, and so on). Write an evaluation of the show.

CULTURAL EVALUATION For many years, the writer of the "Musings" column for the *Boston Globe,* Chet Raymo now writes the blog Science Musings (www.sciencemusings.com). He is the author of twelve books on science, as well as three novels. This essay parallels favorite children's books with breakthroughs in science, suggesting that they share a unique imaginative spirit.

Dr. Seuss and Dr. Einstein: Children's Books and the Scientific Imagination

CHET RAYMO

Some years ago, when an insect called the thrips—singular and plural—was in the news for defoliating sugar maples in New England, I noted in my *Boston Globe* science column that thrips are very strange beasts. Some species of thrips give birth to live young, some lay eggs, and at least one species of switch-hitting thrips has it both ways. Not even the wildest product of Dr. Seuss's imagination, I said—the Moth-Watching Sneth, for example, a bird that's so big it scares people to death, or the Grickily Gractus, a bird that lays eggs on a cactus—is stranger than creatures, such as the thrips, that actually exist.

As if to prove my point, a reader sent me a photograph of a real tropical bird that does indeed lay eggs on a cactus.

What about the Moth-Watching Sneth? Well, the extinct elephant bird of Madagascar stood eight feet tall and weighed a thousand pounds. In its heyday—only a century or so ago—the elephant bird, or Aepyornis, probably scared many a Madagascan half to death.

Pick any Seussian invention, and nature will equal it. In Dr. Seuss's *McElligot's Pool* there's a fish with a kangaroo pouch. Could there possibly be such a fish in the real world? Not a fish, maybe, but in South America there is an animal called the Yapok—a wonderfully Seussian name—that takes its young for a swim in a waterproof pouch.

Dr. Seuss was a botanist and zoologist of the first rank. Never mind that the flora and fauna he described were imaginary. Any kid headed for a career in science could do no better than to start with the plants and animals that populate the books of the madcap master of biology.

One thrips, two thrips, red thrips, blue thrips. The eggshell of an elephant bird, cut in half, would make a splendid salad bowl. Is it Seuss, or is it reality? You see, the boundary between the so-called "real" world and the world of the imagination begins to blur. And that is just as it should be if a child is to grow up with a proper attitude toward science.

Do black holes, those strange products of the astronomer's imagination, really exist? What about electrons, invisibly small, fidgeting in their atomic shells? How about the dervish dance of DNA as it unzips down the middle to reproduce itself? No one has ever seen these things, at least not directly. Like the Gractus and the Sneth, they are wonderful inventions of the imagination.

Of course, we are convinced that black holes, electrons, and unzipping DNA are real, because of the way those things connect with other things we know about the world and because certain experiments—a myriad of exacting experiments—turn out in certain ways. But it is important to remember that the world of science is a made-up world, a world of let's pretend, no less so than the strange flora and fauna of Dr. Seuss. The physicist Michael Faraday once said, "Nothing is too wonderful to be true." To be a good scientist, or to have a scientific attitude toward the world, one must be able to imagine wonderful things—even things that seem too wonderful to be true.

Creative science depends crucially upon habits of mind that are most readily acquired by children: curiosity; voracious observation; sensitivity to rules and variations within the rules; and fantasy. Children's books that instill these habits of mind sustain science.

I am not talking about so-called "science books for children." I am not talking about "fact" books. I would argue that many science books written especially for children may actually diminish the very habits of mind that make for good science.

I used to occasionally review children's science books for a journal called *Appraisal.* Most of the offerings I was sent for review were packed full of useful information. What most of these books do not convey is the extraordinary adventure story of how the information was obtained, why we understand it to be true, or how it might embellish the landscape of the mind. For many children—and adults, too—science is information, a mass of facts. But facts are not science any more than a table is carpentry. Science is an attitude toward the world—curious, skeptical, undogmatic, forward-looking. . . .

We live in an age of information. We are inundated by it. Too much information can swamp the boat of wonder, especially for a child. Which is why it is important that information be conveyed to children in a way that enhances the wonder of the world. For example, there are several fine information books for children about bats. But how much richer is that information when it is presented this way:

> A bat is born
> Naked and blind and pale.
> His mother makes a pocket of her tail
> And catches him. He clings to her long fur
> By his thumbs and toes and teeth.
> And then the mother dances through the night
> Doubling and looping, soaring, somersaulting—
> Her baby hangs on underneath.

There is every bit as much information in Randall Jarrell's *The Bat-Poet* as in the typical informational book. But, oh, what information!

If a child is led to believe that science is a bunch of facts, then science will not inform the child's life, nor will science enhance the child's cultural and imaginative landscape. By all means let's have books for kids that communicate what we know—or think we know—about the world; the more factual information we accumulate about the world, the more interesting the world becomes. But the scientific attitude—ah, that's something else. There is no better time to communicate the scientific attitude than during childhood, and no better way than with quality children's books.

Consider these lines of Jarrell's *The Bat-Poet:*

> The mother eats the moths and gnats she catches
> In full flight; in full flight
> The mother drinks the water of the pond
> She skims across.

That wonderful line—"In full flight; in full flight"—conveys the single most important fact about bats: their extraordinary aviator skills. By repeating the phrase, Jarrell not only teaches us a bat fact but also helps us experience what it means to be a bat.

Curiosity, voracious seeing, sensitivity to rules and variations within the rules, and fantasy. These are habits of mind crucial for science that are best learned during childhood. Let us consider them one by one.

Curiosity

Albert Einstein wrote: "The most beautiful experience we can have is the mysterious. It is the fundamental emotion which stands at the cradle of true art and true science." At first, this might seem a strange thought as it applies to science. We are frequently asked to believe that science takes mystery out of the world. Nothing could be further from the truth. Mystery invites curiosity. Unless we perceive the world as mysterious, we shall never be curious about what makes the world tick.

My favorite books about curiosity are the children's books of Maurice Sendak, precisely because of their successful evocation of mystery. Sendak's illustrations convey the spooky sense of entwined order and chaos, good and menace that we find in nature. In *In the Night Kitchen* Mickey hears a thump in the night. Down he falls, out of his pajamas, into the curious world of the night kitchen. The night kitchen is full of familiar things—the city skyline in the background consists of boxes and cans from the pantry—yet nothing is quite the same as in the daylight world. Mickey takes charge. He molds; he shapes; he rearranges. He contrives clothes from bread dough, and a dough airplane, too. He takes a dip in a bottle of milk. The night kitchen is the awake world turned topsy-turvy.

Mickey's adventure is a dream, of course, but so what? The American social philosopher Lewis Mumford said: "If man had not encountered dragons and hippogriffs in dreams, he might never have conceived of the atom." It is an extraordinary thought, that science depends upon the dreaming mind. The dreamer, says Mumford, puts things together in ways never experienced in the awake world—joining the head, wings, and claws of a bird with the hind quarters of a horse—to make something fabulous and new: a hippogriff. In the dream world, space and time dissolve; near and far, past and future, familiar and monstrous merge in novel ways. In science, too, we invent unseen worlds by combining familiar things in an unfamiliar fashion. We imagine atoms, for example, as combining characteristics of billiard balls, musical instruments, and water waves, all on a scale that is invisibly small. According to Mumford, dreams taught us how to imagine the unseen world.

In science we talk about "dreaming up" theories, and we move from the dreamed-up worlds of the night kitchen, Middle-Earth, Narnia, and Oz to dreamed-up worlds that challenge the adult imagination. An asteroid hurtles out of space and lays waste a monster race of reptiles that has ruled the earth for two hundred million years. A black hole at the center of the Milky Way galaxy swallows ten million stars. A universe begins in a blinding flash from a pinprick of infinite energy. How did we learn to imagine such things? Mumford believed that dreams released human imagination from bondage to the immediate environment and to the present moment. He imagined early humans pestered and tantalized by dreams, sometimes confusing the images of darkness and sleep with those of waking life, subject to misleading hallucinations, disordered memories, unaccountable impulses, but also animated now and then by images of joyous possibility. These are exactly the characteristics I admire in Sendak's works. As long as children are reading such books, I have no fear for curiosity.

Voracious Observation

I love books that stretch a child's powers of observation. Graeme Base's *Animalia*. The books of Kit Williams. Richly textured books. Books hiding secrets. Of these, my favorites are the books in Mitsumasa *Anno's Journey* series—Bayeux tapestries that hide a hundred observational surprises. The more you look, the more you see, ad infinitum. Texture is everything.

The texture of a book can be too simple, or too complex. It can be uninteresting, or hopelessly cluttered. The nineteenth-century physicist James Clerk Maxwell said: "It is a universal condition of the enjoyable that the mind must believe in the existence of a discoverable law, yet have a mystery to move in." Anno's books have a rich textural complexity, but they are structured by discoverable law. As often as I have perused these books, with children and alone, I have found new elements of law, subtly hidden, shaping the whole. With such books the child practices the very qualities of mind that led Maxwell to the laws of electromagnetism.

Rules and Variations within the Rules

If there is one thing that defines science, this is it. The Greeks called it the problem of the One and the Many. They observed that the world is capable of infinite variation yet somehow remains the same. And that's what science is—the discovery of things that stay the same in the midst of variation.

The human mind rebels from too much constancy and from too much chaos, preferring instead a balance of sameness and novelty. Endless variation within a simple set of rules is the recipe for the perfect game: patty-cake, ring-around-the-rosy, blackjack, chess, science. We learn this first in the nursery, with the rhyme on mother's or father's knee:

Jack and Jill
Went up the hill,
To fetch a pail of water;
Jack fell down,
And broke his crown
And Jill came tumbling after.
Then up Jack got,
And home did trot,
As fast as he could caper;
To old Dame Dob,
Who patched his nob
With vinegar and brown paper.

The nursery song initiates the child into a kind of playful activity for which science is the natural culmination. Rhyme is a special activity marked off from ordinary experience by the parent's lap and the book. Presumably, the infant recognizes rhyme as a special use of language. The language of the rhyme is more highly structured than ordinary discourse, by rhyme, rhythm, and alliteration. In a chaos of unarticulated sound and dimly perceived meanings, the nursery song evokes a feeling of recognition and order. "Ah, this is familiar" is the emotion the child must feel. "This makes sense." The semantic aspect of the song is not the important thing. The rhyme creates order. Its perfection is limited and temporary, but it is enough to provide security and pleasure. The order of the rhyme is an end in itself, and the child will be quick to set even a minor deviation straight with "That's not the way it goes." We do not begin to understand why the human mind responds this way, but in the nursery rhyme we are touching upon a quality of mind that drives science.

Tension between rules and the breaking of rules is a common theme of children's books. Chris Van Allsburg's award-winning *JUMANJI* tells the story of a board game that two children find in the park. The game has three simple rules regarding the game pieces, rolling the dice to move through the jungle to the Golden City, and the object of the game. And a final rule: once the game is started, it will not be over until one player reaches the Golden City. And now comes the fun—and terror—as the children find themselves swept along by the rules of the game. Is it a dream? Is it life?

A side effect of those children's science books which stress factual information is a conviction on the part of the child that science is all rules, all order, all comprehensibility. Nothing could be further from the truth. The rules of science exist within a matrix of ignorance. The chaos and incomprehensibility of the natural world is not exhausted by science. As Thomas Huxley said, the point of science is to reduce the fundamentally incomprehensible things in nature to the smallest possible number. We haven't the foggiest notion what things such as electric charge, or gravity, or space, or time are. These are fundamentally incomprehensible. Why they exist we haven't a clue. We are content if we can describe a multitude of other things in terms of these fundamental incomprehensibilities. Science is an activity that takes place on the shore of an infinite sea of mystery.

Fantasy

The physicist Bruce Lindsay defined science this way: "Science is a game in which we pretend that things are not wholly what they seem in order that we may make sense out of them in terms of mental processes peculiar to us as human beings. . . . Science strives to understand by the construction of theories, which are imaginative pictures of things as they might be, and, if they were, they would lead logically to that which we find in actual experience." In other words, a scientific theory is a kind of fantasy that is required to match the world in a particularly strict sort of way. We have ample testimony from great scientists of the importance of fantasy to creative scientific thought. Einstein said: "When I examine myself and my methods of thought, I come to the conclusion that the gift of fantasy has meant more to me than any talent for abstract, positive thinking."

In the nineteenth century, educators often opposed encouraging a child's gift for fantasy. Knowledge imparted to children by Victorians was required to be "useful," as opposed to "frivolous." Victorian children who wanted to read romances, or fairy tales, had to do so by candlelight in the night closet or in the privacy of the park. What a sad, sad notion of what it means to grow up! I would more quickly welcome into my science classes the child who has traveled in Middle-Earth and Narnia than the child who stayed home and read nothing but "useful" information. The eminent essayist Lewis Thomas said of childhood: "It is the time when the human brain can set to work on language, on taste, on poetry and music, with centers at its disposal that may not be available later on in life. If we did not have childhood, and were able to somehow jump catlike from infancy to adulthood, I doubt very much that we would turn out human." And, he might have added, we would certainly not turn out to be scientists.

Let's not be too overly concerned about providing science facts to children. A child absorbs quite enough science facts from school and television, from computers and the other rich technologies at the child's disposal. If we want to raise children who will grow up to understand science, who will be citizens who are curious, skeptical, undogmatic, imaginative, optimistic, and forward-looking, then let's turn the Victorian rule on its head and put into the hands of children books that feed imagination and fantasy. There is no better time to acquire scientific habits of mind, and no better instigator than quality children's books.

In my *Boston Globe* science column, I had occasion over the years to make reference to Dr. Seuss, Antoine de Saint-Exupéry's *The Little Prince*, Lewis Carroll's *Alice* books, Kenneth Grahame's *The Wind in the Willows*, Felix Salten's *Bambi,* and other children's books. In writing about science I have made reference to children's books more frequently than to adult literary works. This is not an accident. In children's books we are at the roots of science—pure, childlike curiosity, eyes open with wonder to the fresh and new, and powers of invention still unfettered by convention and expectation.

Reading the Genre

1. What qualities does Raymo suggest that all good children's books should have? How does he clearly state his criteria and then apply them? How does he try to convince readers that these are valid criteria? (See "Finding and developing materials," p. 110.)

2. What are the rhetorical benefits and drawbacks of unlikely comparisons, such as that between children's books and advanced science? (See "Compare and contrast," p. 114.)

3. In this article, a scientist is evaluating children's literature. What is the effect of reading an evaluation of a children's text by a serious scientist? How does the writer establish *ethos,* or authority to analyze texts that are not in his field of expertise? How might you do the same thing in your writing?

4. Raymo cites other scientists to both ground and extend his evaluation. To what effect? Find examples of his use of secondary sources, and consider what the use of each of these sources allows Raymo to do as a writer. (See Chapter 38, "Evaluating Sources," p. 415.)

5. **WRITING:** What other things might be learned from children's books? Go to the library and sign out a few books you remember from your childhood. Then write a short report that explores some of the ways these books might be read as scientific, sociological, political, or philosophical texts.

Causal Analysis: Readings

66

CULTURAL ANALYSIS   Pulitzer Prize–winning *New York Times* science writer Natalie Angier is the author of four critically acclaimed books, including the best seller *Woman: An Intimate Geography* (1999). Her most recent, *The Canon: A Whirligig Tour of the Beautiful Basics of Science* (2008), provides a guide to the major theories of science. The following article uses linguistic and psychological research to try to explain a very common phenomenon: swearing.

Almost Before We Spoke, We Swore

Natalie Angier

Incensed by what it sees as a virtual pandemic of verbal vulgarity issuing from the diverse likes of Howard Stern, Bono of U2, and Robert Novak, the United States Senate is poised to consider a bill that would sharply increase the penalty for obscenity on the air.

By raising the fines that would be levied against offending broadcasters some fifteenfold, to a fee of about $500,000 per crudity broadcast, and by threatening to revoke the licenses of repeat polluters, the Senate seeks to return to the public square the gentler tenor of yesteryear, when seldom were heard any scurrilous words, and famous guys were not foul mouthed all day.

Yet researchers who study the evolution of language and the psychology of swearing say that they have no idea what mystic model of linguistic gentility the critics might have in mind. Cursing, they say, is a human universal. Every language, dialect, or patois ever studied, living or dead, spoken by millions or by a small tribe, turns out to have its share of forbidden speech, some variant on comedian George Carlin's famous list of the seven dirty words that are not supposed to be uttered on radio or television.

Young children will memorize the illicit inventory long before they can grasp its sense, said John McWhorter, a scholar of linguistics at the Manhattan Institute and the author of *The Power of Babel*, and literary giants have always constructed their art on its spine.

The Jacobean dramatist Ben Jonson peppered his plays with fackings and "peremptorie Asses," and Shakespeare could hardly quill a stanza without inserting profanities of the day like "zounds" or "sblood"—offensive contractions of "God's wounds" and "God's blood"—or some wondrous sexual pun.

The title *Much Ado About Nothing*, Dr. McWhorter said, is a word play on *Much*

Ado About an O Thing, the *O thing* being a reference to female genitalia.

Even the quintessential Good Book abounds in naughty passages like the men in II Kings 18:27 who, as the comparatively tame King James translation puts it, "eat their own dung, and drink their own piss."

In fact, said Guy Deutscher, a linguist at the University of Leiden in the Netherlands and the author of *The Unfolding of Language: An Evolutionary Tour of Mankind's Greatest Invention,* the earliest writings, which date from 5,000 years ago, include their share of off-color descriptions of the human form and its ever-colorful functions. And the written record is merely a reflection of an oral tradition that Dr. Deutscher and many other psychologists and evolutionary linguists suspect dates from the rise of the human larynx, if not before.

Some researchers are so impressed by the depth and power of strong language that they are using it as a peephole into the architecture of the brain, as a means of probing the tangled, cryptic bonds between the newer, "higher" regions of the brain in charge of intellect, reason, and planning, and the older, more "bestial" neural neighborhoods that give birth to our emotions.

Researchers point out that cursing is often an amalgam of raw, spontaneous feeling and targeted, gimlet-eyed cunning. When one person curses at another, they say, the curser rarely spews obscenities and insults at random, but rather will assess the object of his wrath, and adjust the content of the "uncontrollable" outburst accordingly.

Because cursing calls on the thinking and feeling pathways of the brain in roughly equal measure and with handily assessable fervor, scientists say that by studying the neural circuitry behind it they are gaining new insights into how the different domains of the brain communicate—and all for the sake of a well-venomed retort.

Other investigators have examined the physiology of cursing, how our senses and reflexes react to the sound or sight of an obscene word. They have determined that hearing a curse elicits a literal rise out of people. When electrodermal wires are placed on people's arms and fingertips to study their skin conductance patterns and the subjects then hear a few obscenities spoken clearly and firmly, participants show signs of instant arousal.

Their skin conductance patterns spike, the hairs on their arms rise, their pulse quickens, and their breathing becomes shallow.

Interestingly, said Kate Burridge, a professor of linguistics at Monash University in Melbourne, Australia, a similar reaction occurs among university students and others who pride themselves on being educated when they listen to bad grammar or slang expressions that they regard as irritating, illiterate, or déclassé.

"People can feel very passionate about language," she said, "as though it were a cherished artifact that must be protected at all cost against the depravities of barbarians and lexical aliens."

Dr. Burridge and a colleague at Monash, Keith Allan, are the authors of *Forbidden Words: Taboo and the Censoring of Language,* which will be published early next year [2006] by the Cambridge University Press.

Researchers have also found that obscenities can get under one's goosebumped skin and then refuse to budge. In one study, scientists started with the familiar Stroop test, in which subjects are flashed a series of words written in different colors and are asked to react by calling out the colors of the words rather than the words themselves.

If the subjects see the word *chair* written in yellow letters, they are supposed to say "yellow."

The researchers then inserted a number of obscenities and vulgarities in the standard lineup. Charting participants' immediate and delayed responses, the researchers found that, first of all, people needed significantly more time to trill out the colors of the curse words than they did for neutral terms like *chair.*

The experience of seeing titillating text obviously distracted the participants from the color-coding task at hand. Yet those risqué interpolations left their mark. In subsequent memory quizzes, not only were participants much better at recalling the naughty words than they were the neutrals, but that superior recall also applied to the tints of the tainted words, as well as to their sense.

Yes, it is tough to toil in the shadow of trash. When researchers in another study asked participants to quickly scan lists of words that included obscenities and then to recall as many of the words as possible, the subjects were, once again, best at rehashing the curses—and worst at summoning up whatever unobjectionable entries happened to precede or follow the bad bits.

Yet as much as bad language can deliver a jolt, it can help wash away stress and anger. In some settings, the free flow of foul language may signal not hostility or social pathology, but harmony and tranquillity.

"Studies show that if you're with a group of close friends, the more relaxed you are, the more you swear," Dr. Burridge said. "It's a way of saying: 'I'm so comfortable here I can let off steam. I can say whatever I like.'"

Evidence also suggests that cursing can be an effective means of venting aggression and thereby forestalling physical violence.

With the help of a small army of students and volunteers, Timothy B. Jay, a professor of psychology at Massachusetts College of Liberal Arts in North Adams and the author of *Cursing in America* and *Why We Curse,* has explored the dynamics of cursing in great detail.

The investigators have found, among other things, that men generally curse more than women, unless said women are in a sorority, and that university provosts swear more than librarians or the staff members of the university day care center.

Regardless of who is cursing or what the provocation may be, Dr. Jay said, the rationale for the eruption is often the same.

"Time and again, people have told me that cursing is a coping mechanism for them, a way of reducing stress," he said in a telephone interview. "It's a form of anger management that is often underappreciated."

Indeed, chimpanzees engage in what appears to be a kind of cursing match as a means of venting aggression and avoiding a potentially dangerous physical clash.

Frans de Waal, a professor of primate behavior at Emory University in Atlanta, said that when chimpanzees were angry "they will grunt or spit or make an abrupt, upsweeping gesture that, if a human were to do it, you'd recognize it as aggressive."

Such behaviors are threat gestures, Professor de Waal said, and they are all a good sign.

"A chimpanzee who is really gearing up for a fight doesn't waste time with gestures, but just goes ahead and attacks," he added.

By the same token, he said, nothing is more deadly than a person who is too enraged for expletives—who cleanly and quietly picks up a gun and starts shooting.

Researchers have also examined how words attain the status of forbidden speech and how the evolution of coarse language affects the smoother sheets of civil discourse stacked above it. They have found that what counts as taboo language in a given culture is often a mirror into that culture's fears and fixations.

"In some cultures, swear words are drawn mainly from sex and bodily functions, whereas in others, they're drawn mainly from the domain of religion," Dr. Deutscher said.

In societies where the purity and honor of women is of paramount importance, he said, "it's not surprising that many swear words are variations on the 'son of a whore' theme or refer graphically to the genitalia of the person's mother or sisters."

The very concept of a swear word or an oath originates from the profound importance that ancient cultures placed on swearing by the name of a god or gods. In ancient Babylon, swearing by the name of a god was meant to give absolute certainty against lying, Dr. Deutscher said, "and people believed that swearing falsely by a god would bring the terrible wrath of that god upon them." A warning against any abuse of the sacred oath is reflected in the biblical commandment that one must not "take the Lord's name in vain," and even today courtroom witnesses swear on the Bible that they are telling the whole truth and nothing but.

Among Christians, the stricture against taking the Lord's name in vain extended to casual allusions to God's son or the son's corporeal sufferings—no mention of the blood or the wounds or the body, and that goes for clever contractions, too. Nowadays, the phrase "Oh, golly!" may be considered almost comically wholesome, but it was not always so. "Golly" is a compaction of "God's body" and, thus, was once a profanity.

Yet neither biblical commandment nor the most zealous Victorian censor can elide from the human mind its hand-wringing over the unruly human body, its chronic, embarrassing demands, and its sad decay. Discomfort over body functions never sleeps, Dr. Burridge said, and the need for an ever-fresh selection of euphemisms about dirty subjects has long served as an impressive engine of linguistic invention.

Once a word becomes too closely associated with a specific body function, she said, once it becomes too evocative of what should not be evoked, it starts to enter the realm of the taboo and must be replaced by a new, gauzier euphemism.

For example, the word *toilet* stems from the French word for "little towel" and was originally a pleasantly indirect way of referring to the place where the chamber pot or its equivalent resides. But *toilet* has since come to mean the porcelain fixture itself, and so sounds too blunt to use in polite company. Instead, you ask your tuxedoed waiter for directions to the ladies' room or the restroom or, if you must, the bathroom.

Similarly, the word *coffin* originally meant an ordinary box, but once it became associated with death, that was it for a "shoe coffin" or "thinking outside the coffin." The taboo sense of a word, Dr. Burridge said, "always drives out any other senses it might have had."

Scientists have lately sought to map the neural topography of forbidden speech by studying Tourette's patients who suffer from coprolalia, the pathological and uncontrollable urge to curse. Tourette's syndrome is a neurological disorder of unknown origin characterized predominantly by chronic motor and vocal tics, a constant grimacing or pushing of one's glasses up the bridge of one's nose or emitting a stream of small yips or grunts.

Just a small percentage of Tourette's patients have coprolalia—estimates range from 8 to 30 percent—and patient advocates are dismayed by popular portrayals of Tourette's as a humorous and invariably scatological condition. But for those who do have coprolalia, said Dr. Carlos Singer, director of the division of movement disorders at the University of Miami School of Medicine, the symptom is often the most devastating and humiliating aspect of their condition.

Not only can it be shocking to people to hear a loud volley of expletives erupt for no apparent reason, sometimes from the mouth of a child or young teenager, but the curses can also be provocative and personal, florid slurs against the race, sexual identity, or body size of a passer-by, for example, or deliberate and repeated lewd references to an old lover's name while in the arms of a current partner or spouse.

Reporting in *The Archives of General Psychiatry*, Dr. David A. Silbersweig, a director of neuropsychiatry and neuroimaging at the Weill Medical College of Cornell University, and his colleagues described their use of PET scans to measure cerebral blood flow and identify which regions of the brain are galvanized in Tourette's patients during episodes of tics and coprolalia.

They found strong activation of the basal ganglia, a quartet of neuron clusters deep in the forebrain at roughly the level of the mid-forehead, that are known to help coordinate body movement along with activation of crucial regions of the left rear forebrain that participate in comprehending and generating speech, most notably Broca's area.

The researchers also saw arousal of neural circuits that interact with the limbic system, the wishbone-shape throne of human emotions, and, significantly, of the "executive" realms of the brain, where decisions to act or desist from acting may be carried out: the neural source, scientists said, of whatever conscience, civility, or free will humans can claim.

That the brain's executive overseer is ablaze in an outburst of coprolalia, Dr. Silbersweig said, demonstrates how complex an act the urge to speak the unspeakable may be, and not only in the case of Tourette's. The person is gripped by a desire to curse, to voice something wildly inappropriate. Higher-order linguistic circuits are tapped, to contrive the content of the curse. The brain's impulse control center struggles to short-circuit the collusion between limbic system urge and neocortical craft, and it may succeed for a time.

Yet the urge mounts, until at last the speech pathways fire, the verboten is spoken, and archaic and refined brains alike must shoulder the blame.

Reading the Genre

1. How does the author manage to write an article about swearing with so little swearing in it? What effect does this have on you as a reader? Does it increase your "urge to speak the unspeakable"? If so, why?

2. At its simplest, a causal analysis asks *why something happens.* What claims does Angier make about why people swear? How does she support her claims?

3. Angier uses a range of sources to explore why people swear. List all her sources; then make notes about where each source gets her or his authority and how each source explains the predominance of swearing. Are some sources more reputable than others? Are some sources more persuasive? (See "Find reliable sources," p. 415, and "Analyze claims and evidence," p. 420.)

4. In response to Angier's article, consider a causal analysis of an opposite inclination: Why do people refrain from swearing? What are some of the social, cultural, professional, familial, and personal forces that require people to speak politely? What are some good reasons for using clean language? (See "Find counterarguments," p. 82, and Chapter 30, "High, Middle, and Low Style," p. 366.)

5. **WRITING:** Do the media mold the way people speak? Watch a popular television show or listen to a song. Analyze the language of the television characters, or that of the song lyrics. Can you make inferences about how these texts might influence audiences to speak in the texts' languages? Write a short causal analysis.

CULTURAL ANALYSIS   Alex Williams writes about technology, media, and culture for the *New York Times* and *New York* magazine.

Here I Am Taking My Own Picture

Alex Williams

Morgan Adams, a recent college graduate, decided that her picture on her home page at MySpace.com had lingered a little too long, a full month. To snap a new one she called on the only photographer she thought she could trust: herself.

In her bedroom in Lubbock, Texas, Ms. Adams, 21, tried out a variety of poses—coy, friendly, sultry, goofy—in the kind of performance young people have engaged in privately for generations before a mirror. But Ms. Adams's mirror was a Web cam, and her journey of self-expression, documented in five digital self-portraits, was soon visible to the 56 million registered users of MySpace.

"Everyone's a little narcissistic," Ms. Adams said. "Being able to take pictures of yourself in privacy allows you to do it without inhibitions. Each person takes better pictures of themselves than anyone else can because they know their own bodies, they know their own minds."

The era of cheap, lightweight digital cameras—in cellphones, in computers, in hip pockets, even on key chains—has meant that people who did not consider themselves photography buffs as recently as five years ago are filling ever-larger hard drives with thousands of images from their lives.

And one particular kind of image has especially soared in popularity, particularly among the young: the self-portrait, which has become a kind of folk art for the digital age.

Framing themselves at arm's length, teenagers snap their own pictures and pass the cameras to friends at school or e-mail the images or upload them to the Internet. For a generation raised on a mantra of self-esteem, striking a heroic, sultry, or brooding pose and sharing it with the world comes naturally.

"It's a huge phenomenon," said Matt Polazzo, the coordinator of student affairs at Stuyvesant High School in Manhattan, referring to the compulsive habit of teenagers to snap everything in their lives, especially self-portraits. "Just yesterday I had a girl sitting on the couch in my office," he said. "She took out her cellphone and said,

'Here, I'm going to show you a picture of my best friend,' snapped a picture of herself, and showed it to me, all in one fluid motion."

Art historians say that the popularity of the self-portrait is unprecedented in the century-long history of the snapshot. "I think it is probably a new genre of photography," said Guy Stricherz, the author of *Americans in Kodachrome, 1945–65* (Twin Palms, 2002), which includes snapshots culled from 500 American families. Mr. Stricherz said he reviewed more than 100,000 pictures over 17 years in compiling the book but found fewer than 100 self-portraits. These days you can find as many by clicking through a few home pages on MySpace, Friendster, or similar social networking sites.

Jeff Gluck, a public relations executive, who lives in Woodcliff Lake, New Jersey, and his wife, Elizabeth, often find one of their two oldest daughters, ages 10 and 13, taking pictures of themselves with cellphone cameras. They do it in the back seat of the car or on the sofa watching television. When not mugging for their own cameras, the girls experiment with the family camera. "Many times with our regular digital camera I'll go to download photos at the computer, and I'll find six pictures of one of the kids that they obviously took themselves," Mr. Gluck said.

To a certain extent new technology is driving the new self-portraiture. Cellphone cameras and other digital cameras are sold with wide-angle lenses that allow a picture taken at arm's length to remain in focus. Computers are essentially $1,000 darkrooms that permit sophisticated manipulation of images.

But technology alone can't explain the trend. Even in previous generations when cameras were cheap, they were generally reserved for special occasions. "In 1960 a person just wouldn't take a Kodak Brownie picture of themselves," Mr. Stricherz said. "It would have been considered too self-aggrandizing."

Psychologists and others who study teenagers say the digital self-portraiture is an extension of behavior typical of the young, like trying on different identities, which earlier generations might have expressed through clothing and hairstyles. "Most of what I've been seeing is taking place in the bedroom," said Kathryn C. Montgomery, a professor of communication at American University, referring to teenage self-portraits. Dr. Montgomery studies the relation of teenagers to the digital media. "It's a locus of teen life where they are forming their identities, and now it's also a private studio where they can develop who they are. What better tool could they have than one that allows them to take pictures of themselves and manipulate them like never before?"

To Jeffrey Jensen Arnett, a developmental psychologist, digital self-portraiture is a high-tech way of expressing an impulse among teenagers and young adults that psychologists call "the imaginary audience."

"This is the idea that adolescents think people are more interested in them than they actually are, that people are always looking at them and taking note of what they are doing, even if it is just walking across the school cafeteria," said Dr. Arnett, who is a Fulbright scholar at the University of Copenhagen.

To Dr. Arnett, the role-playing evident in many self-portraits found online is "a form of pretend: the adolescent version of children dressing up." Others speculate that today's young people are different from earlier generations because they are more comfortable with public self-exposure.

"When I was a kid I didn't want my picture taken," said Jim Taylor, a trend consultant at the Harrison Group in Waterbury, Connecticut. "But these kids are fabulous self-marketers."

He added: "They see celebrities expressing their self-worth and want to join the party. This is a free forum to do so."

"Self-branding is a big deal for kids, and self-produced entertainment is a big deal," Mr. Taylor said. In their pictures, ordinary young women metamorphose into glamour queens or pinup girls, thanks to a few well-rehearsed come-hither poses and mood lighting reminiscent of an old Hollywood studio portrait. Average boys turn themselves into brooding antiheroes by gazing intently into their camera lens in a darkened room, face half buried in shadow.

"There's always a theatrical quality to their shots," Mr. Taylor said. "Kids love melancholy and sadness. There is lots of obvious symbolism about whether they see themselves as an actress, a model, a Christ figure, or a Hamlet."

Young people have become so candid in sharing their intimate images online that some parents and lawmakers are concerned. This month the attorney general of Connecticut, Richard Blumenthal, promised an investigation into MySpace, spurred by complaints of parents that minors could have access to sexual images on the site or could post suggestive pictures that could make them vulnerable to sexual predators. Members have included pictures of themselves in scanty attire or suggestive poses. For many, MySpace functions as a dating site.

But the operators of the Web site, which is owned by the News Corporation, the media conglomerate controlled by Rupert Murdoch, insist that a third of the work force is devoted to policing the site for inappropriate material. Offending members can be banned from the network, and MySpace says it will contact law enforcement officials in serious cases.

Not everyone who compulsively snaps self-portraits sees it as a journey of self-discovery. Tim Zebal, 23, an audio engineer in San Francisco, posted on MySpace an arresting shot of himself taken at a dramatic angle, wearing a billowing shirt and framed in a baroque gold mirror. "I had a new camera phone and snapped a picture in the mirror of a bar restroom," Mr. Zebal explained in an e-mail message. "I thought it looked cool. That's it."

Amber Davidson, 19, a freshman at Concordia College in Moorhead, Minnesota, refreshes her self-portrait on MySpace every couple of weeks and puts a lot of thought into it.

"There's been a big increase in creativity over the past couple of years," she said, referring to the self-portraits on the site. "A lot of people get inspired by what they see in other people's pictures."

Her MySpace home page contains five self-portraits created by pointing the camera toward herself, arm outstretched. She composed each shot so that the arm holding the camera is invisible. In one, Ms. Davidson wears a black-and-white spaghetti-strap dress and peers up winsomely at a camera over her head. It took about 15 tries to get it right, she said. "I don't want people to think I'm sitting there taking all these pictures of myself, even though I kind of am."

Since endless experimentation with digital photography costs little or nothing (you just delete the duds), many young camera owners like Ms. Davidson have practiced their art to the point where they have stumbled across sophisticated portraiture techniques of lighting, composition, and camera angle that were once the province of professionals.

Take that shot with the camera held high above the head, so common on MySpace that some members refer to it as "the helicopter shot." It is a fairly sophisticated technique.

Screenshot of the "MySpace Quick Tour" page.

"Shooting from higher up stretches the neck muscles, and there is no double chin," said Ken White, the chairman of the fine-art photography department at the Rochester Institute of Technology, adding that it also accentuates the jaw line. "It is a glamorizing view."

In the era of the blog, when many deem the most trivial and personal information fit for public consumption, the self-reference of the new portraiture feels natural. "In a funny way I don't see this as photography anymore," said Fred Ritchin, an associate professor in the photography and imaging department at the Tisch School of the Arts at New York University. "It's communication. It's all an extension of cellphones, texting, and e-mailing."

Many users consider digital self-portraits whimsical and ultimately disposable.

"People want pictures of a new hairstyle, outfit, or makeup, and they want to show it to their friends," Tom Anderson, the president of MySpace, said in an e-mail message. But, he added, "I suppose all folk art comes from necessity of some sort."

Reading the Genre

1. Williams suggests that self-portraiture is a new online genre. What kinds of portraits does he mention (for example, the "helicopter shot")? Building on the examples Williams offers, can you identify other types of online portraits?

2. In what ways have technological advances allowed for the huge increase in the popularity of these self-portraits? What technologies are involved, and what do these new tools and networking sites allow? (See Chapter 47, "Using Images," p. 504, and Chapter 50, "Designing Print and Online Documents," p. 517.)

3. Williams implies not only that new technologies have led to the ubiquity of these kinds of photos but also that the photos say something important about how technology has influenced a generation. How do the photographs themselves show a shift in our culture? (See Chapter 46, "Understanding Images," p. 500.)

4. Look at another common characteristic of an online networking site such as Facebook (for example, "The Wall"). How do site participants use this feature? Has this feature shaped the way people interact?

5. **WRITING:** Write a list of rules for Facebook users—what this site should be used for, what users should avoid, and so on. Think about all the possible audiences for a person's Facebook page. Choose one specific rule and write a short explanation of why Facebook users should follow it, and what might happen if they don't.

`CAUSAL ANALYSIS`   Lewis Thomas (1913–1993) was a physician, hospital and university administrator, poet, and scholar. Once the dean of the Yale School of Medicine, he won a National Book Award in 1975 for *The Lives of a Cell: Notes of a Biology Watcher* (1974), a collection of essays originally written as columns for the *New England Journal of Medicine.* The following essay comes from his collection *The Medusa and the Snail: More Notes of a Biology Watcher* (1979).

LEWIS THOMAS

The Wonderful Mistake

The greatest single achievement of nature to date was surely the invention of the molecule of DNA. We have had it from the very beginning, built into the first cell to emerge, membranes and all, somewhere in the soupy water of the cooling planet three thousand million years or so ago. All of today's DNA, strung through all the cells of the earth, is simply an extension and elaboration of that first molecule. In a fundamental sense we cannot claim to have made progress, since the method used for growth and replication is essentially unchanged.

But we have made progress in all kinds of other ways. Although it is out of fashion today to talk of progress in evolution if you use that word to mean anything like improvement, implying some sort of value judgment beyond the reach of science, I cannot think of a better term to describe what has happened. After all, to have come all the way from a system of life possessing only one kind of primitive microbial cell, living out colorless lives in hummocks of algal mats, to what we see around us today—the City of Paris, the State of Iowa, Cambridge University, Woods Hole, the succession of travertine-lined waterfalls and lakes like flights of great stairs in Yugoslavia's Plitvice, the horse-chestnut tree in my backyard, and the columns of neurones arranged in modules in the cerebral cortex of vertebrates—*has* to represent improvement. We have come a long way on that old molecule.

We could never have done it with human intelligence, even if molecular biologists had been flown in by satellite at the beginning, laboratories and all, from some other solar system. We have evolved scientists, to be sure, and so we know a lot about DNA, but if our kind of mind had been confronted with the problem of designing a similar replicating molecule, starting from scratch, we'd never have succeeded. We would have made one fatal mistake: our molecule would have been perfect. Given enough time, we would have figured out how to do this, nucleotides, enzymes, and all, to make flawless, exact copies, but it would never have occurred to us, thinking as we do, that the thing had to be able to make errors.

The capacity to blunder slightly is the real marvel of DNA. Without this special attribute, we would still be anaerobic bacteria and there would be no music. Viewed individually, one by one, each of the mutations that have brought us along represents a random, totally spontaneous accident, but it is no accident at all that mutations occur; the molecule of DNA was ordained from the beginning to make small mistakes.

If we had been doing it, we would have found some way to correct this, and evolution would have been stopped in its tracks. Imagine the consternation of human scientists, successfully engaged in the letter-perfect replication of prokaryotes, nonnucleated cells like bacteria, when nucleated cells suddenly turned up. Think of the agitated commissions assembled to explain the scandalous proliferation of trilobites all over the place, the mass firings, the withdrawal of tenure.

To err is human, we say, but we don't like the idea much, and it is harder still to accept the fact that erring is biological as well. We prefer sticking to the point, and insuring ourselves against change. But there it is: we are here by the purest chance, and by mistake at that. Somewhere along the line, nucleotides were edged apart to let new ones in; maybe viruses moved in, carrying along bits of other, foreign genomes; radiation from the sun or from outer space caused tiny cracks in the molecule, and humanity was conceived.

And maybe, given the fundamental instability of the molecule, it had to turn out this way. After all, if you have a mechanism designed to keep changing the ways of living, and if all the new forms have to fit together as they plainly do, and if every improvised new gene representing an embellishment in an individual is likely to be selected for the species, and if you have enough time, maybe the system is simply bound to develop brains sooner or later, and awareness.

Biology needs a better word than *error* for the driving force in evolution. Or maybe *error* will do after all, when you remember that it came from an old root meaning to wander about, looking for something.

Reading the Genre

1. In this essay, Lewis Thomas addresses two very unpopular ideas. First, he suggests that we, as humans, are actually a mistake. Second, he asserts that nature makes such mistakes, and that this is the genius of nature. From these claims, Thomas argues that perhaps we aren't the most important form of life, that maybe nature could have skipped making human beings altogether, and that we would never have been smart enough to build DNA as well as nature has. How does he cushion the impact of these potentially disturbing assertions? (See Chapter 30, "High, Middle, and Low Style," p. 366, and Chapter 30, "Inclusive and Culturally Sensitive Style," p. 374.)

2. How does Thomas adapt his writing for an audience that may not share his extensive understanding of science? (See "Understanding your audience," pp. 47 and 136.)

3. We don't usually think of nature as having "achievements" or making "mistakes." How does Thomas give nature supposedly "human" characteristics, and what effect does this have on his claims?

4. **WRITING:** Write an essay exploring the idea that nature *didn't* make the wonderful mistake of creating humans. What do you think the world would look like without us? Would another species have evolved into our place? Would the environment be different? Describe what the earth would look like without humans, providing logical explanations for how this came about.

EXPLORATORY ESSAY   Neil Swidey writes for the *Boston Globe Magazine,* and his work has won the National Headliner Award and been widely anthologized. His critically acclaimed book *The Assist: Hoops, Hype, and the Game of Their Lives* (2008) follows a Boston high school basketball team as they pursue a state title.

What Makes People Gay?

Neil Swidey

With crystal-blue eyes, wavy hair, and freshly scrubbed faces, the boys look as though they stepped out of a Pottery Barn Kids catalog. They are seven-year-old twins. I'll call them Thomas and Patrick; their parents agreed to let me meet the boys as long as I didn't use their real names.

Spend five seconds with them, and there can be no doubt that they are identical twins—so identical even they can't tell each other apart in photographs. Spend five minutes with them, and their profound differences begin to emerge.

Patrick is social, thoughtful, attentive. He repeatedly addresses me by name. Thomas is physical, spontaneous, a bit distracted. Just minutes after meeting me outside a coffee shop, he punches me in the upper arm, yells, "Gray punch buggy!" and then points to a Volkswagen Beetle cruising past us. It's a hard punch. They horse around like typical brothers, but Patrick's punches are less forceful and his voice is higher. Thomas charges at his brother, arms flexed in front of him like a mini-bodybuilder. The differences are subtle—they're seven-year-old boys, after all—but they are there.

When the twins were two, Patrick found his mother's shoes. He liked wearing them. Thomas tried on his father's once but didn't see the point.

When they were three, Thomas blurted out that toy guns were his favorite things. Patrick piped up that his were the Barbie dolls he discovered at day care.

When the twins were five, Thomas announced he was going to be a monster for Halloween. Patrick said he was going to be a princess. Thomas said he couldn't do that, because other kids would laugh at him. Patrick seemed puzzled. "Then I'll be Batman," he said.

Their mother—intelligent, warm, and open-minded—found herself conflicted. She wanted Patrick—whose playmates have always been girls, never boys—to be himself, but she worried his feminine behavior would expose him to ridicule and pain. She decided to allow him free expression at home while setting some limits in public.

That worked until last year, when a school official called to say Patrick was making his classmates uncomfortable. He kept insisting that he was a girl.

Patrick exhibits behavior called childhood gender nonconformity, or CGN. This doesn't describe a boy who has a doll somewhere in his toy collection or tried on his sister's Snow White outfit once, but rather one who consistently exhibits a host of strongly feminine traits and interests while avoiding boy-typical behavior like rough-and-tumble play. There's been considerable research into this phenomenon, particularly in males, including a study that followed boys from an early age into early adulthood. The data suggest there is a very good chance Patrick will grow up to be homosexual. (Rather than transgender, as some might suspect.) Not all homosexual men show this extremely feminine behavior as young boys. But the research indicates that, of the boys who do exhibit CGN, about 75 percent of them—perhaps more—turn out to be gay or bisexual.

What makes the case of Patrick and Thomas so fascinating is that it calls into question both of the dominant theories in the long-running debate over what makes people gay: nature or nurture, genes or learned behavior. As identical twins, Patrick and Thomas began as genetic clones. From the moment they came out of their mother's womb, their environment was about as close to identical as possible—being fed, changed, and plopped into their car seats the same way, having similar relationships with the same nurturing father and mother. Yet before either boy could talk, one showed highly feminine traits while the other appeared to be "all boy," as the moms at the playgrounds say with apologetic shrugs.

"That my sons were different the second they were born, there is no question about it," says the twins' mother.

So what happened between their identical genetic starting point and their births? They spent nine months in utero. In the hunt for what causes people to be gay or straight, that's now the most interesting and potentially enlightening frontier.

What does it matter where homosexuality comes from? Proving people are born gay would give them wider social acceptance and better protection against discrimination, many gay rights advocates argue. In the last decade, as this "biological" argument has gained momentum, polls find Americans—especially young adults—increasingly tolerant of gays and lesbians. And that's exactly what has groups opposed to homosexuality so concerned. The Family Research Council, a conservative Christian think tank in Washington, D.C., argues in its book *Getting It Straight* that finding people are born gay "would advance the idea that sexual orientation is an innate characteristic, like race; that homosexuals, like African Americans, should be legally protected against 'discrimination'; and that disapproval of homosexuality should be as socially stigmatized as racism. However, it is not true."

Some advocates of gay marriage argue that proving sexual orientation is inborn would make it easier to frame the debate as simply a matter of civil rights. That could be true, but then again, freedom of religion enjoyed federal protection long before inborn traits like race and sex.

For much of the twentieth century, the dominant thinking connected homosexuality to upbringing. Freud, for instance, speculated that overprotective mothers and distant fathers helped make boys gay. It took the American Psychiatric Association until 1973 to remove "homosexuality" from its manual of mental disorders.

Then, in 1991, a neuroscientist in San Diego named Simon LeVay told the world he had found a key difference between the brains of homosexual and heterosexual men he studied. LeVay showed that a tiny clump of neurons of the anterior hypothalamus—which is believed to control sexual behavior—was, on average, more than twice the size in heterosexual men as in homosexual men. LeVay's findings did not speak directly to the nature-vs.-nurture debate—the clumps could, theoretically, have changed size *because* of homosexual behavior. But that seemed unlikely, and the study ended up jump-starting the effort to prove a biological basis for homosexuality.

Later that same year, Boston University psychiatrist Richard Pillard and North-western University psychologist J. Michael Bailey announced the results of their study of male twins. They found that, in identical twins, if one twin was gay, the other had about a 50 percent chance of also being gay. For fraternal twins, the rate was about 20 percent. Because identical twins share their entire genetic makeup while fraternal twins share about half, genes were believed to explain the difference. Most reputable studies find the rate of homosexuality in the general population to be 2 to 4 percent, rather than the popular "1 in 10" estimate.

In 1993 came the biggest news: Dean Hamer's discovery of the "gay gene." In fact, Hamer, a Harvard-trained researcher at the National Cancer Institute, hadn't quite put it that boldly or imprecisely. He found that gay brothers shared a specific region of the X chromosome, called Xq28, at a higher rate than gay men shared with their straight brothers. Hamer and others suggested this finding would eventually transform our understanding of sexual orientation.

That hasn't happened yet. But the clear focus of sexual-orientation research has shifted to biological causes, and there hasn't been much science produced to support the old theories tying homosexuality to upbringing. Freud may have been seeing the effect rather than the cause, since a father faced with a very feminine son might well become more distant or hostile, leading the boy's mother to become more protective. In recent years, researchers who suspect that homosexuality is inborn—whether because of genetics or events happening in the womb—have looked everywhere for clues: Prenatal hormones. Birth order. Finger length. Fingerprints. Stress. Sweat. Eye blinks. Spatial relations. Hearing. Handedness. Even "gay" sheep.

LeVay, who is gay, says that when he published his study fourteen years ago, some gays and lesbians criticized him for doing research that might lead to homosexuality once again being lumped in with diseases and disorders. "If anything, the reverse has happened," says LeVay, who is now sixty-one and no longer active in the lab. He says the hunt for a biological basis for homosexuality, which involves many researchers who are themselves gay or lesbian, "has contributed to the status of gay people in society."

These studies have been small and underfunded, and the results have often been modest. Still, because there's been so much of this disparate research, "all sort of pointing in the same direction, makes it pretty clear there are biological processes significantly influencing sexual orientation," says LeVay. "But it's also kind of frustrating that it's still a bunch of hints, that nothing is really as crystal clear as you would like."

Just in the last few months, though, the hints have grown stronger.

In May, Swedish researchers reported finding important differences in how the brains of straight men and gay men responded to two compounds suspected of being pheromones—those scent-related chemicals that are key to sexual arousal in animals. The first compound came from women's urine, the second from male sweat. Brain scans showed that when straight men smelled the female urine compound, their hypothalamus lit up. That didn't happen with gay men. Instead, their hypothalamus lit up when they smelled the male-sweat compound, which was the same way straight women had responded. This research once again connecting the hypothalamus to sexual orientation comes on the heels of work with sheep. About 8 percent of domestic rams are exclusively interested in sex with other rams. Researchers found that a clump of neurons similar to the one LeVay identified in human brains was also smaller in gay rams than straight ones. (Again, it's conceivable that these differences could be showing effect rather than cause.)

In June, scientists in Vienna announced that they had isolated a master genetic switch for sexual orientation in the fruit fly. Once they flicked the switch, the genetically altered female flies rebuffed overtures from males and instead attempted to mate with other females, adopting the elaborate courting dance and mating songs that males use.

And now, a large-scale, five-year genetic study of gay brothers is underway in North America. The study received $2.5 million from the National Institutes of Health, which is unusual. Government funders tend to steer clear of sexual orientation research, aware that even small grants are apt to be met with outrage from conservative congressmen looking to make the most of their C-SPAN face time. Relying on a robust sample of 1,000 gay-brother pairs and the latest advancements in genetic screening, this study promises to bring some clarity to the murky area of what role genes may play in homosexuality.

This accumulating biological evidence, combined with the prospect of more on the horizon, is having an effect. Last month, the Rev. Rob Schenck, a prominent Washington, D.C., evangelical leader, told a large gathering of young evangelicals that he believes homosexuality is not a choice but rather a predisposition, something "deeply rooted" in people. Schenck told me that his conversion came about after he'd spoken extensively with genetic researchers and psychologists. He argues that evangelicals should continue to oppose homosexual behavior, but that "many evangelicals are living in a sort of state of denial about the advance of this conversation." His message: "If it's inevitable that this scientific evidence is coming, we have to be prepared with a loving response. If we don't have one, we won't have any credibility." . . .

Let's get back to Thomas and Patrick. Because it's unclear why twin brothers with identical genetic starting points and similar post-birth environments would take such divergent paths, it's helpful to return to the beginning.

Males and females have a fundamental genetic difference—females have two X chromosomes, and males have an X and a Y. Still, right after conception, it's hard to tell male and female zygotes apart, except for that tucked-away chromosomal difference. Normally, the changes take shape at a key point of fetal development, when the male brain is masculinized by sex hormones. The female brain is the default. The brain will stay on the female path as long as it is protected from exposure to hormones. The hormonal theory of homosexuality holds that, just as exposure to circulating sex hormones determines whether a fetus will be male or female, such exposure must also influence sexual orientation.

The cases of children born with disorders of "sexual differentiation" offer insight. William Reiner, a psychiatrist and urologist with the University of Oklahoma, has evaluated more than a hundred of these cases. For decades, the standard medical response to boys born with severely inadequate penises (or none at all) was to castrate the boy and have his parents raise him as a girl. But Reiner has found that nurture—even when it involves surgery soon after birth—cannot trump nature. Of the boys with inadequate penises who were raised as girls, he says, "I haven't found one who is sexually attracted to males." The majority of them have transitioned back to being males and report being attracted to females.

During fetal development, sexual identity is set before the sexual organs are formed, Reiner says. Perhaps it's the same for sexual orientation. In his research, of all the babies with X and Y chromosomes who were raised as girls, the only ones he has found who report having female identities and being attracted to males are those who did not have "receptors" to let the male sex hormones do their masculinizing in the womb.

What does this all mean? "Exposure to male hormones in utero dramatically raises the chances of being sexually attracted to females," Reiner says. "We can infer that the absence of male hormone exposure may have something to do with attraction to males."

Michael Bailey says Reiner's findings represent a major breakthrough, showing that "whatever causes sexual orientation is strongly influenced by prenatal biology." Bailey and Reiner say the answer is probably not as simple as just exposure to sex hormones. After all, the exposure levels in some of the people Reiner studies are abnormal enough to produce huge differences in sexual organs. Yet, sexual organs in straight and gay people are, on average, the same. More likely, hormones are interacting with other factors.

Canadian researchers have consistently documented a "big-brother effect," finding that the chances of a boy being gay increase with each additional older brother he has. (Birth order does not appear to play a role with lesbians.) So, a male with three older brothers is three times more likely to be gay than one with no older brothers, though there's still a better than 90 percent chance he will be straight. They argue that this results from a complex interaction involving hormones, antigens, and the mother's immune system.

By now, there is substantial evidence showing correlation—though not causation—between sexual orientation and traits that are set when a baby is in the womb. Take finger length. In general, men have shorter index fingers in relation to their ring fingers; in women, the lengths are generally about the same. Researchers have found that lesbians generally have ratios closer to males. Other studies have shown masculinized results for lesbians in inner-ear functions and eye-blink reactions to sudden loud noises, and feminized patterns for gay men on certain cognitive tasks like spatial perception and remembering the placement of objects.

New York University researcher Lynn S. Hall, who has studied traits determined in the womb, speculates that Patrick was somehow prenatally stressed, probably during the first trimester, when the brain is really developing, particularly the structures like the hypothalamus that influence sexual behavior. This stress might have been based on his position in the womb or the blood flow to him or any of a number of other factors not in his mother's control. Yet more evidence that identical twins have womb experiences far from identical can be found in their often differing birth weights. Patrick was born a pound lighter than Thomas.

Taken together, the research suggests that early on in the womb, as the fetus's brain develops in either the male or female direction, something fundamental to sexual orientation is happening. Nobody's sure what's causing it. But here's where genes may be involved, perhaps by regulating hormone exposure or by dictating the size of that key clump of neurons in the hypothalamus. Before researchers can sort that out, they'll need to return to the question of whether, in fact, there is a "gay gene." . . .

In the course of reporting this story, I experienced a good deal of whiplash. Just when I would become swayed by the evidence supporting one discreet theory, I would stumble onto new evidence casting some doubt on it. Ultimately, I accepted this as unavoidable terrain in the hunt for the basis of sexual orientation. This is, after all, a research field built on underfunded, idiosyncratic studies that are met with full-barreled responses from opposing and well-funded advocacy groups determined to make the results from the lab hew to the scripts they've honed for the talk-show circuit.

You can't really blame the advocacy groups. The stakes are high. In the end, homosexuality remains such a divisive issue that only thoroughly tested research will get society to accept what science has to say about its origin. Critics of funding for sexual orientation research say that it isn't curing cancer, and they're right. But we devote a lot more dollars to studying other issues that aren't curing cancer and have less resonance in society.

Still, no matter how imperfect these studies are, when you put them all together and examine them closely, the message is clear: While postbirth development may well play a supporting role, the roots of homosexuality, at least in men, appear to be in place by the time a child is born. After spending years sifting through all the available data, British researchers Glenn Wilson and Qazi Rahman come to an even bolder conclusion in their book *Born Gay: The Psychobiology of Sex Orientation,* in which they write: "Sexual orientation is something we are born with and not 'acquired' from our social environment."

Meanwhile, the mother of twins Patrick and Thomas has done her own sifting and come to her own conclusions. She says her son's feminine behavior suggests he will grow up to be gay, and she has no problem with that. She just worries about what happens to him between now and then.

After that fateful call from Patrick's school, she says, "I knew I had to talk to my son, and I had no clue what to say." Ultimately, she told him that although he could play however he wanted at home, he couldn't tell his classmates he was a girl, because they'd think he was lying. And she told him that some older boys might be mean to him and even hit him if he continued to claim he was a girl.

Then she asked him, "Do you think that you can convince yourself that you are a boy?"

"Yes, Mom," he said. "It's going to be like when I was trying to learn to read, and then one day I opened the book and I could read."

His mother's heart sank. She could tell that he wanted more than anything to please her. "Basically, he was saying there must be a miracle—that one day I wake up and I'm a boy. That's the only way he could imagine it could happen."

In the year since that conversation, Patrick's behavior has become somewhat less feminine. His mother hopes it's just because his interests are evolving and not because he's suppressing them.

"I can now imagine him being completely straight, which I couldn't a year ago," she says. "I can imagine him being gay, which seems to be statistically most likely."

She says she's fine with either outcome, just as long as he's happy and free from harm. She takes heart in how much more accepting today's society is. "By the time my boys are twenty, the world will have changed even more."

By then, there might even be enough consensus for researchers to forget about finger lengths and fruit flies and gay sheep, and move on to a new mystery.

Reading the Genre

1. Find passages where it is obvious that Swidey is carefully handling material that may be sensitive. How does he maintain his impartiality? How is he able to address readers across a range of perspectives? (See Chapter 31, "Inclusive and Culturally Sensitive Style," p. 374.)

2. Why is the title question important? What is at stake? Why is it important, rhetorically, to show all that is at stake?

3. Create a simple outline of this essay, including all the locations, the people Swidey introduces, and the major statements Swidey makes in his writing. How does this outline help you understand the organization of the essay? In what other ways might the essay be organized? (See Chapter 24, "Outlines," p. 342.)

4. What major source of evidence does Swidey examine in this essay? How does his evidence differ from that used in other causal analysis essays? How does this change his argument? (See Chapter 37, "Doing Field Research," p. 412.)

5. **WRITING:** Swidey does not provide full citations for the studies mentioned in this essay. Research this material online, find the proper citations, and cite the sources in either MLA or APA style. Create a bibliographical reference for the studies as well. Finally, summarize one of these studies in a few short sentences. (See Chapter 40, "Summarizing Sources," p. 424; Chapter 44, "MLA Documentation and Format," p. 437; and Chapter 45, "APA Documentation and Format," p. 474.)

CAUSAL ANALYSIS   Gardiner Harris and Anahad O'Connor write science, medicine, and health features and news stories for the *New York Times*. O'Connor is also the author of the book *Never Shower in a Thunderstorm: Surprising Facts and Misleading Myths about Our Health and the World We Live In* (2007). The following essay—which first appeared in the *New York Times* in 2005 and subsequently was chosen for the anthology *Best American Science Writing 2006*—investigates the causal controversy around autism and childhood vaccinations.

On Autism's Cause, It's Parents vs. Research

Gardiner Harris and Anahad O'Connor

Kristen Ehresmann, a Minnesota Department of Health official, had just told a State Senate hearing that vaccines with microscopic amounts of mercury were safe. Libby Rupp, a mother of a three-year-old girl with autism, was incredulous.

"How did my daughter get so much mercury in her?" Ms. Rupp asked Ms. Ehresmann after her testimony.

"Fish?" Ms. Ehresmann suggested.

"She never eats it," Ms. Rupp answered.

"Do you drink tap water?"

"It's all filtered."

Ms. Ehresmann's colleague, Patricia Segal-Freeman, spoke up. "Well, do you breathe the air?" Ms. Segal-Freeman asked, with a resigned smile. Several parents looked angrily at Ms. Ehresmann and Ms. Segal-Freeman, who left.

Ms. Rupp remained, shaking with anger. "That anyone could defend mercury in vaccines," she said, "makes my blood boil."

Public health officials like Ms. Ehresmann, who herself has a son with autism, have been trying for years to convince parents like Ms. Rupp that there is no link between thimerosal—a mercury-containing preservative once used routinely in vaccines—and autism.

They have failed.

The Centers for Disease Control and Prevention, the Food and Drug Administration, the Institute of Medicine, the World Health Organization and the American Academy of Pediatrics have all largely dismissed the notion that thimerosal causes or contributes to autism. Five major studies have found no link.

Yet despite all evidence to the contrary, the number of parents who blame thimerosal for their children's autism has only increased. And in recent months, these parents have used their numbers, their passion and their organizing skills to become a potent national force. The issue has become one of the most fractious and divisive in pediatric medicine.

"This is like nothing I've ever seen before," Dr. Melinda Wharton, deputy director of the National Immunization Program, told a gathering of immunization officials in Washington in March. "It's an era where it appears that science isn't enough."

Parents have filed more than 4,800 lawsuits—200 from February to April alone—pushed for state and federal legislation banning thimerosal and taken out full-page advertisements in major newspapers. They have also gained the support of politicians, including Senator Joseph I. Lieberman, Democrat of Connecticut, and Representatives Dan Burton, Republican of Indiana, and Dave Weldon, Republican of Florida. And Robert F. Kennedy Jr. wrote an article in the June 16 issue of *Rolling Stone* magazine arguing that most studies of the issue are flawed and that public health officials are conspiring with drug makers to cover up the damage caused by thimerosal.

"We're not looking like a fringe group anymore," said Becky Lourey, a Minnesota state senator and a sponsor of a proposed thimerosal ban. Such a ban passed the New York State Legislature this week.

But scientists and public health officials say they are alarmed by the surge of attention to an idea without scientific merit. The antithimerosal campaign, they say, is causing some parents to stay away from vaccines, placing their children at risk for illnesses like measles and polio.

"It's really terrifying, the scientific illiteracy that supports these suspicions," said Dr. Marie McCormick, chairwoman of an Institute of Medicine panel that examined the controversy in February 2004.

Experts say they are also concerned about a raft of unproven, costly and potentially harmful treatments—including strict diets, supplements and a detoxifying technique called chelation—that are being sold for tens of thousands of dollars to desperate parents of autistic children as a cure for "mercury poisoning."

In one case, a doctor forced children to sit in a 160-degree sauna, swallow 60 to 70 supplements a day and have so much blood drawn that one child passed out.

Hundreds of doctors list their names on a Web site endorsing chelation to treat autism, even though experts say that no evidence supports its use with that disorder. The treatment carries risks of liver and kidney damage, skin rashes and nutritional deficiencies, they say.

In recent months, the fight over thimerosal has become even more bitter. In response to a barrage of threatening letters and phone calls, the Centers for Disease Control has increased security and instructed employees on safety issues, including how to respond if pies are thrown in their faces. One vaccine expert at the centers wrote in an internal e-mail message that she felt safer working at a malaria field station in

Kenya than she did at the agency's offices in Atlanta.

Thimerosal was for decades the favored preservative for use in vaccines. By weight, it is about 50 percent ethyl mercury, a form of mercury most scientists consider to be less toxic than methyl mercury, the type found in fish. The amount of ethyl mercury included in each childhood vaccine was once roughly equal to the amount of methyl mercury found in the average tuna sandwich.

In 1999, a Food and Drug Administration scientist added up all the mercury that American infants got with a full immunization schedule and concluded that the amount exceeded a government guideline. Some health authorities counseled no action, because there was no evidence that thimerosal at the doses given was harmful and removing it might cause alarm. Others were not so certain that thimerosal was harmless.

In July 1999, the American Academy of Pediatrics and the Public Health Service released a joint statement urging vaccine makers to remove thimerosal as quickly as possible. By 2001, no vaccine routinely administered to children in the United States had more than half of a microgram of mercury—about what is found in an infant's daily supply of breast milk.

Despite the change, government agencies say that vaccines with thimerosal are just as safe as those without, and adult flu vaccines still contain the preservative.

But the 1999 advisory alarmed many parents whose children suffered from autism, a lifelong disorder marked by repetitive, sometimes self-destructive behaviors and an inability to form social relationships. In 10 to 25 percent of cases, autism seems to descend on young children seemingly overnight, sometime between their first and second birthdays.

Diagnoses of autism have risen sharply in recent years, from roughly 1 case for every 10,000 births in the 1980s to 1 in 166 births in 2003.

Most scientists believe that the illness is influenced strongly by genetics but that some unknown environmental factor may also play a role.

Dr. Tom Insel, director of the National Institute for Mental Health, said: "Is it cell phones? Ultrasound? Diet sodas? Every parent has a theory. At this point, we just don't know."

In 2000, a group of parents joined together to found SafeMinds, one of several organizations that argue that thimerosal is that environmental culprit. Their cause has been championed by politicians like Mr. Burton.

"My grandson received nine shots in one day, seven of which contained thimerosal, which is 50 percent mercury as you know, and he became autistic a short time later," he said in an interview.

In a series of House hearings held from 2000 through 2004, Mr. Burton called the leading experts who assert that vaccines cause autism to testify. They included a chemistry professor at the University of

Kentucky who says that dental fillings cause or exacerbate autism and other diseases and a doctor from Baton Rouge, Louisiana, who says that God spoke to her through an eighty-seven-year-old priest and told her that vaccines caused autism.

Also testifying were Dr. Mark Geier and his son, David Geier, the experts whose work is most frequently cited by parents.

Dr. Geier has called the use of thimerosal in vaccines the world's "greatest catastrophe that's ever happened, regardless of cause."

He and his son live and work in a two-story house in suburban Maryland. Past the kitchen and down the stairs is a room with cast-off, unplugged laboratory equipment, wall-to-wall carpeting and faux wood paneling that Dr. Geier calls "a world-class lab—every bit as good as anything at NIH."

Dr. Geier has been examining issues of vaccine safety since at least 1971, when he was a lab assistant at the National Institutes of Health, or NIH. His résumé lists scores of publications, many of which suggest that vaccines cause injury or disease.

He has also testified in more than 90 vaccine cases, he said, although a judge in a vaccine case in 2003 ruled that Dr. Geier was "a professional witness in areas for which he has no training, expertise, and experience."

In other cases, judges have called Dr. Geier's testimony "intellectually dishonest," "not reliable," and "wholly unqualified."

The six published studies by Dr. Geier and David Geier on the relationship between autism and thimerosal are largely based on complaints sent to the Disease Control Centers by people who suspect that their children were harmed by vaccines.

In the first study, the Geiers compared the number of complaints associated with a thimerosal-containing vaccine, given from 1992 to 2000, with the complaints that resulted from a thimerosal-free version given from 1997 to 2000. The more thimerosal a child received, they concluded, the more likely an autism complaint was filed. Four other studies used similar methods and came to similar conclusions.

Dr. Geier said in an interview that the link between thimerosal and autism was clear.

Public health officials, he said, are "just trying to cover it up."

Scientists say that the Geiers' studies are tainted by faulty methodology.

"The problem with the Geiers' research is that they start with the answers and work backwards," said Dr. Steven Black, director of the Kaiser Permanente Vaccine Study Center in Oakland, California. "They are doing voodoo science."

Dr. Julie L. Gerberding, the director of the Disease Control Centers, said the agency was not withholding information about any potentially damaging effects of thimerosal.

"There's certainly not a conspiracy here," she said. "And we would never consider not acknowledging information or evidence that would have a bearing on children's health."

In 2003, spurred by parents' demands, the CDC asked the Institute of Medicine, an arm of the National Academy of Sciences and the nation's most prestigious medical advisory group, to review the evidence on thimerosal and autism.

In a report last year, a panel convened by the institute dismissed the Geiers' work as having such serious flaws that their studies were "uninterpretable." Some of the Geiers' mathematical formulas, the committee found, "provided no information," and the Geiers used basic scientific terms like "attributable risk" incorrectly.

In contrast, the committee found five studies that examined hundreds of thousands of health records of children in the United States, Britain, Denmark, and Sweden to be persuasive.

A study by the World Health Organization, for example, examined the health records of 109,863 children born in Britain from 1988 to 1997 and found that children who had received the most thimerosal in vaccines had the lowest incidence of developmental problems like autism.

Another study examined the records of 467,450 Danish children born from 1990 to 1996. It found that after 1992, when the country's only thimerosal-containing vaccine was replaced by one free of the preservative, autism rates rose rather than fell.

In one of the most comprehensive studies, a 2003 report by CDC, scientists examined the medical records of more than 125,000 children born in the United States from 1991 to 1999. It found no difference in autism rates among children exposed to various amounts of thimerosal.

Parent groups, led by SafeMinds, replied that documents obtained from the Disease Control Centers showed that early versions of the study had found a link between thimerosal and autism.

But CDC researchers said that it was not unusual for studies to evolve as more data and controls were added. The early versions of the study, they said, failed to control for factors like low birth weight, which increases the risk of developmental delays.

The Institute of Medicine said that it saw "nothing inherently troubling" with the CDC's adjustments and concluded that thimerosal did not cause autism. Further studies, the institute said, would not be "useful."

Since the report's release, scientists and health officials have been bombarded with hostile e-mail messages and phone calls. Dr. McCormick, the chairwoman of the institute's panel, said she had received threatening mail claiming that she was part of a conspiracy. Harvard University has increased security at her office, she said.

An e-mail message to the CDC on November 28 stated, "Forgiveness is between them and God. It is my job to arrange a meeting," according to records obtained by the *New York Times* after the filing of an open records request.

Another e-mail message, sent to the CDC on August 20, said, "I'd like to know how you people sleep straight in bed at night knowing all the lies you tell & the lives you know full well you destroy with the poisons you push & protect with your lies." Lyn Redwood of SafeMinds said that such e-mail messages did not represent her organization or other advocacy groups.

In response to the threats, CDC officials have contacted the Federal Bureau of Investigation and heightened security at the Disease Control Centers. Some officials said that the threats had led them to look for other jobs.

In *Evidence of Harm*, a book published earlier this year that is sympathetic to the notion that thimerosal causes autism, the author, David Kirby, wrote that the thimerosal theory would stand or fall within the next year or two.

Because autism is usually diagnosed sometime between a child's third and fourth birthdays and thimerosal was largely removed from childhood vaccines in 2001, the incidence of autism should fall this year, he said.

No such decline followed thimerosal's removal from vaccines during the 1990s in Denmark, Sweden, or Canada, researchers say.

But the debate over autism and vaccines is not likely to end soon.

"It doesn't seem to matter what the studies and the data show," said Ms. Ehresmann, the Minnesota immunization official. "And that's really scary for us because if science doesn't count, how do we make decisions? How do we communicate with parents?"

Reading the Genre

1. What does this essay say about how much people *want* to understand causes? What happens when believed-in causes are challenged or disproved? What does this reveal about the persuasive power of a causal explanation?

2. What does this essay reveal about the powerful *ethos,* or authority, of science? When new data emerges from scientific studies, scientific hypotheses based on earlier evidence often need to be updated and changed. But how does this affect the people who believed these hypotheses? (See "Consider and control your ethos," p. 77, and "Consider its use of rhetorical appeals," p. 231.)

3. How can this be a causal analysis essay if it proposes no answers? Even without proposing definitive answers or explanations, is this essay persuasive? How?

4. It is difficult to prove scientific causality. But what special challenges are posed when you are trying to show that a cause is *not* plausible? (See "Respond to opposing claims and points of view," p. 70.)

5. **WRITING:** Design two advertisements: one composed by the "antithimerosal" campaign that warns against mercury in vaccines; the other by scientists refuting inconclusive data linking thimerosal and autism. As you write, think about the differences in purpose, tone, and argumentation strategies in the two advertisements.

Proposal: Readings

67

PROPOSAL FOR CHANGE   As the federal government's official spokesperson on pressing public health issues and initiatives, the surgeon general of the United States is most familiar to Americans from the warnings printed on cigarette and other product packaging (following a surgeon general's 1964 report on the harmful, cancer-causing effects of smoking, the warnings began to be placed on cigarette packaging). The following selection is excerpted from "Underage Drinking: A Call to Action" on the surgeon general's Web site: www.surgeongeneral.gov/topics/underagedrinking.

Prevention and Reduction of Alcohol Use and Alcohol Use Disorders in Adolescents

Surgeon General of the United States

To succeed, prevention and reduction efforts must take into account the dynamic developmental processes of adolescence, the influence of an adolescent's environment, and the role of individual characteristics in the adolescent's decision to drink. The goals of interventions aimed at underage alcohol use[1] are to:

- Change societal acceptance, norms, and expectations surrounding underage drinking.
- Prevent adolescents from starting to drink.
- Delay initiation of drinking.
- Intervene early, especially with high-risk youth.[2]

---

[1] The ultimate goal is to increase the age of initiation to the minimum legal drinking age of 21, thereby eliminating drinking by individuals under 21 and its consequences; however, underage drinking is so strongly embedded in the Nation's culture that the more realistic goals of increasing the average age of initiation and reducing underage drinking and its negative consequences are included as incremental steps.

[2] Examples of high-risk youth include children with externalizing disorders, children from families with a history of alcohol dependence, youth who exhibit a special predilection for sensation seeking, and youth who have experienced trauma. These are risk factors not only for alcohol use but for other substance abuse and mental disorders as well.

- Reduce drinking and its negative consequences, including progression to alcohol use disorders (AUDs), when initiation already has occurred.
- Identify adolescents who have developed AUDs and who would benefit from additional interventions, including treatment and recovery support services.

In essence, these efforts form a continuum designed to help children and adolescents make sound choices about alcohol use. Scientific research provides the foundation for the design of interventions that accomplish these goals and the means for determining which interventions are effective.

Prevention efforts have typically approached the issue of underage drinking through two avenues: by seeking to change the adolescent and by seeking to change the adolescent's environment. Interventions aimed at adolescents themselves seek to change expectations, attitudes, and intentions; impart knowledge and skills; and provide the necessary motivation to better enable adolescents to resist influences that would lead them to drink. Environmental interventions seek to reduce opportunities for underage drinking (i.e., the availability of and access to alcohol for adolescent consumption). Examples include (1) increasing enforcement of and penalties for violating the minimum legal drinking age for youth who drink or attempt to purchase alcohol, for merchants who sell to youth, and for people who provide alcohol to underage youth, and (2) reducing community tolerance for underage alcohol use.

Adopting a Developmental Approach

A developmental approach to interventions retains the same fundamental goals as the traditional approach and, in addition, incorporates an understanding of the dynamic, complex nature of adolescent development. The objective of this approach is to ensure the emergence of a self-reliant, competent, and healthy adult at the end of the adolescent maturation process. It focuses on identifying and countering, weakening, or eliminating risk factors for underage alcohol use while identifying and strengthening protective factors—all based on the adolescent's maturational stage, internal characteristics, and the characteristics of the external environment.

The developmental approach addresses the multilayered environment, or social systems, in which adolescents exist. It promotes creating opportunities for positive growth and development by recognizing youth for their assets and abilities and by engaging them in their communities through such activities as volunteering, sports, music, academics, and leadership (Benson et al. 1998; Lerner 2002; Scales et al. 2000). There is evidence that youth who spend more time engaged in these types of activities are less likely to engage in risky behaviors, such as alcohol use.

Integrated Structures to Protect the Adolescent

A scaffold is a temporary, supportive structure used in the construction of buildings and other large structures. In this context, the term *scaffolding* (Gauvain 2001; Vygotsky 1978; Wood et al. 1976) is used to represent the structured process through which positive development is facilitated and risk is minimized by providing protection from the natural risk-taking, sensation-seeking tendencies of the adolescent. It is a fitting metaphor for the supports and protections that parents and society provide children and youth to help them function in a more mature way until they are ready to function without that extra support. Through scaffolding, parents and societies can provide young people—who can be viewed as "adults under construction"—with supports that ensure their safe and healthy maturation from birth to adulthood (e.g., curfews that change as children get older and are ready for greater responsibility).

Throughout childhood and especially during adolescence, effective scaffolding requires frequent readjustment because individuals and their situations are continually changing. This external support system, or scaffold, around the adolescent promotes healthy development and provides protection from alcohol use and other risky behaviors by facilitating good decision-making, mitigating risk factors, and buffering against potentially destructive outside influences that draw adolescents to alcohol use. *Buffering* refers to protecting adolescents by intercepting or moderating adverse pressures or influences on them so that they are not overwhelmed and can rely on their own adaptive capacities for self-protection.

Ideally, effective scaffolding is:

- *Developmentally based and culturally appropriate:* The protective extent of the scaffold matches the child's developmental stage and maturation level, is culturally appropriate, and is modified as needed, especially during significant transition points in the adolescent's life.
- *Comprehensive:* Scaffolding is multifaceted, consisting of elements constructed by parents, school, community, and society. Scaffolding is the responsibility of the Nation as a whole, for which underage alcohol use is a public health and safety problem.
- *Integrated:* The various components of the scaffold (e.g., community, school, and parents) are aligned, complement and reinforce each other, and create synergy. When some weaken, others are strengthened.
- *Evolving:* The scaffold is modified as the child matures to remain developmentally appropriate to the adolescent's maturational level to encourage the development of autonomy and, ultimately, the adoption of adult roles. The scaffold should protect, but not suffocate, allowing adolescents to interact with, and contribute to, the world in which they live and ultimately achieve the developmental goals of independence and self-reliance.
- *Initiated early:* The scaffold is initiated early, before puberty begins. However, it is better to construct a scaffold later than not at all.
- *Long-term:* Some form of scaffold should remain in place throughout adolescence, but elements should be carefully removed to facilitate the development of independence and self-reliance.

A shift in significant support structures, such as parental divorce or a move to a new town, can increase the risk for alcohol use and may require that additional elements be added to strengthen the scaffolding, at least temporarily.

A developmental approach to underage drinking recognizes that not all adolescents drink, and those who do drink differ in their drinking patterns (the way in which they tend to drink—e.g., daily drinking, bingeing, weekends only) and their drinking trajectories (how and when they started drinking and how their drinking plays out over time). No single trajectory or pattern of consumption describes the course of alcohol use for all or even most young people (Schulenberg et al. 1996a, 1996b). The trajectories and patterns of consumption vary considerably as adolescents grow into young adults and may be altered by their experiences, including treatment for AUDs (Chung et al. 2003). Developmental differences in consumption trajectories and patterns may have important implications for interventions, determining, for example, what types of messages are relevant to specific groups of young people. Some interventions have proved effective for youth who have not initiated alcohol use but not for youth who have (Perry et al. 1996, 2002).

Intervening with Adolescents Who Have Alcohol Problems, Including AUDs

Based on their responses to a survey conducted in 2004, approximately 3.7 million or 9.8 percent of American youth ages 12–20 met criteria for AUDs and/or received treatment at a specialty facility[3] for an alcohol problem. Interventions for youth with AUDs are an essential component of the protective structure society should provide for its adolescents and one end of the continuum of interventions that prevents and reduces underage alcohol use. Of the 3.7 million, only 232,000 received treatment in a specialty facility, suggesting an unmet need for screening,[4] referral, and treatment of adolescent AUDs and associated behavioral problems. Contributing

---

[3] *Specialty treatment* is defined as treatment received at hospitals (inpatient only), drug or alcohol rehabilitation facilities) (inpatient or outpatient), or mental health centers. It excludes treatment in an emergency room, private doctor's office, self-help group, prison or jail, or hospital as an outpatient.

[4] *Screening* refers to the process of evaluating members of a population (e.g., all patients in a physician's practice) to estimate their likelihood of using alcohol and/or having alcohol-related problems.

factors may include the cost of intervention, lack of insurance coverage, limited access to care, and lack of awareness of the problem. For example, not all pediatricians systematically screen adolescent patients for substance abuse (Kulig and American Academy of Pediatrics Committee on Substance Abuse 2005). Furthermore, pediatric health care providers underestimate alcohol use and AUDs among adolescents (Wilson et al. 2004). In addition, a subset of young people receives much of their medical care in an emergency department where it is unlikely they will be asked about their alcohol use. Further, limited availability of developmentally and culturally appropriate treatment and, in rural areas, the need to travel long distances to receive care may present additional barriers to intervention.

When adequate screening is in place, adolescents with alcohol-related problems, including those who do not meet formal diagnostic criteria, can be identified, referred for, and provided with appropriate interventions (including brief interventions) to prevent them from progressing to deeper alcohol involvement. However, diagnosing AUDs among adolescents is a challenging task. Criteria used to diagnose AUDs in adolescents were derived largely from clinical and research experience with adults (Chung et al. 2005). Yet, numerous developmental differences between adolescents and adults may affect the applicability of AUD criteria to youth. Developmental differences in alcohol use patterns indicate the need to adapt existing criteria to make them relevant to, and properly scaled for, an adolescent's stage of maturation (Brown 1999; Chung and Martin 2001, 2005; Martin et al. 1996). Current diagnostic criteria may overestimate problems in some adolescents while failing to capture hazardous practices in others (Martin and Winters 1998). Of primary importance is the need for a more valid diagnostic system for assessing the nature and magnitude of adolescent problem drinking that is appropriate to an adolescent's stage of maturation.

Early evidence on the effectiveness of brief motivational interventions in reducing or eliminating alcohol-related problems in adolescents indicates that they may be effective in reducing both drinking and its consequences, such as drunk driving (reviewed in Larimer and Cronce 2002; see also Tevyaw and Monti 2004). However, further analysis is necessary to determine both the duration of effects and which adolescents are likely to benefit from this type of intervention based on their drinking patterns, trajectories, and behaviors. As appropriate, adolescents can be referred for more extensive and/or intensive treatment for their AUDs.

Most current specialized treatment services are not optimally designed for access and engagement by youth (Brown 2001). Consequently, alternative treatment formats, attention to developmental transitions, and social marketing are needed to more adequately address alcohol use and alcohol-related problems emerging in adolescence (Brown 2001; Kypri et al. 2004; O'Leary et al. 2002). Further, treatment for adolescents frequently requires integrating interventions for alcohol use, other drug use, mental disorders, and family problems. Some of the most promising interventions for adolescents with AUDs have incorporated multiple components and systems, such as family-based intervention, group or individual cognitive–behavioral therapy, and therapeutic community interventions (see, e.g., Swensen et al. 2005 and Waldron and Kaminer 2004).

References

Benson, P.; Leffert, N.; Scales, P.; et al. Beyond the "village" rhetoric: Creating healthy communities for children and adolescents. *Applied Developmental Science* 2:138–159, 1998.

Brown, S.A. "A Double-Developmental Model of Adolescent Substance Abuse." Paper presented at the Annual Scientific Meeting of the Research Society on Alcoholism, Santa Barbara, CA, 1999.

Brown, S.A. Facilitating change for adolescent alcohol problems: A multiple options approach. In: Wagner, E.F., and Waldron, H.B., eds. *Innovations in Adolescent Substance Abuse Intervention*. New York: Pergamon, 2001, pp. 169–187.

Chung, T., and Martin, C.S. Classification and course of alcohol problems among adolescents in addictions treatment programs. *Alcoholism: Clinical and Experimental Research* 25:1734–1742, 2001.

Chung, T., and Martin, C.S. What were they thinking? Adolescents' interpretations of DSM-IV alcohol dependence symptom queries and implications for diagnostic validity. *Drug and Alcohol Dependence* 80:191–200, 2005.

Chung, T.; Martin, C.S.; Grella, C.E.; et al. Course of alcohol problems in treated adolescents. *Alcoholism: Clinical and Experimental Research* 27:253–261, 2003.

Chung, T.; Martin, C.S.; and Winters, K.C. Diagnosis, course, and assessment of alcohol abuse and dependence in adolescents. In: Galanter, M., ed. *Recent Developments in Alcoholism, Vol. 17: Alcohol Problems in Adolescents and Young Adults: Epidemiology, Neurobiology, Prevention, Treatment.* New York: Springer, 2005, pp. 5–27.

Gauvain, M. *The Social Context of Cognitive Development.* New York: Guilford, 2001.

Kulig, J.W., and the American Academy of Pediatrics Committee on Substance Abuse. Tobacco, alcohol, and other drugs: The role of the pediatrician in prevention, identification, and management of substance abuse. *Pediatrics* 115:816–821, 2005.

Kypri, K.; McCarthy, D.M.; Coe, M.T.; et al. Transition to independent living and substance involvement of treated and high-risk youth. *Journal of Child and Adolescent Substance Abuse* 13:85–100, 2004.

Larimer, M.E., and Cronce, J.M. Identification, prevention and treatment: A review of individual-focused strategies to reduce problematic alcohol consumption by college students. *Journal of Studies on Alcohol Supplement* No 14:148–163, 2002.

Lerner, R.M. Promoting healthy adolescent behavior and development: Issues in design and evaluation of effective youth programs. *Journal of Pediatric Nursing* 17:338–344, 2002.

Martin, C.S.; Langenbucher, J.W.; Kaczynski, N.A.; et al. Staging in the onset of DSM-IV alcohol symptoms in adolescents: Survival/hazard analyses. *Journal of Studies on Alcohol* 57:549–558, 1996.

Martin, C.S., and Winters, K.C. Diagnosis and assessment of alcohol use disorders among adolescents. *Alcohol Health & Research World* 22(2):95–105, 1998.

O'Leary, T.A.; Brown, S.A.; Colby, S.M.; et al. Treating adolescents together or individually? Issues in adolescent substance abuse interventions. *Alcoholism: Clinical and Experimental Research* 26:890–899, 2002.

Perry, C.L.; Williams, C.L; Komro, K.A.; et al. Project Northland: Long-term outcomes of community action to reduce adolescent alcohol use. *Health Education Research* 17:117–132, 2002.

Perry, C.L.; Williams, C.L.; Veblen-Mortenson, S.; et al. Project Northland: Outcomes of a communitywide alcohol use prevention program during early
adolescence. *American Journal of Public Health* 86:956–965, 1996.

Scales, P.; Benson, P.; Leffert, N.; et al. The contribution of developmental assets
to the prediction of thriving among adolescents. *Applied Developmental
Science* 4:27–46, 2000.

Schulenberg, J.; O'Malley, P.M.; Bachman, J.G.; et al. Getting drunk and growing
up: Trajectories of frequent binge drinking during the transition to young
adulthood. *Journal of Studies on Alcohol* 57:289–304. 1996*b*.

Schulenberg, J.E.; Wadsworth, K.N.; O'Malley, P.M.; et al. Adolescent risk factors for binge drinking during the transition to young adulthood: Variable-
and pattern-centered approaches to change. *Developmental Psychology*
32:659–674, 1996*a*.

Swensen, C.C.; Henggeler, S.W.; Taylor, L.S.; et al. *Multisystemic Therapy and
Neighborhood Partnerships: Reducing Adolescent Violence and Substance
Abuse.* New York: Guilford, 2005.

Tevyaw, T.O., and Monti, P.M. Motivational enhancement and other brief interventions for adolescent substance abuse: Foundations, applications, and
evaluations. *Addiction* 99(Suppl. 2):63–75, 2004.

Vygotsky, L.S. *Mind and Society: The Development of Higher Mental Processes.*
Cambridge, MA: Harvard University Press, 1978.

Waldron, H.B., and Kaminer, Y. On the learning curve: The emerging evidence
supporting cognitive-behavioral therapies for adolescent substance abuse.
Addiction 99(Suppl. 2):93–105, 2004.

Wilson, C.R.; Sherritt, L.; Gates, E.; et al. Are clinical impressions of adolescent
substance use accurate? *Pediatrics* 114(5):e536–540, 2004.

Wood, D.J., Bruner, J., and Ross, G. The role of tutoring in problem solving.
Journal of Child Psychology and Psychiatry 17:89–100, 1976.

Reading the Genre

1. How is this article organized? How are lists used to prioritize information, to distinguish issues, and to define problems?

2. How does this proposal incorporate research? How is evidence used to support claims and findings?

3. Who is the audience for this essay? Make a list of people who might be the ideal readers for this report. (See "Understanding your audience," p. 167.)

4. Create a list of other public health issues that you think the surgeon general should turn his or her attention to; then propose some possible solutions to a few of these problems.

5. **WRITING:** Rewrite this report as a pamphlet for a parent or as a book for a child. How would you change this essay to reach these different audiences?

PROPOSAL FOR CHANGE   Laura Pappano is an award-winning journalist, and Eileen McDonagh teaches political science at Northeastern University. Together, they write a blog hosted by the news and opinion site, the Huffington Post (www.huffingtonpost.com/eileen-mcdonagh-and-laura-pappano). The following essay is from their book *Playing with the Boys: Why Separate Is Not Equal in Sports* (2008).

EILEEN MCDONAGH AND LAURA PAPPANO

Time to Change the Rules

Sports matter precisely because they are more than play. Organized athletics reveal our beliefs and biases and offer a proving ground for the lessons we care about. Sports culture may be steeped in tradition and resistant to reinterpretation. But we must try. We must be able to recast our athletic heroes as girls and women. We must reimagine games and rules and opportunities so that women and men can compete more often on the same field.

The idea of change in sport is as old as the notion of tradition in sport. Regardless of how organic it feels or for how long it has been woven into nationalistic rituals, sport is human-made. Athletic rules change constantly, seeking ways to draw larger audiences, speed up play, or improve player safety. On the eve of Wimbledon in 2003, for example, one newspaper polled tennis fans and concluded "millions are switching off 'boring' tennis" because it had become a contest of power serves. The newspaper survey of tennis aficionados, not mere average citizens, revealed half of respondents believed the solution was to adjust the game by reducing the pressure inside tennis balls to make them slower.[1]

There is, in other words, nothing "pure" or unalterable about sports. The practice of realigning conferences or jumping divisions is a constant in organized athletics. Players are traded and teams carry on. It should not be impossible to set goals at end marks other than winning a championship or selling more tickets. It should be possible to make gender equity a goal too.

Sport holds a distinguished place in our society. In his analysis of American fitness from 1890 to 1940 Donald J. Mrozek observes that "the genteel preacher, doctor, or teacher came to tolerate the public display and physical assertiveness of organized sport and athletics by seeing with them new means for ingraining the principles of ethical conduct."[2] At the very moment organized sport could have been rejected as a crude intrusion into American life, it had the fortune of being seized on by the upper-middle class and cast as a noble pursuit, an enterprise that developed physical health and moral character. As a result, Mrozek asserts, organized sport has become "a key building block of the mass culture."[3]

Sport today, despite its dark side, remains idealized as a vessel of positive social values. Players, fans, and parents may misbehave at sporting events, but we continue to emphasize the positive lessons. We prefer the romanticized image of athletics as a wholesome contest in which the rules are plain, the play fair, and the victors gracious. The clarity of games, whether Saturday morning youth soccer or the U.S. Open in tennis, is welcomed in a world in which things are not often as they seem and the final outcome is elusive.

Despite the starry-eyed glamour afforded American sport, despite the good to individual lives, it has been a barrier to gender equity. The time has come to acknowledge this and rethink the structure of American sport to support fair play and a just society. While many point to the progress women have made in terms of athletic achievement and public visibility, it does not erase the larger fact: females have been accommodated and tolerated, not treated as equals and promoted. There have been small adjustments and concessions to "let the girls play," but organized sport has resisted deep change. The solution is not to "let" females play, but to open our eyes to inequalities that have become routine business in organized sport that are barriers to women athletes.

We need reform at several levels. It is not work for one segment of society, but for all, from the personal to the governmental, from attitudes of coaches to institutional rules. Here are ten recommendations intended as a starting point.

1. *Accept a new, gender-neutral view of sports.*   We must challenge the stereotype that males are naturally superior athletes and consider the individual first. There are more athletic differences among individuals than between athletes which are based only on gender. This means challenging biases that label some sports as female and others as male. Girls can race cars; boys can figure-skate. Parents, teachers, neighbors, community leaders, and others whose impressions shape attitudes from youth must recognize and challenge ingrained stereotypes. Support children in playing whatever sport they choose; encourage girls to play sports that are not traditionally considered female and boys to play in sports that are not traditionally male.

2. *Increase opportunities for coed sports at every level.* We need more events in which males and females play together. At the professional level, we must have more models of sex-integrated sporting events, even if they are initially special promotional events outside of regular circuit play. At recreational, youth, middle and high school levels, we must stop the reflexive sex segregation of sports. There must be more coed teams and more coed opportunities for competition. This means dividing teams by ability with the goal of increasing participation so that more individuals—even those males who are not stellar athletes—may find an appropriate level of competition.

3. *Gender-blind sports rules.* The International Olympic Committee, as well as governing bodies of various men's and women's sports, should eliminate rule differences between male and female versions of a sport which reflect outmoded beliefs about male and female capabilities or that merely serve to differentiate male and female play. Wherever reasonable, the size of play areas, the length of games and races, the points needed to win, or other measures in a sport should be the same for males and females.

4. *Require parity in ticket prices, promotion, and salaries at educational institutions.* We must close the gap between pay for coaches of male teams and coaches of female teams. In addition, there should be no difference in ticket prices between men's and women's college and high school sporting events. College promotions offices should be required to put as much media effort into promoting women's sporting events as they do promoting men's.

5. *Equal television time for women's sports.* Much as the federal government requires broadcasters to devote regularly scheduled time to educational broadcasting for children for the privilege of using the airwaves, broadcasters should be required to devote equal time to programs on women's athletics or to covering women's events. As has happened with children's programming, these demands will likely yield new media stars and capture for broadcasters a new pool of viewers.

6. *Better print and online news coverage for women's sports.* Too many newspapers and mainstream online news and sports sites still cover women's sport events as charity work. The stories of female athletes and competition are just as compelling as stories about male athletes. The more people learn about an athlete, the more they will care and seek coverage. More television coverage of women's sports will drive increased interest in and reporting on female athletes. If sports editors value women's athletics as more than the occasional soft feature, people will look for those stories. They are looking for them now, and they're missing.

7. *Women must "speak" sports.* Athletics are important in our society and women opt out at their peril. Just as it is important to vote and be informed about local, national, and international political events, following sports can promote one's inclusion in business, professional, and everyday public life. Many women are already sports fans, consumers, and participants. They are already benefiting from sports as a key feminist tool.

8. *Feminist power play: bringing athletics into the network.*   Men long ago created a power network that includes leaders in business, politics—and sports. Powerful women gather around business and political issues, but we must widen the circle so that there are more frequent and visible networking crossovers among high-profile female athletes, coaches, and team owners, and politicians and business leaders. We must help each other. Ruth Ann Marshall, president of the Americas for MasterCard, for example, decided to have MasterCard sponsor LPGA players like Dottie Pepper and sponsor the Women's World Cup soccer. Such forward-thinking acts must be replicated by women in power. This is not charity. Raising the profile of female athletes and business and political leaders broadens public recognition for women and normalizes female competence and power.

9. *If you can, buy the team—or at least a ticket.*   We need women to support women's athletics. Buy a season ticket to the WNBA franchise. Attend and support female athletic events. Take your children to see women play. If you can afford it, buy a team. More women must be at the owner's table, whether in women's leagues (precious few choices at the moment) or in men's. We must drive change from outside as well as from within. Even an act as simple as having your March Madness office pool include the Women's NCAA basketball tournament—not just the men's—raises awareness of compelling women's play. There is no apologetic stance needed: the women have game and more people need to know about it.

10. *Strengthen Title IX.*   Title IX may have seemed appropriate when it was passed in 1972, but it never demanded equality. We now need financial equality, even if that means dramatically scaling back men's college football and basketball programs, some of which hardly resemble programs suitable for educational institutions. If the NFL or the NBA wants a development league, they should build it. Colleges should value men's and women's Olympic sports as part of their educational mission. Title IX also must be more aggressively enforced. And finally, Title IX must *not* permit coercive sex segregation that prevents girls from "playing with the boys."

Sports: The Next Frontier

In the United States, the act of defining sex difference has defined inequality. The long-standing images of women as weak and physically inferior to males has ensured stark sex differentiation and in the past barred females from higher education, kept them from the right to vote, and created barriers in the workplace. In many cases, women embraced these limitations, agreeing it was not their "place" to occupy the same social and economic space as men.

Integrating higher education, permitting women to vote, and outlawing sex bias at work have been crucial steps not just for women, but also for American society. Organized athletics represents the next goal in the quest for equal participation. Familiar arguments of female physical and biological differences drive sex-separate athletic programs, differentiated male and female rules (not based on actual physical differences), and sex-differentiated expectations.

In fact, the barriers female athletes face today are not chiefly physical but social and cultural. One has only to look internationally to see the limiting power of social gender bias. When Lima Azima finished last in the 100-meter race at the World Track and Field Championships in Paris in August 2003, no one blamed her athletic ability. Her victory was in overcoming impressive obstacles to become the first Afghan woman ever to compete in a major worldwide sports event. She wore long baggy pants to other runners' sleek, form-fitting uniforms. She struggled with the starting blocks, had never worn proper running shoes (Adidas donated shoes for the race), and had not been permitted to train outdoors or in front of men. Merely participating was success.[4]

In Bangladesh, the women's soccer team has faced protests from conservative Muslim groups that consider their play immoral. In October 2004, the women's team played despite a demonstration by 500 activists in Dhaka carrying placards reading, among other slogans: "Stop un-Islamic activities, protect sanctity of womanhood." Moulana Abdur Rashid, deputy chief of the Islamic Constitution

Movement, warned that "the national sport council will be put under siege . . . if the satanic women's football league is not abandoned immediately."[5]

The pervasive belief that athletics will keep women from being womanly persists. Research at the University of Nigeria found 51 percent of women were concerned that playing a sport would lead them to develop masculine features and therefore they chose not to participate. Many worried that athletics could affect menstruation and reproduction, and that they could be injured, which kept parents from encouraging daughters to play sports.[6]

Females in some minority groups avoid sports because of similar cultural messages. For example, only 43 percent of Hispanic high school sophomore girls play at least one interscholastic sport, compared with 52 percent of non-Hispanic sophomore girls. The issue is not money but cultural habits in which girls are not encouraged to stay after school for sports because they are expected at home to help with family obligations. Raul Hodgers, athletic director at Desert View High School in Tucson, Arizona (the school is 80 percent Hispanic), noted that "most of these girls are athletically inclined, but it is difficult to acclimate parents to the idea of kids staying after school."[7] And he was referring to girls, not boys.

In some parts of the developing world the demands of daily survival make sports appear trivial, while in other developing nations women are restricted to private spheres of home and child rearing, excluding them from public realms of work and sport.[8] And yet it is clear that athletics can be potent diplomatic and ideological tools.

The Chinese have earned international attention for athletics, winning 32 Gold Medals at the 2004 Athens Olympics, second only to the Americans. The Chinese government urged all Chinese citizens to learn from those athletic victories. "The excellent performance by China's athletes again shows the spirit of the Chinese nation's unremitting efforts to improve itself," the government said in broadcasts on state-run television. "The motherland is proud of you, and the people are proud of you."[9]

Nationalism

The rise of China's athletic profile on the international stage (NBA star Yao Ming has also helped) is seen as clear evidence of a nation on the road to economic dominance. Interestingly, success of Chinese women athletes, in part, has been attributed to a cultural norm in which an athlete's Chinese identity is viewed as more important than her gender identity. "Any polarization of males versus females is therefore overwhelmed by feelings of 'China versus the world,'" noted one researcher. "This is a phenomenon starkly at variance with the historical 'male versus female' dichotomy common in Western sporting nations, but is closer to the situation that existed in much of Eastern Europe and Cuban sport."[10]

It may be socially convenient to differentiate sports by sex. However, it thwarts power sharing and equality between the sexes. When Little League lawyers and physicians in 1974 argued to a New Jersey civil rights hearing officer that "boys like to be with boys and girls like to be with girls" in their failed quest to keep girls off the diamond, they echoed a cultural belief: regardless of whether boys and girls can or should play together, many don't want to.[11]

Although girls are now permitted to play Little League, and modest numbers actually do, most choose softball instead. Talk with parents and you hear similar sentiments: their daughters don't want to play with boys and boys don't want to play with girls. Whether the sport is baseball, basketball, ice hockey, wrestling, or soccer, the presumption is that athletes prefer to compete with players of their own sex. Adults, even in social tennis, gravitate to same-sex play. Organized sport truly is the most sex-segregated secular institution in our society. More than a reflection of actual physical differences between males and females, it reveals cultural norms and our present comfort zone. We have been conditioned—and our children are being conditioned—to believe this is *the right way* to play.

Sharing power depends on sharing turf in the Oval Office, Congress, state houses, local government, boardrooms, CEO suites—and on the playing field. Opening power structures to greater male-female cooperation means including more females in athletic opportunities with males, inviting more women to the business golf outing, seeing more females pick-and-roll in a pick-up, recreational league, or after-work basketball game.

This must start when children are young. Just as the drive for increasing racial and ethnic diversity is considered critical to preparing children for the future, we must teach children from the time they step onto the gymnasium floor on Saturday mornings to play Itty Bitty Basketball that girls and boys can pass to one another, and either can drive to the hoop.

The Family and Community

This requires a new way of thinking and an active effort by parents and youth sports leaders. It is critical we get out of the gender role habits that dominate in sports and the rest of life. It matters for players and for fans. It matters for athletes, coaches, organizers, media members, and sponsors. The challenge, in other words, demands a break from a sex-segregated past that stretches back well more than a century.

The Government

It is recognized now that women can and should have educational opportunities equal with men. This, in turn, serves as a foundation for equal employment opportunities. As a nation we want women to enter nontraditional educational and employment fields, through government and foundation-sponsored programs aimed at encouraging women to enter such fields as math, science, and engineering.

Sports

We must do the same thing in sports. The family, the community, and government must press girls to explore nontraditional sports. We need role models. Girls must see women playing football and being referees in high-profile professional sports, including football, basketball (there's just one), and baseball. Just as the government encourages sex integration—rather than sex segregation—in math, science, and engineering, it must encourage sex integration in athletic programs. Sports is the next battleground in the fight for gender equality. The roots of sex discrimination must be challenged head-on. There are physical biological differences between the sexes. But they are not as great as we have supposed, and the female difference is not necessarily a lacking. Women are not inherently weak and in need of protection.

Not all women will support this drive. In every era, as women sought to gain equal access to education, to voting and workplace rights, other women were their fiercest adversaries. Women didn't want to take on male roles that meant learning, earning, and having a voice in our democracy. We know there is no justice without responsibility. More than ever we need women's voices in the halls of power, at the helms of corporations, and being celebrated for their athletic prowess. Women are starting to gain recognition for physical ability, mental acuity, and the ability to compete. And, yes, "*thank God* we ain't what we was."

However, we are not yet what we ought to be. Females playing sports with males must become standard practice, not the exception. And as surprising, if not difficult, as this idea may be for some, it is an idea that is gaining ground. When sports writer Dave Anderson, for example, speculated about how Tiger Woods's infant daughter, Sam Alexis, might handle her father's legacy, he noted that "maybe she'll want to try to win the most majors on the women's Tour, *if not the men's Tour*."[12] *Exactly.* Playing with the boys should be an option, if not the norm, for her and for all girls and women, if we are to become *what we ought to be.*

Notes

1. Anthony King, "Wimbledon Fans Falling Out of Love with the Power Game," *Daily Telegraph,* June 23, 2003, 7.
2. Donald Mrozek, "Sport in American Life: From National Health to Personal Fulfillment, 1890–1940," in Kathryn Grover, ed., *Fitness in American Culture: Images of Health, Sport, and the Body, 1830–1940* (Rochester, NY: Margaret Woodbury Strong Museum, 1989), 19.
3. Mrozek, "Sport in American Life," 24.
4. "Runners Make History," *Syracuse Post-Standard,* August 21, 2004, 6; "Track and Field," *Syracuse Post-Standard,* August 24, 2003, D2.
5. "Bangladesh Group Protests against Women's Soccer," *Gleaner* (Kingston, Jamaica), October 18, 2004, 12.
6. S. U. Anyanwu, "Issues and Patterns of Women's Participation in Sport in Nigeria," *International Review for Sport Sociology* 15 (1980): 878–895. Cited in R. Chappell, "Sport in Developing Countries: Opportunities for Girls and Women," *Women in Sport and Physical Activity Journal* 8, no. 2 (1999): 1.
7. MaryJo Sylwester, "Hispanic Girls in Sports Held Back by Tradition," *USA Today,* March 29, 2005, 1.
8. Robert Chappell, *Sport in Developing Countries* (Roehampton University, 2007).
9. Chinese Athletes Cash in on Medalist Status: China's Communist Rulers Cast Olympians as Model Workers," www.msnbc.msn.com/id/5867721.
10. James Riordan, "Chinese Women and Sport Success, Sexuality, Suspicion," *Women in Sports and Physical Activity Journal* 9, no. 1 (2000): 87.
11. Dr. Thomas Johnson, psychiatrist from San Diego, testifying in support of Little League. Summary of proceedings for hearing, State of New Jersey, Department of Law and Public Safety, Division on Civil Rights, November 8, 1973, 3, National Organization for Women papers, National Task Force on Sports file (31.10), Schlesinger Library, Radcliffe Institute for Advanced Study.
12. Dave Anderson, "Now Woods May Be Compared to Nicklaus as a Father," *New York Times,* Thursday, June 21, 2007, E16, emphasis added.

Reading the Genre

1. In a report, it is important both to identify an issue and to show the significance of the issue. How do McDonagh and Pappano define the issue at the heart of this essay? What do they argue about how far-reaching this problem is?

2. What audience do the authors target in this essay? Is their intended audience male or female? How wide or specific is the audience? How might their audience create change? How does the authors' choice of audience affect the essay? (See "Understanding your audience," p. 167.)

3. How does the section entitled "Sports: The Next Frontier" build on the recommendations in this proposal? Is it important for proposal writers to open up larger questions, consider wider implications, and test their ideas? How does doing so alter their arguments?

4. Review the authors' use of headings and subheadings in this excerpt. What is the rhetorical purpose of these headings? How do you think the authors made decisions about what words and phrases to use for these headings? (See Chapter 50, "Designing Print and Online Documents," p. 517.)

5. **WRITING:** Imagining that you have been recruited to help McDonagh and Pappano accomplish their goals, choose just one of the ten suggestions from this essay and develop a concrete plan—at least five strategies—that will actually help to implement this suggestion. Make sure that your recommendations are reasonable, specific, and realistic. Use clear language to describe how the plan can be followed.

PROPOSAL FOR CHANGE   The Union of Concerned Scientists (UCS) describes itself on the UCS Web site as "*the* reliable source for independent scientific analysis." This huge organization, made up of more than 200,000 citizens and scientists, undertakes ambitious scientific research and applies it to environmental problems. Recent UCS initiatives include global warming and clean energy research, and a project to ensure scientific integrity in pollution studies. The following proposal explains complicated scientific research on global warming to a broad audience and is emblematic of much of the work the UCS does to urge citizens and politicians to act on environmental issues.

Global Warming 101: A Target for U.S. Emissions Reductions

Union of Concerned Scientists

Contents

1. Setting a Reasonable Target

2. Dividing Up the Work

3. Defining the U.S. Share of Global Emissions Reductions

4. Evaluating Existing Proposals

5. The Way Forward

Substantial scientific evidence indicates that an increase in the global average temperature of more than two degrees Celsius (°C) above pre-industrial levels (i.e., those that existed prior to 1860) poses severe risks to natural systems and human health and well-being. Sustained warming of this magnitude could, for example, result in the extinction of many species and extensive melting of the Greenland and West Antarctic ice sheets—causing global sea level to rise between 12 and 40 feet. In light of this evidence, policy makers in the European Union have committed their countries to a long-term goal of limiting warming to 2°C above pre-industrial levels.

The United States has agreed in principle to work with more than 180 other nations under the United Nations Framework Convention on Climate Change to bring about the "stabilization of greenhouse gas concentrations in the atmosphere

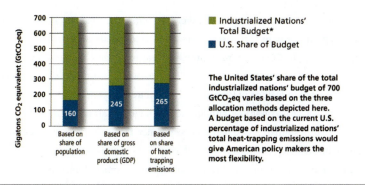

The United States' share of the total industrialized nations' budget of 700 GtCO2eq varies based on the three allocation methods depicted here. A budget based on the current U.S. percentage of industrialized nations' total heat-trapping emissions would give American policy makers the most flexibility.

*All heat-trapping emissions, including those from land use and land cover changes. The budget assumes industrialized nations' emissions peak in 2010 and developing nations' emissions peak in 2020.

Figure 1.   *Defining the U.S. Share of the Industrialized World's Cumulative Emissions Budget (2000–2050)*

at a level that would prevent dangerous anthropogenic [human-caused] interference with the climate system." Though the federal government has done little to live up to that agreement thus far, there is now growing momentum to pursue deep reductions in emissions of carbon dioxide (CO_2) and other heat-trapping gases that cause global warming. California, Florida, Hawaii, Minnesota, New Jersey, Oregon, and Washington have all enacted laws or established policies setting global warming pollution reduction targets, while states in both the Northeast and West have signed agreements to achieve regional targets. Now the U.S. Congress is considering several bills that propose a variety of global warming emissions reduction targets.

Setting a Reasonable Target

A proper evaluation of the adequacy of these bills must consider what is needed to avoid the potentially dangerous consequences of temperatures rising more than 2°C. Scientific studies indicate that, to have a reasonable chance of preventing temperatures from rising above this level, we must stabilize the concentration of heat-trapping gases in the atmosphere at or below 450 parts per million CO_2-equivalent (450 ppm CO_2eq—a measurement that expresses the concentration of all heat-trapping gases in terms of CO_2). This "stabilization target" would provide a roughly 50 percent chance of keeping the global average temperature from rising more than 2°C, or 3.6 degrees Fahrenheit, above pre-industrial levels, and a 67 percent chance of rising less than 3°C. Therefore, any policy that seeks to avoid dangerous climate change should set a maximum stabilization target of 450 ppm CO_2eq.

To meet this target, worldwide cumulative emissions of heat-trapping gases must be limited to approximately 1,700 gigatons (Gt) CO_2eq for the period 2000–2050—of which approximately 330 GtCO_2eq has already been emitted. Staying within this 1,700 GtCO_2eq "global cumulative emissions budget" will require aggressive reductions in worldwide emissions (i.e., those of industrialized and developing nations combined).

Dividing Up the Work

If we assume the world's developing nations pursue the most aggressive reductions that can reasonably be expected of them, the world's industrialized nations will have to reduce their emissions an average of 70 to 80 percent below 2000 levels by 2050. In addition, industrialized nations' cumulative emissions over this period must be no more than 700 GtCO_2eq (approximately 40 percent of the global budget).

This 70 to 80 percent range for reductions by 2050 assumes that industrialized nations' emissions will peak in 2010 before starting to decline, and that those from developing nations will peak between 2020 and 2025. A delay in the peak of either group would require increasingly steep and unrealistic global reduction rates in order to stay within the cumulative emissions budget for 2000–2050.

Defining the U.S. Share of Global Emissions Reductions

There are several ways to determine the United States' share of the industrialized nations' emissions budget, including allocations based on the current U.S. share (among industrialized countries) of population, gross domestic product (GDP), and heat-trapping emissions. Using these criteria, the U.S. cumulative emissions budget ranges from 160 to 265 $GtCO_2eq$ for the period 2000–2050, of which approximately 45 $GtCO_2eq$ has already been emitted (Figure 1).

Given our aggressive assumptions about reductions by other nations and the fact that 450 ppm CO_2eq represents the upper limit needed to avoid a potentially dangerous temperature increase, the United States should reduce its emissions at least 80 percent below 2000 levels by 2050.

The costs of delay are high. To meet this minimum target, the United States must reduce its emissions an average of 4 percent per year starting in 2010.[1] If, however, U.S. emissions continue to increase until 2020—even on a "low-growth" path projected by the Energy Information Administration (EIA)—the United States would have to make much sharper cuts later: approximately 8 percent per year on average from 2020 to 2050, or about double the annual reductions that would be required if we started promptly. The earlier we start, the more flexibility we will have later (Figure 2).

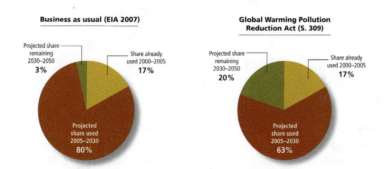

Business as usual (EIA 2007)

Projected share remaining 2030–2050 **3%**

Share already used 2000–2005 **17%**

Projected share used 2005–2030 **80%**

Global Warming Pollution Reduction Act (S. 309)

Projected share remaining 2030–2050 **20%**

Share already used 2000–2005 **17%**

Projected share used 2005–2030 **63%**

Under a "business as usual" scenario projected by the Energy Information Administration, the United States would use nearly all of its emissions budget by 2030, requiring unrealistically drastic cuts thereafter to achieve the 450 ppm CO_2eq stabilization target by 2050. In contrast, the emissions cuts required by S. 309 (the Global Warming Pollution Reduction Act) would allow reductions to proceed in a more gradual fashion, providing greater flexibility in the method and timing of reductions.

Figure 2.   *Spending the U.S. Cumulative Emissions Budget*

[1] *Equivalent to an average absolute reduction of 0.16 $GtCO_2eq$ per year (or about 2 percent of current levels).*

Evaluating Existing Proposals

Of the current climate policy proposals before the U.S. Congress, only the Global Warming Pollution Reduction Act (S. 309) and the Safe Climate Act (H.R. 1590) would require reductions consistent with staying below the upper limit of the U.S. cumulative emissions budget (265 GtCO$_2$eq) (Figure 3a). All of the other bills under consideration—the Lieberman-Warner proposal, the Global Warming Reduction

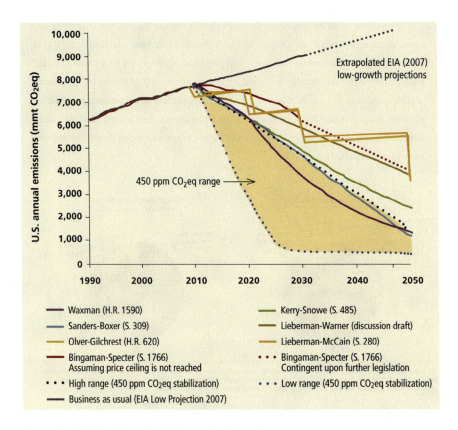

Figure 3a.   *U.S. Emissions Reductions under Federal Proposals*

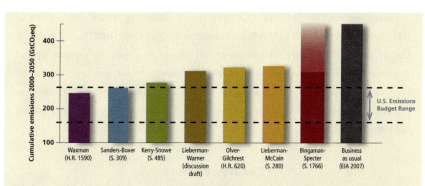

Only two current climate policy proposals (H.R. 1590 and S. 309) would stay within the emissions budget of 160 to 265 GtCO₂eq defined in this analysis, and even these proposals would result in emissions well above the low end of the range. For S. 1766, the potential range of cumulative emissions for 2000–2050 is provided.*

FIGURE 3b. *Cumulative U.S. Emissions in 2050 under Federal Proposals*
The lower portion of the bar indicates cumulative emissions for S. 1766 under the best-case scenario, in which the bill's price ceiling is never triggered, all emissions reduction targets out to 2030 are met, and all of the conditions needed to achieve the 2050 target are met, including international action, a recommendation by the president to Congress, and additional congressional legislation. This scenario also assumes that the 2050 target reduces total (economy-wide) U.S. emissions 60 percent below 2006 levels, even though earlier targets reduce emissions for only 85 percent of the economy. The color gradient in the upper portion of the bar represents the uncertainty in the additional cumulative emissions that would occur if the bill's price ceiling were triggered. (The darker the color, the more likely it is that total cumulative emissions would reach that level.) The gradient is for illustrative purposes only and does not represent explicit modeling of the price ceiling's effect on emissions decisions. The range depicted here assumes that if the price cap is triggered, the total cumulative emissions could approach those projected by the EIA under a low-growth "business as usual" scenario.

Act (S. 485), the Climate Stewardship Act (H.R. 620), and the Low Carbon Economy Act (S. 1766)—would exceed that limit. The amounts by which these bills would go over the budget may not appear to be great, but if every nation went over its budget by a similar amount, the result would be a greatly increased risk of dangerous climate change.

Furthermore, no proposal currently before Congress would come close to the proposed lower end of the U.S. emissions budget (160 $GtCO_2eq$). Several of the proposals do provide for congressional review and periodic reports by the National Academy of Sciences to ensure U.S. targets remain consistent with the goal of preventing the global average temperature from rising 2°C above pre-industrial levels. These periodic reviews are an essential element of any robust federal climate policy.

The Way Forward

It is clear that the United States must quickly overcome its current impasse on climate policy if we are to avoid the risks of dangerous climate change. Many solutions are already available, including greater energy efficiency, increased use of renewable energy, and reductions in deforestation. These changes can be encouraged by a wide range of market-based and complementary policies including cap-and-trade programs, renewable electricity standards, efficiency standards for electricity and vehicles, and incentives for cleaner technologies and international cooperation on emissions reductions.

For the United States to be fully engaged in the fight against global warming, however, Congress must support legislation that requires the deep reductions in heat-trapping emissions needed to stay within the emissions budget described here and preserve a climate safe for future generations.

Reading the Genre

1. Who is the primary audience for this article? Might there be a secondary audience too? That is, in addition to the people whom the authors are encouraging to make changes, what other groups might they be hoping to persuade?

2. In many proposals, it is important to establish exactly *who* has the responsibility to create change. How do the authors argue that the United States is responsible for responding to this problem, even though it is also a global problem?

3. Recall the three rhetorical appeals discussed in Chapter 8, "Rhetorical Analysis." (See "Consider its use of rhetorical appeals," p. 231.) Which rhetorical appeals are used most in this essay? Look especially at the charts, graphs, and other visual evidence provided.

4. How does this article compare and contrast prior proposals? What techniques are used in these comparisons? (See "Examine prior solutions," p. 170.)

5. **WRITING:** Create your own comparison of proposals. Choose a problem for which others have proposed solutions. For instance, research a topic such as immigration, health care, or welfare reform. Review recent proposals that address these issues, and compare these ideas, as the Union of Concerned Scientists do with the emission reduction bills proposed in the U.S. Congress. Your comparison can be presented in the form of a chart or written as a summary. Then, based on this comparison, propose your own unique solutions.

PROPOSAL FOR CHANGE   Robert D. Bullard is director of the Environmental Justice Resource Center at Clark University. In his book *Dumping in Dixie* (1990), he introduced the concept of "environmental justice," arguing that minorities bear the bulk of the burden of pollution and other environmental problems, while having less access to the benefits of services such as health care and to open spaces in the form of parkland. His latest book is *The Black Metropolis in the Twenty-First Century: Race, Power, and Politics of Place* (2007), and he is currently working on a study of how the health and welfare of African Americans has been endangered by government policies and decisions. The following essay appears in *The Covenant with Black America* (2006).

ROBERT D. BULLARD

Assuring Environmental Justice for All

All communities are not created equal. If a community happens to be poor, black, or of color, it receives less protection than does an affluent white community. The environmental justice framework defines "environment" as where we live, work, play, worship, and go to school, as well as the physical and natural world. Environmental justice is built on the principle that all Americans have a right to equal protection of our nation's environmental, health, housing, transportation, employment, and civil rights laws and regulations. Environmental protection is a basic human right.[1]

The environmental justice movement has come a long way since its humble beginning in Warren County, North Carolina, where a PCB landfill ignited protests and over 500 arrests. Those protests also led the United Church of Christ's Commission for Racial Justice in 1987 to produce *Toxic Wastes and Race*,[2] the first national study to correlate waste facility sites and demographic characteristics. Race was found to be the most potent variable in predicting where these facilities were located—more powerful than poverty, land values, and homeownership. In 1990, *Dumping in Dixie: Race, Class, and Environmental Quality*[3]—the first book on environmental racism—

documented discriminatory policies and practices that allowed polluting facilities to be concentrated in black communities.

In 1992, after much prodding from environmental justice advocates, the U.S. Environmental Protection Agency (EPA) finally acknowledged its mandate to protect all Americans.[4] And on February 11, 1994, environmental justice reached the White House, when President Bill Clinton signed Executive Order 12898, "Federal Actions to Address Environmental Justice in Minority Populations and Low-Income Populations."[5] The order mandated federal government agencies to incorporate environmental justice into all of their works and programs.

Today, millions of Americans are concerned about the threat of exposure to chemical and biological agents. The tragic events of September 11, 2001 (terrorist attacks on the World Trade Center in New York, the Pentagon in Washington, and the plane crash in rural Pennsylvania), and the anthrax scare heightened concern and worry about disaster preparedness.

Toxic chemical assaults, however, are not new for too many African Americans and other people of color who are forced to live next to and often on the fence line with chemical industries that spew their poisons into the air, water, and ground. These residents experience a form of "toxic terror" 24 hours a day and seven days a week. When chemical accidents occur, government and industry officials tell residents to "shelter in place."[6]

Hurricane Katrina exposed the world to the naked reality of environmental racism. *Environmental racism* refers to any policy, practice, or directive that differentially affects or disadvantages (whether intended or unintended) individuals, groups, or communities based on race or color.[7] Environmental racism combines with public policies and industry practices to provide benefits for whites while shifting costs to people of color.[8] Katrina presented in living color clear links among race, poverty, land use, environmental risk, and unequal protection.[9] Poverty impacts health because it determines how many resources poor people have and defines the amount of environmental risks they will be exposed to in their immediate environment.[10]

Race maps closely with the geography of environmental risks and devastation: Katrina laid bare the "dirty little secret" of poverty in America.[11] The U.S. poverty rate is 12.5 percent.[12] Blacks, who are disproportionately poor, comprise a significantly large share of the three Gulf Coast states hardest hit by Katrina—Louisiana, Mississippi, and Alabama. Blacks comprise 32.5 percent of the population in Louisiana, 36.3 percent in Mississippi, and 26 percent in Alabama. New Orleans is nearly 68 percent black;[13] about 28 percent of its residents live below the poverty level, more than 80 percent of whom are black. The African American population in the coastal Mississippi counties where Katrina struck ranged from 25 percent to 87 percent black.

Before Katrina, New Orleans was struggling with a wide range of environmental justice and health concerns, including an older housing stock with lots of lead paint. More than 50 percent (some studies place this figure at around 70 percent) of children living in the inner-city neighborhoods of New Orleans had blood lead levels above the current guideline of 10 micrograms per deciliter (μg/dL), which is defined as the "level of concern" by the Centers for Disease Control and Prevention.[14] Childhood lead poisoning in some New Orleans black neighborhoods was as high as 67 percent.

Environmental health problems related to environmental exposure were hot-button issues in New Orleans long before Katrina's floodwaters emptied out the city. New Orleans' location on the Mississippi River Industrial Corridor increased its vulnerability to environmental threats. Dozens of toxic "time bombs" along this chemical corridor—the 85-mile stretch from Baton Rouge to New Orleans—made "Cancer Alley" a major environmental justice battleground.[15]

There are questions about what a "new" New Orleans should look like. There is even talk about some "low-lying" neighborhoods, inhabited largely by African

Americans, not being rebuilt, such as the sealed-off Lower Ninth Ward. It is no accident that blacks tend to live in the lowest-lying areas of the city.[16] Residents fear environmental reasons—location in flood plain and environmental contamination and new zoning codes—may be used to kill off their neighborhoods. Black residents have deep-seated fears and resentment that they will once again be left out of rebuilding, with decisions driven more by race than by topography. Some of New Orleans' white power elites—heads of law firms, tourist businesses, and conservation groups—have a vision and plan for the recovery, restoration, and rebuilding of New Orleans: "smaller and more upscale."[17]

Before rebuilding and reconstruction in New Orleans and the Gulf Coast can begin in earnest, mountains of debris and toxic wastes must be cleaned up and disposed of in an environmentally sound way. Katrina left behind "a complex array of environmental health problems."[18] Katrina dumped over 63 million cubic yards of debris in Louisiana and 62.5 million cubic yards of debris in Mississippi. In contrast, Hurricane Andrew generated 20 million cubic yards of debris in 1992. Louisiana officials are faced with the challenge of disposing of mountains of debris from Katrina. Some of the disposal methods have come under fire from environmentalists, environmental justice leaders, and the EPA.

The Army Corps of Engineers is charged with cleaning up miles of sediments laced with cancer-causing chemicals, toxic metals, industrial compounds, petroleum products, and banned insecticides—all at levels that pose potential cancer risks or other long-term hazards.[19] This is likely to be the "mother of all toxic cleanups."[20] Much of the contaminated topsoil where 110,000 New Orleans flooded homes sit can be scooped up and replaced with clean soil. However, cleaning up the muck that seeped into houses is a major challenge.

Health officials are now seeing a large number of evacuees afflicted with "Katrina cough," an illness believed to be linked to mold and dust.[21] Individuals who otherwise do not have allergies have been coming down with the illness. It is especially worrisome for people with health problems—AIDS, asthma, and other serious respiratory illnesses—who may reenter their homes. Molds are not just an irritant; they can trigger episodes and set up life-threatening infections when normal immune systems are weakened. Mold spores are known triggers of asthma attacks—an illness that disproportionately affects African Americans.

Generally, government air quality tests focus on toxins, such as benzene, in areas where Katrina caused oil spills. The government does not have regulatory standards for either indoor or outdoor levels of mold spores. Independent tests conducted by the Natural Resources Defense Council (NRDC) in mid-November found dangerously high mold counts in New Orleans air.[22] The spore counts outdoors in most flooded neighborhoods tested by NRDC—New Orleans East, the Lower Ninth Ward, Chalmette, Uptown, Mid-City, and the Garden District—showed levels as high as 77,000 spores per cubic meter at one site in Chalmette and 81,000 spores per cubic meter at another site in the Uptown area. The National Allergy Bureau of the American Academy of Allergy and Immunology considers any outdoor mold spore level of greater than 50,000 spores per cubic meter to be a serious health threat.

Hurricane Katrina and its aftermath are just the tip of the environmental racism iceberg; the bright side is that they are instructive and inform what we must do. To assure environmental justice for all, we must address all of the inequities that result from human settlement, industrial facility siting, and industrial development. We must educate and assist groups in organizing and mobilizing, empowering ourselves to take charge of our lives, our communities, and our surroundings. We must address power imbalances and the lack of political enfranchisement; we must redirect our resources so that we can create healthy, livable, and sustainable communities for *all* of us.

Power rests in all of us; when we operate as a collective, that's when we are most powerful and move forward as a unit. Katrina can be the issue that mobilizes us, organizes us, and creates the catalyst that unites us to work for justice in environmental protection, justice in terms of enforcement of regulations, and justice in terms of our children's being able to live, play, and go to school in environments that are not hazardous to their health.

As we said in the beginning: the environment is everything—where we live, work, play, and go to school, as well as the physical and natural world. We cannot separate the physical environment from the cultural environment. We have to talk about making sure that justice is integrated throughout all of the stuff that we do.

THE FACTS ON ENVIRONMENTAL JUSTICE

Childhood Lead Poisoning

- Lead poisoning continues to be the number-one environmental health threat to children of color in the United States, especially poor children and children living in inner cities.[23]
- Black children are five times more likely than white children to have lead poisoning.[24]
- One in seven black children living in older housing has elevated blood lead levels.[25]
- About 22 percent of African American children living in pre-1946 housing are lead poisoned, compared with 6 percent of white children living in comparable types of housing.[26]
- Recent studies suggest that a young person's lead burden is linked to lower IQ, lower high school graduation rates, and increased delinquency.[27]
- Lead poisoning causes about 2 to 3 points of IQ lost for each 10 μg/dL lead level (μg/dL = 10 micrograms of lead in a deciliter—one-tenth of a liter—of blood).[28]

Toxic Neighborhoods

- Nationally, three out of five African and Latino Americans live in communities with abandoned toxic waste sites.[29]
- The U.S. General Accounting Office (now known as the Government Accountability Office) estimates that there are between 130,000 and 450,000 brownfields (abandoned waste sites) scattered across the urban landscape from New York to California—most of which are located in or near low-income, working-class, and people-of-color communities.[30]
- Over 870,000 of the 1.9 million (46 percent) housing units for the poor—mostly minorities—sit within a mile of factories that reported toxic emissions to the Environmental Protection Agency.[31]

- More than 600,000 students—mostly African American—in Massachusetts, New York, New Jersey, Michigan, and California attended nearly 1,200 public schools located within one-half mile of federal Superfund or state-identified contaminated sites.[32]
- More than 68 percent of black Americans live within 30 miles of a coal-fired power plant—the distance within which the maximum effects of the smoke-stack plume are expected to occur—compared with 56 percent of white Americans.[33]

Katrina Toxic Contamination and Health Threats

- Katrina caused six major oil spills, releasing 7.4 million gallons of oil, or 61 percent as much as the 11 million gallons that leaked into Alaska's Prince William Sound from the Exxon *Valdez* in 1989.[34]
- The storm hit 60 underground storage tanks, five Superfund sites, and 466 industrial facilities that stored highly dangerous chemicals before the storm; it disabled more than 1,000 drinking-water systems, creating a "toxic soup" with *E. coli* in the floodwaters far exceeding EPA's safe levels.[35]
- Katrina left behind an estimated 22 million tons of debris, with more than half—12 million tons—left in Orleans Parish.[36]
- Flooded homes containing over one million pieces of "white goods," such as refrigerators, stoves, and freezers, require disposal.[37]
- An additional 350,000 automobiles must be drained of oil and gasoline and then recycled; 60,000 boats may need to be destroyed; and 300,000 under-ground fuel tanks and 42,000 tons of hazardous waste must be collected and properly disposed of at licensed facilities.[38]
- Government officials peg the numbers of cars lost in New Orleans alone at 145,000.[39]

Flooded Homes

- An estimated 140,000 to 160,000 homes in Louisiana may need to be demolished and disposed of.[40]
- More than 110,000 of New Orleans' 180,000 houses were flooded, and one-half sat for days or weeks in more than six feet of water.[41]
- As many as 30,000 to 50,000 homes in New Orleans may have to be demolished, while many others could be saved with extensive repairs.[42]

Flooded Schools

- Katrina displaced more than an estimated 350,000 school children in the Gulf Coast—187,000 in Louisiana, 160,000 in Mississippi, and 3,118 in Alabama.[43]
- The powerful storm closed the New Orleans school system and left a trail of toxic muck in classrooms and on playgrounds. Over 93 percent of New Orleans' 125,000 public school children are African American.[44]

What the Community Can Do

Hurricane Katrina exposed the systematic weakness of the nation's emergency preparedness and response to disasters. The powerful storm also exposed the racial divide in the way the U.S. government responds to natural and manmade disasters in this country. It is time for *all* Americans to receive equal environmental protection. African Americans must demand that government agencies charged with protecting them use uniform cleanup standards to ensure equal protection of public health and environmental justice: (1) what gets cleaned up, (2) where the waste is disposed, (3) what gets rebuilt, and (4) where it gets rebuilt are key environmental and social equity issues.

Because of the enormous human suffering and environmental devastation, the rebuilding of New Orleans and the Louisiana, Mississippi, and Alabama Gulf Coast region will test the nation's ability and commitment to address lingering social inequality and institutional barriers that created and maintained the racial divide of "two Americas," one black and poor and the other white and affluent.

What Every Individual Can Do Now

- Do not forget the victims of Katrina. The rebuilding effort will go on for several years. Write to your congressional representatives and demand follow-up action and support.
- Educate yourself, your family, and your friends about issues of environmental justice.
- Find out about air quality, water quality, and toxic waste sites in your community.
- When you hear about environmental concerns in your communities, help to organize meetings, attend all gatherings, and encourage others to do the same.
- Make sure your home is free from the hazards of lead poisoning.
- Most of all: *Hold all leaders and elected officials responsible and demand that they change current policy.*

What Works Now

Officials at all levels of government must equally protect all citizens. It is unjust to allow African Americans to live in hazardous conditions while warning and saving their white neighbors. Allowing waivers of environmental standards could compound the harm already caused by previous disasters and current ones such as Katrina; they undermine health protection of the most vulnerable members of our society.

A defined role for HBCUs [Historically Black Colleges and Universities] in close proximity to brownfields redevelopment and related pilot programs should be included in the remediation process from local to federal levels. Many of the nation's 105 HBCUs are located in or near communities suffering from environmental problems. Urban universities, with their multiple social and physical sciences specialists, are natural partners in land use decision-making in environmental remediation.

Manage Debris

Hurricane Betsy struck the State of Louisiana and the City of New Orleans in 1965, hitting the mostly black and poor New Orleans' Lower Ninth Ward especially hard. Debris was buried in the Agricultural Street Landfill—located in a predominately black New Orleans neighborhood.[45] Over 390 homes were built on the northern portion of the 95-acre landfill site from 1976 to 1986. The Agricultural Street Landfill neighborhood was added to the National Priorities List as a Superfund site in 1994 because of toxic contaminants such as metals, polycyclic aromatic hydrocarbons (PAHs), volatile organic compounds, and pesticides.

The actual cleanup began in 1998 and was completed in 2001. The Concerned Citizens of Agriculture Street Landfill filed a class-action suit against the city for damages and cost of relocation. It took nine years to bring this case to court.[46] The case was still pending when Katrina struck.

Weeks after Katrina hit, the Louisiana Department of Environmental Quality (LDEQ) allowed New Orleans to open the 200-acre Old Gentilly Landfill to dump construction and demolition waste from the storm.[47] Federal regulators had ordered the unlined landfill closed in the 1980s. LDEQ officials insist that the old landfill meets all standards, while residents and environmentalists disagree, questioning the safety and suitability of dumping at the old landfill. Even some high-ranking elected officials have expressed fear that reopening the Old Gentilly Landfill could create an ecological nightmare.[48] The landfill caught fire four days after environmentalists filed a lawsuit to block the dumping.[49]

Wastes and debris from Katrina should be recycled and disposed of using methods that meet existing environmental and health standards. It is equally imperative that cleanup standards, building codes, and land use designations not be used as tools to discriminate against and ultimately kill off "low-lying" black neighborhoods.

Involve Impacted Communities in Environmental Decision-Making

Promote Environmental Justice–Driven Community Development

Impacted residents must be involved in all environmental health decisions made regarding the cleanup, recovery, and rebuilding of damaged communities and brownfields. The EPA and other federal agencies must work closely with the local communities most affected by environmental problems in decisions on cleanup, recovery, and rebuilding to ensure a democratic and safe process.

Local officials must also strengthen policy requirements and enforcement mechanisms to safeguard environmental health for all brownfields projects. (A brownfield is a property that the expansion, redevelopment, or reuse of may be complicated by the presence or potential presence of a hazardous substance, pollutant, or contaminant.)[50] Hurricane Katrina has created brownfields across the

Gulf Coast region. Removing health risks must be the main priority of all brownfields action plans.

Government agencies, community members, and environmental justice organizations should all become involved in and support one another in redeveloping local neighborhoods to integrate brownfields priorities into long-range neighborhood redevelopment plans. This will allow for the use of Tax Increment Finance (TIF) funds accrued by the redevelopment process to fund the cleanup and redevelopment of brownfields sites for community-determined uses.

Institute Anti-Displacement Provisions in Brownfields Redevelopment

City officials should not only prevent displacement, but must also support community-driven planning and programming activities that minimize or eliminate displacement of incumbent residents. Government funding should support efforts to expand opportunities for community-based organizations to purchase and redevelop properties in their neighborhoods, in partnership with African American business entrepreneurs through existing brownfields redevelopment programs. Government agencies at all levels—particularly at the local and regional levels—should provide tax benefits and subsidies typically given to private institutions.

A Final Word

The environmental justice movement demands an end to environmental racism and development policies and practices that endanger the health of the environment and displace people from their homes and neighborhoods. African Americans and other people of color have a right to a clean, safe, just, healthy, and sustainable environment. Unless the issue of environmental justice is addressed squarely in the aftermath of Hurricane Katrina, there will not be any black New Orleans neighborhoods to recover or redevelop.

Endnotes

1. Robert D. Bullard, *The Quest for Environmental Justice: Human Rights and the Politics of Pollution* (San Francisco: Sierra Club Books, 2005).

2. Commission for Racial Justice, *Toxic Wastes and Race in the United States: A National Report on the Racial and Socio-economic Characteristics of Communities with Hazardous Waste Sites* (New York: United Church of Christ, 1987).

3. Bullard, *Dumping in Dixie: Race, Class, and Environmental Quality* (Boulder, CO: Westview Press, 1990), chapter 1.

4. U.S. EPA, *Environmental Equity: Reducing Risk for All Communities* (Washington, DC: EPA, 1992).

5. William J. Clinton, "Federal Actions to Address Environmental Justice in Minority Populations and Low-Income Populations, Exec. Order No. 12898," *Federal Register*, 59, No. 32, February 11, 1994, available at http://www.epa.gov/compliance/resources/policies/ej/exec_order_12898.pdf#search='executive%20order%2012898' and at http://www.fs.fed.us/land/envjust.html.

6. Bullard, "It's Not Just Pollution," *Our Planet*, Vol. 12, No. 2, 2001: 22–24.

7. Bullard, *Confronting Environmental Racism: Voices from the Grassroots* (Boston: South End Press, 1993).

8. *See* Robert D. Bullard, ed., *Confronting Environmental Racism: Voices from the Grassroots* (Boston: South End, 1993); Bullard, "The Threat of Environmental Racism," *Natural Resources & Environment* 7 (Winter, 1993): 23–26; Bunyan Bryant and Paul Mohai, eds., *Race and the Incidence of Environmental Hazards* (Boulder, CO: Westview Press, 1992); Regina Austin and Michael Schill, "Black, Brown, Poor, and Poisoned: Minority Grassroots Environmentalism and the Quest for Eco-Justice," *The Kansas Journal of Law and Public Policy* 1 (1991): 69–82; Kelly C. Colquette and Elizabeth A. Henry Robertson, "Environmental Racism: The Causes, Consequences, and Commendations," *Tulane Environmental Law Journal* 5 (1991): 153–207; and Rachel D. Godsil, "Remedying Environmental Racism," *Michigan Law Review* 90 (1991): 394–427.

9. *See* Bullard, *Unequal Protection: Environmental Justice and Communities of Color* (San Francisco: Sierra Club Books, 1994).

10. Kenneth Olden, "The Complex Interaction of Poverty, Pollution, Health Status," *The Scientist*, Vol. 12, No. 2, (February 1998): 7. *See* NIEHS: Division of Extramural

Research and Training: Health Disparities Research, available at http://www.niehs.nih
.gov/dert/programs/translat/hd/ko-art.htm.

11. Mark Sauer, "Dirty Little Secret: Disaster Laid Bare the Prevalence of Poverty in
America," *The San Diego Union-Tribune,* September 18, 2005.

12. U.S. Bureau of the Census, "People: Poverty," available at http://factfinder.census
.gov/jsp/saff/SAFFInfo.jsp?_pageId=tp8_poverty.

13. U.S. Bureau of the Census, "Orleans Parish, Louisiana," *State and County Quick Facts,*
2000, available at http://quickfacts.census.gov/qfd/states/22/22071.html.

14. Felicia A. Rabito, LuAnn E. White, and Charles Shorter, "From Research to Policy:
Targeting the Primary Prevention of Childhood Lead Poisoning," *Public Health Reports*
119 (May/June 2004).

15. *See* Beverly Wright, "Living and Dying in Louisiana's Cancer Alley," in Robert
D. Bullard, *The Quest for Environmental Justice,* pp. 87–107.

16. Jason DeParle, "Broken Levees, Unbroken Barriers: What Happens to a Race
Deferred," *The New York Times,* September 4, 2005.

17. Evan Thomas and Arian Campo-Flores, "The Battle to Rebuild," *Newsweek,* October 3,
2005, available at http://www.msnbc.msn.com/id/9469300/site/newsweek.

18. Centers for Disease Control and Prevention and EPA, *Environmental Health Needs
and Habitability Assessment,* Atlanta: Joint Task Force Hurricane Katrina Response,
Initial Assessment (September 17, 2005), found at http://www.bt.cdc.gov/disasters/
hurricanes/katrina/pdf/envassessment.pdf#search='centers%20for%20disease%
20control%20katrina%20contamination'.

19. Randy Lee Loftis, "Extreme Cleanup on Tap in New Orleans," *The Dallas Morning News,*
November 6, 2005, available at http://www.dallasnews.com/sharedcontent/dws/dn/
latestnews/stories/110605dntswtoxic.c3d4a5d.html.

20. "The Mother of All Toxic Cleanups," *Business Week,* September 26, 2005, available at
http://www.businessweek.com/magazine/content/05_39/b3952055.htm.

21. Scott Gold and Ann M. Simmons, "Katrina Cough Floats Around," *The Los Angeles
Times,* November 4, 2005, available at http://www.latimes.com/news/nationworld/
nation/la-na-cough4nov04,0,7514027.story?coll=la-home-headlines.

22. Natural Resources Defense Council, "New Private Testing Shows Dangerously High
Mold Counts in New Orleans Air," Press Release, November 16, 2005, available at
http://www.nrdc.org/media/pressreleases/051116.asp.

23. National Institute of Environmental Health Sciences, *Environmental Diseases from A to Z*, NIH Publication No. 96-4145, available at http://www.niehs.nih.gov.

24. Alliance for Healthy Homes, "Children at Risk, Disparities in Risk: Childhood Lead Poisoning," http://www.afhh.org/chil_ar_disparities.htm.

25. Trust for America's Health, "Browse by Topic: Health Disparities—Lead," http://healthyamericans.org.

26. *Ibid.*

27. *See* U.S. Centers for Disease Control and Prevention (2000), MMWR, 49 (RR-14): 1–13; *see also* National Institutes of Health (NIH), National Institute of Environmental Health Sciences (NIEHS), Health Disparities Research, http://www.niehs.nih.gov/oc/factsheets/disparity/home.htm.

28. Peter Montague, "Pediatricians Urge a Precautionary Approach to Toxic Lead," September 29, 2005, *Rachel's Democracy and Health News*, #827 (September 2005), http://www.rachel.org/bulletin/bulletin.cfm?Issue_ID=2513.

29. Commission for Racial Justice, *op. cit.*

30. R. Twombly, "Urban Uprising," *Environmental Health Perspective*, Vol. 105 (July 1997): 696–701.

31. "Study: Public Housing Is Too Often Located Near Toxic Sites," *The Dallas Morning News*, October 3, 2000, available at http://www.cnn.com/2000/NATURE/10/03/toxicneighbors.ap/.

32. "Child-Proofing Our Communities Campaign," *Poisoned Schools: Invisible Threats, Visible Actions* (Falls Church, VA: Center for Health, Environment, and Justice, March 2001); *see also* http://www.childproofing.org/mapindex.html.

33. *See* the Air of Injustice report on the Clear the Air Web site at http://cta.policy.net/proactive/newsroom/release.vtml?id=23901.

34. Marla Cone and Ashley Powers, "EPA Warns Muck Left by Floodwaters Is Highly Contaminated," *The Los Angeles Times*, September 16, 2005; *Associated Press*, "Katrina and the Environment," September 16, 2005, available at http://wwwcbsnews.com/stories/2005/09/16/Katrina/main855409.shtml.

35. Marla Cone, "Floodwaters a Soup of Pathogens, EPA Finds," *The Los Angeles Times*, September 8, 2005, p. A18.

36. Ted Griggs, "Rebuilding to Be Slow, Expensive," *The Advocate*, September 11, 2005, p. 12A.

37. *Ibid.*

38. James Varney and Jan Moller, "Huge Task of Cleaning Up Louisiana Will Take at Least a Year," Newhouse News Service, October 2, 2005, available at http://www.newhousenews .com/archive/varney100305.html.

39. *Ibid.*

40. U.S. EPA and Louisiana Department of Environmental Quality, "News Release: Top State and Federal Environmental Officials Discuss Progress and Tasks Ahead After Katrina," September 30, 2005, available at http://www.deq.state.la.us/news/pdf/ administratorjohnson.pdf#search='katrina%20debris%20350%2C000%20automobiles'.

41. *Ibid.*

42. *Ibid.*

43. Marnie Hunter, "Schools Take in Displaced Students," CNN.com, September 12, 2005, found at http://www.cnn.com/2005/EDUCATION/09/07/katrina.schools/.

44. Annie Schleicher, "School Bells Ring for Children Displaced by Hurricane Katrina," *The NewsHour with Jim Lehrer,* September 7, 2005, found at http://www.pbs.org/ newshour/extra/features/july-dec05/katrina_9-07.html.

45. Alicia Lyttle, "Agricultural Street Landfill Environmental Justice Case Study," University of Michigan School of Natural Resource and Environment, found at http://www.umich .edu/~snre492/Jones/agstreet.htm.

46. Bullard, *The Quest for Environmental Justice, op. cit.*

47. Cain Burdeau, "New Orleans Area Becoming a Dumping Ground," *The Associated Press,* October 31, 2005.

48. Gordon Russell, "Landfill Reopening Is Raising New Stink," *The Times-Picayune,* November 21, 2005, available at http://www.nola.com/news/t-p/frontpage/index.ssf?/ base/news-4/1132559045240640.xml.

49. WDSU, "Hurricane Debris Catches Fire at Old Gentilly Landfill," November 4, 2005, available at http://www.wdsu.com/news/4611257/detail.html?rss=no&psp=news.

50. http://www.epa.gov/brownfields/about.htm.

Reading the Genre

1. Review the organization of this essay. List the headings and subheadings, and consider the structuring decisions Bullard made in each section. How do the layout and organization fit with the purposes and tone of the different sections of the essay? (See "Creating a structure," p. 172, and Chapter 50, "Designing Print and Online Documents," p. 517.)

2. What are the key terms in this essay? How are they defined, and how important are they to Bullard's efforts to persuade his audience?

3. Bullard stresses the urgency and timeliness of this issue. How effective are these appeals, and how are they conveyed? In what ways is timing essential to all proposals?

4. How do the endnotes in this essay bolster Bullard's argument? Review the endnotes: What do you notice about the sources he has used? Does he use different types of source material for different purposes?

5. **WRITING:** What charts, figures, or images could be used to strengthen this proposal? Search online for pictures, illustrations, maps, charts, and other visuals that could be incorporated into this essay. What would need to be changed or added to the writing to fully integrate this new visual information? (See Chapter 42, "Integrating Sources into Your Work," p. 431.)

PROPOSAL IDENTIFYING A PROBLEM Philosopher and political economist Francis Fukuyama is the author of several books, most notably *The End of History and the Last Man* (1992), in which he argued that after the collapse of Communism and the end of the cold war, the ideological conflict and inequality that characterize human history would end. The essay that follows is taken from a more recent work, *Our Posthuman Future: Consequences of the Biotechnology Revolution* (2002), in which his earlier thesis has changed—he worries, now, that conflict will arise as humans create new inequalities. In the following essay, Fukuyama examines two classic science fiction novels and asks what can be learned from them.

FRANCIS FUKUYAMA

A Tale of Two Dystopias

The threat to man does not come in the first instance from the potentially lethal machines and apparatus of technology. The actual threat has always afflicted man in his essence. The rule of enframing (*Gestell*) threatens man with the possibility that it could be denied to him to enter into a more original revealing and hence to experience the call of a more primal truth.

—Martin Heidegger, *The Question Concerning Technology*[1]

I was born in 1952, right in the middle of the American baby boom. For any person growing up as I did in the middle decades of the twentieth century, the future and its terrifying possibilities were defined by two books, George Orwell's *1984* (first published in 1949) and Aldous Huxley's *Brave New World* (published in 1932).

The two books were far more prescient than anyone realized at the time, because they were centered on two different technologies that would in fact emerge and shape the world over the next two generations. The novel *1984* was about what we now call information technology: central to the success of the vast, totalitarian empire that had been set up over Oceania was a device called the telescreen, a wall-sized flat-panel display that could simultaneously send and receive images from each individual household to a hovering Big Brother. The telescreen was what permitted the vast centralization of social life under the Ministry of Truth and the Ministry of Love, for it allowed the government to banish privacy by monitoring every word and deed over a massive network of wires.

Brave New World, by contrast, was about the other big technological revolution about to take place, that of biotechnology. Bokanovskification, the hatching of people not in wombs but, as we now say, in vitro; the drug soma, which gave people instant happiness; the Feelies, in which sensation was simulated by implanted electrodes; and the modification of behavior through constant subliminal repetition and, when that didn't work, through the administration of various artificial hormones were what gave this book its particularly creepy ambiance.

With at least a half century separating us from the publication of these books, we can see that while the technological predictions they made were startlingly accurate, the political predictions of the first book, *1984,* were entirely wrong. The year 1984 came and went, with the United States still locked in a Cold War struggle with the Soviet Union. That year saw the introduction of a new model of the IBM personal computer and the beginning of what became the PC revolution. As Peter Huber has argued, the personal computer, linked to the Internet, was in fact the realization of Orwell's telescreen.[2] But instead of becoming an instrument of centralization and tyranny, it led to just the opposite: the democratization of access to information and the decentralization of politics. Instead of Big Brother watching everyone, people could use the PC and Internet to watch Big Brother, as governments everywhere were driven to publish more information on their own activities.

Just five years after 1984, in a series of dramatic events that would earlier have seemed like political science fiction, the Soviet Union and its empire collapsed, and the totalitarian threat that Orwell had so vividly evoked vanished. People were again quick to point out that these two events—the collapse of totalitarian empires and the emergence of the personal computer, as well as other forms of inexpensive information technology, from TVs and radios to faxes and e-mail—were not unrelated. Totalitarian rule depended on a regime's ability to maintain a monopoly over information, and once modern information technology made that impossible, the regime's power was undermined.

The political prescience of the other great dystopia, *Brave New World,* remains to be seen. Many of the technologies that Huxley envisioned, like in vitro fertilization, surrogate motherhood, psychotropic drugs, and genetic engineering for the manufacture of children, are already here or just over the horizon. But this revolution has only just begun; the daily avalanche of announcements of new breakthroughs in biomedical technology and achievements such as the completion of the Human Genome Project in the year 2000 portend much more serious changes to come.

Of the nightmares evoked by these two books, *Brave New World*'s always struck me as more subtle and more challenging. It is easy to see what's wrong with the world of *1984:* the protagonist, Winston Smith, is known to hate rats above all things, so Big Brother devises a cage in which rats can bite at Smith's face in order to get him to betray his lover. This is the world of classical tyranny, technologically empowered but not so different from what we have tragically seen and known in human history.

In *Brave New World,* by contrast, the evil is not so obvious because no one is hurt; indeed, this is a world in which everyone gets what they want. As one of the characters notes, "The Controllers realized that force was no good," and that people would have to be seduced rather than compelled to live in an orderly society. In this world, disease and social conflict have been abolished, there is no depression, madness, loneliness, or emotional distress, sex is good and readily available. There is even a government ministry to ensure that the length of time between the appearance of a desire and its satisfaction is kept to a minimum. No one takes religion seriously any longer, no one is introspective or has unrequited longings, the biological family has been abolished, no one reads Shakespeare. But no one (save John the Savage, the book's protagonist) misses these things, either, since they are happy and healthy.

Since the novel's publication, there have probably been several million high school essays written in answer to the question, "What's wrong with this picture?" The answer given (on papers that get A's, at any rate) usually runs something like this: the people in *Brave New World* may be healthy and happy, but they have ceased to be *human beings*. They no longer struggle, aspire, love, feel pain, make difficult moral choices, have families, or do any of the things that we traditionally associate with being human. They no longer have the characteristics that give us human dignity. Indeed, there is no such thing as the human race any longer, since they have been bred by the Controllers into separate castes of Alphas, Betas, Epsilons, and Gammas who are as distant from each other as humans are from animals. Their world has become unnatural in the most profound sense imaginable, because *human nature* has been altered. In the words of bioethicist Leon Kass, "Unlike the man reduced by disease or slavery, the people dehumanized à la *Brave New World* are not miserable, don't know that they are dehumanized, and, what is worse, would not care if they knew. They are, indeed, happy slaves with a slavish happiness."[3]

But while this kind of answer is usually adequate to satisfy the typical high school English teacher, it does not (as Kass goes on to note) probe nearly deeply enough. For one can then ask, What is so important about being a human being in the traditional way that Huxley defines it? After all, what the human race is today is the product of an evolutionary process that has been going on for millions of years, one that with any luck will continue well into the future. There are no fixed human characteristics, except for a general capability to choose what we want to be, to modify ourselves in accordance with our desires. So who is to tell us that being human and having dignity means sticking with a set of emotional responses that are the accidental by-product of our evolutionary history? There is no such thing as a biological family, no such thing as human nature or a "normal" human being, and even if there were, why should that be a guide for what is right and just? Huxley is telling us, in effect, that we should continue to feel pain, be depressed or lonely, or suffer from debilitating disease, all because that is what human beings have done for most of their existence as a species. Certainly, no one ever got elected to Congress on such a platform. Instead of taking these characteristics and saying that they are the basis for "human dignity," why don't we simply accept our destiny as creatures who modify themselves?

Huxley suggests that one source for a definition of what it means to be a human being is religion. In *Brave New World,* religion has been abolished and Christianity is a distant memory. The Christian tradition maintains that man is created in God's image, which is the source of human dignity. To use biotechnology to engage in what another Christian writer, C. S. Lewis, called the "abolition of man" is thus a violation of God's will. But I don't think that a careful reading of Huxley or Lewis leads to the conclusion that either writer believed religion to be the *only* grounds on which one could understand the meaning of being human. Both writers suggest that nature itself, and in particular human nature, has a special role in defining for us what is right and wrong, just and unjust, important and unimportant. So our final judgment on "what's wrong" with Huxley's brave new world stands or falls with our view of how important human nature is as a source of values.

The aim of this book is to argue that Huxley was right, that the most significant threat posed by contemporary biotechnology is the possibility that it will alter human nature and thereby move us into a "posthuman" stage of history. This is important, I will argue, because human nature exists, is a meaningful concept, and has provided a stable continuity to our experience as a species. It is, conjointly with religion, what defines our most basic values. Human nature shapes and constrains the possible kinds of political regimes, so a technology powerful enough to reshape what we are will have possibly malign consequences for liberal democracy and the nature of politics itself.

It may be that, as in the case of *1984,* we will eventually find biotechnology's consequences are completely and surprisingly benign, and that we were wrong to lose sleep over it. It may be that the technology will in the end prove much less powerful than it seems today, or that people will be moderate and careful in their application of it. But one of the reasons I am not quite so sanguine is that biotechnology, in contrast to many other scientific advances, mixes obvious benefits with subtle harms in one seamless package.

Nuclear weapons and nuclear energy were perceived as dangerous from the start, and therefore were subject to strict regulation from the moment the Manhattan Project created the first atomic bomb in 1945. Observers like Bill Joy have worried about nanotechnology—that is, molecular-scale self-replicating machines capable of reproducing out of control and destroying their creators.[4] But such threats are actually the easiest to deal with because they are so obvious. If you are likely to be killed by a machine you've created, you take measures to protect yourself. And so far we've had a reasonable record in keeping our machines under control.

There may be products of biotechnology that will be similarly obvious in the dangers they pose to mankind—for example, superbugs, new viruses, or genetically modified foods that produce toxic reactions. Like nuclear weapons or nanotechnology, these are in a way the easiest to deal with because once we have identified them as dangerous, we can treat them as a straightforward threat. The more typical threats raised by biotechnology, on the other hand, are those captured so well by Huxley, and are summed up in the title of an article by novelist Tom Wolfe, "Sorry, but Your Soul Just Died."[5] Medical technology offers us in many cases a devil's bargain: longer life, but with reduced mental capacity; freedom from depression, together with freedom from creativity or spirit; therapies that blur the line between what we achieve on our own and what we achieve because of the levels of various chemicals in our brains.

Consider the following three scenarios, all of which are distinct possibilities that may unfold over the next generation or two.

The first has to do with new drugs. As a result of advances in neuropharmacology, psychologists discover that human personality is much more plastic than formerly believed. It is already the case that psychotropic drugs such as Prozac and Ritalin can affect traits like self-esteem and the ability to concentrate, but they tend to produce a host of unwanted side effects and hence are shunned except in cases of clear therapeutic need. But in the future, knowledge of genomics permits pharmaceutical companies to tailor drugs very specifically to the genetic profiles of individual patients and greatly minimize unintended side effects. Stolid people can become vivacious; introspective ones extroverted; you can adopt one personality on Wednesday and another for the weekend. There is no longer any excuse for anyone to be depressed or unhappy; even "normally" happy people can make themselves happier without worries of addiction, hangovers, or long-term brain damage.

In the second scenario, advances in stem cell research allow scientists to regenerate virtually any tissue in the body, such that life expectancies are pushed well above 100 years. If you need a new heart or liver, you just grow one inside the chest cavity of a pig or cow; brain damage from Alzheimer's and stroke can be reversed. The only problem is that there are many subtle and some not-so-subtle aspects of human aging that the biotech industry hasn't quite figured out how to fix: people grow mentally rigid and increasingly fixed in their views as they age, and try as they might, they can't make themselves sexually attractive to each other and continue to long for partners of reproductive age. Worst of all, they just refuse to get out of the way, not just of their children, but their grandchildren and great-grandchildren. On the other hand, so few people have children or any connection with traditional reproduction that it scarcely seems to matter.

In a third scenario, the wealthy routinely screen embryos before implantation so as to optimize the kind of children they have. You can increasingly tell the social background of a young person by his or her looks and intelligence; if someone doesn't live up to social expectations, he tends to blame bad genetic choices by his parents rather than himself. Human genes have been transferred to animals and even to plants, for research purposes and to produce new medical products; and animal genes have been added to certain embryos to increase their physical endurance or resistance to disease. Scientists have not dared to produce a full-scale chimera, half human and half ape, though they could; but young people begin to suspect that classmates who do much less well than they do are in fact genetically not fully human. Because, in fact, they aren't.

Sorry, but your soul just died . . .

Toward the very end of his life, Thomas Jefferson wrote, "The general spread of the light of science has already laid open to every view the palpable truth, that the mass of mankind has not been born with saddles on their backs, nor a favored few booted and spurred, ready to ride them legitimately, by the grace of God."[6] The political equality enshrined in the Declaration of Independence rests on the empirical fact of natural human equality. We vary greatly as individuals and by culture, but we share a common humanity that allows every human being to potentially communicate with and enter into a moral relationship with every other human being on the planet. The ultimate question raised by biotechnology is, What will happen to political rights once we are able to, in effect, breed some people with saddles on their backs, and others with boots and spurs?

A Straightforward Solution

What should we do in response to biotechnology that in the future will mix great potential benefits with threats that are either physical and overt or spiritual and subtle? The answer is obvious: *We should use the power of the state to regulate it.* And if this proves to be beyond the power of any individual nation-state to regulate, it needs to be regulated on an international basis. We need to start thinking concretely now about how to build institutions that can discriminate between good and bad uses of biotechnology, and effectively enforce these rules both nationally and internationally.

This obvious answer is not obvious to many of the participants in the current biotechnology debate. The discussion remains mired at a relatively abstract level about the ethics of procedures like cloning or stem cell research, and divided into one camp that would like to permit everything and another camp that would like to ban wide areas of research and practice. The broader debate is of course an important one, but events are moving so rapidly that we will soon need more practical guidance on how we can direct future developments so that the technology remains man's servant rather than his master. Since it seems very unlikely that we will either permit everything or ban research that is highly promising, we need to find a middle ground.

The creation of new regulatory institutions is not something that should be undertaken lightly, given the inefficiencies that surround all efforts at regulation. For the past three decades, there has been a commendable worldwide movement to deregulate large sectors of every nation's economy, from airlines to telecommunications, and more broadly to reduce the size and scope of government. The global economy that has emerged as a result is a far more efficient generator of wealth and technological innovation. Excessive regulation in the past has led many to become instinctively hostile to state intervention in any form, and it is this knee-jerk aversion to regulation that will be one of the chief obstacles to getting human biotechnology under political control.

But it is important to discriminate: what works for one sector of the economy will not work for another. Information technology, for example, produces many social benefits and relatively few harms and therefore has appropriately gotten by with a fairly minimal degree of government regulation. Nuclear materials and toxic waste, on the other hand, are subject to strict national and international controls because unregulated trade in them would clearly be dangerous.

One of the biggest problems in making the case for regulating human bio-technology is the common view that even if it were desirable to stop technological advance, it is impossible to do so. If the United States or any other single country tries to ban human cloning or germ-line genetic engineering or any other proce-dure, people who wanted to do these things would simply move to a more favorable jurisdiction where they were permitted. Globalization and international competi-tion in biomedical research ensure that countries that hobble themselves by putting ethical constraints on their scientific communities or biotechnology industries will be punished.

The idea that it is impossible to stop or control the advance of technology is simply wrong.... We in fact control all sorts of technologies and many types of sci-entific research: people are no more free to experiment in the development of new biological warfare agents than they are to experiment on human subjects without the latter's informed consent. The fact that there are some individuals or organiza-tions that violate these rules, or that there are countries where the rules are either nonexistent or poorly enforced, is no excuse for not making the rules in the first place. People get away with robbery and murder, after all, which is not a reason to legalize theft and homicide.

We need at all costs to avoid a defeatist attitude with regard to technology that says that since we can't do anything to stop or shape developments we don't like, we shouldn't bother trying in the first place. Putting in place a regulatory system that would permit societies to control human biotechnology will not be easy: it will require legislators in countries around the world to step up to the plate and make difficult decisions on complex scientific issues. The shape and form of the institu-tions designed to implement new rules is a wide-open question; designing them to be minimally obstructive of positive developments while giving them effective enforcement capabilities is a significant challenge. Even more challenging will be the creation of common rules at an international level, the forging of a consensus among countries with different cultures and views on the underlying ethical questions. But political tasks of comparable complexity have been successfully undertaken in the past.

Notes

1. Martin Heidegger, *Basic Writings* (New York: Harper and Row, 1957), p. 308.
2. Peter Huber, *Orwell's Revenge: The 1984 Palimpsest* (New York: Free Press, 1994), pp. 222–228.
3. Leon Kass, *Toward a More Natural Science: Biology and Human Affairs* (New York: Free Press, 1985), p. 35.
4. Bill Joy, "Why the Future Doesn't Need Us," *Wired* 8 (2000): 238–246.
5. Tom Wolfe, "Sorry, but Your Soul Just Died," *Forbes ASAP,* December 2, 1996.
6. Letter to Roger C. Weightman, June 24, 1826, in *The Life and Selected Writings of Thomas Jefferson,* Thomas Jefferson (New York: Modern Library, 1944), pp. 729–730.

Reading the Genre

1. How does Fukuyama help the reader understand his argument, even if the audience has never read the books he writes about? How do the books *1984* and *Brave New World* and the examples of a future world they provide, help him explore his topic?

2. Fukuyama offers a "straightforward solution." But can you also list the counterarguments he discusses, and all the difficulties that stand in the way of his solution? Why does he choose to look at all these problems? Does this approach diminish the strength of his argument? (See "Respond to opposing claims," p. 70; "Find counterarguments," p. 82; and "Address counterpoints when necessary," p. 85.)

3. How does the author establish his ethos? Consider how he describes himself and his expertise, how he argues, and how he incorporates the expert voices of others. (See "Consider and control your ethos," p. 77, and Chapter 42, "Integrating Sources into Your Work," p. 431.)

4. What is the rhetorical effect of the three future scenarios that Fukuyama describes? What is he attempting to persuade the reader to feel about these possibilities? How does he accomplish that goal?

5. **WRITING:** Try your hand at science fiction, creating a future scenario like the ones Fukuyama suggests. Write the scenario in the second person, addressing the readers directly as "you" and telling them what their lives will be like in the year 2050. Imagine a future in which one element of current culture has become much more extreme and prevalent. Here are some possibilities: What havoc will global warming have caused? How will humans interact with computers, and with other human beings? Reflect on the ways that these scenarios might function as arguments—how might they convince us to act *now* to avoid future problems?

Literary Analysis: Readings

TEXTUAL ANALYSIS Camille Paglia is a culture critic and professor of humanities and media studies at the University of the Arts, in Philadelphia. She writes a monthly column for Salon.com and is a contributing editor at *Interview* magazine. This essay on Joni Mitchell comes from her most recent book, *Break, Blow, Burn: Camille Paglia Reads Forty-Three of the World's Best Poems* (2005). Mitchell is the only songwriter among this group of the world's best poets; Paglia defends her choice of the singer and, through her analysis of the song "Woodstock," reveals the complexity of Mitchell's writing. The song lyrics are reprinted before the essay.

JONI MITCHELL

Woodstock

I came upon a child of God
He was walking along the road
And I asked him, where are you going
And this he told me

I'm going on down to Yasgur's farm   5
I'm going to join in a rock 'n' roll band
I'm going to camp out on the land
And try and get my soul free

We are stardust
We are golden   10
And we've got to get ourselves
Back to the garden

Then can I walk beside you
I have come here to lose the smog
And I feel to be a cog   15
In something turning

Well, maybe it is just the time of year
Or maybe it's the time of man
I don't know who I am
But life is for learning   20

We are stardust
We are golden
And we've got to get ourselves
Back to the garden

By the time we got to Woodstock   25
We were half a million strong
And everywhere there was song
And celebration

And I dreamed I saw the bombers
Riding shotgun in the sky   30
And they were turning into butterflies
Above our nation

We are stardust
    million-year-old carbon
We are golden   35
    caught in the devil's bargain
And we've got to get ourselves
Back to the garden

CAMILLE PAGLIA

"Woodstock"

In the 1960s, young people who might once have become poets took up the guitar and turned troubadour. The best rock lyrics of that decade and the next were based on the ballad tradition, where anonymous songs with universal themes of love and strife had been refined over centuries by the shapely symmetry of the four-line stanza. But few lyrics, stripped of melody, make a successful transition to the printed page. Joni Mitchell's "Woodstock" is a rare exception. This is an important modern poem—possibly the most popular and influential poem composed in English since Sylvia Plath's "Daddy."

"Woodstock" is known worldwide as a lively, hard-driving hit single by Crosby, Stills, Nash, and Young (from their 1970 *Déjà Vu* album). This virtuoso rock band, which had actually performed at the Woodstock Music Festival in August 1969, treats Mitchell's lyric uncritically as a rousing anthem for the hippie counterculture. Their "Woodstock" is a stomping hoedown. But Joni Mitchell's interpretation of the song on her album *Ladies of the Canyon* (also 1970), where she accompanies herself on electric piano, is completely different. With its slow, jazz-inflected pacing, her "Woodstock" is a moody and at times heartbreakingly melancholy art song. It shows the heady visions of the sixties counterculture already receding and evaporating.

In the sleeve notes and other published sources, the verses of "Woodstock" are run together with few or no stanza breaks. Hence the song's wonderfully economical structure is insufficiently appreciated. My tentative transcription follows the sleeve in omitting punctuation but restores the ballad form by dividing lines where rhymes occur. "Woodstock" is organized in nesting triads: its nine stanzas fall into three parts, each climaxing in a one-stanza refrain. In Mitchell's recording, the three refrains are signaled by the entrance of background scat singers—her own voice overdubbed. At the end, this eerie chorus contributes two off-rhymed lines that I insert in italics.

Mitchell the poet and artist has cast herself in the lyric as a wanderer on the road to Woodstock, beckoning as a promised land for those fleeing an oppressive society. She meets another traveler, whose story takes up the rest of part one (1–12). Hence "Woodstock" opens with precisely the same donnée as does Shelley's "Ozymandias" ("I met a traveller from an antique land / Who said . . ."). Responding with her own story, Mitchell's persona repeats her companion's hymnlike summation ("We are stardust / We are golden") to indicate her understanding and acceptance of its message (13–24). Now comrades, they arrive at Woodstock and merge with a community of astounding size. From that assembly rises a mystical dream of peace on earth and of mankind's reconnection to nature (25–38).

The song's treatment by a male supergroup automatically altered it. The four musicians, bellying up front and center, are buddies—the merry, nomadic "rock 'n' roll band" whom the lyric's young man yearns to join (6). But Mitchell's radical gender drama is missing. Presented in her voice, the lyric's protagonist is Everywoman. The wayfarers' chance encounter on the road to Woodstock is thus a reunion of Adam and Eve searching for Eden—the "garden" of the song's master metaphor (12). They long to recover their innocence, to restart human history. The song's utopian political project contains a call for reform of sexual relations. Following Walt Whitman or Jack Kerouac, the modern woman writer takes to the road, as cloistered Emily Dickinson could never do. She and her casual companion are peers on life's journey. Free love—"hooking up" in sixties slang—exalts spontaneity over the coercion of contract.

The rambler is "a child of God," like Jesus' disciples on the road to Emmaus, because he desires salvation—but not through organized religion (1). He has shed his old identity and abandoned family, friends, property, and career. Like her, he is a refugee. Indifferent to his social status, she honors him in the moment. And she asks no favors or deference as a woman. Her question—"where are you going"—implies. Where is this generation headed (3)? Is it progressing, or drifting? Does it aim to achieve, or merely to experience? And if the latter, how can raw sensation be bequeathed to posterity without the framing of intellect or art?

He's on his way to "Yasgur's farm"—the festival site on six hundred acres of rolling pastureland in upstate New York, a working dairy farm owned by the paternal Max Yasgur (5). It is nowhere near the real Woodstock, an art colony town seventy miles away. Most of those who flocked to the three-day Woodstock festival were the white, middle-class children of an affluent, industrialized nation cut off from its agrarian roots. In Mitchell's song, their goal, "Yasgur's farm," becomes a hippie reworking of Yahweh's garden. The young man planning "to camp out on the land" to free his soul is a survivalist searching for primal nature (7–8). Michael Wadleigh's epic documentary film *Woodstock* (1970) records the violent gale and torrents of rain on the second day that turned the field into a morass. The "rock 'n' roll band" coveted by the traveler is ultimately the festival audience itself, united in music—an adoptive family of brothers and sisters who were rocked by lightning and who rolled in the mud.

"We are stardust / We are golden": the refrain is a humanistic profession of faith in possibility (9–10). Mankind was created not by a stern overlord but by sacred nature itself. It's as if the earth were pollinated by meteor showers. To be golden means to be blessed by luck: divinity is within. "We've got to get ourselves / Back to the garden": Woodstock pilgrims need no Good Shepherd or mediating priesthood (11–12). When perception is adjusted, the earth is paradise now. The woman wanderer is touched by the stranger's sense of mission: "Then can I walk beside you" (13)? Woman as equal partner rejects the burden of suspicion and guilt for man's Fall. She too is a truth seeker: she has "come here to lose the smog"—the smoke that gets in our eyes from romantic love and from the cult of competition and celebrity in our polluted metropolises (14). She feels egotistic preoccupations lifting as she becomes "a cog / In something turning"—the great wheel of karma or of astrological cycle (15–16). (Woodstock was initially called an "Aquarian Exposition" to mark the dawning of the harmonious Age of Aquarius.)

The impulse for migration to Woodstock could be "just the time of year," when summer juices surge and vacationers flock to mountains or sea (17). But if it's "the time of man" (a gender-neutral term), Woodstock's mass movement is an epochal transformation (18). The lyric's apocalyptic theme can be understood as a healing amelioration of the modernist pessimism of Yeats's "The Second Coming" — a poem that Mitchell would daringly rewrite for a 1991 album. Yeats's sinister beast slouching toward Bethlehem has become a generation embarked on a spiritual quest.

"I don't know who I am": the road to Woodstock leads to self-knowledge or self-deception (19). As a name, "Woodstock" is fortuitously organic, with associations of forest and stalk or lineage: streaming toward their open-air sanctuary, the pilgrims are nature's stock, fleeing a synthetic culture of plastics and pesticides. (In her raffish hit song "Big Yellow Taxi," Mitchell says, "They paved paradise / And put up a parking lot / . . . Hey farmer farmer / Put away that DDT now.") The festival-goers believe, rightly or wrongly, that music is prophetic truth. "Life is for learning," for expansion of consciousness rather than accumulation of wealth or power, "the devil's bargain" (compare Wordsworth's "sordid boon"; 20, 36). The returning refrain hammers the point home: we own everything in nature's garden but are blinded by ambition and greed.

The lyric seems to take breath when the pair, with near ecstasy, realize their journey has been shared by so many others: "By the time we got to Woodstock / We were half a million strong" (25–26). The first "we" is two; the second, by heady alchemy, has become a vast multitude. It's as if Adam and Eve are seeing the future—the birth of Woodstock nation, forged of Romantic ideals of reverence for nature and the brotherhood of man. As the two melt into the half million, there is an exhilarating sense of personal grievances and traumas set aside for a common cause. The crowd is "strong" in its coalescence, however momentary. "Everywhere there was song / And celebration": duty and the work ethic yield to the pleasure principle, as music breaks down barriers and inhibitions (27–28). The group triumphs, for good or ill.

The artist's "I" reemerges from the surging "we" of the Woodstock moment: "I dreamed I saw the bombers / Riding shotgun in the sky / And they were turning into butterflies / Above our nation" (29–32). Is this a shamanistic or psychedelic hallucination? Or is it a magic metamorphosis produced by the roaring engine of rock, with its droning amps and bone-shuddering vibration, eddying up from the earth? The bombers are the war machine then deployed in Vietnam. During her childhood, Joni Mitchell's father was a flight lieutenant in the Royal Canadian Air Force. Thus "Woodstock" aligns the modern military with mythic father figures and sky gods, as in William Blake's engraving *The Ancient of Days,* where Yahweh, crouched in a dark cloud, launches spears of sunlight from his rigidly out-thrust down-stretched hand.

"Riding shotgun" means guarding a stagecoach in the Wild West. Why are the bombers on alert—to smite foreign enemies, or to monitor domestic subversives? Rebel children are the nation's new frontier. The bombers, Pharaoh's pursuing chariots, can destroy but not create; they helplessly follow social change from a distance. Their alteration to butterflies "above our nation" suggests an erasure of borders, restoring the continental expanse of pre-Columbian North America. It's as if mistrust and aggression could be wished away and nationalistic rivalries purged around the world. The impossibility of this lovely dream does not negate its value. Perhaps the armored warplanes are chrysalises hatching evolved new men, the pilots floating down on parachutes to join the festival of peace. But we cannot live as flitting butterflies. Civilization requires internal and external protections and is far more complex and productive than the sixties credo of Flower Power ever comprehended.

In spatial design, "Woodstock" tracks along the wanderers' narrow path, then suddenly expands horizontally at its destination, where the half million have gathered. Buoyed by "song," the lyric now swells vertically to the sky, where it bewitches and exorcizes its harassers. Finally, it sweeps backward in time to take in geology: we are "million-year-old carbon" (34). Our Darwinian origins are a primeval swamp of lizards and plants, crushed to a fertile matrix. We are kin to rocks and minerals, the lowest of the low in Judeo-Christianity's great chain of being. What injects life into the song's stardust and carbon is not the Lord's breath but music. By affirming our shared genetic past, furthermore, Mitchell's metaphor conflates the races: we are carbon copies of one another. If at the cellular level we're all carbon black, then racial differences are trivial and superficial. And carbon under pressure transmutes to the visionary clarity of diamond.

The grandeur of Mitchell's lyric, with its vast expanse of space and time, is somewhat obscured in its carefree performance by Crosby, Stills, Nash, and Young, who are true believers in the revolutionary promise of Woodstock nation. By literally re-creating the "song and celebration," their bouncy, infectious rock rendition permits no alternative view of the festival, even though by the time their record was released, the disastrous Altamont concert had already occurred, exposing the fragility of Woodstock's aspirations. (*Gimme Shelter,* the Maysles brothers' 1970 documentary on the all-day festival at Altamont Speedway near San Francisco, captures the discord and violence leading to a murder in front of the stage.) CSN&Y's evangelical version of "Woodstock" was meant to convert its listeners to pacifism and solidarity. But six months after release of their single, the group had bitterly broken up. They themselves couldn't hold it together. And Mitchell's love affairs with two band members (Crosby and Nash) also ended.

In the hesitations and ravaged vibrato of her recording of "Woodstock," Joni Mitchell confides her doubts about her own splendid vision. Partly because she did not perform at Woodstock, her version has more distance and detachment. Her delivery makes lavish use of dynamics, so that we feel affirmation, then a fading of confidence and will. This "Woodstock" is a harrowing lament for hopes dashed and energies tragically wasted. It's an elegy for an entire generation, flamingly altruistic yet hedonistic and self-absorbed, bold yet naive, abundantly gifted yet plagued by self-destruction. These contradictions were on massive display at Woodstock, where the music was pitifully dependent on capitalist technology and where the noble experiment in pure democracy was sometimes indistinguishable from squalid regression to the primal horde.

An extended coda begins, as if the song doesn't want to end. The lyrics dissolve into pure music — Woodstock's essence. The coda, with its broken syllables, is a crooning lullaby that turns into a warning wail. Mitchell is skeptical about groups; she longs to join but sees the traps. When her voice falls away, her reverberating piano goes on by stops and starts. The entire power of "Woodstock" is that what is imagined in it was *not* achieved. Woodstock the festival has become a haunting memory. Mitchell's final notes hang, quaver, and fade. Cold reality triumphs over art's beautiful dreams.

Reading the Genre

1. Paglia closely reads every line and word of the song "Woodstock." How does this reading allow her to suggest that the song is telling one particular story? Do you think there could be other meanings, or do you think Paglia got it right? (See "Examine the text closely, p. 199, and Chapter 19, "Smart Reading," p. 317.)

2. Is Paglia's reading shaped by the fact that a woman wrote this song? How important is it in literary analysis to consider a text's author, and why?

3. Paglia writes about the different recorded performances of the song. In what ways does the song's meaning change when the song is performed by different bands, with different instrumentation, or in different venues?

4. How does Paglia describe the social context in which the song was written? What would change if the song were written and performed today? (See "Finding and developing materials," p. 198.)

5. **WRITING:** Read lyrics written by one of your favorite artists (song lyrics are readily available online). Do a close, line-by-line and word-by-word analysis of the song. Using this close reading, what assertions can you make about the subject of the song? Support these claims by finding out more about who the author is, how and where the song has been performed, and the social context in which the song was written. (See Chapter 36, "Finding Print and Online Sources," p. 406.)

ANALYSIS OF A GENRE   Alison Gillmor writes articles and reviews for CBC.ca and the *Winnipeg Free Press* and is a frequent writer for the Canadian magazine *The Walrus*, from which this essay comes. In this piece, Gillmor examines the recent popularity of books about dogs, identifying emerging common themes among these books and describing how our culture's images of dogs seem to have changed.

The Walrus

Posted: April 2007
From: Alison Gillmor

It's a Dog's Life: *They're Not Just Pets Anymore—They're Teachers, Preachers, Shrinks, and Philosophers*

The heroic dog is a much-cherished image in our culture, but while we admire trained search-and-rescue dogs, we really crave stories about gifted amateurs—regular pets who run into burning buildings or jump into icy rivers to save the young or the injured. Recently, psychologists at the University of Western Ontario devised an experiment to test whether dogs actually do understand human emergencies. The first simulation involved an owner feigning a heart attack; the second replicated the classic master-trapped-under-a-fallen-bookcase scenario. The researchers found an increase in anxious doggy hovering but no actual rescue attempts. "There is a tendency to bond with our animals and to believe, or want to believe, that they are highly intelligent, that they understand when we're talking to them or when we're gesturing to them," explained researcher Bill Roberts. "I think that's probably the root of people believing animals are more intelligent than they actually are."

We expect our dogs to rescue us. But Lassie barking when Timmy falls down the well is no longer enough. According to the litter of dog memoirs that have crowded bookstores and bestseller lists, dogs are now giving our plugged-in kids authentic childhoods, getting feckless twentysomethings to grow up, keeping marriages together, consoling the newly divorced and the terminally ill, even shepherding boomers out of middle-aged, middle-class ruts. Dogs can comfort a soldier stationed in Iraq (*From Baghdad, With Love*), offer a canine entree to other countries (*Ella in Europe*), or help their owners lose weight (*The Dog Diet, A Memoir*). Occasionally they give business advice (*Short Tails and Treats from Three Dog Bakery*). More and more, they are expected to provide the emotional and spiritual "life lessons" that used to come from teachers, preachers, shrinks, and philosophers. The phrase "unconditional love" pops up often in these books.

There are probably dry, statistical, socioeconomic reasons for our current obsession with dogs. In an urban, accelerated, mobile culture, the affection of an animal is reassuringly physical and direct. Another reason — one we're less willing to acknowledge — is that dogs are blank slates, *tabulae rasae* onto which we can write ourselves. Jon Katz, the author of several dog books as well as the Heavy Petting column for *Slate*, suggests that people find in dogs whatever they need. In *The New Work of Dogs: Tending to Life, Love, and Family* (Random House, 2004), Katz argues that people can "perceive in their dogs any trait or emotion they like, unencumbered by the dogs' own voices." Katz, a self-described "dog-love rationalist," believes that loving a dog can be an "incalculably rewarding experience," but he counsels us to be aware of what we're asking of dogs and why we're asking it.

One would think that writers would be especially conscious of this sensible stance, but a quick look at current dog books suggests that many are not. The rapidly expanding market for anything dog-related — along with the phenomenal success of John Grogan's *Marley & Me: Life and Love with the World's Worst Dog* (William Morrow, 2005) — means that publishers are rushing to grab any manuscript that can be sent out with a wagging tail on its cover. Some of these books function at the same harmless level as dog-park bragging, but unfortunately dogs' best qualities are also those that make them magnets for lousy prose. To paraphrase the late British dog trainer Barbara Woodhouse: There are no bad dogs, just bad dog writers. Dogs' sweet, snouty faces can easily lead people into sentimentality, and their decent, frank, four-square personalities make it tempting to fall into certainty — and sentimentality and certainty are rarely good for writers. It takes a real act of authorial will to turn away from those big puppy eyes, but the best dog writers manage, tackling the mysteries of the human-canine connection with contrariness, caution, and a careful delineation of where dog nature ends and human speculation begins.

One way to get around the warm-and-fuzzies is to take the usual conventions of the dog narrative and give them a good shake. Take Scottish writer Thomas Healy, who wouldn't know a feel-good story if one smacked him in the face. His memoir, *I Have*

Heard You Calling in the Night (Harcourt, 2006), is crafted with the stylized bluntness one might expect of a poetic man who hangs out at boxing clubs. Healy grew up in a tough corner of Glasgow in the 1950s, "when the Gorbals was the Gorbals." A self-described hard man, he drinks and brawls. (At one point he gets a badly infected hand, only to find that someone else's tooth is lodged in his knuckles.) In the 1980s, with his fortieth birthday approaching, he acquires a Doberman puppy that he names Martin—a dignified name for a dignified dog. Healy is not quite sure what makes him decide to buy Martin, and people who know him are taken aback. "They had not thought I was a doggy sort of man. Well, neither had I." In the end, he sees it as a kind of providence.

The memoir's title is taken from a hymn sung at a Catholic ordination service Healy attends one night, and there is a thin, tough line of spiritual grace running through the book. Healy believes that Martin saves him, not by being an angel in canine form but simply by being. Healy realizes that he can't drink until he blacks out because there will be no one to feed Martin. He can't pick fights and go to jail because there will be no one to walk Martin. Healy's redemption is neither quick nor easy—he has many setbacks, including a spectacular lapse that sees him getting blind drunk on something called scrumpy. This may be a story about a dog rescuing a man, but it's an unusually stark and unsentimental one, and all the better for it.

New York writer Abigail Thomas, author of *A Three Dog Life* (Harcourt, 2006), also subverts expectations. A phrase that comes up frequently in goopy dog books is "living in the moment"—the notion that a dog's happy talent for focusing on whatever is in front of its nose can help humans stop fretting needlessly about the future and the past. Thomas has good reason to be wary about living in the moment: her husband, Rich, lives with a traumatic brain injury that has robbed him of his short- and long-term memory. As she explains in this plainspoken memoir, he "is lodged in a single moment and it never tips into the next."

Seven years into Thomas's marriage, Rich was walking their dog, Harry, when the leash broke and Harry bolted onto Riverside Drive. Rich ran after the dog and was hit by a car. The dog that inadvertently caused the accident helps Thomas deal with its terrible aftermath, but she refuses to turn it into a literary situation: "There is no room for irony here, no room for guilt or second-guessing. That would be a diversion, and indulgence. These are hard facts to be faced head-on." Thomas's three dogs all help with this task. Their warmth and simple routines comfort her and give structure to what might otherwise be shapeless days.

Healy and Thomas kick against the tendency to give dog stories aggressively uplifting messages, eschewing the jollier writers' "if only dogs could talk" premise. If dogs really could talk, they might have something to say about the platitudes being put forward in their names. In *10 Secrets My Dog Taught Me* (Rodale, 2005), Carlo De Vito offers some syntactically challenged life lessons ("Simplicity is the stripping away of the things that occupy us instead of what make us whole") that he claims to have learned from Exley, his German shorthair pointer. The sentiments attributed to Exley would make any self-respecting dog pine for the days when its ancestors ran behind coaches in Dalmatia or chased wolves in the Pyrenees. That may have been hard work, but it was clean; a dog knew where it stood at the end of the day.

Increasingly, the image of dogs in contemporary North American culture is stranded somewhere between their sharp-toothed primal past and the luxe lure of Burberry canine couture. It wasn't always like this. In *The Dog and I* (Penguin, 2006), veteran Canadian journalist Roy MacGregor measures out his life in the dogs he has walked—Buddy, Cindy, Bumps, Bandit, Cricket, and Willow. While this gentle memoir portrays dogs as stalwart creatures and wonderful companions, it makes no extravagant emotional demands on their good natures. MacGregor is old enough to remember when dogs were just dogs. They lived outside, "or, if they were lucky, in a shed," and were fed random table scraps. As MacGregor grows older, his dogs are promoted to warmer, comfier berths, but they remain animals.

This separate status is no longer enough for many North American pet owners, who are increasingly turning dogs into people by ascribing to animals their own motives, feelings, beliefs, and neuroses. A related trend involves turning people into dogs. A populist misreading of scientific research into the social behaviors of dogs and their instincts as pack animals and predators has created a bizarre form of behaviorism in which human families are replicating wolfpack dynamics so that Rover can feel securely slotted into a canine hierarchy.

This top-dog approach accounts for the strange suburban spectacle of that nice guy down the street suddenly grabbing the family pet by the throat and flipping it on its back in order to establish dominance—a training move known as the "alpha roll." This controversial technique was first advanced by the Monks of New Skete, an Eastern Orthodox order that describes the raising of German shepherds in upstate New York in their 1978 book, *How To Be Your Dog's Best Friend*. (They have since recanted.) Cesar Millan, the celebrity "dog whisperer" on the National Geographic Channel, is the current dominance guru. Defenders say that he taps into canine instinct; critics suggest that his alpha-male act has little to do with wolf behavior, nothing to do with domesticated-dog behavior, and a lot to do with macho human posturing.

With all this confusing overlap going on, it's a relief to come across dog memoirs that clearly delineate human roles and animal roles. These works understand that dogs are dogs and people are people; that the needs of dogs and humans are often different and conflicting. This matter-of-factness in no way discounts the relationship between humans and animals; if anything, the bonds between the two are all the more astonishing because they force us to reach across the species gap.

The goofball protagonist of John Grogan's *Marley & Me* defines dogginess. Easy to love but hard to anthropomorphize, Marley is bouncy, messy, drooly, and humpy, prone to inscrutable but unstoppable canine instincts that drive him to swallow speaker components and dig through drywall. Marley isn't actually the world's worst dog; he's just overly enthusiastic, a quality that carries both advantages and disadvantages as Marley helps his master and mistress, John and wife Jenny, form a family. John and Jenny start out as two independent professionals with time and money to spare. Their clothes are intact, their furniture clean, their garden free of trenches. They spend Sunday mornings drinking coffee and reading newspapers. Then, after five-week-old Marley moves in, their lives start careening toward the responsibilities of dog ownership, then parenthood, and finally the quotidian joys and sorrows of domestic life. All along, Marley is teaching the Grogans something important—mostly that a high tolerance for chaos, catastrophe, and expense is a good foundation for family happiness.

Of course, Marley "teaches" the Grogans about the meaning of life and family the same way he does almost everything—by accident. Some dog tales read like self-help books, making it seem as if dogs are on a mission to solve the problems of the North American middle class. Fortunately, good analytic writers find that dog ownership breeds more questions than answers. Susan Cheever, for instance, grew up in a, well, *Cheeveresque* home that favored large sporting dogs bought from

WASP-y breeders and named after eighteenth-century ancestors. As an adult, she finds herself in the piquant position of acquiring a miniature dachshund named Cutie. In an essay anthologized in *Woman's Best Friend: Women Writers on the Dogs in Their Lives* (Seal Press, 2006), she muses on this unlikely event and on the ethics of the animal-human bond: "I have become increasingly haunted by our treatment of the animals in our lives. . . . What does it mean to own a living creature? What responsibilities does that entail?" She also realizes, with a clear-eyed view of Cutie's priorities, that he is not about to rescue her from this moral wrangling: "Cutie doesn't seem concerned about the questions his presence poses for me. All he wants is to have his back scratched."

Roger Grenier's thoughts also run to doubts in *The Difficulty of Being a Dog* (University of Chicago Press, 2000), a collection of infinitely delicate observations on the condition of dogness. Originally published in Paris in 1998 as *Les larmes d'Ulysse* (The Tears of Ulysses), this small volume was a bestseller in France, partly because the French love their dogs—they bring them to cafés, remember—and partly because Grenier's writing is intellectually stringent enough to be discussed at dinner parties. Grenier is a novelist and essayist who has worked for many years at the publishing house Éditions Gallimard. His musings on dogs are learned, literary, and existential. (Albert Camus once dog-sat for him.) If Grenier suggests that the experience of loving a dog is life-affirming, he means it in the very Gallic sense that life is lived more keenly in the knowledge of death. Dogs help with this, in short, because they generally predecease their owners: "Because dogs inflict the suffering of loss upon us, the French sometimes call them 'beasts of sorrow,' *bêtes de chagrin*," Grenier points out, making it quite clear that this is not *Chicken Soup for the Dog Lover's Soul*.

While Grenier derives great joy from strolling the Rue du Bac with his dog Ulysses, he often finds himself looking at the situation from the other end of the leash, wondering what dogs' psychologically entangled relationships with humans might cost them. Being a man of letters, he summons literary sources, quoting Rainer Maria Rilke, who says of dogs, "Their determination to acknowledge us forces them to live at the very limits of their nature." French writer Antoine de Rivarol puts it this way: "We have dragged [domestic animals] far from their own realm without transporting them into ours." Grenier sees dogs as tragic exiles. For him, the bond between animals and humans is this slightly melancholic sense of loss and alienation.

In a very real, evolutionary sense, dogs were made by people. Once wide-ranging wolves, they have been domesticated into the warmer, softer creatures that lie next to our beds at night. We are still shaping dogs today, making them into what we want and need them to be and accepting precious little responsibility for doing so. The dog-book writers in North America—with noteworthy exceptions—set up dogs as soul-mates, spirit guides, and savants. If dogs could read these inflated images, they would probably look sad-eared and embarrassed, the way they do when their owners dress them up for Halloween. Fortunately, dogs remain unaware of their current celebrity status; they just carry on doing what they do. It's the humans, as usual, making all the fuss.

Reading the Genre

1. How does Gillmor's use of the anecdote about the University of Western Ontario study affect the literary analysis that follows? Do you think that knowing this information from the start of the essay has an effect on readers? (See "Draw on previous research," p. 188.)

2. What does Gillmor want us to believe about the dog-human relationships portrayed in the books she writes about? How does she manage to stick with her thesis even as she considers viewpoints she doesn't agree with? (See Chapter 22, "Thesis," p. 336.)

3. Using a highlighter, identify the sections in which Gillmor summarizes each book she discusses. Can you identify patterns in the style of her summaries? With two different color highlighters, also highlight all paraphrases and all direct quotations. Look for patterns in how Gillmor uses these forms. (See Chapters 40–42 on using sources.)

4. Create four columns on a blank sheet of paper, and title each column with one of the four roles that Gillmor identifies in her subtitle: "teachers, preachers, shrinks, and philosophers." Find examples of each of these roles in her analysis, and describe these examples under the headings.

5. **WRITING:** Analyze the representation of a famous animal—Lassie, Benji, Mr. Ed, M.V.P., Air Bud, Cujo, Washoe, White Fang, Winn-Dixie, Old Yeller, Willy, Alex (the parrot), or another famous animal of your choice. Make observations about this animal's talents and its interactions with humans, and then draw some conclusions about the way humans "write themselves" through these animals. Is this animal a teacher, a preacher, a shrink, or a philosopher?

ANALYSIS OF A GENRE   Writer and social critic Naomi Wolf's first book, *The Beauty Myth* (1990), was an international best seller about the ways that a culture's norm or ideal of "beauty" is imposed on women. Her subsequent articles and books have touched on the issues of adolescent sexuality, pregnancy and childbirth, and the state of democracy in the United States. Wolf currently maintains a blog for the online news and commentary site, the Huffington Post. The *Gossip Girl* series of books that Wolf writes about in this article (first published in the *New York Times*) has been made into a successful—and equally controversial—television show.

Young Adult Fiction: Wild Things

Naomi Wolf

These books look cute. They come in matched paperback sets with catchy titles, and stay for weeks on the children's books best-seller list. They carry no rating or recommended age range on the cover, but their intended audience—teenage girls—can't be in doubt. They feature sleek, conventionally beautiful girls lounging, getting in or out of limos, laughing, and striking poses. Any parent—including me—might put them in the Barnes & Noble basket without a second glance.

Yet if that parent opened one, he or she might be in for a surprise. The *Gossip Girl, A-List,* and *Clique* series—the most successful in a crowded field of *Au Pairs, It Girls,* and other copycat series—represent a new kind of young adult fiction, and feature a different kind of heroine. In these novels, which have dominated the field of popular girls' fiction in recent years, Carol Gilligan's question about whether girls can have "a different voice" has been answered—in a scary way.

In Lisi Harrison's *Clique* novels, set in suburban Westchester, the characters are twelve and thirteen years old, but there are no girlish identity crises, no submissiveness to parents or anyone else. These girls are empowered. But they are empowered to hire party planners, humiliate the "sluts" in their classes ("'I'm sorry, I'm having a hard time understanding what you're saying,' Massie snapped. 'I don't speak Slut'"), and draw up a petition calling for the cafeteria ladies serving their lunch to get manicures.

The *Clique* novels are all about status. But sex saturates the *Gossip Girl* books, by Cecily von Ziegesar, which are about seventeen- and eighteen-year-old private school girls in Manhattan. This is not the frank sexual exploration found in a Judy Blume novel, but teenage sexuality via Juicy Couture, blasé and entirely commodified. In *Nothing Can Keep Us Together,* Nate has sex with Serena in a Bergdorf's dressing room: "Nate was practically bursting as he followed Serena. . . . He grabbed her camisole and yanked it away from her body, ripping it entirely in half. . . . 'Remember when we were in the tub at my house, the summer before 10th grade?' . . . 'Yes!' 'Oh, yes!' . . . Nate began to cry as soon as it was over. The Viagra had worn off just in time."

The *A-List* novels, by Zoey Dean (a pseudonym for a married writing team hired by the media packager 17th Street Productions, which created all three series and sold them to Little, Brown), are spinoffs of the *Gossip Girl* series. Now we're on the West Coast, among a group of seniors from Beverly Hills High. Here is Anna, in Las Vegas for the weekend with her posse: "Was there any bliss quite like the first five minutes in a hot tub? Well, yes, actually. Ben. Sex with Ben had been that kind of bliss. . . . Would sex with Scott offer that kind of bliss?" Her best friend, Cyn, also has feelings for Scott: "She'd shed a lot of her usual wild-child ways as soon as they'd hooked up. No more stealing guys with wedding rings away from their wives just because she could. . . . No more getting wasted at parties and dirty dancing with handsome waiters. . . . No more taking E," or ecstasy, at nightclubs.

But anything can get old eventually. Cyn offers Anna this world-weary roman-tic guidance: "We used to jump each other, like, three times a night. When we went out to the movies, we'd sit by a wall and do it during the boring parts." She recommends "semi-sex"—not oral sex, because "that is so over"—behind a statue at MoMA.

Unfortunately for girls, these novels reproduce the dilemma they experience all the time: they are expected to compete with pornography, but can still be labeled sluts. In *Invasion of the Boy Snatchers,* the fourth novel in the *Clique* series, Lisi Harrison reproduces misogynist scenarios of other girls shaming and humiliating a girl who is deemed "slutty"—Nina, an exchange student from Spain. When Harrison writes that Nina's "massive boobs jiggled," you know she is doomed to the Westchester equivalent of a scarlet letter.

Though *Rainbow Party* got all the attention last year—that was the novel about oral sex in which the characters even sounded like porn stars: Hunter, Rod, and Rusty—kids didn't buy it, literally. In spite of a shiny, irresistible cover showing a row of candy-colored lipsticks, it was a book more reported about than read.

But teenagers, or their parents, do buy the bad-girls books—the *Clique, Gossip Girl,* and *A-List* series have all sold more than a million copies. And while the tacky sex scenes in them are annoying, they aren't really the problem. The problem is a value system in which meanness rules, parents check out, conformity is everything, and stressed-out adult values are presumed to be meaningful to teenagers. The books have a kitsch quality—they package corruption with a cute overlay.

In the world of the *A-List* or *Clique* girl, inverting Austen (and Alcott), the rich are right and good simply by virtue of their wealth. Seventh graders have Palm Pilots, red Coach clutches, Visas, and cellphones in Prada messenger bags. Success and failure are entirely signaled by material possessions—specifically, by brands. You know the new girl in the *Clique* novel *Best Friends for Never* is living in social limbo when she shops at J. Crew and wears Keds, and her mother drives a dreaded Taurus rather than a Lexus. In *Back in Black* the group of *A-List* teenagers spends a weekend at "the Palms Hotel and Casino"; brands are so prominent you wonder if there are product placement deals: "Vanity Fair always prepared giveaway baskets. . . . Last year's had contained a Dell portable jukebox, a bottle of Angel perfume by Thierry Mugler, and a PalmOne Treo 600 Smartphone." (The copyright page of the latest *Gossip Girl* book lists credits for the clothing featured on the cover: "gold sequined top—Iris Singer, peach dress—Bibelot@Susan Greenstadt," and so on.)

In these novels, the world of wealthy parents is characteristically seen as corrupt and opportunistic—but the kids have no problem with that. In the *A-List* novels, power is all about favors: "Orlando Bloom was next door with Jude Law, and Sam knew him from a dinner party her father had hosted to raise money for the Kerry campaign." As Anna challenges a young would-be writer, Scott, "Do you think you only got published in *The Times* because your mother called in a favor?"

The mockery the books direct toward their subjects is not the subversion of adult convention traditionally found in young adult novels. Instead they scorn anyone who is pathetic enough not to fit in. In the *Clique* novels, the "pretty committee," dominated by the lead bitch-goddess, Massie, is made up of the cool kids of their elite girls school. They terrorize the "losers" below them in the social hierarchy: it's like *Lord of the Flies* set in the local mall, without the moral revulsion.

The girls move through the school in what has become, in movies like *Mean Girls* and *Clueless,* a set piece for nasty cool-girl drama: they are "striking and confident in their matching costumes. . . . like a gang of sexy fembots on a mission to take over suburbia." In the classic tradition of young adult fiction, Massie would be the villain, and Claire, the newcomer who first appears as an L.B.R., or "Loser Beyond Repair," would be the heroine: she is the one girl with spunk, curiosity, and age-appropriate preoccupations. Claire and her family live in the guesthouse of the wealthy Block family; Claire's mother is friends with Massie's mother, but her father seems to be employed by Massie's father in an uneasily dependent relationship. In Jane Austen or Charlotte Brontë, that economic dependency on the "great house" would signal that the heroine stands in opposition to the values of that mansion. Yet Claire's whole journey, in class terms, is to gravitate into the mansion. She abandons her world of innocence and integrity—in which children respect parents, are honest, and like candy—to embrace her eventual success as one of the school's elite, lying to and manipulating parents, having contempt for teachers, and humiliating social rivals.

Over the course of the series, Claire learns to value her own poorer but closer-knit family less than she did before. Indeed, she pushes her father into greater economic dependence on the rich patrons, absorbing Massie's shopping tastes and learning to disdain her mother's clothing. Veronica and Betty morph into mistresses of the universe, wearing underwear to school with the words "kiss it" on the rear.

Since women have been writing for and about girls, the core of the tradition has been the opposition between the rebel and the popular, often wealthy antiheroine. Sara Crewe in Frances Hodgson Burnett's *Little Princess* loses her social standing and is tormented by the school's alpha girls, but by the end of the story we see them brought low. In *Little Women*, Jo March's criticism of "ladylike" social norms is challenged by an invitation to a ball; while Meg, the eldest girl, is taken in by the wealthy daughters of the house and given a makeover—which is meant to reveal not her victory as a character but her weakness.

This tradition carried on powerfully through the twentieth century. Even modern remakes, like *Clueless*, show the popular, superficial girl undergoing a humbling and an awakening, as she begins to question her allegiance to conformity and status.

In the *Clique* and *Gossip Girl* novels, meanwhile, every day is Freaky Friday. The girls try on adult values and customs as though they were going to wear them forever. The narratives offer the perks of the adult world not as escapist fantasy but in a creepily photorealistic way, just as the book jackets show real girls polished to an unreal gloss. It's not surprising that Cecily von Ziegesar matter-of-factly told an interviewer that she sees her books as "aspirational" (which she seemed to think was a good thing).

The great reads of adolescence have classically been critiques of the corrupt or banal adult world. It's sad if the point of reading for many girls now is no longer to take the adult world apart but to squeeze into it all the more compliantly. Sex and shopping take their places on a barren stage, as though, even for teenagers, these are the only dramas left.

Reading the Genre

1. How does Wolf balance her explanation of what the books are about with her evaluation of their message? How does she provide evidence for claims such as "The problem is a value system in which meanness rules, parents check out, conformity is everything, and stressed-out adult values are presumed to be meaningful to teenagers"? (See "Read for claims, reasons, and evidence," p. 319, and Chapter 39, "Critical Reading and Note-Taking Strategies," p. 420.)

2. Draw a cover for one of these books, creating an image of the characters and their world, based on the information that Wolf offers about the books. Are there more details you'd like to see, so that you can better picture these people? Compare your image with an actual cover from one of these books (easily found online). Does the effort of creating these sorts of images help readers better evaluate a literary analysis essay? (See "Use images to tell a story," p. 15, and Chapter 46, "Understanding Images," p. 500.)

3. How does Wolf focus her analysis on the specific audience for these books? Can you think of other books that have such a specific audience (age, gender, and so on) and that so clearly speak to the "values" of this group?

4. **WRITING:** Young adult (YA) fiction is a genre — a group of similar texts with similar conventions. The "rich, mean-girl fiction" that Wolf writes about is a subgenre — a group of books *within* a genre that are even more similar. List as many other genres of fiction as you can, and then try to list as many subgenres as you can. (See "Focus on its genre," p. 200.)

TEXTUAL ANALYSIS Joyce Carol Oates has published more than a hundred books of fiction, poetry, short stories, and essays, including *Black Water* (1992), *Where Are You Going, Where Have You Been: Selected Early Stories* (1993), *We Were the Mulvaneys* (1996), *Blonde* (2000), *The Gravedigger's Daughter* (2008), and *A Fair Maiden* (2009). Her work has won many awards, and she teaches humanities and creative writing at Princeton University. In the following analysis, from an essay collection titled *Uncensored: Views and Reviews* (2005), Oates explores the novels of Michael Connelly and other works of the "noir crime fiction" genre. Michael Connelly's most recent novel in the series Oates writes about is titled *The Brass Verdict* (2008).

JOYCE CAROL OATES

L.A. Noir: Michael Connelly

A Darkness More Than Night
Michael Connelly

Los Angeles has long been celebrated as the *noir* dream-factory of America. If, per capita, the city and its environs may be less riddled with corruption and violence than Youngstown, Ohio, or Camden, New Jersey, it possesses a redeeming ironic glamor missing from such sublunary locales. This western edge of our continent seems more truly to have "pandered in whispers to the last and greatest of all human dreams" than the eastern island of which, in the famous concluding passage of *The Great Gatsby*, F. Scott Fitzgerald spoke with such melancholy lyricism. Southern California has been the inspiration for a number of *noir* writers of distinction, from the most influential of "hard-boiled" detective novelists Raymond Chandler (*The Big Sleep*, 1939; *Farewell, My Lovely*, 1940) and the more literary Ross MacDonald (*The*

Moving Target, 1949) to our contemporaries Joseph Wambaugh, James Ellroy, and Michael Connelly.

Chandler and MacDonald wrote what are essentially romances, about heroic private investigators involved in murder investigations. (In real life, private investigators are virtually never involved in murder investigations.) Wambaugh, Ellroy, and Connelly write more realistic crime novels of that popular sub-genre known as the police procedural, which was virtually created in the 1950s by Ed McBain (pseudonym of Evan Hunter) in his 87th Precinct series. In the classic police procedural, investigators are professional detectives, not private investigators or gifted, charming amateurs. The detailed procedure of a crime investigation, which constitutes the backbone of a typical Michael Connelly novel, can be assumed to be authentic, if not so minutely detailed as a forensics procedural by Patricia Cornwell, a former pathologist. In Connelly's novels we follow investigations from the often intimate perspective of a canny detective named Harry ("Hieronymus") Bosch, of the Hollywood division of the LAPD; Bosch's precinct is one Connelly came to know well during his thirteen years as a crime reporter for the *Los Angeles Times* in the late 1980s. (Connelly grew up in Fort Lauderdale, where he came of age during the South Florida high-profile cocaine-driven violence of the 1970s; as a young reporter for papers in Daytona Beach and Fort Lauderdale, he was assigned to police beats.) What is most appealing about Bosch is that, far from being a fantasy hero, he's a flawed, deeply troubled and isolated man; a professional police officer who has the grudging respect of most of his colleagues but has been suspended from duty at least twice (for shooting an unarmed suspect in a serial murder case, for an impulsive assault against one of his superiors), and who seems perpetually on the brink of burn-out or implosion. A colleague says of Bosch that he has "haunted eyes" and, in *A Darkness More Than Night,* he's even a suspect in a gruesomely elaborate murder.

Aptly named for Hieronymus Bosch, the fifteenth-century Dutch painter of nightmare moral allegories, whose Christian mysticism reveled in scenes of serio-comic sadism, Bosch too is an "avenging angel" with a powerful wish to see sinners punished. Bosch is far from being an idealist but, in his misanthrope way, he's an idealist who still believes in the possibility, if not the probability, of justice—through his own exertions. The background Connelly provides for Bosch is brief and instructive: Bosch's mother, a prostitute, was murdered when he was a child, and, during the Vietnam War, Bosch served in a special branch of the U.S. Army trained to enter the labyrinthine tunnel-networks dug by the Vietcong. Both experiences have left psychic damage, making Bosch into an obsessive who can't let go of a case. A colleague named McCaleb, a former F.B.I. profiler, perceives Bosch as a special breed of cop who sees his job not as a mere skill or craft but as a vocation; such cops take on the responsibility of speaking for the dead:

> There was a sacred bond cast between victim and cop that formed at the crime scene and could not be severed. It was what ultimately pushed them into the chase and enabled them to overcome all obstacles in their path. . . . It had been [McCaleb's] experience that these cop/angels were the best investigators he ever worked with. He also came to believe that they traveled closest to that unseen edge, beneath which lies the abyss.

Nietzsche's famous aphorism in *Beyond Good and Evil* might stand as an epigraph for Michael Connelly's fiction: "Whoever battles with monsters had better see that it does not turn him into a monster. And if you gaze too long into an abyss, the abyss will gaze into you."[1]

(It's interesting to note that Connelly modeled his fictitious detective on fellow *noir* novelist James Ellroy, whose mother was murdered in Los Angeles when Ellroy was ten, and whose subsequent career as a writer of crime fiction of Dostoyevskian passion and scope clearly springs from that childhood trauma.)[2]

Michael Connelly began his highly successful career with *The Black Echo* (1992), which introduced Harry Bosch, and quickly followed up with three Bosch novels, *The Black Ice, The Concrete Blonde,* and *The Last Coyote* (perhaps Connelly's strongest novel, in which Bosch, suspended from the LAPD, investigates the murder of his mother); Connelly then alternated Bosch novels (*Angels Flight, Trunk Music*) with densely plotted mystery-thrillers (*The Poet, Blood Work, Void Moon*) that continue the preoccupations of the Bosch novels, in particular the complicity between criminal and pursuer. Occasionally, as in *Trunk Music* and *Void Moon*, Connelly shifts his locale (to Las Vegas), but his base is Los Angeles in its infinite variety, and his subjects are timely as L.A. headlines: Hollywood murders, racism and race riots, drug-dealing, violence and corruption within the LAPD, sadistic sexual crimes, incest and child rape and murder, pedophilia on the Internet.

A Darkness More Than Night, Connelly's tenth novel, is something of an experiment: Connelly brings together Bosch with the less distinctive hero of *Blood Work,* F.B.I. profiler Terry McCaleb, now retired to a tenuous private life as a husband and father living on Catalina Island, and the even less distinctive journalist Jack McEvoy of *The Poet.* McEvoy has hardly more than a walk-on role here, as a journalist duped by a corrupt source, but McCaleb is given equal billing with Bosch. In this *noir* landscape, McCaleb is an unlikely player: a reasonable, decent, fair-minded individual who's a devoted family man and who has recently had a heart transplant, disqualifying him from scenes of physical bravado and action. Where Bosch, an isolate, broods compulsively upon the past—his wife, appropriately named Eleanor Wish, whom he loves very much, has left their marriage under mysterious circumstances—McCaleb has found a new center to his life in his infant daughter, so tenderly noted in the novel that the reader fears for McCaleb's vulnerability: "He felt a kind of love he had never felt before."

But it remains Bosch, here as elsewhere, who propels the narrative and gives to *A Darkness More Than Night* its air of suspenseful urgency. Divided into two centers of moral consciousness—Bosch's and McCaleb's—the novel has a tricky double plot involving a high-profile murder trial in which Bosch is the primary prosecution witness (a Hollywood director is accused of having strangled a young actress and subsequently arranged her body to suggest a lurid auto-erotic accident), and an LAPD investigation into the murder of a low-level criminal (whose body has been arranged to suggest a re-enactment of a sadistic bondage scene out of Hieronymus Bosch's *A*

Garden of Earthly Delights). By so dividing his novel Connelly allows Bosch and McCaleb to regard each other, like uneasy brothers. And when, after Bosch saves McCaleb's life, McCaleb calmly informs Bosch, "I'm not going to be your friend any more," the revelation is as startling as any in the novel and, for Bosch, more upsetting. For *A Darkness More Than Night* hasn't been so much about the pursuit of evil as the cultivation of conscience: how to live, amid evil, a decent life? How, policing violence, to avoid committing violence? In his rejection Bosch takes strength from a sense of kinship with Los Angeles: "A city of lost light. His city. . . . The city of the second chance."

In the latter half of the American twentieth century, "crime" seemed to have acquired a mythopoetic status. In writing of crime, one is writing of American life *in extremis*. Crime detection, criminal trials, the enforcement or, more likely, the thwarting of justice—these have become crucial cultural issues, beyond mere entertainment; to anatomize a high-profile crime, in as much detail as possible, has become a way of decoding the American soul. This goes to the root of our childlike, or primitive, conviction that death can't ever be "natural"—always it must have an agent, someone specific to blame and to punish. The fantasy exerts a powerful fascination for, if we can locate the agent of death, we can forestall death. The most talented of crime writers, like Michael Connelly, work with genre formulae as poets work with "fixed" yet malleable forms like sonnets and sestinas; they affix their signatures to the archetype. It's an art of scrupulous realism conjoined with the abiding fantasy of a resolution in which the terrifying mysteries of mankind's inhumanity to man, suffering, dying, death are explained and dispelled. As McCaleb, crossing by boat to Catalina Island at night, assures his worried wife: "I'll be all right. I can see in the dark."

Notes

1. Aphorism 146. Nietzsche, Friedrich. *Beyond Good and Evil.* London: Oxford U. Press, 1917. p. 68.
2. See Michael Connelly's interview in *Talking Murder: Interviews With 20 Mystery Writers,* edited by Charles L. P. Silet (Ontario Review Press, 1999).

Reading the Genre

1. Oates begins this essay by comparing Connelly's works to other crime and detective fiction. Draw a family tree that shows the connections among the authors of these works. How does the explanation of these connections help to introduce the reader to Connelly and his style of writing?

2. Create a chronological list of both Connelly's jobs and his books (as well as the books' themes). How have he and his writing changed over time? How important is it for the reader to understand this history? If you haven't read the books in question, how does an understanding of similar authors and of Connelly's past works help you understand the essay? (See "Finding and developing material," p. 198.)

3. How does Oates show that location is important to understanding *A Darkness More Than Night*? How does Los Angeles figure in the stories, and in her review? Can you think of other novels in which location is also so important?

4. Compare Oates's description of the Bosch character to some of the works of the painter Hieronymus Bosch—for instance, the painting *The Last Judgment*. Does this painting help you understand why Oates suggests that the policeman hero of Connelly's novels (Harry Bosch) is "aptly named"? How could she extend her analysis of the allusion between the novel's hero and the famous Dutch painter?

5. **WRITING:** If a written text references a work of art, understanding the reference then depends on viewing the artwork. Following are some famous pairings of poetry and art:

   - William Carlos Williams's poem "The Great Figure" inspired Charles Henry Demuth to paint *I Saw the Figure Five in Gold*.

   - Edward Hopper's painting *House by the Railroad* inspired the poet Edward Hirsch to write "Edward Hopper and the House by the Railroad."

   - Paul Cezanne's painting *L'Estaque* inspired the poem "Cezanne's Ports" by Allen Ginsberg.

   Select a written text that references a work of art, and then research and write about the connections between the two works. How does seeing *both* texts offer more to the audience than would either text alone?

TEXTUAL ANALYSIS   Geraldine DeLuca teaches English at Brooklyn College and is the cofounder and coeditor of *The Lion and the Unicorn*, a journal devoted to the "serious, ongoing discussion of literature for children." The following analysis honors Charles Schulz, the creator of the *Peanuts* comic strip, and seeks to connect his life and his work. This essay can be seen as a form of biographical criticism—literary analysis that focuses on the facts of an author's life and family background to gain insights into his or her writing. A sample *Peanuts* strip precedes the analysis. The title of this article comes from the Emily Dickinson poem of the same name, which can be found on page 209.

"I felt a Funeral, in my Brain": The Fragile Comedy of Charles Schulz

GERALDINE DELUCA

I was never a devoted follower of the Peanuts comic strip, yet I'm moved by the news of Charles Schulz's death. Here was a man in love with his work and the characters he'd created. In a career that lasted nearly fifty years, he never missed a daily deadline. . . . Last night, on the eve of publication of his final strip, he died. His work and his life ended on the same day. . . .

Despite his success, Charles Schulz struggled all his life with depression and anxiety. "I suppose I have always felt apprehensive and anxious," he once said. "I have compared it to the feeling that you have when you get up on the morning of a funeral."

—"Sy Safransky's Notebook"

My own reaction to Schulz's death was similar to Safransky's. The *Peanuts* strip was not something I followed particularly, but I found myself upset for days when Schulz died. Partly it may have been that I was reeling from the recent, unexpected death of my sister and felt, as I've read in a poem somewhere, that the door to my brain had been blown open. My defenses were down. And maybe I was sad because I recognized that his were too, always, that he was suffering just as we were, and keeping the faith. Perhaps that is one reason why we loved him, because, as Linus says, he was the "Charlie Browniest," the most vulnerable, because he lived in a psychic universe in which he woke each day to a funeral, and out of that depression and anxiety, he drew his wonderful strip.

By most measures, Schulz's life was a great success story. He had a reasonable childhood with loving if restrained parents. His father, like Charlie Brown's, was a barber. His strip was early on appreciated, and his work grew steadily. He married and had children. He got divorced, but then he married again and had a happy relationship with his second wife. He had a daily and a Sunday strip, and he collaborated with like-minded souls (Bill Melendez, Lee Mendelson, Vince Guaraldi) to make videos that were faithful to his low-key sensibility. *Peanuts* artifacts proliferated throughout the country; he made many millions of dollars, and every day, until a few months before his death, he did what he loved: he drew his strip. "You don't work all your life to get to do something," he told his biographer, Rheta Grimsley Johnson, "so that you can have time not to do it" (41).

The defining trauma of his life seems to have been the loss of his mother. She died of cancer in 1943, shortly after he was drafted into the army. Her illness was protracted and painful, and the last time he saw her was on a weekend pass during basic training. She told him that they should say goodbye because they would probably not see each other again, and she died the next day (Johnson 51). Although he spent most of his tour of duty in Kentucky, in 1945 he was shipped to Europe where, moving across France, Germany, and Austria, he participated in the liberation of Dachau, Munich, and Berchtesgaden. Another loss, less tragic, but still weighty to Schulz, was his rejection by the young woman who became in the strip Charlie Brown's unrequited love, "the little red haired girl."

Lucy would say, "Get over it." But what kind of therapist is she? And why is she the therapist to begin with? Perhaps because, despite the hip surface of the strip, therapy is not the route to salvation in *Peanuts*. Schulz's characters do not get over great losses. They do not change. In *The Gospel according to Peanuts,* Robert Short suggests a view of life that was probably more congenial to Schulz, which is that we are flawed souls who occasionally have a redemptive experience, a moment of release, of joy, but then we revert to our old patterns and we suffer again. It was in Schulz's nature to suffer. He was shy, even agoraphobic, Johnson says. He was known to get off planes before take-off. What seemed to help him was a small congregation, a carefully charted life, the routine of his work. When he returned from the war, he began attending church services and studying the Bible; he began drawing cartoons, and his artist's thin skin kept him close to those painful states of feeling that are so well depicted in his strip.

The world of *Peanuts* is a suburban pastoral where none of the characters has reached puberty, all the love is unrequited, and sexual experience remains unknown. The kids spend their time playing baseball; flying kites; attending ordinary, boring schools. From time to time, they stage Christmas pageants that affirm after all, despite shameless displays of acquisitiveness, that the true meaning of Christmas is not aluminum trees and excesses of presents but a scrawny evergreen and the birth of Christ. But moments of such serenity don't override the failure, exasperation, unfulfilled desire, greed, and existential dread that haunt Schulz's characters. There is much that they don't understand that pulls on them. Despite their sheltered lives, there are hints of mortality. Snoopy periodically comments on the falling leaves, here in pointedly heroic terms—as if to say, see what happens when you step into the world: "The first leaf to make the courageous leap! The first leaf to depart from home! The first leaf to plunge into the unknown! / The first leaf to die!!" (Short 110). In a tender scene, Charlie Brown and Linus crouch before a seedling together, and Charlie Brown says, "It's a shame that we won't be around to see it when it's fully grown." "Why," Linus asks, "where are we going?" (Short 56).

The characters are offshoots of Schulz's psyche, humor figures, defined mostly by a single trait, an unruly pantheon of narcissists whose legs rotate toward and away from wholeness. Because they are children, their outrageous behavior charms us. They seem to speak from just below the surface where the unconscious intrudes upon consciousness. Driven by their desires and fears, they blurt out their truths or hold onto their blanket or take pratfalls or fall asleep at their desks. They move in bands, and they alternately insult and embrace one another. Like many comic characters, they are rigid, self-absorbed, stuck. Sometimes they hug each other or get kissed by the dog or find a lost library book, and they declare a moment of happiness. But then they assume their worried look again.

The drawings are deceptively simple and enormously expressive. Round, oversized faces, distinguished by the curve of a cheek or a hairdo, are composed of two dots for eyes, dashes for eyebrows, a line for a mouth that turns into a kidney-shaped opening when they howl. The compact little bodies literally get blown away. They spin in the air like pinwheels. They get tangled in kite strings and hang upside down from trees. Sometimes they stand behind a wall, two heads projecting—Charlie Brown and Linus—contemplating life's dilemmas. Sometimes they insult each other—Lucy figures largely here—and then one walks away, leaving a blank space where the other now stands alone.

Short calls attention to the acuteness of Schulz's vision in defining a moral universe. His strips often read like parables, and this was evident from their inception. The first *Peanuts* strip appeared on October 2, 1950. It was a renaming by Schulz's editors of a strip called *Li'l Folks,* and the drawing is rudimentary compared to the more evolved, precise style that developed in the next few years. But the strip goes to the heart of the human condition. Charlie Brown is walking toward Shermy and another child. Shermy says, "Well! Here comes ol' Charlie Brown! / Good ol' Charlie Brown. Yes sir! / Good ol' Charlie Brown. / How I hate him!" Charlie Brown is wearing a little smile, apparently unaware that hatred is being directed his way. But on some level, given who he is, he must feel it. And Shermy, who watches him, looks caught and perplexed by his own feeling.

Johnson says that Schulz regretted this famous first strip because he thought hatred was an "inappropriate emotion" (x). But the strip's power lies in the truth of those feelings of unexamined hatred that children discover early and carry around. And if the polite, affable Schulz worried about what he was saying, the artist in him followed a deeper vision and keener sense of honesty. His strip is full of inappropriate emotions. That is part of its brilliance. To Short, it is as if Schulz "speaks in tongues," a conduit for little gems that his own more censorious part would find discomfiting but that he knows enough to publish.

At the heart of the strip are the characters who seem to mirror Schulz's personality most closely, the three males, Charlie Brown, Snoopy, and Linus. Charlie Brown, Schulz says, is "everyman." "When I was small," he writes, "I believed that my face was so bland that people would not recognize me if they saw me someplace other than where they normally would. . . . It was this weird kind of thinking that prompted Charlie Brown's round ordinary face" (*Peanuts: A Golden Celebration* 14). While he is often the butt of jokes, a melancholy soul who seems to stand outside the circle, he also carries moral weight. When his sister Sally (who is frequently depicted working on her homework) writes in script, "Christmas is getting all you can get while the getting is good," Charlie Brown says, "**Giving!** The only real joy is **giving!**" This understanding is part of his heavy burden of consciousness, and most of the time he doesn't know what to do with it.

Snoopy, by contrast, is happy. He is a dog, first of all, and perhaps for that reason, relieved of some of the dour knowledge that plagues Charlie Brown. And he is a dog who ponders his own contentment, who requires only that his dog dish be filled with food. When characters yell at him, he is as likely as not to kiss them. In his relatively carefree state, he can create discomfort in others, like his tiny friend Woodstock the bird, whom he often knocks around without knowing it. Unlike Charlie Brown, Snoopy is resistant to insult. When Lucy tells him that his manuscript "A Sad Story" is "a dumb story," he thinks to himself, "that's what makes it so sad" (*Peanuts: AGC* 138). Happiness, Schulz implies through Snoopy, involves a certain degree of obliviousness, a thick skin, so to speak. And it is in Snoopy that Schulz invests the artist part of himself. Sitting on top of his dog-house, suggesting the small-scale, domestic nature of Schulz's work, Snoopy taps out his corny stories. He is the dreamer, the world famous hockey star, the world famous astronaut, and most notably the World War One Flying Ace, battling his nemesis, the Red Baron. He is insulated from the perceptions that trouble his owner, Charlie Brown. And he has the outlet of his art.

The blanket-carrying Linus represents the philosopher in Schulz, the seeker, the man of faith. Early on in the strip, Linus confuses Halloween with Christmas and introduces the Great Pumpkin. In the video *It's the Great Pumpkin, Charlie Brown,* he tells Sally that the Great Pumpkin will come to his pumpkin patch because it is a "sincere" patch, free of hypocrisy. The Great Pumpkin respects sincerity, Linus says. And when he comes, he'll bring toys to all the children. Sally, who claims to love him and who, to Linus's distress, calls him her "sweet Babboo," is furious with him when it turns out that the Great Pumpkin isn't coming, that there will be no presents. So she finally departs in a huff, leaving him alone with his belief, a troubled-looking child who nonetheless often demonstrates the preacherly eloquence, inner calm, and spacy imagination of a visionary.

The girls, on the other hand, have a more aggressive energy. Lucy, of course, can be relentlessly terrible. Schulz writes that "Lucy comes from the part of me that's capable of saying mean and sarcastic things" (*Peanuts: AGC* 25). To say the least. She is the devouring mother, the one who wants to tell everyone exactly what she thinks of them. Whereas Charlie Brown swallows his anger and gets depressed, Lucy lashes out to defend against her own anxieties. Other people's happiness makes her uncomfortable because it contrasts with her own inherently irascible state, and she tries to argue characters out of their good moods. When she sees Snoopy gaily dancing, she yells, "**Stop it!** Stop it this instant! With all the trouble there is in this world, you have no right to be so happy!" (*Peanuts: AGC* 24). When Charlie Brown's little sister Sally is born, Lucy is furious that Charlie Brown is pleased. She tells him, "I suppose it's never occurred to you that over-population is a serious problem?!" (*Go Fly a Kite, Charlie Brown*). "It's the wrong time" for new babies, she tells Linus. He stands with his blanket pressed against his face, his dot eyes pondering her position. Then he turns to her and replies, "What are you gonna do with all those babies who are lined up waiting to be born? / You just can't tell them to go away and **wait** for another thousand years, can you? **Can you?**" (*Go Fly a Kite*). When she fails to discourage Charlie Brown on the grounds of overpopulation and world strife, she finds a more personal approach:

> You think having a baby sister is great, don't you?/From now on you're going to have to **share** the affection of your mother and dad! But you think you won't mind that, don't you! / You think It'll be fifty-fifty, don't you? Well, it won't! With a baby sister, it'll be fifty-one–forty-nine! Maybe even **sixty-forty!** (*Go Fly a Kite*)

Her weak spot is Schroeder, the Beethoven enthusiast. She leans on his toy piano, grotesquely vying for his attention, grinning her awful grin, at times even throwing his piano up a tree or down a sewer, so that he'll have to notice her. Lucy is the control freak, the merciless, insatiable one who doesn't trust, whose own strategies never get her the love she wants.

Occasionally she has a sweeter moment, most notably when talking to Rerun, whom she calls Rerun because he's just another baby brother, a re-run of Linus. Rerun doesn't seem to suffer Lucy's wrath. She treats him patiently, like a parent with her youngest child. And to her credit, when Linus falls asleep in the pumpkin patch—long after she has put on her witch mask and led the charge against him for being so stupid as to wait out there all night—Lucy is the one who gets out of bed and brings him home. So she is not completely without scruples. Perhaps the best one can say about her is that she offers intermittent positive reinforcement, creating in a character like Linus the look of a child whose hair is always standing on end.

The other girls, Sally, Marcie, and Peppermint Patty, seem a little further from Schulz's nerve endings. They express his exasperation and bewilderment with the daily insults and injustices of life, but they seem to be "other," constructs of a social world rather than manifestations of Schulz's psyche. Sally is frequently depicted in school settings, always trying unsuccessfully and with little sense of ethics to make her way there. When she has to do yet another science project, she steals Woodstock's newly constructed home and offers it as a prehistoric bird's nest. When she gets a C on her coat hanger sculpture, she protests,

> Was I judged on the piece of sculpture itself? If so, is it not true that time alone can judge a work of art? / Or was I judged on my talent? If so, is it right that I be judged on a part of life over which I have no control? . . . Was I judged on what I had learned about this project? If so, then were not you, my teacher, also being judged on your ability to transmit your knowledge to me? Are you willing to share my C? (*Peanuts: AGC* 89)

Schulz says he based this strip on a similar experience of his son's, and he used Sally to dramatize it, "for she is a character who expresses indignation well, and who is completely bewildered by all the things she has to go through in school" (*Peanuts: AGC* 89). Sometimes she stands outside the school and talks to the building because maybe that's what it feels like to talk to teachers: like talking to a wall.

Marcie and Peppermint Patty are often written into the same strips, and they too are likely to be found in school. Marcie is very smart, very well behaved, hopeless at sports, and Schulz muses that "she seems to have to put up with some kind of pressure from home to be a good student" (*Around* 30). Peppermint Patty, by contrast, is a great athlete and an unsuccessful student. She was introduced as a character from another school on the working-class side of town when Schulz decided that Charlie Brown needed an opposing baseball team. In the videos, she has a hip, tough way of talking, she wears Birkenstock-type sandals, and she calls Charlie Brown "Chuck."

> Her most notable trait is that she always falls asleep in school. About her history, Schulz speculates: We have received some vague hints that Peppermint Patty does not have a mother and that her father travels a little bit, which means that Patty sometimes stays up quite late at night because she doesn't like being home alone, which is why she is sleepy the next day. But, we really don't know what happened to her mother. Was there a breakup in the marriage, or did her mother die? We don't know. I wonder if we will ever find out. (*Around* 30)

Schulz writes that the "narcolepsy people" at Stanford University told him that Peppermint Patty should be sent to a sleep-disorder center. The suggestion reflects the tension in the strip between the artist's particular, freewheeling vision and the social function he is perceived to serve for his readers. If Peppermint Patty is falling asleep, is it enough to say that she goes to bed too late or that she's tuning out because she thinks her teacher hates her? To his readership, she may stand for children who are ignored or discriminated against in school—children with disabilities, children whose family situations or social worlds make learning more difficult. If her father leaves her alone at night, shouldn't the child welfare people be notified? Schulz seemed to understand that he bore a responsibility to take care of his characters because his readers included so many children. He must have recognized that he was perceived as a small, consistent moral voice in an often immoral universe. But he was writing stories, not case studies. If Peppermint Patty falls asleep in school, then that's what she does. Kids fall asleep in school all the time. She is a fictional character. So mostly he demurred gracefully because it was his nature not to want to offend, and then he did what he wanted.

And out of his deep sympathy for the condition of children, Schulz created interesting, psychologically astute strips around Peppermint Patty. When she gets an F on her test, she tells Franklin, the boy who sits in front of her, that the reason she fails all the time is that she has a big nose and the teacher doesn't like her looks. "Your paper is blank," Franklin points out. But that's irrelevant to her. If the teacher doesn't like your looks, why bother writing the test? In another series of strips, Schulz reinforces this notion of teacher prejudice and affirms Patty's way of seeing. The studious Marcie, who pays attention to things like contests, tells Peppermint Patty that she, Patty, has won the "All-City School Essay Contest." "You wrote about looking at clouds, remember? Anyway, you won. . . . Congratulations." In the next strip, Peppermint Patty says to Charlie Brown:

> Explain this, if you can, Chuck. Everyone in our class had to write an essay on what we did during Christmas vacation. / When I got mine back, the teacher had given me a 'D minus.' Well, I'm used to that, right, Chuck? Right! / Now, guess what. All those essays went into a city essay contest, and I won! Explain that, Chuck.

Snoopy, lying on his doghouse, thinks, "Never listen to reviewers" (*Peanuts: AGC* 137). So, like other characters, but more pointedly because she seems to be "at risk," a motherless child, one who, for whatever reason, is not doing well in school, Peppermint Patty represents the promise of the unpromising child. And Schulz stands up for her not by having her diagnosed and fixed but by reminding us of the value of her eccentricity. She may not perform in conventional ways, but, perhaps for that very reason, she notices the clouds.

This is not to say, of course, that there are not children who need intervention and special help, but that doesn't seem to be the way things work in Schulz's world. In a spiritual sense, he seemed to say, we are radically unfixable. And as far as his strip is concerned, comedy thrives on eccentricity, on the tension between the "normal" center toward which the characters are supposed to be integrating themselves and their aberrations. In the correspondence course in drawing that Schulz took when he was a young man, he a got a C− in "Drawing of Children." Despite our best knowledge and all the experts who would tell us how to be, life unfurls itself in surprising ways. And to be normal or to succeed all the time is, he points out, not funny. Failure is funny. A character in a ridiculous situation is funny. Repetition is funny. Never learning from one's mistakes is funny. The success of his strip rested on his being able to do endless turns on a rather restricted repertoire, finding in the situation of a group of children who essentially never learn continued ways to explore the dilemma of being human.

Schulz appealed to a huge and wide-ranging audience. He had the most successful comic strip in newspaper history. *Peanuts* was carried in 2,600 newspapers across 75 countries and was translated into 21 languages. He regarded himself as writing for adults. Yet many of the small books compiled from those strips became *Weekly Reader* books for children, and he respected that audience as well. His videos too were remarkably successful. Nat Gertler writes of *A Charlie Brown Christmas*:

> This unlikely piece, which the network brass feared too slow-moving, too religious, too innocent, and sounding too much of jazz and amateur kid voices, pulled in an unbelievable 45 share and won an Emmy and a Peabody. Suddenly . . . CBS decided that *Peanuts* was a good thing after all. (Gertler)

Schulz appealed to what was "cool" in our culture, and yet he quoted the Bible regularly. He had simply found himself a permanent place in the American sensibility, drawn from a homely and authentic vision that he never seemed to compromise.

It is a commonplace to say that comedy derives from pain, that the artist flees from life and then writes about it. That certainly seems to be the case with

Schulz. And one senses in his strip the great pleasure he derived from letting his art unfold freely, year after year, to an appreciative audience. You're not crazy, he told us. If you think your life is bad, climb into my imagination for a moment. You're bound to feel better. His success didn't ease the depression, the agoraphobia, and his wife learned to travel without him. To friends who moved across the country, he could only say goodbye. As he got older, he even stopped listening to music because its beauty was too painful to bear. The strip keeps trying to define that elusive state, happiness, but as Lucy tells Snoopy, "Just because you're happy today, doesn't mean you'll be happy tomorrow! / Happiness isn't everything, you know! / It'll never bring you peace of mind" (*Peanuts: AGC* 25). And what will bring peace of mind? Maybe getting lost in one's work, transmuting all that angst into art. And still, even if one feels relaxed on going to bed, one may wake as if to face a funeral.

Works Cited

Gertler, Nat. "Bill Melendez: A Brief Biography." *Peanuts Book List*. Web.

Johnson, Rheta Grimsley. *Good Grief: The Story of Charles M. Schulz*. Kansas City: Andrews and McMeel/United Features Syndicate, 1995. Print.

Safransky, Sy. "Sy Safransky's Notebook." *The Sun* [Chapel Hill, NC] August 2000: 47. Print.

Schulz, Charles M. *Around the World in 45 Years*. Kansas City: Andrews and McMeel/United Features Syndicate, 1994. Print.

———. *Go Fly a Kite, Charlie Brown*. 1959. New York: Holt, Rinehart and Winston, 1960. Print.

———. *Peanuts: A Golden Celebration: The Art and the Story of the World's Best-Loved Comic Strip*. Ed. David Larkin. New York: HarperCollins, 1999. Print.

Short, Robert L. *The Gospel According to Peanuts*. Richmond, VA: John Knox P, 1964. Print.

Reading the Genre

1. This essay might be seen as a form of encomium—an essay that honors the memory of someone who has died. How does DeLuca honor Schulz? By memorializing him, does she also place his work in a particular light?

2. DeLuca sets up parallels between characters in the comic strip and aspects of Charles Schulz's life and personality: How are these comparisons structured, and how does she make them persuasive? (See Chapter 19, "Smart Reading," p. 317.)

3. What major themes does DeLuca identify in *Peanuts*? In what way does she focus on and explore these themes? How is her essay organized around these themes? (See Chapter 23, "Organization," p. 340.)

4. DeLuca describes a *Peanuts* strip so that we understand it without seeing it. How does she manage this, and then use these examples to ground her analysis? See the example on page 850, and describe it for someone who can't see it. (See "Focus on its meanings, themes, and interpretations," p. 199.)

5. **WRITING:** Choose any comic strip from your local newspaper and follow it for a week. Or visit the comic's Web site and look at the seven most recent strips. What is the dominant theme of this comic? Choose three examples of action, dialogue, or imagery from the strips that illustrate this theme, and describe these things for readers who cannot see the strips themselves. Use these examples to support your thesis about the theme of the comic.

69

Rhetorical Analysis: Readings

DISCOURSE ANALYSIS   Deborah Tannen is a professor in the linguistics department at Georgetown University, and her book *You Just Don't Understand: Women and Men in Conversation* (2001) was on best-seller lists for years. The following essay is adapted from her most recent book, *You're Wearing That? Understanding Mothers and Daughters in Conversation* (2006). She has also written books about the ways people talk at work, with friends, and in the press, politics, and law. This rhetorical analysis is also a sociolinguistic analysis, or discourse analysis—a study of the ways language is used and how conversation structures relationships.

Oh, Mom. Oh, Honey.: Why Do You Have to Say That?

Deborah Tannen

The five years I recently spent researching and writing a book about mothers and daughters also turned out to be the last years of my mother's life. In her late eighties and early nineties, she gradually weakened, and I spent more time with her, caring for her more intimately than I ever had before. This experience — together with her death before I finished writing — transformed my thinking about mother-daughter relationships and the book that ultimately emerged.

All along I had in mind the questions a journalist had asked during an interview about my research. "What is it about mothers and daughters?" she blurted out. "Why are our conversations so complicated, our relationships so fraught?" These questions became more urgent and more personal, as I asked myself: What had made my relationship with my mother so volatile? Why had I often ricocheted between extremes of love and anger? And what had made it possible for my love to swell and my anger to dissipate in the last years of her life?

Though much of what I discovered about mothers and daughters is also true of mothers and sons, fathers and daughters, and fathers and sons, there is a special intensity to the mother-daughter relationship because talk — particularly talk about personal topics — plays a larger and more complex role in girls' and women's social lives than in boys' and men's. For girls and women, talk is the glue that holds a relationship together — and the explosive that can blow it apart. That's why you can think you're having a perfectly amiable chat, then suddenly find yourself wounded by the shrapnel from an exploded conversation.

Daughters often object to remarks that would seem harmless to outsiders, like this one described by a student of mine, Kathryn Ann Harrison:

"Are you going to quarter those tomatoes?" her mother asked as Kathryn was preparing a salad. Stiffening, Kathryn replied, "Well, I was. Is that wrong?"

"No, no," her mother replied. "It's just that personally, I would slice them." Kathryn said tersely, "Fine." But as she sliced the tomatoes, she thought, can't I do anything without my mother letting me know she thinks I should do it some other way?

I'm willing to wager that Kathryn's mother thought she had merely asked a question about a tomato. But Kathryn bristled because she heard the implication, "You don't know what you're doing. I know better."

I'm a linguist. I study how people talk to each other, and how the ways we talk affect our relationships. My books are filled with examples of conversations that I record or recall or that others record for me or report to me. For each example, I begin by explaining the perspective that I understand immediately because I share it: in mother-daughter talk, the daughter's, because I'm a daughter but not a mother. Then I figure out the logic of the other's perspective. Writing this book forced me to look at conversations from my mother's point of view.

I interviewed dozens of women of varied geographic, racial, and cultural backgrounds, and I had informal conversations or e-mail exchanges with countless others. The complaint I heard most often from daughters was, "My mother is always criticizing me." The corresponding complaint from mothers was, "I can't open my mouth. She takes everything as criticism." Both are right, but each sees only her perspective.

One daughter said, for example, "My mother's eyesight is failing, but she can still spot a pimple from across the room." Her mother doesn't realize that her comments—and her scrutiny—make the pimple bigger.

Mothers subject their daughters to a level of scrutiny people usually reserve for themselves. A mother's gaze is like a magnifying glass held between the sun's rays and kindling. It concentrates the rays of imperfection on her daughter's yearning for approval. The result can be a conflagration—whoosh.

This I knew: Because a mother's opinion matters so much, she has enormous power. Her smallest comment—or no comment at all, just a look—can fill a daughter with hurt and consequently anger. But this I learned: Mothers, who have spent decades watching out for their children, often persist in commenting because they can't get their adult children to do what is (they believe) obviously right. Where the daughter sees power, the mother feels powerless. Daughters and mothers, I found, both overestimate the other's power—and underestimate their own.

The power that mothers and daughters hold over each other derives, in part, from their closeness. Every relationship requires a search for the right balance of closeness and distance, but the struggle is especially intense between mothers and daughters. Just about every woman I spoke to used the word *close,* as in "We're very close" or "We're not as close as I'd like (or she'd like) to be."

In addition to the closeness/distance yardstick—and inextricable from it—is a yardstick that measures sameness and difference. Mothers and daughters search for themselves in the other as if hunting for treasure, as if finding sameness affirms who they are. This can be pleasant: After her mother's death, one woman noticed that she wipes down the sink, cuts an onion, and holds a knife just as her mother used to do. She found this comforting because it meant her mother was still with her.

Sameness, however, can also make us cringe. One mother thought she was being particularly supportive when she assured her daughter, "I know what you mean," and described a matching experience of her own. But one day her daughter cut her off: "Stop saying you know because you've had the same experience. You don't know. This is my experience. The world is different now." She felt her mother was denying the uniqueness of her experience—offering too much sameness.

"I sound just like my mother" is usually said with distaste—as is the wry observation, "Mirror mirror on the wall, I am my mother after all."

When visiting my parents a few years ago, I was sitting across from my mother when she asked, "Do you like your hair long?"

I laughed, and she asked what was funny. I explained that in my research, I had come across many examples of mothers who criticize their daughters' hair. "I wasn't criticizing," she said, looking hurt. I let the matter drop. A little later, I asked, "Mom, what do you think of my hair?" Without hesitation, she said, "I think it's a little too long."

Hair is one of what I call the Big Three that mothers and daughters critique (the other two are clothing and weight). Many women I talked to, on hearing the topic of my book, immediately retrieved offending remarks that they had archived, such as, "I'm so glad you're not wearing your hair in that frumpy way anymore"; another had asked, "You did that to your hair on purpose?" Yet another told her daughter, after seeing her on television at an important presidential event, "You needed a haircut."

I would never walk up to a stranger and say, "I think you'd look better if you got your hair out of your eyes," but her mother might feel entitled, if not obligated, to say it, knowing that women are judged by appearance—and that mothers are judged by their daughters' appearance, because daughters represent their mothers to the world. Women must choose hairstyles, like styles of dress, from such a wide range of options, it's inevitable that others—mothers included—will think their choices could be improved. Ironically, mothers are more likely to notice and mention flaws, and their comments are more likely to wound.

But it works both ways. As one mother put it, "My daughters can turn my day black in a millisecond." For one thing, daughters often treat their mothers more callously than they would anyone else. For example, a daughter invited her mother to join a dinner party because a guest had bowed out. But when the guest's plans changed again at the last minute, her daughter simply uninvited her mother. To the daughter, her mother was both readily available and expendable.

There's another way that a mother can be a lightning rod in the storm of family emotions. Many mothers told me that they can sense and absorb their daughters' emotions instantly ("If she feels down, I feel down") and that their daughters can sense theirs. Most told me this to illustrate the closeness they cherish. But daughters sometimes resent the expectation that they have this sixth sense — and act on it.

For example, a woman was driving her mother to the airport following a visit, when her mother said petulantly, "I had to carry my own suitcase to the car." The daughter asked, "Why didn't you tell me your luggage was ready?" Her mother replied, "You knew I was getting ready." If closeness requires you to hear — and obey — something that wasn't even said, it's not surprising that a daughter might crave more distance.

Daughters want their mothers to see and value what they value in themselves; that's why a question that would be harmless in one context can be hurtful in another. For example, a woman said that she told her mother of a successful presentation she had made, and her mother asked, "What did you wear?" The woman exclaimed, in exasperation, "Who cares what I wore?!" In fact, the woman cared. She had given a lot of thought to selecting the right outfit. But her mother's focus on clothing — rather than the content of her talk — seemed to undercut her professional achievement.

Some mothers are ambivalent about their daughters' success because it creates distance: A daughter may take a path her mother can't follow. And mothers can envy daughters who have taken paths their mothers would have liked to take, if given the chance. On the other hand, a mother may seem to devalue her daughter's choices simply because she doesn't understand the life her daughter chose. I think that was the case with my mother and me.

My mother visited me shortly after I had taken a teaching position at Georgetown University, and I was eager to show her my new home and new life. She had disapproved of me during my rebellious youth, and had been distraught when my first marriage ended six years before. Now I was a professor; clearly I had turned out all right. I was sure she'd be proud of me — and she was. When I showed her my office with my name on the door and my publications on the shelf, she seemed pleased and approving.

Then she asked, "Do you think you would have accomplished all this if you had stayed married?" "Absolutely not," I said. "If I'd stayed married, I wouldn't have gone to grad school to get my PhD."

"Well," she replied, "if you'd stayed married you wouldn't have had to." Ouch. With her casual remark, my mother had reduced all I had accomplished to the consolation prize.

I have told this story many times, knowing I could count on listeners to gasp at this proof that my mother belittled my achievements. But now I think she was simply reflecting the world she had grown up in, where there was one and only one measure by which women were judged successful or pitiable: marriage. She probably didn't know what to make of my life, which was so different from any she could have imagined for herself. I don't think she intended to denigrate what I had done and become, but the lens through which she viewed the world could not encompass the one I had chosen. Reframing how I look at it takes the sting out of this memory.

Reframing is often key to dissipating anger. One woman found that this technique could transform holiday visits from painful to pleasurable. For example, while visiting, she showed her mother a new purchase: two pairs of socks, one black and one navy. The next day she wore one pair, and her mother asked, "Are you sure you're not wearing one of each color?" In the past, her mother's question would have set her off, as she wondered, "What kind of incompetent do you think I am?" This time she focused on the caring: Who else would worry about the color of her socks? Looked at this way, the question was touching.

If a daughter can recognize that seeming criticism truly expresses concern, a mother can acknowledge that concern truly implies criticism — and bite her tongue. A woman who told me that this worked for her gave me an example: One day her daughter announced, "I joined Weight Watchers and already lost two pounds." In the past, the mother would have said, "That's great" and added, "You have to keep it up." This time she replied, "That's great" — and stopped there.

Years ago, I was surprised when my mother told me, after I began a letter to her "Dearest Mom," that she had waited her whole life to hear me say that. I thought this peculiar to her until a young woman named Rachael sent me copies of e-mails she had received from her mother. In one, her mother responded to Rachael's effusive Mother's Day card: "Oh, Rachael!!!!! That was so WONDERFUL!!! It almost made me cry. I've waited 25 years, 3 months, and 7 days to hear something like that."

Helping to care for my mother toward the end of her life, and writing this book at the same time, I came to understand the emotion behind these parallel reactions. Caring about someone as much as you care about yourself, and the critical eye that comes with it, are two strands that cannot be separated. Both engender a passion that makes the mother-daughter relationship perilous — and precious.

Reading the Genre

1. In addition to rhetorical analysis, this essay offers a discourse analysis—a study of language use. How does Tannen present the evidence that she will analyze? How do you think she chose this evidence? (See "Read for claims, reasons, and evidence," p. 319, and Chapter 39, "Critical Reading and Note-Taking Strategies," p. 420.)

2. Think about Tannen's categories for analysis—such as *yardsticks*, *techniques*, and topics like the *Big Three*. How do these categories allow her to analyze what is said, how it is said, and how people deal with what is said?

3. How does Tannen address the danger of stereotypes in this essay? How does this essay consider race, class, and gender differences? Identify parts of this essay where Tannen considers individuality. (See Chapter 31, "Inclusive and Culturally Sensitive Style," p. 374.)

4. This essay has many quotes. Closely review how Tannen handles these quotations. What kinds of signal words does she use to introduce and summarize quotes? How does her language add meaning to the quotes? (See Chapter 42, "Integrating Sources into Your Work," p. 431.)

5. **WRITING:** Do some field work. Sit at a busy table in a cafeteria, restaurant, or food court, and take notes about what is said and how. Get permission from everyone you observe, and then take detailed notes. Using your notes, make observations about how the people you observed interacted, based on what they said and how they said it. How do people talk about food? How do families interact? How do food workers relate to customers? (See Chapter 37, "Doing Field Research," p. 406.)

CULTURAL ANALYSIS   Eric Weiner is a foreign correspondent for National Public Radio and the *New York Times* and the author of the travel book *The Geography of Bliss: One Grump's Search for the Happiest Places in the World* (2008). Weiner has also written for *New Republic*, Slate.com, and the *Los Angeles Times*.

Slate.com

Posted: Friday, March 25, 2005, at 4:17 AM PT
From: Eric Weiner

How They Do It: Euromail
What Germans Can Teach Us about E-mail

North America and Europe are two continents divided by a common technology: e-mail. Techno-optimists assure us that e-mail—along with the Internet and satellite TV—makes the world smaller. That may be true in a technical sense. I can send a message from my home in Miami to a German friend in Berlin and it will arrive almost instantly. But somewhere over the Atlantic, the messages get garbled. In fact, two distinct forms of e-mail have emerged: Euromail and Amerimail.

Amerimail is informal and chatty. It's likely to begin with a breezy "Hi" and end with a "Bye." The chances of Amerimail containing a smiley face or an "xoxo" are disturbingly high. We Americans are reluctant to dive into the meat of an e-mail; we feel compelled to first inform hapless recipients about our vacation on the Cape which was really excellent except the jellyfish were biting and the kids caught this nasty bug so we had to skip the whale watching trip but about that investors' meeting in New York. . . . Amerimail is a bundle of contradictions: rambling and yet direct; deferential, yet arrogant. In other words, Amerimail *is* America.

Euromail is stiff and cold, often beginning with a formal "Dear Mr. X" and ending with a brusque "Sincerely." You won't find any mention of kids or the weather or jellyfish in Euromail. It's all business. It's also slow. Your correspondent might take days, even weeks, to answer a message. Euromail is also less confrontational in tone, rarely filled with the overt nastiness that characterizes American e-mail disagreements. In other words, Euromail is exactly like the Europeans themselves. (I am, of course, generalizing. German e-mail style is not exactly the same as Italian or Greek, but they have more in common with each other than they do with American mail.)

These are more than mere stylistic differences. Communication matters. Which model should the rest of the world adopt: Euromail or Amerimail?

A California-based e-mail consulting firm called People-onthego sheds some light on the e-mail divide. It recently asked about 100 executives on both sides of the Atlantic whether they noticed differences in e-mail styles. Most said yes. Here are a few of their observations:

"Americans tend to write [e-mails] exactly as they speak."

"Europeans are less obsessive about checking e-mail."

"In general, Americans are much more responsive to e-mail—they respond faster and provide more information."

One respondent noted that Europeans tend to segregate their e-mail accounts. Rarely do they send personal messages on their business accounts, or vice versa. These differences can't be explained merely by differing comfort levels with technology. Other forms of electronic communication, such as SMS text messaging, are more popular in Europe than in the United States.

The fact is, Europeans and Americans approach e-mail in a fundamentally different way. Here is the key point: For Europeans, e-mail has replaced the business letter. For Americans, it has replaced the telephone. That's why we tend to unleash what e-mail consultant Tim Burress calls a "brain dump": unloading the content of our cerebral cortex onto the screen and hitting the send button. "It makes Europeans go ballistic," he says.

Susanne Khawand, a German high-tech executive, has been on the receiving end of American brain dumps, and she says it's not pretty. "I feel like saying, 'Why don't you just call me instead of writing five e-mails back and forth,'" she says. Americans are so overwhelmed by their bulging inboxes that "you can't rely on getting an answer. You don't even know if they read it." In Germany, she says, it might take a few days, or even weeks, for an answer, but one always arrives.

Maybe that's because, on average, Europeans receive fewer e-mails and spend less time tending their inboxes. An international survey of business owners in twenty-four countries (conducted by the accounting firm Grant Thornton) found that people in Greece and Russia spend the least amount of time dealing with e-mail every day:

forty-eight minutes on average. Americans, by comparison, spend two hours per day, among the highest in the world. (Only Filipinos spend more time on e-mail, 2.1 hours.) The survey also found that European executives are skeptical of e-mail's ability to boost their bottom line.

It's not clear why European and American e-mail styles have evolved separately, but I suspect the reasons lie within deep cultural differences. Americans tend to be impulsive and crave instant gratification. So we send e-mails rapid-fire, and get antsy if we don't receive a reply quickly. Europeans tend to be more methodical and plodding. They send (and reply to) e-mails only after great deliberation.

For all their Continental fastidiousness, Europeans can be remarkably lax about e-mail security, says Bill Young, an executive vice president with the Strickland Group. Europeans are more likely to include trade secrets and business strategies in e-mails, he says, much to the frustration of their American colleagues. This is probably because identity theft—and other types of hacking—are much less of a problem in Europe than in the United States. Privacy laws are much stricter in Europe.

So, which is better: Euromail or Amerimail? Personally, I'm a convert—or a defector, if you prefer—to the former. I realize it's not popular these days to suggest we have anything to learn from Europeans, but I'm fed up with an inbox cluttered with rambling, barely cogent missives from friends and colleagues. If the alternative is a few stiffly written, politely worded bits of Euromail, then I say . . . bring it on.

Reading the Genre

1. Why does Weiner suggest that it is worthwhile to examine something like e-mail style? Why does this issue matter?

2. Create a list of the key distinctions between Euromail and Amerimail. How does Weiner use these distinctions to formulate a comparison between the two forms and to represent one as better than the other? (See "Compare and contrast," p. 114.)

3. Weiner asserts that the differences between e-mail styles suggest "deep cultural differences." What are these stylistic and cultural differences? Do you think he makes a convincing link between these cultural differences and differences in e-mail style? How does he support his assertions with research? (See Chapters 38 and 39.)

4. By the end of his essay, Weiner has compared Amerimail unfavorably with Euromail. Go back and look at his comparisons, and try to come up with ways to argue *for* the virtues of Amerimail.

5. **WRITING:** Draft an e-mail to a professor, asking for an extension on an upcoming assignment. Then draft an e-mail to a family member or friend, making plans for an upcoming holiday. Write these e-mails in Amerimail style, and then in Euromail style. Then look at both versions of each e-mail and consider the differences between them, as well as the virtues and drawbacks of each style for each audience.

ANALYSIS OF AN ADVERTISEMENT   Renowned teacher and cultural critic Stanley Fish has written a number of books, most recently *Save the World on Your Own Time* (2008). He has taught at many colleges and universities, and though famous as a literary theorist, he also teaches law. The following article first appeared in the *New York Times*.

New York Times.com

Posted: May 4, 2008, 4:47 pm
From: Stanley Fish

The Other Car

Six years ago my wife and I traded in two cars for two new-used ones. Twice in a few weeks, one of us drove an old car up a ramp to the cavernous second floor of the dealership and just left it there. Well, not quite, for later we reported to each other the same experience. Each of us walked away, but then looked back, realizing that this familiar friend would be gone from our lives forever and, more poignantly, that we were abandoning a faithful, if increasingly troublesome, retainer.

These feelings were of course irrational. Inanimate objects do not have emotions (Stephen King's Christine and Arthur Clarke's HAL are cautionary exceptions), and it makes no sense to experience guilt at having mistreated them (can you in fact mistreat, except in a technical sense, a machine?), but I am sure that we were not unique in our self-reproaches and misgivings.

Avis Rent-a-Car certainly agrees with me, for that company is now running a series of commercials featuring older cars that are being neglected and fear being discarded in favor of the shiny new and with-it high-tech vehicles available, on demand, for around 45 dollars a day. The genius of the commercials is that they foreground the sexuality that informs the relationship between the car owner and the object of his/her affection.

It is of course a commonplace to note that sex is a staple of automobile advertising, but in most ads the idea is that a car with the right curves will attract the girl with the right curves; the piece of machinery is instrumental to the effort to attain the object of desire. But in the Avis ads, the piece of machinery *is* the object of desire (there is a hint of the human-cyborg union promised at the end of the first *Star Trek* movie), and the very act of desiring it constitutes infidelity.

In three of these ads, infidelity is not a metaphor; it is literally what is going on; and the parallels between car-adultery and husband/wife adultery are delineated with such precision, point for point, that the experience of watching is uncomfortable for anyone who has been on either the giving or receiving end in this age-old scenario.

My favorite (and a favorite on the blogosphere) is entitled "Look Back." It features, in the starring and tragic role, a battered red Saab 900 (I own a black one). The scene opens on a sparsely populated airport parking lot. A well-dressed man is getting himself together in preparation for boarding. He puts some trash on the dashboard, gets out of the car, kicks the door shut (wince!), and puts a coffee cup on the roof.

While all this is happening, the car is speaking in a mournful male voice. It/he says, "So, he's going away with Avis, again. He'll get something with the GPS so that he can find his lattes and his driving range. If that's the way he wants it, fine." But this moment of bravado-dignity doesn't last. As the philandering driver walks away, he pauses and rummages in his pocket, concerned that he may have left something in the old clunker. Hope revives, and the Saab says, "Did he just look back? I think he looked back."

The last shot is of the parking lot, empty except for the forlorn automobile sitting there with an abandoned coffee cup, which it cannot see, on its abandoned "head." Another voice—here's where the traditional commercial kicks in—chimes in cheerfully, "One more reason why Avis should be your other car."

One viewer who rates the ad on the internet likes it, but complains that "the gender of the voice of the vehicle should be the opposite gender of the owner." No, these ads are indifferent to gender. Lust is lust and betrayal is betrayal, whether the relationship is gay or straight.

In another ad ("Three Days"), the straying partner is a woman who has just returned from a three-day vacation. As she settles into the front seat, the car, a tired-looking, sickly green thing, spots the Avis receipt in her handbag, just as a wife or husband might spy a telltale matchbook from a restaurant in a town neither of them has ever visited. The car voice-over comes on, and it is sarcastic: "Who does she think she's kidding. You know what she's been doing in Miami. You sit here staring at a cement wall, alone, and she has the gall to just show up three days later and pretend that she doesn't smell like 'new car.' " (Another gender reversal: it's usually the woman who smells perfume on the man.) The ad ends with more sarcasm: "She was with a Prius hybrid. Oh, suddenly, she's an environmentalist?"

In the third ad, "Conference," the cuckolded vehicle is a Buick, sitting, iced-over, in a parking lot. A flier for a New Mexico resort is on the seat. The Buick speaks: "He said he had to go to Sante Fe for work. Big Conference. Right! You know what's happening. He's driving around with another car. He'll say he was with a client. He was probably with that red Cadillac CTS from Avis, again." Just before the word *again* (the equivalent in this series of Poe's "nevermore") is intoned, a piece of ice, obviously a tear, falls from the Buick's tail light.

When the hucksterish voice of the company spokesperson chirps, "With dozens of the hottest cars to choose from, there's a reason Avis is your other car," the effect is jarring because the dramatization has been so affecting. We care about these people—I mean cars—and the intrusion of the profit motive is unwelcome.

Strange to say, these are not good ads precisely because they are so good. The point of a commercial is to make the viewer fall in love with the product, in this case the hot cars Avis is pimping. But the viewers of these commercials are more likely to give their affections to the product's victims, for it is from their point of view that the narrative has been presented.

While Avis's intention is, no doubt, to advance its corporate fortunes through these commercials, the image the ads project is less than flattering. Avis comes across as the supplier of temptation, the enabler of seduction, a corporate madame. Its stable of "hot cars" lure men and women to default on their responsibilities, to throw away the tried and true, to surrender to the meretricious glitter of the new. But these wiles are defeated by the sympathy we are made to feel for those who have been harmed by them.

Who would have thought that in the early years of the twenty-first century, advertising would give us a morality tale of such power?

I still wonder whenever I see a car that looks like one of those I have discarded whether it is in fact mine. Forgive me.

Reading the Genre

1. What are the rhetorical appeals that Fish identifies in the advertisements? What is the dominant rhetorical appeal of the ads? How is this appeal made, and what is the desired effect? (See "Consider its use of rhetorical appeals," p. 231.)

2. The online version of this article includes hypertext links to all three of the ads that Fish analyzes. What do these links add to the essay? Do we need to be able to see the advertisements ourselves to understand Fish's analysis? (See "Make the text accessible to readers," p. 235.)

3. Fish wants to make a statement about the specific rhetorical appeals used in these commercials. Look at another series of advertisements—perhaps a series of ads for a large company like Apple or Volkswagen that sells consumer goods. In this series of ads, what rhetorical appeals are used?

4. These ads give emotions, thoughts, and voice to inanimate objects. In this way, the advertisements' creators get to imagine an emotional world that doesn't exist—they write monologues for neglected cars. Write a similar monologue from the perspective of the rental car. How does it feel to be shiny and new? How does it feel to be used only temporarily, never committed to or owned? How might you create a monologue from the perspective of a new car that might be used, inversely, to sell used cars?

5. **WRITING:** In groups, in pairs, or on your own, write an advertisement for a new product, using a monologue written from the perspective of the old product it will replace. What would the old product say that might make you desire the new product instead of it?

ANALYSIS OF TWO TELEVISION SHOWS Shayla Thiel Stern teaches journalism and mass communication at the University of Minnesota in Minneapolis. She is the author of *Instant Identity: Adolescent Girls and the World of Instant Messaging* (2007), which, according to Thiel Stern's Web site (www.shaylathielstern.com/research.html), "investigates how gender and identity are articulated by girls as they use Instant Messaging with their peers and examines the cultural implications of IM as they relate to this generation." This essay originally appeared on FlowTV, a Web site about "the changing landscape of contemporary media" (www.flowtv.org).

FlowTV

Posted: August 21, 2008
From: Shayla Thiel Stern

Familiar Zip Code, New Bodies: A Critical Analysis of the Feminine Body in *90210*

When *Beverly Hills, 90210* premiered, I was still in high school, and I still remember my initial reaction to the show as the film rolled on the actors in West Beverly High:

Who in the world are these really old people?

Indeed, being from small-town Midwestern America, I had not seen teens the bleach-blonde likes of Tori Spelling, who was actually younger than I was despite looking far older, but all of the "teens" on this show just looked at least twenty-five to me—way too old to be playing high schoolers. (And in fact, it turned out some were. Luke Perry, who played Dylan McKay, and Ian Ziering, who played Steve Sanders, were in their mid-twenties when the show first debuted, and Gabrielle Carteris, who played Andrea Zuckerman, was actually twenty-nine.)

So it felt like déjà vu when I saw a promo announcing that *90210*—a latter-day spinoff of *Beverly Hills, 90210*—would debut on September 2. The girls in the advertisement—certainly the one sitting in a Jacuzzi between a pair of male legs—had to be fairly close to thirty. (I'd like to hope that hot tub parties aren't starting in the middle teens now, though I'm sure I'm still a naive small-town Midwesterner at heart.)

If you have never heard of *90210* in either form, I'll quickly get you up to speed: The Aaron Spelling–produced show (yes, he was Tori's dad) premiered on Fox in the fall of 1990 as one of the first-ever teen soaps, and initially centered on Brandon and Brenda Walsh, twins whose parents uprooted them from Minneapolis, Minnesota, to

The cast of the original Beverly Hills, 90210.

flashy Beverly Hills, California, where they befriended surfers and children of Holly-wood execs and former stars, and wormed their way into the intricate social scene while dealing with issues like drug abuse, accidental gun violence, racism, teen preg-nancy, and date rape. The wildly popular show, which was geared toward the teen and twenties demographic, lasted ten seasons.

Beverly Hills, 90210 was one of the first of a genre of soap operas featuring beautiful teens living in a fantasy environment, and arguably, a cultural touchstone.[1]

It also seemed to spawn a genre of shows casting beautiful young people, who are supposed to be teens, but actually look ten years older than your average teen. Think about James Van Der Beek on *Dawson's Creek,* Scott Wolf on *Party of Five,* Kristin Kreuk on *Smallville,* Charisma Carpenter on *Buffy the Vampire Slayer,* and every single "teen" character on *One Tree Hill.* Even though they might have been adolescents at the time they started playing their signature roles, they did not look it.

The question then becomes, why do producers repeat this casting tactic, when it could serve to make the shows even less realistic in the eyes of the viewers they hope to attract?

This is a complicated question, but I believe the answers are less complicated. First, in the new *90210* debuting next month, consumerism is a clear motivation. . . . Dior, Dolce and Gabbana, and Tiffany appear almost subliminally in the trailer.

If you are wearing Dior and Dolce, you are probably not an average sixteen-year-old girl, even a girl from the 90210 zip code. These are sophisticated clothes, designed to look good on very thin women in their late twenties and older . . . apparently like the "girls" on the new *90210*. These particular actresses can succeed in selling a lifestyle and a luxury brand name in their twentysomething bodies so much better than they could have in their sixteen-year-old bodies. (As a counterpoint, imagine Lane from the early *Gilmore Girls* shows in similar fashion.)

Second—and others (Katherine Sweeney[2] in *Maiden USA*, M. Gigi Durham[3] in *The Lolita Effect*, and Emily White[4] in *Fast Girls*, to name a few) have made this point previously in more scholarly terms—it would be downright creepy to see average-looking fourteen- to eighteen-year-olds placed in the sexualized world that is a teen soap opera. Imagine girls—such as your fourteen-year-old niece, or if you need to envision a more famous high school freshman, Dakota Fanning perhaps—cavorting in a Jacuzzi, seducing older men, wearing stilettos and micro-minis. In order for audiences to derive (guilty) pleasure from watching these situations in *90210,* producers must represent adolescent girls as women in their mid-twenties. While our culture has seen (and in some cases, embraced) the sexualization of increasingly younger starlets over the past ten years, we still might not be at that extreme point.

However, I would argue that this is just a fairly easy critique of media representation of the adolescent girls. There is a more troubling underlying current here to examine, and that is the realization of how the feminine body, and specifically the adolescent female body, exists within cultural discourse, and how it has changed over a relatively short span of time. We can see this clearly in the two versions of *90210*. It is absolutely striking to note how different the young women cast in the roles in the 2008 version of *90210* look than their predecessors in 1990. Granted, fashions and trends change. But put the high-waisted, baggy acid-washed jeans aside and focus on bodies and faces. Notice how the bodies of the 1990s females in the cast are proportioned. They have hips, wider thighs, vaguely pronounced muscles, and heads that appear to belong on top of their bodies. By the standards of 1990, these actresses were thin and pretty.

The cast of the new 90210.

Without the aid of Photoshop (which was released just after the first *90210* episode aired), these young women—old as they looked to audiences at the time— probably would have looked ridiculous decked out in the clothing we see on the stars of the new *90210.* They would not have been good for the consumerist, fashion-fetish aspect of the program at all. Furthermore, despite the "racy" episode in which Brenda loses her virginity to Dylan, members of the original cast were hardly sexualized at all; this episode pales in comparison to even the trailer for the new *90210,* where the actresses appear to be lounging in a dark bedroom with another (male) character making out with an unseen partner behind them.

And it is not only the adolescent girls from Beverly High who must undergo a cultural aging process to become culturally intelligible to the 2008 teen soap audience. The mothers, teachers, and other adults in their lives must as well—though theirs is reverse-aging. Cindy Walsh, the mother from the original series who was played by Carol Potter, appeared to be in her middle to late forties, and dressed modestly enough for audiences not to even wonder whether she had a yoga-body underneath. Lori Loughlin, who plays Debbie Wilson, the mother of the Kansas-transplanted teens in the new series, is actually forty-four in real life, but she looks nearly as beautiful and thin as the high school girls, making most of the women on the show appear to be close to age thirty in the promotional materials.

In borrowing from the theory of Susan Bordo, the women from both shows demonstrate how in a very short but increasingly mediated point in history, women's and girls' bodies are shaped and inscribed by the culture surrounding them.[5] Through Pilates, cosmetic surgery, low-carb diets, hair straightening, skin lightening, Botox, and so many other means, women have mirrored media representations of "perfect" women and shaped their bodies to fit the representation. While Photoshop almost certainly plays a role in the perfection process of promotional photos, however, it does not stop women and girls in reality from attempting to alter their bodies and faces to conform to this fantasy portrayal.

The old and new versions of *90210* exemplify this idea perfectly. And in the new version, all of the female bodies portrayed must be old/young/perfect enough for this cultural moment to enable a plot that allows audiences to feel enticed without feeling dirty, guilty, or simply disgusted.

Of course, it is important that we not discount the notion of agency—the notion that audiences can make what they will of this new show. Many of us found the original to be campy and ridiculous, and we reveled in the ridiculousness. Certainly audiences have the power to do the same with the next, and in our brave new media-ted world, we might even enjoy the recaps of this new version on *Television Without Pity* more than watching the actual program. However, Bordo's point cannot be lost in the argument for media pleasure or resistant readings of cultural texts like *90210*. When dominant cultural discourses that relegate girls and women to the passive, stereotypical roles of consumer and sex object actually lead to both physical and cultural change, we should take notice.

Notes

1. "Even on Television, Puberty Can't Last Forever." *New York Times* May 3, 2000. Retrieved Aug. 10, 2008.
2. Sweeney, Katherine. *Maiden U.S.A.* NY: Peter Lang Pubs, 2008.
3. Durham, M. Gigi. *The Lolita Effect.* NY: Overlook Press, 2008.
4. White, Emily. *Fast Girls*. NY: Penguin, 2007.
5. Bordo, Susan. *Unbearable weight: Feminism, Western culture, and the body.* Berkeley, CA: University of California Press, 1993.

Reading the Genre

1. How does Stern make her article accessible to readers who may not be familiar with either the new or the old version of *90210*? How does she use comparisons to other shows to help the reader understand the genre of the show she is talking about? (See "Focus on its genre," p. 200.)

2. How does Stern cite the analysis of other writers in her essay? How does she use her source material to support her ideas? (See Chapter 38, "Evaluating Sources," p. 415, and Chapter 42, "Integrating Sources into Your Work," p. 431.)

3. How does Stern extend her analysis of this television show into an argument about the images of women in popular culture? What is that argument? (See "Make a difference," p. 228.)

4. **WRITING:** Using the main points of Stern's essay, supported by the ideas of Bordo that Stern uses, analyze another show from this genre with regard to representations of young women, or representations that challenge what seem to be dominant images.

CULTURAL ANALYSIS   Laurie Fendrich is an artist, an art critic, and a professor of fine arts at Hofstra University. Her articles about both art and art education have been published in the *New York Times* and *ArtNews* magazine, and her drawings and paintings have been exhibited in museums and galleries in the United States and Canada.

The Beauty of the Platitude

LAURIE FENDRICH

Platitudes—hackneyed declarative sentences that assert the truth—are maligned for a reason. Ordinarily found in speech (most people know enough to avoid them in writing), platitudes assert everything—and nothing—all at once. Because they've been uttered so many times previously, and in so many trivial conversations, they tend to arrive stillborn, no more than a clump of meaningless words. Their form, stiff and unbendable by nature, permits little if any wiggle room for play. Just as greetings like "Hello" are conversation-starters, platitudes like, "Life is a process of change," or the one that's most particularly grating to me as an artist—"Art is a form of communication"—are conversation-stoppers.

For the educated, who are on call 24/7 to be as clever and quick-witted as possible, to be caught uttering a platitude is as embarrassing as being caught making a grammatical error. Once it's slipped out of the mouth (by accident, of course), the only recourse is to quickly smother the mortifying moment by piling on a few sentences making it clear the platitude was meant ironically.

Sometimes platitudes are a way for the speaker to assert his or her power over others. For example, "Education is the key"—a particularly popular platitude in today's lexicon—frequently masks a hidden agenda. It doesn't mean, "Education will make you successful in life," as much as it means, "If only you'd come around to my position, you'd be right." To say, "Education is the key" is often no more than code for the command, "Think like I do."

Then there are the platitudes that, although clearly intended on takeoff to mean well, and to comfort the suffering, can accidentally land very roughly.

One of my colleagues, a classicist who teaches courses in etymology, told me he can't stand it when people say, "Death is a part of life." Whenever he hears those words, he says, he always thinks, "No it's not. It's death. That's why it's got its own word." This little platitude is particularly fascinating because it easily can be turned on its head to become, "Life is a part of death." Since only a mortician could possibly take comfort from these words, however, this particular baby never got off the ground.

Not all platitudes are bad. Like WD-40, the handiest and most efficient grease for opening that pesky stuck drawer, some platitudes open stuck conversations. Moreover, they lend a human loveliness, if not a liveliness, to speech. They work beautifully when people can't find any way to end a bad conversation.

For example, a long tale of woe, coming from a nice but bothersome neighbor, can be abruptly and satisfactorily ended with the gentle platitude, "Well, you know, life is a process of growth and change." Repugnant and new-agey as it might seem to an intelligent soul to utter this sentence, it can be a powerful, yet delicate, deus ex machina when applied with care. The conversation instantaneously leaps from wallowing in muck to a happier plane where, not so surprisingly, it all works out for the best.

Reading the Genre

1. How many specific types of platitude does Fendrich identify? How does her identification of types of platitude lend an organization to this short essay? (See "Develop a structure," p. 233.)

2. Write a paragraph about education using as many platitudes as you can think of. Reread this paragraph and find one platitude that seems to say something important. What exactly does the platitude mean, and how does it help you write about education?

3. Watch an athlete or entertainer being interviewed (online or on television), and identify the platitudes he or she uses. Why would athletes and entertainers use these platitudes? Underneath the platitudes, do you sense that the interviewee really wants to say something different? (See Chapter 32, "Vigorous, clear, economical style," p. 328.)

4. **WRITING:** Building on question 3, rewrite an interview with a famous athlete or entertainer, replacing platitudes with the statements you believe this star would *really* like to make. Then develop a list of interview questions for this person that might lead the interviewee to give answers that aren't "conversation-stoppers."

MEDIA ANALYSIS   John Jordan, an associate professor of communication at the University of Wisconsin–Milwaukee, has published many articles on issues concerning the media and contemporary culture. This essay, analyzing the rhetorical techniques of sports announcers and commentators, was originally posted to the cultural studies Web site FlowTV (www.flowtv.org).

FlowTV

Posted: October 27, 2007
From: John W. Jordan

Sports Commentary and the Problem of Television Knowledge

John Frankenheimer's 1998 film, *Ronin,* contains a truly sublime moment that illustrates the raw power of athleticism as an audio/visual spectacle. In one narratively insignificant scene, the camera follows a figure skater, played by former Olympic champion Katarina Witt, as she rehearses her routine. Rachmaninoff plays over the empty stadium's speakers as Witt gracefully strides and leaps across the ice. Audible above the music are the more jarring sounds of her skates grinding into the ice as she gathers energy for her next maneuver. The scene becomes a study in contrasts, and the cumulative effect is enthralling; the violent noise of Witt's skates belying the smooth grace of her movements, the sights and sounds of an exceptional athlete engaged in the perfection of her sport.

I have watched, but never really been a fan of, figure skating on television, and was surprised by my attraction to this scene. What made it so compelling compared to its television counterpart, I later realized, was the conspicuous absence of the omnipresent sports commentators. Their overly enthusiastic discourse on lutzes and Biellmanns, and their pontifications about how a particular jump was "sending a message" to the other competitors, drowned out the beauty of the skating with a flood of technical jargon. The film allowed me to experience the skater on her own terms while television insisted that I engage skating on the commentators' terms. Obviously, sports commentary is not limited to figure skating; all televised sports exhibit similar tendencies for over-discussion. For example, no quarterback can complete a pass without the audience being told what kind of a pass it was by a former quarterback-turned-commentator who then analogizes the play to one from his own playing past.

Watching sports on television is less about observing the athletic spectacle of graceful competition than it is witnessing the construction of a televisual compendium of sports knowledge for which the game is merely the backdrop.

Given the ubiquity of sports commentary on television, there must be some perceived purpose behind it. But what might that purpose be? More importantly, what does it say about television sports audiences and the regard in which they are held by television networks that no sporting activity can be conveyed to the public without commentary? Why are television audiences not allowed to experience televised sports with only the natural sounds of the event? Inquiring about the role of commentating in televised sports engages how television creates knowledge and situates audiences with respect to sports. What we find is that television sports commentary turns sports from a visceral spectacle into a technical oration, and for no discernible benefit.

The most generous view of television sports commentary suggests that its purpose is to provide otherwise inaccessible information to viewers in a timely manner so as to enhance their viewing experience. And commentary can and does fulfill this function. With research staff on hand and their own well of experience, television commentators can draw out those interesting bits of history and trivia that, at the right moment in a game, can both inform and entertain their audiences with explanations of obscure rulings or contextualizations of significant plays. But commentators are not held in reserve off-camera until this information is needed; they are thrust into the foreground and seemingly required to speak even when there isn't really much to say. They are the vanguard of the over-verbalizing forces of modern television. But information dissemination is not the same as conveying understanding, and it is the difference between those two that generates the knowledge problematic for television.

Any quality assessment of information is subjective, but one needn't be a cynic to question the instructional value of much of the sports commentary on television. John Madden's teleprompter circles around and discussion of the sweat stains of defensive linemen may be amusing, but certainly stretch the consideration of what counts as sports commentary. Similarly, tennis commentator Mary Carillo's extended stories about Roger Federer's attendance at a New York fashion show, with which she regaled audiences during play at this year's U.S. Open, certainly make it fair to question the information value of such details over more pertinent information about the actual play on the court. Even those who applaud these digressions admit that the commentators are known more for their personalities than for their ability to provide quality information to audiences (e.g., Maffei, 2006). But I'm not describing only those instances when commentary moves from the trivial to the tangential; too much substantive information can also distract the viewer by asking them to give more attention to the commentator than to what is being commented on.

For those "in the know," technical jargon indeed may be neither impenetrable nor detrimental to their viewing enjoyment, much in the same way that casual fans may appreciate Madden's and Carillo's meanderings through sensibility. But television is not a democratic but a tyrannical medium—we can only observe what it gives us. When the commentary is present, we must all accept it or mute it; there can be no in-between. The coverage interpellates the viewer as someone needing this data in order to enjoy the sporting event. Familiarity is rewarded, but not knowledge—the latter is claimed as the medium's province. The audience is positioned as not being knowledgeable enough about the sport to enjoy it on its own terms or with only minimal informational assistance. Consequently, the commentary is a rhetoric of entertainment more than instruction. The unfortunate consequence of this assumption is that commentators believe that any factoid or story they convey—no matter its relation to what is taking place on the field of play—is of interest to the home viewer. Audiences have few means available for escaping or challenging their position in this dynamic. The forceful manner of the medium seldom creates an opportunity for audiences to assess this claim independent of the commentary and its self-established justification.

On a very few occasions, however, a different perspective has been available, and is helpful for situating sports commentary within the politics of the audience's relationship to television. On December 20, 1980, NBC experimented with an "announcerless" broadcast of an NFL game between the New York Jets and the Miami Dolphins. Viewers at home heard only the natural sounds of the game, similar to what the fans in the stadium heard that night. The game earned respectable ratings, but the format was not continued because network executives considered it a "one-time gimmick" (Rubinstein, 2000). A quarter of a century later, following a media lockout by the Canadian Football League, several weeks' worth of announcerless games were broadcast to fans, and their ratings were dramatically higher than games which featured commentary ("King Kaufman's," 2005). Fans, it would seem, are both capable of and willing to experience sports on television without the informational assistance of commentators or their anecdotes, and while these instances may be too few to support the claim that viewers prefer announcerless broadcasts, they do warrant additional thought along these lines.

If any event on television could be broadcast without worrying about the audience's ability to understand and appreciate what they are seeing, relying on the audience's existing level of familiarity with the concept, it certainly would be a sports event. And yet, sports are the most heavily commented events on television, to the point where it is not uncommon for there to be more commentators for an event than there are actual competitors on the field. If the explanation for this circumstance is that the audience needs educating, then there are significant issues both with the quality of this education and the manner in which it is provided. Sports commentary on television, in its current form, is not simply too often distracting and trivial; its self-insistence is detrimental to fans' ability to experience the events they have tuned in to watch. The technical knowledge hurled at television sports audiences shifts them from a position of being able to appreciate the athlete's skills at the visceral level to a position where technical understanding is rewarded. Sports commentary as such is television's vestigial organ, the unnecessary remnant that points out how the medium has not completely evolved into the modern media sphere. With the Internet in particular, the mythos of the uninformed audience is challenged. This is not to say that Internet audiences are smarter or better educated about the sports that they are watching, merely that they have access to a wealth of information and are far less reliant on commentators to provide it to them, as countless fan and media sites across the Web demonstrate. The realization needed here by networks is that, when it comes to sports, television is a medium of stimulation much more than it is a medium of information. Perhaps it would be best if television sports coverage were reshaped as a medium of appreciation, where the visceral impact of sport is conveyed more cleanly and directly. In the current media age, commentating is the province of audiences eager to make their own voices heard, not to simply listen to intermediaries who drift increasingly into shouting outrages in an attempt to garner attention and justify their airtime. Television should handle the transmission of the natural sites and sounds of the games and the commentary should be left to the fans to discover and generate for themselves.

References

King Kaufman's sports daily. (2005, August 31). Retrieved September 15, 2007, from
        http://www.salon.com/news/sports/col/kaufman/2005/08/31/wednesday/
Maffei, John. (2006, June 22). These voices don't mince words. *North County Times.*
        Retrieved September 15, 2007, from http://www.nctimes.com/articles/2006/06/23/
        sports/maffei/22_00_516_22_06.txt
Rubinstein, Julian. (2000, September 3). Monday night football's hail Mary. *New York
        Times Magazine.* Retrieved September 15, 2007, from http://www.julianrubinstein
        .com/football.html

Reading the Genre

1. How does Jordan focus his essay on purpose and audience? How are the two connected? What are the purposes of sports commentary? How does this commentary give audiences what they want or need? (See Chapter 19, "Smart Reading," p. 317.)

2. Why might commentators be wrong about the purposes of what they say, and wrong about what their audiences want and need? How important is it for the audience to recognize when a speaker is getting things wrong? (See "Consider the audiences of the text," p. 230, and Chapter 30, "High, Middle, and Low Style," p. 366.)

3. Who is Jordan's audience for this essay? Is he writing for sports fans? If you are a fan, do you feel he speaks to you? If you aren't a fan, what do you think about this article?

4. Jordan ends the essay with a proposal. Does this proposal seem like a reasonable possibility? Is this essay an argument for change in sports commentary, or a critique of something that isn't likely to change? Should the main purpose of this article be to argue or to analyze?

5. **WRITING:** Watch a national sporting event, and then write an analysis of the roles of the different commentators and the on-screen visual information. To prepare, list all the names of the broadcast's voices and faces, and try to define their roles or functions. Then review the commentary the viewer is given through on-screen data, visuals, and interviews; list all the "otherwise inaccessible information" that fans are given; and consider the ways that each element instructs or entertains. Use these notes to construct your short analysis of sports commentary. As you do so, consider how other televised events—such as news or financial programming—are also saturated with information.

ANALYSIS OF WEB SITES   Darren Crovitz teaches English and English education at Kennesaw State University, and his articles on media and education issues have been published in many scholarly journals. In the following analysis of Internet advertisements, Crovitz effectively scrutinizes the textual, visual, and interactive elements of these Web pages.

Scrutinizing the Cybersell: Teen-Targeted Web Sites as Texts

DARREN CROVITZ

Over the last decade, analyzing and assessing online information has become a regular part of many English classes. We now expect students to become familiar with the advantages and disadvantages of Internet research, including how to evaluate the credibility of Web sites and the information they contain. As online environments become more sophisticated, however, we might consider expanding students' critical-thinking opportunities beyond the concerns of traditional research. While media literacy has been a part of our field for several decades, the explosion in Web-based content and communication in the last few years combined with youth culture's embrace of these developments makes it vital that we consider the academic potential of these new texts.

Take a moment to consider the thousands of products marketed to young people—the wide spectrum of snack foods, soft drinks, candy, toys, games, clothes, and gadgets competing for their money and attention. Now consider that many of these products have a slick Web site devoted to grabbing and holding a kid's attention and associating that product or brand with what's cool. Corporations are no longer limited to the old-media advertising strategies of print, radio, and TV. Digital advances in image, sound, video, animation, and design now allow companies to embed their product pitch within an interactive cyberreality, allowing a particular target consumer—suburban teenage boys, for instance—to be represented, defined, and influenced.

It may be tempting to shake our heads at this latest development in consumer culture while also considering it beyond the scope of an English class. Because these sites specifically target students, however, they are a rich opportunity to help young people learn about rhetorical analysis and the need to weigh messages that are immediately relevant to their lives. In doing so, we address a primary need of multimodal literacy ("to understand how [such] works make meaning, how they are based on conventions, and how they are created for and respond to specific communities or audiences") while centering our practice in real examples of language and image use in their world ("NCTE," par. 16). While classroom analysis of how advertising works to manipulate an audience is nothing new, viewed within the broader field of media and digital literacy these skills take on increased importance. "If our children are to be able to navigate their lives through this multi-media culture," explain Elizabeth Thoman and Tessa Jolls in "Literacy for the 21st Century: An Overview and Orientation Guide to Media Literacy Education," they will need more than the conventional skills of reading and writing print texts: "they need to be fluent in 'reading' and 'writing' the language of images and sounds" as well (6). . . .

With both pre-service and experienced English teachers at Kennesaw State University, I have used product Web sites as a means of linking traditional concepts of persuasion (e.g., the Aristotelian appeals) to the realm of new media. As a way into this topic, we look closely at a number of Web sites aimed at selling to young people, two of which are described in detail in this article. Our first task as a class becomes an assessment of how these sites use multimodal strategies to define a target audience and convey a particular message. That is, we want to ask how these Web sites seek to define young audiences—in terms of appearance, hobbies and interests, and lifestyle—while positioning a product as integral to their world. . . .

Please note: These sites feature advanced graphics, sound effects, online game areas, and embedded video, so they require a fairly up-to-date computer system with speakers to experience them fully.

Example One: SlimJim.com

In the last few years, the ConAgra Foods Corporation has made a significant effort to market its Slim Jim meat snacks to adolescent males. Part of this media push has been an interactive Web presence in which Slim Jims are presented as part of a hypermasculine philosophy characterized by the concept of "snap moments" (derived from the shouted catchphrase "Snap into a Slim Jim!") during which boys overcome fear to accomplish "extreme feats" ("Snap!"). Past Slim Jim spokespersons have included professional wrestler Randy "The Macho Man" Savage and the Fairy Snapmother, a "tattooed punk rocker with wings" who uses a tough-love approach to help boys become men. Television ads featuring the latter character are purposely designed with an edgy humor in the style of MTV's *Jackass,* a program renowned for its controversial and often-dangerous stunts.

Slim Jim's emphasis on rough humor and its focus on teenage boys as a target audience are also reflected in its high-end interactive Web site. As a class we start with the assumption that the site is a "text" that can be "read" for meaning, and we begin the discussion with a set of questions derived from the fields of visual and media literacy:

- What specific choices were made in designing this page, and for what effect?
- What do choices in sound, graphics, colors, layout, and design convey?
- What choices are evident in the actual language used on the page?
- What do these elements remind us of? What possible associations can be made?
- Who is the target audience for this page? How do we know?
- What is not on the page, and why?

The discussion is based on the assumption that *nothing is an accident* in this text, that all design elements have a purpose and so communicate some kind of meaning. (Given that the site is clearly a sophisticated effort likely constructed at considerable cost, this is not much of a stretch.) Students have had in-depth discussions about the connotations of the site's colors (predominantly red, black, and yellow) along with the omnipresent "whip/crack" sound effects and the comedic use of a meat snack as a weapon. The site is heavy on parody and includes a video timeline of "great moments in Snap history" and a record of the first Snap moment:

> According to historians, the first human Snap occurred when cavemen decided to club their fears away, and hunt wooly mammoths and mastodons and stuff. As today's civilization has moved past such practices, we've had to find other ways to Snap through. Like by hucking ourselves off of large mountain peaks, or jumping the Great Wall of China. At Slim

> Jim, we are proud to stand behind those who attempt to Snap in such endeavors. Even if they fail miserably in the process. ("About Us," par. 1)

In its tone and style, this mock history adopts a satirical pose, locating Slim Jim in the world of extreme sports and teen lingo. Or rather, it *attempts* to accomplish these things, as students have pointed out. Cross-marketing with Mountain Dew and the Dew Action Tour, which features sports such as BMX biking and skateboarding, purposely associates Slim Jims with an "edgy," alternative youth crowd. Likewise, the tongue-in-cheek idiom represented above can be viewed as a corporate co-opting of cultural language, an attempt to gain credibility with the target audience that can easily backfire. (One of the more humorous examples of this misappropriation occurred in a recent McDonald's Internet banner ad, in which a young man gazes at a hamburger with a thought caption that reads, "I'd hit it." Most students are well aware of the sexual connotations—apparently lost on McDonald's executives—of this streetwise phrase.)

. . . The latest ad campaign deals with hunting the "snapalope," a small deerlike creature made from Slim Jim sticks; it features an extensive, interactive faux Web site (the "Snapalope Hunting Association of America" [SHAA] at http://www.shaa.com) devoted to this activity. [We] could examine how the features on this site play on genre expectations for such organizational texts, from the multipart "S.H.A.A. Hunting Guide" and the "message from our president" to the group's fake logo. Though intentionally ironic, the SHAA site is part of a larger Internet hoax phenomenon that itself offers much potential for analysis. One of the highlights of the hoax-site genre is probably POP! The First Male Human Pregnancy (http://www.malepregnancy.com), a sharply produced site that uses corporate and scientific imagery, rhetoric, and design to create an overwhelming impression of legitimacy. Similarly, the Dihydrogen Monoxide Research Division (http://www.dhmo.org) adopts the look and language of a public-health page while serving as "an unbiased data clearinghouse" about this purportedly dangerous chemical compound. Such sham sites can range from the harmless to the purposely provocative to the criminal, but all rely on adopting the language, structure, and appearance of certain genres to create a patina of credibility. When we consider the prevalence of Web and e-mail fraud—much of which depends on convincing a victim that he or she is actually visiting a safe and familiar site rather than a bogus one—the ability to discern and evaluate such textual deception becomes even more crucial.

From another perspective, the Slim Jim Web site raises questions of gender identity and cultural roles that [we] might consider. Slim Jim is doing more than selling snacks in a funny way; it's also reinforcing a narrow definition of manhood characterized by stereotypes and silly, if not risky, behavior. . . .

Example Two: Doritos.com

Frito-Lay's Doritos Web site is a great example of a multimodal, multilayered, persuasive text aimed at young people. As with the Slim Jim site, the site features high-end graphics, sound, and video layered over more traditional text-and-image messaging. The version we used in class has been changed . . . but the following description illustrates the company's approach to marketing to teens and the direction of our class discussions.

Visitors are greeted immediately by simultaneous sound, image, and motion as the Doritos logo—a vaguely triangular shape formed by a flame pattern reminiscent of an EKG heartbeat—materializes suddenly from a dark red background. Stylized Doritos bags whip across the screen along with navigation links that snap into place. Elements of the page are in constant movement, inviting interactivity. The style is techno-frenetic; mousing over items on the screen produces a highlighted visual effect and an electrical fusion sound. Students have discussed the peculiar visual sensibility at work on the Doritos site—a post-apocalyptic, urban, grungy-yet-slick style—and the constant jittery motion that seems an echo of the quick-cut camera work of MTV programming. This comparison often leads to a discussion about the presumed short attention spans of teenagers and how the site plays on and possibly reinforces this stereotype.

Throughout the Doritos Web site, Frito-Lay explicitly targets a teenage market. Clicking on any of the flavored Doritos bags on the main page will take viewers to a different page featuring embedded video and images of young people engaged in various kinds of leisure activities. For instance, "Nacho Cheese" flavor takes us to a scene of three teens dancing to a hip-hop tune emitted from a boom box, which in turn receives its pulsing energy from a bag of Doritos.

The representation presented here—of how cool teens look, what they wear, and what they like—is ripe for analysis. . . . What we're looking at is an artificial construction rather than a real scene of teen life: The people dancing on screen are actors, chosen for a particular reason. The same goes for their clothing, their dancing style, and the music they are listening to. Frito-Lay is attempting to define its target audience with a specific, visual example while simultaneously locating its product as central to this vision. Once we are able to see this scene as only one *interpretation* of teen life, it becomes easier to imagine the choices that lie behind this scene, and to begin pondering "why." . . .

[We can] consider the implications of gender and ethnicity in this evoked scene, with its focus on a blonde girl, obviously Anglo, dancing in an urban style before a background audience of an African American male and a dark-haired girl. Similarly, the text on the page ("Rock your mouth with the high-decibel nacho cheese flavor that started a snacking revolution") draws on counter-culture connotations in musical and social history in service of a product pitch. . . .

The other Doritos flavors on the site have similar depictions of young people immersed in cool activities . . . or at least "cool" as defined by the Frito-Lay marketing department. As they get the hang of reading these pages, students inevitably note the ethnic assumptions at work in some of these representations. For instance, on the interactive page for "Spicy Nacho" flavor, a Latina teen "tags" a wall with the Doritos logo before tossing the spray can to the viewer; the can replaces our mouse pointer and suddenly we can add our graffiti to the page. Other pages on the site depict a low-rider Cadillac against a rap beat; a female African American DJ operating a couple of turntables; a grungy Anglo male rocking out on air guitar; and a Hispanic teen juggling a soccer ball. All of these scenes attempt to connect with a young target audience and in turn can be evaluated as multilayered texts seeking to define what cool looks like. Many other aspects of this sophisticated site can be examined through a rhetorical lens. In a section titled "Join," visitors are invited to become members of "Club Doritos," which "gets you access to awesome sweepstakes, great offers, and more!" Current members of the club can click a link to "Manage your profile," a phrase that echoes the language of online networking sites such as MySpace and Facebook that are immensely popular with teenagers. . . .

Final Thoughts

On average, young people now spend about three hours each day on the Internet, as much time as they do watching television (Davis). And just as TV can be watched from a noncritical, passive perspective, so too can teens surf the Web— or build Web sites—without analyzing or evaluating the information they encounter, treating at face value that which has been constructed for an intended effect. Since "[m]ost media messages are organized to gain profit and/or power," it becomes essential that [young people] gain practice in critiquing such texts

(Thoman and Jolls 15). We want them to have the capacity to deal proactively and thoughtfully with all manner of online branding, selling, and messaging, rather than simply reacting. . . .

Works Cited

"About Us." *SlimJim.com*. Web. 10 Sept. 2006.

Davis, Wendy. "Web Ties TV in Race for Teens' Eyeballs." *Online Media Daily*. 14 June 2006. Web. 10 Oct. 2006.

"NCTE Guideline: Multimodal Literacies." *NCTE*. Nov. 2005. Web. 22 May 2007.

"Snap! Slim Jim's Fairy Snapmother Flies into Convenience Stores." ConAgra Foods News Release. *ConAgra Foods*. 15 Nov. 2005. Web. 22 May 2007.

Thoman, Elizabeth, and Tessa Jolls. "Literacy for the 21st Century: An Overview and Orientation Guide to Media Literacy Education." *Center for Media Literacy*. 2005. Web. 15 Oct. 2006.

Reading the Genre

1. A key term in this essay is *multimodal literacy*. How would you define this term? How does Crovitz himself develop a rhetorical analysis that is "multi-modal"?

2. Crovitz shows that analysis of these sites is tricky, not only because they are deceptive but also because this deception is supposed to be noticed. What are the dilemmas in analyzing a text that is, in Crovitz's words, "tongue-in-cheek"?

3. How does Crovitz describe the interactive nature of these sites? How is this different from a straightforward visual analysis? What can be learned from this essay about describing and analyzing Web sites? (See "Make the text accessible to readers," p. 235.)

4. What does Crovitz's essay have to teach us about the ethics of advertising? What are his arguments about the content of these sites? (See Chapter 39, "Critical Reading and Note-Taking Strategies," p. 420.)

5. **WRITING:** Visit a site Crovitz mentions in his essay, or find another parody site on your own. Using the six questions that Crovitz offers for analysis, critique the site.

Acknowledgments (continued from p. iv)

Deb Aronson. "The Nurture of Nature." Originally published in *Science and Spirit,* July 2003. Reprinted by permission of the author.

Emily Bazelon. "Hitting Bottom: Why America Should Outlaw Spanking." From Slate .com, posted Thursday, January 25, 2007. Copyright © 2008 Slate.com and Washingtonpost. Newsweek Interactive Co. LLC. Reprinted by permission. All rights reserved.

Sharon Begley. "Learning to Love Climate 'Adaptation.'" From *Newsweek,* December 22, 2007 issue, page A20. Copyright © 2007 Newsweek, Inc. All rights reserved. Used by permission and protected by the Copyright Laws of the United States. The printing, copying, redistribution, or retransmission of the Material without express written permission is prohibited. www.newsweek.com.

David Bianculli. "A Gladiator of Mockery, Stephen Colbert Is Dismantling American Society from the Inside." From *The Phoenix,* November 11, 2007. Reprinted by permission of David Bianculli, TV Critic, NPR's "Fresh Air" and TV Worth Watching. www.tvworthwatching.com.

Jane E. Brody. "Gene-Altered Food: A Case Against Panic." From the *New York Times,* Health & Fitness Section, December 5, 2000 issue, page 8. Copyright © 2000 The New York Times. All rights reserved. Used by permission and protected by the Copyright Laws of the United States. The printing, copying, redistribution, or retransmission of the material without the express written permission is prohibited. www.nytimes.com.

David Brower. "Let the River Run Through It." From *Sierra,* March/April 1997. Reprinted by permission of the Estate of David Brower.

Carrie Brownstein. "So I Thought I Could Dance." Posted on Carrie Brownstein's blog, MonitorMix, September, 2008. www.npr.org/blog/monitormix/. Reprinted by permission of Carrie Brownstein.

Robert Bruegmann. "How Sprawl Got a Bad Name." From *American Enterprise,* Volume 17, Issue 5, June 15, 2006, p. 6. Reprinted by permission of the author.

Frank Bruni. "Life in The Fast Food Lane." From the *New York Times,* May 24, 2006. Copyright © 2006 The New York Times. All rights reserved. Used by permission and protected by the Copyright Laws of the United States. The reprinting, redistribution, or retransmission of the Material without express written permission is prohibited. www.nytimes.com.

Robert D. Bullard. "Assuring Environmental Justice For All." From *The Covenant With Black America.* Reprinted by permission of Robert D. Bullard.

"Carter II" lyrics (8 lines). By Tristan G. Jones, X, Dwayne Carter.

Jeanette Catsoulis. Excerpt from review of *Eragon: A Boy and His Dragon.* From the *New York Times,* Performing Arts Section, December 15, 2006 issue, page E20. Copyright © 2006 by The New York Times. All rights reserved. Used by permission and protected by the Copyright Laws of the United States. The printing, copying, redistribution, or retransmission of the Material without express written permission is prohibited. www.nytimes.com.

Clive Crook. "John Kenneth Galbraith, Revisited." From *National Journal,* May 15, 2006. Originally published in *The Atlantic* Online, May 6, 2006. www.theatlantic

Douglas Kellner. "Contradictions of Michael Jordan." Excerpt from *Media Spectacle* by Douglas Kellner. Copyright © 2003 by Douglas Kellner. Reprinted by permission of Routledge, an imprint of Taylor & Francis Books UK. All rights reserved.

Naomi Klein. "Pay to Be Saved: The Future of Disaster Response." First published in *The Nation,* August 29, 2006. © Naomi Klein. Reprinted by permission of Klein Lewis Productions.

Andrew and Judith Kleinfeld. "Go Ahead, Call Us Cowboys." From the *Wall Street Journal.* Copyright 2004 by Dow Jones & Company, Inc. Reproduced with permission of Dow Jones & Company, Inc. in the formats of Text and Other Book by Copyright Clearance Center.

E. Philip Krider. "Benjamin Franklin and Lightning Rods." From *Physics Today,* January 2006, p. 42. Copyright © 2006 American Institute of Physics. Reprinted by permission of the American Institute of Physics, Inc.

Robert Kuttner. "College Rankings or Junk Science?" From *The American Prospect Online:* February 27, 2006. The American Prospect, 200 L Street NW, Suite 717, Washington, DC 20036. Reprinted with permission from Robert Kuttner. All rights reserved.

Laura Layton. "Uranus's Changing Rings." *Astronomy,* December 28, 2005, p. 29. Copyright © 2007 Astronomy magazine, Kalmbach Publishing Company. Reprinted by permission.

Elaine Liner. "Dumpster Diving." Posted on the "Phantom Professor" blog, January 3, 2006. Reprinted by permission of the author.

Eileen McDonagh and Lauren Pappano. "Time to Change the Rules." From *Playing with the Boys: Why Separate Is Not Equal in Sports.* Copyright © 2008. By permission of Oxford University Press, Inc.

Ellen McGrath. "Is Depression Contagious?" From *Psychology Today,* July/August 2003. Copyright © 2003 Sussex Publishers, LLC. Reprinted with permission of the publisher.

Liz Miller. "Size Doesn't Matter: *Brokeback Mountain.*" From bookslut.com/Bookslut Literary Magazine Web, January 2006. Reprinted by permission of the author.

Joni Mitchell. "WOODSTOCK," Words and Music by JONI MITCHELL © 1968 (Renewed) CRAZY CROW MUSIC. All Rights Administered by SONY/ATV MUSIC PUBLISHING, 8 Music Square West, Nashville, TN 37203. All Rights Reserved. Used by permission of ALFRED PUBLISHING CO., INC.

Gabriela Montell. "Do Good Looks Equal Good Evaluations?" From *The Chronicle of Higher Education,* October 15, 2003. Reprinted by permission of the publisher.

James Morris. "My Favorite Wasteland." From *The Wilson Quarterly,* Autumn 2005. Reprinted by permission of the author.

Walter S. Mossberg and Catherine Boehret. "A Gold Standard for PCs." Originally published in the *Wall Street Journal,* November 30, 2005. Copyright 2005 by Dow Jones & Company, Inc. Reproduced with permission of Dow Jones & Company in the formats of Text and Other Book by Copyright Clearance Center. All rights reserved.

"Move Around." Words and Music by Byron Thomas and Christopher Dorsey. Copyright © 2006 FRESH IS THE WORD, SONGS OF UNIVERSAL, INC. and CHOPPER

Page 126: © Columbia/Courtesy of the Everett Collection.

Page 129: Courtesy of the EPA.

Page 132: © Loretta Rae/Corbis.

Page 137: Stephen Schauer/Getty Images.

Page 143: Mary Evans Picture Library/Everett Collection.

Page 145: Anne R. Carey and Gia Kereselide, USA TODAY. June 30, 2006. Reprinted with permission.

Page 154: © Bettmann/CORBIS.

Page 155: © John Springer Collection/CORBIS.

Page 156: © Bettmann/CORBIS.

Page 157: © Bettmann/CORBIS.

Page 161: Reprinted with permission of AdBusters.

Page 165: Lauren Greenfield/VII/AP.

Page 168: David Young-Wolff/PhotoEdit.

Page 169: © CORBIS.

Page 174: Massachusetts Turnpike Authority. Used with permission.

Page 184: Tyler Brett and Tony Romano (T&T). Reprinted with permission.

Page 187: Courtesy of Kayla Mohammadi. Reprinted with permission.

Page 196: Top: MIRAMAX/The Kobal Collection/Jill Sabella. Bottom: HBO/Courtesy of Everett Collection.

Page 207: PhotoFest. © United Artists.

Page 217: Focus Features/The Kobal Collection.

Pages 218–20: Library of Congress Prints and Photographs Division, Washington, D.C.

Page 226: Courtesy of Dell, Inc.

Page 227: George Nikitin/Associated Press.

Page 229: Masi Oka © 2007 America's Milk Processors.

Page 235: Courtesy of the Navy Environmental Health Center.

Page 255: © Bill Aron/PhotoEdit, Inc.

Page 256: Jim Zook/© Images.com/Corbis.

Page 261: © George Steinmetz/Corbis.

Page 264: NSDAP/The Kobal Collection.

Page 267: Ziga Soleil/Getty Images.

Page 273: Mario Villafuerte/Bloomberg/Landov.

Page 279: © Bob Daemmrich/The Image Works.

Page 281: © Hulton-Deutsch Collection/Corbis.

Page 285: Jerome Tisne/Getty Images.

Page 291: © Reuters/Christian Charisius/Landov.

Page 299: © Hulton-Deutsch Collection/Corbis.

Page 309: Photo by Jacob Botter. Reprinted with permission.

Page 310: Library of Congress.

Page 312: Wikipedia image used with permission under the terms of the GNU Free Documentation License.

Page 313: *CSI Miami* photo credit: CBS/Robert Voets/Landov.

Page 313: Stefan Lovgren/National Geographic Image Collection.

Index